ADVANCED EDU

ADVANCED EDUCATIONAL PSYCHOLOGY

Second Edition

S.K. MANGAL

*Formerly, Professor and Head
Department of Postgraduate Studies,
and Principal, C.R. College of Education
Rohtak, Haryana*

PHI Learning Private Limited
Delhi-110092
2017

₹ 325.00

ADVANCED EDUCATIONAL PSYCHOLOGY, 2nd ed.
by S.K. Mangal

ISBN-978-81-203-2038-3

The export rights of this book are vested solely with the publisher.

Thirty-fourth Printing (Second Edition) ... ... **January, 2017**

Published by Asoke K. Ghosh, PHI Learning Private Limited, Rimjhim House, 111, Patparganj Industrial Estate, Delhi-110092 and Printed by Rajkamal Electric Press, Plot No. 2, Phase IV, HSIDC, Kundli-131028, Sonepat, Haryana.

Contents

Preface

It gives me immense pleasure to write the preface of the second edition of the text, 'Advanced Educational Psychology'. Right from its first publication in the year 1993 and the continuous reprint in the subsequent years, it has been widely appreciated and warmly acknowledged by a vast family of its readers comprising the students and the faculty members of the disciplines psychology, education and teacher preparation of the universities in India and abroad. The candidates preparing for the various State and National level competitive examinations for admission to courses or for joining government services including the most coveted one like IAS (especially those who opt psychology as one of the optional paper) and its allied services have also found this text a quite helping hand in their venture.

In the recent times there has been a lot of change in the syllabi of the universities and competitive examinations. To meet their requirements, a few chapters namely, Psychology of Individual Differences, Transfer of Learning or Training, Emotional Development and Emotional Intelligence, and Learning Disabilities and Learning Disabled Children, have been added.

Also, a few topics like factors affecting growth and development, outcomes of learning, factors affecting learning, Gagne's theory of learning, Carl Roger's theory of experiential learning, creative thinking, critical thinking, training or development of thinking, and factors affecting problem solving, have been included.

In addition to these elaborations, the subject matter of the text also has been thoroughly checked and revised to make it more readable and useful to its readers.

It is therefore hoped that the text will serve the interest and purpose of its readers in a more comprehensive and a useful way. Any suggestion for further improvement will be highly appreciated and thankfully acknowledged by the writer as well as the publisher.

In the end, I feel it my utmost duty to extend my thanks to all my students, colleagues and host of my readers for having provided me due incentives and suggestions to bring out the revised edition in the present form. I am also indebted to the ideas of the various scholars whose writings have been the source of inspiration and backbone for writing this book.

Special thanks are also due to Shri Asoke K. Ghosh, Managing Director, Prentice-Hall of India and the publishing team who have always proved themselves a constant source of inspiration for encouraging creative and useful publications in the field of education and psychology.

With warm wishes to the readers.

S.K. MANGAL

Preface to the First Edition

Educational Psychology, the science of education, aims at improving the processes and products of education. It supplies the means and ways as well as the science and technology for helping the teachers, the teacher-trainers, the educational planners, the administrators and counselling personnels in their respective areas of activity so that they will be able to assist the younger generation in their pursuit of education. That is why its study is made compulsory at all levels of the teacher-training programme, guidance, administration and courses of education, ranging from elementary and high school to undergraduate, postgraduate and research levels.

Though there are a number of undergraduate level books available on the subject, there is a dearth of advanced level texts which are suited to the educational framework and the teaching-learning situations prevalent in our country. The problem is particularly acute as we have a large number of universities and postgraduation centres where educational psychology is being taught and good texts on the subject are not available. This text is therefore meant to fill this gap.

This text differs from many other Indian texts not only because of its vast coverage of the topics, but also because it gives the latest developments in the various areas of educational psychology. Besides, the book is written in a lucid and an engaging style, to assist the readers grasp the subject better.

The initial chapters provide the meaning, nature and scope as also methods and systems of psychology and its branch, educational psychology. The systems or schools of psychology have been covered in such a way as to give both the historical perspective and the contemporary situation. In view of their enormous importance, the systems propagated by Freud, Adler, Jung and Piaget have been discussed in separate chapters. Since growth and development, motivation and attention have vital links with the process of learning, these have been covered in the chapters preceding learning. While dealing with the nature and theories of learning, due care has been taken to make the students understand facts essential for human learning in a given situation. The educational implications of all the theories of learning have also been given so as to help the students make use of these theories.

The indepth discussion on the theories of learning is followed by a systematic treatment on memory, including types of memory, and an analysis of the meaning of forgetting.

The cognitive aspects have been grouped together and covered in the chapters on intelligence, creativity, and psychology of thinking, reasoning and problem solving. In this context, an attempt has been made to provide the latest developments in the field, e.g. Gardner's theory of multiple intelligence, the raging controversy about the misuse of IQ results, Arieti's theory of creativity and effective steps in problem solving, and so on.

The chapter on personality has been placed deliberately after dealing with those aspects relating to the personality development of children, covered in earlier chapters. Besides analysing the major concepts, theories and viewpoints on personality, the current researches and findings also find a place here.

The chapter dealing with exceptional children covers the major types of exceptional children. Here the characteristics, means of identification, etymology of their behaviour alongwith their specific needs, problems, remedial education and other aspects have been discussed in relation to the settings and situations prevalent in our country. Finally, an important aspect of human behaviour, namely, adjustment, its meaning and relevance have been discussed in the last chapter.

The text is sufficiently illustrated with examples, diagrams and tables to facilitate the readers in understanding the topics discussed. At the end of each chapter, besides providing a summary for recollection of the topics discussed, appropriate references and suggested readings have been given to enable the readers delve deeper into the subject.

I am indebted to the various authors, research workers and educational psychologists whose views and opinions have been incorporated in the text. Many of my students have been a great source of inspiration to me during the last three decades of my association with them. I also wish to sincerely thank my wife, Uma Mangal, who has been a constant source of inspiration and timely help to me while I was writing the text. Besides, I would like to thank Shri N.R. Sharma for typing the manuscript. Finally, I wish to thank the Publishers, Prentice-Hall of India, for the meticulous processing of the manuscript, both during the editorial as well as in the production stages.

Any comments or suggestions for improving the contents would be warmly appreciated.

S.K. MANGAL

Chapter 1

Psychology—Meaning, Nature and Scope

INTRODUCTION

The subject psychology has been becoming increasingly popular day by day. The number of colleges and the students opting for the study of this subject is going up every year in almost all the universities in India. This fast growing subject is an offshoot of Philosophy. With the passage of time, the content of Psychology has acquired a scientific nature and it is no longer based on speculation. The gradual change of this subject from Philosophy to Science has been responsible for the changes in its meaning and concept from time to time as may be evident from the following discussion.

DEFINING PSYCHOLOGY

1. *In terms of the study of the soul.* The earliest attempts at defining psychology owe their origin to the most mysterious and philosophical concept, namely, that of soul. Etymologically, the very word 'psychology' means the study of the soul as it is derived from the two Greek words *psyche*, meaning soul and *logos*, signifying a rational course of study.

2. *In terms of the study of the mind.* What is soul? How can it be studied? The inability to find clear answers to such questions led some ancient Greek philosophers to define psychology as the "study of the mind". Although the word mind was less mysterious and vague than soul, yet it also faced the same questions, namely: What is mind? How can it be studied? Consequently, this definition was also rejected.

3. *In terms of the study of consciousness.* The failure to define the terms soul and mind persuaded the philosophers and psychologists to search for some other suitable definitions.

William James in his book *Principles of Psychology* published in 1890 defined psychology as "the description and explanation of state of consciousness as such".

Wilhelm Wundt (1832–1920) who established the first psychology

1

laboratory at the University of Leipzig, in Germany and his disciple Edward Bradford Titchener also defined psychology as *the science of consciousness.* According to these psychologists, the description and explanation of the states of consciousness is the task of psychology which is usually done by the instrument of 'introspection'—the process of looking within.

This definition was also rejected on the following grounds:

(a) It has a very narrow range on account of its not talking about the subconscious and unconscious activities of the mind.

(b) Being entirely subjective, the introspection method for the study of the conscious activities of the mind was an unscientific method.

(c) It could not include the study of the consciousness of animals.

4. *In terms of the study of behaviour.* From the nineteenth century onwards, with the advent of the modern era of scientific investigation and thought, psychology began to be defined in terms of the study of behaviour.

William McDougall, a British psychologist, was the first to define psychology as the science of behaviour. In his book *Physiological Psychology* published in 1905 he wrote:

Psychology may be best and most comprehensively defined as the positive science of the conduct of living creatures.

Later, in 1908, in his book *Introduction to Social Psychology*, he added the word 'behaviour' to his definition and finally in 1949 in his book *An Outline of Psychology* gave the following meaningful definition:

Psychology is a science which aims to give us better understanding and control of the behaviour of the organism as a whole.

In the same period, Pillsbury (1911) gave the same behavioural definition of the term psychology: "Psychology may be most satisfactorily defined as the Science of human behaviour".

However, in later years, in 1913, J.B. Watson, the father of the behaviourist school, elaborated the concept of the term behaviour including in it both human and animal behaviour and defined psychology as "the science of behaviour" (taking into account human as well as animal behaviour).

Taking clues from the earlier work, contemporary psychologists and various other writers have explained and defined psychology as the science of behaviour using a somewhat different vocabulary.

N.L. Munn (1967) says:

Psychology is a science and the properly trained psychologist is a scientist or at least a practitioner who uses scientific methods and information resulting from scientific investigation.

Similarly, according to Desiderato, Howieson and Jackson (1976):

Psychology can be broadly defined as the investigation of human and animal behaviour and of the mental and physiological processes associated with the behaviour.

Conclusion

The foregoing discussion on the definitions of Psychology clearly shows that the meaning and concept of this subject has changed frequently depending upon whether it was based on philosophical or scientific thinking. Commenting on this aspect, Woodworth (1948) says:

> First psychology lost its soul, then its mind, then it lost its consciousness. It still
> has behaviour of a sort.

Although even at this final stage there seems to be no agreement over a universal definition of Psychology, yet the definitions may be generally viewed in the light of behaviour. It may then be concluded that Psychology is a science of behaviour or a scientific study of behavioural activities and experiences. The questions which remain unanswered at this stage are:

(a) What do we actually mean by the term 'behaviour'?

(b) What is the nature of Psychology? Is it a science? If yes, then what kind of science is it?

Meaning of the Term Behaviour

The term 'behaviour' is taken in its totality, connoting a wide and comprehensive meaning. "Any manifestation of life is activity," says Woodworth (1948), and behaviour is a collective name for these activities. Therefore, the term 'behaviour' includes all the motor or conative activities like walking, swimming, dancing etc.; cognitive activities, e.g., thinking, reasoning, imagining etc., and affective activities like feeling happy, sad, angry, etc.

This includes not only the conscious behaviour and activities of the human mind but also the subconscious and unconscious and hence covers not only the overt but also the covert behaviour involving all inner experiences and mental processes.

It is not limited to the study of human behaviour. The behaviour of animals, insects, birds and even plants also comes within the purview of Psychology. Therefore, when we talk about the study of behaviour in Psychology, we mean the study of behaviour of all living organisms.

In a nutshell then, the term behaviour refers to the entire life activities and experiences of all living organisms.

NATURE OF PSYCHOLOGY

It is an accepted reality that the nature of Psychology is quite scientific. This fact has been properly recognized by eminent psychologists and thinkers as may be inferred from the definitions of Psychology, in terms of the scientific study or science of behaviour, already given. Let us, however, try to analyze why Psychology should be called a science. In general, we may term a subject scientific, if it

1. possesses a body of facts which can be supported through universal laws and principles;

2. emphasizes the search for truth;
3. does not believe in hearsay, stereotypes or superstition;
4. believes in cause and effect relationships;
5. adopts the method of objective investigation, systematic and controlled observation and a scientific approach;
6. stands for the generalization, verifiability and modification of the observed results or deduced phenomena;
7. helps in predicting future developments; and
8. is able to turn its theory into practice by having an applied aspect.

Let us summarize the nature of psychology in the light of the above-mentioned criteria.

1. Psychology possesses a well-organized theory which is supported by the relevant psychological laws and principles.
2. It has its applied aspect in the form of various branches of applied psychology like industrial, legal, clinical and educational psychology.
3. It believes that every behaviour has its roots, and factors causing, influencing or nurturing it.
4. Subjective ideas and opinions are not considered significant in the study of behaviour in psychology. It emphasizes the search for truth by advocating objectivity, reliability and validity in the assessment of behaviour.
5. The methods and techniques employed in the study of behaviour in psychology are quite scientific. Steps like the analysis of behaviour, formulation of hypotheses, objective observations or controlled experimentation, deduction, verification and generalization of the results etc. provide the solid base for the scientific method and approach in psychology.
6. The results of the study of behaviour are always open to verification under similar conditions by other experimenters and observers. These results may be accepted, modified, or altered in the light of the latest data and findings.
7. The established facts, principles and laws of behaviour in Psychology enjoy universal applicability in practical life, in other bodies of knowledge and future researches in its own sphere.
8. An appropriate description and quantification of behaviour is possible through psychology. We may make dependable predictions about the organism in the light of its studied behaviour.

On the basis of the above characteristics, it may be established beyond doubt that Psychology qualifies as a science. Its nature is quite scientific and not philosophical or esoteric as it used to be in the olden days.

What Kind of Science is Psychology?

We can divide all the sciences into two broad categories—the positive and the normative. While physical and life sciences are termed as *positive sciences,* subjects like logic, philosophy and ethics are included in the category of *normative sciences.*

In contrast to normative sciences, positive sciences study facts *as they are* and have little or no concern with what *ought to be.* Psychology in this sense easily falls in the category of positive sciences.

What Kind of Positive Science is Psychology?

The question that arises is: Can we equate Psychology, the science of behaviour with the positive sciences like Physics, Chemistry, Botany, Zoology, Astronomy and Mathematics? The answer lies in the negative. In comparison to these sciences, Psychology is not so perfect and developed a science. In fact, it is a behavioural science which deals with the behaviour of an organism. This behaviour is quite dynamic and unpredictable. Methods of its study are also not as absolute and objective as those adopted by the natural sciences. On the other hand, physical or chemical reactions studied by the natural sciences are always predictable on account of the nature of the material involved and the study processes. As a result, the studies in natural sciences are bound to be more exact, accurate and objective than the studies of behaviour in psychology.

It is, therefore, not correct to place Psychology in the same category as the physical and natural sciences. Although constant efforts are being made to make its techniques and approach as objective, exact and accurate as possible, Psychology has not yet attained the position and status of these sciences. Thus it may, in the true sense of the term, be called a developing positive science rather than a developed positive science. Hence, in the ultimate analysis, for understanding the nature and meaning of the subject, we can define psychology as a *developing positive science of behaviour.*

SCOPE OF PSYCHOLOGY

The scope of a subject can usually be discussed under two heads:

1. The limits of its operations and applications.
2. The branches, topics and the subject matter it deals with.

The field of operation and applications of psychology are too wide. It studies, describes and explains the behaviour of living organisms. Here the terms 'behaviour' and 'living organism' carry unusually wide meanings. Behaviour is used to include all types of life activities and experiences—whether conative, cognitive or affective, implicit or explicit, conscious, subconscious or unconscious of a living organism. Also, the term living organism is employed to include all living creatures inhabiting the earth irrespective of species, caste, colour, age, sex, mental or physical state. Thus, the normal, the abnormal, the young and the old belonging to different stock, spheres and walks of human life are all studied by this science. Moreover, studies in psychology are not confined to human behaviour alone but they also encompass the behaviour of animals, insects, birds and even plants.

In this way, wherever life exists and there are living organisms, Psychology may be needed for the study of their activities and experiences. We know that the living organisms as well as their life activities are countless and no limit can, therefore, be imposed upon the fields of operation and application of Psychology.

BRANCHES AND FIELDS OF PSYCHOLOGY

For the sake of convenience and specialised study psychology may be divided into different branches. First, we divide it into two broad categories, namely, Pure Psychology and Applied Psychology.

Pure psychology provides the framework and theory of the subject. Its contents deal with the formulation of psychological principles and theories and it also suggests various methods and techniques for the analysis, assessment, modification and improvement of behaviour.

In applied psychology, the theory generated or enunciated through pure psychology finds it practical expression. Here we discuss the application of psychological rules, principles, theories and techniques with reference to real-life situations.

The above-mentioned pure and applied aspects of psychology can be further grouped into various branches. Let us first consider some of the branches of pure psychology.

BRANCHES OF PURE PSYCHOLOGY

General Psychology

This is a relatively large field of psychology which deals with the fundamental rules, principles and theories of Psychology in relation to the study of behaviour of normal adult human beings.

Abnormal Psychology

This is the branch of psychology which describes and explains the behaviour of abnormal people in relation to their environment. The causes, symptoms and syndromes, description and treatment of the abnormalities of behaviour form the subject matter of this branch.

Social Psychology

This branch of psychology deals with group behaviour and inter-relationships of people among themselves. Group dynamics, likes and dislikes, interests and attitudes, social distance and prejudices of the people in their personal and social relationships are studied by this branch.

Experimental Psychology

This branch of psychology describes and explains the ways and means of carrying out psychological experiments along scientific lines under controlled or laboratory situations for the study of mental processes and behaviour. It takes up animals, birds and human beings as the subjects of these experiments.

Physiological Psychology

This branch of psychology describes and explains the biological and physio-logical basis of behaviour. The internal environment and physiological structure of the body, particularly the brain, nervous system, and functioning of the glands in relation to the conative, cognitive and affective behaviour of human beings comprise its subject matter.

Parapsychology

This new branch of psychology deals with extra-sensory perception, precognition, cases of claimed rebirth, telepathy and allied phenomena.

Geopsychology

This branch or field of psychology describes and explains the relation of physical environment, particularly weather, climate, soil, and landscape with behaviour.

Developmental Psychology

This branch or field of psychology describes and explains the processes and products of growth and development in relation to the behaviour of an individual from birth to old age. For added convenience, it is further sub-divided into branches such as Child Psychology, Adolescent Psychology and Adult Psychology.

BRANCHES OF APPLIED PSYCHOLOGY

Educational Psychology

This is the branch of applied psychology which seeks to apply the psychological principles, theories and techniques to human behaviour in educational situations. The subject matter of this branch covers psychological ways and means of improving all aspects of the teaching–learning process including the learner, the learning process, learning material, learning environment and the teacher.

Clinical Psychology

This branch of applied psychology describes and explains the causes of mental illness or abnormal behaviour of a patient attending a clinic or hospital and suggests individual or group therapy for the treatment and effective adjustment of the affected person in society.

Industrial Psychology

This branch of applied psychology seeks application of the psychological principles, theories and techniques for the study of human behaviour in relation to the industrial environment. It studies the topics and the ways and means of ascertaining the tastes and interests of consumers, advertising and sale of products, selection, training and placement of personnel, solution of labour problems, establishment of harmonious relations between the employers and the employees, strengthening the morale of the workers and increasing production etc.

Legal Psychology

It is the branch of applied psychology which studies the behaviour of clients, criminals, witnesses etc. in their respective surroundings with the application of psychological principles and techniques. It contains the subject matter for improving the ways and means of detection of crimes, identification and apprehension of false witnesses and other complex issues. The root causes of any crime, offence, dispute or legal case can be properly understood through the use of this branch of psychology and subsequently proper corrective and rehabilitative measures can be decided upon.

Military Psychology

This branch of psychology is concerned with the use of psychological principles and techniques in the field of military activities. How to maintain the morale of the soldiers and citizens during wartime, how to fight the enemy's propaganda and intelligence activities, how to secure recruitment of better personnel for the armed forces, and how to improve the fighting capabilities and organizational climate and leadership in the armed forces are some of the various topics that are dealt with by this branch of psychology.

Political Psychology

This branch of psychology deals with the use of psychological principles and techniques in studying politics and deriving political gains. The knowledge of the dynamics of group behaviour, judgment of public opinion, qualities of leadership, psychology of propaganda and suggestion, the art of diplomacy etc. are some of the key concepts that find place in the subject matter of Political Psychology.

In short, Psychology, by studying, explaining and understanding behaviour has proved quite useful in many walks of our life. Its use and scope in our daily life are varied. For instance, it has

1. contributed significantly to the improvement of the processes and products of education;
2. highlighted the importance of good behaviour to the patients, removed a lot of superstitions and provided valuable therapies in the field of medicines;
3. underlined the importance of the knowledge of consumer psychology and harmonious inter-personal relationship in the field of commerce and industry;
4. helped in detection of crime and dealing with criminals;

5. proved useful to the leaders and the politicians in developing qualities of leadership for leading the masses;
6. provided valuable help in relation to guidance and educational, personal as well as vocational counselling;
7. contributed substantially in the field of military science for improving the resources and operations; and
8. finally, it has helped human beings to learn the art of understanding their own behaviour, seeking adjustment with themselves and with others, and enhancing as well as actualizing their potentialities to the full.

SUMMARY

Psychology, defined first in its history of evolution as the study of the soul has been known progressively as the study of the mind, study of consciousness and finally as the study of behaviour. Today, it is considered as the science of behaviour in its comprehensive meaning and covering all types of behaviour of all living organisms.

Psychology is quite scientific in nature. It believes in the relationship of cause and effect, uses observation, experimentation and other scientific methods for its study, possesses a universally accepted body of facts and believes in modification and alterations in its principles through future researches and findings. It is, however, not as perfect and developed a science as the other natural and physical sciences. In fact, it is a developing behavioural science which is in the process of becoming as objective, exact and accurate as possible to come on par with the developed sciences. Therefore, it is termed as a *developing positive science of behaviour.*

The scope of psychology is very wide. It studies, describes and explains the behaviour of all living organisms. As living organisms and their life activities are countless, no limit can be imposed upon the scope of this subject. It has many branches and fields of study, like General Psychology, Abnormal Psychology, Social Psychology, Experimental Psychology, Physiological Psychology, Para-psychology, Geo-psychology, Developmental Psychology, Clinical Psychology, Industrial Psychology, Legal Psychology, Military Psychology, Political Psychology and so on.

REFERENCES

Desiderato Otells, Howieson, D.B. and Jackson, J.H., *Investigating Behaviour— Principles of Psychology*, New York: Harper & Row, 1976, p. 5.

James, W., *Principles of Psychology*, 2 vols., New York: Henry Holt, 1890.

————, *Psychology*, New York: Collier, 1962.

McDougall, W., *Psychology—The study of behaviour*, New York: Henry Holt, 1912.

————, *An Outline of Psychology*, 13th ed., London: Methuen, 1949, p. 38.

Munn, N.L., *Introduction to Psychology*, Delhi: 1967.

Pillsbury, W.B., *Essentials of Psychology*, New York: Macmillan, 1911.

Watson, J.B., Psychology as a behaviourist views it, *Psycho. rev.*, vol. 20, 1913.

————, *Psychology from the Stand-point of a behaviourist*, Philadelphia: J.B. Lippincott, 1919.

————, *Behaviourism*, London: Kegan Paul, 1930.

Woodworth, R.S., *Psychology*, London: Methuen, 1945.

————, *Contemporary Schools of Psychology*, London: Methuen, 1948.

SUGGESTED READINGS

Guildford, J.B. (Ed.), *Fields of Psychology*, New York: Van Nostrand, 1966.

Keller, F.S., *The Definitions of Psychology*, New York: Appleton Century, 1937.

Chapter 2

Educational Psychology— Meaning, Nature and Scope

WHAT IS EDUCATIONAL PSYCHOLOGY?

As already discussed, Educational Psychology is one of the many branches of Psychology dealing mainly with the problems, processes and products of education. It is an attempt to apply the knowledge of psychology in the field of education. Here we try to study human behaviour, particularly the behaviour of the learner in relation to his educational environment. In other words, Educational Psychology may be defined as that branch of psychology which studies the behaviour of the learner in relation to his educational needs and his environment. Educational Psychology has been defined by various psychologists and scholars. For the sake of understanding what educational psychology is, let us analyze a few important definitions.

Skinner (1958):

> Educational psychology is that branch of psychology which deals with teaching and learning.

Crow and Crow (1973):

> Educational psychology describes and explains the learning experiences of an individual from birth through old age.

Peel (1956):

> Educational psychology is the science of education.

The definition given by Skinner considers Educational Psychology to be the psychology of teaching and learning, i.e. psychology applied in the field of education for improving the methods and products of the teaching–learning process. Education in its applied form is centred around the process of teaching and learning and it is this which helps the teacher in better teaching and the learner in better learning.

The definition given by L.D. Crow and Alice Crow describes Educational Psychology as that subject area of the curriculum through which one can study the development of an individual in terms of his learning achievement during his life-span. How he goes on learning as a result of interaction with his environment and how he can learn effectively is covered by Educational Psychology.

Learning, however, on account of its close association with experience, often said to be a great teacher, is never independent of teaching. Therefore, what we find in the process of development is nothing but a planned spontaneous scheme of teaching and learning. All our efforts and energies in the field of education are directed to planning and devising the appropriate means of better teaching and effective learning. Educational Psychology is mainly meant for solving the practical problems related to the field of education, especially the process of teaching and learning.

It is these considerations which led E.A. Peel to define and describe Educational Psychology as the science of education, i.e. a discipline which can be used to improve the processes and products of education in a scientific way. Let us now briefly analyse the definition given by Peel.

IS EDUCATIONAL PSYCHOLOGY A SCIENCE OF EDUCATION?

Science and technology have made it possible for us to carry out all our tasks efficiently, effectively and speedily. With the help of minimum input in terms of labour, energy and time, science helps us to derive maximum output in terms of the quality and quantity of the finished products or outcomes. Science and technology have thus made our life quite comfortable.

Let us try to evaluate educational psychology against this criterion. What role can it play in the field of education? Does it help the persons connected with the task of arranging and providing education or getting the fruits of education in the same way as science and technology help those connected with other tasks in our day-to-day life? Surely it does. It helps in realizing the objectives of education in a better way. Education aims at shaping the behaviour of the students in a desirable way and bringing about all-round development in their personality. The task is carried out through the process of formal or informal teaching and learning. Educational psychology comes in here for planning the process of teaching and learning by adopting the scientific principle of minimum input for maximum output. As a result, with the help of Educational Psychology, a teacher can teach effectively by making minimum use of his energy in terms of time and labour; similarly, the students can learn effectively by spending less of their time and effort.

Educational Psychology thus helps to carry out the processes and produce the results of education. It supplies the necessary knowledge and skills, especially for the teacher, to realize the objectives of education. It equips the teacher by supplying the essential scientific skills, technological expertise and advice in moulding and shaping the behaviour of his students for the desirable all-round development of their personality much in the same way as the persons connected with the actual construction of a bridge are helped by an engineer or mechanic equipped with the essential civil, mechanical or electrical technology. Educational

Psychology thus plays the same role as other sciences or technology in helping the teachers and other persons connected with the building of the future of the youngsters in their charge. Thus we are justified in describing Educational Psychology as the science and technology of education.

NATURE OF EDUCATIONAL PSYCHOLOGY

In the foregoing discussion, we have substantiated Peel's definition of Educational Psychology as the science of education, and established beyond doubt that the nature of Educational Psychology is nothing but scientific.

Moreover, in discussing the nature of Psychology, we have clearly shown that the basic nature of the subject is scientific. Since Educational Psychology is an offshoot and part and parcel of Psychology, its nature cannot be different from the main subject. The following points further confirm the nature of Educational Psychology as scientific.

1. Educational Psychology possesses a well-organized, systematic and universally accepted body of facts supported by the relevant psychological laws and principles.

2. It is constantly in search of the truth, i.e. studying the behaviour of the learner in relation to his educational environment. Moreover, the findings of such study are never taken as absolute and permanent. The results of any study in Educational Psychology can be challenged and are modified or altered in terms of the latest explanations and findings.

3. It employs scientific methods and adopts a scientific approach for studying the learner's behaviour. Setting of hypotheses, objective observation, controlled experimentation, clinical investigation, and generalization based on adequate similar evidences provide enough reasons for its studies to be termed scientific.

4. The processes and products of these studies are sufficiently scientific as a high degree of logical viability, objectivity, reliability and validity is maintained in carrying out the study and research in the field of Educational Psychology.

5. Educational Psychology does not accept hearsay and does not take anything for granted. It emphasizes that essentially there is some definite cause linked with a behaviour and the causes of this behaviour are not related to supernatural phenomena.

6. Educational Psychology is mostly concerned with the 'what' and the 'why' of happenings in the present instead of caring for the past. Therefore, in its study, it focuses attention on problems like the present behaviour of the learner, the causes of such behaviour, and the repercussions if it were to continue unchanged.

7. It is a positive science rather than a normative science and like the sciences, it does not concern itself with values and ideals. Therefore, instead of answering questions like "what ought to be", e.g. why education should be provided and what type of education is to be provided to the children, youth or adults, it focuses attention on

providing the key to the 'how', 'when' and 'where' of education for proving its worth as a science and technology.

8. The generalizations arrived at and conclusions reached through the study of Educational Psychology are sufficiently reliable and thus like the sciences, these can be used for predictions of behaviour in similar situations. R.B. Cattell, the modern psychologist, believed so much in the predictable quality of these studies that he persisted in defining personality as the attribute which permits a prediction of what a person will do in a given situation.

This discussion shows that Educational Psychology is sufficiently scientific. As compared to the natural sciences like physics, chemistry and biology, and applied sciences like engineering and medicine, it is not so perfect and developed a science. In fact, it is an applied behavioural science, which deals with the behaviour of the learner in the educational environment. Since the learner's behaviour is dynamic and unpredictable, and the methods of its study are also not absolute and objective, educational psychology cannot claim the status of a developed positive science like other natural or applied sciences. Although we accept its nature as quite scientific, yet we cannot term it as a developed positive science and have to satisfy ourselves with saying that it is a developing positive science of the learner's behaviour.

SCOPE OF EDUCATIONAL PSYCHOLOGY

Educational Psychology is the science of education which mainly deals with the problems of teaching and learning and helps the teacher in his task of modifying the learner's behaviour and bringing about an all-round development of his personality. Therefore, while in psychology the scope of study and the field of operation are extended to cover the behaviour of all living organisms related to all their life activities, in Educational Psychology, the scope of such behavioural study has to be limited within the confines of the teaching-learning process, i.e. studying the behaviour of the learners in relation to their educational environment, specifically for the satisfaction of their educational needs and the all-round development of their personality. Specifically, thus, the subject matter of Educational Psychology must be centred around the process of teaching and learning for enabling the teacher and learners to do their jobs as satisfactorily as possible.

Let us first see the different issues that may be involved in an ongoing teaching-learning process. For improving the processes and products of the system related to teaching and learning, we will have to improve all the ingredients of this phenomenon. For this purpose, the basic questions involved in the teaching-learning process must be satisfactorily attended to:

Who is being taught or educated?

By whom is he to be taught or educated?

Why is education to be provided to the child or what are the values or objectives that are to be aimed at through the teaching-learning process?

What is to be taught or what learning experience is to be imparted to the learner for achieving the desired educational objectives?

How, when and where should these learning experiences be satisfactorily provided to the learner for achieving the desired educational objectives?

Educational Psychology seeks to provide satisfactory solutions and answers to all the questions raised above except the why of education as this is purely the concern of Educational Philosophy, a matter to be decided by society or the government. Therefore, all texts of Educational Psychology, are loaded with material related to the other six basic questions. Let us try to clarify and answer them.

Who is being Educated?

The individuality and personality of the learner must be known before he is taught or subjected to behaviour modification. Therefore, topics and contents like the following which are helpful in exploring the individuality of the learner are to be included in the study of Educational Psychology:

The process and pattern of growth and development during different stages of an individual's life, his instincts and other innate abilities, the learned and acquired abilities, individual differences in terms of abilities and capacities and their measures such as the extent of interests, aptitudes, attitudes, intelligence, creativity are also important for personality appraisal.

By Whom is the Learner to be Taught

In order to achieve the desired success in any teaching–learning process, the role of the teacher can never be minimized. In fact, much depends on the competency and capability of the teacher for carrying out the desired task. Not everybody can be entrusted with the crucial task of behaviour modification and personality development of a number of children studying in a class or school. One has to make oneself capable by equipping oneself for it. For this purpose, the teacher himself must be acquainted with his own self, the expectations from him in terms of personality, characteristics, role playing and work habits. Consequently, he is required to pay attention to the following aspects which have been included in a text of educational psychology:

1. Personality traits and characteristics of good teachers
2. Duties and responsibilities of a teacher
3. Measures for knowing and doing away with his own conflicts, anxiety and tension
4. Teacher's motivation, level of aspiration, adjustment and mental health.

What is to be Taught?

Whereas the aims and objectives of providing education to the children at one or the other developmental stage are decided by Educational Philosophy depending on the needs and wishes of the society or government, Educational Psychology plays its role in deciding the type of learning experiences suitable for the children at each developmental stage by keeping in view the differences in their potentialities. The subject matter of Educational psychology thus definitely covers the topics helpful in suggesting principles, methods and techniques for the selection of the learning experiences appropriate to each developmental stage of the children. It enunciates how to organize the contents or topics gradewise for giving them the shape of a syllabus or curriculum. How to cater for the individual differences and individuality of the children in framing the syllabi or curricula is also taken care of by educational psychology. The subject tries to encompass the essential knowledge and skills for equipping the teachers to plan, select and arrange learning experiences to the children suitable for their age, grade and also meeting their specific individual potentialities.

How are the Learning Experiences to be Provided?

Who is being taught, and what is to be taught and for what purpose? After answering these questions another question which arises is, how should the child be given the learning experiences planned for different stages of his growth? In other words, what is to be done for the proper and effective communication between the teacher and the taught? What should be the appropriate methods and techniques of imparting education to the children? How can children be helped in the acquisition of useful learning experiences for the desirable modification in their behaviour and appropriate development of their personality? Educational Psychology tries to provide satisfactory solutions for all these questions by including relevant topics such as the following:

1. Nature, laws and theories of learning
2. Remembering and forgetting
3. Means of effective learning and memorization
4. Transfer of learning or training
5. Sensation and perception
6. Concept formation
7. Interest and attitude formation thinking, reasoning and problem solving behaviour etc.

When and Where are the Learning Experiences to be Provided?

Every time and place or environmental situation is not suitable for a particular piece of instruction or the sharing of a learning experience. The effectiveness of a teaching-learning programme depends largely on the suitability of the teaching-learning situations in terms of time, place and other environmental factors. Educational psychology helps the teacher and the learners to understand the suitability and appropriateness of a teaching-learning situation for the effective realization of the teaching-learning objectives. It also helps them to modify the teaching-learning situation to achieve the desired results by giving place in its study to topics such as the following:

1. Classroom climate
2. Institutional/organizational climate
3. Individual, self, supervised and group study
4. Factors affecting attention
5. Role of rewards and punishment

6. Group behaviour and group dynamics
7. Guidance and counselling.

In the discussion so far, we have tried to outline the general scope of Educational Psychology. However, the scope of a fast growing subject like Educational Psychology cannot be limited in such a way. Educational Psychology being a science of education has to supply the necessary knowledge and skills for carrying out all the tasks of education. Education cannot be static and fixed or unchanging as it has to be planned according to the changing circumstances and needs of a particular society or nation. To meet the emerging problems and demands in the field of education, Educational Psychology has to work hard to keep evolving new concepts, principles and techniques. The subject matter of Educational Psychology as also its field of operation is, therefore, expanding day by day and in view of this, it is not possible to limit the scope of this subject. It would, in fact, be unwise to do so. Such a step would not only hamper the progress of this fast growing and developing science of behaviour but would also hinder the realization of the objectives of education. Hence, it is only right not to strictly define the scope of Educational psychology so as to leave the way open for its further expansion and declare it as having no limits to effectively fulfil the aims and objectives of education.

SUMMARY

Educational psychology as one of the branches of psychology tries to study the behaviour of the learner in relation to his educational environment. It has been variously defined. Most of the definitions centre around the fact that educational psychology as a specialized branch of psychology concerns itself with suggesting ways and means of improving the processes and products of education, enabling the teachers to teach effectively and the learners to learn effectively by putting in the minimum effort. It is thus designated as the science of education. It has simplified the tasks and improved the efficiency of the teacher or all those connected with the processes and products of education by supplying them with the essential knowledge and skills in much the same way as science and technology has helped in making possible maximum output through minimum input in terms of time and labour in our day to day activities.

The nature of educational psychology is regarded as scientific because like the sciences, it possesses a well organized, systematic and universally accepted body of facts; remains constantly in search of truth through research and experimentation; employs scientific methods in its study, and the results of its study are subject to further verification and modification.

However, as it is not so perfect a science as the natural and applied sciences, it is defined as a developing positive science of the learners' behaviour.

The scope of Educational Psychology is both limited and extensive. It is limited in the sense that Educational Psychology must concern itself only with the study of the behaviour of the learner in the educational environment. It must include the topics and contents which are specifically meant for improving the processes and products of education mainly centred around the teaching-learning process. As a result, its study has to include only those topics and subject material which help in

1. knowing the learner;
2. enabling the teacher to know his self, his strengths and limitations and to acquire essential teacher-like traits;
3. selection and organization of proper learning experiences suited to the individuality and developmental stages of the learner;
4. suggesting suitable methods and techniques for providing the desired learning experiences; and
5. in arranging proper learning situations.

However, its scope may be considered extensive in the sense that all that is needed for providing solutions to the problems and demands of our educational system must find place in the study of Educational Psychology. Since the problems and demands are unending and the process of education is dynamic, we cannot expect rigidity in terms of a strict delineation and definition of the scope of Educational Psychology. It needs to be left unfettered for the inclusion of what is needed in it for better serving the cause of education.

REFERENCES

Cattell, R.B., Quoted by C.S. Hall and G. Lindzey, *Theories of Personality*, New York: Wiley, 1970, p. 386.

Crow, L.D. and Alice Crow, *Educational Psychology*, New Delhi: Eurasia Publishing House, 1973, p. 7.

Peel, E.A., *The Psychological Basis of Education*, London: Oliver and Boyd, 1956, p. 8.

Skinner, C.E. (Ed.), *Essentials of Educational Psychology*, Englewood Cliffs, New Jersey: Prentice-Hall, 1958, p. 1.

SUGGESTED READINGS

Bigge, M.L. and Hunt, M.P., *Psychological Foundation of Education*, New York: Harper & Row, 1968.

Cronbach, L.J., *Educational Psychology*, New York: American Book Co., 1948.

Gates, A.I., et al., *Educational Psychology*, 3rd ed., New York: Macmillan, 1948.

George, J. Mouley, *Psychology of Effective Teaching*, New York: Holt, Rinehart and Winston, 1968.

Morris, E. Eson, *Psychological Foundation of Education*, New York: Holt, Rinehart and Winston, 1972.

Smith, M. Daniel, *Educational Psychology*, New York: Allyn & Bacon, 1978.

Sorenson, H., *Psychology in Education*, New York: McGraw-Hill, 1964.

Stephens, J.M., *Educational Psychology*, New York: Holt, Rinehart and Winston, 1956.

Travers, R.M., *Educational Psychology*, New York: Macmillan, 1973.

Chapter 3

Methods of Educational Psychology

INTRODUCTION

Educational Psychology is the scientific study of the behaviour of the learner in relation to his educational environment. Behaviour in all its aspects can be studied scientifically through a single technique or approach known as *observation*. This leads us to the simple conclusion that observation may be regarded as the only method or technique for conducting studies of behaviour. This single technique or approach, however, gives rise to several methods or approaches, depending upon the conditions in which observations have to be recorded, the procedure adopted and tools used. We shall discuss this aspect now.

1. Observation of one's own behaviour by looking within or looking inward may be adopted as one of the approaches. Such an approach is known as the method of *introspection.*
2. Sometimes behavioural events are observed and recorded under natural conditions by some person or persons. Such observation approach is termed as *naturalistic observation* or simply as *observation.*
3. Observation and recording of behavioural events under controlled conditions is known as *experimentation.*
4. When these are conducted outside the laboratories in real-life settings by adopting the survey technique, the method is named as the *normative survey method* or the *field survey method.*
5. In case the observation is made through recording a case history, i.e. reconstruction of an individual's biography, the approach may be termed as the *case study* or *case history method,* and if we use psychoanalysis for interpreting the behaviour of a person through the expression of his unconscious behaviour then the method may be termed as the *psychoanalytic method.*
6. If the case history material and process of psychoanalysis is used for the diagnosis and treatment of the behavioural problems, the method is termed as the *clinical method.*
7. In the situation where physical devices are used to observe and measure psychological experiences, the approach may be termed as the *psycho-physical method.*

The various modes of observations may thus give rise to a number of methods and approaches like introspection, naturalistic observation, experimentation, normative survey or field survey, psychoanalytic, clinical and psychophysical methods. Let us discuss all these approaches that help us to investigate the behaviour of a learner.

INTROSPECTION METHOD

This is the oldest known method for the study of behaviour. In the early days of the evolution of Psychology, behaviour was studied only through a kind of self-examination of inner observation called *introspection*.

The word 'introspection' is made up of two Latin words, *intro* meaning "within" or "inward", and *spiere,* meaning to "look". Hence, introspection means looking within or looking inward. In introspection, then, one is required to get inside one's own mind. It is a sort of self-observation in which one perceives, analyses and reports one's own feelings and, in fact, everything that takes place in one's mind during the course of a mental act. For example, when in a state of anxiety, fear or anger, one may be asked to determine by one's own observation what one sensed, thought or felt at the time of experiencing that emotion.

Merits

Introspection—the observation and reporting of one's own mental processes—is considered important on account of its unique nature. It is a simple and readily available method. One's mental processes are always present and can be introspected at any time. Introspection is, therefore, able to give us a direct and immediate insight into one's own mental processes without involving any extra expenditure of material or apparatus. Moreover, introspection provides adequate knowledge of the inner or covert experiences and thus the inner behaviour of an individual in the form of thought or feeling can be revealed through introspection.

Drawbacks and Limitations

Introspection as a method of studying behaviour, however, suffers from some serious drawbacks and limitations:

1. In introspection one needs to observe or examine one's mental processes carefully in the form of thoughts, feelings and sensations. The state of one's mental processes is continuously changing. Therefore, when one concentrates on introspecting a particular phase of one's mental activity that phase passes off. For example, when one gets angry at something and afterwards sits down to introspect calmly or to self-examine, the state of anger is sure to have passed off and so what one tries to observe is not what is happening at that time with oneself but what had happened some time before.

2. Introspection as a method of serious study lacks in reliability, validity and objectivity for the following reasons:

(a) The results lack reliable communicability and repeatability because any one investigator can never be sure that what he feels or senses is the same as is experienced by other investigators. If we invite introspection reports on the nature of the sensation of green for example, these reports are bound to differ. Some will insist that green is a unitary sensation, whereas others may say that green is a mixed sensation involving yellow and blue. We have no means for the objective observation of the introspection phenomenon. Moreover, in introspection one studies one's own behaviour or mental process. It is not possible, to verify self-observation as one's own mind cannot be studied by others in introspection.

(b) It is next to impossible to acquire validity and exactness in self-observation or examination of one's own mental process. The mind in perceiving its own functions tries to divide itself into two halves—the subject and the object. The object of observation and the instrument of observation are of course one and the same. This automatically affects the validity and exactness of the observation process and the perceived results. A man who is angry or afraid cannot observe exactly what is going on in his mind and remain unchanged in his emotional state of anger or fear. The consciousness on his part is sure to affect his mental or emotional state which is the object of observation.

3. The scope of introspection as a method of studying behaviour is rather limited. It can only be applied satisfactorily in the case of adult normal human beings. The behaviour of children, abnormal human beings, animals etc., cannot be studied by this method.

Conclusion

Thus, if we try to evaluate the introspection method, we find that it is based on self-speculation, lacks reliable communicability, replicability and reasonable exactness or precision. It is neither sufficiently scientific, practicable nor simple enough to handle. It cannot therefore be taken as an adequate or sufficient single method for psychological studies. The conclusions arrived at by this method need to be supported by specific scientific findings through some other objective and reliable method.

OBSERVATION METHOD

Observation as a method of studying behaviour consists of the perception of an individual's behaviour under natural conditions by other individuals and the interpretation and analysis of this perceived behaviour by them. It is thus essentially a way of 'perceiving the behaviour as it is'. By this method we can infer the mental processes of others through observation of their external behaviour. In fact, it is an indirect approach to the study of the mental process. If some one frowns, howls, grinds his teeth, closes his fists, by observing the external signs of his behaviour, we can say that he is angry. But to study this behaviour concerning anger in natural conditions, one has to wait for the event to occur. Similarly, to study the behaviour of students in a crowd or during a strike, and the behaviour of a delinquent or problem child, the psychologist has to wait till the particular behaviour occurs and then use all his resources to observe, record, analyse and interpret the behaviour from what he has perceived under natural conditions.

Merits

The observation method occupies a prominent place in the study of human behaviour. It is natural, flexible and economical. Its results are reliable and can be verified. The natural observation method is particularly suitable for studying the developmental characteristics of individual children's habits, interests and other personality traits. For example, the effects of the absence of one or both parents on a child's development can be determined properly through observation of his development. Similarly, a clinical psychologist may be able to collect the required data about the abnormal behaviour of an individual by observing him under natural conditions of his day to day life.

Drawbacks and Limitations

The observation method cannot be termed as sufficiently objective, reliable and valid for the following reasons:

1. It can prove useful only for collecting data on the observable behaviour of an individual. It is impossible, to observe what is happening in the mind of others, and so reasoning can only be through external behaviour. It is possible that a person may be expert at hiding his feelings and emotions and disguising his evil nature under the cover of artificial sobriety. In such cases the method of observation fails to judge the true nature of the individual concerned.

2. Subjectivity factors on the part of the investigator as well as in the process of observation also affect the results of observation. There may be distortions of observable factors depending upon the observer's degree of care in observation. His interests, values, and prejudices may also distort the contents and results of the observation. He may lay extra emphasis on one part of one's behaviour and may altogether neglect some other very important aspect. The interpretations of the recorded events may also be similarly coloured. One may read one's own thoughts, feelings and tendencies into others' minds. The lacunae resulting from such subjectivity may, however, be corrected to a certain extent by having as many observers as possible for observing the same phenomenon and employing scientific instruments such as a tape recorder, or a video camera etc., for recording the events.

3. Another serious limitation of the observation method is that the behaviour observed is dependent on the time and place and on the individual or group of people involved. It lacks replicability as each natural situation can occur only once.

4. Another important limitation of the observation method lies in its inability to establish a proper cause and effect relationship. If two phenomena, say poverty and delinquent behaviour, invariably occur together, it cannot be established that poverty is the sufficient and necessary cause of delinquent behaviour or vice versa.

EXPERIMENTAL METHOD

The experimental method is considered the most scientific and objective method of studying behaviour. It lays emphasis on performing experiments. The word 'experiment' comes from a Latin word experimentum meaning 'a trial' or 'test'. Therefore, in experimentation we try or put to the test the material or phenomenon whose characteristics or consequences which we wish to ascertain. In the sciences, while conducting such experiments in the laboratory or outside in a natural environment we may want to learn the effect of friction on motion, the effect of sunlight on growth of plants, etc. In educational psychology also, we perform such experiments in the psychological laboratory, class-rooms or outside the class-rooms in physical or social settings to study the cause and effect relationship regarding the nature of human behaviour, i.e. the effect of anxiety, drugs or stresses on human behaviour, the effect of intelligence, or participation in co-curricular activities, on the academic performance of students, etc. In performing all such experiments we try to establish certain cause and effect relationships through objective observations of the actions performed and the subsequent changes produced under pre-arranged or rigidly controlled conditions. From these observations certain conclusions are drawn and theories or principles are formulated. The essential features of the experimental method are:

1. Experiments performed in this method essentially require two persons, the experimenter and the subject or the person whose behaviour is to be observed.
2. These experiments are always conducted on living organisms in contrast to experiments in the physical sciences which are generally conducted on inorganic or dead subjects.
3. The key factor in this method is the control of the conditions or variables. By this control we can eliminate irrelevant conditions or variables and isolate the relevant ones. We thus become able to observe the causal relationship between two phenomena, keeping all other conditions almost constant. For example, if we try to study the effect of intelligence on academic achievement by the experimental method, we will need to determine the causative relation between the two phenomena (variables)—intelligence, and academic achievement. One of these variables, the effect of which we want to study, will be called the *independent variable* and the other the *dependent variable*. Thus the independent variable stands for the cause, and the dependent variable is the effect of that cause. Other conditions like study habits, sex, socio-economic conditions, parental education, home environment, health, past learning, memory, etc., which exercise a good impact upon

one's achievement besides one's intelligence are termed *intervening variables*. In experimentation, all such intervening variables are to be controlled, i.e. they are to be made constant or equalized and the effect of only one independent variable, e.g. intelligence in the present case, on one or more dependent variables is studied. For this we try to change and vary the independent variable. This brings about concomitant changes in the dependent variable or variables. These changes are objectively observed and measured on the basis of which certain conclusions are reached.

As already emphasized, in the experimental method experiments can be performed in the psychological laboratory or in the class-rooms or outside the class-rooms under rigidly controlled conditions. Let us discuss how these experiments are performed.

Experiments in the Laboratory Set-up

Just like other physical or natural sciences, experiments can be performed in Psychology or Educational Psychology for studying the behaviour in the actual laboratory set-up. Thorndike's experiments on cats, Pavlov's experiments on dogs, Skinner's experiments on rats and pigeons and similar other experiments to study the behaviour related to learning, transfer of learning, memory, attention, perception etc., are all examples of such laboratory experiments. Let us illustrate the process of conducting these experiments with an example.

Title: Effect of knowledge of results on performance.

Name of the subject: Sex and Age: Education:
Date and Time: Name of the experimenter:

Hypothesis: The knowledge of results acts as an incentive or motivating force for improvement in performance.

Apparatus and material: A sheet of white paper, a ruler and a pencil.

Plan of the study: The study involves the task of drawing a straight line of a certain length, say 12 cm, on a sheet of white paper with the following details:

1. Telling the subject about the measurement of the line he draws after each trial.
2. Not informing or letting him know the results of his performance.

Instructions: The subject will be provided with detailed instructions for conducting the experiment.

TABLE 3.1   Observation Record

Length of line drawn in centimetres without and with the knowledge of results.

Trial Nos.	1	2	3	4	5	6	7	8	9	10
Without knowledge of results (WKR)	10.1	9.8	10.4	11.3	11.8	12.5	10.4	10.8	11.4	12.7
With knowledge of results (WR)	10.2	11.5	11.8	12.8	12.6	11.9	12.2	12.0	12.2	12.1

TABLE 3.2   Interpretation of Results

Error or difference from actual length in centimetres under two conditions.

Trial Nos.	1	2	3	4	5	6	7	8	9	10	Total
Difference from actual length (under WKR)	1.9	2.2	1.6	0.9	0.2	0.5	1.6	1.2	0.6	0.7	11.4
Difference from actual length (under WR)	1.8	0.5	0.2	0.8	0.6	0.1	0.2	0.0	0.2	0.1	4.5

It may be seen that the total difference from actual length estimated by the subject under the first condition (without knowledge of results) during the first ten trials is much higher than that estimated under the second condition (with knowledge of results). Whereas it is 11.4 cm in the former case, it is only 4.5 cm in the latter. It can easily be inferred from the above findings that there is a definite improvement in the performance of the subject through feed-back, i.e. the knowledge of results.

Experiments Outside the Laboratory Set-up

In Educational Psychology, experiments can also be conducted without involving the usual psychological laboratory set up. However, for such studies, there is need of some specific experimental designs for controlling the variables and measuring their effects. A few of such designs are:

1. *The control test or single-group design.*   In these designs it is not necessary to have two different individuals or groups of subjects for the experiment. Here a single individual or group of individuals can work as the subject for the experiment. The subject, whether an individual or a group of individuals, is first objectively observed under normal conditions and then under different sets of changed conditions. Conclusions are then drawn by comparing the differences. Suppose we wish to study the effect of the fear stimulus. In the psychological laboratory, all necessary arrangements of instruments and material necessary for the study of the fear responses of the subject in the form of changes in respiration, pulse and heart-beat, blood pressure, functioning of the digestive and other internal systems, facial expression etc., will be made. The initial readings regarding all these functions under normal conditions when there is no fear stimulus present will be taken from the related instruments. The subject will then be exposed to sudden fear stimuli like a snake, a loud noise, darkness etc., and then the changes in the readings as a result of the intensity of fear responses will be recorded from the various instruments. The difference in the second and initial readings will then indicate the different degrees of intensity of the fear which could be aroused on account of the different types of fear stimuli in a particular individual.

As another illustration, we may conduct an experiment to ascertain whether a group of students can do better in an intelligence test under the influence of a specific drug like benzedrine sulphate, caffeine or *brahmi.*

For this investigation, we will take only one group of some students, preferably of the same age, sex and state of health. The procedure of the experiment will comprise the following steps:

(a) These students can be given sugar capsules after which they can be put through some intelligence test. This will provide the initial testing under normal conditions.

(b) Some time later, they can be given drug capsules and tested on the same intelligence test. This will make a test under changed conditions.

(c) The I.Q. scores under these two situations are noted down and the difference is calculated. If any significant difference is found, it will be attributed to the influence of the drug.

2. *Control-group design.* The control test or the single group design method has a serious drawback known as the *positive practice effect.* If an individual is subjected to a certain kind of fear stimulus, it will surely affect the responses on his further exposure to fear stimuli. If a group is subjected to a certain drug, then it will automatically carry its effect or influence at the time of the introduction of some other drugs at the later stage. Control group designs help in minimising such a practice effect.

In the control group design two separate groups, known as the experimental group, and the control group, participate in the experiment. They are equated or matched on various traits like age, sex, intelligence and other personality characteristics. There is a one-to-one correspondence in the two equated groups. Now the control group is given sugar capsules and tested on some intelligence test. At the same time, the experimental group is given the drug capsule and tested on the same intelligence test. The differences in the intelligence scores of the groups are then calculated. In case some significant differences are found, they are attributed to the effect of the drug.

3. *Multiple-group design.* Sometimes, we have to experiment with more than two groups for arriving at the appropriate conclusion. For example, if we want to study the effect of knowledge of English on the speed with which people subsequently learn French, we decide to teach English to a group of students and then see whether they learn French more easily. But more easily than whom? Certainly we will need another group, or groups for comparison. Group A, consisting of students who have learnt the English language is called the experimental group. Group B may function as a control group for comparison, since it did not learn English earlier. If group A learns French faster than Group B, can we attribute the difference in speed to the earlier study of English? Certainly not. It may be that practice on account of learning any subject or language may have the same positive transfer effect. To rule out these possibilities it is essential to add some more control groups like C and D. Now if group A demonstrates a clear superiority over the other three groups, then and only then may we infer that learning English facilitates learning French. For illustration, the working of a multiple group design for data collection in the present case may be tabulated as shown.

Group	Subject for test held in the month of August	Test held in the month of February
A	English	French
B	No test	French
C	Any subject (say Mathematics)	French
D	Russian	French

4. *Designs involving rotation.* This experiment involves presenting two or more stimulating situations to the experimental subjects in as many sequences as necessary to control the serial effects of fatigue or practice. For example, if we want to determine the relative influence of two specified conditions A and B (say praise and blame) on a group of subjects, we will not measure all the subjects under condition A and then under condition B. Condition A might cause fatigue or so train the subjects that the measures under condition B would not be independent of the fatigue or training effects. Here two alternatives can be adopted:

(a) We may obtain half the measures for condition A, all the measures for condition B, and then the other half of the measures for condition A. This technique is sometimes called the A B B A order.

(b) Another alternative is to separate the subjects into two equated groups, one of which receives treatment A and then B, whereas the other group receives treatment B and then A. Both sets of A results and both sets of B results may then be combined and the difference between them calculated.

Limitations of the Experimental Method

1. The Experimental method advocates the study of behaviour under completely controlled rigid conditions. These conditions demand the creation of artificial situations or environment and the behaviour studied under these conditions may be or is usually different from the spontaneous or natural behaviour. Therefore, the experimental method fails to study behaviour in natural conditions as may be possible through natural observation.

2. The second limitation or difficulty lies in exercising actual control or handling of the independent variable and the intervening variables. It is very difficult to know and control all of the intervening variables. Similarly we cannot always control the independent variable. Therefore, it is not always possible to create the desired conditions in the laboratory and consequently, in the absence of these controlled conditions, the success of this method becomes quite uncertain.

3. In the experimental method we often make use of animals or birds as subjects for experimentation. It is also debatable whether experimental results obtained from such sources are applicable to human beings at all.

4. The scope of the experimental method is limited. All problems of psychology cannot by studied by this method as we cannot perform experiments for all the problems that may come up in the diverse subject matter of psychology.

5. The dynamic nature and unpredictability of human behaviour does not always allow the independent variable to lead to change in the dependent variable. Human behaviour is not a mechanical behaviour. The anger or fear producing stimuli or variables may or may not yield the required responses as desired under experiment and hence it is not possible to get uniform responses or changes in the dependent variables on account of the concomitant changes in the independent variable.

6. The experimental method is a costly and time consuming method. Moreover, the conduct of experiments under this method requires specialized knowledge and skills. In the absence of such specialized abilities, it is not possible to use this method.

DIFFERENTIAL METHOD

The differential method is based on individual differences. Therefore, all the measures applied to the calculation of individual differences are included in this method. The differential method is also named as the normative survey method or the field survey method as the investigator has to go to the field to make his investigations. It is sometimes called the statistical method for the reason that statistical techniques become the major devices for the study of the individual differences. Now, the question that arises is, how do differential methods differ from experimental methods? It may be felt that the differentce between the experimental and differential methods is only arbitrary and artificial, since the procedure of finding the effects on dependent variables by the application of the independent variables is the same. This, however, is not true as T.G. Andrews (1958) comments:

> Differentiation between experiments and differential methods may appear quite artificial, and it is true that all psychologists will not agree to such an apparently artificial classification scheme. Nevertheless, it should always be made clear that the independent variables resulting from individual differences are never under the investigator's control to the same degree that experimental variables are.

Thus, differential methods differ from the experimental approach in that the investigator cannot intentionally manipulate the variables and each of these is studied as an independent variable. For instance, in studying the relationship of achievement with intelligence, it is not possible to manipulate intelligence. Therefore, we have to take each individual and study his achievement in relation to his intelligence. After that, we can try to arrive at certain conclusions with the help of statistical techniques.

The key concept in using the differential methods is their technique of studying differences within the same individual or between individuals in different groups. Usually for this purpose four types of main approaches or designs are used. These are:

1. Correlation Approach
2. Field Survey Approach
3. Longitudinal Approach
4. Cross-sectional Approach.

In the Correlation Approach, the psychologist takes people as they are and studies what they usually do, without changing the conditions under which they respond to the tests or perform the desired tasks. For example, in the above case of finding the relationship of achievement with intelligence, the intelligence as well as the achievement, say academic achievement of each individual can be found with the help of intelligence as well as achievement tests. The subjects will naturally differ from one another and by using the statistical technique of correlation, the desired relationship can be ascertained.

In the Field Survey Approach, the differences with regard to a particular trait pattern or characteristics among the individuals are discovered by conducting the field survey and taking adequate samples, from the studied population. For example, in 'studying the individual differences with regard to adjustment patterns or job satisfaction among high school teachers working in government and non-government schools', the use of the differential method would require (a) the taking of adequate samples of both categories of teachers, (b) finding out the adjustment or job satisfaction scores of the teachers included in these groups, and (c) analysing the differences, if any, in the pattern of adjustment or job satisfaction.

In the Longitudinal Approach, the differences in an individual or group of some individuals are studied over a long span of time. For example, by learning the pattern of growth and development with regard to physical, mental, emotional, social or moral dimensions of personality, we can study a particular infant or a number of infants as they normally grow and develop through successive ages. However, this type of study would require quite a long span as the researcher has to wait for the normal course of development to occur.

The Cross-sectional Approach is the alternative for studying or discovering the normal trend where instead of studying one or more infants at their successive ages we can take different infants of varying ages for studying them simultaneously to determine the pattern of growth and development at different ages. In all the above approaches meant to discover differences, the researcher is required to take the help of the statistical methods for analysing his data and interpreting his research findings with regard to the differences among individuals, groups and methods of treatment.

CLINICAL METHOD

Whereas experimental and differential methods are generally used to investigate general behavioural facts, the clinical method is directed towards the study of individual behaviour. The clinical set-up or environment is associated with health care and treatment of the individuals who come for advice and treatment of their physical and mental disorders. Clinical methods also remind us of all those methods which deal with the task of investigating the root causes of a problem or exceptional behaviour and suggesting as well as providing proper environment and possible treatment.

The concept of a clinical method is included in the concept of clinical psychology which is the art and technology of dealing with the adjustment problems of the individual for purposes of his optimum social adjustment and welfare. The analysis of this definition may help us to observe some of the characteristics of the nature and working of the clinical method:

1. The clinical method is applicable to an individual.
2. The individual has some problems.
3. Methods of both diagnosis and treatment are involved in dealing with these problems.
4. The clinical method is aimed at seeking the maximum adjustment and welfare for the disturbed person.
5. The clinical method is an art as well as a science and technology which means that everybody cannot treat every patient and it takes pleasure in making mankind healthier and better.

Thus, the basic elements in this method of psychological investigation are the diagnosis and treatment of the problem or mental illness of an individual.

Method of Diagnosis

Diagnosis by the clinical method requires a symptomatic account of the overall situation in order to ascertain the root cause of an illness or behavioural problem. For such diagnosis, one has to look into the past events or experiences of the individuals, their impact and reactions, the present environment and adjustment problems, and the total personality make-up, etc. For ascertaining all about these aspects the following techniques are generally employed.

1. *Adequate physical check-up.* The individual suffering from a behavioural problem must be made to go through a detailed physical check-up to ascertain whether the behaviour exhibited is of a functional or of an organic nature. In case there are no physical causes for the behaviour in question, then and only then should it be diagnosed as a subject for psychological treatment.

2. *Making out the case history.* For finding the clues or delving into the events from the earlier experiences of the individual which may be responsible for the present behaviour, the psychologist then tries to use the case history technique.

In this technique, information is collected from the memory of the individual, his parents, the members of his family, his relatives, guardians, neighbours, friends, teachers, doctors and from the available records and reports concerning the individual's past. For collecting the relevant information the following sources may be used:

    (a) *Identifying data.* This may contain the name of the individual, his father's name, his residential address, date of birth, caste, religion, nature of exceptional or abnormal behaviour, etc.

   (b) *Environmental background.* This may contain information about the members of the individual's family, his parents, their relationship with each other, and behaviour with the subject (individual) of the study, the educational and socio-economic status of the family, the accidents and incidents which may have occurred in the family, the types of neighbourhood, friends and socio-cultural environment, the type of school education and school or job situation environment etc., he may have passed through.

   (c) *Developmental history.* This may contain the history of the growth and developmental process of the individual in relation to the treatment, behaviour and environmental facilities available from birth onwards, history of his mental and physical health, education and occupation, social and emotional adjustment, sex-life etc.

   (d) *History of exceptional/abnormal behaviour.* This may contain all the relevant information regarding the development of the behaviour in question up to the present stage.

3. *The clinical interview.* Additional but very important information may be obtained by the investigator by arranging a clinical interview with the individual. For this purpose, he may carefully plan appropriate questions and persuade the individual to give free and frank responses by establishing the necessary rapport. For understanding the inner working of the individual's mind, he may be given the opportunity to talk about himself in this interview session. From these responses, the investigator may draw conclusions for the diagnosis of the root cause of the behaviour.

4. *Direct observation of behaviour.* Direct observation of the behaviour of the individual by the investigator in the natural set-up, living and working conditions may prove quite useful in knowing the nature and causes of the behaviour. In the case of children, direct observation of the subject at play may provide a useful means of understanding him, his behaviour and his problem.

5. *Using tests and measuring devices.* Certain testing and measuring devices may also be used to ascertain the interests, abilities, attitudes, aptitudes and the total personality of the individual and relevant information may thus be obtained for understanding the individual and his behaviour.

Method of Treatment

In order to serve the welfare of the individual, diagnosis should be followed by treatment. For the treatment of a behavioural problem, efforts are to be made to bring about a change in the behaviour of the individual by his adjustment with himself and with his environment and thus ultimately restore his normal mental health. This can be usually accomplished in two ways:

   1. Modifying the environmental forces
   2. Modifying the individual's attitude.

The physical and socio-cultural environment of the individual needs to be modified in such a way that he may not be subjected to further disharmony and maladjustment. Rather, he should be able to get a pleasant and encouraging environment characterized by wholesome and harmonious relationships with other social beings and he should get enough opportunity for the fulfilment of his basic needs. For this purpose the following measures may be adopted:

1. He may be physically removed from one situation and placed in another, like a boarding house, foster home or with guardians and adopted parents.
2. The attitude of the parents, teachers and others toward him may be changed.
3. More adequate recreational facilities, better living conditions, work placement and working conditions may be provided or some suitable measures for the sublimation and catharsis of repressed desires and wishes may be taken.

A complete modification of the individual's philosophy of life is required for bringing about a change in his behaviour. He must be made to harmonise his thinking, feeling and doing. For this purpose, the following measures may be adopted:

1. Guidance and counselling
2. Psychoanalysis
3. Techniques like auto-suggestion hypnosis, psychodrama and role-playing
4. Therapies like psychotherapy, group therapy, play therapy, occupation therapy, attitude therapy etc.

Conclusion

The above discussion regarding the nature and working of the clinical methods may lead us to conclude that clinical methods in all their shapes and forms are always concerned with the diagnoses and treatment of adjustment problems or mental and psychological illness of the individual. It is, however, not necessary that clinical methods should always be used to study or treat the mental illness or abnormal behaviour of an individual. The real purpose of clinical findings is to help in conducting an intensive and thorough study of the behaviour of the individual. Therefore, it does not matter whether we carry out the study of a normal or abnormal behaviour with the help of a clinical set-up. There is no bar to study the behaviour of normal persons or even exceptional individuals like high achievers, creative geniuses, saints, social workers and leaders by employing clinical methods of collecting relevant information through various means. Whether an individual requires treatment or follow-up depends upon the case under clinical study. A clinical study thus does not necessarily require resort to methods of treatment. The treatment can be affected only when the individual under study needs it. Therefore, broadly speaking, clinical methods may be taken as the methods of studying the behaviour of an individual in all possible detail relevant to the purpose of the study.

Merits and Demerits of Clinical Methods

The chief merit of the clinical methods is that they can be safely employed to study the particular or specific behaviour of an individual. No two individuals are alike in their behaviour patterns and a real study of human behaviour can, therefore, only be made through a personal and individual study of every human being. Clinical methods provide an intensive study involving all possible details regarding individual behaviour. Therefore, as far as true investigation of individual behaviour is concerned, no method can match the efficiency and usefulness of the clinical methods. Their usefulness is further enhanced when they provide valuable information regarding the adjustment or behavioural problem of the individual and subsequent suggestions and measures for the treatment and solution of these problems. Clinical methods, thus render signal service to mankind.

Their main limitation or drawback is that their proper use demands a lot from the clinical researcher. He should be mature and technically proficient in handling such studies. He cannot involve his own self and personality make-up while diagnosing and treating the individual in his charge. The other limitation is related to the very restricted scope of such studies as the effort put into, and the findings of these studies cannot be generalized. These are meant only for individual cases and end with the diagnosis and treatment of the individual cases under study.

PSYCHO-PHYSICAL METHODS

The branch of psychology which is concerned with the study of the relationship between physical and psychological phenomenon is called *psycho-physics*. In this sense, the term 'psycho-physical methods' may be used to refer to all those methods in which attempts are made to employ physical devices for the scientific measurement of some psychological experiences like the sensations of weight, brightness, loudness and other such dimensions. Other complicated psychological phenomena like sleep or span of memory etc. can also be studied by psycho-physical methods.

Three classical psycho-physical methods devised by the German physio-logist and physicist Gustav Fechner (1801–1887), the father of psycho-physics are still in vogue. They are:

1. The method of minimal changes or the method of limits.
2. The method of constant stimuli or the method of right and wrong responses.
3. The method of average or mean error.

These methods are primarily employed to measure the absolute threshold and the difference threshold. Both the absolute threshold and the difference threshold are statistical concepts and are measured in much the same way.

The absolute threshold may be defined as the minimum value of a physical stimulus that reliably produces sensation. Absolute threshold, thus, separates the sounds we can hear from those we cannot, the odours we can smell from those we cannot, the brightness of the light we can see from that we cannot, and so on.

The difference threshold may be defined as the minimum difference in value between two stimuli which can be perceived by the subject. For example, when one experiences a particular weight put in one's hand, how much minimum weight has to be added to it so that the total becomes just distinguishable as different from the first. Let us now give a brief idea of the three psycho-physical methods mentioned above.

The Method of Minimal Changes or the Methods of Limits

This method may be used for finding out the absolute threshold and difference threshold. The procedure may be outlined as below:

1. The subject is exposed to a particular sensation. For example, he may be asked to report whether he can see the object lying at a particular distance (say 80 cm) or not.
2. If he cannot see the object, the distance is gradually decreased until the subject reports that he is able to see the object. Suppose at the distance of 77 cm he says no but at the distance of 76 cm he says yes then both these values at which the subject's response changed from no to yes about the visibility of the object will be noted down by the experimenter.
3. In the next round, the object may be placed at a distance much nearer than the absolute threshold, say 70 cm in the present case. This distance may then be gradually increased till the subject reports that he does not see the object. The successive values at which the subject's response changes from yes to no is noted down. Let these values be 75 and 76 cm in the present case.
4. All these values pertaining to minimal changes in the value of the absolute threshold or difference threshold in both descending and ascending series of trials are then noted down. The process is repeated many times. After the completion of several ascending and descending series, the experimenter, may compute the average of all these minimal values. (The limits of the intensity of the sensory stimuli which produce a change from 0 to 100 per cent in terms of the feeling or sensation). In the present example, we may compute the average of the values, 77, 76, 75 and 76 etc., yielding the value $\dfrac{77 + 76 + 75 + 76}{4}$, i.e. 76 cm, as a minimal value of the distance at which the subject may be able to see the experimental object.

The absolute threshold concerning auditory intensity may also be similarly determined. In an ascending series of trials, the experimenter, while beginning with a clearly sub-threshold value, may progressively raise the intensity of the sound until the subject reports that he hears it. In the descending series of trials, he may gradually decrease the intensity of sound till the subject reports that he does not hear the sound. The average of all these values, in the several ascending and descending series, at which the subject's response changed about his hearing of the sound is then calculated to be designated as the absolute threshold.

The Method of Constant Stimuli (The Method of Right and Wrong Responses)

In this method the value of the intensity of the sensory stimulus is not gradually increased or decreased as in the case of the method of limits but the sensory stimuli of varying intensity are presented to the subject at random. The stimuli include at least one sample which is well above the probable threshold value and another sample which is well below it. The subject is then asked to indicate whether or not he detects each of these randomly presented stimuli. The responses of the subject in the form of yes or no are then noted down by the experimenter and ultimately the probability of the yes response is related to intensity of the stimuli. All the values related to the yes responses are then averaged out to give the required threshold.

The Method of Average Error

This method is also called the method of mean error or the adjustment method. In performing experiments by this method, the subject is presented with some stimulus of a standard intensity. He may then be asked to adjust a variable stimulus to this standard by making a number of attempts. In doing so he will probably miss the standard by a certain margin. This is referred to as the error. The average of these error is noted down. It is subtracted or added to the standard value (depending upon the positive or negative sign of the value of the computed average error) for giving the subject's absolute threshold of sensitivity to the stimulus.

Conclusion Regarding Methods

Which of the foregoing methods is the most suitable in studying the problems of educational psychology is a difficult question to answer. All these methods have their own strengths and weaknesses and have some unique characteristics which make them highly specific in particular situations. However, a wise investigator must keep in mind the factors of objectivity, reliability and validity for the solution of the problem in hand. He should possess a keen insight into the nature of his subjects, their problems, environmental surroundings and the resources at his disposal and accordingly select the proper method or methods to keep himself as scientific and objective as possible to derive the best possible results from his study.

SUMMARY

The study of behaviour in Educational Psychology can be made through the observation of a learner's behaviour. This observation may be carried out in various forms by employing a variety of methods.

Introspection is a sort of self-observation in which one perceives, analyses and reports one's own feelings and, in fact, every thing that takes place in one's mind during the course of a mental act. Although it provides a simple, inexpensive and readily available method for studying one's behaviour, it is considered to be an unscientific method.

Natural observation provides a way of studying the behaviour of an individual, by another individual, under the most natural conditions. Valuable data for studying human behaviour can be collected by this method. However, this can also not be termed as sufficiently objective, reliable and valid for studying human behaviour.

Experimental method is considered to be the most scientific and objective method for studying behaviour. Here we try to study the cause and effect relationship regarding human behaviour by performing experiments, i.e. objective observations under rigidly controlled laboratory-like conditions. The key factor in this method is the controlling of conditions or variables. There are three types of variables: independent, dependent and intervening. Independent variable stands for the cause and dependent for the effect of that cause. The other conditions or factors that influence the cause and effect relationship are called intervening variables. In an experiment all such variables need to be controlled. For exercising such control, we may make use of various experimental designs like control test or single group design, control group design, matching group design and design involving rotation, depending upon the demands of the experiment and availability of resources.

Differential method is a method based on individual differences, it is also called the normative survey method. Here we study the behaviour of several individuals to find out the relative differences. Correlation, longitudinal and cross-sectional studies of behaviour are included in this method and statistical measures are also used for the necessary analysis and interpretation of collected data through the normative survey techniques.

Clinical method helps in diagnosis and treatment of the problem or exceptional behaviour of an individual. Diagnosis may be carried out through an adequate physical checkup, building up of a comprehensive case history (looking into past experiences or finding out reasons for the present behaviour), arranging a clinical interview, using relevant tests and measuring devices, and observing the client's behaviour in a real, natural set-up. Treatment is usually accomplished in two ways: (a) by modifying the environmental forces, and (b) by modifying the individual's attitude so that he is adjusted to his self and to his environment.

Psycho-physical methods employ physical devices for the scientific measurement of some psychological experiences like sensations of weight, brightness, loudness and other such dimensions. The popular psycho-physical methods are (a) the method of minimal changes or the method of limits, (b) the method of constant stimuli or the method of right and wrong responses, and (c) the method of average or mean error. All these psycho-physical methods are primarily employed to measure the absolute threshold (minimum value of a physical stimulus that reliably produces sensation) and the difference threshold (minimum difference in value between two stimuli that can be perceived by the subject).

REFERENCE

Andrews, T.G. (Ed.), *Methods of Psychology*, New York: Wiley, 1958, p. 17.

SUGGESTED READINGS

Boring, E.G., *A History of Experimental Psychology*, 2nd ed., New York: Appleton-Century-Crofts, 1950.

Horney, K., *New Ways in Psychoanalysis*, New York: W.W. Norton & Co., 1939.

Sidman, M., *Tactics of Scientific Research*, New York: Basic Books, 1960.

Wilson, E.B., Jr., *An Introduction to Scientific Research*, New York: McGraw-Hill, 1952.

Woodworth, R.S., *Experimental Psychology* (rev. ed.), New York: Holt, 1954.

Chapter 4

Systems or Schools of Psychology and Their Bearing on Education

INTRODUCTION

As we have already seen, psychology owes its origin to philosophy. However, as time elapsed psychologists attempted to discard the approaches and methods based on speculation and provided a scientific base to the subject for the study of behaviour. These efforts gave birth to a number of schools or systems of psychology such as structuralism, functionalism, behaviourism, Gestaltism, psychoanalysis, individual psychology, analytical psychology, humanist psychology, transpersonal psychology and cognitive psychology, etc. The emergence of these systems or schools of thought not only influenced the development of various trends and approaches for assessment of behaviour but also affected the processes and products of education. In the present chapter we aim to briefly trace the history of evolution of the different systems of psychology to show their impact or bearing on education.

STRUCTURALISM

Wilhelm Wundt (1832–1920), a German Professor, was mainly responsible for the evolution of this school of psychology. He opened the world's first psychological laboratory in Leipzig in 1879 with the sole purpose of the systematic study of the mind. For this, he focused his experiments on conscious experience involving one's thoughts, feelings, sensations, perceptions and ideas. As he focused his attention on the analysis of the components of consciousness (the supposed structure of the mind), his approach to psychology is called as *structuralism*. Wundt and his students conducted experiments in the laboratory by using the art of introspection or self-observation. The subjects were usually asked to report exactly what they were experiencing at the moment when they were exposed to stimuli such as light, colour, sound or the feel of an object. The psychologists performing the experiments also acted as subjects for the observations and recording of their own perceptions and feelings and then presenting their analyses of the activities of the mind.

The Leipzig laboratory produced most of the leading psychologists. One of its well-known products was Edward Bradford Titchener (1867–1927), a British by birth, who became professor of psychology at Cornell University. According to him, psychology may be regarded as the science of consciousness or the study of experience. Consciousness or experience can be broken or analysed into three basic elements: physical sensations, feelings and images such as memories and dreams. For example, when we report the perception experiences of a banana, we try to combine visual sensation (what we see) with feelings (our like or dislike for the banana) and with images (past experiences with other bananas). Through his studies Titchener concluded that the structure of the human mind was made up of more than 30,000 separate sensations, feelings, and images, and nothing else.

In this way, Wundt and his followers like Titchener, known as structuralists, tried to provide a systematic study of the mind through the study of its structure (identifying the basic units of consciousness or experience along with the combinations in which they occur) by adopting introspection as the main technique.

Criticism

Structuralism is criticised on the following grounds:

1. As a system of psychology, structuralism is regarded as a very limited system which is unable to cover all aspects of human behaviour. The isolation of such important topics as motivation, individual differences and abnormal behaviour etc., clearly reveals the limited scope of this system.

2. According to this system, function involves structures, and structures of the mind can be explained through its parts, not its process. Such explanation involving the division of the human mind into individual elements, as Paplia and Olds (1987) have observed, may appear quite unnatural and untenable. For example, it is difficult for a structuralist to say "this is an apple" because (a) such a statement fails to analyze the apple into its various elements—that it is small, round, green or red in colour, smooth-skinned, etc.; and (b) because referring to the object simply as an apple rather than in terms of the elements that an observer could see would be interpreting the object, not describing it.

3. The introspection method used by the structuralists for studying behaviour can neither be regarded as objective, reliable nor valid since each introspectionist may be found to describe his own sensory experiences in his own subjective way. This was the reason why Titchener, the structuralist, doubted if psychology could ever be a science of behaviour and according to him biology alone could be a science of behaviour.

Merits of Structuralism and Its Contribution to Education

1. Structuralism helped in establishing psychology as an independent and organised discipline by separating it from philosophy and metaphysics.

2. It provided introspection as a method of studying behaviour. Despite wide-spread criticism, introspection is still regarded as one of the important methods for studying behaviour. What goes on inside one's mind during the course of a mental act can be experienced or explained only by the individual himself, and introspection is the only suitable technique that can be employed in extracting such reports. Consequently, studies in Educational Psychology can benefit from the use of this method.

3. Structuralism is credited with having taken the initiative in establishing the first psychological laboratory and employing the technique of systematic observation of the activities of the mind. It has resulted in making psychology a subject of scientific study and experimentation. What we find today in the field of psychology and Educational Psychology in terms of laboratory as well as field experiments can then safely be claimed as a positive contribution of the school of structuralism.

FUNCTIONALISM

William James (1842–1910), the father of psychology in USA, is regarded as one of the pioneers of the functional school of psychology. Strongly influenced by the Darwinian theory and his own interest in anatomy, physiology and medicine, he adopted a biological approach to the study of the mind and led the field away from structuralism. He declared that something was definitely wrong in Wundt's and Titchener's approach. He claimed that consciousness or experience cannot be broken up into elements, and there is no way to separate ideas, thoughts, sensations or perceptions. Structuralism does not reveal anything about what the mind really does or how it goes about doing it. Knowing the composition or structure of the mind is not as important as understanding its activities or functions. Therefore, William James, through his doctrine of functionalism, advocated the theory of mental life and behaviour. He considered the mind to be a recent development in the evolutionary process, the function of which was to aid man's adjustment to his environment. The consciousness or mental life, according to him, is a continuous and flowing unity, a stream that carries the organism in its adaptation to the environment. Our minds are constantly forging associations, revising experiences, starting, stopping, jumping back and forth in time for adding to our functional abilities to adapt to our environment. Elaborating his viewpoint, he further concluded that habits are nothing but functions of the nervous system. When we repeat an activity a number of times, our nervous systems are altered so that the next time we engage in it we do so automatically without much conscious thought.

During the subsequent years in the 19th and 20th centuries, ideas propagated by William James were consolidated on a more scientific footing by functionalists like John Dewey (1859–1952), James Rowland Angell (1869–1949), J.M. Cattell, Edward L. Thorndike (1874–1949) and R.S. Woodworth (1869–1962).

Merits of Functionalism and its Contribution to Education

Functionalism, regarded as a more scientific and more practical system of psychology than structuralism, helped in making the system of education as practicable and useful as possible by the following contributions:

1. It laid emphasis on functionability of the contents of the curriculum by advocating that only those things should be taught to the children which they could apply in everyday life.

2. The methods and techniques of learning were made more functionable through the ideas propagated by this system. Functionalists like Dewey felt that the emphasis of education and teaching methods should not be on the subject matter but on the needs of the students. Such learner-centred approaches in the methods of teaching opened the way for the discovery of new methods and devices in the teaching-learning process.

3. This system widened the scope of psychology and educational psychology by developing a variety of new methods beyond introspection for studying behaviour mainly based on scientific enquiry, systematic data collection and objective interpretation and by including in its sphere the study of many useful topics not covered by structuralism.

4. The field of measurement and evaluation related to psychology and education has also been enriched by functionalism with the introduction of certain valuable techniques and devices like the questionnaire, inventory, mental tests, and various other means for the objective description of behaviour.

5. Functionalism opened the way for the study of psychology in terms of the adjustment of the organism to its environment. The study and problems of the individual, normal as well as abnormal, were incorporated in the subject matter of psychology and educational psychology.

6. Functionalism paved the way for applied research in response to the application of psychology to the practical problems, particularly in the field of educational psychology. John Dewey, a strong advocate of functionalism, proved the relevance of the psychology of learning and motivation etc., by establishing his own school and integrating theory with practice. Such practical attempts combined with the theoretical ideas have been responsible for revolutionizing the modern system of education to a great extent.

BEHAVIOURISM

John B. Watson (1878–1950) put forward an entirely new doctrine, named *behaviourism* which was quite contrary to structuralism and functionalism. He concluded that the whole idea of consciousness is absurd. Consciousness cannot be proved by any scientific test, for consciousness cannot be seen, touched, or exhibited in a test tube. Even if it exists it cannot be studied scientifically, because admittedly it is subjected only to private inspection. Therefore, if we intend to make psychology a science of behaviour, we should concentrate only on the observable and measurable behaviour. We have to discard altogether not only the concept of consciousness but also all mentalistic notions like soul, mind, mental life, images and ideas, etc.

Consequently, behaviourism as a method of studying behaviour focused its attention totally on the overt or observable behaviour. For this purpose, it tried to reduce all of man's activity, including his thinking, feeling and volition to the level of that behaviour which could be observed and objectively recorded. Thus, a behaviourist is not interested in the feeling of fear (because it is not measurable) but pays attention to the changes in heart rate and blood pressure which are the effects of fear and can be objectively measured. The theory of behaviourism as propagated by Watson was in fact based on the findings of the Russian psychologist Ivan Pavlov (1849–1936), the propagator of the theory of classical conditioning.

In his classic experiment, Pavlov conditioned a dog to salivate at the sound of a bell by substituting that sound for the sight and smell of meat and concluded that all behaviour is a response to some stimulus in the environment. Watson tried to apply this approach in the field of human behaviour. In the famous experiment with an 11-month old baby named Albert, he conditioned the baby's behaviour to fear a rat by substituting the rat with a sudden loud noise. He concluded that behaviour is merely the response to some environmental stimulus. How we behave and why we behave in a particular way can be successfully demonstrated and explained through habit formation or conditioning. Thus conditioning through environmental influences and not hereditary endowments or innate differences is responsible for shaping the behaviour of a child.

Behaviourism, thus, tried to project human beings as little more than rather complex machines which respond in a particular fashion to a particular kind of stimulus. The behaviour of an individual may, thus, be supposed to be controlled by environmental forces, and not by hereditary endowments or innate differences.

His strong convictions about the stimulus response automatization and environmental influences made Watson assert boldly in 1926:

> Give me a dozen healthy infants, well informed and my own specified world
> to bring them up in and I will guarantee to take any one at random and train
> him to become any type of specialist I might select—doctor, lawyer, artist,
> merchant chief and yes, even beggar-man and thief, regardless of his talents,
> penchants, tendencies, abilities, vocations and race of his ancestors.

The doctrine of behaviourism propounded by Watson and his disciples, thus, ushered a new era in the field of psychology by making it somewhat materialistic, mechanistic, deterministic and objective like most of the physical and natural sciences. However, it suffered from a number of drawbacks, limitations and shortcomings. For this reason it has been subjected to criticism and has been modified and refined in a number of ways by contemporary psychologists like Lashley, Tolman, Hull and Skinner. While Lashley devoted himself to neuro-physiology and Tolman believed in purposive behaviourism, B.F. Skinner, a leading American behaviourist of the present age, emphasized a system of learning known as *operant conditioning*, quite different from the type of conditioning advocated by Pavlov and Watson. The task of behaviour modification he advocated and the teaching machines he popularized by using the principles of reward, wield significant influence in the fields of psychology, education and medicine.

Merits of Behaviourism and its Contribution to Education

1. Behaviourists in the study of behaviour rejected the notions of structuralists for figuring out what people were feeling or seeing or the functionalists' notion of how and why they were thinking. Instead, they focused on what was actually being done by the people and observed by the observer or investigator. In this way, they introduced the scientific method for studying behaviour, which is essentially based on the objective observation of the behaviour and the events. Behaviourism thus helped in replacing introspective measures with the scientific and objective measures.

2. Behaviourists, while giving second place to hereditary characteristics, highlighted the role of environment in shaping and modifying the behaviour of children. It helped in revolutionizing all the programmes and methods related to education, training and rehabilitation by emphasizing a greater need to provide the best possible learning situations and environment for better growth and development of the child.

3. The approach to dealing with abnormal and mentally sick persons as well as delinquent, maladjusted, backward and problem children was also drastically changed on account of the experimental findings of the behaviourists. In particular, the techniques of shaping behaviour and the behaviour modification programmes advocated by the behaviourists ushered a new era into this field.

4. Since behaviourists did not believe in entities like the '*mind*', and the mind-body problem, the mental approach to human behaviour was altogether discarded. As a result, all concepts related to the doctrine of mentalism like sensation, emotion, perception were dropped from psychology and education texts, giving way to new concepts like stimulus, response, habits, learning, and conditioning.

5. Behaviourism helped in extending the scope of educational psychology to include the study of animals as a way to learn more about human nature.

6. Behaviourism advocated the use of reinforcement, and rewards (in place of punishment and unpleasant experiences) as inducement for the acquisition of desirable behaviour and for giving up the undesirable.

7. Behaviourism highlighted the role of motivation and definition of the aims and purposes in learning and shaping of behaviour.

8. Behaviourism gave rise to new ideas and innovations in the field of learning and instruction like programmed learning and individualized self instructional programmes involving teaching machines and computer-assisted instruction.

GESTALT PSYCHOLOGY

The reaction against structuralism and functionalism was not confined to the USA. In Germany it gave birth to a new school called *Gestalt psychology*, quite distinct from behaviourism. The most prominent members of this school were Max Wertheimer (1880–1943), Kurt Koffka (1886–1941), Wolfgang Kohler (1887–1967), and Kurt Lewin (1890–1947).

'Gestalt' is a German word, the nearest English translation of which is configuration or, more simply, an organised whole in contrast to a collection of parts. Therefore, Gestalt psychology is opposed to the atomistic and molecular approach to behaviour. According to it, an individual perceives the thing as a whole and not as a mere collection of its constituents or elements. To a Gestalt psychologist, the meaning of sensation or perception is always related to the total situation, and perception always involves a problem of organisation. A thing is perceived as a relationship within a field which includes that thing, the viewer, and a complex background incorporating the viewer's purpose and previous experiences. Gestaltists also rejected the mechanistic approach to behaviour as advocated by the behaviourists through a simple stimulus–response connection. They asserted that a sort of organisation definitely exists between the stimulus and response which helps in forming a new gestalt or an organised whole. For example, when one looks at a tree what one sees is a tree. Even though a tree consists of colour, brightness and a form but when perceived by the mind all these components become a pattern, or a gestalt. The Gestaltists further claim that when the components of a thing are brought together by the mind, something new (even more valuable and comprehensive than the original components) may emerge, reinforcing the statement: "the whole is different from the sum of its parts". As a result, human behaviour is characterized as an intelligent behaviour rather than a simple stimulus–response mechanism. An individual perceives the situation as a whole and after seeing and evaluating the different relationships in relation to the available environment, takes the proper decision in an intelligent way although quite often he does so impulsively. Gestalt psychology used the term 'insight' to describe this type of human behaviour and summarized the behavioural process as consisting of the following three steps:

1. Perception of the situation as a whole.
2. Seeing and judging the relationships between various factors involved in the situation.
3. Taking an immediate decision and behaving accordingly.

Gestalt psychology, in this way, stood in strong opposition to traditional psychology comprising structuralism, functionalism and behaviourism. Specifically, it deplored the brick and mortar concept of structuralism—i.e. elements, or 'bricks' bound by association or 'mortar' and were equally dissatisfied with the stimulus–response conditioning or machine-like explanation of human behaviour.

Merits of Gestalt Psychology and its Contribution to Education

1. Gestaltists maintained that the whole is always greater than its consti-
    tuents or parts. This proposition influenced the field of education in
    many aspects as we now discuss.

(a) In the construction and organisation of the curricula and syllabi, due
    consideration is being given to the Gestalt principle. The concerned
    subject matter of a particular subject is always organised as a whole
    and the curriculum comprising different subjects and activities is so
    framed as to reflect unity and cohesiveness among them.
(b) Stress is being laid on an inter-disciplinary approach in education.
(c) The Gestalt approach has been duly acknowledged in methodology
    and techniques of teaching and learning. This has resulted in
    presenting the learning material in a Gestalt form (as an organised
    whole) and then proceeding to the parts.
(d) Due stress on the Gestalt (organised and combined) efforts on the part
    of teachers, administrators, parents and other members of society is
    being laid in the education and welfare of children.

2. Gestaltists laid great emphasis on the role of motivation, and definite
    goals and purposes in any type of learning. This has resulted in
    providing a central role to motivation in any scheme of learning and
    education. The emphasis on setting clear-cut objectives, defining them
    in definite behavioural terms and linking education with the needs
    and motives of the learner may be said to be some of the great
    contributions of Gestalt psychology.
3. Gestaltism has a notable feature that it makes the task of perception,
    learning and problem solving an intelligent task rather than a
    piecemeal molecular function or a mere stimulus–response mechanical
    process. It has provided a scientific and progressive method of
    problem solving based on the cognitive abilities of the learners.
4. Gestaltism has necessitated research in the field of organisational
    climate, institutional planning, group dynamics etc., for organising the
    factors in the environment of the learner into a meaningful whole so as
    to put in the best efforts for managing the affairs of education and
    welfare of the individuals.

SCHOOL OF PSYCHOANALYSIS

Psychoanalysis as a system or school of psychology was the brain-child of
Sigmund Freud (1856–1939), a Viennese physician. This movement put forward
views quite contrary to structuralism, functionalism, behaviourism or gestaltism for
explaining human behaviour. Freud, the father of this movement presented a new
dimension in the field of psychology. The influence of psychoanalysis in terms of
the totality of human behaviour including the conscious, sub-conscious and
unconscious behaviour, structure of the psyche, the concept of repression, catharsis

in the form of revealing the unconscious, the psycho-sexual development and giving sex its rightful place in the realm of human behaviour, will always remain praise-worthy and memorable.

In course of later developments in the psychoanalytical movement, an association for the development of psychoanalysis was formed in 1902. The personalities associated with this school became famous either by virtue of their efforts in advocating Freud's point of view or because of the establishment of their own psychoanalytic systems based upon their own views. Two systems, namely, individual psychology established by Alfred Adler (1870–1937) and analytical psychology established by Carl Jung (1875–1961) are worthy of note. In these systems, an effort was made to provide some general urge as a substitute for sex which, in their opinion, was given excessive importance by Freud. Adler provided a substitute in the form of the self-assertion or the power-seeking motive and laid emphasis on the individuality of the subject by advocating the proposition of the life-style. Jung, on the other hand, replaced the sex urge with the more comprehensive term 'libido' or the 'life urge'. We shall discuss these systems in detail later.

The other notable neo-Freudians or rather, neo-Adlerians of the modern age have been Freud's daughter Anna, Karen Horney, Harry Stack Sullivan, Erich Fromm, Erik Erickson and Heinz Hartmann, etc. The efforts of these researchers have led to modifications in the traditional psycho-analytical approach, particularly in terms of playing down of the role of sex and stressing the role of society.

SYNTHESIS OF SCHOOLS: THE RECENT TREND IN CONTEMPORARY PSYCHOLOGY

In the foregoing discussion, we have seen that there has been a practice or tradition among the adherents of different schools like structuralism, functionalism, behaviourism, Gestaltism, and psychoanalysis to focus on the weaknesses of other schools and spend a great deal of energy to prove a contrary point. Quite opposite to this trend, the psychology of today witnesses an eclectic approach in dealing with human behaviour by accepting the fact that the various viewpoints or schools help in one way or the other in studying the complex human behaviour by throwing light on its different aspects.

However, behaviourism and psychoanalysis are the two major forces at work in the field of contemporary psychology. The other major forces in the field may be further termed as humanist psychology, transpersonal psychology and cognitive psychology. We have already talked about the former two aspects, now let us discuss the remaining ones.

Humanist Psychology

This new school of psychology reflects the recent trends of humanism in psychology. Abraham Maslow, Carl Rogers, Rollo May, Arthur Combs, Gordon Allport and other eminent workers have contributed to its growth. Humanist psychology gives more value to the human being by not considering him merely as a sophisticated machine or a victim of the conflict between the ego and the id. It considers him as a purposeful being, capable of adapting himself to his environment and choosing his own course of action in order to achieve the goals which he has selected for himself. These goals may be as simple as the satisfaction of a common physical need or as lofty as the attainment of self-realization or personal fulfilment.

Humanist psychology emphasizes such distinctively human aspects of personality as the existence of free will and freedom of choice and man's search for unique goals and values to guide his behaviour and to give a personal meaning to his existence.

Transpersonal Psychology

Transpersonal psychology is one of the latest approaches prevalent in contemporary psychology. The work of Abraham Maslow in terms of self-actualization, by harnessing one's fullest potential may be said to be the cornerstone of this school of psychology. It focuses its attention on the study of personal experiences that seem to transcend ordinary existence. In other words, what we think and how we feel in our altered states of awareness is the subject area of transpersonal psychology. These states may be reached during states of severe stress and distress or in moments of great excitement and happiness. They may be aroused during periods of sleep or deep concentration. Experimentally, they may be induced with the help of some specific drugs, religious conversations, yoga and transcendental meditation, etc.

Cognitive Psychology

This new school of contemporary psychology is the result of the wave of intellectualism demonstrating faith in man's higher cognitive abilities and capacity to adapt to his environment and struggle for perfection. The roots of this psychology may be discovered in the cognitive outlook of the gestaltists who advocated an overall mental functioning and insight in place of a molecular and mechanistic approach for the study of human behaviour.

The main theme of this new school is cognitive revolution (sometimes referred to as the 'white-box' theory) which postulates that internal processes are the subject matter of psychology. This contrasts with behaviourism (sometimes called the 'black-box' theory). By referring to it as it as the black box theory, it is implied that behaviourists are concerned with the output or response (R) of the organism in a certain situation, and to some degree with the input or stimulus (S) but do not consider what transpires between the stimulus and the response. This unexplored element is represented by a 'black box' which intervenes between S and R.

Cognitive psychology studies man's thinking, memory, language, development, perception, imagery and other mental processes in order to peep into the higher human mental functions like insight, creativity and problem solving. Cognitive psychologists are totally opposed to the stimulus–response approach of the behaviourists. They maintain that there is more to learning and behaving than just single responses to stimuli. The human mind does not accept an information from its environment in exactly the form and style it is conveyed to him. The conveyed information is compared with the information already stored in the mind, it is then analysed and often enlarged upon and given a quite new form. Finally, it is subjected to interpretation and then used or stored according to the need of the time.

Cognitive psychology thus presents the system's viewpoint to explain the behavioural mechanism. In this system, whatever is conveyed through stimuli in the environment is the 'input'. The cognitive functioning of the human mind is the 'process' and the result of the cognitive functioning is the 'output' or the 'product'.

Cognitive psychology is gaining in popularity day by day. Edward Tolman, one of the founder cognitive psychologists, has made notable contributions in the field of learning, thinking and creative functioning. While explaining the problem-solving behaviour of the higher organisms, he stated that the organism tries to set up mental hypotheses about the ways to solve problems and then sets out to test these hypotheses through purposeful behaviour.

Jean Piaget, Swiss psychologist, who has been the most prominent among the contemporary cognitive psychologists, has shown keen interest in the study of development of cognitive abilities and operation of cognitive processes in children. He has outlined a definite pattern and stages of development of cognitive abilities depending upon the biological readiness of the children. We will discuss his work in detail in one of the later chapters.

SUMMARY

Different psychologists at different times have expressed their views to explain the why and how of human behaviour. This has led to establishment of different schools of thought or systems of psychology affecting the products and processes of education.

Structuralism is one of the oldest schools of thought. It was propagated by Wilhelm Wundt (1832–1920), of Germany. The other notable psychologist of this school was E.B. Titchener of USA. Structuralism emphasized the systematic study of the mind through the study of its structure (identifying the basic units of consciousness or experience along with the combinations in which they occur) by adopting introspection as the main technique. Besides separating psychology from philosophy and metaphysics, this school of thought is notable for introducing introspection as one of the methods for the study of behaviour.

Functionalism was initiated by William James (1842–1910), the father of American psychology. The other notable psychologists belonging to this school were John Dewey, James Angele, E.L. Thorndike and R.S. Woodworth. It considers the mind to be a recent development, still in an evolutionary phase, the function of which is to aid man's adjustment to his environment. It also emphasizes that habits are nothing but functions of the nervous system. Thus, because this school of thought lays much emphasis on the functional aspects, it is known as functionalism. It has influenced the system of education by advocating the use of functionable curricula, methods and techniques of learning and providing scientific methods and techniques for the objective study and description of human behaviour.

Behaviourism as a school of thought owes its origin to J.B. Watson (1878–1958). The other notable psychologists of this school are Ivan Pavlov, Lashley, Tolman, Hull and Skinner. As a school of thought it focuses its attention totally on the overt or observable behaviour for its objective observation and considers environmental forces to be the sole factor in shaping one's personality and influencing one's behaviour. It revolutionized the field of education by strongly emphasizing the need of proper environmental organisation (with least emphasis on what has been done by hereditary forces) for better growth and development of the child. It introduced the scientific method for the study of behaviour necessarily based on the objective observation of the behaviour and events. The techniques of shaping behaviour and behavioural modifications, the use of reinforcement (rewards) in place of punishment and unpleasant experiences, etc., have been the other useful contributions of this school of thought in the field of education.

Gestalt psychology owes its origin to a group of German psychologists, namely, Wertheimer, Koffka, Köhler and Kurt Lewin. It emphasizes the role of configuration or organisation in the perceptual field and highlights the role of insight and understanding in learning or problem solving. As a result, this school of thought paved the way for organising the subject matter and curricula as a whole in relation to various learning areas and experiences, proceeding from the whole to the parts etc. It has emphasized the need for making the task of learning or problem solving an intelligent task, based on insight and understanding rather than unintelligent repetition and mechanical reproduction.

Psychoanalysis propagated by Sigmund Freud (1856–1939) has been responsible for putting forward many new ideas like the unconscious and subconscious mind, the concept of repression and catharsis, psycho-sexual development, sex as an urge responsible for all types of behaviour, and psychoanalysis as a method of studying behaviour etc. It has highlighted the role of earlier experiences and the need for better education to the child in the formative years. In later years, as a reaction to Freuds overemphasis on sex, Alfred Adler (1870–1937) and Carl Jung (1875–1961), both students of Freud tried to found their own schools of thought, viz. individual psychology and analytical *psychology*. While Adler tried to replace Freud's sex urge with the power motive, Jung provided the urge for self actualization as the sole motive governing one's behaviour.

Recent trends in contemporary psychology have witnessed many schools of thought. The better known among these are: behaviourism, psychoanalysis, humanist psychology, transpersonal psychology and cognitive psychology.

Humanist psychology advocated by contemporary psychologists like Maslow, Rogers, Arthur Combs, Gordon Allport reflects the recent human trends in psychology.

Transpersonal psychology deals with what we think and how we feel in our altered states of awareness.

Cognitive psychology has its roots in the cognitive outlook of the Gestaltists. The names of psychologists like Edward Tolman and Jean Piaget are associated with the propagation of the ideas of this school of thought. It highlights the role of man's higher cognitive abilities and capacities to adapt to his environment and lays stress on studying the cognitive development and functioning of a man through his behaviour.

REFERENCES

Freud, S., *A General Introduction to Psychoanalysis*, New York: Liveright, 1935.

Paplia, D.E. and Olds, S.W., *Psychology*, New York: McGraw-Hill, 1987, p. 8.

Skinner, B.F., *About Behaviourism*, New York: Alfred Knopf, 1974.

Wertheimer, M., *A Brief History of Psychology*, New York: Holt, Rinehart & Winston, 1970.

Woodworth, R.S., *Contemporary Schools of Psychology*, London, Methuen, 1948.

SUGGESTED READINGS

Chaplin, J.P. and Krawiec, T.S., *Systems and Theories of Psychology*, 3rd ed., New York: Holt, Rinehart & Winston, 1974.

Heidbreder, Edna, *Seven Psychologies*, Ludhiana: Kalyani Publishers, 1971.

Herrnsteen, R.J. and Boring, E.G., *A Source Book on the History of Psychology*, Cambridge (Mass.): Harvard University Press, 1965.

Marks, R.W. (Ed.), *Great Ideas in Psychology*, New York: Bantam, 1966.

Murphy, G., *An Historical Introduction to Modern Psychology*, 4th ed., New York: Harcourt, Brace & Jovanovich, 1975.

Nordby, V.J. and Hall, C.S., *A Guide to Psychologists and Their Concepts*, San Francisco: W.H. Freeman & Co., 1974.

Chapter 5

Psychoanalysis—Freud's System of Psychology

INTRODUCTION

Psychoanalysis as a system or school of psychology was the brainchild of Sigmund Freud (1856–1939), a Viennese physician. This school put forward altogether different views, quite contrary to structuralism, functionalism, behaviourism or gestaltism to explain human behaviour. For the first time, this system presented a beautiful blend of theory and practice. On the theoretical side it presented a theory to understand and explain the human psyche and on the practical side it provided a method known as psychoanalysis for the study of human behaviour, and also as a therapy for treating the mentally ill. Let us first discuss some of the major concepts and ideas basic to the development of the psychoanalytic theory and then discuss the application of the theory through the psychoanalytic method of studying behaviour and as therapy for treating the mentally ill.

STRUCTURE OF THE PSYCHE OR MIND

Freud, while explaining the structure of the human psyche or mind, divided it in two different parts, first by arranging it into three layers as the *conscious*, the *subconscious* and the *unconscious* and second, by postulating three other components, viz., 'id', 'ego', and 'super ego'. Let us try to understand these terms.

The Concept of Conscious, Subconscious and Unconscious Mind

If we were to compare the human mind to an ocean, pond or a river, then the upper layer or the surface would represent the conscious mind, the main bed would be identified with the subconscious, and the bottom would form the unconscious.

The conscious mind lies just above the surface of the water like the tip of an iceberg and occupies only one tenth of our total psyche or mental life. The ideas, thoughts and images that we are aware of at any moment of our mental life are said to lie within this upper layer of our mind. Just beneath the conscious layer lies the subconscious mind. This middle portion of our mind stores all types of information just beneath the surface of awareness dormant or untapped which can be easily brought to the level of consciousness at a moment's notice whenever required. Thus in the middle bed or layer of the human mind there lie all experiences or knowledge which have been gained or learned by an individual through various types of experiences or training.

Below the subconscious mind lies the unconscious, the most important part of our mind. It is related to the vast part of our mental life which is hidden and usually inaccessible to the conscious. It contains all the repressed wishes, desires, feelings, drives and motives, many of which relate to sex and aggression. All these repressed and forbidden desires and ideas are not destined to lie permanently in the unconscious. They usually strive and agitate to come up to the subconscious or the conscious layers of the mind, sometimes in disguised forms, in dreams and in reveries. This hidden treasure of mental life belonging to the unconscious is thus responsible for most of our behaviour and in fact, as Freud asserts, what we do and how we behave is always determined by the forces residing in our unconscious and not by the choices of the conscious mind. Not to speak of normal behaviour, the causes and forms of abnormal behaviour and mental illness are also decided by what is hidden in the unconscious and, therefore, the task of the psychotherapist consists of a search for the relevant in the unconscious and bringing it up into the conscious.

The Concept of Id, Ego and Super Ego

Freud further invented three more concepts, the *Id, Ego* and *Super ego* for explaining the structure of the psyche and used them in providing a two-tier, tripartite division of the psyche as may be understood diagrammatically from Figure 5.1.

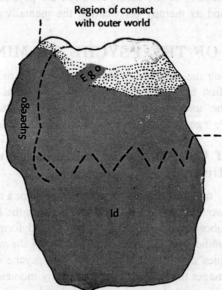

Figure 5.1 Structure of the human mind compared to an iceberg. (In the figure the *blank* area represents the conscious, the *dotted* area indicates the subconscious and the *dark* area shows the unconscious.)

The Id represents the animal in man and is seated in the unconscious. It is the source of mental energy and of all instinctive energy of the individual. It is present at birth and has the qualities of a spoiled child: i.e., it must get what it wants, when it wants it. In this way Id is quite selfish and unethical. It knows no reality, follows no rules and considers only the satisfaction of its own needs and drives. It operates according to the pleasure principle—the pursuit of pleasure and the avoidance of pain and in practice it does so by attempting to discharge the energy of the psyche quite irresponsibly.

However, for the sake of the welfare of the individual and of society, the blind Id cannot be allowed to discharge the useful psyche energy in such thoughtless and irresponsible ways and so two other wings of the human psyche system, namely, the ego and the super ego come into play.

The super ego is the direct antithesis of Id and represents the ethical and moral aspect of the psyche. It usually develops in the child at the age of five and is referred to as 'conscience', or the judgment from within. Like Id, it is also seated in the unconscious but is not governed by man's instinctive tendencies or primitive drives. It is idealistic in nature, and perfection is its goal, rather than pleasure-seeking or destruction.

The Ego develops out of the Id and acts as an intermediary between three sets of forces, i.e., the instinctive, irrational demands of the Id, realities of the external world and the ethical, moral demands of the Super ego. It is extended to all the three layers of the mind for exercising its balancing role, i.e., to control the Id in terms of reality and to appease the Super ego.

PSYCHODYNAMICS—BEHAVIOURAL PROCESS

How does the psyche system develop and operate in an individual for shaping his personality and determining his behaviour? The question can be answered through the following concepts and views expressed by Freud.

Life and Death Instincts

Freud believed in the role of instinct in driving human behaviour. He postulated two main instincts namely the life instinct and the death instinct, as the source of all the psyche energy available in man.

One's life instinct is engaged in the service of one's life and its main aims are survival and the propagation of the species. It is manifested through sex and love. Freud gave the name 'libido' to the driving force of the life instinct and made it synonymous with the sex urge and sexuality of human beings. The libido believes in the pleasure principle. Since all physical pleasure, aroused from any of the organs in the body and through any functions, as advocated by Freud, is ultimately sexual in nature, the sex urge or sex motive may be regarded as the dynamic force and centre of all human behaviour at all ages.

The concept of the other instinct, called the death instinct, relates to the impulse for destruction. It is manifested through acts of aggression, cruelty and even of suicide. Freud held that when one's life instinct is not allowed to function or to govern one's behaviour, the death instinct comes into the picture for operating behaviour. For example, when one is not permitted to seek sexual gratification or derive pleasure, one is bound to lose one's balance, suffer frustration which may consequently lead to the destruction of one's self or of others.

Infantile Sexuality and Psycho-Sexual Development

According to Freud, sex is the life urge or fundamental motive in life. All physical pleasures arising from any of the organs or any of the functions are ultimately sexual in nature. Sexuality is not the characteristic only of the adults. Children from the very beginning have sexual desires also. This, he termed as 'infantile sexuality'. A child passes through the following different stages with respect to his psycho-sexual development:

1. *The oral stage.* According to Freud, the mouth represents the first sex organ for providing pleasure to the child. The beginning is made with the pleasure received from the mother's nipple or the bottle. Thereafter, the child derives pleasure by putting anything, candy, a stick, his own thumb, etc. into his mouth.

2. *The anal stage.* At this stage, the interest of the child shifts from the mouth as the erogenous zone to the organs of elimination, i.e. the anus or the urethra. He derives pleasure by holding back or letting go of the body's waste material through the anus or the urethra. This stage, generally, ranges from two to three years.

3. *The phallic stage.* This phase starts from the age of four years with the shifting of the child's interest from the eliminating organs to the genitals. At this stage children come to note the biological differences between the sexes and derive pleasure by playing with and manipulating the genital organs. This stage, according to Freud, may give rise to a number of complexes like deprivation and Electra complexes in girls and castration and *Oedipus* complexes in boys. The deprivation complex is the result of the feeling generated in the minds of the little girls that they have been deprived of the male organ by their mothers. Castration complex is generated in boys through their fear of being deprived of the male organs certainly as a result of the threat received from elders that the organ would be cut off if they did not give up the habit of playing with it. About the Oedipus and Electra phases, Freud says that they are the result of the sexual attraction or pleasure that children experience in the company of the parent of the opposite sex. In case the parent of the same sex frustrates the desire, expresses his or her resentment and is not friendly to the boy or girl, the child may develop Oedipus or Electra complex by loving the opposite sex parent more and rather hating the like sex parent.

4. *The latency stage.* This period starts from six years in the case of girls and seven to eight years in the case of boys and extends up to the onset of puberty. At this stage, boys and girls prefer to be in the company of their own sex and even neglect or hate members of the opposite sex.

5. *The genital stage.* Puberty is the starting point of the genital stage. The adolescent boy and girl now feels a strange feeling of strong sensation in the

genitals and attraction towards the members of the opposite sex. At this stage they may feel pleasure by self-stimulation of the genitals, may fall in love with their own self by taking interest in beautifying and adorning their bodies and may be drawn quite close to members of the opposite sex even to the extent of indulging in sexual intercourse.

The Flow of Libido

The libido, in Freud's system, represents that life maintaining energy which aims to seek pleasure through sexual gratification. It can be equated to a river and its flow determines the type of behaviour or personality make-up of an individual.

1. If its flow is outward, causing satisfactory sexual gratification and pleasurable sensations from outside objects, the behaviour tends to be quite normal.
2. If its flow is inward, it can develop in the inculcation of a spirit of 'self-love' leading to self-indulgence and narcissism.
3. If its path is blocked, then it may become stagnant. In such cases the libido may be said to have been arrested or fixed on an object or stage of development. For example, if a child does not get enough stimulation and pleasure by sucking etc., at the oral stage, his libido may get fixed at this stage and consequently in the later years of his life he may be seen excessively interested in eating, drinking or stimulating the mouth in any manner.
4. In case the flow of the libido is so blocked that it gets repressed or flows backward then the person may develop a regressed personality. Such persons tend to behave in the manner and ways related to that developmental stage at which they suffer frustration over the satisfaction of their pleasure seeking desires.
5. When the flow of the libido is blocked, condemned or repressed through the authority exercised by the ego in deference to the super ego, it may cause severe anxiety and conflicts in the individual causing neurotic or psychotic behaviour.
6. In case the flow of the libido is deflected, it may lead an individual to seek sex gratification through other socially desirable sublimated ways and to develop his personality accordingly.

Anxiety, Conflicts and Disintegration of Personality

Anxiety and conflicts lead an individual to develop into an abnormal personality. Freud describes anxiety as a painful emotional experience, representing a threat or danger to the individual concerned. Whereas in the state of fear the source of tension is known, in case of anxiety one cannot relate it to an external object. In a real sense, the sources of free floating anxiety are related to earlier traumatic experiences. Very often it is the result of undischarged sexual impulses—a blocked up libido.

Blocking up or repression of the libido or sexual urge, according to Freud, does not end only in a free floating anxiety but also gives birth to severe conflicts leading to mental illness and abnormal behaviour. All conflicts in one way or the other represent clashes of the authority and roles of one's id, ego and super ego. Id, by its nature wants immediate gratification of its desires and appetites. Super ego as the antithesis of id, tries to censor and push them back into the unconscious. Repression leads to the formation of certain complexes, creates a source of anxiety and develops an agitating force to fight with the super ego. The ego plays a role of moderator. In case the super ego is too strong and dominates the ego of the individual, the anxiety and conflict may give birth to a psychotic personality but in case the super ego is not so rigid, then the expression of the repressed libido may result in a less severe form of personality disintegration like neurosis or milder symptoms like headache, backache, restlessness, lack of sleep and appetite.

PSYCHOANALYSIS AS A THERAPY

Besides providing a method of studying behaviour in the name of psychoanalytic method, Freud's theory of psycho-analysis has also contributed a therapy, i.e. the practical technique of treating mental illness. This therapy involves the following main steps.

Establishing Rapport

Attempts are made to establish a reciprocal emotional bond of mutual trust and faith between the analyst and the patient. Freud named this type of rapport as transference. When it is established, the patient begins to identify himself completely with the analyst by respecting and having full faith in him. The analyst also in turn becomes generous and capable enough to help him.

Analysis

This step is meant to find out the causes of the patient's problem. According to Freud, the behavioural problem or mental illness is the result of repressed wishes and desires dumped into the unconscious. For treatment, this unconscious needs to be explored. Freud suggested techniques like free association, dream analysis and the analysis of daily psychopathology for this exploration.

1. *Free association.* In this technique, the affected individual is made to lie on a soft coach and say anything that comes into his or her mind no matter how trivial or ridiculous it may seem.

2. *Dream analysis.* According to Freud, the dream is essentially a disguised satisfaction of desires that have been repressed during the waking life. These repressed desires or experiences are released symbolically in dreams. The analysis of these dreams can reveal the unconscious mind and thus lead to the root of the abnormalities.

3. *Analysis of the daily psychopathology.* The repressed desires or experiences lying in the unconscious can also be revealed through day to day psychopathology in terms of slips of the tongue and slips of the pen, forgotten names and forgotten appointments, lost gifts and misled possessions.

Synthesis

After discovering the reasons or roots of the trouble, attempts are made to restructure and restore the balance of the psyche. This requires the whole story to be put before the patient. The patient is made to come out of the trouble by accepting the exposure of the contents of the unconscious, and having them synthesized in a realistic way with the help of suggestions put forward by the analyst.

Breaking the Rapport

Finally, the rapport or the temporary emotional bond formed during the course of the treatment is broken to enable the patient to face the realities of life without the support of the analyst.

CRITICISM OF FREUD'S SYSTEM OF PSYCHOANALYSIS

Although Freud's work in the study of human behaviour is compared with the discovery of Copernicus that the earth was not the centre of the universe or with the Darwin's theory that monkeys and chimpanzees are the forefathers of man, yet it came in for severe criticism during and after his lifetime. The shortcomings of his system are enumerated briefly as follows:

1. His system reflects his medical background and consequently he has tried to emphasize man only as a natural or biological and not as a cultural entity. His assertion that man is a selfish pleasure-seeking animal is only one side of the story. Every man has an animal within him but he does not always live or strive only for the derivation of pleasure. He is also a social being and can make sacrifice and live for others.

2. Freud, in his study of human behaviour, has not been sufficiently scientific and objective. Many times he has concluded and generalized on the basis of a single study or case of mental illness and for that reason, many of his views and findings lack general applicability. For example, his theory of Oedipus and Electra complexes emphasizing hatred for the parent of the same sex and love for the parent of the opposite sex have not been found universally true, as we can find an altogether different type of attitude and relationship between parents and children depending upon the treatment received by the children under different environmental situations.

3. The most severe criticism suffered by Freud's system is concerned with his overemphasis of the role of sex in human life. Freud seems to overgeneralize everything in terms of sex as he declares that "the world

revolves round the sexes, not around the axis". His views on infantile sexuality are regarded as robbing the child of his divine nature and unique innocence. Certainly Freud has taken a very biased and erroneous stand by reducing human behaviour to a function of a single unitary motive, i.e. the sex motive.

The complex human behaviour cannot be interpreted in such a generalized unitary fashion. There are so many motives or urges that come into play for determining human behaviour at a particular time in a particular situation. However, we should not also do an injustice to Freud by denigrating and underplaying the importance of sex in human life. Sex, according to Freud, should be taken to be synonymous with anything which gives us sensation and pleasure. Sex is refined, beautiful, full of love and affection and helps us to derive pleasure and maintain the stream of our life. Therefore, sexuality or the sex motive must be interpreted in a wide sense for deriving all physical and mental pleasure and maintaining the process of life and not merely in terms of the sexual act or copulation.

4. Freud took the unconscious as a dumping ground of all the discarded or repressed wishes and a safe abode for all evils and vices in man responsible for giving birth to many conflicts, tensions and mental illness. However, it is not all that can be said for the unconscious. The unconscious can play a vital part in storing all that is good, beautiful and divine in man and thus lead a person to playing a more useful and constructive role in life in terms of creation, sacrifice and striving for the higher ideals.

5. Freud laid too much emphasis on the role of early childhood experiences in the determination of the course of one's life as well as one's overall personality. Although the impact of these early experiences cannot be ignored, what happens afterwards should also not be underestimated. If the views propagated by Freud are to be accepted blindly, then we are reduced to mere puppets in the hands of our early childhood traumatic experiences, the memory of which is stored in our unconscious. However, as may be experimentally verified, this is not true; our personality make-up or behaviour is not determined only by what happens with us in our childhood but also by the events or circumstances that we face in our adult life.

CONTRIBUTION TO EDUCATION

Although as happens with any new ideology, much is said against the system advocated by Freud, it has many things on the credit side. Its contribution to education can be summarized as follows:

1. Prior to Freud, behaviour was taken to mean conscious behaviour only. The concept and scope of the term 'behaviour' was thus widened and enlarged with the introduction of unconscious and pre-conscious

behaviour. Consequently, the sphere and scope of psychology in general, and educational psychology in particular was expended with the introduction of the system of psychoanalysis.

2. Freud's system of psychoanalysis has provided a very good method for the study of human behaviour.

3. Freud was a medical man and consequently his system propagated the biological approach as opposed to the mechanical approaches adopted by the behaviourists. It resulted in a change of outlook towards human beings and especially towards children. By emphasizing the emotional or affective side of behaviour and the inner nature of man and highlighting the role of instincts, needs, and wishes, Freud's system ushered in an era of child-centred education.

4. The ill effects of unnecessary restrictions, and the importance of earlier childhood experiences was adequately highlighted by Freud's system of psychoanalysis. It has given an impetus to the movement of early childhood education, incorporating the giving of maximum freedom to children for expression of their biological urges and minimum interference in the course of their natural growth and development.

5. The discovery of the unconscious and its importance in determining behaviour has helped in determining the causes of behavioural deviations. In education, this has helped in understanding the exceptional children, planning their education and the taking of all possible precautionary measures for preventing their becoming problem children or maladjusted personalities.

6. Freud's psychoanalysis has contributed significantly to providing education for mental health. By revealing the role of the unconscious, psycho-sexual development, the role of early childhood experiences, psychology of conflicts, anxiety or defence mechanisms etc., it has led to the diagnosis of mental illness. Psycho-analysis as a therapy has provided a method of treatment for the mentally ill and disturbed. The causes and symptoms suggested in psychoanalysis may thus prove helpful to the teachers and parents to remain vigilant for the preservation of mental health and the promotion of timely treatment of the behavioural problems and mental illness of children.

7. Psychoanalysis has highlighted the importance of the process of catharsis for releasing pent-up emotions, repressed desires and wishes. It has brought out the necessity of making adequate provision of cocurricular activities, hobbies and freedom of expression for children in any scheme of formal education and training.

8. Freud's psychoanalysis has also contributed considerably to high-lighting the role of sex in one's life in terms of shaping one's personality and determining one's behaviour. It in fact opened a new chapter in the history of sex education by (a) discussing the stages of psycho-sexual development, (b) emphasizing the need for spontaneous expression of the sex instinct, and (c) changing the general attitude towards sex by treating it as a natural, essential, biological function instead of regarding it as shameful, dirty or bad.

SUMMARY

Psycho-analysis—Freud's system of psychology represents a fine blend of theory and practice for the understanding and shaping of human behaviour.

The psychoanalytic theory put forward by Freud provides the theoretical framework for understanding human behaviour. Briefly it involves the following concepts:

Structure of the psyche or mind. Freud provides a two-tier tripartite division of the psyche, first, by breaking it into three layers as the conscious, the subconscious and the unconscious and second by postulating three more concepts of Id (the most selfish, unethical and basic component of man's animal nature), Super ego (the ethical-moral aspect of the psyche) and the Ego (the real self, the balancing force between id and super ego).

Life and death instincts. Instincts, the life instinct and the death instinct, play a decisive role in shaping human behaviour. The goal of the life instinct is survival and the propagation of the species. Libido, or sexual urge is the energy force of the life instinct. Most of our behaviour is governed by the sex motive. In case.one is not permitted to seek the gratification of sex, one is bound to behave under the direction of the death instinct, leading towards the destruction of one's own self or causing harm to others.

Infantile sexuality and psycho-sexual development. Sex is the life urge, there-fore, not only of adults but also of infants who manifest sexual desire by sucking the breast of their mother and feeling satisfied. Freud termed this as infantile sexuality. Growing with such need for sex gratification the individual's psycho-sexual development is said to pass through certain distinctive stages like the oral stage, the anal stages, the phallic stage, the latency stage and the genital stage. At each of these five stages of psycho-sexual development, the child seeks sex gratification through some distinct peculiar means, which is unique to that particular stage, i.e. sucking behaviour, seeking sex gratification through the use of the mouth at the infantile stage. In case the child is denied proper sex gratification through the specified ways of his stages, he is bound to suffer at the later stages turning him into a disorganised personality showing maladaptive behaviour.

The flow of libido. Libido, the life maintaining energy which aims at seeking pleasure through sex gratification, may work as the determinant of one's personality make-up. In case the flow of this energy in terms of the satisfaction of the sexual urge is normal and satisfactory, the behaviour remains satisfactory and normal. But in case this flow is repressed, blocked or damned up, it ends not only in free floating anxiety but also gives birth to severe conflicts leading to mental illness and abnormal behaviour.

Psychoanalysis as a method (of studying behaviour) and a therapy (treating mental illness or abnormal behaviour) is said to involve steps like (a) establishing rapport with the subject, (b) analysis of the behaviour of the subject to uncover the underlying causes of the abnormality by adopting techniques like free association, dream analysis, and analysis of daily psychopathology, (c) synthesis for restructuring and restoring the lost balance of the psyche and (d) breaking the rapport in order to enable the patient to face the realities of life without the support of the analyst.

Criticism of Freud's System of Psychoanalysis. Freud's system of psychoanalysis has been criticised mainly on the following grounds:

1. It treats mankind to be selfish, pleasure seeking and animal-like rather than social and humane.
2. It often overgeneralizes on the basis of a single study.
3. It overemphasises the role of sex in human life.
4. It attaches too much importance to the role of the unconscious as a determinant of behaviour.
5. It exaggerates the role of early childhood experiences for setting out the course of one's life.

Contribution to Education. Freud's system of psychoanalysis has made the following contributions to education:

1. It has given a good method for the study of behaviour.
2. It has provided a good therapy for treatment of mental illness and abnormal behaviour.
3. It has highlighted the importance of good education and a healthy environment in the early years by emphasising the role of childhood experiences.
4. Freud's concept of the unconscious has helped in understanding the cause of maladaptive behaviour.
5. His emphasis on the role of sex in one's life has brought out the necessity of providing proper sex education to children.
6. Freud's system of psychoanalysis has called for the provision of proper extracurricular activities and suitable hobbies etc. in the school programmes for the release of repressed or blocked libidinal energy and pent-up feelings.

REFERENCES

Freud, S., *The Ego and the Id*, London: Hogarth Press, 1923.

_____, *Inhibition, Symptoms and Anxiety*, London: Hogarth Press, 1926.

_____, *Introductory Lectures on Psychoanalysis*, London: Allen & Unwin, 1929.

_____, *A General Introduction to Psychoanalysis*, New York: Liveright, 1935.

_____, *The Problem of Anxiety*, New York: W.W. Norton & Co., 1936.

_____, *Beyond the Pleasure Principle*, New York: Liveright, 1950.

_____, *An Outline of Psychoanalysis*, London: Hogarth Press, 1953.

_____, *Three Essays on the Theory of Sexuality*, New York: Basic Books, 1962.

_____, *Psychopathology of Everyday Life*, New York: W.W. Norton & Co., 1971.

SUGGESTED READINGS

Alexander, F. and French, T.M., *Psychological Therapy*, New York: Ronald Press, 1946.

Brill, A.A., *Psychoanalysis*, New York: Saunders, 1922.

Hall, C.S. and Lindzey, G., *Theories of Personality*, 3rd ed., New York: Wiley, 1978.

Jones, E., *The Life and Work of Sigmund Freud* (Lionel Trilling and Steven Marcus, Eds.), Garden City, New York: Anchor Books, 1963.

Levin, M.J., *Psychology—A Biographical Approach*, New York: McGraw-Hill, 1978.

Previn, Lawrence, A., *Personality*, New York: Wiley, 1984.

Richman, J. (Ed.), *A General Selection from the Works of Sigmund Freud*, Garden City, New York: Anchor Books, 1957.

Roazen, P., *Freud and His Followers*, New York: Alfred Knopf, 1975.

Stagner, Ross, *Psychology of Personality*, New York: McGraw-Hill, 1974.

Symonds, P., *The Dynamics of Human Adjustment*, New York: Appleton, 1946.

Woodworth, R.S., *Contemporary Schools of Psychology* (Rev. ed.), London: Methuen, 1965.

Chapter 6

Adler's System of Individual Psychology

INTRODUCTION

Born in Vienna in 1870, Alfred Adler began his career as an ophthalmologist. He joined Freud's school of psychoanalysis in 1902 and became one of his prize pupils. He broke away from Freud mainly over the latter's overemphasis on sex and founded a new school of psychology. His system is called *Individual Psychology* because it lays emphasis on the individuality of human beings in terms of their unique characteristics at the time of birth, the availability of an exclusive environment for growth and development and adoption of a specific style of life to achieve power and attain perfection.

WHAT THE SYSTEM TELLS

Adler, in his system for explaining behaviour, replaced the life instinct or sex motive advocated by Freud with the motive to seek power or attain superiority and perfection. According to him, for the satisfaction of the power motive, one follows one's own path in one's own way and thus develops a unique style of life, depending upon the order of birth, early life experiences and the requirements of the creative self. Success or failure in the satisfaction of the power motive by adopting his own style turns a person into an adjusted or a maladjusted personality. The individual then further learn the ways of striving and making adjustments and this is how, according to Adler's system, one behaves and leads one's life.

MAJOR CONCEPTS OF INDIVIDUAL PSYCHOLOGY

Power Motive and Striving for Superiority and Perfection

How and why one behaves in a particular fashion may be explained in terms of one's striving for the satisfaction of one's urge to dominate, to gain superiority and to achieve perfection in one field or the other. This urge to dominate or to strive for superiority or perfection, as Adler says, is innate. It is part of one's life and in fact may be termed as life itself.

63

Why, one may ask, did Adler select the power motive as the only motive to explain human behaviour? The genesis of this may be traced to the experiences to which a child is exposed in his early childhood.

1. Every child is born as a helpless mass, entirely dependent upon grown ups for the satisfaction of his needs. Consequently, he may have a burning desire to seek power, to dominate and to attain superiority in order to overcome and compensate for his feelings of inadequacy and inferiority.
2. He may be brought up in such a way that he may develop attitudes for ruling and dominating over others and as a manifestation of this trait, he may crave for superiority and the desire to surpass others.
3. He may be the victim of negligence or develop some inferiority feelings. The urge to strive for superiority helps him overcome his feelings of inferiority and inadequacy.

Style of Life

If one wants to live, one has to strive to or establish superiority in one way or the other and consequently one has to adopt one's own style of life. This style of one's life has been the key point in Adler's system of individual psychology. One is known and judged by one's style of life. According to Adler, all human beings have the same goal—that of gaining superiority over others but may adopt different ways and means to fulfil their power motive, strive for superiority and reach the goal of perfection. The manner in which they strive and the ways and means they adopt collectively constitute the style of life. Accordingly, one person may try to become superior through developing as a political leader; an other may strive to become a renowned author, writer, artist, scientist or wrestler. One's style of life thus depends on the areas or fields in which one chooses to strive for superiority. The whole of one's time schedule, habits of work, personal and social contacts, comprising one's style of life then, will naturally be tailored to the ways and means one chooses for striving towards superiority and perfection.

Adler has mentioned four types of life styles for the development of personality, namely, (a) the ruling type, (b) the go-getting type, (c) the escaping type, and (d) the struggling type.

What makes them develop these distinct styles of life may be influenced by the following factors:

1. *The order of birth.* According to Adler, the order, place and position of the child in the family when he is born is to a great extent responsible for fashioning his style of life.

2. *The type of children.* Adler has pointed out that different types of children pick up different styles of life for their personality development. For example, the pampered child may adopt a life-style to get his wishes accepted and for him to be treated as prince. On the other hand, the unwanted or neglected child may either turn into a timid, shy and insecure person or become a drunkard and criminal.

3. *Fictional finalism.* The style of one's life also depends upon the mechanism of fictional finalism which means that men live by many purely fictional ideas which do not necessarily conform to reality. We can cite examples such as the following: "Stars or lines on our palm decide our future or destiny", "Female child is a curse to the family", "Women are made to be governed or ruled by men", and so on. The belief in such fictional ideas is sure to affect the philosophy and style of one's life.

4. Compensation for inferiority. In many cases, one's style of life is fashioned in relation to some compensatory behaviour for a particular kind of inferiority. For example, the life-style of Demosthenes who became the world's greatest orator was the outcome of the compensation for the inferiority he suffered on account of his stuttering as a child. Similarly, the conquering style of Napolean was fashioned as a compensation for the feeling of inferiority he suffered because of his small physical stature.

5. The creative self. The creative power of the individual is responsible, to a great extent, for determining and shaping his style of life. According to Adler, it is the creative self which gives meaning to life by creating goals as well as suggesting means to achieve the goal. This creative self grows and develops in an individual out of his hereditary endowments and environmental experiences. He tends to solve problems and act according to the dictates of his creative self. His style of life is, therefore, said to be fashioned in accordance with the development of his creative self.

6. Social interest. Man is a social creature and his style of life is also determined through the varying social interests he shows in maintaining social relationships, extending cooperation, sympathy and kindness and thus in a wider sense helping society to attain the goal of perfection. Striving for superiority, in this case, becomes a socialized rather than a selfish need and the life style gets fashioned through one's innate social interests.

How Adler's System Operates

Based on the above-mentioned tenets, the operation of Adler's system of studying behaviour or personality make-up can be outlined as follows:

1. There is a strong inner urge in all human beings to seek power or strive for superiority. As the child grows and develops, this urge is also increased.
2. Besides this, hereditary, constitutional and other environmental factors operating during the first four or five years may give rise to many complexes, particularly feelings of inferiority in the child. To overcome or compensate for inferiority, one may resort to seeking power or striving for superiority.
3. The creative self, or the need for creative expression, may also force the individual to strive for superiority or perfection.

All the above-mentioned situations may force the individual to seek power or strive for superiority and perfection. For the fulfilments of this urge, he may then adopt a relevant life style suiting his specific environmental situation. He continues to strive for superiority by picking up the means and material through his life style. In doing so, he may succeed, or fail depending upon the inner and outer forces operating in such effort. In case of failure he often has to slightly modify his goals or style of life in keeping with his self or his environment. If he succeeds in such adjustment, he remains normal, otherwise he may drift towards mild or severe mental illness, needing urgent suitable treatment to bring about a change in his life style and goals of life.

Merits and Contribution to Education

Adler was a practical psychologist and he laid more emphasis on the problems of children, their proper education and adequate upbringing. He was so interested in applying his day to day psychology to the field of education that he himself started an Institute of Pedagogy at Vienna, with its branches at different places. He also directed his energies to provide guidance and counselling to parents and teachers to help them in providing better education and upbringing to their wards at home and at school. It is for these reasons that he is often remembered as a pedagogist and child psycho-therapist. The contributions of his system of psychology may be summarised as follows:

1. Adler played down the Freudian concept of sex urge as the only motive behind human behaviour. He replaced it with the urge to seek power or to attain superiority or perfection. In other words, he brought into the realm of psychology a useful urge or motive, namely the power motive or self-assertion. Every individual, from the very beginning, wants to satisfy this inner urge by asserting himself and wishing to be more powerful, to dominate somebody and be recognised as superior and of some value or importance. Parents and teachers must be very careful in recognizing this inner craving of children in the course of their upbringing and education. Every child should be given due recognition and the opportunity to do something and feel important. His distinctive self should not be attacked, but given due respect and means for proper expression.

2. Adler's system opposed the Freudian overemphasis on the unconscious, rather, it asserted that man lives and behaves through his conscious and is not merely a toy in the hands of his unconscious. He is always conscious of his strengths and weaknesses and strives to achieve his goals with full awareness. These views provided an impetus to all conscious efforts on the part of students, parents and teachers to strive for realization of the goals of life as perfectly as possible rather than to become mere instruments in the hands of the unconscious.

3. Adler's assertion that every man acts and behaves according to his own style of life helped in the growth of individualistic tendencies in education. It underscored the need to know and study every child as a separate individual and to plan his education and the development of his personality through ways and means suited to his individual self. 'Child centred education' and 'individualized instruction' are thus the direct outcome of Adler's work.

4. Adler's system emphasized the importance of the first four or five years of one's life in the shaping of one's personality. He tried to make the parents and teachers understand the possible impact of the birth order, size of the family and methods of rearing on the bahaviour and personality of the children. He warned them to be very cautious in rearing as well as in educating their children so that they do not develop an inferiority complex or unwarranted need for compensatory behaviour which might give rise to some mental illness or behavioural problem. A few of his findings and suggestions in this regard are worth mentioning:

(a) Every precaution and all preventive measures should be taken to safeguard the children so that they do not become physically or mentally handicapped. In case this happens, the child should be so treated and reared that he is not subjected to feelings of inferiority. He may be provided with other channels along which to strive for superiority and thus compensate for this deficiency. But, in doing so, he should not be made conscious or aware of his handicap.

(b) No child should be reared so as to develop as a pampered child. Every child should be brought up in such a way that while showing affection and tenderness to him and meeting his needs, he is made to stand on his own feet and learn to strive for superiority by using his own strength.

(c) No child should be brought up in such a way that he feels, neglected, unwanted or insulted. Every child needs due attention and respect for his self and sense of security, for his proper growth and development. In case the environmental situation at home does not provide what is needed by the child, alternative arrangement in terms of a foster home, greater care and affection by the teacher and members of society, should be provided so that he does not turn into a problem child.

(d) As far as possible, negative means like nagging, warning, reprimanding, putting blame, scolding, severely beating and whipping etc., for making the child behave in some specific and desirable ways should be avoided as these do not yield favourable results and only deepen the child's feeling of inferiority and discourage him from striving for supremacy. Therefore, Adler feels positive measures in the form of praise, rewards and incentives should be used for shaping the behaviour of children.

(e) In no case, should the parents and teachers encourage rivalry and unhealthy competition among the children as this may enhance the feelings of inferiority, insecurity and anxiety and give rise to serious behavioural problems.

5. Adler rendered a great service by emphasizing the role of social interests and other social determinants in shaping one's style of life and personality make-up. This helped in providing due recognition to the various social agencies for acting as means of imparting education to the youngsters as well as realising the need for mutual cooperation, cohesion, group dynamics and organisation of an improved environment for the better growth and development of children's personalities.

6. Adler's emphasis on the role of the creative self in the shaping of one's personality and unique style of life opened up a new dimension in the field of education. It gave due importance to the identification and nurturing of the creative faculties in the child.

7. Adler's system laid stress on prevention, early diagnosis and timely treatment of behavioural problems of the children so that these do not grow into severe mental illnesses or threats to the individual and to society. The trend for understanding the real cause of behavioural problems, treating every case on an individual basis, paying due attention, providing timely care and realizing the need for a well established guidance clinic are some of the well-known contributions of Adler's system of individual psychology.

SUMMARY

The system of psychology propagated by Alfred Adler, a prize disciple of Freud, is known as Individual Psychology. The operation of this system revolves around the following two key concepts:

Power motive. Every individual has a strong urge to seek power or attain superiority and perfection in one field or the other. This power-seeking behaviour is either a compensatory behaviour for overcoming feelings of inferiority and inadequacy or may be a sort of reinforcement behaviour the roots of which may lie in the individual's earlier experiences.

Style of life. To fulfil the motive of seeking power or achieving perfection, one has to choose one's own style of life, i.e. ways and means for striving towards superiority and reaching the goal of perfection. Adler names four personality types depending upon the different life styles viz., the ruling type, the getting type, the escaping type, and the struggling type. Why and how one chooses a particular type of life style depends on one's individual make-up and earlier experiences. These are influenced by factors such as, (a) the order of birth, (b) the manner in which one has been brought up during childhood, (c) fictional finalism, i.e. the deep-rooted beliefs in some ideas prevalent in society, (d) compensation for inferiority, (e) the demands of one's creative self, and (f) one's innate social interests.

How the system of individual psychology operates. Persuaded and motivated to seek power or superiority (on account of seeking compensation, reinforcement or satisfaction of one's creative self), one is forced to adopt the relevant life style suited to one's environmental situation. One continues to struggle for achieving one's goals through the ways and means provided by one's life style. While striving, however, one has to maintain a proper balance between one's needs and efforts. In case one succeeds in making such an adjustment, one remains normal, otherwise one may drift towards maladaptive behaviour.

Merits and contribution to education. The major contributions of individual psychology may be summarized as:

1. Emphasizing the need of paying due respect to the phenomenal self of the child and providing the means for self-expression and self-actualization.
2. Giving conscious behaviour and deliberate effort a major share in striving towards the realization of life's goals.
3. Giving impetus to 'child centred education' and 'individualized instruction'.
4. Emphasizing the importance of the first four or five years of life in the shaping of personality and for this purpose devoting due attention to the rearing as well as education of children during this period, taking care to ensure that they do not imbibe inferiority or guilt feelings.
5. Giving due recognition to various social agencies and social activities for shaping the behaviour and personality of children.
6. Providing due importance to the identification and nurturing of creativity.
7. Stressing the need for prevention, early diagnosis and timely treatment of behavioural problems of children and realizing the need of a guidance clinic in the school.

REFERENCES

Adler, A., *The Neurotic Constitution*, London: Kegan Paul, 1921.

————, *Understanding Human Nature*, London: Allen & Unwin, 1928.

————, *The Education of Children*, New York: Greenberg, 1930.

————, *What Life Should Mean to You*, New York: Grosset and Dunlop, 1937.

————, *The Practice and Theory of Individual Psychology*, Totowa, N.J: Littlefield Adams, 1968.

————, *The Science of Living*, Garden City, New York: Anchor Books, 1969.

————, Hall, C.S. and Lindzey, G., *Theories of Personality*, 3rd ed., New York: Wiley, 1978.

SUGGESTED READINGS

Levin, M.J., *Psychology—A Biographical Approach*, New York: McGraw-Hill, 1978.

Stagner, R., *Psychology of Personality*, New York: McGraw-Hill, 1974.

Symonds, P., *The Dynamics of Human Adjustment*, New York: Appleton, 1946.

Wexberg, E., *Individual Psychology* (Trans. by W.B. Wolf), London: Allen & Unwin, 1929.

————, *Individual Psychology and Sex*, London: Cape, 1931.

Woodworth, R.S., *Contemporary Schools and Psychology* (Rev. ed.), London: Methuen, 1965.

Chapter 7

Analytical Psychology— Jung's System of Psychology

INTRODUCTION

Carl Gustav Jung, physician by profession, was born in the Swiss village of Kesswell in 1875. He came in close contact with Freud and became his staunch supporter and follower to the extent that Freud declared him as 'crown prince' and 'beloved son'. However, in the years that followed, very serious ideological differences (mainly on account of Freud's overemphasis on sex) developed between the two to such an extent that Jung established a separate school of thought called *Analytical Psychology* for experimenting with and propagating his ideas. Let us try to understand Jung's system of analytical psychology through some of the main psychological concepts.

STRUCTURE OF THE PSYCHE OR MIND

Jung, like Freud, accepted the existence of the unconscious besides the conscious in the structure of one's psyche. However, he differed a great deal in his concept of the unconscious. According to Jung, one's mind consists of the following parts:

Conscious Mind

The upper layer of one's mind consists of the memories, thoughts and feelings that result from one's consciousness. It is in fact the seat of one's ego and conscious behaviour. It is only a fraction of the human mind. Below it lies one's vast unconscious divided into two parts—the personal unconscious and the collective unconscious.

Personal Unconscious

The layer of the mind concerning the personal unconsciousness lies beneath but in very close contact with the conscious. It is highly individualistic and personal in nature. It contains all the repressed desires, ideas, feelings, fears, guilts, anxieties, forgotten incidents, dreams, fantasies and other private experiences which might occur in the lifetime of an individual.

70

Collective Unconscious

Beneath the layer of the personal unconscious lies the collective unconscious. This is neither personal nor private but is universal to all individuals. According to Jung, the modes of thinking, feeling and doing as held by one's ancestors being transferred from generation to generation become part and parcel of one's unconscious. The individuals who inherit such vast stores of ancestral characteristics or racial memory, then are conditioned to perceive the world in the same way as the previous generations did. One's collective unconscious thus contains the experiences of the whole race gathered over millions of ancestral years specifically in the form of universal ideas or images called archetypes. Since the entire human race has the same origin and common ancestral history, these archetypes or images held and contained in our unconscious are the same. That is why these are called the racial or collective unconscious. Let us try to learn more about these archetypes.

Archetypes. Archetypes are the roots and bases of the collective unconscious. They represent the eternally inherited ideas and forms which are common to every generation and culture since the dawn of mankind. They may either be handed down with the evolving brain in the form of inherited neural patterns or may be acquired through direct and indirect experiences. They are available in abundance in old myths and fairy tales and folklore in religious and cultural traditions in enduring literature and art. A variety of archetypes exist, like the mother archetype, the father archetype, the hero and the persona, the anima and the animus, and the shadow and the self. Let us briefly discuss these archetypes.

The mother archetype: It is an eternal idea or image which is inherited from generation to generation and is common and universal to all cultures and races. The image of the mother always appears to be pious, warm, loving, protective and nourishing.

The father archetype: In contrast to the mother archetype, the father archetype reflects strength, authority and power. In all cultures where the earth, plants and rivers are equated with the mother image, the sun, sky, oceans, lightning and thunder, are associated with the father image.

The hero archetype: This is well known to us through our concept of a person who is an ideal, and often unselfish, figure in every respect. Similarly, in every culture or race we find many other eternal ideas which are quite universal and identical like the image of God, birth and death, demon and devil, saints and wise men, and the existence of some energy force moving this world.

Whereas the archetypes discussed above may be regarded as primary roots, archetypes like persona, the anima and animus are known as the secondary and tertiary roots.

PERSONA: This signifies the mask we wear to face society irrespective of our real personality. It represents a role or part played by us like the role of father or son, of wife or mother, of servant or master, of coward or courageous person chosen to meet a particular social situation. One has to wear different masks at different times to cope with the existing social situation. Not learning to play these roles, developing personal or excessive identification with one role (overemphasis on the persona), according to Jung, may lead to personality problems.

ANIMA: This is associated with the female characteristics and *animus* with the image of maleness. Jung declared that every male has a female in him and every female a male in her, meaning thereby that characteristics of both anima and animus lie within every individual. The presence of both male and female characteristics in the individual may be due to the plain fact of their living together from times immemorial.

THE SHADOW: This signifies the archetype that resembles the concept of Freud's Id. Consequently, it may represent all that is bad or mean in man. In the words of Jung, "it personifies everything that the subject refuses to acknowledge about himself." Symbolically, we can refer to it as the *devil* or *satan* in man who does not care for morality or social norms. However, as Jung clarifies, the shadow should not be considered as merely an enemy or the worst side of one's personality. It has a positive side also in one's creative expression.

The self as archetype was highly emphasized by Jung. The concept of self is a universal idea that can be found in all primitive philosophies and religions. In Hinduism, we know it as *atma*, well known for its individuality, the integrating force of one's personality and component of the universal cosmos, *brahm*. Self in Jung's system carries a wide connotation. It works as (a) an archetype—one of the most important bases of the collective unconscious; (b) an integrating force for all the components of one's psyche, i.e. conscious and unconscious, male and female, good and bad, etc., and (c) a centre of one's personality and the originator as well as balancing force of one's behaviour.

In his topology of the mind, Jung does not deny that the conscious mind is operative in the outside world but he lays greater emphasis on the inner world and the deep-rooted unconscious. However, his unconscious, whether personal or collective, is quite different from that of Freud in the following manner:

1. It is not merely the dumping ground of the suppressed ideas and desires of the conscious.
2. It is not evolved out of the conscious. On the contrary, the conscious has been evolved out of the unconscious. Consciousness cannot create itself—it arises from unknown depths of the unconscious.
3. It consists, not only of the unconscious of one's personal nature but also of the collective and racial nature. On the lines of Charles Darwin, Jung (1959) put forward the idea of evolutionary growth of the human mind:

The psyche is not of today, its ancestry goes back many millions of years. Individual consciousness is only for flowers and fruit of the season, sprung from the perennial rhizome (stem and root system) beneath the earth.

Thus the picture of the human psyche (see Figure 7.1) may be composed of various archetypes as the roots (resting in the deep interior), stemming out into the personal unconscious and blossoming out in the open as the conscious.

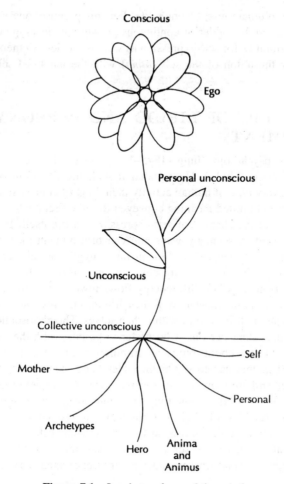

Figure 7.1 Jung's topology of the mind.

RELIGION, CREATIVITY, AND MOTIVE OF SELF-ACTUALIZATION

For explaining how and why we behave in a particular way, while freud laid down the idea of the sex urge or the sex motive and Adler, the motive of power seeking or striving for supremacy, Jung advocated the motive of self-actualization. According to him man is not merely a biological entity or social animal seeking gratification for his sex urge or power motive but being a developed and distinctive creation of the Almighty he always aims for some higher goals in his life. Jung believes that altruism is as innate in man as egoism. Religion is the need of human beings and morality is deep-seated in their collective unconscious. Therefore, man has a greater need for the spontaneous religious forms of expression. Similarly, there is an innate creative spark in every individual the basis of which also lies in the unconscious depths of his mind. These inner creative aspects of one's mind also need some forms of expression. In this way, one has a strong inner urge or motive to express one's talents or abilities or to make self-actualization the ultimate goal of one's life. For this purpose, one wants to climb higher and higher on the ladder of continuous growth and development by getting maximum opportunities for self-expression as well as the development of one's self and wishing for the union of the self (*atma*) with the universal self (cosmos or *brahm*).

THE CONCEPT OF LIBIDO AND PERSONALITY DEVELOPMENT

In his system of psychology, Jung (1875–1961) assigned a very comprehensive meaning to the term 'libido'. He equated it with the life urge or life energy responsible for every type of human activity including, of course, sex gratification, i.e. the narrower and limited meaning conveyed through Freud's libido. In fact, for Jung, libido was not the channel of self-expression but life itself. In an individual it can manifest itself in so many ways and can turn him into a writer, scientist, artist, mathematician as needed by him in his struggle for self-actualization.

Libido, the life energy, as Jung observes, may flow both ways—inward or outward. The persons in whom life energy flows inward are termed as *introverts*. These persons seek the manifestation of their life through inner activities by going inward and digging up things from within themselves. The philosophers, scientists, writers, and similar other persons, who prefer to be busy with their own thoughts and are not bothered about physical stimulation and the realities of their environment fall in this category. On the other hand, persons in whom the life energy flows outward are termed as *extroverts*. Such people seek the manifestation of their life through activities related with the outer world. They are successful at adjusting to the realities of their environment, are socially active and more interested in leaving a good impression on others. Their behaviour is influenced more by physical stimulation or sensory experiences than by their inner thoughts and ideas. Politicians, social workers, lawyers, insurance agents, salesmen, etc., fall in this category.

Based on the characteristics of introvert and extrovert personalities mentioned above, we should not think that a person is exclusively introvert or extrovert. According to Jung, both introvert and extrovert tendencies are ordinarily present in the personality of an individual but one of them is found to be dominant, thus making the person into a particular type. Moreover, an individual may also be seen to shift from one orientation—introvert or extrovert, to the other. For example, an introvert may behave in a gregarious fashion in response to some particular environmental situation and vice-versa. Similarly, it may also be seen that a person may appear to be belonging to a particular type of introversion or extroversion but in actual sense he may be just the opposite type.

Going further into the task of classifying the individuals by definite personality types, Jung associated a person's introvert and extrovert orientations with four main behavioural functions, namely, thinking, feeling, sensation and intuition, resulting in the following eight personality types:

1. The Introverted Thinking Type
2. The Extroverted Thinking Type

3. The Introverted Feeling Type
4. The Extroverted Feeling Type
5. The Introverted Sensational Type
6. The Extroverted Sensational Type
7. The Introverted Intuitive Type
8. The Extroverted Intuitive Type

This eight-fold division of personality types along with their main behavioural characteristics can be illustrated as in Table 7.1.

Table 7.1 Jung's Description of Personality Types

I			E
I	*Introverted thinking type*	*Extroverted thinking type*	E
	← THINKING →		
	Characteristics (i) More theoretical, detached and aloof (ii) Afraid of external realities (iii) Tactless and cold (iv) Absorbed in his own intellectual pursuit	*Characteristics* (i) Realistic and practical (ii) Supports theory with facts (iii) Propagates his views with insistence and vehemence	
I	*Introvert intuitive type*	*Extrovert intuitive type*	E
	Characteristics (i) More subjective and more concerned with probabilities than actualities (ii) Moody, unstable, and temperamental (iii) Behaves like the theoretical scientists and prophets (iv) Quite unstable in their friendship or loyalty	*Characteristics* (i) More outwardly, optimistic and change-seeker (ii) Attracted by future possibilities of gain and can take risk or gamble (iii) Quite set in intuitive judgement of the future course of activities	Intution
I	*Introvert sensational type*	*Extrovert sensational type*	E
Sensation	*Characteristics* (i) Possesses refined tastes and interests but quite choosy and fussy about the things he likes (ii) Learn and thin as he does not eat well (iii) Dissatisfied, broody and rather sad in the general appearance (iv) Better in writing than speaking and interested in books and magazines	*Characteristics* (i) Good eaters accepting any thing eatable at any moment (ii) Easily bored and demand constant emotional sensation (iii) Carefree, friendly and talkative (iv) No patience for abstract or theoretical ideas	
I	*Introvert feeling type*	*Extrovert feeling type*	E
	← FEELING →		
	Characteristics (i) Day dreamer (ii) Strong feelings, likes and dislikes (iii) Does not express his feelings to others and goes on suffering internally (iv) May feel strongly but does not resort to any step	*Characteristics* (i) More social (ii) Objective in his outlook and admires things of others (iii) helpful nature and feels for the suffering of others (iv) Expresses his feelings externally instead of suffering internally.	

DREAMS AND NEUROSES

Jung agrees with Freud in saying that dreams originate from one's unconscious but does not consider them as a mere representation of repressed or concealed desires. According to him, dreams are not past-oriented but are more present-oriented and forward looking. They are concerned with what is being done by us at present in our waking life and have two-dimensional foundations—the compensatory as well as the prospective. In performing a compensatory task, what has been left incomplete or the solution that has not come up during our waking state may be supplied and supplemented by our unconscious through dreams. In performing a prospective function, dreams, with the help of the unconscious, predict future events and anticipate the future conscious achievements.

One's dreams are not, thus, merely a means for unreal wish fulfilment. They work as true companions or guides to one's conscious mind to meet its day to day difficulties and planning wisely in anticipation of one's future.

According to Jung, the individual may have two types of dreams, springing from the personal unconscious and the collective unconscious. Whereas dreams from the personal unconscious can be interpreted objectively, the dreams from the collective or racial unconscious are to be interpreted subjectively since they usually deal with the dreamer's own attributes and tendencies.

Neurosis

Jung has a quite distinctive view about the causes of neurotic behaviour and its overall implications. According to him, neurosis represents regression or going back as a result of serious obstacle in the flow of libido or imbalances created in the mind through disharmony between one's conscious and unconscious. According to Jung, the causes of neuroses do not lie in the past but in the present as a neurosis represents loss of self-confidence on account of one's inability to cope with the demands of one's present environment. Also, when there is a serious conflict between one's unconscious and the conscious, (the conscious self advocating morality and the unconscious holding out for amorality) the inner self gets torn between the two, resulting in a split personality and abnormal behaviour.

However, Jung, like Freud, did not consider neurosis as a completely negative or dark side of one's personality. He considered it as an attempt on the part of the neurotic to lift himself. In neurosis one gets valuable opportunities to communicate with one's inner self and to think out better ways and means for achieving the higher aim of self-actualization.

JUNG'S PSYCHOTHERAPY

Jung's system of analytical psychology advocates self-actualization as the ultimate aim of human life and, consequently, the therapy suggested by him for the cure of mental illness is centred round the key concept of making the patient first understand what is wrong with his self and then helping him in integrating it. When this happens, the blockage in the natural libidinal flow can be removed and the balance of the psyche is restored by bringing about a reconciliation between the conflicting desires of one's conscious and unconscious. Jung put forward the technique of controlled association for this in contrast to the method of free association advocated by Freud.

In the technique of controlled association, the patient is not required to say freely what he feels or knows but is guided or helped in doing so through the content or words of an association test. In the actual procedure, the analyst makes use of a word association test consisting of some meaningful words related to the problem and the life history of the patient. The patient is asked to say whatever comes to his mind or to associate the words by listening to a particular word of the association test. The responses of the patient are then analysed by the analyst to understand the underlying causes of the behavioural problems of the patient. In addition to the data gathered through the responses of the word association test, the dreams of the patient are also analysed to obtain clues to the roots of the problem lying in one's personal or racial unconscious.

When the analysis is over, the analyst helps the patient to gain an insight into himself. For this purpose, the patient is made to understand the significance of the material belonging to his personal and racial unconscious as revealed by him through the word association and his dreams. Gradually, the patient becomes aware of the unrealistic demands of the unconscious, the obstacle in the path of his adaptation to his environment and integration of his self.

After this stage the treatment follows the process of synthesis. The goal of such synthesis is to bring about an integration of the self, a reconciliation between one's conscious and unconscious in view of the realities of life on the one hand and actualization of the creative potentialities of the unconscious on the other. For this purpose, the analyst may provide helpful suggestions to the patient or the patient may be guided to seek an independent solution so that the conflict between the conscious and unconscious may be successfully resolved and he may be able to strive well for achieving the higher goal of self-actualization.

Merits of Jung's Psychotherapy and its Contribution to Education

Jung's system of analytical psychology definitely carries many philosophical, psychological and educational values. It has provided more meaning and value to human life by advocating self-actualization as its ultimate goal rather than mere sex gratification or power seeking as advocated by Freud and Adler respectively. Furthermore, he gave a new dimension to the realm of the unconscious by advocating the existence of the collective or racial unconscious. Our behaviour, to a great extent, is not merely dominated by our own desires and wishes resting in our unconscious but by the silent impressions or impacts of all our thinking and feelings rooted in the culture of our particular race and humanity in general. Thus, what we can think or feel collectively or universally as human beings, has its very existence in our unconscious. This is an inherited treasure which is passed from generation to generation and that is why our psyche is as primitive and old as human civilization itself and what we have today may be the result of thousands of years of evolution in much the same way as the organic evolution propounded by Darwin.

The other notable contribution of Jung's system is the categorization of people into definite personality types based on the outward or inward flow of their libido, i.e. life energy. His other contributions like emphasis on the moral, social and cultural values as against the animal nature stressed by Freud, and the need of the realization of creative aspects inherent in man and integration of his self have essentially been quite helpful in the field of education. The main contributions of his system may be outlined below.

1. Jung considered the nature of man to be basically good as it was supposed to be dominated by the racial unconscious consisting of valuable social, cultural and moral qualities quite earnestly transferred from generation to generation. The function of education thus, according to him, consists in drawing out the best available in the vast store-house of the unconscious of the individual. The children thus are guided and encouraged to maximize or actualize potentialities inherent in them and for this purpose, maximum opportunities in the form of suitable methods and appropriate environment should be provided to them at home and at school.

2. He underlined the need to ascertain the introvert or extrovert natures of the individuals for correct planning of their education, to help in their proper growth and development as well as to adjust to their self and their environment. The need to guide the children so that they do not drift towards the extreme end of extroversion or introversion or develop into imbalanced personalities by developing one aspect of behaviour or personality at the cost of the others was also emphasized. The extrovert children should be guided to devote some time to introspection, meditation and communication with the inner self and the introverts should be encouraged to come out and have proper contacts with the outside world, widen their interests and develop relationships with other children and adults.

3. The educational activities and educational system should be so planned and designed as to help the children to seek the ultimate aim of man's life i.e., self-actualization.

4. Since an essential creative spark is present in every child, appropriate opportunities should be provided to him through formal and informal education for actualizing his creative potentialities.

5. According to Jung, religion has a positive influence on the integration of one's personality by helping one to fully understand one's own self, harmonizing the conflicting desires, giving inner peace, enhancing faith and providing a healing touch to the wounded self. Religious or moral education should, therefore, be provided through formal as well as informal agencies of education.

6. One's education and the process of growth and development should be so planned that one is not distanced from the basic tenets of one's culture or racial characteristics. Moreover, education should make one realistic in terms of adapting to oneself and to one's environment.

7. Jung's system contributed the word association test as one of the methods to discover personality traits of an individual.

8. Jung's system advocated that the system and scheme of education be so planned as to provide the maximum opportunity for development of the self in complete harmony with the development of others and of society or human race as a whole so that the forces operative in one's personal unconscious and racial unconscious may play their part in their own way for the complete and full development of one's individuality with reference to one's social context.

SUMMARY

The school of thought or system of psychology developed by Carl Jung, the famous psychologist, is known as analytical psychology. The major concepts of this system may be summarized as follows:

Structure of the psyche.   The structure of one's mind consists of one's conscious, the personal unconscious and the collective unconscious. The conscious is the seat of one's ego and conscious behaviour. Beneath it lies the personal unconscious—containing all the repressed material connected with one's private and personal life. The collective unconscious lies beneath the layer of one's personal unconscious. It is common and universal to all individuals and contains the experiences of the whole race collected over millions of years specifically in the form of universal ideas or images called archetypes.

Motive of self-actualization.   Jung advocated the motive of self-actualization in place of Freud's sex motive and Adler's power motive as the basis of human behaviour. According to him the urge for self-expression or exhibiting one's talent or abilities or seeking the highest goal of one's life by merging one's self with the universal self (the cosmos or *brahm*) is the real motive behind one's struggle in life. Depending upon the extent to which this urge is satisfied, the individual remains satisfied and his behaviour is termed normal. Once the equilibrium is disturbed, he falls into the trap of maladjustment and his behaviour becomes maladaptive.

Libido and personality development.   Jung extended the meaning of the term 'libido' by equating it with the life urge or life energy responsible for every type of human activity including, of course, sex gratification. Its normal flow makes an individual normal while its repression, blockage or damming up may lead to abnormalities. In the case of normal flow also a person may be an introvert or an extrovert. However, in practice, Jung feels nobody is exclusively introvert or extrovert. Usually people have both the characteristics and tendencies and depending on which trait is dominant, they may be classified as introvert or extrovert. Later on, Jung extended his two-fold classification of definite personality types to eight personality types.

Dreams.   In Jung's opinion one's dreams are not merely a means of artificial wish fulfilment. They work as a true companion to one's conscious mind for solving one's day to day difficulties and may be utilized in planning wisely in anticipation of one's future.

Neuroses. Neurosis, according to him represents regression ongoing back, as a result of a serious obstacle in the flow of the libido or imbalances created in the mind through disharmony between one's conscious and unconscious. For the genesis of the causes the present is more important than the past. It represents one's lack of ability to cope with one's environment. Once one's confidence in oneself is restored one can be reset in one's striving for self-actualization.

Jung's psychotherapy. The therapy suggested by Jung is centred round the key concept of making the patient first understand what is wrong with his self and then to help him in integrating his self. The technique of controlled association (in contrast to the method of free association used by Freud) is used for analysing the problem behaviour. The patient is then helped to obtain an insight into his problem and afterwards attempts are made to help him to re-establish the harmony of his self with his environment, i.e. to seek an independent solution of his problem.

Contribution of Jung's system to education. Jung's system contributed significantly to education by emphasizing the need to

1. plan and design the education of children for maximum actualization of their potentialities;
2. set the goal of education as higher than self actualization—the integration of the self with the greater self i.e., the cosmos or *brahm*;
3. realize the need and importance of religious or moral education for integration and welfare of the individual's self;
4. ensure that the process of education does not remove one from one's cultural roots or racial characteristics;
5. developing one's individuality in complete harmony with the development of others in society or mankind as a whole; and
6. take care of education and development of the children with their introvert and extrovert nature in view and guarding against their becoming extreme introvert, or extreme extrovert.

SUGGESTED READINGS

Hall, C. S. and Lindzey, G., *Theories of Personality*, 3rd ed., New York: John Wiley, 1978.

Jung, C.G., Psychology Types, London: Harcourt Brace, 1923.

————, *Contributions to Analytical Psychology*, London: Kegan Paul, 1928.

————, *Integration of Personality*, London: Kegan Paul, 1940.

————, *Development of Personality*, London: Routledge & Kegan Paul, 1948.

————, Conscious, unconscious and individuation, in G. Adler, M. Fordham, and H. Read (Eds.), *The Collected Works of C.G. Jung*, London: Routledge, 1959.

Jung, C.G., *The archetypes and the collected unconscious*, in G. Adler, M. Fordham, and H. Read (Eds.), *The Collected Works of C.G. Jung*, London: Routledge, 1959.

Levin, M.J., *Psychology: A Biographical Approach*, New York: McGraw-Hill, 1978.

Ross, T.A., *Introduction to Analytical Psychotherapy*, London: Arnold, 1921.

Stagner, Ross, *Psychology of Personality*, New York: McGraw-Hill, 1974.

Symonds, P., *The Dynamics of Human Adjustment*, New York: Appelton, 1946.

Thorpe, L.P. and Katz, B., *The Psychology of Abnormal Behaviour*, New York: Ronald Press, 1961.

Van, Teslaar, J.S., *An Outline of Psychoanalysis*, New York: The Modern Library, 1925.

Woodworth, R.S., *Contemporary Schools of Psychology* (Rev. ed.), London: Methuen, 1965.

Chapter 8

Piaget's Developmental Psychology and Its Bearing on Education

INTRODUCTION

Jean Piaget, a Swiss biologist, had profound interest in epistemology, a branch of philosophy concerned with the nature of knowledge. Later, he developed a keen interest in child and cognitive psychology. In 1920, he associated himself with the Binet Testing Laboratory in Paris which was engaged in the task of developing intelligence tests to be used in the French school system. Here he got the opportunity to think about the nature of the development of intellectual abilities in children. His biological orientation made him define and understand intelligence in quite a different way and study the process of intellectual development in terms of maturation by stages. He opposed Binet's idea of defining intelligence in terms of the number of correct responses to the items contained in a particular intelligence test. Instead, he defined intelligence as the ability to adjust, adapt or deal efficiently with, one's environment. Intelligence changes and develops as the organism matures biologically and as it gains from experiences. Thus according to Piaget, intelligence may be regarded to represent all those dynamic traits which help an individual to create optimal conditions for his survival under existing circumstances.

So keen was his interest in the study of cognitive and child psychology that he along with his wife (a former student of his at the Rousseau Institute) devoted almost all the previous years of their early married life to studying the intellectual development of their own three children by making them the subjects of their laboratory studies. As a result, today his theory of intellectual development has no parallel in the history of research in the field of developmental, cognitive and child psychology. For understanding this theory concerning the stages of intellectual development, let us first try to understand the major theoretical premise on which the theory stands.

PIAGET'S THEORETICAL NOTIONS

Piaget designed a proper framework to understand the structure, functioning and development of the cognitive network of the human mind. He postulated that, like physical organs of the human body, there are two aspects of the human mind: One is referred to as cognitive structure and the other as cognitive functioning.

Cognitive Structure

Unlike other creatures, the human baby is born with a few practical instincts and reflexes such as sucking, looking, reaching and grasping. Therefore, the initial cognitive structure of infants is supposed to incorporate only those cognitive abilities or potentials which help them to do such acts such as look, reach out or grasp. Piaget named these abilities or potentials as *schemas*. Let us understand the meaning conveyed by the term 'schema' more clearly by referring to a particular schema like the 'sucking schema'. It refers to one's general cognitive ability or potential to suck objects. This schema is more than a single manifestation of the sucking reflex. It can be thought of as a cognitive structure that makes all acts of sucking possible. However, the description of this act of sucking differs in relation to contents i.e., specific responses to specific stimuli such as the mother's nipple, a spoon, a toy etc. We thus conclude that a schema represents a unit of one's cognitive structure in the shape of a general potential to perform a particular class of behaviours (like sucking, grasping, calculating etc.), the content of which is related to the conditions that prevail during any particular manifestation of that general potential.

The various schemas with their contents thus form the basic structure of the human mind. The earlier schemas represent those reflexes and instincts that are biologically inherited. However, as a child grows, with the interaction of physical and social environment, he is able to form different schemas, resulting in changes and modifications in his cognitive structure.

Cognitive Functioning

The structure of an organism is said to play a decisive role in its functioning. Therefore, what is available to an individual in terms of his schemas decides how he is going to respond to the stimuli present in his physical or social environment. On the other hand, the individual has to adapt to his environment for survival as well as proper growth and development. The key to his cognitive development thus lies in his constant interaction with an adaptation to his physical and social environment. The task of such adaptation is carried out through the processes of assimilation and accommodation.

Assimilation refers to a kind of matching between the already existing cognitive structures and the environmental needs as they arise. In a situation where a six-month old infant is given a new toy it is likely to respond by putting the toy in its mouth. This is assimilation, as what the child did was to assimilate, incorporate or fit ideas about the new toy into already existing cognitive structures about old toys. His cognitive structure about old toys revolved around the sucking schema, therefore, he at once responded by performing the act of sucking.

Now, in case the new toy is too big to be picked up and placed in the mouth, it will certainly need a change or modification in the already existing cognitive structure. The child will have to change his old ways of thinking and behaving in order to adapt or adjust to the new situation. Consequently, now instead of sucking, the child may respond by pushing or grasping the toy. This is called *accommodation* as one tries to accommodate or adjust to new ways of thinking and behaving in place of assimilating or behaving in the same old fashion. Thus, whereas in the process of assimilation, one's responses are supposed to bank upon one's past experiences and already compiled stock of information, in the process of accommodation one has to learn new ways of thinking and behaving by making changes or modifications in one's existing cognitive structure. For instance, when the child is offered milk in a tumbler instead of the feeding bottle, first he tries his old way of behaving i.e., sucking. Afterwards, as a result of accommodation he picks up the new ways and consequently makes the necessary modification in his old cognitive structure.

Parallel to the concept of the processes of assimilation and accommodation linked with the process of the child's cognitive development, Piaget postulated the concept of *equilibration*. He asserted that the process of assimilation or accommodation helps the organism to adjust or maintain a harmonious relationship between himself and his environment. This adjustment mechanism was called equilibration by Piaget. It can be defined as an innate tendency or continuous drive on the part of an organism to organise its experiences (through assimilation or accommodation) for obtaining optimal adaptation to the changing demands of its environment by maintaining a proper balance between its cognitive structure and the changing demands of its environment. In fact, it is the need of seeking optimal adaptation or maintaining balance between himself and his environment that makes an individual feel uncomfortable and start reorganising his cognitive structure for equipping himself with new ways of thinking and behaving.

In this way Piaget highlighted the role of the following factors in one's cognitive make-up and its functioning:

1. The biologically inherited reflexes and mental dispositions as the fundamental cognitive structure.
2. The changes and development brought about in the cognitive structure through maturation (i.e., the process of natural growth).
3. The changes and development in the cognitive structure brought about through experiences (interaction with the physical and social environment) involving the processes of assimilation, accommodation and equilibration.

STAGES OF INTELLECTUAL DEVELOPMENT

As already pointed out, Piaget, on account of his biological background, traced the initiation of human cognitive development in terms of biologically inherited ways of interacting with the environment. He further postulated that the changes and developments in one's cognitive structure are brought about by interaction with one's physical and social environment. This task is carried out through the mechanism of equilibration, resulting in constant organisation of one's cognitive structure by the interplay of accommodation and assimilation. This task of constant organisation of the mental structure is an individual phenomenon; we may, therefore, find wide differences between children in terms of possession of cognitive abilities. However, as Piaget concluded, this organisation of the mental structure in all children always takes place in a particular order involving definite stages of intellectual development. Thus, although children of the same age may differ in terms of possession of mental abilities, the order, in which the abilities evolve, and the pattern of development are quite constant and universal. Let us discuss this pattern of intellectual development in terms of the four developmental stages suggested by Piaget.

Sensori-motor Stage (From birth to about two years)

Piaget called the first stage of intellectual development the sensori-motor stage because (a) it is characterized by the absence of language, and (b) it is limited to direct sensory and motor interactions with the environment. The cognitive development occurs along the following pattern:

1. At birth the infant exhibits a limited number of uncoordinated reflexes such as sucking, looking, reaching and grasping.

2. During the next four months the uncoordinated reflexes are coordinated into simple schemas providing the child with a general potential to perform certain classes of behaviour. For example, the infant now tries to suck anything which is put into his mouth, stares at whatever he sees, reaches for everything and grasps all that is put into his hands.

3. By the age of 8 months the infant is able to react to objects outside himself. He begins to realize that the objects around him are separate from himself and they have their independent and permanent existence. Prior to such development his view of the environmental objects is quite transitory, i.e. what is out of sight is purely out of mind. For example, if the infant is playing with a toy and you pick it up, hide it somewhere while allowing the child to watch your act of hiding the toy, he will at once forget about it. For him the toy placed under a blanket or hidden somewhere has disappeared and is no more. With the passage of time, gradually the concept of object permanence evolves in the cognitive structure of the infant. He begins to realize that the objects continue to exist even though he cannot see or experience them. Thus he begins to search for the objects that are hidden. For example, if you hide a toy in the blanket the infant will try to lift the blanket and search for the toy. In case you have shifted it somewhere, he will proceed to investigate its whereabouts under the assumption that the object has its permanent identity. When he does so we may infer that the child has been able to see or experience the object in his mind by making its mental image. Now he can proceed to the next stage of intellectual development involving the symbolic world of language by leaving behind the pure sensory or motor exploration.

Pre-operational Stage (about 2 to 7 years)

While stepping into this stage, the child begins to replace direct action in the form of sensory or motor exploration with symbols. The learning of the language provides him with a good tool for thinking. He begins to utter words to ask for something rather than just reaching out to get it. In addition to words, his thinking is also characterized by other symbolic representations or images of the things in the environment. This stage can be further sub-divided into (1) the pre-conceptual phase (approximately two to four years) and (2) the intuitive phase (approximately four to seven years).

1. *Pre-conceptual phase.* This is the period of the rudimentary concept formation and is characterized by the following features:

    (a) In the early part of this stage, the children seem to identify objects by their names and put them into certain classes. However, they usually make mistakes in this process of identification and concept formation. For example, they think all men are '*daddy*', all women are '*mummy*' and all dogs are '*montu*'.

    (b) Their mode of thinking and reasoning is quite illogical at this stage. It is neither inductive nor deductive but rather transductive in nature. For example, the child at this stage would reason like: as "cows are big animals with four legs and a long tail. This animal is also big and has four legs and a long tail, therefore it is a cow".

    (c) Their thinking is sometimes too imaginative and far removed from reality. It may be seen in their play activities when a block of wood is turned into a riding horse or motor cycle and a doll into a baby. Moreover, at this stage they are unable to distinguish between living and non-living objects. For them the doll in their hands is a live baby who can cry, smile and sleep. Similarly the dreams they have are, for them, real and concrete events.

    (d) The other major characteristic of the intellectual structure of the child at this stage is concerned with his egocentric nature. By egocentric Piaget means that the child can see the world only from his own standpoint. He considers that the sun and moon are following him, the rain falls to delight him, and obviously what exists in the external environment is specifically meant for him. He cannot think that people may have different opinions and differ in their modes of thinking and conclusions. He considers himself as the centre of a world of people who are supposed to perceive the things the way he does.

2. *Intuitive phase* (approximately four to seven years). At this stage the child progresses towards the formation of various concepts at a more advanced level. For example, now he will agree that apples, oranges and bananas are all fruits despite the difference in their shape, colour or taste. But what he thinks or solves at this stage is carried out intuitively, rather than in accordance with any logical rule. Consequently, as Piaget concludes, the child's thinking at this stage in not logical and is full of contradictions. It is clearly reflected in the absence in him of the two main cognitive characteristics namely, reversibility (ability to reverse) and conservation (ability to see an object as permanent even though its length, width or shape changes). When a child realizes that not only has he a brother but his brother also has a brother in him, it can be said that the child has developed the reversible quality in his cognitive operations. However, at the pre-operational stage children are seen not to possess the reversible characteristic in their mental functioning. For them moving from A to B may not carry the same meaning as moving from B to A.

The thinking of pre-operational children at the intuitive stage is marked by an inability to conserve in terms of quantity as well as number as may be understood through the following experiments:

Experiment No. 1. A child belonging to the pre-operational age say five years old is shown two identical containers filled with the same quantity of coloured water. The child will agree that both have the same amount. Now the experimentor pours the water from one of the containers into a taller but narrower container and asks the child to compare the amount of water in this taller container with the amount in one of the old containers.

The inability to conserve in terms of quantity makes the child think that there is more water in the taller container even when the child has observed that the same amount of water has been poured into it (see Figure 8.1). The child in

Experimental stage–1 (Two containers of the same shape and size)

Experimental stage–2 (Containers differing in size and shape)

Figure 8.1 Experiment demonstrating inability for conservation in terms of quantity.

this experiment is likely to say that the taller container has more water because the level of the water is higher in this container. According to Piaget this happens because the child at this stage fails to realize that the amount or quantity of a material does not change with the change in the shape or appearance of its container. In other words, the child belonging to the pre-operational stage shows a marked inability to conserve continuous quantity.

Experiment No. 2. A child is shown two sets of beads arranged in one-to-one correspondence. The child is asked if the beads in the two rows are equal in number. The child would say that there are. The beads in one row are then spaced further apart (or spaced closer together) and the child is then asked to tell which row has more beads.

Here with reference to Figure 8.2 the child belonging to the pre-operational

Figure 8.2   Experiment demonstrating inability for conservation in terms of number.

stage is likely to say that the bottom row has more beads. What leads the child to think in such an illogical manner? The answer according to Piaget lies in the fact that the concept of the conservation of numbers is not yet developed in the child. He is therefore, unable to realize the simple fact that a mere change in appearance or arrangement of some objects cannot increase or decrease their number. As a conclusion it may be said in connection with intellectual development of the child belonging to the pre-operational stage that although the child's cognitive structure or thinking is seen to be operated through symbols instead of motor and sensory actions, yet his thinking at this stage is characterized as illogical and full of contradictions.

Concrete Operational Stage (about seven to eleven years)

This stage shows marked developments in the cognitive functioning of the child.

1.   The child now learns to deal with concepts and ideas that exist only in mental terms. He can now think about things and figure out discrepancies and relationships.
2.   He begins to think in terms of a set of interrelated principles rather than single bits of knowledge. As a result he can think in terms of systems.
3.   His thinking becomes more logical and systematic. He can now make use of inductive and deductive approaches in terms of reasoning and arriving at conclusions.
4.   The child now develops the ability to conserve both in terms of quantity and number of objects. He can now very well think that the change in appearance of an object does not alter either its quantity or its number.
5.   The thinking of the child is no longer 'rigid' and 'irreversible'. A female child who has a sister now clearly realizes that her sister also has a sister.
6.   The child now is no longer ego-centric in his thinking. He does not think of himself as the centre of the external world and does not perceive the world only from his own standpoint. He does not find it difficult to appreciate that other people have experiences, views and ideas that differ from his own.
7.   The child now develops the abilities to deal adequately with classes. He can classify objects. He develops the ability of serialisation like arranging things from largest to smallest and vice versa. The number concept is also developed, but it all happens in a very simple concrete form.

8. The child now learns to carry out rather complex operations or tackle problems as long as they are concrete and not abstract. For example, the child now realizes the importance of cardinal numbers and ordinal numbers. He can operate symbolically by combining, reversing and forming associations among different objects.

In this way, the child reaches a satisfactory level in terms of intellectual development by his thinking becoming quite systematic and logical. However, what is done or thought by him at this stage is done purely on a concrete level. His thought processes are limited to real events observed or the actual objects operated by him. He is unable to think in abstract terms. In this way the concrete operation stage can actually be a pre-preparation for the final stage of formal operations mainly concerned with abstractions.

Formal Operation Stage (about 12 to 15 years)

The intellectual development and functioning takes a very sophisticated shape at this stage as the child learns to deal with abstraction by logical thinking. Actually he learns to utilize the tool of symbolism as effectively as possible in the process of thought and problem solving. The child now gets interested in forms. He begins to construct relationships between concrete operations and between symbols. Generalizations and framing of rules by operating in abstract terms become quite possible at this stage. The child now begins to appreciate that some hypothetical problems can be solved mentally by applying the same rules as would be applied to concrete problems. He begins to look at problems in many ways and explore various solutions but in a very systematic and logical way. For example, if a child of this stage is shown five colourless, odourless liquids in test tubes and is asked to find out what combination of the five will produce a brown liquid, he is likely to discover the possible combination by adopting a systematic approach, e.g., combining the first and second, then first and third, then first and fourth and so on. Thus it is quite distinctive in comparison to the children belonging to earlier stages of cognitive development who will simply resort to trial and error for finding the solution.

Moreover, the child's thinking at this stage does not remain only concrete but becomes hypothetical, with considerations given to the most unusual ideas. Hence the creative aspects in the child are very much visible during this age not only in terms of concrete operations but also in terms of abstraction and pure imagination. For example, previous to this stage, if we were to ask a child to imagine he has three fathers, he might reply that it is no use imagining such a thing as one can only have one father. However, in the formal operational stage such thoughts involving unusual ideas are possible. Here one can imagine figures and shapes and can fly in the air without wings as is often done by children when studying poetry, algebra and geometry.

The other noticeable characteristic of this stage, as Piaget found, was the child's interest in dealing with things that do not exist in reality instead of the things concerning the present which are actually perceived by him.

In fact, Piaget was of the opinion that the thought processes and the intellectual functioning of a child at the formal operational period reflect the beginning of the most advanced stage in the functioning of his cognitive system. It provides a ladder to reach the limits of a person's intellectual development and actualize his potentiality to the maximum in the available circumstances. The high order of intellectual functioning developed through this stage, according to Piaget, is usually characterized by the presence of the most sophisticated cognitive abilities like the ability to (a) build up multiple hypotheses and a number of alternate solutions; (b) verify all possible solutions in a systematic and logical way; (c) generalize and arrive at abstract rules that cover many specific situations.

In this way, according to Piaget, after the expiry of the formal operation stage the child may reach full intellectual potential. He may discover the solutions of problems through mental manipulation of symbols by adopting a logical and systematic procedure known as scientific thinking and problem solving rather than a reflexive, motor or sensory manipulation as is done at the sensory motor stage; or by exposing his thinking operationally in more concrete terms as done at the concrete operation stage. It thus represents a stage which helps the child to attain mental maturity with respect to the development of his cognitive abilities.

CRITICAL EVALUATION OF PIAGET'S THEORY

Piaget's theory on intellectual development has been questioned and challenged on the following grounds:

1. Piaget's views on the pattern of intellectual development are not as uniform and universal as claimed by him. He based his theory on detailed observations of European children as they grew up in 1920s, 1930s and 1940s. The subsequent researches in Europe and outside have demonstrated significant deviations from the chronological ages linked with different stages of intellectual development by Piaget.
2. The Piagetian view that thinking proceeds in distinct stages has also been seriously challenged. It has been found that cognitive performance at particular ages is usually very inconsistent.
3. Piaget's claim that children below the age of concrete operations are incapable of logical thinking and are egocentric has been refuted by a number of research studies. It has been established that children are able to both think logically and show sensitivity and concern for the feelings and viewpoints of others at very early ages.
4. The claim that a child is unable to perform an intellectual task like conservation at ages below those specified by Piaget has also been questioned. A number of studies have shown that it is possible to train children to carry out not only tasks like conservation but also very typical complex formal operations at ages below those specified by Piaget.
5. Piaget has linked biological maturation with the development of cognitive abilities and thus made a certain stage of maturation necessary for learning the cognitive task related to that maturation age. He is thus often blamed for being a pure nativist who gives singular importance to

biological maturation for the intellectual development of the child. However, this criticism is one-sided, as Piaget believes that maturation works only as the framework for intellectual development and the necessary material and means are supplied by one's physical and social environment. His stand on this issue may become quite clear through the following assertion of Inhelder and Piaget (1958):

> The maturation of the nervous system can do no more than determine the totality of possibilities and impossibilities at a given stage. A particular social environment remains indispensable for the realization of these possibilities. It follows that their realization can be accelerated or retarded as a function of cultural and educational conditions.

If we examine the nature of the criticism levelled against Piaget's theory we find that most of it is one-sided. For example, as is clear from the above quotation, it is not true that Piaget's theory does not take the environmental experiences into account. Similarly, we can visualize that, while laying down different stages of cognitive development, Piaget does not mean that all children belonging to all cultures essentially pass through these stages in the chronological periods specified by him. As he gives due recognition to the forces of biological inheritance, maturation and environmental experiences in the formation and functioning of one's cognitive structure, the possibility in terms of variation in ages for reaching a particular stage of intellectual development cannot be ruled out. Consequently the actual age at which certain types of mental abilities appear varies from child to child or from culture to culture. Irrespective of this acknowledgement linked with the individual differences with regard to intellectual development, the contribution of Piaget's theory can never be underrated. Whatever points we may raise against the universality and validity of his theory, it would always be remembered that intellectual development involves stages as specified by Piaget and occurs in the same order irrespective of the individual and environmental differences or geographical and cultural barriers.

APPRECIATION AND CONTRIBUTION TO EDUCATION

Piaget, an acknowledged international authority in the field of child psychology and cognitive development, has contributed a great deal to the theory and practice of education. His contributions may be briefly summarized as follows:

1. Piaget interpreted and defined intelligence in a practical way. From birth onwards, the individual has to struggle for survival and seek adjustment with his environment. Intelligence in terms of his cognitive structure and its functioning helps him in this task. Therefore, the intelligence of an individual can only be assessed in terms of the nature of adjustment (balance between him and his environment) he is making at a particular time under the prevailing circumstances. This means that one's intelligence is a dynamic function. It really has some purposes or functions and it is these functions that help us to measure the intelligence

of a person. Interpreting intelligence in this way has led to intelligence tests being devised with emphasis on the mechanism of adaptation on the one hand, and maintenance of the balance between abilities and environmental demands for the development and welfare of the child on the other.

2. Piaget's theory has highlighted the importance of drives and motivation in the field of learning and development. It has utilized the concept of equilibration for this purpose by defining it as the continuous drive towards equilibrium or balance between the organism and its environment. Piaget's equilibration can be equated with Freud's sex gratification and Jung's self-actualization for activating one's behaviour.

3. Piaget's theory provides valuable information and advice on curriculum planning and structuring the schemes of studies. Since children of a particular region tend to reach a particular stage in their intellectual development at a particular age, what is to be planned in terms of their curriculum or scheme of studies must always be in tune with the expected level of their maturation and mental abilities. In other words, an ideal curriculum should provide the appropriate experiences at the proper time. For example, it is no use teaching world geography to students studying in first or second standard because at that age they have not yet acquired the necessary concepts like country, state, or even city. Therefore, it is more appropriate to teach them local geography such as their neighbourhood, school, classroom and so on. Similarly, teaching algebra to the students of fourth or fifth standard is pointless as children of this age may not have acquired the ability to deal with abstractions.

   Piaget's theory may help in this direction by providing a suitable framework of the learning experiences in view of the cognitive development of the children and the needs of society.

4. The knowledge of Piaget's theory may prove quite valuable to teachers and parents for making them aware of the nature of the thought processes of the children at a particular level of maturation or chronological age. They may also get some idea of the changes that take place in the cognitive structure and functioning of their children. This type of knowledge may prove quite beneficial to them in dealing with the children and planning their training and education.

5. The major contribution of Piaget's theory is its analysis and suggestion of the optimal conditions for an individual's learning and development by introducing the concept of assimilation, accommodation and equilibration. According to Piaget, learning and development are the net result of interaction between a person's cognitive structure and his environmental experiences. For optimal learning to take place, the experiences or information presented must be of such a form and nature that it can be assimilated into the present cognitive structures, but at the same time different enough to necessitate a change in those structures calling for accommodation and resulting in new learning. Consequently, if the new information or learning is completely unrelated to previous

learning, it will certainly not fit in with the present cognitive structure and so would not be understood. On the other hand, if it is too simple or unchallenging, it will be completely assimilated and hardly any need for further learning will arise. Therefore, according to Piaget's theory, for acquiring learning it is essential that experiences or material presented to the learner are somewhat new and moderately challenging to initiate the phenomenon of accommodation but at the same time these experiences should be sufficiently linked and related with one's old learning so that they may be reasonably easy for being assimilated and understood by the learner.

6. Since the Piagetian theory considers both physical and social experiences as quite indispensable for one's intellectual development, it has placed a major responsibility on parents, teachers and others directly or indirectly connected with the education and welfare of children to arrange for the most appropriate and stimulating environment for their children.

7. Piaget's theory may be said to have the following implications vis-a-vis the children of nursery and elementary school:

    (a) Since the children of this age are able to think only in concrete terms, it is advisable to allow them to experiment with materials in order to accommodate new understanding and to acquire new learning by themselves. For instance, to give the idea of the fractions 1/4, it would be best to cut an apple into four equal parts and then show one piece physically to show that the meaning of the fraction 1/4 is 'one out of four parts'.

    (b) The teacher must try to emphasize discovery learning rather than teaching or telling each and every part of information to the students. They should try to set up environments in which the students can have a wide variety of experiences for self or discovery-learning.

8. Piagetian theory conveys that symbolic thinking adopted by children in their thought process after the sensory motor stage is not limited to the use of language only. There may be children who prefer to use images, relationships and other symbols instead of language as a tool for their thinking and may make better progress in terms of further learning and cognitive advancement. Therefore, the teaching–learning process should not be limited to the use of verbal communication, but should involve other symbolic expression and means for the communication of ideas suited to the circumstances and nature of the learner.

9. The last but not the least contribution of Piagetian theory is its emphasis on the individualization of education. It has advocated the need of child-centred education by saying that the educational experiences must be built around the learner's cognitive structure. What is suitable, appropriate and challenging to his cognitive structure must be given for him to acquire new experiences and develop his cognitive abilities. Since cognitive structures are sure to vary from child to child, in providing education, we have to think in terms of tailoring the educational material according to each child's cognitive structure. For this purpose the teacher

has to know the level of functioning of each student's cognitive structure and then plan for his further learning and intellectual development accordingly.

SUMMARY

Jean Piaget, a Swiss biologist, developed a keen interest in child and cognitive psychology, particularly in the nature of the development of intellectual abilities in growing children.

Based on his studies, Piaget stated that the child is born with a few practical instincts and reflexes like sucking, looking, reaching and grasping etc., and these inborn traits make him perform related tasks. The cognitive abilities related to the performing of such tasks were termed *schemas* (the basic functional units of one's cognitive structure) by Piaget. The schemas available to an individual child decide how he is going to respond to the stimuli present in his physical or social environment.

In the course of the child's intellectual development, significant changes are brought about in his initial cognitive structure (composed of the basic schemas). These changes are the result of maturation, the process of natural growth, and the experiences like interaction with the physical and social environment involving the processes of assimilation, accommodation and equilibration. The constant organisation or evolution of the mental structure, although an individual phenomenon, takes place in all children in a particular order involving definite stages of intellectual development, viz., the sensori-motor stage, pre-operational stage, concrete operational stage and formal operation stage.

The Sensori-motor stage (birth to 2 years) is characterized by the absence of language and limited to the child's direct sensory and motor interaction with his environment. During this stage, the child acquires the concept of object permanence, the realization that people and objects do not cease to exist when they are out of his sight.

At *the pre-operation stage* (2 to 7 years), the child's direct action in the form of sensory or motor explorations is replaced by words, or with other symbolic representations or images about things in the environment. His thought process at this stage usually displays a high degree of egocentrism, or inability to consider others' points of view.

During *the concrete operational stage* (7 to 11 years), children begin to think logically but are unable to think in abstract terms. Their thought processes are limited to concrete objects and events. However, they are able to understand the cognitive concept such as number, classification and conservation.

During *the formal operation stage* (12 years to 15 years or later), individuals are able to think abstractly, test hypotheses and deal with problems that are not physically present in their environment. Actually this stage reflects the most advanced period in the functioning of the cognitive system. The individual here may reach the intellectual potential to discover the solutions to problems through mental manipulation of symbols by adopting a logical and systematic way known as scientific thinking and problem solving.

Piaget, in this way, is noted for having enumerated the definite developmental stages of the orderly evolution of human intelligence regardless of the individual and environmental differences or geographical and cultural barriers. The other contributions of his theory in the field of education are that it helps in

1. understanding one's intelligence as the function of one's ability to adapt or adjust to one's environment;
2. providing a suitable framework of the learning experiences in view of the cognitive development of children and the needs of society;
3. acquainting us with the thought processes of children at a particular level of their maturation or chronological age;
4. emphasizing the organization of optimal conditions for an individual's learning and development in the light of the processes of assimilation, accommodation and equilibration;
5. stressing the importance of the variety of aid material other than verbal communication and concrete objects involving useful symbolic expressions; and
6. emphasizing the need for tailoring the education of a child according to the level of functioning of his cognitive structure.

REFERENCES

Inhelder, B. and Piaget, J., *The Growth of Logical Thinking from Childhood to Adolescence* (Trans. by Anne Parson and Stanley Milgram), New York: Basic Books, 1958.

Papalia, D.E. and Olds, S.W., *Psychology*, New York: McGraw-Hill, 1987.

Piaget, J., *Judgement and Reasoning in the Child*, New York: Harcourt & Brace, 1926.

————, *The Child's Conception of the World*, New York: Harcourt & Brace, 1929.

————, *The Moral Judgement of the Child*, New York: Harcourt & Brace, 1932.

————, *The Origins of Intelligence in Children*, New York: International Universities Press, 1952.

————, *The Construction of Reality in the Child*, New York: Basic Books, 1954.

————, *Psychology of Intelligence*, Totowa, N.J.: Littlefield Adams, 1966.

Piaget, J. and Inhelder, B., *The Psychology of the Child* (Trans. by Helen Weaver), New York: Basic Books, 1969.

————, Piaget's Theory, in P.H. Mussen (Ed.), *Carmichael's Manual of Child Psychology*, Vol. 1, New York: Wiley, 1970.

SUGGESTED READINGS

Hergerhahn, B.R., *An Introduction to Theories of Learning*, Englewood Cliffs, N.J.: Prentice Hall, 1976.

Levin, M.J., *Psychology: A biographical approach*, New York: McGraw-Hill, 1978.

Chapter 9

Psychology of Growth and Development

MEANING OF GROWTH AND DEVELOPMENT

Change is the law of nature. Animate or inanimate objects are all subject to change. Animate objects are distinguished from inanimate objects chiefly by their potentiality to maintain the flow and cycle of life. Seeds, after germinating in the soil grow as saplings and then as specific plants or trees which in turn flower and produce seeds or fruits for further germination. Similar is the case with birds, animals and human beings who can reproduce their own kind by the transmission of specific characteristics of the species through sexual union between the male and the female.

As far as the human being is concerned, life starts with the conception in the mother's womb as a result of the process of fertilization of the ovum (egg cell) of the mother by the sperm cell of the father. The mother's womb then becomes the site and the means for the growth and development of the new life and it is only after about nine months that the baby is able to come into the world as a newborn. The period spent in the mother's womb is termed as pre-natal period and is usually not included in the computation of one's chronological age. In all animals, including human beings, the pre-natal period resembles the time taken by a germinating seed to come out of the soil, which then grows and develops into a full-fledged plant or tree. *The processes by which a germinating seed or conceived organism is turned into the mature plant or full-fledged being are collectively termed growth and development.* The processes of growth and development are thus the medium and the means for bringing about changes in the organisms. The terms growth and development are often used interchangably and regarded as synonymous terms. In general, they refer to the changes produced by the interaction of one's genetic and environmental factors as well as to the changes in the physical, mental, social, emotional and moral aspects involving one's individuality. However, they differ in a sense and are capable of conveying different meanings as will become evident from the following discussion.

Distinction between Growth and Development

The changes in various dimensions of one's personality are mainly of two types—

96

quantitative and qualitative. While the term 'growth' may be limited to the changes in the quantitative aspect, i.e. increase in size, length, height and weight and expansion of vocabulary etc., the term 'development' implies the overall changes occurring in both the quantitative as well as the qualitative aspects. Therefore, development as a term carries a wider and more comprehensive meaning than the term growth.

Since growth is limited to the description of quantitative changes, its scope is confined to those aspects or dimensions of one's personality in which quantitative changes occur. As a result, in dealing with those aspects or dimensions of personality where both the quantitative and qualitative changes are involved, the term growth is not employed. On the other hand, development as a compre-hensive term, related to all types of changes, can be employed to describe the changes in all dimensions of one's personality whether physical, mental, social, moral or any other. That is why whereas we come across descriptions like physical growth and development, mental growth and development in the titles of the texts, we seldom come across these in the case of the social, emotional and moral aspects of personality. Here we usually drop the term growth and refer simply to social, emotional and moral development since the quantitative changes in these aspects are not as directly observable and measurable as in the physical and mental aspects. Therefore, when we talk of development in one or the other dimension of one's personality, it is clear that we are describing and explaining the overall changes in the structure and functioning of that particular aspect. For example, when we study physical development we do not aim to describe the changes in the size and proportions of the physical organs in a solely physical sense but also to point out the impact of these physical changes in terms of improvement in the working or functioning of the physical organs. The term growth, on the other hand, carries a limited and narrower meaning. It is a sub-system of the development as it is concerned merely with the quantitative changes in comparison to the overall changes described and explained by the process of development. This does not continue throughout one's life. It stops when maturity has been attained while development is a continuous process. Starting right from conception it does not end with the attainment of maturity but continues throughout the entire life span of an individual.

Development is said to be a complex process in comparison to the process of growth. The results of growth in terms of quantitative changes are very specific, fairly easy to observe and measurable. The results of development, in comparison, are quite complex and difficult as far as their actual assessment and measurement is concerned.

Thus, the terms growth and development, both imply changes in one's behaviour and personality make-up. Development related to the overall changes, structural as well as functional, carries a comprehensive meaning and consequently we would prefer to describe the trends of changes during the life span of an individual in various dimensions of personality as well as discussing the principles and theories to highlight the pattern and mechanism of these changes.

Stages of Growth and Development

As pointed out earlier, Life's journey begins with conception in the womb of the mother. The approximate nine month period spent in mother's womb is known as the pre-natal period. A child is said to be born when it (fetus) emerges from the internal environment (womb) and has its first contact with the external environment. It is called the post-natal period—and is in fact the beginning of computation of chronological age. The period between the birth and two years— is called the infancy period followed by the phase of childhood lasting for about 10 to 12 years. This is followed by the period of adolescence when one attains puberty (sexual maturity) and is capable of reproduction. In true sense it is the transition period between childhood and adulthood. On attaining maturity in all aspects, viz., physical, mental, emotional and social, one attains the status of an adult, lasting for a long period before one becomes senescent or begins to show signs of ageing.

The above-mentioned specific titles of infant, child, adolescent, adult, or old person are specifically related to distinct stages of growth and development into which the human life span is hypothetically divided. Each of these stages is said to extend over a somewhat definite period in years. This division, though arbitrary, gives an idea of the age-linked developmental stages (see Table 9.1).

Table 9.1   Age Span for the Human Developmental Stages

Period or stages of development	Approximate age
1. Infancy	From birth to 2 years
2. Childhood	From 3rd year to 12 years
(a) Pre-childhood	From 3rd year to 6 years
(b) Later childhood	From 7th year to 12 years or in a strict sense up to the onset of puberty
3. Adolescence	From 13th year to 19 years or in a strict sense from onset of puberty till the attainment of maturity
4. Adulthood	From 20th year to 60 years or in a strict sense from attaining maturity to the age one ceases to produce one's own kind
5. Old age or ageing	From 61 years or in a strict sense from the end of the reproduction capability till death

During all these developmental stages, human beings exhibit typical behavioural characteristics in all dimensions of behaviour and personality make-up which are specific to each stage. There are, however, individual variations, and no one is similar to others in all aspects of behaviour and dimensions of person-ality. A study of the pattern of growth and development exhibited by individuals while passing through the above-mentioned stages provides very useful data for parents and teachers to plan the development and education of children. In the pages that follow, we shall discuss the salient features of this pattern.

Principles of Development

Development, although an individual phenomenon, has been found to follow a logical and sequential pattern from conception onward. It seems that it is operated by some general rules or principles. These rules or principles may be named as the principles of development. Let us now discuss these principles briefly.

1. *Principle of continuity.* Development follows the principle of continuity which means that in one's life it is a never-ending process. It starts with conception and ends with death. The changes, however small and gradual, continue to take place in all dimensions of one's personality throughout one's life.

2. *Principle of lack of uniformity in the developmental rate.* Development, though continuous, does not exhibit steadiness and uniformity in terms of the rate of development in various dimensions of personality or in the developmental periods and stages of life. In passing through the developmental stages, the changes are often so silent and gradual as to be almost invisible over a long duration but sometimes they are as fast as to be noticed quite easily. Thus, instead of steadiness, development usually takes place in fits and starts showing almost no change at one time and a sudden spurt at another, as for example, shooting up in height and sudden change in social interest, intellectual curiosity and emotional make-up.

3. *Principle of individual difference.* Every organism is a distinct creation in itself. Therefore, the development which it undergoes in terms of the rate and outcome in various dimensions is quite unique and specific.

4. *Principle of uniformity of pattern.* Although there seems to be a clear lack of uniformity in terms of the rate of development and also there are distinct individual differences with regard to the process and outcome of the various stages of development, yet it follows a definite pattern in one or the other dimension which is uniform and universal with respect to the individuals of a species. For instance, the development of language follows a somewhat definite sequence quite common to all human beings. This is true of other cognitive abilities, and physical and psycho-social development follows a somewhat uniform sequence spread over different developmental stages and periods of one's life.

5. *The principle of proceeding from general to specific responses.* While developing in relation to any aspect of personality, the child first picks up or exhibits general responses and learns to show specific and goal-directed responses afterwards. For example, a baby starts by waving his arms in a general random movement and afterwards these general motor responses are converted into specific responses like grasping or reaching out. Similarly, when a newborn infant cries, his whole body is involved in doing so but as he develops, it is limited to the vocal cords, facial expressions and eyes etc. In the development of language, the child begins with generalized responses, such as by calling all men daddy and all women mummy but as he grows and develops, he begins to use these names only for his father and mother.

6. *Principle of integration.* By observing the principle of proceeding from the

general to the specific or from the whole to the parts, it does not mean that only the specific responses are aimed for the ultimate consequences of one's development. Rather, it is a sort of integration that is ultimately desired. Throwing light on this principle Kuppuswami (1963) observes—"Development thus involves a movement from the whole to parts and from the parts to the whole" and in this way it is the integration of the whole and its parts as well as the specific and general responses that enables a child to develop satisfactorily in relation to various aspects or dimensions of his personality.

7. *Principle of interrelation.* The various aspects or dimensions of one's growth and development are interrelated. What is achieved or not achieved in one or the other dimension in the course of the gradual and continuous process of development surely affects the development in other dimensions. A healthy body tends to develop a healthy mind and an emotionally stable and socially conscious personality. Inadequate physical or mental development may, on the other hand, result in a socially or emotionally maladjusted personality. This is why all efforts in education are always directed towards achieving harmonious growth and development in all aspects and dimensions of one's personality.

8. *Principle of interaction.* The process of development involves active interaction between the forces within the individual and the forces belonging to his environment. What is inherited by the organism at the time of conception is first influenced by the stimulation received in the womb of the mother and after birth, by the forces of the physical and socio-psychological environment for its development. Therefore, at any stage of growth and development, the individual's behaviour or personality make-up is nothing but an end-product of the constant interaction between his hereditary endowment and environmental set-up.

9. *Principle of cephalocaudal and proximodistal tendencies.* Cephalocaudal and proximodistal tendencies are found to be followed in maintaining the orderly sequence and direction of development.

According to the cephalocaudal tendency, development proceeds in the direction of the longitudinal axis (head to foot). That is why, before it becomes able to stand, the child first gains control over his head and arms and then on his legs. In terms of the proximodistal tendency, development proceeds from the near to the distant and the parts of the body near the centre develop before the extremities. That is why, in the beginning the child is seen to exercise control over the large fundamental muscles of the arm and the hand and only afterwards over the smaller muscles of the fingers.

10. *Principle of predictability.* Development is predictable, which means that with the help of the uniformity of the pattern and sequence of development, we can, to a great extent, forecast the general nature and behaviour of a child in one or more aspects or dimensions at any particular stage of its growth and development. That is why we can discuss in developmental psychology the general nature of the development at different stages such as infancy, childhood, and adolescence. Not only is such prediction possible along general lines but it is also possible to predict the range within which the future development of an individual child is going to fall. For example, with the knowledge of the development of the bones of a child it is possible to predict his adult structure and size. Similarly, the appraisal of one's mental ability, emotionality and sociability can tell us a lot about the future trends of one's development.

11. *Principle of spiral versus linear advancement.* The path followed in development by the child is not straight and linear and development at any stage never takes place with a constant or steady pace. At a particular stage of his development, after the child had developed to a certain level, there is likely to be a period of rest for consolidation of the developmental progress achieved till then. In advancing further, therefore, development turns back and then moves forward again in a spiral pattern as illustrated in Figure 9.1.

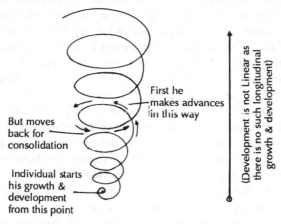

Figure 9.1   Spiral pattern of movement in development (as opposed to linear).

EDUCATIONAL IMPLICATION OF THE PRINCIPLES OF GROWTH AND DEVELOPMENT

The knowledge of the above-mentioned principles of growth and development may prove beneficial to us in a number of ways described below.

1. Development is a continuous and non-stop process at all periods and stages of human life. Therefore, we should never give up our efforts to achieve perfection in terms of development in the different dimensions of out personality.

2. The principle and knowledge of individual differences reminds us to understand the wide individual differences that surface at all periods of growth and development among children. Each child should be helped along the developmental process within the sphere of his own strengths and limitations.

3. The principles related to growth and development suggest a pattern or trend for the advancement of children on the developmental path. This knowledge can help us know as to what can be expected in terms of the proper growth and development at a particular developmental stage

and we can then plan accordingly to achieve it by organising the environmental experiences.

4. Principles like "proceeding from general to specific responses", and the principle of "integration" help us to plan the learning processes and arrange suitable learning experiences so as to achieve maximum gains in terms of growth and development.

5. The principle of interrelation and interdependence directs us to strive from the very beginning for the all round harmonious growth and development of the personalities of our children and cautions us not to encourage the development of a particular aspect at the cost of another.

6. The principle of spiral advancement of development helps us to make adequate arrangement for the subsequent progress and consolidation of the progress achieved during specific developmental stages.

7. The cephalocaudal and proximodistal tendencies as suggested by the principle of developmental direction help us to arrange the suitable learning experiences, processes and environmental set-up so as to accommodate and help the youngsters to grow and develop according to the trend and nature of these tendencies.

8. The principle of interaction reminds us to recognise the joint responsibility of heredity and environment in the development of personality. Accordingly, although they can develop within the limits of their genetic make-up, yet to attain maximum development, we have to arrange for the best environmental settings and experiences for our children. The environment that we provide should always be conducive to developing their potentialities and never prove to be an obstacle in the way of the adjustment of their self with their environment.

FACTORS INFLUENCING GROWTH AND DEVELOPMENT

Right from conception, the beginning of life in a mother's womb, the growth and development of human beings is influenced by a variety of factors categorized broadly as internal and external. Let us try to throw some light on these factors.

Internal Factors

All those factors which lie within the individual are called *internal factors*. These factors include:

1. Heredity factors
2. Biological or Constitutional factors
3. Intelligence
4. Emotional factors
5. Social nature

Let us discuss the influence of these internal factors on the growth and development of children.

1. *Heredity factors.* Heredity factors play their part at the time of conception in the mother's womb. What is transferred to the offspring from its immediate parents in the form of genes and chromosomes at this time, constitutes the hereditary contribution. This contribution is the real starting point and basis for all the growth and development that take place later in the life of the child. The height, weight, colour of the eyes and the skin, the characteristics of the hair, are all decided by these hereditary influences. The physical structure, nervous system and other things related to one's constitutional make-up, body chemistry and physical development are, to a great extent, decided by hereditary factors. Hereditary factors, in fact, as emphasized earlier, lay the foundation and it is the quality of this foundation that is helpful in the future growth and development. If hereditary contributions are satisfactory, then with minimum efforts of the environmental forces, we get satisfactory results. However, in case the hereditary contribution is quite meagre, then we have to make tremendous efforts for achieving desired success in terms of a child's satisfactory growth and development.

2. *Biological and constitutional factors.* A child's constitutional make-up somatic structure, physique and body chemistry influence his growth and development throughout his life. This can be substantiated in the following manner:

(a) A child who is physically weak or have internal deformities cannot be expected to achieve satisfactory results in terms of his normal physical growth and development. He usually suffers from illness which not only hamper his physical growth but also affect his development in other spheres—mental, social and emotional.

(b) The nervous system which controls the body movement, affects the growth and development of a child in cognitive spheres.

(c) The endocrine or ductless glands are potent factors affecting the growth and development of an individual from his birth. The chemistry of the body is governed by these glands. Each of these glands secretes its own chemicals known as *harmones*. These harmones reach the blood stream, and get circulated throughout the body. They influence all those tissues on which depend the function of body system, emotional actions and even thoughts and, therefore, the functioning of the ductless glands exercises a great influence on various aspects—physical, social, mental, emotional and moral—of a person's growth and development. For a balanced growth and development, the normal functioning of these glands is essential. In case there is over activity (hyperactivity) or under activity (hypoactivity) of these glands, it results in serious abnormality in growth and development. For example, imbalance in pituitary gland may lead to an abnormal increase or decrease in height.

(d) Defective constitutional make-up like ugly face, short stature and any other deformity of the body may give birth to feelings of inferiority in a child. Moreover, he may face adjustment problems in the social environment and, consequently, may lag behind in the race of growth and development pertaining to various aspects of his personality.

3. *Intelligence.* Intelligence, as the ability to learn, adjust and take right decision at right time, has a significant role in the overall growth and development of a child. It affects his social behaviour, moral judgement and emotional growth. An intelligent person is said to exercise reasonable control over his emotions, and is found to carry on well with his personal and social adjustment. Thus, the physical, social, emotional, moral and language development of a child is greatly influenced and controlled by the level of his intelligence. We cannot expect problem-solving behaviour, creative, imaginative and inventive ability from a child having subnormal intelligence.

4. *Emotional factors.* Emotional factors, e.g. emotional adjustability and maturity, play a big role in influencing a person's overall growth and development. A child who is found to be overwhelmed by negative emotions like fear, anger, jealousy, etc. is adversely affected in his physical, mental, social, moral and language development. If a person cannot exercise a reasonable control over his emotions, he is sure to suffer in terms of his growth and development. He will have to face difficulty in his social adjustment. He may find himself a failure in doing some serious mental activity. Ultimately, he may spoil his physical and mental health.

5. *Social nature.* A person's socialization helps him in achieving adjustment and advancement in other aspects of his growth and development. He may learn from his environment, more by means of his social nature, which may prove to be a boon to him for his proper growth and development.

External Factors

The factors lying outside the individual in his environment are said to be the external factors influencing his growth and development. These factors begin their role of influencing the growth and development just immediately after a baby is conceived. These may include the following.

1. *Environment in the womb of the mother.* What is available to the child for his nourishment in its mother's womb from the time of conception till his birth is quite important from the angle of his growth and development. A few factors associated with this period may be cited as below:

   (a) The physical and mental health of the mother during pregnancy.
   (b) Single child or multiple children getting nourished in the womb.
   (c) The quality and quantity of nutrition received by the embryo within the womb of the mother.
   (d) Whether or not the embryo has been subjected to harmful radiation or rays, etc.
   (e) Normal or abnormal delivery.
   (f) Any damage or accident to the baby in the womb.

2. *Environment available after birth.* Whatever a child gets from different conditions and forces of his environment after his birth, influence his growth and development in many ways. These may be described as follows:

(a) *Accidents and incidents in life.* The growth and development of an individual is greatly influenced by the good and bad incidents and accidents which he happens to meet in his life time. Sometimes, a small injury or an incident may change the entire development course of his life. For example if a child's nervous system is damaged in an accident, it will hamper his mental development and in turn it will affect his development in other spheres—social, emotional, moral and physical.

(b) *The quality of physical environment, medical care and nourishment.* A child's growth and development is greatly influenced by the quality of his physical environment and medical care and nourishment available to him for his living and working. These include open space, balanced diet, good living and working conditions and proper medical care. He will achieve the heights of his growth and development based on the proper availability of these things.

(c) *The quality of the facilities and opportunities provided by the social and cultural forces.* What a child gets from his social and cultural environment for the growth and development of his potentials, influences the entire course of his development. In a true sense, he develops and becomes what he is permitted to and desired by these social and cultural forces. A few of such conditions are pointed out below:

1. Parental and family care received by a child.
2. Economic and social status of the parents and the family.
3. The quality of the neighbourhood and surrounding environment.
4. The quality of schooling received by a child.
5. The quality of peer group relationships and company of a child.
6. The quality of treatment made available to a child and his family with regard to his caste, religion, nationality or citizenship.
7. The quality of educational and vocational facilities and opportunities available to a child.
8. The quality of the government, laws and organization of the society to which a child belongs.
9. The quality of the power and status enjoyed by the country to which a child belongs.

THEORIES OF GROWTH AND DEVELOPMENT

Development involving quantitative as well as qualitative changes in one's structure and its functioning is a process that starts from the earliest stages of any life or organism. The organism, in course of time, reaches its peak to be called mature for its full growth and development. What course or trend this development takes or in what way or to what extent this development occurs in a developing human being has been the subject of extensive study and investigation by eminent psychologists. Consequently, various theories tracing the developmental processes in one or the other dimensions of one's personality at definite developmental stages have emerged. A few of these well-known theories are:

1. Freud's Theory of Psycho-sexual Development.
2. Jean Piaget's Theory of Cognitive Development.
3. Erickson's Theory of Psycho-social Development.
4. Kohlberg's Theory of Moral Development.

As the first two theories have already been discussed, we shall now focus on the other two.

Erickson's Theory of Psycho-social Development

Erik Erickson, the famous psychoanalyst, is credited with developing the theory of psycho-social development which covers normal development over the entire life span of human beings.

Erickson postulated that the development of an individual is the result of his interaction with his social environment. Right from his birth, his social development puts him under specific pressures or conflicts (called crises) by making specific demands at different ages or developmental stages of his life. The individual tries to meet these specific demands or resolve the crises by reacting psychologically in his own way, depending upon his circumstances. The complexity of the demands from society or social environment goes on increasing as the child advances on the ladder of growth and development. So, at each stage of his development, the child faces a new crisis, i.e. an issue that needs to be resolved at that particular stage of development. The way in which the 'crisis' of each stage is resolved has a major bearing on the development of one's personality which in turn is reflected as the positive and negative aspect of one's behaviour. Erickson discovered eight such issues or crises of life arising at different ages or periods of one's development and linked them with the eight stages of one's psycho-social development covering one's entire life span as outlined in Table 9.2.

Table 9.2   Age Span for the Stages of Psycho-social Development

Stage of psycho-social development	Specific age or period
Trust vs. *Mistrust*	Birth to $1^1/_2$ years
Autonomy vs. *Shame and Doubt*	$1^1/_2$ years to 3 years
Initiative vs. *Guilt*	3 to 6 years
Industry vs. *Inferiority*	6 to 12 years
Identity vs. *Role Confusion*	Adolescence (12 to 20 years)
Intimacy vs. *Isolation*	Early adulthood (20 to 45 years)
Generativity vs. *Stagnation*	Middle adulthood (45 to 65 years)
Ego integrity vs. *Despair*	Later adulthood (65 years onwards)

The above division outlines the types of crises that need to be resolved at particular stages or periods of one's life. It also identifies the different stages of psycho-social development, i.e. the personality traits that are likely to develop at a particular stage. For example, one may go on acquiring positive traits like trust independence, initiative, industry and identity, etc., to develop into a meaningful personality. On the other hand, one can develop into a troublesome, confused and doomed personality by failing to successfully resolve the crisis of one's age and developing negative traits like mistrust, shame, doubt, guilt feeling, inferiority and the like. Since these behaviour traits, modes of adjustment or psychological build-up are acquired through one's active interaction with the social environment, the stages of development are referred to as psycho-social development. These different stages of psycho-social development should not be considered to begin suddenly or end abruptly. In fact, one stage evolves into another through the whole life cycle and the crisis of issues not resolved during one stage is supposed to carry over into the stages that follow in some way or the other as revealed through the following discussion:

Stage I: The period of trust vs. *mistrust (Birth to 1¹/₂ years).* In the first one and a half years of life, the infant is confronted with the crisis termed *trust* vs. *mistrust*. During this period the baby is completely dependent upon its mother or caretaker for the satisfaction of its needs. The way it is nourished, handled, protected and kept safe and comfortable at this stage may provide the baby with a sense of security or insecurity, a feeling of trust or mistrust in the mother or caretaker and ultimately in its surroundings. The sense of trust or mistrust with regard to the environment gained in this way at this stage of development may then be carried over to the stages of development to follow and consequently reflected in the developing personality.

Stage II: The period of autonomy vs. *shame and doubt (1¹/₂ to 3 years).* Having gained a primary sense of trust and security with regard to his environment, in the second and third years of his life, the child now passes through the second stage of psycho-social development. With the newly developed motor or physical skills and language ability, the child now engages in exploring his environment and experimenting with his strengths and limitations for achieving a sense of auto-nomy and independence. The child now needs proper safety measures against the risks involved in activities like walking, running, pulling, and handling the objects of his environment or in terms of learning undesirable language but this does not mean that he should be denied a reasonable degree of freedom to acquire a sense of independence. Within the bounds of safety, he must be provided adequate opportunities for the acquisition of a sense of autonomy and knowledge about his limitations.

Children who are denied the opportunity to develop a sense of independence by over-protective, harsh or restrictive parents begin to doubt their ability and ultimately begin to feel embarrassed or ashamed in the presence of others. However, the development of the sense of doubt and shame within reasonable limits is not harmful. A healthy sense of doubt helps the child to set his own limits and the development of shame helps him to develop a sense of right and wrong. Therefore, at this stage of psycho-social development, the child needs to be helped in striking a balance between the conflicting needs of his social environment to acquire a sense of autonomy and develop a sense of doubt and shame for the adequate development of his personality.

Stage III: The period of initiative vs. *guilt (3 to 6 years).*   The third stage of psycho-social development between three to six years of age is characterized by the crisis of initiative versus guilt. Equipped with the sense of trust and autonomy the child now begins to take initiative in interacting with his environment. He asks questions about each and everything, explores his environment ceaselessly, and engages in planning and carrying out activities of various kinds. The extent to which the initiative for carrying out physical and mental exploration is encouraged or discouraged by the parents and the available social environment, goes a long way in developing ability in the child to initiate plan and carry out these activities in later life.

In case the child is discouraged from taking the initiative by his parents and guardians not having faith in him, or is pulled down by unhealthy criticism, punishment or rebuke for minor failures, the child is sure to develop a sense of guilt leading to hesitation, indecision and lack of initiative in planning and carrying out his life activities. Although in case of failure he feels a reasonable amount of guilt for having failed to take the initiative at the right time or made mistakes in planning and carrying out his activities, this enables him to learn from his failures. However, to allow this to develop into a guilty conscience is harmful to the development of the child's personality. Therefore, there is a need to resolve the crisis of *initiative* vs. *guilt* at this stage of psycho-social development and it can be properly done if we allow the child to experiment with his initiative by properly supervising and guiding his activities and encouraging him to develop a habit of self-evaluation of the results of his initiative.

Stage IV: Period of industry vs. *inferiority (6 to 12 years).*   Generally, by this age children begin to attend to school where they are made to learn various skills and the teachers as well as the school environment generate pressures on them to work hard in order to perform well. Parents also now begin to make demands upon the children to lend their hand with household duties or in some cases saddle them with occupational responsibilities. They have also to compete with their peers in terms of competence and productivity in school and other social situation. Now, in case the child performs well in school, home or in other social environments or is admired for his intellectual or motor pursuits he will be likely to develop a sense of industry filled with a sense of achievement. Such a child will conse-quently be motivated to work harder and achieve more in terms of competency and productivity. On the other hand, if his performance remains inferior to that of his peers or he does not satisfy his teachers and parents with his performance, he may begin to look down upon himself and develop a sense of inferiority.

The teachers and the school environment thus play a very significant role in helping the child out of the industry versus inferiority crisis. For the child, the school becomes the place where success and failure are defined. Therefore, it is the duty of the teachers and school authorities to structure their classroom and school environment in such a way as to help the students to maintain a positive attitude and view themselves as capable and valuable individuals.

Stage V: The period of identity vs. *role confusion (12 to 19 years).*   This stage, beginning with the advent of puberty, is marked with the crisis of *identity* vs. *role* confusion. Equipped with the sense of trust, autonomy, initiative and industry, adolescents begin to search for their own personal identity. The sudden changes in their bodies and mental functioning and the altered demands of society compel them to ask questions of themselves like, who am I? What have I become? Am I the same person I used to be? What am I supposed to do and in which manner am I to behave?

Erickson asserts that at this stage, the adolescent's search by questioning and redefining his own socio-psychological identity established during earlier stages is definitely linked with (a) his sudden and rapid bodily changes, and (b) anxiety and pressures related to his need to make decisions about his future education and career. Consequently, the adolescent tries to search for his new role and identity. He experiments with various sexual, occupational and educational roles to understand who he is and what he can be.

The extent to which an individual is able to develop a sense of identity will depend upon the degree of success he achieves in resolving the crisis related to all the previous stages. Failure in resolving the crises of those periods would be likely, at this stage, to result in role confusion and consequently the individual will not be able to find himself. He may then feel completely bewildered, not knowing what to do and how to behave on his own. He may be unable to make the decision about his educational or professional career or about making friends. The lack of self-identification and role confusion may also lead to overidentification with villains and clowns, showing a type of childish and impulsive behaviour or developing conformity in taste and style and intolerance of others. On the other hand, if the psycho-social development of the adolescent results in his achieving a sense of identity, it will result in the individual of the adolescent results in his achieving a sense of identity, it will result in the individual developing the required confidence in his ability to do things, make him properly balanced in terms of emotional reactions and will place him in harmony with his environment.

Teachers and parents can play a very constructive role in helping adolescents through this identity versus confusion crisis. The adolescents, craving for identity must be fully recognized and it should be clearly understood that adolescents want to be identified as adults and must, therefore, be treated as such and not as children as many teachers and parents tend to do. They should never be belittled or humiliated in front of their peers or anyone else for that matter. They must be assigned responsibilities independently or collectively and be trusted for their promises and conduct.

Stage VI: The period of intimacy vs. isolation (20 to 45 years). This is the sixth stage of psycho-social development, and spans the years of early adulthood. During this stage the individual tends to develop a sense of intimacy or commitment to a close relationship with another person.

Throwing light on this aspect Erickson (1950), writes:

> Thus the young adult, emerging from the search for and the insistence on identity, is eager and willing to fuse his identity with that of others. He is ready for intimacy, that is, the capacity to commit himself to concrete affiliations and partnerships and to develop the ethical strength to abide by such commitments even though they may call for significant sacrifices and compromises.

Thus, during this stage, the individual seeks to form close personal attachments by merging his identity with that of another person. The relationships develop into such a close involvement that he tends to risk even the loss of his ego or image as is evidenced in the harmonious relationships between husband and wife and intimate friends, and in the ideal relationship between a teacher and his pupil. The ultimate sense of intimacy is clearly visible in terms of the mutual identity experienced at the time of simultaneous organs in sexual intercourse with a loved partner of the opposite sex. Another form of such intimacy is seen in sacrifices made for one's close friends or for members of one's family.

The opposite of intimacy is isolation. When one fails to develop an adequate sense of intimacy by merging one's identity with that of another person or when relations deteriorate for one reason or another, one tends to develop a sense of isolation—a pulling away from relationships and breaking off of ties. Alternatives have to be developed for intimate relationships. It is essential to maintain equilibrium in such cases as the deviation from or denial of intimate relationships is costly in terms of a normal and happy life. This does not mean, however, that isolation is altogether undesirable or harmful. A certain degree of isolation is crucial to the maintenance of one's individuality and the development of one's personality in the desired direction, but if it exceeds certain limits, it may become a serious handicap to the establishment and maintenance of close ties and may lead to loneliness and self-absorption. The crisis of *intimacy* vs. *isolation* needs to be resolved by striking a balance between the two contradictory needs—the need for intimacy and the need to maintain one's individuality. The degree to which one succeeds in resolving this crisis is said to secure one's adjustment with one's self and the world one lives in.

Stage VII: ***The period of creativity* vs. *stagnation (middle adulthood—45 to 65 years).***   An individual's life up to this stage is taken up with trying to establish himself in a professional career. Now, he needs to satisfy his need for generativity, a concern to establish and guide the next generation. This is realized through nurturing his own children, guiding and directing other young people and by engaging in some kind of creative, productive or fruitful activity that may prove beneficial to society. Instead of caring only for himself or for those in his family or friends who are close to him, he participates in the welfare of the future generation as represented by his own children, pupils, subordinates and young people in general. This is, in fact, an effort at extension of one's self and its merger with self or others in society.

As opposed to the sense of generativity, there is a tendency on the part of the individual to become egoistic and selfish. This leads to stagnation and personal impoverishment. Although it would be quite natural to pause in one's life's work to reflect upon, evaluate and consolidate one's achievements and to regroup one's energies for future productivity, an excess of this hiatus may result in self-indulgence and psychological invalidism. A balanced adjustment between the extremes of the need for generativity and the need for inactivity is thus required so that in the time of inactivity one may become more energetic and be able to put renewed efforts into rendering service to society and future generation.

Stage VIII: The period of ego-integrity* vs. *despair (old age, about 65 onwards). This stage of psycho-social development is associated with later adulthood or old age. Although the precise commencement of old age cannot be determined because some people remain physically and mentally active well into their eighties and nineties, others feel, look and act old even in their fifties, yet biologically speaking, old age may be said to begin when people cease to reproduce.

During this last stage of psycho-social development one is confronted with the final crisis of one's life span, termed *ego-integrity* vs. *despair.* Ego-integrity refers to the integration or culmination of the successful resolution of all the seven previous crises in the course of one's life. The successful resolution of the previous crises provides a sense of fulfilment and satisfaction to one's ego. When one reflects on one's past and feels satisfied over what has been done, one is sure to develop a positive outlook about oneself and the world around. A person with a developed sense of ego-integrity is at peace with the life he has lived and has no major regrets over what could have been or for what should have been done differently. On the other hand, persons who have not been able to successfully resolve the previous crises of the developmental stages are sure to feel differently. They look back on their lives with despair and feel dissatisfied with the way they have lived their lives. The thought that they now have no time left for changing the course of their lives and doing what should have been done, makes them feel miserable and, consequently, they are doomed to develop a deep sense of despair. These people can become desperately afraid of death. On the other hand, people who have no regrets for the way their lives have been lived and who have an admiration or love for their ego are easily able to accept the inevitability of their death and live life as fully as they can till their last breath.

At the same time, despair is not the absolute negative aspect of one's personality. To feel satisfied or dissatisfied about one or the other issue is common and natural. One may regret many mistakes and deficiencies of one's life, but this should not be stretched to the point where one develops a sense of disaffection with one's ego and begins to hate oneself and then sink into a state of utter depression. It is, therefore, essential to strike a balance between the conflicting needs of ego–integrity and despair and to successfully resolve the final crisis of one's life resulting in a well-balanced optimistic outlook for oneself and the outside world in order to live the remaining days of one's life as gracefully and productively as possible.

In a summarised form, Erickson's stages of psycho-social development covering entire life span of an individual may be represented in the following manner.

Infant
Trust vs. *Mistrust*
Needs maximum comfort with minimal uncertainty to trust himself/herself, others, and the environment

Toddler
Autonomy vs. *Shame and Doubt*
Works to master physical environment while maintaining self-esteem

Preschooler
Initiative vs. *Guilt*
Begins to initiate, not imitate, activities; develops conscience and
sexual identity

School-Age Child
Industry vs. *Inferiority*
Tries to develop a sense of self-worth by refining skills

Adolescent
Identity vs. *Role Confusion*
Tries integrating many roles (child, sibling, student, athlete, worker)
into a self-image under role model and peer pressure

Young Adult
Intimacy vs. *Isolation*
Learns to make personal commitment to another as spouse, parent or partner

Middle-Age Adult
Generativity vs. *Stagnation*
Seeks satisfaction through productivity in career, family, and civic interests

Older Adult
Integrity vs. *Despair*
Reviews life accomplishments, deals with loss and preparation for death

Kohlberg's Theory of Moral Development

Lawrence Kohlberg, a psychologist belonging to the University of Harvard is
known for putting forward a theory of the development of moral judgement in the
individual, right from the years of early childhood. He has based his theory of
moral development on the findings of his studies conducted on hundreds of
children from different cultures.

He differs from the popular view that children imbibe the sense and methods
of moral judgement from their parents and elders by way of learning. According
to him *as soon as we talk with children about morality, we find that they have
many ways of making judgements which are not internalized from the outside, and
which do not come in any direct and obvious way from parents, teachers and even
peers* (Kohlberg, 1968). Going further he clarified that internal or cognitive
processes like thinking and reasoning also play a major role in one's moral development, i.e. the way children make moral judgement depends on their level of
intellectual development as well as on their upbringing and learning experiences.

For studying the process of moral development in human beings, Kohlberg
first defined *moral development as the development of an individual's sense of
justice*. For estimating one's sense of justice he concentrated on one's views on
morality with the help of a test of moral judgement consisting of a set of moral
dilemmas. For instance, should a man who cannot afford the medicine his dying
wife needs, steal it? Should a doctor mercy-kill a fatally ill person suffering terrible
pain? Is it better to save the life of one important person or a lot of unimportant
persons? With the help of the responses he got from his subjects he came to the

conclusion that like the Piagetial stages of cognitive development, there also exist universal stages in the development of moral values, and the movement from one stage to another depends on cognitive abilities rather than the simple acquisition of moral values of one's parents, elders and peers. He then identified three levels of moral development, each containing two stages as shown in Table 9.3.

Table 9.3   Kohlberg's Six Stages of Moral Development

Level I	Premoral (Age 4 to 10 years)
Stage 1:	The stage of obedience for avoiding punishment
Stage 2:	The stage of conforming to obtain rewards and favours in return
Level II	Conventional morality (Age 10 to 13 years)
Stage 3:	The stage of maintaining mutual relations and approval of others
Stage 4:	The stage of obedience for avoiding censure by higher authority or social systems
Level III	Self accepted moral principles (Age 13 or not until middle or later adulthood or never)
Stage 5:	Stage of conforming to the democratically accepted law and mores of community welfare
Stage 6:	Stage of conforming to the universal ethical principles and the call of one's conscience

Let us now briefly discuss these levels and stages of morality.

Premoral level (4 to 10 years).   The child begins to make judgements about what is right or wrong, good or bad. However, the standards by which he measures the morality are those of others. He is persuaded to take such judgement either to avoid punishment or to earn rewards. Development of morality at this level usually follows the following two stages:

Stage 1:   In the beginning, the child's morality is controlled by the fear of punishment. He tries to obey his parents and elders purely to avoid reproof and punishment.

Stage 2:   In the second stage of the premoral level, children's moral judgement is based on self-interest and considerations of what others can do for them in return. Here they value a thing because it has some practical utility for them. They obey the orders of their parents and elders and abide by some rules and regulations, because it serves their interests.

Conventional morality level (10 to 13 years).   At this stage also, children's moral judgement is controlled by the likes and dislikes of others—the conventions, rules and regulations and the law and order system maintained within society. Stealing or mercy-killing would thus be judged wrong because it is considered wrong by society at large and by the legal system. In this way, the conventional level of morality may be regarded as the level where the child identifies with authority. It is characterized by the following two stages:

Stage 3:   In the early years of the second level of moral development, the child's moral judgement is based on the desire to obtain approval of others and avoid being disliked by being declared a good boy or a good girl. For this purpose he begins to judge the intentions and likes or dislikes of others and acts accordingly.

Stage 4: In the later years of the conventional morality level, children's moral judgements are governed by conventions as well as the laws and mores of the social system. The standards of others are now so established that it becomes a convention to follow them. The children now follow the rules and regulations of society and take decisions about things being right or wrong with a view to avoiding censure by the elders, authorities or the social system.

Self-accepted moral principles level (Age 13 or during late adulthood). This marks the highest level of attainment of true morality as the controlling force for making moral judgements now rests with the individual himself. He does not value a thing or conform to an idea merely because of consideration of the views of others, conventions or the law and order system of society but because it fits into the framework of his self-accepted moral principles. This level is also characterized by two separate stages:

Stage 5: At this stage the individual's moral judgements are internalized in such a form that he responds positively to authority only if he agrees with the principles upon which the demands of authority are based. The individual at this stage begins to think in rational terms, valuing the rights of human beings and the welfare of society. For example, at this stage in deference to the rights of the human being, the decision about mercy-killing may be left to the individual who is suffering, and if so needed, the concerned laws may be amended for the welfare of society at large.

Stage 6: At this stage, the controlling forces for making moral judgements are highly internalized. The decisions of the individual are now based upon his conscience and the belief in universal principles of respect, justice and equality. He does what he, as an individual thinks right regardless of legal restrictions or the opinion of others. Thus, at this stage people act according to the inner voice of their conscience and lead a life that they can without self-condemnation or feeling of guilt or shame.

From the above discussion of the stages of moral development, it is clear that although children begin to think about morality in terms of justice or right and wrong at a very early age, yet they have to wait until adolescence or adulthood for the dawning of the stage of true morality. Also, it is not essential that all people pass through the third level of moral development. Most adults are not able to cross the second level and few can reach stage 5, and among these there are very few who, being intellectually quite sound, can think rationally and base their moral judgement purely on the dictates of their conscience at the risk of life and property.

SUMMARY

The terms 'growth' and 'development' both represent the processes that result in changes in an organism right from the beginning of its life. However, the term development is more comprehensive than growth as it is related to the overall changes, structural as well as functional, in all aspects of one's personality namely, physical, mental, emotional, social and moral taking place continuously right from conception till death.

The course of one's life from conception till death is divided into certain specific stages referred to as the stages of growth and development, namely, infancy, childhood, adolescence, adulthood and old age. Each of these stages chronologically extends over a rather definite period in years and is characterized by typical norms of behavioural characteristics which are specific to the particular stages in all the different dimensions of the make-up of one's personality.

Moreover, development in general, from conception onward in various dimensions of one's personality is found to follow some basic rules known as the principles of development. The knowledge of these principles of growth and development proves quite useful to parents and teachers for ensuring the harmonious growth and development of the personalities of their children. For example, the principle of individual difference reminds them to plan the education and care for the development of the children, keeping their wide individual differences in mind. Similarly, principles like general to specific, whole to parts, the integration of general and specific as well as whole and parts help them to plan the learning processes and arrange suitable learning experiences for achieving maximum gains in terms of growth and development.

The factors influencing a person's growth and development may be classified as *internal factors* and *external factors.* The internal factors (lying within the individual) may include hereditary factors, biological or constitutional factors, his intelligence, emotional make-up and social nature. The external factors may be traced in a person's environment right from conception and, therefore, it may be categorized as the environment available in the mother's womb (internal environment) and environment available after birth (external environment) for a child's growth and development.

Various theories have been put forward by different psychologists from time to time for tracing the developmental processes in one or the other dimension of one's personality.

Freud's Theory of Psycho-sexual Development points out five distinct stages of development, viz. psychosexual stages: oral, anal, phallic, latent and genital (described earlier in Chapter 5). These stages are separated from each other on the basis of the shift in the areas of sex gratification known as erogenous zones. Failure to be appropriately gratified at a particular stage may result in a fixation at that stage.

Piaget's Theory of Cognitive Development identifies four distinct stages of children's intellectual development: sensory-motor, pre-operational, concrete operational, and formal operational (discussed in Chapter 8). A child's cognitive abilities develop as he progresses from stage to stage. For example, in the concrete operation stage he begins to think logically but is unable to think abstractly. During the formal operational stage, he begins to think abstractly and deal with problems that are not physically present.

Erickson's Theory of Psycho-social Development brings out eight stages spread over the whole span of human life. These are *trust* vs. *mistrust* (birth to 1 year), *autonomy* vs. *shame and doubt* (1 to 13 years), *initiative* vs. *guilt* (3 to 6 years), *industry* vs. *inferiority* (6 to 12 years), *identity* vs. *role confusion* (12 to 19 years), *intimacy* vs. *isolation* (20 to 45 years), *generativity* vs. *stagnation* (45 to 65 years) and *ego-integrity* vs. *despair* (65 years onwards). Each of these stages is associated with a distinctive crisis of life faced by the individual at that particular stage. How well one will be developed and acquire positive or negative aspects of behaviour depends upon the manner in which these crises of life are resolved by him.

Kohlberg's Theory of Moral development relates an individual's moral development to his cognitive development. Kohlberg identified three levels of moral development: *premoral* (4 to 10 years), *conventional morality* (10 to 13 years) and *self-accepted moral principles* (age 13 or sometime afterwards). Each of these levels was described to consist of two stages. In this way he tried to describe moral development as a function of the development of one's sense of justice evolving progressively through the six stages covered at the three levels of morality at different periods of one's life. He also asserted that many of us are not able to cross the second level of moral development. Therein lies the varying individual perception in terms of the quality and level of morality depending upon cognitive development as well as on upbringing and social experiences.

REFERENCES

Erickson, E., *Childhood and Society*, New York: Norton, 1950, p. 263.

_____, *Identity: Youth and Crises*, New York: Norton, 1968.

Freud, S., *An Outline of Psychoanalysis*, London: Hogarth Press, 1953.

_____, *Three Essays on the Theory of Sexuality*, New York: Basic Books, 1962.

Kohlberg, L., The development of moral character and moral ideology, in M. Hoffman and L. Hoffman (Eds.), *Review of Child Development Research*, Vol. I, New York: Russell Sage Foundation, 1964.

_____, The child as a moral philosopher, *Psychology Today*, Vol. 2, pp. 25–30, 1968.

_____, Moral stages and moralization: The cognitive developmental approach, In: T. Lickona (Ed.), *Moral Development and Behaviour*, New York: Holt, Rinehart and Winston, 1976.

Kohlberg, L. and Turiel, E., *Research and Moral Development: A cognitive developmental approach*, New York: Wiley, 1971.

Kuppuswami, B. (Ed.), *Advanced Educational Psychology*, Jalandhar: University Publications, 1963.

Piaget, J., *The Origins of Intelligence in Children*, New York: International University Press, 1952.

_____, *Psychology of Intelligence*, Totawa, N.J., Little-field Adams, 1968.

SUGGESTED READINGS

Carmichael, L. (Ed.), *Manual of Child Psychology*, New York: Wiley, 1946.

Crow, L.D. and Crow, Alice, *Educational Psychology*, New Delhi: Eurasia Publishing House, 1973.

Hurlock, E.B., *Child Psychology*, Tokyo: McGraw-Hill, 1959.

Inhelder, B. and Piaget, J., *The Growth of Logical Thinking from Childhood to Adolescence* (Trans. by Anne Parsons and Stanley Milgram), New York: Basic Books, 1958.

Levin, M.J., *Psychology: A biographical approach*, New York: McGraw-Hill, 1978.

Mangal, S.K., *Educational Psychology*, Ludhiana: Prakash Brothers, 1989.

Marry, F.K. and Marry, R.V., *From Infancy to Adolescence*, New York: Harper and Brothers, 1940.

Paplia, D.E. and Olds, S.W., *Psychology*, New York: McGraw-Hill, 1987.

Chapter 10

Psychology of Individual Differences

MEANING AND DEFINITION OF INDIVIDUAL DIFFERENCES

There seems to be no end to the variations, deviations and differences present among the creations of the Almighty in the form of living or non-living. We can see different types of soils, rocks, stones around us on this very earth. The quality and characteristics of the water we drink, get variated from place to place and region to region. Apart from non-living, such variations and differences are equally found among the living beings. We can see countless varieties of plants, insects, birds and animals on the earth. Some are named as fruits, some as vegetables, some as pulses or some as grains, depending upon their common or varying characteristics. It is true that there are some characteristics common or otherwise, that help in grouping a class of objects or living beings in one category or species and thereby separating them also from others. It helps us in differentiating and distinguishing a particular type of living or non-living being from others. As a result we can confidently say that this particular bird is a crow and that is a parrot or a peacock.

However, with such classification or grouping, it should not be assumed that members of the same species are alike in all aspects. Apparently all cows, buffaloes, parrots and peacocks may seem to be alike on account of their common resemblance as well as qualities and characteristics peculiar to their species. However one's cow is not the same as another's. Inspite of having all the common qualities and characteristics unique to their kind, all cows differ from one another in many aspects.

As a conclusion, it must be clearly understood that whatever lies around us in the form of non-living or living beings differ from each other in many aspects. These differences and variations become more intense and remarkable as we draw our attention closer and closer to human beings as one of the ultimate creation of the almighty in the history of evolution. We, as human beings quite distinctly differ in size, shape, appearance, speed of reaction and innumerable other aspects of our personality make up and behaviour. Among us some are healthy and enthusiastic, while others are weak and irritable. Some are blue eyed and black haired while others have black eyes and grey hair. Some are known as girls or women while others are named as boys or men. Some learn quickly and others slowly, some remember well while others forget, some respond quickly and some others slowly. In this way no one among us is just the same as another. The sons and daughters of the same parents or even identical twins are not exactly the same as their counterparts. Every one of us is a typical human being in oneself.

Being alike in some aspects we are definitely different in many ways. We, inspite of belonging to a common species known as human beings have our own individuality which contributes for the variance and differences found among ourselves. These differences in human beings, are referred to as "individual differences" in the languages of sociology and psychology. Let us learn more about it in order to build up a definition. For this purpose let us take a look at the two different explanations given for this term in the "Dictionary of Education" by Carter B. Good (1959).

1. Individual differences stand for "the variations or deviations among individuals in regard to a single characteristic or a number of characteristics".
2. Individual differences stand for "those differences which in their totality, distinguish one individual from another".

The above two dictionary meanings of the term individual differences, now can help us in building a workable definition with reference to whatever we discussed earlier in this chapter, in the following words:

The differences among individuals that distinguish or separate them from one another and make one as a unique individual, may be termed as individual differences.

Types or Varieties of Individual Differences

Whatever differences or variations exist among the human beings, may be generally grouped or classified into two broad categories, namely: (i) Physical or physiological differences, and (ii) Psychological differences.

While physical or physiological differences among us are related with the differences created on account of the differences or variations in terms of physical or physiological makeup of our bodies, the psychological makeup or conditions generate differences among us in terms of varying intellectual potentialities, interests, attitudes, aptitudes, emotional, social and moral development etc.

In this way, the two broad classifications of differences can be divided into specific sub-categories. Otherwise also it is advisable to understand the total pattern of individual differences existing among us through a number of specific categories or divisions. Consequently, let us try to discuss the variation or differences among us by dividing these into the following specific types or varieties:

1. *Physical differences.* Individuals differ in height, weight, colour of skin, colour of eyes and hair, size of hands and heads, arms, feet, mouth and nose, length of waistline, structure and functioning of internal organs, facial expression,

mannerisms of speech and walk, hair style and other such native or acquired physical characteristics.

2. Mental differences. People differ in intellectual abilities and capacities like reasoning and thinking, power of imagination, creative expression, concentration etc. In the field of general intelligences also we find tremendous difference between individuals. On the basis of these differences they are usually classified as idiot, imbecile, moron, border line, normal, bright, very superior and genius.

3. Differences in motor ability. There exist a wide difference in motor abilities such as reacting time, speed of action, steadiness, rate of muscular moment, manual dexterity and resistance to fatigue etc.

4. Differences in achievement. Differences exist in achievement and in knowledge even among individuals who have almost the same amount of intelligence and have been subjected to equal amount of schooling and experience.

5. Emotional differences. In some individuals, positive emotions like love, affection and amusement and the like are prominent whereas, in some, negative emotions are more powerful. Individuals also differ in the manner they express their emotions. Some are emotionally stable and mature, while others are emotionally unstable and immature. In this way there exist wide emotional differences among individuals.

6. Differences in interests and aptitudes. Variations occur among the individuals in relation to the specific tastes and interests. Some take interest in meeting people, attending social functions and are very fond of picnics and group excursions; others feel happy in solitude, avoid social gatherings and are interested in meditation or enjoy company of books. In a similar way, people are found to have different aptitudes. Some have mechanical aptitude, while the others have scholastic, musical or artistic aptitudes.

7. Difference in attitudes, beliefs and opinions. Individuals are found to possess varying attitudes towards different people, groups, objects and ideas. Their attitudes may be positive, negative or of somewhat indifferent nature. Similarly they differ in respect of beliefs, opinions, and ideas. Some believe in one thing, others in another. Some are conservative and rigid while the others are progressive, liberal and dynamic.

8. Learning differences. Individual differences are found in the field of learning also. Some learn more easily and are able to make use of their learning more comfortably than others. For some, one method of learning or memorization is more suitable, while for others, a different method suits. In the same way suitability of learning environment also depends upon the individual nature of the learner. Thus there are wide individual differences in relation to learning.

9. Differences in social and moral development. Individuals differ in respect of their social and moral development. Some are found to be adjusted properly in the social situations and lead a happy social life while others are *socially* *handicapped*, unsocial or antisocial. Similarly, people are found to differ in respect of ethical and moral sense.

All the above mentioned varieties of individual differences lead us to conclude that as a whole the personality of an individual is unique in itself. In all the dimensions and aspects of behaviour and personality traits the individuals differ from each other and thus no one can be said to be exactly similar to another.

Distribution of Individual Differences

It might be clear now that we all do differ from one another in one way or the other in so many aspects. However, at this point the question may emerge as to how much we are likely to differ, what should be the range or limitations of the differences existing among us? Do these variations or differences follow some pattern? How are these differences distributed over a large number of our population? Let us seek answers for such questions.

Answer to all such questions lies in the fact that distribution of almost all the things in nature follows the pattern of a normal curve. Height, weight, beauty, wealth, intelligence and similar other attributes of our personality are distributed in our population in a normal way. Let us know what this normal distribution means. Let us consider simple practical situations all around us in our day-to-day life. We find that most of us are quite average in possession of attributes of our personality. Majority of us possess average weight, height, wealth, beauty and intelligence etc. There are very few who are too fatty like Tuntun or Aaga (the fatty film personalities) or too thin like Johny Walker. Similarly while we seldom come across the beauty like Noor Jahan, Padmavati or Cleopatra, we also rarely find too ugly figures. Mostly there are normal or average beautiful figures all around us. This is equally applicable to the distribution of intelligence. Most of us have normal intelligence ranging between 90 to 110 IQs. Persons having IQs more than 140 or 150 (Genius) as well as possessing IQs less than 60 or 40 (Idiots or Imbeciles) are rarely found.

In this way, it can be easily concluded that a majority among us consists of averages or normals in terms of possession of all the attributes of our personality. How many of us are above or below average in a given population can be understood with the help of a distribution pattern shown by normal curve. Let us try to draw such a normal curve on the basis of a hypothetical data related with the distribution of achievement scores (a attribute of the personality) over a given population of examinees.

For having a large sample of population of the examinees let us take up the record of the last year's XII Class annual examination of a school in Haryana. We may have the total scores of all the examinees appearing in the said examination arranged serially according to their roll numbers. Out of this huge data, we can randomly select for our study the total scores of 10,000 students for our study. Now calculate the average score or mean value of the sample. For this purpose, we will add individual total marks of these 10,000 students and then divide it by 10,000 to get the mean or average score for the sample. If we try to analyse the total marks earned by this population of 10,000, we will find that majority of them have either earned the mean average score or lie quite nearest to this value. There are very few who have got distinction marks or very low marks. In case we try to plot the total scores earned by these 10,000 students on a sheet of graph paper by taking scores on x-axis and number of students (frequencies) on the y-axis, we will have a bell-shaped curve like below (shown in Figure 10.1).

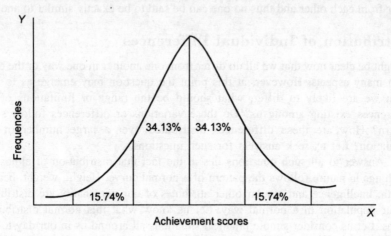

Figure 10.1   The distribution of achievement scores in a population of examinees.

Let us analyse the pattern of distribution of achievement scores in the population of examinees.

1.   As revealed by this curve, we can find that the majority (34.13% + 34.13%, i.e. 68.26%) of students have either got marks equal to the mean average value or lying quite nearer to this value. This sub-population of 6,826 out of 10,000 thus can be declared as normal, i.e. the students who possess normal or average academic achievement abilities.

2.   The curve shows that 15.74% of the students have earned more marks than the average. This 15.74% sub-population of the students, i.e. 1574 out of 10,000 is named as above average in terms of their academic achievements. A similar percentage, i.e. 15.74% of the students also lie on the other side of the mean value. It shows that there are 15.74% students i.e. 1,574 out of 10,000, who have got less marks than the average value. These students are named as below average or sub-normals in respect of their academic achievement in class XII final examination.

3.   The normal curve thus shows the pattern of distribution of an attribute in a given population. Here it has demonstrated that out of 10,000, the majority of 68.26%, i.e. 6,826 out of 10,000 consist of averages. There are only 15.74%, i.e. 1,574 out of 10,000, who are below average and a similar percentage 15.74%, i.e. 1,574 out of 10,000, who are labelled as above average.

Thus we can conclude that individual differences among us always follow the pattern of a normal curve.

It is true that we do differ from each other and no one is like another. However, majority of us, that is, 68.26%, are quite average, i.e. possess average typical value in terms of possession of personality attributes. A very few of us deviate from this average value and classified as quite above or below average or normal in terms of other personality attributes.

Determinants of Individual Differences

Why do we differ from each other in so many ways? What is it that is responsible for such differences and variations among us? Are these differences present in the individuals right from their birth or even at the time of conception, or do they creep in afterwards? Educationalists, sociologists and psychologists have tried to seek answer to these questions through their studies and researches. They have in turn concluded that both the hereditary as well as environmental factors are jointly responsible for differences and variations among us. How does it happen? In what ways do hereditary and environmental influences contribute towards such variations? To seek answer to such questions let us analyse in detail, the concepts 'heredity' and 'environment' along with their contributions singly or together for creating individual differences.

Let us learn about one's heredity.

What is Heredity?

A cat gives birth to a kitten, a cow to a calf and a human being to a baby. The members of each of these species resemble one another and possess characteristics common to their respective species. Now the question arises as to what is it that is responsible for a particular type of body, shape and other similar characteristics in the members of one species. On further observation, we find that there are individual differences even in the members of the same species. A child resembles his sisters, brothers, parents, grand-parents, and other members of the family more than the people not related to him at all. What is it that causes such similarities and dissimilarities? The answer usually referred to is heredity which means that an offspring inherits most of the personality traits of his parents and forefathers which make him resemble them. It is in this sense that Douglas and Holland (1947) defined heredity in the following words:

> One's heredity consists of all the structures, physical characteristics, functions
> or capacities derived from parents, other ancestry or species.

When does a child inherit such personality characteristics from his parents or forefathers and how is this process of inheritance performed? What helps in such inheritance? These are some of the basic questions which need some clarifications at this stage. For answers let us try to understand how life begins.

How Life Begins: Life in actual sense begins with the conception, approximately, nine months before birth. The mechanism of conception is explained below:

The male and female reproductive organs produce germ cells. In the males their testes produce the male germ cells, the spermatozoa, while in the females, their ovaries produce the female germ cells, the ova. 'Life' is the result of the union of these male and female cells.

As a result of coitus at the time of mating, the male germ cells, numerous in quantity, try to come into contact with female germ cells. The male germ cells are deposited at the mouth of the uterus and try to make contact with the single ovum (normally only one ovum is produced in each menstrual cycle). Out of so many spermatozoa, in a normal case, only one sperm (single male cell) is able to establish contact with the ovum (single female cell) situated in the ovarian duct of the mother and makes it fertile. This process is called fertilization. The fertilized Ovum is technically known as zygote, the starting single cell structure of a new life.

Human life thus starts from a single cell produced by the union of two germ cells, one from each parent and gradually develops into a complicated composition of trillions of body cells and yet containing the same genetic material that was inherited at the time of conception.

The zygote i.e. the fertilized ovum consists of a semi-fluid mass called cytoplasm and within the cytoplasm there is a nucleus which contains chromosomes. Chromosomes always exist in pairs. In human zygote there are 23 pairs of chromosomes (46 individual chromosomes) 23 of which are contributed by the father and 23 by the mother and this is why the transmission of hereditary characteristics from the mother and the father is said to be equal.

Chromosomes possess a thread like structure and are made up of very small units called genes. It is estimated that there are more than 1,000 genes in each human chromosome cell. The possibility regarding the combination of 23,000 characteristics each from mother and father, may help us to understand the reasons for uniqueness of each individual.

Regardless of their minute size, the composition of genes has been determined in terms of "DNA" and "RNA". DNA stands for deoxyribonucleic acid and is said to be a basic chemical substance primarily responsible for genetic inheritance. RNA stands for ribonucleic acid and it acts as an active assistant to DNA for carrying out the genetic code message from parent to offspring.

Thus, what we get from our ancestral stock through our parents at the time of fertilization of the ovum of the mother by the sperm of the father is in the form of chromosomes, genes and their respective classical constituents. The inheritance of traits at the time of conception makes up the native capital and endowment of an individual that are present with him in the form of sum total of the traits basically present in the fertilized ovum. These are called the heredity factors present in an individual.

The Role of Genes

In search of hereditary functions of genes through his experiments on garden peas and fruitflies, Gregor Mendel hypothesized that some genes are *dominant* and others *recessive.* Like chromosomes, genes also occur in pairs. Each of the pairs

During mating each passes on his or her chromosome to child.

The father's role is merely that of passing on half of his chromosomes by way of a sperm.

The mother although she also acts as incubator and nourisher for the egg contributes no more to the child's heredity than does the father.

These 46 chromosomes comprise everything that determine the heredity of the child.

Figure 10.2 Transmission of chromosomes at the time of conception.

is donated by one of the parents. An offspring thus may be found to derive a gene pair in one of the following forms:

1. a dominant gene from one of the parents and a recessive gene from the other.
2. dominant genes from both the parents.
3. recessive genes from both the parents.

In simple meaning a dominant gene must exhibit its dominance over the recessive ones. For example, if one parent gives a dominant gene for brown eyes and the other provides a recessive gene for blue (a recessive gene), the offspring will have brown eyes (characteristic of the dominant gene).

However, the fact that a particular trait is recessive in one generation in no way rules out the possibility of its occurrence in the future. To be precise, in the above example of mutation between brown and blue genes resulting into brown eyes, the recessive blue gene may lie in wait. If that offspring is copulated with another gene in some one else for blue eyes, (even if he or she may not possess blue eyes) their offspring, the third generation, might have blue eyes.

The idea behind the role of genes, specified as above, may thus provide us a solid support (besides the chance pairing of 23 chromosomes and 23,000 genes from the egg and sperm cells) for explaining the variations and dissimilarities in height, weight, intelligence, blood type, eye colour, and the colour and texture of the skin and hair and similar other important characteristics found in the parents and their offsprings as well as among the offsprings of the same parents.

What is Environment?

From the above discussion, it is clear that a child inherits the traits and characteristics of its parents and forefathers through genes at the time of conception. Therefore, what it possesses at the time of conception is all due to heredity. After conception, how he develops is the outcome of interaction between his hereditary characteristics and environment. The forces of environment begin to play their part and influence the growth and development of the individual, right from the time of fertilization of the ovum by sperm. Therefore, from the environmental point of view, not only what happens after birth is important but also what goes on inside the womb of the mother after conception has equal significance.

The above point of view has given birth to several meanings and definitions of environment as the following:

Borning, Langfield and Weld (1961):

> The environment is every thing that affects the individual except his genes.

Woodworth and Marquis (1948):

> Environment covers all the outside factors that have acted on the individual since he began life.

Before birth, the mother's womb is the place where these forces play their part. The foetus gets its nourishment from the blood stream of its mother. The physiological and psychological states of the mother during pregnancy, her habits and interests, all influence the development of the foetus. After birth, the child is exposed to numerous environmental forces that are purely external. These can be divided into two parts—physical forces and social or cultural forces. Food, water, climate, physical atmosphere of the home, school, village or city, the natural resources available are included in the physical forces: while the parents, members of the family, friends and class mates, neighbours, teachers, the members of the community and the society, the means of mass communication and recreation, religious places, clubs, libraries etc. are included in social forces.

These different environmental forces have a desirable impact on the physical, social, emotional, intellectual, moral and aesthetic development of the individual. Their influence is a continuous one which begins with the emergence of life and follows till death.

ROLE OF HEREDITY IN GENERATING INDIVIDUAL DIFFERENCES

Hereditary factors begin their influence right from the time of conception of the child through the transmission of chromosomes and genes of its ancestral stock from its immediate parents. The role of these factors in providing uniqueness to the personality of the born child and in proving to be a significant factor in generating individual differences can be explained as follows:

1. *Heredity determines the sex of the child.* As already understood, there exist 23 pairs of chromosomes in the sperm and the ovum. Out of these the first twenty-two pairs of chromosomes are called autosomes. The autosomes are responsible for deciding and determining the growth and development of most of the characteristics and structural composition of our body. The remaining twenty-third pair is the sex chromosome. Whether the baby to be born should be a boy or a girl and what sex-linked characteristics should it possess, are decided by the mechanism of sex chromosomes of the father and the mother. Let us have a deeper understanding of this mechanism.

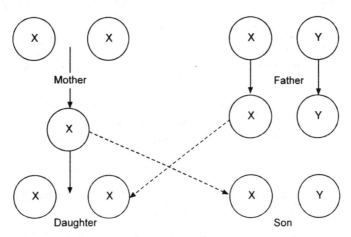

Figure 10.3 Determination of sex—boy or girl?

There are two different types of sex chromosomes, X chromosome (usually big in size) and Y chromosome (comparatively smaller than X). In a male child one member of the sex chromosome is X chromosome (contributed by the mother) and the other is 'Y' (contributed by the father). In a female child, both these sex chromosomes, one from each parent, are X chromosomes.

All eggs have X chromosomes, but sperm cells may contain either type. Therefore, a mother's role in the determination of her baby's sex is quite neutral. At the time of conception she can contribute only one type of sex chromosome, i.e. X-chromosome. Much depends upon the possibility of the type of sex chromosomes X or Y that may be transmitted by the sperm cell of the father. If X chromosome is transmitted, the child will be female and if Y chromosome is transmitted it will result in a male child. Thus, the father is biologically more accountable for determination of the sex of his baby to be.

2. *Heredity contributes significantly towards physical constitution.* Most of the attributes related to our body make-up, its constitution and functioning are well decided and guided by heredity. Some children have blue eyes, others have black or brown. Certainly, this difference is actually brought out by their genetic differences. Same is the case with the colour and texture of the skin and hair, height, facial outlook and appearances, blood types, finger prints etc. The son or the daughter of a Japanese or a Chinese national can easily be recognized on the basis of physical structure inherited by them from their parents. An Afghan or a German boy or girl will definitely have well built body structure and tall stature in comparison to an average Indian boy or a girl. This difference is definitely created by means of their respective heredity contributions.

Besides such differences in the physical constitution, structure and body make-up, hereditary factors are also said to be the sole cause for some diseases like tuberculosis, cancer, haemophilia, schizophrenia and other abnormalities. These diseases are the result of defect in genes and chromosome and are passed on to subsequent generations.

Along with other necessary physical aspects, the physiological set up of our mind (composed of our spinal cord, brain and nervous system) is also well inherited by the child.

However, sometimes the role of heredity as a determinant of physical constitution or bodily make-up becomes questionable, especially in situations in which the

(a) parents are of black colour while the child is white;

(b) parents are extraordinarily genius while the child is an idiot;

(c) child does not inherit the blindness, lameness or mental disorder of his parents; and

(d) child does not resemble any of his sisters or brothers.

If we try to seek clarification for these, then we will realise that in fact, variations are the result of chance factors that work as follows:

(i) It is purely by chance that a particular sperm fuses with a particular ovum to form a zygote. Moreover, in zygote there are 23 pairs of chromosomes, 23 of which are contributed by the sperm of the father and 23 by the ovum of the mother. Which chromosomes from ovum will be paired with which chromosomes from sperm depends upon chance. A number of permutations and combinations are possible for the fusion of these chromosomes. That explains why no two individuals are perfectly identical.

(ii) What an individual gets from heredity is determined by the genes which he receives through his parents. The traits of the ancestors, besides those genes of immediate parents are also transmitted to the offsprings through genes (which are part of chromosomes). Therefore, it is possible that a child possesses certain traits that are traceable to one or more of his ancestors, even though they may not be found in either of his parents.

3. *Contribution of heredity towards the birth of twins and the related individual differences.* Sometimes there are births of twins and multiples. Very often they are found to differ much from their siblings in many aspects. Not only are the twins found to differ from their counterparts inspite of their commonness in their hereditary stocks, but also they are different as individuals. How does this happen? The mechanism of multiple births may be said to be an important determinant for the individual differences among twins and siblings etc. Let us try to seek answers for these questions through the following description related to the birth of twins and multiples.

Normally at the time of fertilization, a single ovum is fertilized by a sperm of the male. It results in the birth of a single offspring at one time. But sometimes this normal function is disturbed when two or more ova get fertilized resulting in the birth of two or more offsprings at a time. There are two distinctly different types of twins namely Identical twins and Fraternal twins.

Identical twins. Usually fertilization of one ovum produces one offspring. Sometimes however, when the ovum splits as a result of fertilization the two parts fail to unite together. The result is that each part develops into a complete individual. The twins formed thus are called identical because they carry exactly the same genes. They possess almost the same characteristics and are definitely of the same sex.

Fraternal twins. Normally, in a woman during each menstrual period, only one ovum is matured but it may happen that two or more ova may mature simultaneously and get fertilized simultaneously by two different sperms. The result is that two different zygotes are produced. The individuals thus produced are known as the fraternal twins or non-identical twins. They have different combination of chromosomes and genes as both ova are fertilized by different sperms. Fraternal twins therefore, are sure to differ in many traits. They need not belong to the same sex.

The above information about twins and multiples helps us draw a conclusion about the role of hereditary factors in bringing individual differences as the following:

1. Twins are bound to differ from siblings as they are inherited from different sets of chromosomes and genes.
2. Fraternal twins differ from each other on account of the inheritance of different combination of genes and chromosomes.
3. As far as identical twins are concerned, they may exhibit too much of similarities and resemblances on account of their common heredity stocks. However, it is not essential for them to be quite identical. They may also exhibit their individualities, differences and variations in one way or other. These can be attributed to a great extent to the

environmental influences after their conception or birth. However, the role of heredity cannot be denied as in spite of being identical twins, they may receive at the time of conception somewhat a different type of composition of genes and chromosomes quite capable of creating differences in their genetic structure resulting in two different types of personalities.

ROLE OF ENVIRONMENT AS DETERMINANT OF INDIVIDUAL DIFFERENCES

As discussed earlier, hereditary factors are transmitted to the offsprings at the time of their conception by the immediate parents, through their respective chromosomes and genes. In this way, actually the role of heredity ends with conception. What goes on inside the womb after conception are thus internal environmental influences. These forces play their role approximately for 9 months till the birth of the child and are in fact responsible in many ways for shaping the individual. In its true sense they differ not only from mother to mother but also from one child to another of the same mother. Let us now try to understand the influence of internal environment.

A foetus gets its nourishment in the womb indirectly through the mother. Therefore, whatever the mother eats or drinks have an impact on the growth and development of the child. Not only the quality of her diet but also the environment available to her during pregnancy is quite important for the baby. If the mother remains tense, worried, anxious and emotionally upset or mentally perturbed, then it may eventually have an adverse effect on the growth and development of the baby.

Individual differences in children are thus certainly caused by the variations and differences existed in the physical and mental health of their mothers during pregnancy. It is said that about Mahabharat you might be knowing Abhimanyu had learnt the art of entering into Chakravyuh when he was in his mother's womb. It may seem an exaggeration but it is certain that what happens with the mother and the child from time of conception till birth is responsible for generating significant individual differences.

At the time of delivery also, the environment available to the mother and the child affects the well-being, growth and development of the child. Here, the individual differences may be caused by situations like premature or mature delivery, normal delivery or a caesarean delivery, hygienic or unhygienic conditions, and the general atmosphere at the time of delivery.

After birth, all things related to the external environment—physical, sociological, cultural and psychological—influence and affect each and every aspect of the growth and development of the child. In every step and at all times, these external environmental influences available to each child are quite different in nature as well as in effect. One may argue that children of the same parents or members of the same family have the same environment. But this is never possible, no matter how hard one may try. Even a mother cannot claim paying equal attention, care and affection to all her children. While in most Indian homes male children get preferred treatment over female children, two even real brothers also may not be treated in the same way by their own parents. The same is also true in the case of students being taught by the same set of teachers in the same set-up. No teacher can provide exactly the same treatment to all of his students. Thus as reality speaks, all children cannot be brought up in the same home, cannot reside in the same neighbourhood, cannot get education in the same institution or get the same social, cultural, physical and psychological set up. Hence, individuals are bound to differ significantly from each other in various ways.

Looking at from another angle, we find that there lies tremendous energy and strength in all types of environmental forces. They can mould, make or mar, build or destroy, help or obstruct any individual. We are just a toy, a product or a victim of these mighty forces. This is why when two children of the same parent or even identical twins are brought up in different environmental set up, they may turn up into two entirely opposite personalities. While a bad company or a negative environment may turn an innocent child into a devil, a devil or dacoit like Balmiki may turn a saint with the help of a positive and a favourable environment. On this earth, there are positive and negative, favourable and unfavourable, healthy and unhealthy, proper and improper environmental conditions that can determine the directions of a child's future. These conditions create big variations and differences among children as they grow up. Within the society we can find that the privileged, rich, educated, genius, belonging to the urban belt, flourish, those belonging to the underprivileged suffer adversely in the cruel hands of unfavourable environmental forces. In this way, when in our society we cannot remove inequalities, disharmonies and differences, how can we expect the absence of variations or differences in the individualities of human beings. Since all these inequalities in any society are always the creation of the environmental forces, it can be safely concluded that environment plays a very significant role in creating individual differences.

RELATIVE IMPORTANCE OF HEREDITY AND ENVIRONMENT AS DETERMINANTS OF INDIVIDUAL DIFFERENCES

We have already discussed and analysed separately the role of heredity and environment in creating differences and variations among human beings. Now the question arises as to which one of them is more responsible or more important from the angle of creating such variations and differences?

Arguments in favour of heredity and environment showing the relative importance of one or the other, have given birth to controversy. The hereditarians claim that heredity is everything. They point out that it decides and sets everything about the personality of an individual. No amount of education or training can change an individual from what he is or what he has inherited from his ancestors. According to them, the function of education or environment in the making of a personality can be compared to polishing or painting a wooden furniture. Any polish or paint cannot change the basic qualities of the wood used in the furniture. It can only improve its appearance and increase its life span.

The environmentalists are of the opinion that heredity does not in any way, affect the growth and development of an individual. Man is the product of his environment. He is what his environment has made him to be. There is nothing like fixed hereditary characteristics or inherited qualities. What a man has done, another man can also do if he gets favourable opportunities. Thinking on these lines, Watson, one of the prominent environmentalists declared, "Give me any child, I will make him what you desire."

Both the hereditarians and the environmentalists have also tried to collect a fund of experimental evidences in support of their view points.

Dr. Pasricha (1963) has made a beautiful concluding remark about these experiments. She writes,

> It is quite customary for the Psychologists wedded to either size viz. heredity and environment, to perform experiments and quote findings in favour of either of the factors. It has also been found that the findings of these experiments can be interpreted either way and can be easily made to support the opposite view. When analysed in an objective manner, it indicates clearly that the two are so closely interwoven that it is difficult to separate the effect of one from that of the other.

That is why, it will be quite erroneous on our part if we try to vote exclusively in favour of either heredity or environment as the sole determinant of individual differences. However, from every angle, it will be quite safe to conclude that differences or variations are the joint product of interaction between the hereditary endowments and environmental influences. In support of this view point we can place the following arguments:

1. The supposition that a particular trait in an individual is exclusively the product of his heredity or environment, does not hold ground. The individual's personality is the product of both heredity and environment. McIver and Page (1949) have aptly put forward their views as:

> Every phenomenon of life is the product of both. Each is as necessary to the result as the other. Neither can ever be eliminated and neither can ever be isolated.

2. The controversial arguments regarding the relative importance of heredity and environment are quite useless. The question whether heredity is more important than environment or vice versa, is of similar nature as to ask whether the seed or the soil is more important for the proper growth of a plant. The seed and the soil do not work independently; they are indeed mutually dependent. A seed has the power to grow into a plant but how well it grows depends on the soil into which it is sown. The plant cannot grow without either the seed or the soil. It needs both. Also it is useless to say that one of them contributes more than the other, in the proper development of the plant.

In a similar way, it is hard to make any statement in favour of either heredity or environment in the process of development of an organism. Both are equally important and indispensable. Also, it is wrong to assume that they are opposed to each other. They complement and support each other. The remark made by Garrett (1968) is worth quoting in this context:

> Nothing is more certain than that heredity and environment are co-acting influences and that both are essential to achievement.

3. In judging the relationship between heredity and environment it can be said that it is absurd to use the term *'heredity or environment'*. The 'either' and 'or' relationship between these two terms do not exist. It is always *'heredity and environment'*. But now the question arises whether the relationship between them is simply of an additive nature or not. The personality of an individual is not just the sum total of his heredity and environment. As Woodworth and Marquis (1948) put it,

> The relation of heredity and environment is not like addition, but more like multiplication. The individual does not equal heredity + environment, but does equal heredity × environment.

They further declare that the individual is a joint product of his heredity and environment just in the same way as the area of a rectangle is the joint product of its length and breadth. Like the base of a rectangle, heredity provides us the structure on which, with the help of favourable environment, desired construction can be made. The native powers and energies of an individual, like the seed, lie in heredity but it is up to the environment to extract these energies and to enable to reach up to their maximum limits.

4. Let us also study the relationship between heredity and environment from another angle. As a gift from heredity, we get our working capital but it is the environment which gives us the opportunity to invest it.

The capital as well as the opportunities for its proper development are essential for success in business. There are instances where individuals starting from a very meagre amount have been able to earn in millions. Therefore, the extreme view of hereditarians like Galton "Thus far shalt thou go and no further", is not correct. However, if we take it for granted, then can we go 'thus far' without the cooperation of environment?

Since we all have inherited different stock, at the time of starting our journey of life and also have got different environmental backing and opportunities, variation and differences among us bound to exist. Neither heredit nor environmental influences can be exclusively declared as the sole factor causing individual differences. Therefore, it is always safe to conclude that one's heredity, his environment and the interaction between these two are the true determinants of individual differences. This conclusion holds good for all types of variations and differences among human beings.

The idea of 'individual differences' has a great implication in the field of Education, in the following manner.

Educational Implications of the Psychology of Individual Differences

The notion that individuals differ in various abilities, capacities and personality characteristics recessitates the adoption of individual tendencies in Education. It compels the teachers to realize the following facts:

1. In any group there are individuals who deviate from the norms of the group. Along with the average, the presence of very superior and extremely dull is equally possible in his class.
2. Every teacher should try to have the desired knowledge of the abilities, capacities, interests, attitudes, aptitudes and other personality traits of his pupils and in the light of this knowledge should render individual guidance to children for the maximum utilization of their potentialities.
3. It is wrong to expect uniformity in gaining proficiency or success in a particular field from a group of students. On account of their subnormal intelligence, previous background, lack of proper interest, aptitude and attitude some students have to lag behind in some or other area of achievement.
4. All students cannot be benefited by one particular method of instruction and a uniform and rigid curriculum.

Provisions for 'individual differences' in Schools

Realization of the above facts or some more of their nature makes us think that we must have some provision for the wide individual differences among our pupils in our schools. Emphasizing this need Crow and Crow (1973) write,

> Since we supposedly are teaching individuals, not groups of individuals, it is the function of the school within its budgetary personnel and curricular limitations to provide adequate schooling for every learner no matter how much he differs from every other learner.

How can we accomplish this task is a pertinent question to be asked at this stage. In fact, to provide adequate schooling or learning experience for every learner according to his individuality is not a simple task. However, the following suggestions can be helpful for any teacher:

1. *Proper knowledge of the individual's potentialities.* The first step in making provisions for individual differences is to know the abilities, capacities, interests, aptitudes and other personality traits of individual pupils. For this purpose, frequent assessment in the form of intelligence tests, cumulative record card, interest inventories, attitude scales, aptitude tests and measures for assessing personality traits shall be carried out.

2. *Ability grouping.* In the light of the results derived from various tests of knowing individual differences in terms of individual potentialities in various dimensions, the students in a class or area of activity can be divided into homogenous groups. Such division can prove beneficial in adjusting the method of instruction to varying individual differences.

3. *Adjusting the curriculum.* To meet the requirement of varying individual differences among the pupils the curriculum should be as flexible and differentiated as possible. It should have the provision for a number of diversified courses and cocurricular experiences so that the pupils may get opportunity to study and work in the areas of their own interests and abilities. It should provide adjustment to suit the local requirements and potentialities of students of different groups.

4. *Adjusting the methods of teaching.* Considering the varying individual differences, adjustment with regard to the adaptation of methods of teaching is very effective. Every teacher should be somewhat free to formulate his own plan and strategy and adopt different instructional procedures which he finds most suited to different pupils. He should follow different procedures or methods of instruction to suit the requirements of varying ability groups of his pupils.

5. *Adopting special programmes or methods for individualizing instruction.* Schools may also adopt some special programme or methods of teaching like Dalton plan, the Winnekta plan, the project Method or use programmed learning material for enabling the students to learn at their own individual pace.

6. *Other measures of individualizing instruction.* For the purpose of individualizing instruction a few practical measures can also prove beneficial.

1. The student strength of the class or section should be made as small as possible.
2. The teacher should try to pay individual attention to the group under instruction.
3. The teacher should keep in view the individual difference of his students while engaging them in drill or practice work in the class-room or assigning home-task.
4. In case where ability grouping is not possible and more specifically under the prevalent system of class teaching, special coaching and guidance programme for both the dull and the gifted children are most helpful.

Thus, the problem of individual differences can be tackled with multi-dimensional tasks. The teacher, school authorities, the parents and the Government as well as voluntary agencies—all should join hands to meet the individual requirements of children who possess tremendous individual differences.

SUMMARY

There exist wide individual differences among human beings. By these individual differences, we mean differences among individuals that distinguish or separate them from one another. As a result of these, individuals differ from each other in so many aspects like physique, somatic structure, functioning of internal and external organs, growth and development in various dimensions, personality traits and ways of behaving and reacting to stimuli.

Distribution of such individual differences among human beings follows the pattern of a normal curve. As a consequence, majority that is, 68.26% of us are quite average in terms of possession of one or the other personality attributes. A very few of us deviate too much from this average value making themselves exceptional or special individuals among the total population.

Both heredity and environmental forces are said to be the sole determinants of the wide individual differences found in human beings. We, at the time of conception (fertilization of the ovum by the sperm), differ in respect of the possession of chromosomes, genes and their respective classical constituents. As a result, some of us are boys and some are girls, some are blue and some are black eyed, a few of us suffer from inborn or hereditary diseases while others are not. After conception what goes on inside and outside a mother's womb (approximately for nine months) and after birth, our interaction with the environmental forces, physical, social, cultural and educational opportunities available to us for our growth and development—all these create individual differences. Therefore, what exists among us in terms of our individual differences is the joint responsibility of both the hereditary and environmental forces.

The knowledge of the existing wide individual differences among the learners carry quite significant educational implications. It has helped the learners to know themselves in terms of their potentialities and teachers and parents to realise that they have to teach and care for their children in terms of their individualities. It has led to the individualization of instruction and educational programmes to suit the needs, interests and potentialities of individual learners. The curricula methods of teaching, man and material resources and other things in any scheme of education and institutional set up are thus going to be organized in close tune with the psychology of individual differences.

REFERENCES

Boring, E.C., Langfield, H.S., and Weld, H.P. (Ed.), *Foundations of Psychology*, New York, John Willey & Sons, 1961 (Ind. Edi.).

Crow, L.D. and Crow, A., *Educational Psychology*, New Delhi, Eurasia Publishing House, 1973 (3rd Ind. Reprint).

Douglas, O.B. and Holland, B.F., *Fundamentals of Educational Psychology*, New York, The Macmillan Co., 1947, p. 51.

Garret, H.E., *General Psychology*, New Delhi, Eurasia Publishing House, 1968 (Ind. Reprint).

Good, Carter, V., *Dictionary of Education*, McGraw Hill, 1959.

McIver, R.M. and Page, C.H., *Society: An Introductory Analysis*, London, Macmillan & Co. 1949.

Parischa, Prem, *Educational Psychology*, Delhi, University Publishers, 1963.

Woodworth, R.S. and Marquis, D.G., *Psychology*, New York, Henry Holt & Co., 1948.

SUGGESTED READINGS

Crow, L.D. and Crow, A., *Child Psychology*, New York, Barney & Noble, 1969 (Reprint).

McDougall, William, *An Outline of Psychology*, London, Methuen & Co., 1949.

Ross, J.S., *Groundwork of Educational Psychology*, London, George, G. Harrap & Co., 1951.

Slavin, R.E., *Educational Psychology*, New Jersey, Prentice Hall, 1991.

Stern, C., *Principles of Human Genetics*, San Francisco, W.H. Freeman & Co., 1973.

Chapter 11

Psychology of Motivation

WHAT IS MOTIVATION?

We see a girl getting bruises and cuts and quite often falling down while learning cycling, but she tries to improve her performance by continued practice. Similarly, an athlete may be seen to rise quite early in the morning and regularly visit the track or field for continued practice irrespective of the odds of the seasons. A student may be seen to burn the midnight oil as the examination approaches.

What makes the above girl, the athelete and the student behave in a particular manner? The answer to such questions on the why and how of behaviour lies in the key word 'motivation'. They behave as they do because they are motivated to do so. *Motivation, thus, may be regarded as something which prompts, compels and energises an individual to act or behave in a particular manner at a particular time for attaining some specific goal or purpose.* But what exactly is responsible for the motivation of an individual? What are the real activating forces that push and pull an individual to move or act for achieving a specific goal? Psychologists have tried to provide the answer by identifying these activating forces as needs, drives and motives.

NEEDS

Needs are general wants or desires. Every human being has to strive for the satisfaction of his basic needs if he has to maintain or improve or fulfil himself in the world.

Nothing can be said about the number of the individual needs. While some scholars hold that the number of individual needs is infinite, others have provided a definite number, e.g. Murray has given a list of 37 needs. In this text, for the sake of proper understanding and clarity, we would like to divide human needs into two broad categories, namely, biological needs and socio-psychological needs.

Biological Needs

All our bodily or organic needs fall into this category. They may be further categorized as follows:

1. In the first category of biological needs, we have the need for oxygen, water and food. These needs are most fundamental for our survival and

existence. We cannot even imagine survival beyond a limited period if we are deprived of these.

2. In the chain of our survival and existence the other category of biological needs includes needs such as the need for (a) rest when tired, (b) action when rested, (c) regular elimination of waste products from the body, (d) having an even internal body temperature, (e) sleep after periods of wakefulness, (f) protection from threats of the physical environment like hazards of weather, natural calamities, wild animals, etc.

3. In the third category of biological needs, we can place the need for satisfaction of the sex urge or desire to seek sex-experiences. Although the sex urge is not essential for the survival of an individual, it is the strongest human urge in the satisfaction of which lies his proper growth, development, adjustment and well-being. Moreover, the satisfaction of this need and normal sexual behaviour is most essential for a happy domestic life and the continuity and survival of the human species.

4. In the last category of biological needs, are the needs associated with the demands of our senses. These sensory needs include the need for physical contact, sensory stimulation and stimulus variability and manipulation. Although we may not die if deprived of these needs, they are considered to be essential for our general welfare and optimal growth.

Socio-psychological Needs

Under this category, we can list all those needs that are associated with the socio-cultural environment of an individual. They are acquired through social learning. Although such needs are not linked with the survival of the organism or the species, yet deprivation of these may lead to a psychological state, thereby seriously affecting its survival and welfare. For the sake of clarity these needs may be classified in the following manner:

1. *The need for freedom or gaining independence.* Nature has created us as free and independent individuals and requires us to remain so. Therefore, all human beings have an urge to remain free and independent.

2. *The need for security.* Every one of us needs to feel secure not only from physical dangers but also from the socio-psychological angles, we need desirable emotional, social and economic security for our well-being.

3. *The need for love and affection.* Every one of us, irrespective of age, caste, colour and creed, has a strong desire to love and to be loved. Depending upon one's age and circumstances, it may vary in intensity and nature, but a sort of emotional craving for the satisfaction of this need is exhibited universally by all living organisms.

4. *The need to achieve.* Every human being has a strong desire to achieve some or the other goals like money, fame, reputation, degree, positions of merit, medals, a good spouse, spiritual attainment, etc., not only to raise his status in the eyes of others but also for the satisfaction he would get from his own accomplishment.

5. *The need for recognition or social approval.* Each one of us has an inherent desire to gain recognition, appreciation and esteem in the eyes of others. An artist may thus desire to be known for his art, a young woman may desire to be appreciated for her beauty, good manners or housekeeping especially by their peers. A student may show this desire by excelling over other students of his class and thus gaining the required social status, prestige or approval from his fellow students, teachers and parents.

6. *The need for company.* Man is called a social animal in the sense that he has a strong urge to be with his own kind and maintain social relations with them. The real impact of this need can be felt by those individuals who are faced with social rejection or solitary confinement.

7. *The need for self-assertion.* Every one of us has an inherent desire to get an opportunity to rule or dominate over others. It may vary in intensity from person to person but it is exhibited by all of us in one or the other situation irrespective of age, strength and status. Some may show it in dealing with their juniors, servants, life partner of children while others may exhibit it towards their pets and even inanimate things like dolls or pictures This need to assert oneself gives birth to an important motive called the power motive which works as a strong determinant of one's personality and behaviour.

8. *The need for self-expression or self-actualization.* We all have an inherent craving for the expression of our self and actualization of our own potentialities. An individual may have a poet, musician or painter hidden within him and thus may have a strong desire to have his talent exhibited or nurtured. In this way we want to get adequate opportunities for the expression and development of our potentialities and so we strive to this end and are not happy until we get the opportunities for such self-expression and self-actualization.

DRIVES

A need gives rise to a drive which may be defined as an aroused awareness, tendency or a state of heightened tension that sets off reactions in an individual and sustains them for increasing his general activity level. The existence of a need moves or drives the individual from within and directs his activities to a goal that may bring about the satisfaction of that need. The strength of a drive depends upon the strength of the stimuli generated by the related need.

Drives of any nature are divided into two categories. In the first category are the biological or primary drives such as hunger, thirst, escape from pain and the sex drive. In the second category are the socio-psychological or secondary drives such as fear or anxiety, desire for approval, struggle for achievement, aggression and dependence. These drives are not related to physiological needs and therefore do not arise from imbalances in the body's internal functioning. They arise from socio-psychological needs and are said to be acquired through social learning as a result of one's interaction with the socio-cultural environment. These drives move an individual to act for the satisfaction of his socio-psychological needs which in turn reinforce the behaviour so that it may be maintained and continued. Contrary to the socio-psychological or secondary drives, primary or biological drives are basically unlearned in nature and rise from biological needs as a result of a biological mechanism called *homeostasis*.

The term 'homeostasis' was coined by W.B. Cannon, a prominent Harvard University physiologist. Cannon (1932) suggested that our body system constantly works toward an optimum level of functioning, maintaining a normal state of balance between input and output. For example, when the blood sugar level drops, the brain, glands, stomach organs, and other body parts send out signals which activate a hunger drive and make one feel hungry. After food has been consumed by the individual's body, it returns to a state of balance. This maintenance of an overall physiological balance is homeostasis. When there is an imbalance, there is a need to restore the balance and a drive arises which in turn serves as an instigator of behaviour.

The term 'homeostasis' used by Cannon with reference to body chemistry now has been broadened to include any behaviour that upsets the balance of an individual. The denial or failure in the satisfaction of any basic need may bring about an imbalanced psychological state, giving rise to a primary or secondary drive for initiating a particular kind of behaviour.

DRIVES AND INCENTIVES

Drives are also influenced and guided by incentives. Praise, appreciation, rewards, bonus, fulfilment of one's need and achievement of the desired objectives are some examples of incentives.

An incentive works as a reinforcing agent as it adds more force to a drive. A piece of toffee, chocolate, an ice cream or a toy may act as an incentive for a boy and as a result he may be further motivated to act or behave in a desirable way. Similarly a favourite food may provide an incentive for an individual to eat or a favourite movie may compel an individual to go and see it. Drives, whether primary or secondary, are thus greatly affected and directed by incentives. These incentives work more forcefully in case the organism has been deprived of that particular incentive for a length of time.

MOTIVES

In their search for the origin of a motivated behaviour, psychologists, start from the basic needs—biological or socio-psychological. A particular need gives rise to an activating force or a drive that moves an individual to act or behave in a particular fashion at a particular time. Drives thus work as the basic activating forces behind behaviour. However, in psychological as well as day-to-day language we usually come across statement like: What was the motive behind this crime? What may be the motive of an individual to criticise or blame us? These statements clearly indicate that a motive works as a basic activating force behind a particular behaviour. It makes one wonder why the terms 'drive and 'motive' which carry the same meaning are often employed interchangeably. However, psychologists while explaining the mechanism of behaviour have now started to concentrate on the term motive instead of the old term drive. For clarity, they have tried to define it in the following ways. According to *Fisher* (Labhsingh and Tiwari, 1971):

> A motive is an inclination or impulsion to action plus some degree of orientation or direction.

Rosen, Fox and Gregory (1972):

> A motive may be defined as a readiness or disposition to respond in some ways and not others to a variety of situations.

Carroll (1969):

> A need gives rise to one or more motives. A motive is a rather specific process which has been learned. It is directed towards a goal.

All these definitions lead us to generalize that:

1. Motive is an inner state of mind or an aroused feeling generated through basic needs or drives which compel an individual to respond by creating a kind of tension or urge to act.
2. It is a preparation for responding in some selective manner for the satisfaction of the related need and is a goal-directed activity, pursued till the attainment of the goal.
3. A change in goal may bring about changes in the nature and strength of the motive, while attainment of the goal helps in the release of tension aroused by a specific motive.
4. Motive may be considered to be a learned response or tendency and also an innate disposition.

Motive may thus be considered to be an energetic force or tendency (learned or innate) working within the individual to compel, persuade or inspire him to act either for the satisfaction of his basic needs or the attainment of some specific purpose. There are a variety of motives based on the basic human needs. For understanding the nature and role of these motives, let us briefly discuss a few important ones.

Hunger Motive

Our body's need for food is the basis of this motive. The longer we are deprived of the food, the greater the intensity of this motive. More often, a growling stomach or hunger pangs caused by the contraction of the stomach are taken as hunger signals. This may be quite misleading because these symptoms may be produced by temporal conditioning caused by eating at a more or less fixed time every day. On the basis of laboratory findings, it has been now agreed that the physiological key to hunger lies in the chemical composition of the blood and a structure in the brain called the hypothalamus. The sugar, glucose which is present in our blood helps to provide energy to the body. It can be stored in the liver only in small quantities and for a short time. When the amount of glucose in the blood, the blood-sugar level, drops below a certain point, a message is sent to the hypothalamus which in turn alerts the body to its need for food. After eating, when the blood-sugar level has risen, the hypothalamus works for inhibition of the hunger messages. Two areas of the hypothalamus that are involved in the hunger mechanism have been identified. The lateral hypothalamus controls the 'on' switch and thus sends out hunger signals, while the ventromedial hypothalamus performs the task of inhibition by controlling the 'off' switch.

The physical mechanism of hunger as explained above tries to throw light on the working of the hunger motive and the eating behaviour. However, our eating behaviour is too complex to depend only on blood sugar levels and the hypothalamus. Recent researches have suggested that number of other parts of the brain such as the limbic system and the temporal lobe may also play a major role in the human hunger drive. It has also now been experimentally proved that besides the chemical composition and brain mechanism, certain other personal, social, cultural and psychological factors like choice or preference for a specific food, one's biological predisposition, boredom, loneliness, nervousness, insecurity, anxiety, depression, socio-cultural demands, acquired food habits and similar other factors also govern the eating behaviour of human beings.

Thirst Motive

This drive or motive arises from the need for quenching thirst. It is found to be stronger than the food motive as we can exist longer without food than we can without water. In the case of this motive, the apparent signals like hunger pangs in the hunger motive come from the sensation of dryness in the mouth and throat. However, as we have seen with hunger, the thirst motive goes much deeper than that. The physiological key to the thirst motive, like the hunger motive, lies in the imbalance of fluid in the body tissues and the hypothalamus. Imbalance of fluid in the body has been linked to the level of salt (sodium chloride) in the blood stream as salt caused dehydration. A high level of salt in the blood upsets the fluid balance in the tissues which in turn calls for the supply of fluid to them. This message is conveyed to the lateral hypothalamus and the thirst drive is activated. After getting the supply of fluid in the form of a drink, the body's chemical balance is restored. This activates the thirst satiety centre, situated in the hypothalamus which in turn switches off the thirst drive.

In this way, it may be seen that while the chemical imbalance of the body instigates the hunger or thirst motive, the centres for its control lie in the central nervous system particularly the hypothalamus. Similarly it may be seen that the human thirst behaviour depends not only on one's biological predispositions and chemical imbalance of the body tissues and is, to a large extent, a function of social learning. Why we drink, what we drink, when we drink and how we drink somehow or the other, depends upon personal, social and cultural factors and environmental learning.

Sex Motive

The sex motive, although not as essential for an individual's survival as food and water, constitutes a highly powerful psycho-physical motive. Apart from being the medium of survival of the species, its satisfaction results in feeling of immense happiness and well-being in an individual. Whereas the root of the sex motive is purely biological and innate in the non-human animals, it is not so simple in human beings whose sex drive is governed by both the physiological and psychological factors. Therefore, the human sex motive is termed as a complex blend of innate as well as acquired tendencies.

In most animals, sex hormones are undeniably essential in stimulating the sex drive. These hormones, the testosterone in the male and estrogens in the female, are secreted by the testes and the ovaries respectively. Experiments with the removal of testes and ovaries in the case of male and female animals or birds or injection of doses of the male or female sex hormones have clearly demonstrated the extent to which secretion of sex hormones actually determines sexual behaviour in different species.

This dependence on hormones is seen to decrease as we move up the phylogenetic scale from lower animals and birds to monkeys and chimpanzees. Finally, in sexually experienced adult humans, we see still more freedom from hormonal controls. Castrated males and ovariectomized females sometimes experience little or no decline in the sex drive or its satisfaction. Females may also remain sexually active after the natural decline in ovarian function that occurs with age in the form of menopause.

In addition to the dependence on hormones, females of most species, excluding humans are sexually receptive only at certain times—when they are in heat or, in more technical language, during the oestrus cycle. During this period, the ovaries secrete and release a greater quantity of oestrogen into the blood stream as a result of which the female becomes receptive to the advances of the males. This period coincides with the occurrence of ovulation in the females and consequently may result in pregnancy.

In human beings, although pregnancy is possible only in the oestrus periods, the sex drive is not dependent upon their occurrence. In general, human females and males can be sexually motivated at any time quite independently of the period of fertility and hormone production. Much of their motivation in the form of sexual arousal and behaviour is rooted in earlier experiences and social learning and controlled by lesions in the hypothalamus, the subcortical structure in the brain.

On account of the involvement of the cortical areas of the brain, the sources for the instigation of the sex drive and sexual arousal are highly varied in human beings. Sometimes this may be emotional feelings about the sex partner and at other times it may be a visual, auditory, or tactile sensation, a picture or a fantasy. In practice, the sex game is more psychological than biological or organic. For example, a smell of one's choice or even a little moonlight can work wonders in stimulating the sex drive in humans. The other variables related to one's socio-cultural environment, sexual experience and learning also play a significant role in guiding and deciding the mode and nature of the sex drive and behaviour in human beings independently of their fertility period and secretion of hormones.

Maternal Motive

The behaviour involving the care and protection of offspring by the females of a species is called maternal behaviour and the motive that energises a female to engage in such behaviour is called the maternal drive or motive. The maternal drive is stimulated both by biological as well as psychological factors interrelated with learning. Hormones also play an important role in activating the maternal drive. The hormone progesterone has been found to be important in maintaining pregnancy. Another hormone, prolactin, produced by the pituitary gland, directs the mammary glands to secrete milk for the newborn.

Maternal behaviour in the later period is controlled and guided by the learning components of the natural maternal drive. The stimuli responsible for activating the maternal drive and behaviour spring from a variety of sources: from one's physical environment, or socio-cultural background, from one's mother and grandmother, from observing the behaviour of friends and neighbours, from books, movies and television etc. One's own physical and mental health may also contribute in this direction. However, much depends upon the impact of social learning and earlier experiences which leave an indelible impression on the mind of the mother justifying the finding that being a good and loving mother depends considerably on one's having had a good and loving mother for oneself.

Aggression Motive

The aggression motive is related to those behaviours that are intended to inflict physical or psychological harm on others. Various views have been expressed about the origin and working of this motive. Those believing in the instinctive theory like Freud, Lorenz and Ardrey held that the aggression motive is linked with an innate independent instinctual tendency in human beings which expresses itself in destructive and violent activities. However, this innate drive concept now stands rejected due to the lack of substantial research.

According to another viewpoint, aggression is a result of frustration. However, later researches have proved that aggression is not always an essential reaction to frustration. Bandura (1973) suggests that frustration generates aggression only in those people who have previously developed aggressive attitudes and actions as a means to cope with their environment. An individual may be aggressive because he has been brought up in the environment where he frequently observed his parents, elders, teachers and peers, showing aggression towards him or towards others. A teacher, parent or a friend, who is rebuking or punishing someone aggressively, essentially provides a model of effective aggression to be imitated by the child. Imitation of aggression does not occur just with live models; violence or aggression shown on television or the cinema screen and described in the pages of magazines and novels may impel an individual towards aggression. This provocation if reinforced, may lead him to adopt aggression as a mode of his usual behaviour.

Affiliation Motive

The affiliation motive springs directly from the affiliation need, a need to be with other people. This need to be with other people has its origin in the herd instinct.

For most animals, the herd instinct is genetically programmed as a result of which they live together in packs, flocks or groups and so receive better care and protection for their welfare and survival. In human beings also the desire to be in a group may stem from the herd instinct for the fear and anxiety concerning welfare and survival. However, the arousal of the affiliation motive in their case is a somewhat complex phenomenon. It is very often stimulated by some other needs or motives like the social approval motive, the recognition motive, the power motive and the achievement motive. As these needs or motives are connected with the socio-psychological make-up of the individuals, the affiliation motive must be considered to be an offshoot of early experiences and social learning.

Whether an individual adopts an isolated lifestyle or an affiliated lifestyle, depends upon his experiences and interaction with his environment from earliest childhood. For example, children who are raised in close-knit families, show a stronger affiliation motive than those coming from more loosely knit families. Neglected children or destitutes, on the other hand, may lack intensity of the affiliation motive. In this way, patterns of affiliated behaviour and strength of the affiliation motive may vary from individual to individual based on earlier experiences and social learning.

Achievement Motive

The need to achieve is the spring-board of the achievement motive. This desire is as basic and natural as the other biological or socio-psychological needs. However, in a competitive society or set-up the desire to excel over others or achieve a higher level than one's peers is intensified which in turn may lead to a stronger drive or motive to achieve something or everything that is essential to beat the others in the race and consequently experience a sense of pride and pleasure in the achievement. The type of motivation produced by such desire for achievement is called the achievement motivation and has been defined in various ways. Two such definitions are now given.

Atkinson and Feather (1966):

> The achievement motive is conceived as a latest disposition which is manifested in overt striving only when the individual perceives performance as instrumental to a sense of personal accomplishment.

Irving Sarnoff (Mangal, 1989):

> Achievement motive is defined in terms of the way an individual orients himself towards objects or conditions that he does not possess. If he values those objects and conditions, and he feels that he ought to possess them he may be regarded as having an achievement motive.

Based on these definitions, we can say that the achievement motive moves or drives an individual to strive to gain mastery of difficult and challenging situations or performances in the pursuit of excellence. It comes into the picture when an individual knows that his performance will be evaluated, that the consequence of his actions will lead either to success or failure and that good performance will produce a feeling of pride in accomplishment. The achievement motive may thus be considered to be a disposition to approach success or the capacity to take pride in accomplishment when success is achieved in an activity.

As for the original and development of the achievement motive, it can be safely said that it is conditioned by one's early training, experiences and subsequent learning. In general, children usually acquire the achievement motive from their parents's lifestyle. Studies have shown that the children whose independent training starts at an early age and who get more autonomy within a cooperative, encouraging and less authoritarian family environment usually develop an achievement-oriented attitude. Later on, the experiences and learning based on the circumstances and situations in his life may lead an individual to provide a level for the intensity of his achievement motive to struggle for attaining the standard of excellence desired by him.

THEORIES OF MOTIVATION

What motivates human behaviour is not a simple question. Psychologists have tried to explain the process and mechanism of motivation in a number of ways. We shall now discuss some of the main viewpoints.

McDougall's Theory of Instinct

The oldest explanation for how and why we behave in a specific manner in a specific situation is given by the Theory of Instinct. Although it was William James who for the first time brought out the concept of instinct to explain behaviour, the credit for developing it into a full fledged theory must be given to William McDougall. According to this theory, our instincts are the springboards of our behaviour. These instincts are innate tendencies or inherited psychological dispositions or even the complex patterns of behaviour that lead to some purposive actions and they don't have to be learned, Emphasizing these views McDougall (1908) writes:

> The human mind has certain innate or inherited tendencies which are the essential springs or motive power of all thoughts and actions, whether individual or collective and are the bases from which the character and will of individuals and of nations are gradually developed under the guidance of intellectual faculties.

Therefore, as McDougall observes, all human behaviour can be explained on the basis of some instinct or the other. McDougall provided a list of 14 instincts and proposed that each instinct is accompanied by a specific emotional disposition (effective experience). The instinct of escape, for example, is accompanied by the emotion of fear, the instinct of combat (pugnacity) by anger, the instinct of repulsion by the emotion of disgust, and so on. He further claimed that all behavioural acts are essentially instinctive and this instinctive behaviour is found to have the following three aspects: (a) cognition (knowing), (b) affection (feeling or experiencing an emotion), and (c) conation (doing or striving). For example, when a child sees a bull coming towards him, he practises an instinctive behaviour by passing through the above-mentioned aspects or cycles. First, he sees the bull, second, he experiences an emotion of fear and third, he tries to run away. Thus, according to McDougall, what we do and how we do it can all be explained through our instinctive behaviour which is governed by our instincts accompanied by our emotional experience.

The theory of instinct proposed by McDougall has been a subject of great controversy and criticism by later psychologists on the following grounds:

1. Since the theory maintains that a behavioural act springs from an instinct, the psychologists believing in this theory began to compile a list of instincts for explaining the countless behavioural acts of human beings. Interestingly, psychological literature was flooded with more than 14 thousand instincts by the end of 1924. This created a lot of confusion and the failure to find a limited number of instincts to account for all human behaviour became the subject of great controversy.

2. Moreover, it was established that all human behaviour cannot be termed instinctive, as most human actions are learned and acquired through interaction with one's environment.

3. The researches by sociologists and anthropologists have emphasized that man is not purely instinctive and his basic nature is not an animal nature. Therefore, his behaviour is not an instinctive behaviour but is definitely shaped by the forces of his social and cultural environment. Had it been operated wholly by instincts, which are common and universal, all of us would have behaved almost identically. The weakness of the instinctive theory thus is fully exposed by its inability to account for the existing individual differences.

4. Researches done in the field of cognitive ability have clearly revealed that behaviour in which the higher intellectuals faculties are involved cannot be explained in terms of instinctive behaviour. The thinking, reasoning and problem solving behaviour cannot be explained as the inert machine-like operation of innate instincts. Although a man interacts with his environment with the help of his innate potentialities for the solution of his problems and satisfaction of his needs, he is definitely helped in doing so by his cognitive abilities supported by the experiences he gains from his environment and, therefore, the how and why of man's behaviour are definitely guided by factors other than the innate instincts and other tendencies he possesses.

In spite of all the criticisms levelled against it, the instinctive theory as a theory of motivation has not altogether lost ground. It is still regarded as an important theory to explain the how and the why of human behaviour. The ethologists like Lorenz and Tibergen, have recently added a new dimension to this theory by evolving the concept of imprinting and species-specific behaviour; occurrence of a particular type of fixed action pattern distinct from chains of reflexes and the usual instinctive behaviour quite independent of any previous experience, imitation or training, etc. The evidences of this species-specific behaviour have been found in behaviour like nesting and care of the young, courtship and sexual behaviour, food seeking, hiding and avoidance of danger, etc., among the different insect, bird, and animal species and races of human beings.

Hull's Drive Reduction Theory

In 1943, Clark Leonard Hull, a professor of psychology at Yale University, developed a theory of motivation named the Drive Reduction Theory. He stressed that biological drives such as hunger, thirst, sex and escape from pain are mainly responsible for initiating and maintaining the primary responses. These drives produce internal tension, an undesirable state that the organism wants to change. In other words, all of his energy is concentrated on his efforts to reduce the heightened tension (drive). Thus a hungry man activated by the need of reducing the tension created through the hunger drive may be compelled to engage in behaviour that would help him to reduce the hunger drive.

The drive reduction theory was supported by other psychologists and its sphere was broadened by including the psychological drives in it. For explaining the mechanism of drive reduction as a source of motivation, the term *homeostasis* already explained in this chapter was also coined. However, the failure of this theory to explain human behaviour especially at the higher cognitive level has reduced its importance as a major motivational theory.

Freud's Psycho-analytic Theory of Motivation

Freud's psychoanalytic theory of motivation is centred around his concepts of instincts and the unconscious. Freud maintained that instincts are the root cause of all activities in a human being. He identified two basic instincts for this purpose. In his book *An Outline of Psycho-analysis* (1953), he asserted that *eros* the life or erotic instinct and the death instinct or the desire to destroy even to the extent of destroying oneself are the ultimate sources of motivation. In fact, the life instinct, the urge for self-preservation, dominates the earlier scenes of one's life. When the life instinct ceases to operate, the death instinct takes over. For example, the person who has failed in a love affair may think of committing suicide. However, what moves or energises the activities of the life instinct is the need for sexual gratification—a means to provide intense pleasure, satisfaction and meaning to one's life. Freud maintained that from birth onwards human beings experience sex gratification and the sex motive, therefore, is quite an important motive that activates human behaviour.

Besides the role played by one's life and death instincts and the sexual urge, the unconscious also is a great determinant and activating force for the cause and operation of one's behaviour. The unconscious, which is 9/10th of one's total mental content according to Freud, remains hidden and usually inaccessible. It consists of one's unfulfilled desires, wishes, ideas and feelings. It is like a great underworld with powerful unseen forces which is responsible, to a great extent, for all that we think, feel and do. Man, as Freud maintains, is but a puppet in the hands of the mighty unconscious and thus he has to behave in the way and manner in which his unconscious dictates. Therefore, the key to the why and how of behaviour lies in the choices made by one's unconscious which are usually the gratification of sex or the seeking of pleasure.

Behaviourists Learning Theories of Motivation

According to the behaviourists' view, how and why we behave in a particular manner is fashioned by the experiences we receive through the acts of learning or training. Many times our behaviour is guided through a simple stimulus—response mechanism as emphasized by Thorndike or operated through the mechanisms of classical or operant conditioning as advocated by Pavlov, Watson and B.F. Skinner. The role of reinforcement as a prime factor for the motivation of behaviour was properly emphasized in Skinner's Theory of Operant Conditioning. He asserted that an organism behaves in the way and manner in which its behaviour is shaped through a particular reinforcement schedule.

Moving in the footprints of Skinner, social learning theorists like Albert Bandura (1977) maintained that human motivation is mainly guided through social rewards like praise. Thus a girl often praised for her skill in the kitchen will turn into a very effective cook and a good housewife. According to him the imitation of other's behaviour, if it results in a reward provides a valuable motivational source for most of us and that is why the concept of modelling is more commonly employed in the world of industry and advertisement.

Adler's Social Urges Theory

Disagreeing with the extreme views of Freud regarding sex as the basis of human motivation, Alfred Adler, a student of Freud advocated that human beings are motivated primarily by social urges. For maintaining one's social self one requires a margin of safety besides simple security in terms of protection from danger. This margin of safety is achieved through domination and superiority. In order not to feel inferior or small, one strives or struggles for superiority. Therefore, the struggle for power, achievement and status or the will to dominate are really an outgrowth of the fundamental need for security. Thus, the motivation of human behaviour may be endorsed through a single basic drive known as the security drive or motive or in terms of a single need, the need for the security to maintain one's social sell.

Goal-oriented Theory of Cognitivism

Unlike the mechanistic and instinctive approaches adopted by other psychologists, the cognitive school of psychology brings the role of cognitive factors in producing human motivation into the limelight. According to this view, human behaviour is purposeful and has a certain end or goal in view. An individual who aspires to reach a goal is helped by his cognitive abilities to develop a desirable drive or motive i.e., tendency to move towards that goal. The achievement of the goal satisfies the individual which in turn reinforces the maintained behaviour.

The cognitive view of motivation was first propounded by the philosopher psychologist William James (1842–1910) who emphasized that the concept of motivation was necessary to bring the psychomotor gap between ideas and actions. This view was further elaborated by psychologists like George Miller who advocated the construction of plans for bridging the psychomotor gap to meet certain ends. Another cue for the involvement of cognitive factors in bringing motivation comes from the theory of cognitive dissonance advocated by American psychologist Leon Festinger. Cognitive dissonance denotes an imbalance between what we believe (cognition) and what we do (conation). It may result in psychological discomfort to us. As a solution, we are motivated to set the imbalance right either by changing in our beliefs or our behaviour. For example, information linking smoking with cancer and heart diseases creates dissonance in chain smokers. They cannot resist the temptation to smoke, even though they are warned that cigarette smoking is injurious to their health. There is, in this situation, an imbalance or dissonance involving the beliefs (cognition) and behaviour. The remedy lies in goal-directed behaviour that is aimed at reducing the dissonance either by stopping the excessive smoking or by refusing to believe the information about the associated danger.

Maslow's Self-actualization Theory

In 1954, Abraham Maslow proposed that a motivational behaviour may satisfy many needs at the same time, thus implying that an act is multi-motivated. Human needs, according to Maslow, arrange themselves in *hierarchies of prepotency*. In other words, the appearance of one need generally depends on the satisfaction of the others. They are closely related to each other and may be arranged from the lowest to the highest development of the personality. He proposed five sets of basic needs that can be arranged in a definite hierarchical order for understanding human motivation as shown in Figure 11.1.

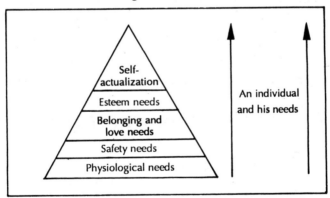

Figure 11.1 Maslow's hierarchical structure of needs.

The physiological needs necessary for survival are at the bottom of the structure while distinctly psychological needs are at the top. Starting from the satisfaction of the physiological needs, every individual strives for the satisfaction of the other needs of a higher order. This striving for one or the other level of needs provides the motivation for his behaviour. A need that has been satisfied is no longer a need. It ceases to be a motivating force and, therefore, the satisfaction of one need leads an individual to try for the satisfaction of other needs. In this way the motivational behaviour of a person is always dominated not by his satisfied needs but by his unsatisfied wants, desires and needs.

The motivational behaviour of most of us fits into the hierarchical structure of needs devised by Maslow and the need of a higher order does not surface until a need of a lower order has been gratified. We can think of the other needs only when the need for food and the other basic physiological needs have been gratified. A hungry person cannot think of casting his vote, doing social service or attaining salvation through remembering God. Similarly, one who is insecure or unsafe may hardly be motivated for the gratification of the need for love or esteem.

But as it happens there is room for exceptions in Maslow's hierarchy of needs to explain human motivation. The history of mankind may point to countless heroes, saints and other great people who always stood up for their ideals, and religious or social values without caring for the satisfaction of biological or other lower needs.

It appears that the effects of the gratification of a need are more stimulating and important than the effects of deprivation. The gratification of needs of the lower order motivates an individual to strive for satisfaction of needs of the higher order. An individual, as Maslow emphasized, can actualize his potentialities as a human being only after fulfilling the higher level needs like love and esteem. However, there may be exceptions to the hierarchical order. One may be more motivated for the satisfaction of one need at the cost of another and therefore a person can reach the top without caring for the satisfaction of needs of the lower order. It is very clear, however, that the need of self-actualization dominates and rules all the other lower level needs. It seems to be the supreme aim of human life and thus works as a master motive for motivating human behaviour. In the words of Maslow *"A musician must make music, an artist must paint, a poet must write poetry, if he is to be ultimately at peace with himself. What a man can be, he must be. He must be true to his own nature. This need we may call self actualization"* (1954). The fulfilment of self-actualization is thus a must for an individual as he will feel discontented and restless unless he strives for what he or she is fitted for.

A CRITICAL ESTIMATE OF THE THEORIES OF MOTIVATION

All the theories stated above try to explain in their own ways why and how we behave in a particular way in a particular situation. All have their strengths and limitations in doing so and no single individual can be said to be competent enough to account for the motivation for all types of behaviour.

Theories like McDougall's instinctive theory, Hull's drive reduction theory, and Freud's psychoanalytic theory give importance to the biological and organic factors in the motivational process. By considering human nature basically as animal nature, these theories in fact provide an *animal model* (the way animals and lower organisms behave) for explaining human behaviour.

The learning theories of the behaviourists including B.F. Skinner and social learning psychologists like Bandura, while completely ignoring the organic and biological factors relied heavily on the functionability of learning experiences and environmental factors to explain the motivation and shaping of human behaviour.

These behaviourists are often criticised for adopting a mechanistic approach and providing a *machine model* in support of their beliefs.

Other psychologists like Adler and Maslow struck a balance by highlighting the importance of both biological factors in the form of needs and urges and learning experiences in the motivational process. However, as we can understand, man is far from being an animal or a machine. Therefore, in this connection, the efforts of cognitive psychologists and humanists like Maslow are worth appreciating. Both these categories of psychologists gave due consideration to the abilities of human beings to strive intelligently for realizing their goals and higher motives. In one's behaviour one is guided through one's cognitive abilities and does not simply act as a puppet in the hands of one's biological functioning or environment.

One cannot, on the other hand, reason or think in a vacuum. One thinks and behaves as required by one's biological make-up and environmental surroundings. Therefore, we cannot isolate the role and influence of any one of the three main constituents namely, biological needs, learning experiences, and cognitive factors in motivating and shaping the behaviour of an individual. Actually, all of them interact and work jointly in the motivation of most of our behaviour. Motivation behaviour regarding eating, for example, is decided by one's biological or organic factors, namely, the bodily need for eating, the learning experience the choice or preference for a particular food and the cognitive factors knowledge about the nutritional value of the food and its suitability to one's body and circumstances, etc. Therefore, in deciding the how and why of one's behaviour we have to seek an eclectic view of all the theories of motivation and consider motivation as an integrated and cumulative product of the interaction among the biological, learned and cognitive components of one's personality.

MEASUREMENT OF MOTIVES

The methods employed for the measurement of motives may be classified as direct, indirect and experimental, depending upon the nature of the adopted measures or techniques.

Direct Methods

In this category we may include all those methods and techniques that permit the subject to express his motives through verbal or other overt behaviour. Here the required information about the motives and the natural behaviour of an individual is gathered directly from the primary source, the subject by asking him to account for his behaviour or through naturalistic objective observation of his behaviour. The major techniques or methods included in this category are questionnaire, inventories, motivation scale, checklist, naturalistic observation, interview, autobiography and other self-description measures.

Indirect Methods

In situations where the subject is either unaware of his motives or is determined not to reveal them, the use of indirect methods is recommended. The material to which the subject is exposed in the indirect measures of studying motives consists of fairly ambiguous or unstructured stimulus situations. Based on the mechanism of projection, the subject is expected to provide clues for his hidden or true motives by responding to these unstructured stimuli. The interpretation of these clues by the experimenter then, may help in the assessment of the subject's true motives.

All the projective techniques like the Rorschach ink blot test, thematic apperception test (TAT), child apperception test, (CAT), the Blacky pictures, drawing completion test, sentence completion technique, word association technique, role-playing and socio-drama, etc., fall in the category of indirect methods of measuring motives.

These projective techniques provide full opportunity to the subject to project his motives and intentions in a structured form through responses in the form of writing stories about the pictures shown or completing a sentence, sketching or drawing, associating a word or playing a role. The interpretation of these structured responses would depend upon the reason for administering the test. For example, if the experimenter is interested in measuring the affiliation or achievement motive, the subject's responses are evaluated in terms of how much affiliation orientation or achievement orientation they display.

Experimental Methods

Experimental methods of measuring motives consist of measures involving objective observations under controlled conditions. For ascertaining the real motives, the experimenter first makes some tentative hypotheses and tests them in the laboratory or laboratory-like conditions to arrive at some objective, reliable and valid conclusions. In addition to the investigation of the origin and causes of a behaviour involving motivation, experimental methods also help in testing the various empirical predictions based on particular motivational hypotheses. For example, one may hypothesize that persons having a strong achievement motive must differ in a number of predictable ways from persons with a weak achievement motive. In experimental testing of this hypothesis, the experimenter may collect scores related to the achievement motive by introducing a projective test like TAT or Rorschach ink blot and subsequently try to demonstrate that subjects who score high in terms of achievement motive are also faster at solving mathematical problems, memorizing poems and performing some typical complex skills.

SUMMARY

Why we behave and how we behave in a particular fashion at a particular moment can be explained in terms of motivation. It is motivation which prompts, compels and energises one to engage in a particular behaviour. The activating forces for the motivation may be termed as needs, drives or motives.

Needs are general wants or desires and are said to be the very basis of our behaviour. They can be broadly classified as biological and socio-psychological needs. Biological needs include all our bodily or organic needs such as the need for oxygen, food, water, rest, sleep and sex, and the like. They are linked with the survival of the organism and the species. Socio-psychological needs like the need for love and affection, security, affiliation, self-assertion and self-actualization are linked with the socio-cultural environment and psychological make-up of an individual. They are considered essential as their deprivation may seriously affect the survival and welfare of an individual.

A need gives rise to a *drive* which activates an individual from within and directs his activities to a goal that may bring about the satisfaction of the need. Biological needs give birth to biological drives such as the hunger, thirst and sex drive and socio-psychological needs produce socio-psychological drives such as the fear, anxiety, approval and achievement drives. Drives are also influenced and guided by incentives like praise, appreciation, reward, bonus etc., as reinforcing agents.

What used to be understood by the word 'drive' has now-a-days been replaced by the more forceful term *motive*. It is defined as an energetic force or tendency (learned or innate) working within the individual to compel, persuade or inspire him to act for the satisfaction of his basic needs or attainment of some specific purposes. Psychologists have identified and named a number of motives.

Hunger motive primarily arises from our body's need for food and the thirst motive from the need for fluid. The need for food or fluid is conveyed to the brain which in turn produces the motivation behaviour involving hunger or thirst. Apart from the biological function, the hunger and thirst motive are also controlled by personal experiences and social learning.

The *sex motive* though having a strong physiological base in the form of hormonal functioning and the oestrus cycle is largely affected by the variables related to one's experience and social learning.

The *maternal motive* (the urge to provide care and protection to offspring) is stimulated both by biological factors and social learning. Motives like the *aggression motive, the affiliation motive* and the *achievement motive* are purely learned as they are linked with the demands of one's environment in terms of social learning.

A number of view-points and theories have been put forward for explaining human motivation. McDougall, through his instinctive theory maintained that all human behaviour could be explained in terms of some instinct or the other associated with these behaviours. Accordingly, Freud picked up two main instincts, namely, the life and the death instincts to account for all human behaviour in his psychoanalytic theory of motivation. He declared sex gratification as the sole motive for energising human behaviour. Adler, while not agreeing with the extreme sex-oriented views of Freud, maintained that human beings are motivated primarily by social urges and therefore human motivation can be explained only in terms of a single drive or motive which he called the security motive. Clark Hull, through his drive reduction theory emphasized that need in the form of stimulation gives birth to a drive or motive which in turn produces motivation.

The learning theories put forward by behaviourists like Thorndike, Watson & Skinner and others emphasized the roles of training and experiences for the shaping and modelling of our behaviour. The social learning theorists like Bandura highlighted the role of social rewards for the motivation of human behaviour. Cognitive psychologists on the other hand, with the help of their goal-oriented theory, advocated the role of cognitive factors in producing human motivation. Psychologists with a humanistic approach like Maslow put forward a hierarchical structure of needs for explaining human motivation. The gratification of lower order needs motivates an individual to strive for the higher order needs. On the top of the hierarchical structure lies the need for self-actualization.

REFERENCES

Atkinson, J.W. and Feather, N.T. (Ed.), *A Theory of Achievement Motivation*, New York: Wiley, 1966, p. 13.

Bandura, A., *Principles of Behaviour Modification*, New York: Holt, Rinehart & Winston, 1969.

_____, *Aggression—A social learning analysis,* Englewood Cliffs, New Jersey: Prentice Hall, 1973.

_____, *Social Learning Theory*, Englewood Cliffs, N.J.: Prentice Hall, 1977.

Fisher, V.E., *An introduction to Abnormal Psychology*, cited by Labh Singh and G.P. Tiwari in *Essential of Abnormal Psychology*, Agra: Vinod Pustak Mandir, 1971, p. 72.

Freud, S., *An Outline of Psychoanalysis,* London: Hogarth Press, 1953.

Hull, C.L., *Principles of Behaviour,* New York: Appleton Century-Crofts, 1943.

Lorenz, K., The evolution of behaviour, *Scientific American,* 67–83, 1958.

McDougall, W., *Social Psychology*, London: Methuen, 1908.

_____, *Social Psychology*, Boston: John Luce, 1921.

Maslow, A., *Motivation and Personality*, New York: Harper & Row, 1954, p. 46.

McClelland, D.C., Atkinson, J.W., Clark, R.A. and Lowell, E.C., *The Achievement Motive*, New York: Appleton, 1953.

Montagu, M.F.A. (Ed.), *Man and Aggression*, New York: Oxford University Press, 1968.

Rosen, E., Fox, Ronald and Gregory, Ean, *Abnormal Psychology,* 3rd ed., Philadelphia: Saunders, 1972, p. 41.

Schachter, S., *The Psychology of Affiliation,* Stanford: Stanford University Press, 1959.

Stacey, C.L. and De Martino, M.E. (Eds.), *Understanding Human Motivation* (rev. ed.), Clevelands: Howard Allen, 1963.

Valley, F.P., *Motivation—Theories and issues,* Monterey, California: Brooks Cole, 1975.

SUGGESTED READINGS

McClelland, D.C., Atkinson, J.W., Clark, R.A. and Lowell, E.C., *The Achievement Motive,* New York: Appleton, 1953.

Montagu, M.F.A. (Ed.), *Man and Aggression,* New York: Oxford University Press, 1968.

Petri, H.L., *Motivation: Theory and research,* 2nd ed., Belmont, CA: Wadsworth, 1985.

Slavin, R.E., *Educational Psychology,* 3rd ed., Englewood Cliffs, N.J.: Prentice-Hall, 1986.

Stipek, D.J., *Motivation to Learn: From theory to practice,* Englewood Cliffs, N.J.: Prentice-Hall, 1988.

Weiner, B., *Human Motivation,* New York: Holt, Rinehart & Winston, 1980.

Chapter 12

Attention

MEANING

We use the word 'attention' frequently in our day-to-day conversation. During lectures in the classroom, a teacher calls for your attention to what he is saying or what he writes on the blackboard. At a railway station or other public places, announcements start with "your attention please" before informing the passengers or other people about the schedules of the trains or some other matter of public interest. Thus attention is taken as a power, capacity or faculty of our mind, which can be turned on or off at will or something in kind or form that can be lent or given to this or that situation. However, this notion, as we shall find out, is misconceived. Attention can never be considered as a force or a faculty of the mind. We must try to understand it in terms of an act, a process or a function. Therefore, the use of this term as a noun is misleading. It may be better understood as a verb like attending or a process involving the act of listening, looking at or concentrating on a topic, object or event for the attainment of a desired result. Let us consider a few definitions provided by eminent authorities in order to understand the proper meaning of this word.

Dumville (1938):

> Attention is the concentration of consciousness upon one subject rather than upon another.

Ross (1951):

> Attention is the process of getting an object of thought clearly before the mind.

Morgan & Gilliland (1942):

> Attention is being keenly alive to some specific factor in our environment. It is a preparatory adjustment for response.

Roediger et al. (1987):

> Attention can be defined as the focusing of perception that leads to a greater awareness of a limited number of stimuli.

Sharma, R.N. (1967):

> Attention can be defined as a process which compels the individual to select some particular stimulus according to his interest and attitude out of the multiplicity of stimuli present in the environment.

All these definitions highlight the following facts:

1. Attention is essentially a process, and not a product.
2. It helps in our awareness or consciousness of our environment.
3. This awareness or consciousness is selective.
4. At any one time, we can concentrate or focus our consciousness on one particular object only.
5. The concentration or focus provided by the process of attention helps us in the clear understanding of the perceived object or phenomenon.
6. In the chain of the stimulus-response behaviour it works as a mediator. Stimuli which are given proper attention yield better response. Therefore, for providing an appropriate response, one has to give proper attention to the stimulus to reach the stage of preparedness or alertness (mental as well as physical) which may be required.
7. Attention is not merely a cognitive function but is essentially determined by emotional and conative factors of interest, attitude and striving.

The foregoing discussion leads us to conclude that attention is a process carried out through cognitive abilities and helped by emotional and conative factors to select something out of the various stimuli present in one's environment and then to bring it to the centre of one's consciousness in order to perceive it clearly for deriving the desired ends.

Selectiveness of Attention

How is it possible for an individual to become capable of selecting one message from the environment and to ignore all others? Psychologists have tried to propound some theories or models of attention to properly answer this question. Broadly these can be divided into two categories—an early selection theory of attention like the Filter theory and the late selection theories.

The Filter theory put forward by Donald Broadbent (1957, 1958) postulated the existence of two general systems—the sensory and the perceptual. Many signals from the environment can be registered simultaneously in the sensory system. In order, however, to make it possible for the perceptual system to attend only to one signal and ignore all others, that is roughly equivalent to conscious attention, the sensory system filters out all unimportant signals before they can reach the perceptual system. As a result of this filtration, extraneous and non-essential signals are excluded from interfering with the selected signals. Since the signal for attention is selected in the initial stages of the process, the filter theory is considered as one of the early selection theories of attention.

The late selection theories e.g., those of Norman (1968) and Schneider and Shiffrin (1977) assert that ignored information is not filtered out at a sensory level. Instead, the information is processed through early stages of perception, and attention to one signal occurs much later, just before conscious awareness. Emphasizing the point further, these theories maintain that although people may still not be conscious of the different signals at that point, some kind of decision-making opens the door to consciousness for the most important or expected signal by ignoring the others.

Signs and Effects of Attention

How can we know that a particular individual is paying attention or not? In this connection much can be said through observation of the symptoms or reactions that accompany the state of preparedness or alertness required by the process of attention. As a person initiates the state of attention, he may turn his head, fix his eyes or set his ears toward the object of attention. Besides this, the muscles and the biological functions of the body may be seen to be specifically preparing for the object of attention. He may adopt a specific posture or hold his breath, or his respiration rate may slow down. In this way, from the observable symptoms in the form of stance, bodily conditions and facial expressions, we may decide whether or not a person is paying attention. However, for drawing more reliable and definite conclusions, the experimenter must try lo avail the introspection analysis report prepared by the subject himself. He should also try to test the validity and reliability of his conclusions by studying attentively the effects of the efforts made by his subject.

Some of these effects of attention may be summarized as follows:

1. Attention helps in bringing about mental alertness and preparedness. As a result one tries to apply one's mental powers as effectively as possible.
2. Attention helps in providing proper deep concentration by focusing one's consciousness upon one object at one time rather than on any others.
3. It makes us better equipped to distinguish or identify the object of attention from others.
4. Attention acts as a reinforcement of the sensory process and helps in the better organisation of the perceptual field for maximum clarity and understanding of the object or phenomenon under observation.
5. Attention provides strength and ability to continue the task of cognitive functioning despite the obstacles presented by the forces of distraction like noise and unfavourable weather conditions.
6. When attention is paid to an object, even the process or phenomenon yields better results in the form of the amount and quality of learning, remembering, transfer of training, thinking, reasoning and problem-solving as well as displaying the inventive abilities and creative functioning.

Types of Attention

Various authors have classified attention in a variety of ways. The classification given by Ross (1951) which seems to be the more acceptable is shown in Table 12.1.

1. *Non-volitional or involuntary attention.* This type of attention is aroused without the will coming into play and we attend to an object or an idea without any conscious effort on our part. A mother's attention to her crying child, attention towards members of the opposite sex, sudden loud noise and bright colours are some examples of non-volitional attention.

Table 12.1 Classification of Attention

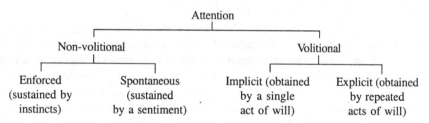

Non-volitional attention as shown in the above table can be aroused by our instincts as also by our sentiments. The attention which is aroused by the instincts is called enforced non-volitional attention. A youngman, when we make an appeal lo his sex instinct or curiosity, becomes quite attentive in his task. The type of attention which he pays at this time can be termed as enforced non-volitional attention.

The other sub-type of non-volitional attention, aroused by the sentiments is called spontaneous non-volitional attention. It is the result of properly developed sentiments. We give somewhat automatic or spontaneous attention towards that object, idea or person around which or whom our sentiments have already been formed.

2. *Volitional or voluntary attention.* Attention is volitional or voluntary when it calls forth the exercise of the will. It demands a conscious effort on our part. It is neither automatic and spontaneous nor given whole-heartedly like volitional attention. Usually in this type of attention, we have a clear-cut goal before us and we make ourselves attentive for its accomplishment. Attention paid at the time of solving an assigned problem of mathematics, answering questions in an examination, consulting the railway time-table before starting on a railway journey are some example of volitional attention.

Volitional attention is further sub-divided into two categories—implicit volitional attention and explicit volitional attention. Whereas in the former, a single act of volition is sufficient to bring about attention, in the latter we need repeated acts of will to sustain it. When a child is assigned some mathematical sums in the class-room, and he does not attend to them, he is warned by the teacher that he will be punished if he does not do his assigned work. This can make him exercise his will power, attend to the assigned task and finish it properly. Here a single act of will is responsible for the arousing of attention. Hence we can take it as an example of implicit volitional attention.

In explicit volitional attention, attention is obtained by repeated acts of will. One has to struggle hard to continue to be attentive. It requires strong will power, application and strong motives to accomplish the task. The attention paid at the time of examination days for the required preparation against heavy odds and distractions, is an apt example of such attention.

Factors or Determinants of Attention

External factors or conditions. External factors or conditions are generally those characteristics outside the situations or stimuli which make the strongest bid to capture our attention. Let us consider these characteristics.

1. *Nature of the stimulus.*   All types of stimuli are not able to bring forth the same degree of attention. A picture attracts attention more readily than words. Among pictures, the pictures of human beings capture more attention than those of animals or objects. Among pictures of human beings, those of great personalities as also of beautiful women or handsome men attract more attention. In this sense coloured pictures are more forceful than two-tone ones. Thus, the most effective stimulus should always be chosen for capturing maximum attention.

2. *Intensity and size of the stimulus.*   In comparison with a weak stimulus, the stronger stimulus attracts more attention. Our attention becomes more easily directed to a loud sound, a bright light or a strong smell. Similarly, a large object in the environment is more likely lo catch our attention than a small object. A large building will be more readily noticed than the small ones.

3. *Contrast, change and variety.*   Change and variety attract attention more easily than sameness and routine. When a teacher is lecturing to his students, the use of maps and charts suddenly attracts their attention. We do not notice the ticking of a clock on the wall but it arrests our attention as soon as it stops. We notice any change in the pattern of attention to which we have become adapted. Actually the factor-contrast or change is highly responsible for capturing attention of the organism and contributes more than the intensity, size or nature of the stimulus. If all the LETTERS on this page were printed in capitals, the capitalized word in this sentence would have no greater attention-getting value than any other word. It is the contrast or change which makes it more forceful.

Novelty also attracts attention. We are compelled to attend to anything that is new or different. So it is always better to introduce change or novelty to break the monotony and secure attention.

4. *Repetition of stimulus.*   Repetition is a factor of great importance in securing attention. We may ignore a stimulus the first time, but when it is repeated several times, it captures our attention. A misspelled word is more likely to be noticed if it occurs twice in the same paragraph than if it occurs only once. In the classroom also, the particular point on which the teacher tries lo draw the attention of the students is raised again and again. While giving the lecture, the important aspects of the speech are often repeated, so that the attention of the audience can be easily directed to the valuable points. But this practice of repetition should be used carefully. Too much repetition of a stimulus may bring diminishing returns.

5. *Movement of the stimulus.*   A moving stimulus catches our attention more quickly than one which is still. In other words, we are more sensitive to objects that move in our field of vision. Most of the

advertisers make use of this fact and try to capture the attention of people through moving electric lights.

Internal factors or conditions. How much and in what way a person will attend to a stimulus depends not only upon the characteristics of that stimulus or the favourable environmental conditions but also upon the person's own interest, motives, basic needs and urges etc. Every person likes to do or attend to those objects or activities that fulfil his own desires or motives and suit his own nature, interest and aptitude. Let us try to see the part played by these inner factors in securing the attention of a person.

1. *Interest and attention.* Interest is a very helpful factor in securing attention. We attend to objects in which we are interested and we do not attend to those in which we have no interest. If we go to the market to buy a book, our attention will be captured more by book shops than by cloth and shoe shops etc. A boy interested in hockey will be more interested in watching a hockey match than football or the volleyball matches being played at the same time on adjacent grounds. A wise teacher is able to draw the attention of his students if he tries to make his lesson interesting by connecting it with their basic needs, drives and interests.

2. *Motives.* The basic drives and urges of the individual are very important in securing his attention. Thirst, hunger, sex, curiosity, fear are some of the important motives that exercise a definite influence upon attention. A hungry person will definitely notice the smell of cooking. The man who fears snakes, will definitely be more attentive to things which resemble a snake. The sex drive occupies a unique place among the different drives. Even the most inattentive student in the class can be made to sit on the edge of his chair if the teacher announces that he is going to talk about the sex-practices of American hippies. Nowadays in the world of advertising, sex is the drive that has been most widely exploited. We can see the shapely girls in bathing suits to sell such unrelated items as tyres, nuts, bolts and tractors.

3. *Mind set.* Besides our interests and motives the mind set is an important factor in securing attention. Mind set means the tendency or bent of the whole mind. A person always attends to those objects towards which his mind has set. A person waiting for a letter from his beloved can recognize her envelope from among a huge pile of envelopes. Similarly, on the day of an examination the slightest thing concerning the examination easily attracts the attention of the students. All this happens because the persons concerned possess a definite bent of mind and consequently their attention is immediately directed towards the related objects.

Span of Attention

While defining attention, we emphasized that in a strict psychological sense only one object, idea, or fact can be the centre of consciousness at one particular moment and consequently we can attend to only one thing at a time. However, it is found with some people that they can attend to more than one, or even many tasks at the same time. While writing a letter they are seen attending to the telephone, keeping track of the time on the wall clock and responding to the approach of somebody else. In other cases, immediately after entering a room or hall, some individuals are able to give a detailed account of the number of chairs and fans, persons present, the pictures on the walls, the colour of the walls or curtains, etc. In this way, they may possess the ability to grasp a number of things, or in other words attend to a number of stimuli in one short exposure. This ability of an individual is evaluated in terms of the span of his attention which varies from person to person and even situation to situation in the same person. Therefore the term 'span of attention' may be defined as the quality, size or extent to which the perceptual field of an individual can be effectively organised in order to enable him to attend to a number of things in a given spell of short duration.

Sir William Hamilton in 1859 tried to perform the first experiments on the span of attention. For his experiments he spread out marbles on the ground before his students and concluded that on an average the span of visual attention is limited to 6–7 marbles, i.e., we are unable to see more than 6–7 marbles at a time. However, if these marbles are arranged in groups or units, we can attend to a greater number of marbles. Further experiments were performed, among others, by later psychologists.

Experiments to study the span of visual attention are done with the help of an instrument known as a tachistroscope and a Falling door type tachistroscope is generally used in college laboratories. It consists of a wooden screen having a window or hole in the middle. Digits, letters or small patterns written or printed on cards are inserted in the apparatus to be seen through the hole or window. The exposure is quite short (generally 1/10 second) which is regulated by a movable falling shutter. The subject is shown the cards through the hole for the fixed exposure time. He may, then be asked to record what he perceived and the number of digits, letters, correctly reproduced may then be considered as the measure of his span of visual attention.

For measurement of the other sensory span of attention, different techniques may be employed. For example, the span of auditory attention may be measured by tapping a number of times and asking the subject how many taps he has heared.

Shifting or Fluctuation of Attention

While paying attention to an object, event or phenomenon, it is not possible for us to hold it continuously with the same intensity for a long duration. In the course of time, the centre of our consciousness either shifts from one stimulus to another or from one part of the same stimulus to another part. This is called the shifting or fluctuation of attention. Fluctuation of attention also involves rapid change in the intensity of attention. The intensity increases or decreases, ranging between the paying of attention, not paying attention, and paying least or less attention.

The reason for the shifting and fluctuation of our attention lies in the division of the field of perception or consciousness at a particular moment.

Consciousness at a particular moment may be divided into two parts, central and marginal. At the time when our attention is on the wall clock and consciousness is focused on it, the other objects and activities going on inside the room remain within the reach of marginal consciousness. This helps us in being partly conscious or aware of them. Both these fields of perception or consciousness are interchangeable. An object of attention at a given moment, may shift to marginal consciousness or even beyond. Consequently the focus of attention generally keeps changing thus making the process of attention quite flexible and dynamic.

The phenomenon of fluctuation of attention was experimentally recorded for the first time in 1875 by the psychologist Urbantschitsch. While testing the auditory sensation he observed that the subject was not able to continuously hear the sound of an alarm clock placed at a distance. At times, he was able to hear the ticking of the clock, but at other times the sound disappeared from his attention.

The study of fluctuation of visual attention can be experimentally made in the psychological laboratory with the help of a device called a Masson's Disc. This disc consists of a circular card-board having four or five patches of ink put in a line along one radius (see Figure 12.1).

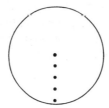

Figure 12.1 Masson's disc.

When the disc is rotated on an electric or mechanically run spindle, each dot appears to the subject to be a circle. The subject is asked to concentrate on any one of the blackish circle on the rotating disc and to report when the circle is clearly seen and when it becomes less clear or blurred. The subject is told to raise his finger when it is clear and put it down when it becomes blurred till it becomes clear again when he raises his finger once more.

Division of Attention

While reading a book, one's attention is centred around the topic or the material in hand. In case a favourite piece of music is being played within the subject's hearing, a number of situations may arise. In one case, the individual may attend to the music and consequently the reading is given up; in another case, he may deliberately try to ignore the music and thus may be able to concentrate on reading. In the third case, there may be confusion where he can neither attend to his reading nor is he able to enjoy the music; in the fourth case, he may be found to be quite capable of paying attention simultaneously to both the stimuli, namely, his reading as well as the music. It is the last situation in which the problem of the division of attention arises. In this case, attention is divided between two tasks. If more than two tasks are attended to and performed simultaneously then the attention will have to be divided among those tasks.

Many researchers have tried to study the effect of the division of attention on the work product. It has been found that the work products suffer less if both the tasks are simple and similar but in the case of difficult and dis-similar tasks, the division of attention proves detrimental. However small the amount may be, the division of attention proves detrimental. However small the amount may be, the division of attention surely results in deterioration in both the quality and quantity of nearly all the tasks attended to and performed simultaneously by an individual. It is rare that no effect is seen as a result of the division of attention. It seems to happen in exceptional instances like those of the famous Late Hardayal and the mathematical wizard Shakuntala Devi or in cases where only one task really requires attention and the remaining tasks can be performed automatically and need little or no attention.

Sustained Attention

If one desires to be successful in the performance of a task, one has to begin with paying attention or concentrating his energies to the operation of that task. But this is the beginning of a process and not the end. After beginning to pay attention, care has to be taken to sustain it for the required length of time. The individual should be wholly absorbed in handling the task, unmindful of anything that might be going on near him, without getting distracted. This is the sustaining of attention. In the words of Woodworth (1945):

> To sustain attention is to concentrate one's activity continuously upon some object or happening or problem.

Thus, in the case of sustained attention, there is no wandering. The individual attention always remains on track and the activity proceeds uninterruptedly and without serious distraction. The most striking examples of such sustained attention are the activities of a hunter who is waiting for the opportune moment to shoot or of an astronomer sitting with his eyes fixed on a particular star while looking through his telescope or of a mathematician working on a problem for a long time.

Truly speaking, if one needs to achieve the required objectives in a reasonable time, one must learn to pay sustained attention. One must concentrate upon the activity which one is involved in. A student who cannot keep his attention fixed for a reasonable length of time is sure to lag behind in his studies. An artist has to strive for sustained attention so that he can finish his desired piece of art. A writer, a poet, a musician—all have to put in sustained attention.

In order to hold attention for a long time, it is essential to capture the genuine interest of the subject in the task which he is doing. All internal as well as external factors for getting attention can also prove helpful in sustaining attention. Every effort must, therefore, be made to make the best use of these factors. Moreover, factors which cause distractions and disrupt attention should be removed. For best results, the individual whose attention is to be sustained should be provided with favourable environmental conditions to work in, and factors, which may disturb him mentally and emotionally should be removed or at least minimized. The will power of the subject must also be adequately developed and he should be made to strive to attain the set objectives and higher ideals of life.

DISTRACTION

When we are attending to an object or activity, there are things in the external environment as well as inside ourselves that tend to intrude and divert our attention from that object or activity. These things which interfere with our attention are called distractors. Distraction, as a psychological term, has been defined by H.R. Bhatia (1968) as follows:

> Distraction may be defined as any stimulus whose presence interferes with the process of attention or draws away attention from the object to which we wish to attend.

The sources of distraction can be roughly divided into external and internal factors. Among the external or environmental factors the more common and prominent are noise, music, improper lighting, uncomfortable seats, unfavourable temperature, inadequate ventilation, defective methods of teaching, improper use of teaching aids, a defective voice or improper behaviour of the teacher etc. The sources of distraction are very diverse and affect an individual according to his own mental set and personality characteristics. The conditions which cause distraction to one individual may prove helpful in sustaining the attention of another.

Therefore, the common notion that unusual environmental conditions always hinder the progress of work is misleading. Some people are found to work better in a noisy environment, for instance, some can concentrate better on studies while the radio is playing. Actually speaking, the source of distraction lies more commonly within the individual himself than in the external environmental conditions. Internal distractions such as emotional disturbance, ill-health, boredom, lack of motivation, feeling of fatigue or preoccupations unrelated to the matter in hand have more effect than the everyday external distractors. If one is in normal health and not suffering from unusual mental worries and emotional disturbances, no power on earth can distract one's attention in case one is determined to pursue one's course. Most of us are in the habit of offering lame excuses in the name of outside distraction, for failures resulting from our unwillingness and lack of determination.

It should not be concluded from the foregoing that external factors of distraction have little significance and so can be ignored. In the presence of external distraction, an individual has to struggle hard to concentrate. He has to put in greater effort to keep the object before his mind. Certainly, there should not be such misutilization of energy which otherwise can be applied to achieve higher aims. Therefore, great care should be taken to do away with all possible environmental causes of distraction. The working situations and environmental conditions should be so modified and adjusted as to provide adequate working facilities and a healthy congenial environment for an individual whose attention in the work we wish to capture and sustain.

SUMMARY

Attention is closely related to the processes and products of learning. It refers to a deliberate and conscious effort on the part of an individual to select one out of the various stimuli present in his environment and bring it to the centre of his consciousness in order to perceive it clearly to achieve a desired result.

Various theories have been put forward to explain the selective nature of one's attention. According to early selection theories like the filter theory, unattended signals are filtered or screened out at the level of the senses before they can reach the perceptual system. Late selection theories on the other hand, deny such filtration at the sensory level and maintain that the attention to one signal or source occurs much later, just before conscious awareness.

Attention is a state of physical as well as mental preparedness and alertness on the part of an individual which may be adjudged through keen observation of his body postures and positions, physiological changes and by studying the yields of the attended learning or problem solving activities.

Normally, we can attend to only one thing at a time. However, there are people who can attend to more than one or even to many tasks at the same time. They are said to possess a larger *span of attention,* i.e., ability to organise a larger perceptual field in a given spell or short duration. The span of attention can be experimentally studied with the help of an instrument called a tachistroscope.

Attention cannot be held continuously with the same intensity for a long duration. In course of time when the centre of consciousness shifts or fluctuates from one object to another or from one part of the same object to another part, it is termed as *shifting or fluctuation of attention.* This study of fluctuation of visual attention can be experimentally made with the help of a device called Masson's Disc.

The phenomenon of *division of attention* is concerned with the task of paying attention simultaneously to a number of stimuli in one's environment. The division of attention adversly affects the products of attention. However, it may be seen that work products suffer less if the tasks being attended to are simple and similar in comparison to difficult and dis-similar tasks.

Attention may be broadly classified as *volitional or voluntary,* i.e., maintained by one's will power and *non-volitional or involuntary,* i.e., without exercise of one's will. While in implicit, volitional attention a single act of volition is sufficient to bring about attention, in explicit volitional attention, we need repeated acts of will to sustain it. Non-Volitional attention also has two categories: *enforced non-volitional* attention aroused by the instincts and *spontaneous non-volitional* attention aroused by the sentiments.

Attention is guided and controlled by *external as well as internal factors.* External factors present in one's environment are: nature of the stimulus, intensity and size of the stimulus, contrast, change and variety, repetition of stimulus, movement of stimulus, etc. Internal factors represent the factors lying within the person himself like interest, motives and mind set.

To obtain better results in learning one has to hold the subject's attention for a desirable length of time without disruption. This needed activity is termed *sustaining of attention.* One has to make serious and deliberate efforts to sustain attention by taking care of all the factors responsible for maintaining attention and eliminating or reducing the forces of distraction.

Distraction represents interference with attention. The source of distraction may be external e.g., noise, improper lighting, uncomfortable seats, etc. and internal, e.g., lack of motivation, emotional disturbances, ill health, boredom or fatigue etc. For achieving useful results, one should try to overcome all such forces of distraction.

REFERENCES

Bhatia, H.R., *Elements of Educational Psychology,* 3rd ed., Calcutta: Orient Longman, 1968, p. 139.

Broadbent, D.E., A mechanical model for human attention and immediate memory, *Psychological Review,* Vol. 64, pp. 205–15, 1957.

————, *Perception and Communication,* Oxford: Pergamon Press, 1958.

Dumville, B., *The Fundamentals of Psychology,* 3rd ed., London: University Tutorial Press, 1938, p. 315.

Morgan, J.B. and Gilliland, A.R., *An Introduction to Psychology,* New York: Macmillan, 1942, p. 128.

Norman, D.A., Toward a theory of memory and attention, *Psychological Review,* Vol. 75, pp. 522–36, 1968.

Roediger, H.L., Rushton, J.P. et al., *Psychology,* 2nd ed., Boston: Little Brown & Co., 1987, p. 161.

Ross, J.S., *Ground Work of Educational Psychology,* London: George G. Harrup & Co., 1951, pp. 170–75.

Schneider, W. and Shiffrin, R.M., Controlled and automatic information processing— Detection, search and attention, *Psychological Review,* Vol. 84, pp. 1–66, 1977.

Sharma, R.N., *Educational Psychology,* Meerut: Rastogi Publications, 1967, p. 392.

Woodworth, R.S., *Psychology,* London: Methuen, 1945, p. 48.

———— (Ed.), *Experimental Psychology,* New York: Holt, 1954.

Chapter 13

Nature and Theories of Learning

NATURE OF LEARNING

Learning occupies a very important place in our life. Most of what we do or do not do is influenced by what we learn and how we learn it. Learning, therefore, provides a key to the structure of our personality and behaviour. An individual starts learning immediately after his birth or in a strict sense even earlier in the womb of the mother. Experience, direct or indirect is found to play a dominant role in moulding and shaping the behaviour of the individual from the very beginning. When he touches a burning matchstick the child gets burnt, and the next time, when he comes across a burning matchstick, he loses no time in withdrawing from it. He learns to avoid not only the burning matchstick but also all burning things. When this happens we say that the child has learned that if one touches a flame, one gets burnt. In the same way from some other experience, he may conclude, for instance, that "green apples are sour", "barking dogs seldom bite", "a bird in hand is better than two in the bush", "be very cautious in believing strangers", etc. All these conclusions derived from experiences, direct or indirect, bring about a change in the behaviour of the individual. These changes in behaviour brought about by experience are commonly known as learning. In this way, *the term learning broadly speaking, stands for all those changes and modifications in the behaviour of the individual which he undergoes during his life time.*

However, this term has not been always interpreted in the same way by the numerous thinkers and psychologists as may be seen from the following definitions:

Gardner Murphy (1968):

> The term learning covers every modification in behaviour to meet environmental requirements.

Henry P. Smith (1962):

> Learning is the acquisition of new behaviour or the strengthening or weakening of old behaviour as the result of experience.

170

Woodworth (1945):

Any activity can be called learning so far as it develops the individual (in any respect, good or bad) and makes him alter behaviour and experiences different from what they would otherwise have been.

Kingsley and R. Garry (1957):

Learning is the process by which behaviour (in the broader sense) is originated or changes through practice or training.

Pressey, Robinson and Horrocks (1967):

Learning is an episode in which a motivated individual attempts to adapt his behaviour so as to succeed in a situation which he perceives as requiring action to attain a goal.

Crow and Crow (1973):

Learning is the acquisition of habits, knowledge and attitudes. It involves new ways of doing things, and it operates in an individual's attempts to overcome obstacles or to adjust to new situations. It represents progressive changes in behaviour . . . . It enables him to satisfy interests to attain goals.

Hilgard (1958):

Learning is the process by which an activity originates or is changed through reaching to an encountered situation, provided that the characteristics of the changes in activity cannot be explained on the basis of native response, tendencies, maturation, or temporary states of the organism (e.g. fatigue or drugs, etc.).

Kimble (1961):

Learning is a relatively permanent change in behavioural potentiality that occurs as a result of reinforced practice.

The above definitions reveal the following facts:

1. Learning is a process and not a product.
2. It involves all those experiences and training of an individual (right from birth) which help him to produce changes in his behaviour.
3. Learning leads to changes in behaviour but this does not necessarily mean that these changes always bring about improvement or positive development. One has an equal chance to drift to the negative side of human personality.
4. Instead of change in existing behaviour or acquisition of new behaviour, learning may also result in discontinuance or abandonment of existing behaviour. Though it is referred to as unlearning, actually unlearning is also a learning process.
5. Learning prepares an individual for any adjustment and adaptation that may be necessary.
6. Learning is purposeful and goal-oriented. In case there is no purpose, there would definitely be hardly any learning.
7. The scope of learning is too wide to be explained in words. It is a very comprehensive process which covers nearly all fields—conative, cognitive and affective—of human behaviour.

8. Learning is universal and continuous. Every creature that lives, learns. In human beings it is not restricted to any particular age, sex, race or culture. It is a continuous, never-ending process that extends from the womb to the tomb.
9. As maintained by Crow and Crow, learning involves new ways of doing things but there is no limit to adopting these ways and means. All learning does not take place in the same manner. Therefore, learning as a process is of different types and involves different methods.
10. As maintained by Hilgard, the concept of learning excludes changes in behaviour on the basis of native response tendencies like instincts and reflexes, etc. Instinctive or species specific programmes cannot be termed as learned behaviour. Similarly, reflexes, the innate involuntary responses to stimulation e.g., blinking at bright lights and the infant's sucking behaviour, cannot be attributed to learning.
11. Learning does not include changes in behaviour on account of maturation, fatigue, illness, or drugs etc.

The last mentioned characteristic reveals that changes in one's behaviour are not always brought about and controlled by learning only. There are other factors like fatigue, drugs, illness, maturation and imprinting, which produce behavioural changes. Can we, then, attribute all such changes in our behaviour to learning? The answer is, no. The reasons are explained in the following discussion:

Learning and Maturation

The changes produced in behviour by maturation are definitely linked with the unfolding and ripening of inherited traits, i.e., the process of natural growth. They are quite independent of activity, practice or experience. In the words of Biggie and Hunt (1968),

> Maturation is a developmental process within which a person, from time to time, manifests different traits, the 'blue-prints' of which have been carried in his cells from the time of his conception.

The resultant behaviour, thus, on account of the process of maturation does not fall in the category of acquired or learned behaviour. However, maturation is closely linked with results of learning and with the process of development. Before certain kinds of learning may take place, one has to have achieved a certain level of maturation. For example, a six-month old baby cannot learn how to control bowel movements because neither his brain nor his body is mature enough to do so. Similarly, a child cannot learn certain speech patterns before a certain degree of maturation has occurred.

Learning and Other Temporary Change-producing Factors

The behavioural changes brought about by factors like fatigue, drugs, illness or emotional situations, are purely transitory in nature. These changes, like physical changes in material objects, are quite unstable. As and when the factor causing a change is removed or restored, the behaviour may revert to its original form.

Hence, the changes in behaviour produced by such factors cannot fall in the category of learning and in comparison to all other factors that lead to changes in human behaviour, the changes brought about by learning, i.e., experience and training, etc. are relatively more enduring and stable.

It is to be noted that we have deliberately used the phrase 'relatively enduring and stable changes' in place of 'absolutely permanent changes' in the behaviour of the learner. It is true that learning brings about changes in behaviour but these changes are not as permanent as the changes brought about by chemical reactions in material objects. The habits we pick up, the interests we develop, the skills we acquire, the knowledge we gain as a result of learning at one or the other occasion can be unlearned, modified or replaced by some other set of similar or different acquired behaviour. Therefore, it is safer to use the term relatively permanent in place of absolutely permanent for the resultant changes in one's behaviour on account of learning and consequently a proper definition of learning may be, *Learning is a process which brings relatively permanent changes in the behaviour of a learner through experience or practice.*

Learning and Imprinting

The term 'imprinting' is often confused with learning. However, it is not proper to label or include the changes in behaviour brought about as a result of imprinting in the category of learned or acquired behaviour. Let us explain this by describing and illustrating the concept of 'imprinting'.

'Imprinting' as a term was first used in the 1930s by the Austrian ethologist Konrad Lorenz for describing the attachment behaviour of new-born birds to the first large moving objects in their environment. He conducted a series of experiments for studying such attachment behaviour. A few of these are described below:

1. In his initial experiments he demonstrated that ducklings and goslings follow the mother soon after hatching perhaps on account of the stimulation provided by her movements and the noises she makes.
2. Afterwards Lorenz used some big objects like a football in place of the mother to be followed by the new-born ducklings and goslings. To his surprise he found that as soon as these birds were hatched, they began to follow the floating ball in the pond.
3. In one of his later experiments he himself worked as a substitute for the football and the mother. For conducting this experiment he first hatched a group of goslings in an incubator and then presented himself as the first moving object they saw. He found that the new-born birds began to follow him wherever he went (see Figure 13.1):

Surprisingly, when the goslings were returned to their real mother at a later stage, they turned away and continued to follow the first perceived moving object i.e., the experimentor, Lorenz. They even showed resentment and gave vent to cries of distress when they were prevented from following him. From such experiments Lorenz concluded that:

Figure 13.1   Experiment on the phenomenon of imprinting.

1. Imprinting represents a sense of strong connection or attachment that is made between the new-born organism and the first object it may have initially responded to. Howsoever, strange this first object may be, they continue to follow it to the extent that they show no attachment to their own mother or any one of their own kind.
2. Imprinting thus represents an inborn perceptual process independent of any training or experience.
3. It is unquestionably a survival mechanism and whatever the first object, it is followed for safety, security, love and attachment. It is like love at first sight, a kind of 'value acquisition', an effective 'imprint' or 'impression' on the tender mind.
4. Imprinting, i.e., connection or attachment is made to the first perceived object within the critical period.
5. It may be taken as an instinctive response or species-specific behaviour i.e., a behaviour pattern common to all members of a particular species and it occurs naturally, depending upon the environmental stimulus which sets it off. In case there is no such stimulus, i.e. moving object, available to the new-born within the critical period, it is doubtful whether the attachment behaviour would be exhibited at all. For example, geese or infant rats, isolated from the natural mother or a mother substitute within the first few days or birth may never develop any significant attachment behaviour (Lorenz, 1952).
6. The critical period, the special and distinct time essential for establishing attachment behaviour, i.e., the process of imprinting, differs from species to species. In baby ducks for example, the ideal time for imprinting is fourteen hours after hatching, in lambs it is one to seven days after birth and in puppies between three and twelve weeks.

Imprinting is thus quite dissimilar and distinct from the actual process of learning. It depends on an instinctive and inborn species-specific behaviour mechanism rather than the experience and training carried out during specific critical periods of the species' lifetime soon after birth.

Types of Learning

Learning, defined as a process of bringing about relatively permanent changes in the behaviour of an organism, may be classified into a number of categories depending upon (a) the domain or specific area of the behaviour in which changes are introduced, or (b) in terms of the methods or techniques that are employed for the introduction of behavioural changes.

If we follow the former criterion, learing can be classified as verbal learning (involving verbal expression), learning of motor skills, (such as walking, dancing, typing, swimming, etc.), affective learning (learning of habits, interest, attitudes, appreciation, etc.), and cognitive learning (learning of concepts, principles, problem solving, etc.).

In terms of the latter criterion, we may categorize learning as trial and error learning, classical conditioning, operant conditioning, chain learning, shaping, learning through generalization, learning through discrimination, serial learning, associate learning, insightful learning, and so on.

An alternative basis adopted by Gagne (1970) for the purpose of classifying learning is worthy of note. By taking into consideration a specific hierarchical order, he classified learning into the following types:

1. Signal learning or classical conditioning
2. S.R. learning or instrumental and operant conditioning
3. Chain learning
4. Verbal associate learning
5. Multiple discrimination
6. Learning of concepts
7. Learning of principles
8. Problem solving.

Various types of such learning are discussed in different parts of this text in the proper context. However, a few are discussed here.

1. *Verbal learning.* Learning of this type helps in the acquisition of verbal behaviour. The language we speak, the communication devices we use, are the result of such learning. Rote learning and rote memorization which is a type of school learning is also included in verbal learning. Signs, pictures, symbols, words, figures, sounds and voices are employed by the individual as essential instruments for engaging in the process of verbal learning.

2. *Motor learning.* The learning of all types of motor skills may be included in this type of learning. Learning swimming, riding a horse, driving a car, flying a plane, playing the piano, hitting a moving target, drawing a geometrical design, adding and multiplying long series of digits, performing experiments and handling various instruments are examples of such learning. Acquisition of various skills through such learning helps in acquiring speed and accuracy in the field of operation of these activities and creates a sort of confidence in the learner to perform with ease and satisfaction. The art of these skills can be acquired through a systematic and planned acquisition and fixation of a series of organised actions or responses by making use of some appropriate learning methods and devices.

3. Concept learning. A concept in the form of a mental image denotes a generalized idea about things, persons or events. For example, our concept of 'tree' is a mental image that throws up the similarities or common properties of all the different trees we know. We will call a thing 'tree' when it has some specific characteristics, the image of which we have already acquired in our mind on account of our previous experience, perception or exercise of imagination. The formation of such concepts on account of previous experience, training or cognitive processes is called concept learning. Concept learning proves very useful in recognizing, naming and identifying things. All our behaviour, verbal, symbolic, motor as well as cognitive, are influenced by our concepts. Thus what we do, say, understand, reason and judge is, to a great extent, controlled by the quality of our concept learning.

4. Problem solving. In the hierarchical order of learning and acquisition of behaviour, problem solving learning denotes a higher type of learning. This learning requires the use of the cognitive abilities like reasoning, thinking, the power of observation, discrimination, generalization, imagination, the ability to infer, draw conclusions and try out novel ways and experimenting, etc. Based on earlier experiences, effect of coaching, training, formal or informal learning and acquisition of knowledge, habits, attitudes, interests and learning, sets, etc., an individual may be motivated to reach an unknown target or to unfold the mystery of an unresolved problem. It is this type of learning which has essentially enabled human beings to contribute significantly to the progress and improvement of society.

In the process of learning one has to adopt an adequate technique in the form of certain methods and processes. In some cases, connections or associations in the form of a stimulus-response mechanism or conditioning may help while in others, organisation of the perceptual field and the use of cognitive abilities may work.

5. Serial learning. Serial learning is a learning situation in which the learner is presented with learning material which exhibits some sequential or serial order. Children encounter it often in school where they are expected to master lists of material such as the alphabet, multiplication tables, the names of all the states in their country, the names of presidents or prime ministers in order, etc. Experiments in the field of serial learning have shown that of the serial learning material, the items presented at the beginning and at the end of the list are easier to remember than those in the middle, and this seems to be true whether the items are non-sense syllables, actual words or longer passages such as a poem.

6. Paired-associate learning. In this learning, learning tasks are presented in such a way that they may be learned by reason of their associations. The name of a village like Kishanpur is remembered on account of its association with the name of Lord Krishna. Ganga, a girl's name may become easy to remember in a paired association with the river Ganges. Much of the verbal or motor learning may, thus, be acquired or remembered by means of the technique of paired or multiple association.

To obtain practice of such paired-associate learning the learner may be presented with a series of paired words or non-sense syllables like the following:

Paired words	Paired non-sense syllables
Dog — Animal	PN — PF
Parrot — Bird	NLP — JDS
Cat — Milk	RJBP — RNYS
Motor — Child	TIPBK — GMPRK

The learner views the pair (two words or syllables) for a brief time, usually less than five seconds. He is then presented with one member of the pair and asked to recall the other. The practice with such procedure then helps in building what is known as associate learning. An example of paired associate learning is the acquisition of foreign language vocabulary items that are paired with their mother-tongue equivalents. The matching items presented in the objective type of questions of the achievement test also emphasize such learning.

OUTCOMES OF LEARNING

Learning, as a useful process, may result in the following outcomes:

1. *Bringing desirable changes in behaviour.* Learning is the process of bringing changes in behaviour. It can help in introducing desired changes in the behaviour of a learner, in all its three domains i.e., cognitive, conative and affective.

2. *Attaining of teaching-learning objectives.* The teaching-learning objectives and teaching learning situation can be effectively reached through the help of learning and consequently a child can be made to acquire essential knowledge, skills, applications, attitudes and interests etc.

3. *Attaining of proper growth and development.* Learning helps in reaching one's maximum in terms of growth and development in various spheres namely physical, mental (cognitive), emotional, social, moral, aesthetic and language.

4. *Attaining balanced development of personality.* Our educational efforts are directed to bring an all-round development in the personality of a child. Learning results in bringing such an all-round development in personality.

5. *Attaining proper adjustment.* Adjustment is a key to success in life. Learning helps an individual to get adjusted to himself and to the environment.

6. *Realizing of the goals of life.* Every man has his own philosophy and style of life and he strives to achieve the goals of his life. Learning process helps an individual to realise his goals.

In this way the process of learning results in varying outcomes which can be said to contribute significantly in the overall improvement and progress of the learner for helping him to lead an adjusted and satisfying life.

FACTORS AFFECTING LEARNING

Learning, as you have studied, can be defined as a process of bringing relatively permanent changes in the behaviour of the learner through experience or practice. An examination of this definition may reveal that learning process is centred around three elements:

1. The learner whose behaviour is to be changed or modified.
2. The type of experience or training required for modification in the learner's behaviour
3. The men and material resources needed for providing desired experiences and training.

Therefore the success or failure in the task of learning in terms of introducing desired modification in the behaviour of a learner will automatically depend upon the quality as well as control and management of the factors associated with the above cited main elements. Let us discuss briefly these factors.

Factors Associated with Learner

Learner is the key figure in any learning task. He has to learn or bring desired modification in his behaviour. How he will learn or what he will achieve, through a particular learning act depends heavily upon his own characteristics and ways of learning. Such things or factors associated with this can be described as follows:

1. *Learner's physical and mental health.* Learning is greatly affected by the learner's physical and mental health maintained by him particularly, at the time of learning. A simple headache or a stomachache can play havoc with the process and products of learning. A child who does not maintain satisfactory physical health, have to suffer adversely in terms of gains in learning. Similarly, the mental state and the health of a learner at the time of learning become potent factors in deciding the out come of his learning. A tense, emotionally and mentally disturbed learner cannot show satisfactory results in learning.

2. *The basic potential of the learner.* The results achieved by the learner through a process of learning depend heavily upon his basic potential to undergo such learning. Such potential may consist of the things given ahead:

(a) Learner's innate abilities and capacities for learning a thing.
(b) Learner's basic potential in terms of general intelligence and specific knowledge, understanding and skills related to a particular learning area.
(c) Learner's basic interests, aptitudes and attitudes related to the learning of a particular thing or area.

3. *The level of aspiration and achievement motivation.* Learning is greatly influenced by the level of aspiration and nature of achievement motivation possessed by a learner. How can we expect learner to achieve a thing for which he has no aspiration?

Also, too much of aspirations make it impossible for an individual to achieve this. A person has to maintain the level of his aspiration and achievement motivation at a reasonable level. That is to say, his aspirations should be neither too high which will result in non-achievement of any of his goals, nor too low as not to try to achieve goals which he is quite capable.

4. *Goals of life.* The philosophy of immediate as well as ultimate goals of one's life affect the process and product of learning. His mode and ways of looking towards things, his inclination towards learning a particular subject and patience and persistence in pursuing his learning despite the heavy odds—all depend up on his goals and philosophy of life.

5. *Readiness and will power.* A learner's readiness and power to learn is a great deciding factor of his results in learning. No power on earth can help a learner if he is not ready to learn. Certainly, if he has a will to learn a thing, then automatically, he will himself find ways for effective learning.

Factors Associated with the Type of Learning Experiences

The type of changes or modifications found in learner's behaviour depends much on the type of learning experience and training received by him for this purpose. This task involves a variety of factors like those given below:

1. *Nature of learning experience.* Learning is influenced by the nature of the subject matter and the learning experiences presented to a learner such as the following:

  (a) Whehter the nature of learning experience is formal or informal, incidental or well-planned, direct or indirect and the like.
  (b) Whether learning experiences are suitably selected on the basis of the principle of child-centredness, principle of activity, criterion of activity, age, grade and experiences of a learner.
  (c) Whether learning experiences are suitably organised for the attainment of desired educational objections or not.

2. *Methodology of learning.* Learning depends upon the methods, techniques and approaches employed for the teaching and learning of the selected contents. Let us weigh the truth of this statement fresh from various angles.

  (a) *Linking the recent learnings with those of the past.* The quality of result in learning, depends much on the abilities of a teacher and a learner to link the present new learning with the past experiences of the learner. Past experiences help the learner to assimilate and understand the new learning.

(b) *Correlating learning in one area with that of another.* Correlation facilitates the task of learning as it allows maximum transfer of training or learning from one area to another. Accordingly, one can expect good results in learning, if learning experiences are given in view of seeking correlation (a) among the different subjects or areas, (b) within the branches or experiences of the same area and (c) with real life happenings and situations.

(c) *Utilization of maximum number of sense.* Senses are said to be the gateway of knowledge and consequently the results in learning are very much influenced by the nature and type of utilization of one's senses in the acquisition of learning experiences. A learner who learns through utilization of his maximum senses like sense of sight, hearing, touch, smell, taste, and also tries to learn by doing things for himself, always has an advantageous edge over others.

(d) *Revision and practice.* Review and practice always brings good results in the achievements of learning. A learner who makes use of sufficient drill work, practice work, revision and review of his learning can be expected to harvest a good yield in terms of his good retention, reproduction and utilization at the proper time.

(e) *Provision of proper feedback and reinforcement.* Learning yields are dependent upon the nature and quality of the reinforcement provided to the learner in his learning task. One must be acquainted with the progress of his learning in terms of his strength and weaknesses and remedial action if needed, may be taken at the proper time. Knowledge of the results and the progress may work for providing immediate reinforcement to the learner. In addition to it, learning process can be suitably designed if we take due care to make planning of proper reinforcement schedules. The results are unmatchable so much so as simple reinforcement techniques in the shapes of approval of the learning response, nodding of the head, smiling, saying good-bye and similar other things bring a magic in terms of a learner's interests and achievements.

(f) *The selection of the suitable learning methods and teaching.* There are sufficient methods and a number of good techniques available for the teaching and learning of different subjects and areas of experiences. The results of learning are always influenced by the nature and quality of the methods and techniques employed for the teaching and learning of a particular content, subject matter or learning experiences like those given in the following:

    (i) Whether or not methods and techniques are helpful in learning by memory or by understanding or reflective level.

    (ii) Whether or not these are teacher-dominated, learner-centred or, allow useful teacher-pupil interaction.

   (iii) Is it possible to proceed on the path of self-learning through them?

Factors Associated with the Men and Material Resources

A learner is helped by the available resources (men and material) for bringing desirable changes in his behaviour. How effectively such changes will take place in his behaviour depend much on the quality and management of these resources. Certain factors which affect learning may be listed in the following manner:

1. Quality of the teacher in terms of his mastery over the subject matter, teaching skills, rich experiences and teacher like qualities and behaviour.
2. Socio-emotional climate available in the institution in the form of teacher-pupil relationships, pupil-pupil relationships and school-staff relationships and the like.
3. Availability of appropriate learning material and facilities like teaching-learning aids, text books, library and laboratory facilities, project works.
4. Availability of proper conducive environment and learning situations like:

- Proper seating arrangement.
- Calm and peaceful environment.
- Management and control of the factors leading to distraction.
- Cooperative and competitive group situations.
- Congenial learning environment at home.
- Provision of proper change, rest and recreation.
- Provision of opportunity for creativity and self expression.

THEORIES OF LEARNING

What goes into the process of learning? How does an individual learn a set of facts and figures, skills, habits, interests, attitudes and similar other things in his life? Such questions have always been a subject of enquiry and investigation for psychologists and, as a result, a number of theories have come into existence. These theories may be broadly classified under two major heads: connectionist or behaviourist theories and cognitive theories.

Connectionist or behaviourist theories belong to the school of behaviourism. They interpret learning in terms of connection or association between stimulus and response. Under this category, we may include theories like Thorndike's theory of trial and error learning, Guthrie's continuity theory of learning, Hull's drive reduction theory of learning, classical and operant conditioning, etc.

Cognitive theories, on the other hand, belong to the school of Gestalt psychology and cognitive psychology. In place of a purely mechanical or instrumental approach these theories emphasize the role of purpose, insight, understanding, reasoning, memory and other cognitive factors in the process of learning. Under this category, theories like the theory of insightful learning, Lewin's field theory of learning, Tolman's sign learning, etc. may be included.

Let us now discuss these behaviourist and cognitive theories of learning.

Trial and Error Theory of Learning

The famous psychologist Edward L. Thorndike (1874–1949) was the initiator of the theory of trial and error learning based on the findings of his experiments on chickens, rats and cats.

In one of his experiments, for instance, he put a hungry cat in a puzzle box. There was only one door which could be opened by correctly manipulating a latch. A fish was placed outside the box. The smell of the fish acted as a strong motive for the hungry cat to come out of the box. The situation is described by Thorndike himself as:

"*It tries to squeeze through every opening; it claws and bites at the bars or wires, it thrusts its paws through any opening and claws at everything it reaches*". In this way, it made a number of random movements and in one of the random movements, the latch was manipulated accidentally. The cat came out and got its reward (see Figure 13.2).

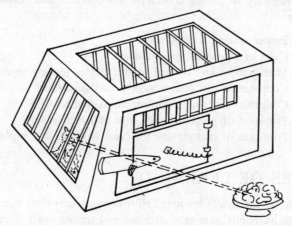

Figure 13.2 An illustration showing Thorndike's cat trying to come out.

In another trial, the process was repeated. The cat was kept hungry and placed in the same puzzle box. The fish and its smell again worked as a motive for it to get out of the box; it again made random movements and frantic efforts. But this time, it took less time to come out. In subsequent trials such incorrect responses, biting, clawing and dashing were gradually reduced and the cat took less time on each succeeding trial. In due course, it was in a position to manipulate the latch as soon as it was put in the box. In this way, gradually, the cat learned the art of opening the door.

The experiment sums up the following stages in the process of learning:

1. *Drive.* In the present experiment it was hunger and was intensified by the sight of the food.

2. *Goal.* To get at the food by getting out of the box.

3. *Block.* The cat was confined in the box with a closed door.

4. *Random movements.* The cat persistently tried to come out of the box without knowing how.

5. *Chance success.* As a result of this striving and random movements the cat, by chance, succeeded in opening the door.

6. *Selection* (of proper movement). Gradually, the cat recognised the correct way to manipulate the latch. It selected the proper way of manipulating the latch out of its random movements.

7. *Fixation.* At last, the cat learned the proper way to open the door by eliminating all the incorrect responses and fixing only the right response. Now it was able to open the door without any error or in other words, learned the correct way of opening the door.

Based upon the experiments mentioned above the major theoretical principles which form the basis of Thorndike's theory of learning are summarized in the discussion which follows.

Learning involves trial and error or selection and connection. Thorndike named the learning of his experimental cat as "trial and error learning". He maintained that learning is the stamping in of the correct responses and stamping out of the incorrect responses through a process of trial and error. In trying to find the correct solution, the cat made many false attempts. It committed error upon error before it hit upon the correct move. In the subsequent trials, it tried to avoid the erroneous moves and to repeat the correct manner of manipulating the latch. Thorndike termed this as learning by selecting and connecting as it provides an opportunity for the selection of the proper responses and to connect or associate them with adequate stimuli.

Learning is the result of the formation of connections. According to Thorndike, learning is the result of the formation of a connection in the nervous system between the stimuli and the responses. Thorndike (1931) writes *that Learning is connecting. The mind is man's connection system.* He believes that there is a definite association between sense, impression, impulse and action. This association is named a bond or connection. Since it is the strengthening or weakening of these bonds or connections, which results in the making or breaking of habits, Thorndike's system is sometimes called "bond psychology" or just "connectionism".

Learning is incremental, not insightful. Through his experiments Thorndike concluded that learning performance is dependent upon the number of trials or opportunities fulfilled by the learner. As we go on increasing the number of trials or practice, our performance gradually improves. Thorndike termed such improvement in performance as *incremental* and so concluded that learning is always *incremental.* It occurs a little bit at a time rather than all at once as is the case in the process of learning explained by the theory of insightful learning. Learning, according to Thorndike, needs several attempts and trials and then occurs in small systematic steps rather than in huge jumps. The solution of a problem does not strike the mind of the animal at once and the time an animal needs to find a solution to a problem depends upon the number of opportunities (trials) it gets to solve it.

Learning is direct, not mediated by ideas. Thorndike did not acknowledge any role to cognition in the process of learning. He asserted that learning is direct and is not mediated by thinking, reasoning or other such mental functions. He maintained that learning is a simple, semi-mechanical phenomenon, a process of establishing a simple connection between sensory stimuli and the appropriate responses and does not involve mediation by any ideas, reasoning or thinking. Exemplifying his views Thorndike (1911) writes.

> The cat does not look over the situation, much less think it over, and then decide what to do. It bursts out at once into the activities helped by instincts and experiences.

Thorndike's Laws of Learning

Thorndike propounded the following laws of learning on the basis of his theoretical notions about the learning process.

1. *The law of readiness.*

> When any conduction unit is ready to conduct, for it to do so is satisfying. When any conduction unit is not in readiness to conduct, for it to conduct is annoying. When any conduction unit is in readiness to conduct, for it not to do so is annoying.

This law is indicative of the learner's state to participate in the learning process. Readiness, according to Thorndike, is preparation for action. It is essential for learning. If the child is ready to learn, he learns more quickly, effectively and with greater satisfaction than if he is not ready to learn. This shows us not to force the child to learn if he is not ready but to also not miss any opportunity of providing learning experiences if the child is prepared to learn. The right moments concerning the learning situation and the learner's state of mind should be recognized and maximum use should be made of this knowledge by the teacher. He should also make an attempt to motivate the students by stimulating their attention, interest and curiosity.

2. *The law of effect.* In the words of Thorndike:

> When a modifiable connection between stimulus and response is made and is accompanied or followed by a satisfying state of affairs, that connection's strength is increased. When made and accompanied or followed by an annoying state of affairs, its strength is decreased.

In other words, learning can be said to have taken place properly when it results in satisfaction and the learner derives pleasure from it. In the situation when the child meets failure or is dissatisfied, the progress of learning is blocked. All pleasant experiences have a lasting influence and are remembered for a long time, while the unpleasant ones are soon forgotton. Therefore, the satisfaction and dissatisfaction, pleasure or displeasure resulting from a learning experience decides the degree of its effectiveness.

This law emphasizes the role of rewards and punishment in the process of learning. Getting a reward as a result of some learning motivates and encourages the child to proceed with increased intensity and enthusiasm while punishment of any kind discourages him and creates a distaste for that learning.

Revised law of effect. Based upon his later researches Thorndike, after 1930 realised that his law of effect was not really correct. He found that while a pleasant or satisfying situation resulted in the strengthening of the connection between stimulus and response, an unpleasant or annoying situation did not necessarily decrease the strength of this connection. From this he concluded that while reinforcements in the form of reward or incentives increase the strength of the S-R connection, unpleasant experiences in the form of pain or punishment do not necessarily weaken it. Thorndike's views regarding the effectiveness of negative measures like punishment in the breaking of undesirable habits and behaviour modification revolutionized the task of rearing and education of children.

3. *The law of exercise.* This law has two sub-parts: the law of use and the law of disuse which may be stated as:

The law of use.

When a modifiable connection is made between a situation and response that connection's strength is, other things being equal, increased.

The law of disuse.

When a modifiable connection is not made between a situation and response, during a length of time, that connection's strength is decreased.

As will be seen, the law of use refers to the strengthening of a connection with practice and the law of disuse to the weakening of connection or forgetting when the practice is discontinued. It can be said in short, that the law of exercise as a whole emphasizes the need for repetition.

Revised law of exercise. After 1930, Thorndike revised not only the law of effect but also the law of exercise. Further work and experiments on the law of exercise demonstrated that both the laws of use and disuse do not work as effectively as propounded by him earlier. He later held that use in the shape of mere repetition does not result in effective strengthening of the connection, nor does the disuse or lack of practice result in the total weakening of the connection. Mechanical use or disuse, therefore, does not necessarily lead to effective learning or total forgetting. Thorndike may thus be said to have discarded the law of use and disuse after 1930.

All these three laws—the law of readiness, the law of effect, and the law of exercise—are significant in many kinds of learning in our life. The laws may be applied to the following proverbs and maxims: "You can lead a horse to the water but you cannot make it drink." "Nothing succeeds like success." "Practice makes a man perfect".

In addition to the laws of readiness, exercise and effect, Thorndike's idea of connectionism led to the enunciation of the following important laws:

1. *Law of multiple response or varied reactions.* This law implies that when an individual is confronted with a new situation he responds in a variety of ways trying first one response and then another before arriving at the correct one.

2. *Law of attitude.* Learning is guided by a total attitude or 'set' of the organism.

The learner performs the task properly if he has developed a healthy attitude towards the task.

3. *Law of analogy.* An individual responds to a new situation on the basis of the responses made by him in similar situations in the past, i.e., he makes responses by comparison or analogy.

The law of analogy propounded by Thorndike led to his famous "identical elements theory" of the transfer of learning or training which states that transfer from one situation of learning to another depends upon the extent and number of elements or components which are common to both situations. It also matches the concept of generalization according to which the similarity of the learning situations or elements increases the likelihood of similar responses.

4. *Law of associative shifting.* This law states that "Any response may be elicited from the learner, of which he is capable, in association with any situation to which he is sensitive". In other words, any response which is possible can be linked with any stimulus. Thorndike clarified his stand through an experiment in which he demonstrated how a cat can be trained to stand up on command. To begin with, a piece of fish is dangled before the cat while you say 'stand up'. After a number of trials, a stage would come when it would not be necessary to show the fish. The oral signal or command alone will then evoke the response. The idea elaborated by this law gave birth to a new theory of learning, known as the *theory of conditioning.*

Thorndike's contribution in the field of learning. Thorndike's theory of trial and error is of great significance in the field of education. It explains the process of learning among animals and human beings on the basis of actual experiments. Not only human learning but animal learning also follows the path of trial and error. A child when confronted with a mathematical problem, tries several possibilities before he arrives at the correct solution. Even discoveries and inventions in the various fields of knowledge are the result of the trial and error process.

For example, Archimedes was confronted with a problem set by his Emperor. There was a 'drive' in that he would be beheaded if he failed to find the solution to the problem. There was a 'block' in that he could not think of any solution. The problem was difficult. He went on experimenting and made a number of attempts (trials) to solve the problem. One day, while having a bath, he met with accidental success and this led to the formulation of the law of floating bodies.

Excessive indulgence in the methods of trial and error, without caring for the development a logical line of thought should not, however, be encouraged under any circumstances. We cannot reduce human learning to a mechanical and random process as advocated by this theory. It must be supported by reason, understanding and insight. Trials and practice coupled with insight, will make the process of learning more effective than either of the methods adopted singly.

Thorndike's laws of learning carry some useful implications. These are:

1.   If one wants to learn something, one should prepare oneself for it by first understanding fully its importance. An instructor or a teacher, on the other hand, in order to teach effectively, must try to prepare the learner by bringing the mechanism of motivation into play.

2. Whatever we want to learn or teach, we must first identify the aspects which are to be remembered and those which may be forgotten. After this, we may try to strengthen the links or connections between the stimuli and responses of those things which are to be remembered, through repetition, drill and reward. For forgetting, the connections should be weakened through disuse and unpleasant results.
3. What is being taught or learnt at any one time should be linked with the past experiences and learning on the one hand and with the future learning on the other, in order to benefit from the mechanism of association, connection or bonds in the process of learning.
4. The learner should try to see the similarities and dissimilarities between the different kinds of responses to stimuli and by comparison and contrast try to apply the learning from one situation to another similar situations.
5. The learner should be encouraged to do his task independently. He must try various solutions of the problem before arriving at the correct one. But in every case he should be careful not to waste his time and energy by proceeding blindly and repeating his mistakes.

In short, Thorndike's theory of trial and error learning and his laws of learning have been a significant contribution to the field of learning. It has made learning purposeful and goal-directed and has emphasized the importance of motivation. It has also given an impetus to drill and practice and highlighted the psychological importance of rewards and praise in the field of learning.

Theory of Classical Conditioning

While studying the functioning of the digestive system, a Russian psychologist named Ivan Pavlov (1849–1936) encountered an unforeseen problem: the dogs in his experiment salivated not only upon actually eating but also when they saw the food, noticed the man who usually brought it, or even heard his footsteps. Pavlov began to study this phenomenon, which he called 'conditioning'. Since the type of conditioning emphasized was a classical one—quite different from the conditioning emphasized by other psychologists at the later stage—it has been renamed classical conditioning. To understand the nature of the process of conditioning, let us discuss the type of experiments performed by Pavlov.

In one of his experiments, Pavlov kept a dog hungry for a few days and then tied him to the experimental table which was fitted with certain mechanically controlled devices. The dog was made comfortable and distractions were excluded as far as it was possible to do so. The observer himself remained hidden from the dog but was able to view the experiment by means of a set of mirrors. Arrangement was made to give food to the dog through an automatic mechanism. He also arranged for a bell to ring every time food was presented to the dog. When the food was put before the dog and the bell was rung, there was automatic secretion of saliva from the mouth of the dog. The activity of presenting the food accompanied with the ringing of the bell was repeated several times and the amount of saliva secreted was measured (see Figure 13.3).

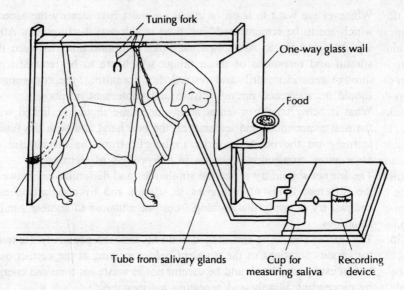

Figure 13.3 Diagrammatic view of the experiment conducted by Pavlov
(Garrett, General Psychology, p. 254).

After several trials the dog was given no food but the bell was rung. In this
case also, the amount of saliva secreted was recorded and measured. It was found
that even the absence of food (the natural stimulus), the ringing of the bell (an
artificial stimulus) caused the dog to secrete the saliva (natural response).
Diagrammatic representation of the experiment is given in Figure 13.4.

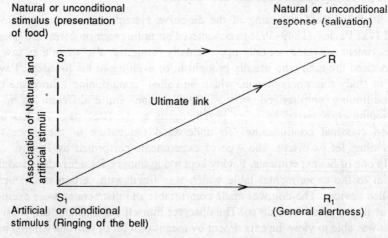

Figure 13.4 Diagrammatic representation of Pavlov's experiment.

The above experiment thus brings to light four essential elements of the
conditioning process. The first element is a natural stimulus, technically known
as unconditioned stimulus (US), i.e., food. It results in a natural response called
the unconditioned response (UR). This response constitutes the second element.

The third element is the artificial stimulus, i.e., the ringing of the bell which is technically known as a conditioned stimulus (CS). It is substituted for the natural stimulus (food). To begin with, the conditioned stimulus does not evoke the desired response, i.e., the conditioned response (CR). The fourth element is the chain of the conditioning process. However, as a result of conditioning, one learns to produce behaviour in the form of a conditioned response to a conditioned stimulus.

The theory of conditioning as advocated by Pavlov, thus, considers learning as habit formation and is based on the principle of association and substitution. It is simply a stimulus-response type of learning where in place of a natural stimulus like food, water, sexual contact, etc., an artificial stimulus like the sound of the bell, sight of light of a definite colour, etc., can evoke a natural response. When both the artificial or natural stimulus (ringing of the bell) and the natural stimulus (food) are brought together several times, the dog becomes schooled or conditioned to respond to this situation. A perfect association occurs between the types of stimuli presented together. As a result, after some time, the natural stimulus can be substituted or replaced by an artificial stimulus and this artificial stimulus is able to evoke the natural response.

John Watson and the Theory of Conditioning

John Watson (1878–1958), the father of behaviourism, supported Pavlov's ideas on coditioned responses. Through his experiments, Watson tried to demonstrate the role of conditioning in producing as well as eliminating emotional responses such as fear.

In one of his experiments, Watson took an eleven month old child named Albert as his subject. The baby was given a rabbit to play with. The baby liked it very much and was pleased to touch its fur. He carefully observed the pleasant responses of the baby. After some time, in the course of the experiment, as soon as the baby touched the rabbit, a loud noise was produced to frighten the baby. The loud noise was repeated every time he tried to touch the rabbit, and this gave rise to a fear response. After some time the baby began to fear the rabbit, even when there was no loud noise when it touched the rabbit. In this way, the baby learned to fear the rabbit through conditioning.

In another experiment, a child named Peter who was afraid of rabbits was used as a subject. At first, the rabbit was placed at a distance from the boy so that it would not pose a threat, but gradually on each successive day, the distance was reduced. Eventually, the rabbit was placed on the table where Peter was eating and then on his lap. Having associated the rabbit with the pleasure of eating, the child lost his fear and began to touch its fur and play with it. Thus through a simple treatment of conditioning the child learned not to fear the rabbit.

From these experiments, Watson, Pavlov and other concluded that all types of learning can be explained in terms of the process of conditioning. What this process is can be understood through the following conclusion:

It is a learning process whereby an artificial or conditioned stimulus is able to function like a natural stimulus when both natural and artificial stimuli are presented together. In this kind of learning, association plays a major role since the individual responds to an artificial stimulus because he associates it with the natural stimulus.

The conditioning theory of learning put forward by Watson and Pavlov actually involves the conditioning of respondent behaviour through a process of stimulus association and substitution. Here the responses of the learner become so conditioned—behaving in the same way or responding similarly to similar situations—that he no longer needs the natural stimuli to evoke the related natural response. As a result, the new substituted stimulus behaves like an original stimulus and is able to evoke the desired response.

Principles of Classical Conditioning

The theory of classical conditioning emphasized by Pavlov and Watson gave birth to a number of important concepts and principles in the field of learning such as:

1. *Extinction.* It was noted by Pavlov that if the conditioned stimulus (ringing of the bell) is presented alone a number of times without the food, the magnitude of the conditioned response of salivation begins to decrease, and so does the probability of its appearing at all. This process of gradual disappearance of the conditioned response or disconnection of the S-R association is called extinction.

2. *Spontaneous recovery.* It was also discovered by Pavlov that after extinction, when a conditioned response is no longer evident, the behaviour often reappears spontaneously but at a reduced intensity. This phenomenon—the reappearance of an apparently extinguished conditioned response (CR) after an interval in which the pairing of conditioned stimulus (CS) and unconditioned stimulus (US) has not been repeated—is called spontaneous recovery. The process of spontaneous recovery shows that somehow, the learning is suppressed rather than forgotten. As time passes, the suppression may become so strong that there would, ultimately be no further possibility of spontaneous recovery.

3. *Stimulus generalisation.* Pavlov's dog provided conditioned response (Salivation) not at the sight of the food but to every stimulus like ringing of the bell, appearance of light, sound of the footsteps of the feeder, etc. associated with its being fed. Similarly Watson's boy Albert showed fear not only of touching a rabbit but also of the mere sight of a rabbit, a white fur coat and even Santa Claus whiskers. Responding to the stimuli in such a generalized way was termed as stimulus generalization with reference to a particular stage of learning behaviour in which an individual once conditioned to respond to a specific stimulus is made to respond in the same way in response to other stimuli of similar nature.

4. *Stimulus discrimination.* Stimulus discrimination is the opposite of stimulus generalization. Here, in sharp contrast to responding in a usual fashion, the subject learns to react differently in different situations. For example, the dog may be made to salivate only at the sight of the green light and not of the red or any other. Going further, the salivation might be elicited at the sight of a particular intensity or brightness of the green light but not at any other. In this way, conditioning through the mechanism of stimulus discrimination one learns to react only to a single specific stimulus out of the multiplicity of stimuli and to distinguish and discriminate one from the others among a variety of stimuli present in our environment.

Implications of Classical Conditioning

In our day to day life, we are usually exposed to simple classical conditioning. Fear, love and hatred towards an object, phenomenon or event are created through conditioning. A father who, when he comes home from office, always rebukes and punishes his child without caring to know the basic reasons may condition his child to fear him, or develop anxiety reactions at the time of his return to home. The child may further develop a feeling of hatred towards his father or even discontent and a hostile attitude towards his home. Similarly, a teacher with his defective methods of teaching or improper behaviour may condition a child to develop a distaste and hatred toward him, the subject he teaches and even the school environment. On the contrary, affection, a loving attitude and sympathetic treatment given to the child by the parents at home or by the teachers at school may produce a desirable impact on him through the process of conditioning.

Most of our learning is associated with the process of conditioning from the beginning. A child learns to call his father 'daddy', his mother 'mummy', and his dog 'Montu' through the process of conditioning, i.e. stimulus—response association and substitution. As a result of stimulus generalization, he may attribute the name of daddy to all adult males, mummy to all adult females and call all dogs by the name Montu. Gradually, he comes to the stage of stimulus discrimination and then learns to discriminate and recognise and attribute different names to different persons, animals and objects. This phenomenon of stimulus generalization and discrimination goes on up to quite a late stage in our life. Often we meet a person and dislike him or her at first sight merely because that individual reminds us of someone else we do not like. We do not like to mix with the people belonging to another faith, religion or caste and often develop a feeling of hatred and animosity towards them even if we have not directly had any unpleasant experience.

What is termed as abnormality in one's behaviour may, to a great extent, be taken as learned. This learned pattern of one's behaviour is acquired through conditioning. For example, a child may be conditioned to develop fear or dislike of dogs. He may become so frightened of dogs after being bitten by one that he is reluctant to venture out alone. In a more complex case, a young woman who has had several unfortunate encounters with the adult males may become so conscious in the presence of any adult male that she is unable to have normal social relations with them leave alone satisfactory sexual ones.

Thus, much of our behaviour in the shape of interests, attitudes, habits, sense of application or criticism, moods and temperaments, is fashioned through conditioning. The process of conditioning, not only helps us in learning what is desirable but also helps in eliminating, avoiding or unlearning of undesirable habits, unhealthy attitudes, superstitions, fear and phobias through deconditioning. An individual who hates a particular person or object may be made to seek pleasure in their company. Another individual who thinks it is a bad sign if a cat crosses his path can be made to give up his superstitious belief.

Operant Conditioning

Although classified and included in the category of conditioning operant conditioning differs significantly from the classical conditioning advocated by Pavlov and Watson. The most outstanding difference lies in the order related with the initiation and response, i.e., stimulus-response mechanism. In classical conditioning the organism is passive. It must wait for something to happen for it to respond. The presence of a stimulus is essential to evoke a response. The behaviour cannot be initiated in the absence of a cause. The child expresses fear only when he hears a loud noise, the dog waits for food to arrive before salivating. In each such instance, the subject has no control over the happening. He is made to behave in response to the stimulus situations. Thus, the behaviour is said to be initiated by the environment, the organism simply responds.

Skinner revolted against the no stimulus–no response mechanism in the evolution of behaviour. He argued that in practical situations in our life, we cannot always wait for things to happen in the environment. Man is not a victim of the environment. He may often manipulate the environment with his own initiative. Therefore, it is not always essential that there must be some known stimuli or cause for evoking a response. Quite often, most of our responses cannot be attributed to the known stimuli. The organism itself initiates the behaviour. A dog, a child, or an individual 'does' something, 'behaves' in some manner, and 'operates' on the environment which is turn responds to the activity. The environment is responding to the activity, rewarding or otherwise largely determines whether the behaviour will be repeated, maintained or avoided.

A question which may be asked at this stage is, from where did Skinner get the cue for such ideas? Definitely, it was from the studies and observations of an earlier psychologist named Edward Lee Thorndike. Through his experiments, for propagating his famous trial and error theory of learning Thorndike concluded that the rewards of a response (like getting food after a chance success through the random movements) leads to repetition of an act and the strengthening of S-R associations. These conclusions made Skinner begin a series of experiments to ascertain the consequences of the rewards in terms of repetition and maintenance of behaviour. Based on the findings of his experiments, he concluded that *"behaviour is shaped and maintained by its consequences. It is operated by the organism and maintained by its results"*. The occurrence of such behaviour was named operant behaviour and the process of learning, that plays a part in learning such behaviour, was termed by him as operant conditioning.

For understanding the basis of Skinner's theory of operant conditioning, let us define and explain some of the concepts used by him.

Respondent and Operant Behaviour

As we have seen, the earlier theories of learning assumed the existence of a known stimulus as a necessary pre-requisite for evoking a response. Skinner, at first, put forward the idea that most of the responses could not be attributed to the known stimuli. He defined two types of responses—the one "elicited" by known stimuli which he called "respondent behaviour" and the other "emitted" by the unknown stimuli which he called "operant behaviour". Examples of respondent behaviour may include all reflexes such as jerking one's hand when jabbed with a pin and the constriction of the pupils on account of bright light or salivation in the presence of food.

In respondent behaviour, the stimulus preceding the response is responsible for causing the behaviour. On the other hand, the stimulus causing operant behaviour is unknown and knowledge of the cause of the behaviour is not important. Here, the consequences of the behaviour are of greater significance and operant behaviour is controlled by the strength of its consequences rather than by the stimuli. Some common examples of such behaviour may include the arbitrary movement of one's hands, arms or legs, a child abandoning one toy in favour of another, eating a meal, writing a letter, standing up and walking about and similar other every day activities.

Operant. Skinner considers an operant as an act which constitutes an organism's doing something, e.g., raising the head, walking about, pushing a lever, etc.

Reinforcer and reinforcement. The concept of reinforcement is identical to the presentation of a reward. A reinforcer is the stimulus the presentation or removal of which increases the probability of a response being repeated. Skinner recognizes two kinds of reinforcers—positive and negative.

A positive reinforcer is any stimulus such as food, water, sexual contact, etc. the introduction or presentation of which increases the likelihood of a particular behaviour. In the educational context, praise, grades, medals, and other prizes awarded to students are examples of positive reinforcers.

A negative reinforcer is any stimulus the removal or withdrawal of which increases the likelihood of a particular behaviour. An electric shock, a loud noise, etc. are said to be negative reinforcers. In the educational context, one example may be a teacher's saying to the students that whoever does drillwork properly in the class would be exempted from homework.

Negative reinforcers and punishment. These two terms should not be taken to have the same meaning. Whereas reinforcers, positive as well as negative strengthen behaviour, punishment weakens it. Punishment has consequences which are not reinforcing or, do not strengthen behaviour and aims at reducing behaviours by imposing unwelcome consequences. On the other hand, negative reinforcers, on the other hand, strengthen desirable behaviour by withdrawing unpleasant experiences. Here it should be noted that for a measure to be called a punisher it should invariably seek to reduce the frequency of a behaviour by the imposition or introduction of unpleasant consequence. For example, in the case of a student who feels pleased about being outside the class instead of feeling bad, to turn him out of the class would not act as a punisher or a means of behaviour modification. Similarly, for students who like being scolded because it gains them their teacher's attention and/or enhances their status among their peers, the scolding instead of working as a punisher is likely to prove to be a reinforcer of their behaviour.

The Schedules of Reinforcement

Skinner put forward the idea of planning of schedules of reinforcement for conditioning the operant behaviour of the organism. Some important schedules are:

1. *Continuous reinforcement schedule.* This is an out and out reinforcement schedule where provision is made to reinforce or reward every correct response of the organism during acquisition of a learning. For example a student may be rewarded for every correct answer he gives to the questions or problems put forth by his teacher.

2. *Fixed interval reinforcement schedule.* In this schedule the organism is rewarded for a response made only after a set interval of time, e.g., every 3 minutes or every 5 minutes. How many times he has given correct responses during this fixed interval of time does not matter; it is only at the expiry of the fixed interval that he is presented with some reinforcement.

3. *Fixed ratio reinforcement schedule.* In this schedule the reinforcement is given after a fixed number of responses. A rat, for example might be given a pellet of food after a certain number of lever presses. A student may be properly rewarded after he answers a fixed number of questions say 3 or 5. The fixed ratio schedule is used in some factories, and by employers of casual workers or labourers where wages are paid on a piece-work basis, i.e., the number of garments sewn or the number of baskets or boxes packed.

4. *Variable reinforcement schedule.* When reinforcement is given at varying intervals of time or after a varying number of responses, it is called a variable reinforcement schedule. In this case, reinforcement is intermittent or irregular. The individual does not know when he is going to be rewarded and consequently he remains motivated throughout the learning process in the hope of reinforcement. The most common example of such a schedule in human behaviour is the reinforcement operation schedules of gambling devices. Here rewards are unpredictable and keep the players well-motivated through occasional returns.

Conclusions about the Various Reinforcement Schedules

Reinforcement and its schedules play a key role in the conditioning of operant behaviour and acquisition of a learning. Where a continuous reinforcement schedule increases the response rate, the discontinuation of reinforcement may result in the extinction of that response or behaviour. A continuous reinforcement schedule, thus, yields the least resistance to extinction and the lowest response rate during learning. Learning of a response, therefore, occurs quickly if every correct response is rewarded, but it is forgotten easily when the reinforcement is stopped. If reinforcement is given after a varying number of correct responses or at varying intervals of time, the response is remarkably resistant to extinction. However, the fixed interval reinforcement schedules are found to provide the lowest yield in terms of performance as the individual may soon learn to respond correctly only when the time or turn of reinforcement arrives. Similarly he may lose interest in getting reinforcement after a fixed interval or fixed number of correct responses.

Weighing all these properly, Skinner suggests a 100 per cent schedule to begin with followed by a fixed interval or fixed ratio schedule to finally arrive at the variable reinforcement schedule for better results in learning or training.

Defining Operant Conditioning

Operant conditioning refers to a kind of learning process where a response is made more probable or more frequent by reinforcement. It helps in the learning of operant behaviour, the behaviour that is not necessarily associated with a known stimulus.

Distinction between Classical and Operant Conditioning

Classical or respondent conditioning is based on respondent behaviour. Specifically, it deals with responses that invariably follow a specific stimulus and are thus elicited, e.g. blinking at a bright light, jumbling at an electric shock, salivation to the taste of food, and so forth. In this greater importance is attached to the stimulus for eliciting the desired response. That is why it is also called a type S conditioning.

On the other hand, operant conditioning helps in conditioning or learning of operant behaviour—behaviour that is emitted (rather than elicited). The organism seems to initiate operant behaviour on his own without a single, explicit, preceding stimulus. In this type of learning, much emphasis is placed on the response rather than the stimulus causing the response. This is why, it is also named as type R conditioning. In type S conditioning, the problem with the trainer or teacher is to select appropriate stimuli for evoking desired response. On the other hand in R type conditioning, out of many responses which an organism is capable of giving, the problem with the trainer or teacher is to evoke only the appropriate responses and then fix them properly with the help of suitable reinforcement.

The difference between these two types of conditioning thus, may be summarized as below:

Classical respondent conditioning	*Operant conditioning*
1. It helps in the learning of respondent behaviour.	1. It helps in the learning of operant behaviour.
2. It is called type S conditioning to emphasize the importance of the stimulus in eliciting desired response.	2. It is called type R conditioning because of the emphasis on the response.
3. In this type of conditioning beginning is being made with the help of specific stimuli that bring certain responses.	3. Here beginning is made with the responses as they occur "naturally" or if they do not occur naturally, shaping them into existence.
4. Here strength of conditioning is usually determined by the magnitude of the conditioned response, i.e., the amount of saliva (as in the case of the classical experiment of Pavlov with the dog).	4. Here strength of conditioning is shown by the response rate i.e. the rate at which an operant response occurs as a result of some reinforcement.

Skinner's Experiments Regarding Operant Conditioning

B.P. Skinner conducted a series of experiments with animals. For conducting the experiments with rats, he designed a special apparatus known as Skinner's Box. It was a modified form of the puzzle box used by Thorndike for his experiments with cats. The darkened sound proof box has a grid floor, a system of light or sound produced at the time of delivery of a pellet of food in the food cup, a lever and a food cup. It is arranged so that when a rat (hungry or thirsty) presses the lever, the feeder mechanism is activated, a light or a special sound is produced and a small pellet of food (or small amount of water) is released into the food cup. For recording the observations of the experiments, the lever is connected to a recording system which produces a graphical plotting of the number of lever presses against the length of time the rat is in the box.

In one of his earlier experiments, Skinner placed a hungry rat in the above described box. In this experiment, pressure on the bar in a certain way by the rat could result in the production of a click and emergence of a food pellet. The click sound acted as a cue or signal to the rat that if it were to respond by going to the food cup, it would be rewarded. The rat was rewarded for each proper pressing of the lever. The lever pressing response having been rewarded, the rat repeated it and was again rewarded which further increased the probability of the repetition of the lever pressing response and so it continued. In this way, ultimately the rat learned to press the lever as desired by the experimenter (see Figure 13.5).

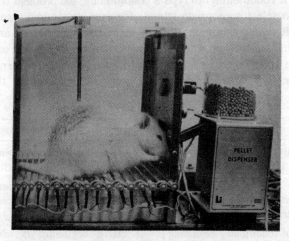

Figure 13.5   A rat in a Skinner Box.

In his experiments with pigeons, Skinner made use of another specific apparatus called the pigeon box. A pigeon in this experiment had to peck at a lighted plastic key mounted on the wall at head height and was consequently rewarded with grain (see Fig. 13.6).

With the help of such experiments, Skinner put forward his theory of operant conditioning for learning not only the simple responses like pressing of the lever but also for learning the most difficult and complex series of responses.

Figure 13.6 A pigeon in an operant conditioning chamber. (In this set-up pecking is the response, the key is the discriminative stimulus, and grain is the reinforcer).

Mechanism of Operant Conditioning

Operant conditioning as emphasized earlier is correlated with operant behaviour. An operant is a set of acts that constitutes some action of an organism. Hence, the process of operant conditioning may start with the responses as they occur naturally or at random. In case they do not occur naturally, then attempts may be made to bring them about. How it can be done is explained later in this chapter under the heading "Shaping".

Once a response as desired by the trainer, experimenter or teacher occurs, it is reinforced through a suitable reinforcer (primary or secondary and positive or negative). In course of time, this response gets conditioned by being constantly reinforced. In Skinner's experiment a pellet of food acted as a positive primary reinforcer for the hungry rat who got the reinforcement after it emitted a certain response (pressing the lever as desired by the experimenter). The secondary reinforcement may also produce the same results as brought about by the primary reinforcement. It is a sort of neutral stimulus which acquires the reinforcing properties (rewarding value) after getting paired or associated with a primary reinforcer (e.g., food or water). The clicking sound and the lighting of a bulb in Skinner's experiment may act as secondary reinforcement if they are coupled with the appearance of a pellet of food.

The important thing in the mechanism of operant conditioning is the emitting of a desired response and its proper management through suitable reinforcement. Here the organism responds in a certain way so as to produce the reinforcing stimulus. The subsequent reinforcement gradually conditions the organism to emit the desired response and thus learn the desired act.

Shaping. There are situations, specially in case of the acquisition of complex behaviour and learning of difficult skills, in which there may be a very remote chance of random occurrence of the responses in a specific or natural way. In such cases, waiting for an organism to behave in a specific way at random (the natural occurrence) may take a lifetime. For example, the chances of a pigeon to dance in a particular manner are extremely remote. The same holds true for a child learning a foreign language or even table manners. In these situations, where the desired responses do not occur at random (or naturally) efforts are directed at eliciting the appropriate responses. This is done by building a chain of responses through a step by step process called "shaping".

In one of his experiments for shaping the behaviour of a pigeon—to teach it to walk in a figure of eight—Skinner watched its activity and gave it a small amount of grain as reward whenever it moved in the proper direction. At first, the pigeon was given the reward for simply turning its head in the right direction, then for taking a step in the right direction, then for making a correct turn, and so on, until it had learned to walk a complete figure of eight.

Shaping in this way, may be used as a successful technique for training individuals to learn difficult and complex behaviour and also for introducing desirable modifications in their behaviour. Behaviour modification techniques and aversive therapy used in treating problem behaviours and abnormality have come into existence through the shaping of the behaviour mechanism.

Chaining. 'Chaining' refers to a process in the shaping of behaviour and the learning of a task where the required behaviour or task is broken down into small steps for its effective learning and subsequent reinforcement. It is a sort of chain reaction where one object sparks the other object in its proximity and that in turn causes sparking in the next object in the chain and so on. In behavioural terms, chaining starts when one response brings the organism into contact with stimuli that both reward the last response and cause the next response. That response in turn causes the organism to experience stimuli that both, reward the response and cause the next response, and so on. The starting of conversation between people is an example of chain behaviour. When we see someone we know, it is an effective stimulus for starting the chain responses. We greet him and he greets in response. His response to our greeting acts not only as a reward for our greeting but also as a stimulus for generating further response, e.g. shaking hands or receiving with outstretched arms, and in this way one generated response gives birth to another response and so on, i.e. behaviour which consists of a chain of responses.

Discrimination and cueing. When you pick up your telephone and hear the dial tone, certain response to the dial tone makes you advance to pushing the buttons, for dialing a number or to stop making use of the telephone. These responses to the dial tone are said to be cues or signals indicating whether operant behaviour should be performed or omitted. Cues or signals thus indicate which behaviour will be reinforced and/which behaviour will be punished. In the Skinner box, the animal learns to press the lever when the light is on and not to press it when the light is off. The light thus becomes a cue or signal for the operant behaviour, i.e., the lever press response. Equipped with this learned signal or cue, the animal picks up the ability to discriminate between stimuli for emitting the learned response. In other words, the animal develops a *discriminative operant* which is an operant response extended to one set of circumstances but not to another.

Discrimination in Skinner's theory may thus be defined as a process of using cues, signals or information to determine when behaviour is likely to be reinforced and/or punished. The process of discrimination has wide applications in the field of instruction and behaviour modification. However, for helping the student learn to discriminate, due care should be taken to provide proper feedback on the correctness or incorrectness of his responses (based on the learned signals and cues).

Generalization. 'Generalization' refers to the ability of an organism dealing with the perception of, and response to, similar stimuli. A child demonstrates this ability when he successfully subtracts four apples from nine apples after learning to subtract four oranges from nine oranges. In this way, generalization may be understood in terms of a learning process where the organism learns to provide similar operant responses, to stimuli similar to but not the same as the training stimulus. In helping the children to learn appropriate generalization due care should be taken by the parents and teachers to reinforce the behaviour of the children only after they demonstrate the ability to generalize correctly. Over generalization like calling all four legged animals as cows should be immediately discouraged and they should be helped to learn correct generalization and discrimination for acquiring the proper concept of things and events surrounding them.

Implications of the Theory of Operant Conditioning

Theory of operant conditioning has revolutionized the field of training or learning by putting forward the following practical ideas and implications:

1. A response or behaviour is not necessarily dependent (contingent) upon a specific known stimulus. It is more correct to think that a behaviour or response is dependent upon its consequences. Therefore, for training an organism to learn a particular behaviour or response, it may be initiated to respond in such a way as to produce the reinforcing stimulus. The individual's behaviour should get the reward and he should in turn, act in such a way that he is rewarded again and so on. Therefore, the learning or training process and environment must be so designed as to create the minimum frustration and the maximum satisfaction in a learner to provide him with proper reinforcement for the desired training or learning.

2. The principle of operant conditioning may be successfully applied in behaviour modification. We have to find something which is rewarding for the individual whose behaviour we wish to modify, wait until the desired behaviour occurs, and immediately reward him when it does. When this is done, the frequency with which the desired response occurs goes up. When the behaviour next occurs, it is again rewarded, and the

rate of response goes up even further. Proceeding in this manner, we can induce the individual to learn the desired behaviour.

3. The development of human personality can be successfully manipulated through operant conditioning. According to Skinner:

We are what we have been rewarded for being. What we call personality is nothing more than consistent behaviour patterns that summarize our reinforcement history. We learn to speak English, for example, because we have been rewarded for approximating the sounds of the English language in our early home environment. If we happened to be brought up in a Japanese or Russian home, we would learn to speak Japanese or Russian because when we approximated sounds in that language, we would have been attended to or rewarded in some other way (Hergenhahn, 1976).

4. The theory of operant conditioning does not attribute motivation to internal processes within the organism. It takes for granted the consequences of a behaviour or response as a source of motivation to further occurrence of that behaviour. Food is a reinforcer to a rat or a pigeon. Knowledge of the correct response is reinforcement to a learner. Secondary reinforcers also prove very important sources of motivation for a learner. Verbal praise, positive facial expressions of the trainer or teacher, a feeling of success, high scores, good grades, prizes, medals and the opportunity to do work one likes are all good motivators. Operant conditioning, thus, provided an external approach to motivation.

5. Operant conditioning emphasizes the importance of schedules in the process of reinforcement of behaviour. In trying to impart or teach a particular behaviour, therefore, great care should be taken for the proper planning of the schedules of reinforcement.

6. This theory advocated the avoidance of punishment for unlearning the undesirable behaviour and for shaping the desirable behaviour. Punishment proves ineffective in the long run. It appears that punishment simply suppresses behaviour and when the threat of punishment is removed, the rate with which the behaviour occurs returns to its original level. Therefore, operant conditioning experiments suggested appropriate alternatives to punishment, in the form of rewarding appropriate behaviour and ignoring inappropriate behaviour, for its gradual extinction.

7. In its most effective application, the theory of operant conditioning has contributed a lot to the development of teaching machines and programmed learning. The theory of operant conditioning has shown that learning proceeds most effectively if:

(a) the learning material is so designed that it produces fewer chances for failure and more opportunities for success;

(b) the learner is given rapid feedback concerning the accuracy of his learning; and

(c) the learner is able to learn at his own pace.

The principles originating from operant conditioning have revolutionized the training and learning programmes. As a result, mechanical learning in the form of teaching machines and computer-assisted instructions have taken root in place of usual classroom instruction.

Theory of Insightful Learning

The views propagated by behaviourists in the form of an association between stimuli and responses for understanding learning faced great difficulty in explaining the learning process or behaviour involving higher cognitive abilities. The chance success through trial and error or association through connectionism and conditioning may account for simple acquisition of knowledge, skills, interests, habits and other personality characteristics, but is not sufficient to account for problem solving, creativity and acquisition of other similar cognitive behaviour including insight (learning that appears to come suddenly).

Dissatisfied with the approach of behaviourists, the cognitive psychologists tried to see learning as a more deliberate and conscious effort of the individual rather than a product of mere habit formation or a stimulus response machine-like mechanism. According to them, in a learning process, the learner does not merely receive or make responses to the stimuli, but definitely processes, i.e., interacts with and does something about what he receives and his response is determined by that processing.

Thinking along these lines, a group of German psychologists called gestalists and particularly Wolfgang Köhler originated a learning theory named insightful learning.

'Gestalt' is a German noun for which there is no English equivalent. So the term was carried over into English psychological literature. The nearest English translation of gestalt is 'configuration' or more simply an 'organised whole' in contrast to a collection of parts. Gestalt psychologists consider the process of learning to be a gestalt—an organised whole. The basic idea of the theory is that a thing cannot be understood by the study of its constituent parts but only by the study of it as a totality or whole.

Infact the focus of Gestalt theory has been the idea of grouping, i.e. characteristics of Stimuli cause us to structure or interpret a visual field or problem in a certain way. The primary factors that determine grouping are:

1. *Proximity* – elements tend to be grouped together according to their nearness.

2. *Similarity* – items similar in some respect tend to be grouped together.

3. *Closure* – items are grouped together if they tend to complete some entity and

4. *Simplicity* – items tend to be organized into simple figures according to symmetry, regularity and smoothness.

These factors, also called the laws of organisation, have been explained in the context of perception and problem solving by Gestalt psychologist.

In practical terms, gestalt psychology is primarily concerned with the nature of perception. According to it, an individual perceives a thing as a whole while the behaviourists and stimulus-response theorists define perception so as to make it analogous with the taking of a photograph. They hold that sensation comes prior to meaning and consider these two acts as separate. But the Gestalt Psychologists do not separate sensation of an object from its meaning. They are of the opinion that unless a person sees some meaning in an object he will pay little or no attention to it, what is more, to the gestalt psychologists, the meaning of sensation or perception is always related to the total situation. According to them perception always involves a problem of organisation. A thing is perceived as a relationship within a field which includes the thing, the viewer and a complex background incorporating the viewer's purposes and previous experience.

Gestalt psychologists tried to interpret learning as a purposive, exploratory and creative enterprise instead of trial and error or a simple stimulus-response mechanism. A learner, while learning, always perceives the situation as a whole and after seeing and evaluating the different relationships takes the proper decision intelligently. He always responds to the proper relationships rather than to specific stimuli. Gestalt Psychology used the term 'insight' to describe the perception of the whole situation by the learner, and his intelligence in responding to the proper relationships. Köhler (1925) used the term 'insight' first of all, to describe the learning of his apes. During the period 1913–1917, he conducted many experiments on chimpanzees in the Canary Islands and embodied his findings in his book (*ibid*). These experiments demonstrated learning by insight. Some of Köhler's experiments are now described.

1. In one experiment, Köhler put the chimpanzee, Sultan, inside a cage and a banana was hung from the roof of the cage. A box was placed inside the cage. The chimpanzee tried to reach the banana by jumping but could not succeed. Suddenly, he got an idea and used the box as a jumping platform by placing it just below the hanging banana.

2. In another experiment, Köhler made this problem more difficult and two or three boxes were required to reach the banana. Moreover, the placing of one box on the other required different specific arrangements.

3. In a more complicated experiment, a banana was placed outside the cage of the chimpanzee. Two sticks, one longer than the other, were placed inside the cage. One was hollow at one end so that the other stick could be thrust into it to form a longer stick. The banana was so kept that it could not be picked up by any one of the sticks. The chimpanzee first tried to reach out to the banana with these sticks one after the other but failed. Suddenly, the animal had a bright idea and joined the two sticks together and reached the banana (see Figure 13.7).

In these experiments, Köhler used many different chimpanzees. Sultan, who was the most intelligent of Köhler's chimpanzees, could solve all the problems. Other chimpanzees could solve the problems only when they saw Sultan solving them.

These experiments demonstrated the role of intelligence and cognitive abilities in higher learning such as problem solving. The apes, somewhat higher animals, did not resort to the blind trial and error mechanism adopted by Thorndike's cat or the simple habit formation as in the case of Pavlov's dog or Watson's Albert. They reacted intelligently by (a) identifying the problem,

Figure 13.7 Köhler's chimpanzee learns to assemble a long stick from two shorter ones.

(b) organising their perceptual field, and (c) using 'insight' (the term coined by Köhler) to reach a solution. Once the situation is perceived as a whole and the perceptual field is properly organised, a problem becomes solvable through flashes of insight.

In human beings we come across such learning a number of times on different occasions. For example, a student may suddenly discover that in the 9's table, the sum of the digits in the answer is always 9 (e.g., $9 \times 5 = 45$, $4 + 5 = 9$ etc.). The student's learning of a new meaningful relationship is then, a result of his insightful learning.

Though Köhler seemed to see insightful learning in terms of a sudden 'aha' or a bolt of lightening, it is found to depend upon factors such as:

- *Experience.* Past experience help in the insightful solution of problems. A child cannot solve the problems of modern mathematics unless he is well acquainted with its symbolic language.

- *Intelligence.* Insightful solution depends upon the basic intelligence of the learner. The more intelligent the individual, the greater will his insight be.

- *Learning situation.* How insightfully an individual will react, depends upon the situation in which he has been placed. Some situations are more conducive to insightful solution than others. As a common observation, insight occurs when the learning situation is so arranged that all the necessary aspects are open to view.

- *Initial efforts.* Insightful learning has to pass through the process of trial and error but this stage does not last long. These initial efforts in the form of a simple trial and error mechanism, open the way for insightful learning.

- *Repetition and generalization.* After obtaining an insightful solution of a particular type of problem, the individual tries to implement it in another situation, demanding a similar type of solution. The solution found in one situation helps him to react insightfully in other identical situations.

Implications of the Theory of Insightful Learning

The greatest contribution of the theory of insightful learning is that it has made learning purposeful and goal-oriented task. It does not involve simple reflexive or automatic machine-like responses. The learner has to be motivated by arousing his interest and curiosity for the learning process and he has to be well acquainted with the specific aims and purposes of the learning.

Moreover, the emphasis, in this theory, on the importance of viewing the situation as a whole has given birth to the important maxim, from the whole to the parts, in the field of learning. If a person wishes to learn or memorise a poem, it should be presented to him as a whole and after being read and understood as a whole, it may be broken into parts or stanzas for being effectively memorized. Similarly, a problem requiring solution should be considered as a whole and after being assessed as a whole, may be tackled for solution on a piecemeal basis.

The theory of insightful learning requires the organisation of the perceptual field and learning material in the form of a 'gestalt' i.e., a whole. Based on this phenomenon, we cannot treat any learning related to a subject or skill as merely a collection of isolated facts, informations or unrelated behavioural acts. This has made significant contributions in the organisation of the curriculum, scheme of studies, work-plan and procedure of planning the schedule of learning or teaching of a skill or a behaviour. What we see to-day in the form of an emphasis on unity and cohesiveness (in the form of gestalt) within the learning acts or experiences in any scheme of studies or learning is nothing but a pattern of learning borrowed from the gestaltist theory of insightful learning.

Guthrie's Contiguous Conditioning

Edwin Ray Guthrie (1886–1959), an earlier behaviourist, was professor of psychology at the University of Washington. While he was influenced by some of the theoretical findings of his contemporaries like selection, connection and associate shifting advocated by Thorndike and classical conditioning propagated by Watson and Pavlov, he took a quite distinctive stand in propounding his own theory of learning. He devised a new model of learning by synthesizing his idea of temporal contiguity (togetherness of stimulus and response) with the Pavolian model of classical conditioning.

The Guthrie-Horton Experiment

Guthrie tried to propagate his theory on the basis of a number of experiments on cats performed in collaboration with G.P. Horton by using a puzzle box (an apparatus similar to that used by Thorndike in his experiments). The experimental situation consisted of placing a cat in the box with a small pole in the middle of the box as a release mechanism. The cat could escape through a door by touching the pole from any side and in any manner. There was an arrangement of food for the cat outside the cage which it could reach after its release. Guthrie and Horton carefully observed approximately eight hundred escapes by a number of cats from a puzzle box and noted that each cat learned to escape from the puzzle box in its own manner. The specific response learned by a particular cat was the one that the cat had hit upon just before it escaped from the box. For example, if a cat used its paw to press the pole, it learned to use its paw in almost the same way for coming out whenever it was put in the box. They also noted that very often the cats after escaping from the box, would ignore the food that was offered to them. Inspite of their lack of interest in the food, however, they were just as quick in their escape from the box the next time they were placed in it irrespective of the way in which they were placed in it, the manner in which they sought their release was the same as was used by them for their first escape. The cats never tried new ways of release. This was referred to as stereotyped behaviour. On the basis of his experiments, Guthrie reached certain conclusions and laid down basic principles for explaining lerning behaviour. These conclusions and principles are discussed in detail in the following pages.

1. *Law of contiguity.* The law of contiguity proposed by Guthrie is the real corner-stone of his unique theory of learning. Guthrie asserted that all rules by which stimuli and responses become associated to give birth to any learning may flow from a single law, the law of contiguity. He gave two explanations for his law:

> A combination of stimuli which has accompanied a movement will on its recurrence tend to be followed by that movement (1952).
> What is being noticed becomes a signal for what is being done (1959).

According to these interpretations stimuli acting at the time of response tend to evoke that response on their recurrence and consequently if something has been done by us in a given situation, then in case we are provided again with that situation, we will tend to do the same thing. It happens on account of the formation of a close association between a stimulus or stimuli and the response and this association is formed on account of contiguity, i.e., the coming together of the stimulus (or pattern of stimuli) and a response.

2. *One trial learning.* Most behaviourists believe in the law of frequency which implies that learning is proportional to the strength of an association which in turn depends upon the frequency with which it has occurred. This is why Thorndike emphasized repetition and drill for a satisfactory state of affairs. Similarly, Watson and Pavlov also emphasized the repetition of the association between conditioned and unconditioned stimuli for the conditioning of a required response. In contradiction to these behaviourists, Guthrie (1942) completely rejected the law of frequency by saying:

A stimulus pattern gains its full associative strength on the association of its first pairing with a response.

In other words, there is no need for repetition of the S-R bond as the association develops its full strength and the learning becomes quite complete after only one pairing between the stimuli and the response. Guthrie thus emphasized one-trial learning in preference to the need for a number of trials for the establishment of an association. In other words, one experience or trial is sufficient to establish an association, i.e., learning.

3. *The recency principle.* Guthrie's theory also rests on the principle of recency which states that what was being done in the past in the presence of a set of stimuli will tend to be done next when that stimulus combination occurs.

4. *Movement-produced stimuli function.* Learning is the result of contiguity between a pattern of stimulation and a response. The stimuli present in one's environment and the responses one makes to them are, however, separated by a fairly long interval of time and, therefore, cannot be thought of as contiguous. There must definitely be some thing to fill in the gap or interval between the occurrence of an external stimulus and the response finally made to it. Guthrie explained this by inventing the term, movement-produced stimuli.

Movement-produced stimuli are those stimuli (distinctly different from the external stimulation that initially caused the movement) which are produced by the movement of our body and are responsible for conditioning the responses to elicit the desired behaviour. Thus, when a response is being initiated by an external stimulus, the body takes on the responsibility of producing the stimulus for the next response and that response can furnish the stimulus for the next one, in the shape of a chain reaction (chaining) for the movements in a desired direction. To throw light on the mechanism of movement-produced stimuli Guthrie (1935) writes:

Such a movement as listening or looking is not over like a flash or an explosion. It takes time. The movement, once started, maintains itself by the stimuli it furnishes. When the telephone bell rings we rise and make our way to the instrument. Long before we have reached the telephone the second has ceased to act as a stimulus. We are kept in action by the stimuli from our own movements toward the telephone. One movement starts another, then a third, the third a fourth, and so on—our movements form series, very often stereotyped in the form of habit. These movements and their movement-produced stimuli make possible a far reaching extension of association or conditioning.

5. *Learning of acts or behaviour.* Our behaviour may involve learning of many skills like driving a car, playing badminton, typing a letter, eating a meal, etc. A skill is made up of many acts and acts are made up of many movements which result from muscular contraction and it is these muscular contractions that are directly predicted by the principle of association. Therefore, learning of a skill or performing an act consists of learning thousands of associations between specific stimuli and specific movements.

While the learning of a single movement (requiring association between a specific stimulus and a specific response or movement) requires only one trial and its degree is not dependent on practice. For example, the skill of typing or playing badminton involves an enormously large number of specific S-R bonds each of which is learned in a single trial. Naturally, it will require time and practice for the establishment of all the necessary connections or bonds and we may therefore, conclude that learning of an act or skill needs practice and it is the practice which helps in attaining proficiency in performing an act or skill. The need of such practice can be better emphasized in the words of Guthrie and Horton (1946):

> Learning of an act does take practice. We assume that the reason for this is that the act names an end result that is attained under varied circumstances and by movements varied to suit the circumstances. Learning an act as distinguished from a movement does require practice because it requires that the proper movement has been associated with its own cues. Even so simple an act as grasping a rattle requires different movements according to the distance and direction and position of the object. One successful experience is not sufficient to equip the infant with an act because the one movement acquired on that occasion might never again be successful.

6. *Role of reinforcement or reward.* It was noticed by Guthrie in the behaviour of the cats that though they often ignored the food placed outside the box, this did not affect their proficiency in coming out of the box. This observation led him to disagree with Thorndike and re-define the role of reward or reinforcement. Reward or reinforcement according to him, is not an essential condition for the re-occurrence of the previous response. In other words, learning is not dependent on reinforcement of behaviour. The law of contiguity, accompanied by the recency principle, is enough to explain the learning behaviour. The animal is likely to repeat the preserved association between being in the puzzle box and moving the pole resulting in its release. Therefore, regardless of the food it gets after its release, the animal would try to repeat the last response which helped it to obtain its release.

Reward or reinforcement like food in this case, according to Guthrie, may simply work as a mechanical arrangement for changing the stimulating conditions and thereby preventing unlearning. In the words of Guthrie (1940):

> The animal learns to escape with its first escape . . . what encountering the food does is not to intensify a previous item of behaviour but to protect that item from being unlearned.

7. *Forgetting and extinction of behaviour.* According to Guthrie's conclusion, extinction or forgetting (weakening or disappearance of the association or bond between a stimulating condition and a response) occurs not due to non-reinforcement but due to the phenomenon of interference. He accepts an extreme form of retroactive inhibition (interference in old learning by new learning) to explain extinction and forgetting. According to him, for the extinction and forgetting of a wrong response of undesirable learning one is required to learn something new in such a way that the old learning is completely knocked out. According to Guthrie (1942):

> Forgetting is not a passive fading of stimulus-response associations contingent upon the lapse of time, but requires active unlearning which consists in learning to do something else under the circumstances.

8. *Role of punishment.* The role played by punishment in learning or forgetting a behaviour was also studied by Guthrie. He accepted the role of punishment in this situation but emphasized that punishment is effective only through its associations resulting in a new response to the same stimuli. In the words of Guthrie (1952):

> It is not the feeling caused by punishment, but the specific action caused by punishment that determines what will be learned. In training a dog to jump through a hoop, the effectiveness of punishment depends on where it is applied, front or rear. It is what the punishment makes the dog do that counts or what it makes a man do, not what it makes him feel.

In this way, punishment works not because it induces certain kinds of painful experiences but because it forces the organism to do something different and thus establishing inhibitory conditioning of unwanted habit resulting in a behaviour incompatible with the punished behaviour. For example, in punishment meted out to a dog which is in the habit of chasing your motorcycle, a slap on the nose or a slap on the rear is equally painful to the dog. However, the slap on the nose in this case would prove more effective because, the slap on the nose will tend to make him stop and jump backward in the presence of the motorcycle, resulting in incompatible behaviour. On the other hand, a slap on the rear will make him continue forward, perhaps with a little more speed and will thus fail in its purpose by eliciting a behaviour not incompatible with the punished behaviour.

Thus, for making punishment effective, we have to arrange things in such a way that stimuli that previously elicited an undesired response, now elicit an unwanted response (incompatible with the punished response) that can make the organism think of changing its ways of behaviour so that it may learn a favourable response, instead of an unfavourable one.

9. Motives and drives. On the basis of his studies, Guthrie concluded that motives and drives occupy an important place in the field of learning as they provide for the maintenance of stimuli for keeping the organism active until a goal is reached. For example, by being hungry or thirsty one is stimulated and this stimulated behaviour is maintained until one gets food or water. Similarly, when one is anxious to achieve a target it stimulates one and the stimulated behaviour is maintained until one gets what one aspires to in terms of money, success or recognition. Drives and motives are, therefore, not only physiological but also socio-psychological and external and in this way any source of stimulation, whether internal or external, capable of maintaining stimuli can be termed as a useful motive or drive for accelerating the movement of the organism to reach a goal.

10. Transfer of training. While rejecting the formal discipline theory outright, Guthrie's theory of learning gives some consideration to Thorndike's identical element theory of transfer. Therefore, according to it similarity between two situations may act as a deciding factor for the probability of a similar response in two situations. Guthrie's theory, however, asserts that transfer in two situations can only take place if the stimulating conditions in both the situations are identical and consequently on account of the variation in the stimulating conditions there is no guarantee that a child who learns something in his study room will be able to reproduce it in the classroom or examination hall.

Summary of Guthrie's Theory of Contiguous Conditioning

Guthrie's theory is based on a single law of learning, that is, the law of contiguity which states that when two events occur together, they are learned. In other words, learning is based on the association or connection between a stimulus and a response and this association occurs simply because of the contiguity, that is, occurrence of the stimulus and response together. For maintaining the chain of contiguity between the external stimuli and the responses finally made by us our body, through its movements, tends to produce the stimulus for subsequent responses in a chain-like mechanism. However, as far as learning in the form of establishing a bond between a stimulating situation and a response is concerned, it occurs in a single trial and this association tends to be continued until there is change in the stimulating conditions or a response is prevented from occurring. The association once made, on this bond once established, makes the organism exhibit the same response (usually in the form of the last movement which helped it to reach a goal like a cat hitting the pole in a particular way to escape from the box) in case it is faced with the same stimulating conditions and when this happens we say the organism has learned the way it should behave to attain its goal.

Contribution and Educational Implications of Guthrie's Theory of Contiguous Conditioning

Guthrie's theory based on a single law of contiguity has wide implications in the field of education:

1. Guthrie's emphasis that learning is complete after only one pairing between the stimuli and the response makes us take care in the organisation of stimulating conditions for eliciting the desired response.

2. The law of contiguity and the recency principle which emerged from this law require that in case we want to revoke a learned response we have to arrange for the occurrence of stimulating conditions identical to the ones in which the response behaviour has been learned. It makes us exercise caution in learning things in the way in which these are going to be utilized by us in the future. For example, if a student teacher is required to teach in the class after becoming a teacher, he must be trained in the actual classroom set up. Similarly, if a student has to be examined in a classroom laboratory or particular examination set up, he can be expected to do better only if he has been taught in conditions in which he is required to demonstrate his performance later on. It enables us to introduce radical changes in the teaching-learning materials, processes and conditions so that the associations made at the time of learning are utilized to the maximum at the time of utilization of the outcomes of learning. The school programme or the task of formal learning must be made so functionable and natural as to coincide with the real life settings so that what is learned at school may prove useful to the learner in real life.

3. Guthrie's theory lays stress on the need of drill and practice as this generates more and more stimuli for eliciting the desired behaviour. According to Guthrie, since learning is complete in terms of the establishment of an association between a stimulus and response, every learning in itself is a unique experience and its transfer from one situation to another cannot properly take place until the two situations are identical. As it is very difficult for stimulating conditions to be identical, we must make the child practise a behaviour under different stimulating conditions. For example, for learning addition of numbers like two and two the child should not learn only from the blackboard or in his note-book but must also learn it through making various associations (in the form of two and two equals four) with the help of concrete objects like chalks, books, pens, apples, etc. in the school or outside the school.

4. Guthrie believes in the interference theory and the mechanism of retroactive inhibition to explain the causes of forgetting. We must, therefore, make sure that the interference caused to the past learning by the new learning is avoided. For minimizing forgetting he advocates that what is being learned should be learned properly and the new learning should be so planned and associated that it may cause least interference to the past learning. A thing to be learned properly needs strengthening of the bond or association between stimuli and response when it is learned the first time. This may necessitate the following:

    (a) Since any behaviour is a complex of movements in response to a complex of stimuli, for evoking a desired response or making the child learn a particular behaviour we must have the support of as many stimuli as possible. The more the stimuli used for evoking a desired response, the less will be the likelihood of a interfering or distracting behaviour.

    (b) In order to evoke a desired response, we must look for all the ways and means for evoking that particular response. All types of drives, motives and means like rewards and punishment must be utilized for evoking and then intensifying the response.

5. Guthrie's theory provided valuable cues and ways for breaking bad habits. For this purpose, Guthrie outlined the following three different techniques:

1. *Threshold technique.* This technique according ot Guthrie (1938) consists of:

Introducing the stimulus at such weak strength that it will not cause the response and then gradually increasing the intensity of the stimulus, always taking care that it is below the 'threshold' of the response.

For instance, suppose there is a boy who does not like to take a bag full of books, note-books, etc. on his shoulder while going to school. If the mother puts the bag on his shoulder, he throws it down and insists that it should be carried by some servant. Now, the technique consists of first putting some eatables and objects of light-weight toys in the bag and ask him to carry it on his shoulder. If he carries it, then we can gradually increase the weights of these and finally replace these things with books and note-books etc. and so break his habit of not carrying the school bag himself.

2. *Fatigue technique.* The fatigue method consists in allowing an individual to perform the task concerning the bad habit repeatedly to the point that he becomes too tired to continue further and thus making him allergic to that task. For example, a little boy who is in the habit of tearing paper unnecessarily may be set right by being allowed or rather forced to tear papers to the point where the task is no longer fun. As a result, the paper will become a cue to doing something other than tearing them. As a result, the child will develop an attitude of avoidance.

3. *Incompatible response technique.* In this technique, an undesired response elicited by particular stimuli is inhibited by a simultaneous presentation of both types of stimuli, the one causing undesired response and the other a stronger stimulus producing a response which is incompatible with the undesired response. For example, if a child is afraid of a dog then he would be allowed to come close to the dog in the presence of his mother, a dominant stimulus for evoking warm relaxed feelings in the child. The pairing of dog and mother will create a feeling of relaxation in the child. Once such relaxation has been experienced by the child, it will pave the way for the child to face the dog alone (without pairing it with his mother) without showing any sign of fear.

All these three techniques can be safely employed by teachers and parents in the task of breaking bad habits as all of them are based on the following general rules:

    (a) first find the cues that are responsible for the undesired responses concerning the bad habit, and then

    (b) practice another response in the presence of these discovered cues for getting rid of the undesired response.

HEBB'S NEUROPHYSIOLOGICAL THEORY OF LEARNING

Donald Hebb, the renowned American psychologist, was initially a staunch believer in Watson's and Pavlov's associationistic points of view for the explanation of learning. But later on, he was greatly influenced by Karl Lashley, who was working at that time in the University of Chicago, and as a result changed his views and propounded a new theory of learning known as Hebb's neuro-physiological theory of learning.

Hebb's neurophysiological approach to learning, as would be seen in the discussion that follows, provides a solid physiological base to the process of learning. According to it the brain and the central nervous system play a key role in learning. Learning results from stimulation and activity of the neurons together with the ability of the brain to organise neural impulses. This approach is said to involve two different streams of thought: one arising from the influence of the S-R theories and the other emanating from the gestalt theories. The S-R influenced approach, often named as the switchboard approach, considers human central nervous system to be a passive switchboard made up of billions of tiny switch-like neurons producing overt responses to sensory inputs. The gestalt approach, on the other hand, advocates the organisational aspect of the brain for making the sensory information or input available to it, more meaningful before invoking an overt response. Let us elaborate some important theoretical aspects of Hebb's theory for understanding its basic nature, foundation and application in the field of education.

Major Theoretical Notions in Hebb's Theory: Formation of Cell Assembly and Development of Phase Sequence

The process of learning, according to Hebb, starts with the process of perception. When we perceive an object or a part of it in the environment, it causes a complex package of neurons (called a cell assembly) to be triggered by our focusing attention on it at a particular moment. The size of this cell assembly depends upon the object or event it represents. For example, the cell assembly related to the engine of a car would definitely be of a smaller number of neurons than the cell assembly of the whole car. However, in perceiving the object as a whole, the different aspects or parts of the same object become neurologically interrelated to form cell assemblies and the firing of the cell assemblies (the complex package of neurons) causes us to experience the thought of the object represented by them.

The subsequent development in one's learning, according to Hebb, is the formation of phase sequences. A phase sequence is a temporarily integrated series of cell assembly activities which when fired make us experience a stream of thought (logically arranged ideas in a sequence). About the development of such phase sequences in the child, Hebb (1972) states:

> Cell assemblies that are active at the same time become interconnected. Common events in the child's environment establish assemblies and then when these events occur together the assemblies become connected (because they are active together). When the baby hears footsteps, let us say, an assembly, is excited; while this is still active he sees a face and feels hands picking him up, which excites other assemblies—so that "footstep assembly" becomes connected with the "face assembly" and the "being picked up assembly". After this has happened, each time the baby hears footsteps only, all three assemblies are excited; the baby then has something like a perception of a mother's face and the contact of her hands before she has come in sight—but since the sensory stimulation have not yet taken place, this is ideation or imagery, not perception.

Types of learning.   According to Hebb, learning can be thought to be of two types. The one, resembling connectionism or associationism, functions on a lower level and is the result of the build up of all assemblies and phase sequences. This type of simple S-R learning can be satisfactorily explained through Guthrie's contiguous learning. The other functions on a relatively higher level are essentially more cognitive. It involves the organisational aspects of the brain and is characterised by insight and creativity. Here the club assemblies and phase sequence developed in the early period of one's life are subjected to rearrangement and desirable organisation for providing better meaning and understanding.

Arousal Level and Performance

Hebb's theory incorporated the arousal theory to explain performance in learning. This theory is concerned with the functioning of the reticular activating system (RAS)—an area located in the brain stem. According to Hebb, a sense receptor on being stimulated provides a neural impulse which in turn is said to perform the cue function as well as the arousal function. The cue function helps the organism to gain information about the environment. In the arousal function, the sensory impulses travelling through the spinal cord to the cortex trigger the RAS. Each increase in the RAS activity makes the level of arousal go higher and higher and this can be measured through an EEG. In general, the RAS prepares the high centre of the brain to receive and act upon environmental information picked up by our sense-receptors. This means that the level of arousal maintained by RAS is directly linked to the performance of an organism in terms of what it receives from the environment as sensory information and how it handles this sensory input. For better functioning and performance in learning, therefore, one has to maintain an optimal level of arousal through the activation of one's RAS. In case it remains low then one would be handicapped not only in receiving the sensory information in a proper way but also in its proper utilization. On the other hand, if it is too high, then it would led to the storing of too much sensory information for analysing by the cortex and thus will result in confusion, conflicting responses and irrelevant behaviour.

How necessary an optimal level of arousal (activated by RAS) is for the best performance in a particular task would depend upon the nature and difficulty level of that task. In general, as Hebb concludes, the difficult task performed in a challenging environment needs a much higher level of arousal in comparison to the simpler and interesting tasks. Therefore, one has to carefully plan for the optimal level of arousal provided by one's RAS in order to ensure a good learning performance in a particular task.

Arousal Level and Reinforcement

Hebb also used his arousal theory to explain the role of reinforcement in learning. Since one's performance is dependent upon the optimal level of arousal by RAS, the secret of the reinforcing behaviour essentially lies in maintaining this level in accordance with the nature of the task and the environment situation. For an individual who finds his arousal level too low, the reinforcement lies in the ways and means to increase it and for one whose arousal level is too high, the reinforcement and reward lies in its decrease. Hebb's theory thus equated increase and decrease in one's level of arousal (or in other words one's drive) with the provision of reinforcement for acquiring better results in one's performance in a particular learning situation.

Memory and Consolidation Theory

Hebb's learning theory threw light on the phenomena of retention, of learning experiences and memory by providing a theory called the consolidation theory. This theory, for the first time, proposed that short-term memory may be somehow translated into long-term memory. Explaining how it could happen, Hebb theorizes that short-term memory triggered by sensory stimulation and maintained by some continuous neural activity somehow causes a structural change in one's nervous system resulting in its consolidation or fixation and thus giving rise to long-term memory.

Through his new theory of learning, Hebb propounded a neurophysiological explanation for the occurrence of the phenomenon of perception, the mechanism of learning and its reinforcement, the performance level, retention of learning experiences in terms of short-term and long-term memory, etc. Its main contribution in the field of learning and education, thus lies in providing a new paradigm and dimension to the approach of learning in addition to what existed as workable paradigms in those days, namely connectionism, associationism and cognitivism.

HULL'S SYSTEMATIC BEHAVIOUR THEORY

Clark L. Hull (1884–1952), a teacher in the Universities of Wisconsin and Yale, is credited with putting forth a systematic mathematical and scientific theory of human behaviour based on conditioning and connectionism of the earlier behaviourists. He built his theory on a logical structure of postulates and theorems.

Hull's theory was first presented in 1943 in his major book '*Principles of Behaviour*'. This theory was extended in 1952 through his last book '*A Behaviour System*'. The system provided in this book for explaining human learning and behaviour consists of 17 postulates and 133 theorems. We shall discuss here a few major concepts and theoretical notions emerging from them.

1. *Change in the traditional S-R notion.* Hull rejected the Guthrie's contiguity approach as well as the S-R formula given by Thorndike. Guthrie emphasized only the contiguity, i.e., togetherness of the stimuli and response, for the formation of an association and Thorndike made it out to be mechanical, a trigger-like function of stimuli-response. Hull introduced the concept of intervening variables (the processes which are thought to be taking place within the organism but are not directly observable) between S and R. Accordingly, when a stimulus (S) impinges on the organism, it results in a sensory neural impulse (s) a kind of stimulus trace. This stimulus trace ultimately causes a motor neural reaction (r) that results in an overt response (R). Thus we may have the formula S-s-r-R instead of the traditional S-R.

However, there are so many other things within the inner mechanism of the organism like his interests, needs and drives and also the reinforcing mechanism that may influence his response or behaviour. Consequently, the traditional S-R formula in Hull's approach was extended to S-O-R incorporating all intervening variables existing between environmental stimulation and overt response.

2. *The concept of reinforcement and drive-stimuli reduction.* Hull maintained that the establishment of a simple S-R connection is not enough for learning. In this regard, he refuted Guthrie's claim that a learning is completed in a single trial. Instead, he maintained that it is stamped through a process of repeated reinforcement like getting food or avoiding pain, etc. However, Hull's reinforcement was different from that of Thorndike or Skinner. Whereas Thorndike used the 'law of effect' for stating his concept of reinforcement and Skinner called it anything that increases the probability of the re-occurrence of a response, Hull viewed it in terms of the reduction of one's need, drive or drive-stimuli. Drive, according to him may be referred to as a state of tension resulting from a need. For example, the thirst drive arises out of our body's need to take in water for its maintenance. If the response or reaction of the organism reduces the need or state of tension or drive, we then have a condition of reinforcement enabling the organism to repeat the S-R association and thus to habitually react in the same way in a particular situation.

Drive stimuli are stimuli that characteristically accompany a certain drive e.g., dryness of the mouth, lips and throat accompanying the thirst drive and hunger pangs accompanying the hunger drive.

During his work, Hull changed his stand twice from need reduction to drive reduction and finally to drive stimulus reduction for associating it with the task of reinforcement for the following two reasons:

1. It was experimentally observed that the behaviour of the hungry rats could be effectively reinforced by saccharine water which is sweet but utterly non-nutritive, i.e. not possessing the capacity to reduce the food need in the least. In this case according to Hull (1952):

   The ingestion of saccharine-sweetened water reduces hunger tension or hunger pains (drive stimulus associated with hunger drive) for a brief period sufficient for a mild reinforcement, much as the tightening of the belt is said to do in hungry men, thus reinforcing that act.

2. Reduction of a drive takes considerable time. For example, if we consider the thirst drive, it takes a long time for the water to go into the mouth, the throat, the stomach, the blood and the effect of its ingestion to be conveyed to the brain to reduce the thirst drive. Reduction of a drive stimulus is a relatively quick process that occurs soon or even immediately after the presentation of a reinforcer. Water is taken by the organism and it soon results in the reduction of the thirst drive stimuli (the dryness of the mouth, lips and throat). The behaviour is reinforced and thus the reinforcement of one's behaviour can be better explained through the concept of drive stimuli reduction than the drive reduction.

Hull thus considered the aim of reinforcement to be the reduction of the drive or drive stimuli. He thought reinforcement to be of two kinds—primary and secondary. Primary reinforcement tended to strengthen a certain behaviour through the satisfaction of basic biological needs, drives or drive stimuli. Secondary reinforcement, on the other hand, is brought about by an originally neutral stimulus like money by association with a primary reinforcing agent like food.

Habit Formation and Habit Strength

According to Hull, when a stimulus emits a certain type of response and it is accompanied by a reinforcer, (capable of reducing the drive or drive stimuli) the association between the stimulus and that response is strengthened. Repetition of the reinforcement, then helps to progressively strengthen the association thus formed. Eventually, it brings about an organisation in the nervous system known as 'habit' or a particular response to a particular stimulus and when this happens we say the behaviour is learned. In this way, Hull reduced learning to habit formation. The success of this learning behaviour is measured through a concept termed as habit strength and symbolized as sHr.

By definition Hull considers habit strength as the strength of the association between a stimulus and a response. It goes up with the number of trials (pairing between a stimulus and a response) provided there is a reinforcement in every trial.

Stimulus generalization. Another concept in Hull's theory is stimulus generalization. It means that if there are two or more similar stimuli, they can elicit the same or nearly the same response from the organism as was elicited by the original stimulus. For example, a child who fears a snake also fears a rope or any other thing which looks like a snake. Based on the characteristic of stimulus generalization, the habit strength sHr will generalize from one stimulus to another to the extent to which the two stimuli are similar. Hull provided the term 'generalized habit strength' symbolized as $s\bar{H}r$ to describe the generalization of habit strength through the phenomenon of stimulus generalization. With this type of the generalization of habit strength he tried to explain the phenomenon of transfer of training (on the lines of Thorndike's Identical Element Theory) by emphasizing that learning performed under similar conditions would be likely to be transferred to the new learning situation.

Reaction potential. Yet another concept elaborated by Hull is that of reaction potential. Reaction potential indicates the potential of an individual to react or respond. He defined it as the probability of the repetition of a learned response at any given moment and provided the following formula to explain its meaning and purpose.

$$\text{Reaction potential} = sEr = sHr \times D \times V \times K$$

where sHr represents the habit strength, D the drive, V the stimulus intensity, and K the incentive.

Accordingly, reaction potential is known to depend upon the following four factors:

1. Habit strength (sHr), i.e. how often the response was rewarded in a particular situation.
2. Strength of the drive (D), potentially present to energize the behaviour of an individual in that situation.
3. Stimulus intensity (V), i.e., the power or the intensity of a stimulus (such as big size, bright colours, loud or appealing sound, or any other strong attraction) to evoke a desired response.

4. The incentive (K), i.e., the degree of the attractiveness of a particular reward present in the situation.

Since all the above four factors are multiplied in contributing towards the building of a reaction potential, if any one had a value of zero, reaction potential would be zero. For example, there could have been many reinforcing pairings between S and R (producing habit strength sHr), but if drive (D) is zero, the organism is not able to detect the stimulus or if the reward or incentive is absent, a learned response will not occur (Hergenhahn, 1976).

Inhibition. Inhibition exercises a regressive effect on the reaction potential by decreasing or sometimes eliminating the possibility of the reoccurrence of a previously learned response. Let us study this concept in detail.

Hull describes two types of inhibitions, reaction inhibition symbolized as *Ir* and conditional inhibition symbolized as *sIr*.

Reactive inhibition is caused by long hours of work, the fatigue associated with muscular activity. It results in inhibition of further response. Reactive inhibition is caused by the internal physiological and biochemical nature of the individual and therefore varies from individual to individual. It causes reduction in the drive level as well as in the reaction potential of an individual to repeat a response or behaviour. The impact of fatigue, however, may vanish as a result of some rest or interruption of work and the inhibition caused on account of physiological factors like fatigue may also disappear. That is why there may be a spontaneous recovery of a learned response after extinction (the non-occurrence of a learned response due to reactive inhibition).

The other inhibition known as conditional inhibition is a result of learning and experience. It rests on psychological and environmental factors instead of internal and physiological factors.

Both of these two types of inhibition work together in exercising the overall effect of reducing or even eliminating the probability of the reoccurrence of a learned response. For example, if a child refuses to learn further, it may be the result of the reactive inhibition, the mental or physical fatigue caused by overwork in terms of learning or it may be the result of psychological or environmental factors such as his dislike of the subject, the method of teaching, the teacher, or other environmental conditions. Similarly, inhibitions may interfere in an individual's response during sex behaviour on account of reaction caused by internal and physiological factors or learned and conditioned inhibitions affected through psychological and environmental factors or by both these two types of inhibitions working together in a particular situation.

Effective reaction potential. Inhibitions, reactive and conditioned, both tend to reduce the level of one's reaction potential. They result in the effective reaction potential symbolised as $s\overline{E}r$. It can be expressed in terms of the following equation:

$$\text{Effective reaction potential } s\overline{E}r = (sHr \times D \times V \times K) - (Ir + sIr)$$
$$= \text{Reaction potential} - \text{Inhibition}$$

Momentary effective reaction potential. In the course of his experiments Hull observed that many of the learned responses were seen to be elicited on some trials but not on others. This led him to present the concept of an oscillation effect symbolized as *sOr*.

He asserted that it happens on account of the variation brought about in the inhibitory potential of an individual from moment to moment depending on several internal and external factors. This continuously changing inhibitory potential was named 'oscillation effect' and was given due weightage in defining the momentary effective reaction potential of an individual for producing a learned response at a particular moment in the following way:

Momentary effective reaction potential

$$s\bar{\bar{E}}r = [(sHr \times D \times V \times K) - I] - sOr$$

This momentary effective reaction potential is responsible for the occurrence of a learned response. Hull provided the following postulates for describing the characteristics of the momentary effective reaction potential in relation to the emittence of a learned response.

1. The value of momentary effective reaction potential must exceed a certain value called reaction threshold (*sLr*) in order to emit a learned response.
2. The probability of a learned response (*p*) is increased to the extent that the value of the momentary effective reaction potential is higher than the value of the reaction threshold.
3. The greater the value of momentary effective reaction potential ($s\bar{\bar{E}}r$), the shorter will be the latency, i.e., the reaction time between the presentation of a stimulus and the elicitation of a learned response.
4. The larger value of the momentary effective reaction potential increases the power of resistance for the extinction of a learned response, i.e., it requires a greater number of non-reinforced responses for extinction.
5. The magnitude of an emitted learned response termed as amplitude (*A*) is directly related to the size of the momentary effective reaction potential.

Summary of Hull's System of Learning

What we have discussed so far about Hull's system of learning, can be systematically summarized as shown in Table 13.1.

Contributions and Educational Implications of Hull's System of Learning

Hull's system of learning is acclaimed and remembered for putting forward a most systematic, scientific and mathematical theory of learning. Hull was able to popularize a very innovative and objective behaviouristic approach to learning which was more effective in comparison to the approach of his predecessors. The significant contributions and educational implications of his theory can be briefly summarized as:

Table 13.1 Hull's System of Learning

Processes	Symbols	Constructs
Reception	Ⓢ ↓	Physical stimulation (external stimulation)
	s	Sensory neural impulse
Interaction	↓	
	r	Motor neural reaction
Summation	↓	
	sHr	Habit strength
Generalization	↓	
	$s\bar{H}r$	Generalized habit strength
		$sHr \times D$ (Drive) $\times V$ (stimulus
Motivation	↓	intensity $\times K$ (incentive)
	sEr	Reaction potential
	|	$sEr - (Ir + sIr)$
		Reactive Conditioned
Inhibition	↓	inhibition inhibition
	$s\bar{E}r$	Effective reaction potential
Oscillation	↓	($s\bar{\bar{E}}r - sOr$)
	$s\dot{\bar{E}}r$	(Momentary effective reaction
Elicitation	↓	potential
	Ⓡ	— A (amplitude of the response)
	Reaction or ⟵	— sTr (response latency)
	response	— n (trials to extinction)
Reinforcement	↓	— p (probability of a response)
	Ⓖ	
	Goal response	
	(reinforcing state of affairs)	

1. Hull's theory rejected the trigger-like mechanism of stimuli-response advocated by Thorndike and introduced the concept of intervening variables between S and R. The things within the individual definitely act and react with what is received in terms of stimuli from the external environment before emitting of an overt response. Hull provided the amended S-O-R formula in place of the traditional S-R approach. He termed the environmental influences upon the individual as 'inputs', and his responses as 'outputs', and what goes from the individual as 'processes'. He asserted that 'input' and 'output' can be measured experimentally and, therefore, behaviour in its processes and products can be subjected to experimental verification.

2. Hull's theory attached sufficient importance to the needs, drives, incentives, reinforcement and adequate motivation for achieving satisfactory results in the process of teaching and learning.

The greatest contribution of Hull's theory lies in its emphasis on linking the learning to the needs of the children. He says that it is the need, drive or drive stimuli that energise an individual to act, behave or learn. Therefore, he advocated the need-based goals of education, including need-based curricula and methods of teaching.

Whereas needs start the process of learning, reinforcement and incentives act as catalytic agents for increasing one's efforts towards achieving the goals of learning. Therefore, in any education process we must involve sufficient possibilities of proper motivation and reinforcement incentives.

3. Hull's theory tried to extend the concept of reinforcement. Prior to this, reinforcement was considered only in terms of rewards and satisfaction but Hull stated that to escape pain or punishment or to reduce need is also a kind of reward and helps in reinforcement.

4. Hull's theory laid great emphasis on the formation of good habits as a means of the learning of desirable behaviour. In practice, Hull reduced the art of learning to mere habit formation and its proper reinforcement. It brought into prominence the role of adequate practice, drill and strengthening of reinforcement. However, he preferred an increase in the number of trials or reinforcement to an increase in the proper quantum of reinforcement and thus advocated continuous and gradual intro-duction of small doses of reinforcement rather than one, single heavy dose.

5. Hull's theory brought into focus the fact that different individuals have different capacities. It presented a systematic and mathematical treat-ment of individual differences. Hull attributed individual differences to the variation of the values of numerical constants in the equations in the postulates. He believed that some numerical constant varied from species to species, from individual to individual and from one physio-logical states to the other in the same individual. If a group participates in a learning situation and everything else is kept constant through experimental controls, then the constant should change in a systematic way from different age groups of the learners. For any group of learners, the constant should not change when identical conditions are introduced. Such views propagated by Hull's theory emphasized the need for planning education according to the individual differences of the learners keeping their respective ages in mind.

6. Hull's theory emphasized the need for proper rest and other measures to reduce the ill-effects of fatigue in any act of learning. The principle of work and appropriate rest, may thus be said to have evolved as a result of the experimental findings of this theory.

7. Hull's theory stood against any inhibition-causing obstacle in the path of learning or emitting the desired response. It stressed the prime need of minimising or removing all types of inhibitions, internal or physiological and external or learned, for achieving good results in the process of teaching and learning or obtaining the desired behaviour in an individual. In a practical class room situation, therefore, a teacher has to be very careful in the proper distribution of the drill and practice work so as to avoid unnecessary fatigue and the resulting inhibition.

Similarly, the principle of change and variety in terms of subjects, teachers and class-rooms etc. may be introduced for bringing down the ill-effects of boredom and fatigue.

8. Hull's system of learning advocated the following chain sequence for improved results in the teaching-learning process:

   (a) *Drive.* This is something which is needed by the learner in order to behave or respond.

   (b) *Cue.* There must be something to which the learner must respond.

   (c) *Response.* The learner must be made to respond or do something in order to learn some act.

   (d) *Reward.* The learner's response must be reinforced or rewarded, thus enabling him to learn what he wants to learn.

Lewin's Field Theory of Learning

Kurt Lewin (1890–1947), a German psychologist eventually settled in the U.S.A., put forward a theory named Lewin's Field Theory in the year 1917. It was based on his doctoral dissertation.

Perception is the key issue in Lewin's theory of learning. It takes learning to be a process of perceptual organisation or reorganisation of one's life space or field involving insight. In addition to the field theory, his system of description is also known as topological psychology or vector psychology. Let us now try to explain some basic concepts utilised by Lewin in propounding his theory.

Topology. Topology is a branch of mathematics which deals with the relative position of geometrical figures in a space. Lewin used the topological concepts for representing the structure of life space in such a way as to define the range of possible perceptions and actions. This can be achieved by showing the arrangement of functional parts of the life space as several regions and their boundaries. While structuring or reorganising one's life space one does it through its division into regions or boundaries.

Vector. The term 'vector' was borrowed by Lewin from mechanics and used for representing a force capable of influencing movements towards or away from a goal. In case there is only one vector (force), then the movement must be in the direction of the vector but if there are two or more vectors (forces) simultaneously acting in different directions, then the resultant vector arising out of the vectors in action will decide the direction and magnitude of movement towards or away from the goal.

Life space. The life space of a person is also known as the psychological field. This field, although influenced and conditioned by one's physical and social environment, cannot be identified with that environment. It is one's psychological world or the space in which one moves psychologically. It contains the totality of one's psychological reality—one's self and what one thinks of or what one gains from one's physical and social environment for determining one's behaviour in a given situation. The life spaces of two persons in an indentical situation may be entirely different. A snake in the corner of a room, not perceived by a person does not exist in his life space, while for his companion, who perceives it, the snake exists. Therefore, one's life space is the space in which one lives psychologically involving one's own perception and depicting one's own view-point. It includes each and every object, person, or idea with which one is concerned at a given time.

The individual in his life space. The individual in his life space represents his totality, mind, body and all that is essential for him to behave as a complete individual in a given situation. It represents his psychological self expressed as 'I', 'my', 'mine', 'me', etc. Diagrammatically, the person may be represented as a point moving about in his life space, affected by pulls and pushes and overcoming the barriers to reaching his goal.

Valence. Lewin describes two types of valences operating in one's life space. When a person is attracted by an object that object is said to have a positive valence. On the other hand, when a person is repelled by an object, the object is said to possess a negative valence. The person is pulled toward a region in his life space along the direction of the positive valence while he tends to move away from a region in his life space that has a negative valence.

Cognitive structure. Lewin used this term as synonymous to insight. It represents the perceptual field or environment including the person as known and understood by the person.

In the light of these concepts and terminology, let us now enumerate what has been conveyed by Lewin's field theory.

Learning—Meaning and Nature

According to Lewin, learning is a relativistic process by which a learner develops a new insight or changes the old views. The development of this new insight or change in the old views can be explained through the structuring or restructuring of one's life space, i.e., the cognitive structure or field of one's perception and understanding. According to Lewin learning therefore, is nothing but a change in one's cognitive structure which is needed for achieving a particular goal or to meet the requirements or needs of an individual in a particular situation.

Lewin's field theory also states that learning is a process responsible for making the life space or field of perception as differentiated as possible. Initially, the life space of a child is less differentiated but as he grows up and learns more, his life space or field of perception becomes more and more differentiated. It gradually becomes more structured and its scope is widened. It shows more sub-regions in it which are connected by well-defined paths. In other words, he begins to make distinctions between reality and unreality at different levels of his life space and to try to act with the knowledge of what leads to what.

Learning and Problem Solving

In problem solving behaviour, a problematic situation faced by an individual represents an unstructured region of his life space. He does not know how to solve the problem or reach the goal. Consequently, he may feel insecure thus giving rise to tension and the need for resolving this tension. This may activate the individual to organise or reorganise the regions of his life space or, in other words, to work for the structuring of his life space or reorganising his field of perception to devise a new insight and understanding to solve his problem. When this is done, the problem can be solved and the method for solving the problem can thus be learnt.

Learning and Repetition

Learning is a required change in one's cognitive structure and this change may occur with repetition, i.e., the situation may require repeated exposures for the required change in the structure to take place. However, it is possible to bring about the required change in the structure with fewer repetitions. In fact, the better organisation and structuring of life space in a particular problematic situation requires new insight or change in the old one instead of mere repetition. Accordingly, the field theory stands against repetition, practice and drill work in the manner advocated by Thorndike and others. According to this theory, excessive repetition does not aid learning. On the contrary, it may lead to a psychological situation with accompanying disorganisation and de-differentiation of the cognitive structure.

Elicitation of Behaviour

How one behaves, is explained by the field theory. The perception of an object or event may give rise to a psychological tension (e.g. desire). Consequently, one may be attracted towards the goal (achieving the desired object). There may also arise some barrier—opposing physical and psychological forces, in the way of the achievement of the goal. Let us assume, for example, that the goal is to gain social recognition and the barrier consists in tendering an apology. The person himself, his goal (+ve valence), the thing he is avoiding (–ve valence), the barrier restricting his movements etc. depicting his life space in this situation may be expressed as in Figure 13.8.

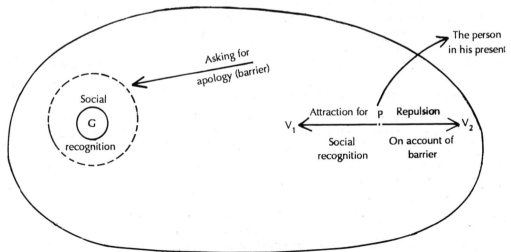

Figure 13.8   Life space of an individual—elicitation of behaviour.

With all the available forces in this situation acting on the individual, he is supposed to structure his life space into an appropriate pattern to achieve the desired goal and consequently his future behaviour will depend on his ability to structure his life space. In case V_1 (the valence representing the attraction of social recognition is greater than V_2 (the valence representing repulsion on account of the barrier of apologising to the group) then the person will structure his life space in such a way as to act for reconciliation with the members of the group by overcoming the barrier, but if $V_2 > V_1$ the person will seek ways and means to remain isolated or cut off from the group.

Motivation

Lewin's theory attaches much importance to motivation in the process of teaching and learning. Lewin takes motivation as attraction towards a goal and clarifies its meaning through the role of valences, the level of aspiration, needs and aroused tension.

1. The perception of an object or event may give birth to a psychological tension (i.e., desire). This, in turn, gives rise to valences (attraction and repulsion of perceived goal objects) acting as environmental forces leading to a motivated behaviour for the satisfaction or resolution of tension.

2. Attractive goals may lose their attraction and motivation may cease if the activity related to them is repeated to the point of satiation.

3. An originally unattractive goal may become attractive through a change in significance of the goal-related activity to the individual. Educational statistics, for example, may seem quite difficult and unattractive to some student teachers but subsequent practice and the possibility of scoring good marks through it may make it look easy and attractive.

4. The choice of goals and attraction toward them is highly influenced by one's previous experiences of success or failure.

5. The level of aspiration also determines one's motivation toward learning in order to reach a particular goal. However, according to Lewin, it should be fixed at a reasonable level as too high or too low a level of aspiration may become a hurdle to arousal of the desired motivation.

Rewards and Punishment

Lewin's theory highlighted the role of both rewards and punishment, in the process of teaching and learning. It also warned against their excessive and improper use. According to Lewin a student, tempted by the rewards may resort to improper methods like cheating in the examination. He, therefore, advocates the putting up of some barriers over the reward situation for avoiding resort to such short-cuts. Punishment should also be carefully introduced as there is a likelihood of the individual withdrawing because of the unpleasantness introduced by the punishment. The activities controlled by the threat of punishment tend to become fearful and abhorred and it is, therefore, the reward which should always be highlighted rather than the punishment.

Success and Failure

What constitutes success or failure in a task for an individual can be explained properly in terms of Lewin's field theory. It says that success or failure, from the psychological angle, depends upon one's ego involvement, the level of aspiration and the psychological satisfaction and resolution of one's aroused tension. Accordingly, success in an easy task may not be a success experience since it does not involve the ego of the person. In the same manner, failure in a very difficult task may not be a failure experience. If we take a broader view, psychological analysis of success on the part of a learner may show the following varied possibilities:

1. Reaching a goal may constitute a success.
2. Getting within the region of the goal may constitute a success experience. For example, a person may lay emphasis on "M.A. appeared" as by doing so he thinks himself to be within reach of the goal.
3. Making some progress in the direction of the goal may also constitute a success experience e.g., if one clears the preliminary examination for the IAS, it may bring one an intense success experience.
4. Selecting a socially approved goal may also in itself constitute a success experience irrespective of the progress and efforts made by the individual for reaching the goal.

The efforts and the results, which provide a success experience to an individual, thus vary in degree depending upon the psychological make-up of the individual.

Memory. Regarding memory and remembering, the field theory put forward the following conclusions:

1. Tasks which do not serve any worthwhile purpose in their completion are not remembered.
2. Ego-involved tasks are retained better than those tasks where ego is not involved.
3. Unsatisfied tasks are remembered better than the finished tasks because of the psychological tensions.
4. Tasks which are linked with the satisfaction of many needs are remembered better than the tasks which lead to the satisfaction of only one need.

Conflicts. Arousal of various types of conflicts in the field theory has been explained with the help of the concepts of negative and positive valences in the form of opposite and almost equal forces operating at a time in the regions of one's life space. Mainly the theory has specified three types of conflicts.

1. *Approach-approach conflict.* This type of conflict, is diagrammatically represented in Figure 13.9.

Here two almost equally strong and equidistant positive valences give birth

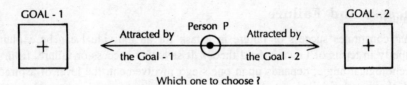

Figure 13.9 Approach-approach conflict.

to the approach-approach type of conflict. This type of conflict arises in situations like the child having to choose between watching a movie of his choice on the video or going on a picnic with his class-mates.

2. *Avoidance-avoidance conflict.* In such conflicts as depicted in Figure 13.10, two almost equally strong and equidistant negative valences work to force the individual to leave the field or escape from the situation. An example of such a conflict is the avoidance of home-work as well as of punishment by a child.

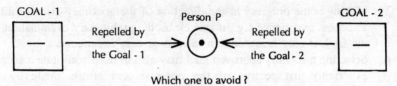

Figure 13.10 Avoidance-avoidance conflict.

3. *Approach-avoidance conflict.* Here, as depicted in Figure 13.11, the person is equally attracted and repelled by the same goal for the desire to attain some object. This type of conflict may arise in the case of a child who is attracted to run a sack race on account of the announced prize for every participant against his not wanting to participate for fear of spoiling his new dress.

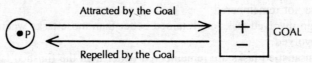

Figure 13.11 Approach-avoidance conflict.

Tolman's Sign Learning

Edward Chace Tolman (1886–1959), an American psychologist propounded a theory of learning in 1932 with the publication of his work *Purposive Behaviour in Animals and Men.* His theory known as Tolman's sign learning or sign-gestalt learning stands midway between the behaviouristic S-R theories and cognitivistic gestalt or cognitive field theories.

His system, known as purposive behaviourism has its roots in behaviourism in the sense that (a) it recognizes the initiation of behaviour through stimulus stimulation, (b) it is opposed to the psychology of consciousness and rejects introspection as a method of studying behaviour, (c) it believes in behaviourism's objective methods of collecting data and interested in precise measurement of behaviour and (d) it has faith in the modification of human behaviour.

Cognitive theorist Tolman has serious differences with the behaviourists on the simple ground of their machine-like approach to human behaviour. He compared the S-R learning system with the operational activities of a telephone exchange—"incoming calls from sense organs" and "outgoing messages to muscles". However, learning according to him, is not so simple an activity undertaken through simple S-R connections of a telephone switch-board but involves complex cognitive activities helped by the brain processes. In his own words:

> (The brain) is far more like a map control-room than it is like an old-fashioned telephone exchange. The stimuli which are allowed in, are not connected by just simple one-to-one switches to the outgoing responses. Rather, the incoming impulses are usually worked over and elaborated in the central control room into a tentative, cognitive like map of the environment. And it is this tentative map, indicating routes and paths and environmental relationships, which finally determines what responses, if any, the animal will finally release (1948).

Main Thoughts and Concepts Propagated by Tolman's Sign Theory

Molar vs. *molecular approach.* Tolman's theory adopted the molar approach in the systematic study of behaviour instead of the molecular approach adopted by the behaviourists like Watson, Skinner, Guthrie and Hull. The chief characteristics of molar behaviour are that (a) it is purposive i.e. always directed toward a goal, (b) it is not mechanical and stereotyped like a spinal reflex and (c) it constitutes a gestalt (a whole or complete) instead of the mere parts or individual "twitches" from which it is supposed to be built up. Consequently, Tolman emphasized studying of behaviour as a complete purposeful exercise, i.e., achievement of the act like a rat running through a maze, a man driving home to dinner, a child hiding from a stranger, etc., instead of studying these acts in the form of certain sequences of muscle twiches.

Presence of intervening variables. Tolman's theory in fact, for the first time in the history of psychology, introduced and highlighted the role of intervening variables. These variables lie midway between the independent variable (stimulus) and the dependent variable (response). Heredity, previous learning, age, special endocrine, drug or vitamin conditions, physiological drives, environmental stimuli, etc., are all examples of intervening variables which, although not objectively observed, are said to be the strong determinants of behaviour. Which type of intervening variable will prove more effective, depends upon the individuality of the individual as well as his internal conditions and psychological state. Sometimes certain innate tendencies and motives like curiosity, exploration and manipulation prove stronger than the physiological drives like hunger. This fact was demonstrated by Tolman through his experiments in which hungry rats were found to take a longer journey through a maze to their food if the longer route happened to be more interesting.

Concept of cognitive maps and sign-gestalts.   Tolman put forward his concept of map-making and sign-learning on the basis of experiments in which rats placed in a complicated maze with food at the end of it were able to find new routes when their initial routes were blocked. They did it not for making simple S.R. connections and repeating the stereotype responses as 'turn left' or 'turn right' but by constructing a mental map of their environment. Actually, what they did was to use their mental or cognitive abilities to lay out a mental map or picture of their environment to recognize what was available to them in a given situation for achieving their goal. Mental mapping, thus, constituted a sort of mental representation or the setting up of certain mental hypotheses in the search for new routes and ways and then testing these hypotheses through intelligent and purposeful behaviour.

In our day to day life, we also make use of such mental mapping to find new ways and solve problems in our daily life by demonstrating our ability to use any of the "many roads to Rome".

In such mental mapping we certainly demonstrate that learning is not a simple routine type S-R mechanism but a process of discovering what leads to what in a given situation. By our own efforts and active exploration we try to discover the golden rule that one event leads to another event or that one sign leads to another (capable of enabling the organism to reorder or reorganise its thinking). This explains why Tolman describes learning as sign learning or sign gestalt learning.

Place learning versus response learning.   According to Tolman, in the process of learning an individual does not learn specific responses to specific stimuli as mentioned by S-R theorists but tries to learn about the places, where things actually lie. He does not learn a fixed movement sequence but an overall path by visualizing a total picture for the achievement of the stipulated target. He then tries to bring about changes in his movements and style of functioning in accordance with the needs of the environment.

Tolman and his associates conducted certain experiments to demonstrate their conclusions about place learning ability. In one of the experiments, using a T maze a rat was first trained to get its food by turning to right. The situation was changed by allowing its entry from the lower end. Consequently it had to change its movements from right to left for getting food (see Figure 13.12). The rat did it, proving that the animal learns places and not the fixed sequence of movements like turning right or left.

In another experiment, the maze in which the rat had learned to run along the correct path was flooded with water. Even when faced with this obstacle, the rat was able to reach its goal by swimming along the correct path. Both these experiments demonstrated the truth of Tolman's findings that it is the place not the fixed responses that are learned by an individual as an outcome of his learning.

Reward Expectancy

Tolman maintained that our learning behaviour is purposive. It is goal-oriented rather than response-oriented. We learn to expect or gain something as a result of

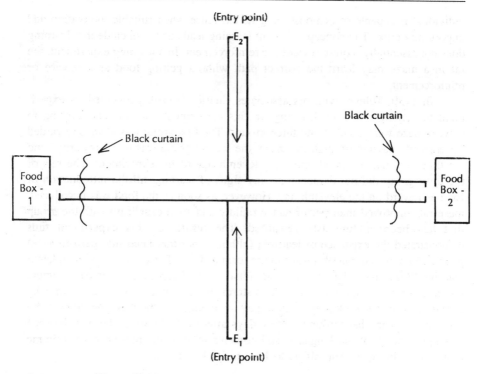

Figure 13.12   An experiment to demonstrate place-learning.

our efforts. Consequently, we may have an expectation that if we go to a certain place or perform a certain act, we may get something, a 'reward' in the language of Tolman. Not getting or getting less than the expected reward may lead to disruption of behaviour, involving frustration. Tolman and his associates conducted a number of experiments to demonstrate the importance of reward expectancy in the process of learning.

In one of their experiments, a group of rats which was trained to run a maze for bran mash was found to show a considerable disruption in their behaviour (in terms of committing more errors) when sunflower seeds were substituted for the bran mash (which was less than the expected reward). In another experiment, a monkey was first allowed to see a banana being placed in one of the two containers. The monkey was quite able to pick up the right container in search of the banana demonstrating his memorization ability. Later on, after removing the monkey from the scene, the experimenter placed a lettuce leaf (the food having less reward value) in one of the containers. When the monkey found the lettuce leaf in place of the expected banana, it exhibited signs of disrupted behaviour, surprise, anger, frustration; rejected the lettuce leaf and began to search vigorously for the expected reward i.e., the banana.

Latent Learning

Tolman also spoke of a type of learning that remains dormant for a considerable length of time in an individual before it is displayed in his behaviour. The individual is capable of demonstrating its existence when suitable motivation and opportunity arise. The concept of latent learning leads us to conclude that learning does not essentially require rewards or reinforcement. In a learning experiment, the rat in a maze may learn the correct path without getting food as a reward or reinforcement.

In 1930, Tolman with his associates Charles Honzik performed an experiment to demonstrate such learning. In this experiment, hungry rats learning to solve a maze were divided into three groups. The first group was always rewarded for correctly passing through the maze, the second group was never rewarded and the third was not rewarded until the eleventh day of the experiment. The rats of the third group did not demonstrate any signs of learning till the introduction of food as reward on the eleventh day. However, as soon as the food was introduced, these rats improved their performance rapidly and soon caught up with the group that had been continuously rewarded. The results of this experiment thus demonstrated the existence of learning (although not translated into performance) prior to the introduction of reward in the form of food. The existence of such latent learning thus remains latent in the individual until a happening in the environment requires him to make use of this hidden stores. In our day-to-day life a person who is engrossed in his work may seem to pay no attention to the dialogue in the radio set playing in the background. A few days afterwards, however, he may be seen to employ much of the language and contents used in the presented programme quite surprising even himself as to how he picked it up.

Types of Learning

Tolman distinguished six types of learning:

1. *Cathexis*. In this type of learning, an association appears to be formed between certain objects and certain drive states. Persons belonging to cold countries where liquors are usually consumed for satisfying the thirst drive, will certainly tend to seek such drinks in preference to a simple glass of water mainly because for them, water has not been associated with the satisfaction of the thirst drive.

2. *Equivalence beliefs*. Sometimes, a sub-goal like scoring of high grades provides the same motivation as might be provided by the main goal like winning love and appreciation etc. The learning performed in such a condition is said to the equivalence beliefs learning.

3. *Field expectancy*. In this type of learning, the learning takes place on account of the expectancy of something occurring in one's environment. Upon seeing a certain sign, for instance, one expects that a certain other sign will follow. The only reward in such a learning is the fulfilment of the expectation. Such learning as may be understood, is not the usual S-R learning but rather S-S or sign-sign learning based on the expectation of signs in one's environment.

4. *Field cognition modes*. This type of learning involves the learning of a strategy, or a way of approaching a problem solving situation by arranging the perceptual field in a specific way for application to each new field with which one is presented.

5. *Drive discrimination.* This type of learning requires the learner to identify and determine his own drive state and respond accordingly. The individual, therefore, has to learn the behaviour needed for satisfying his thirst drive quite differently from the learning of the behaviour needed to satisfy his drive for love and affection.

6. *Motor patterns.* In such learning, the motor patterns are associated with or conditioned by behaviour.

Summary of Tolman's Theory

Tolman's theory truly represents an eclectic approach towards learning. The six kinds of learning it advocated may be seen to have equations with the views of one or the other major theory of learning. The major contribution of this theory is its emphasis on the study of cognitive processes thus making the task of learning an intelligent task rather than a mere telephone like operation or some routine habit formation or conditioning. Tolman, was the first to forcefully argue that all learning is purposeful and goal oriented rather than response oriented. According to him, understanding and map making rather than conditioning or building up S-R connections is the essence of learning. With the number of trials in the way of learning, an individual develops cognitive maps or mental representations (also called sign gestalts) in perfect correlation with the goal he has to achieve and the environment in which he has to strive. These cognitive maps are like various hypotheses the validity of which one has to test one by one to realise one's purpose. A cognitive map becomes effective in influencing one's behaviour only when it helps in meeting one's need or purpose or in getting reinforcement.

However, an organism may be able to learn even if it is not rewarded or its behaviour is not reinforced. This is an unobservable or latent learning which shows its existence in terms of good performance shortly after the introduction of the reward or recognition. Each individual acts according to his cognitive mapping of the environment to reach his goal. The attempts made by him in this direction become significant, showing positive or negative signs as, depending upon the type of reinforcement, each sign leads to another, giving a clear indication of what leads to what; thus the individual ultimately learns to proceed along the correct path. The likelihood of reaching the goal by one of the many routes indicated by the mental mapping and the confirmation of such expectancy through the local signs (reinforcement of the behaviour) makes the individual strive for the new ways and means to proceed on his path to realise his ultimate goal and that is how he learns the ways to solve the problems he is confronted with in a given situation.

Educational implications. The educational implications of Tolman's theory can be outlined as:

1. This theory highlighted the role and importance of purpose in the task of learning. What is to be taught to the child, therefore, should be

purposeful and should lead him towards some clear cut goals and objectives.

2. Tolman's theory emphasized that no learning is wasteful. Attempts at learning are never in vain, although no immediate purpose may appear to be served through such efforts. Such unobservable learning proves beneficial because it surfaces when the need of such learning arises in the accomplishment of a task.

3. This theory clarified that learning is neither a simple straightforward connection between stimuli and responses nor so habitual as to be brought out through repetition and conditioning. It is an intelligent task in which the organiser has to draw a cognitive map of the environment to come out with a proper solution of a problem. Children while learning should not, therefore, be forced to follow a routine or obvious path but should be encouraged to explore as many paths as possible for solving the problems and performing the tasks.

4. A reward or reinforcement is not essential for every step taken towards reaching a goal or learning a particular behaviour. We learn so many things throughout our life for which we are reinforced by no other reward than the satisfaction of the learning itself. Therefore, it is the intrinsic motivation or value of the learning that should be emphasized in the process of teaching and learning rather than some outside reward or high expectation.

5. Since intervening variables like environmental surroundings, drives, previous learning, age, etc. play a major role in influencing the learning process, every effort should be made to take proper note of these variables in any teaching—learning situation to derive the maximum benefit.

GAGNE'S THEORY OF LEARNING

Robert Gagne, the famous American psychologist put forward a theory of learning and instruction incorporating a behaviouristic, eclectic approach to the psychology of learning and teaching. He is specially known for his famous writings "The Conditions of Learning" and "Instructional Technology Foundations". The major theoretical notions and ideas propagated by him through his learning theory may be summarized now.

The Meaning and Concept of Learning

Learning, according to Gagne, may be considered a change in human disposition, or capability which can be retained and which is not simply ascribable to the process of growth. The major task or objective of one's learning is to bring the required change in his way of disposition (tendency to behave in certain ways in given situations) or the capability of performing one task or the other. The result or impact of learning, thus may be subjected to proper measurement since these can be properly observed and inferred by observing the difference in performance of the learner before and after learning. These changes in behaviour or ability and potential of the learner are somewhat enduring, as the learner is capable of utilising and benefitting through the outcomes of such learning. In any case, this is an acquired tendency which cannot be simply associated with the process of natural growth, i.e. maturation etc.

The Outcomes of Learning

Learning, according to Gagne, is supposed to result in the enhancement of a person's performance and capabilities by acquiring new ways of behaving (gaining in terms of knowledge, understanding, skills and change of attitudes etc.). He declared that all types of human learning may result in the development of human capabilities in terms of the following five components:

1. Verbal information
2. Intellectual skills
3. Cognitive strategies
4. Motor skills
5. Attitudes.

Let us know in detail about these outcomes of learning.

1. *Verbal information.* Through one's learning one may acquire different types of information in a verbal form (listening, viewing and reading). One may then make use of this information for one's own purposes or transmit it to others through verbal means (spoken or written). Verbal communication of the acquired information then may prove helpful in many ways to the learner.

2. *Intellectual skills.* Another outcome of learning is that it helps the learner acquire necessary intellectual skills. Gagne (1970) has further classified these intellectual skills into levels or types, e.g. discrimination, concept formation, and rule learning. According to him, these skills assist the learner in "knowing how" in comparison to "knowing that" of (verbal) information, that is, how to convert decimals into fractions, how to interpret various symbols on a page into recognized words, and so on.

3. *Cognitive strategies.* These refer to the internally organized capabilities of a learner, which he acquires through the process of learning. These strategies help him in the tasks related to attending, learning, remembering, thinking and problem solving, leading him to attain his individual and social goals.

4. *Motor skills.* Learning affects the conative domain of a person's behaviour by bringing the required changes in the way he does things through motor activities. His learning to drive a car, swimming, playing a musical instrument or playing a game are all the outcomes of acquisition and development of his motor skills.

5. *Attitudes.* Learning helps the learner to bring significant changes in the affective domain of his behaviour, particularly in terms of the change in his disposition or attitude that is, his attitude towards things, persons or events.

These outcomes can be illustrated as in the form of a Table 13.1.

Table 13.1   Illustrating Gagne's Outcomes of Learning

Learning outcomes	Example of human performance made possible by the related learning outcome
1. Verbal Information	Stating Newton's laws of motion.
2. Intellectual skills	Exhibited in the following manner:
(i) Discrimination	Distinguishing printed letter 'd' from 'b'.
(ii) Concept formation	Naming apple as fruit and distinguishing it from other fruits.
(iii) Generalization of rule or principle	Demonstrating and concluding that matter expands after heating.
3. Cognitive strategy	Thinking and discovering a novel strategy for the purification of water.
4. Motor skill	Learning to play harmonium.
5. Attitude	Choosing teaching as a noble profession.

Types of Learning (Gagne's hierarchical structure of learning)

Gagne maintained that all learnings are not alike and, consequently, he divided human learning into eight types or categories arranged in hierarchy. He gave them a hierarchical order based on their internal connections since one type of learning provides a prerequisite for the next higher order learning. These eight types of learning in their hierarchical order can be presented in the form of a Table 13.2 as follows:

While presenting such a hierarchical order, Gagne tried to guide the process of learning and instructional organisation by emphasizing that in learning, the lower steps of hierarchy must be mastered before the higher steps can be learned. Gagne's theory of learning provides a genuine basis for the proper organisation and sequencing of instruction.

Conditions or Events of Learning

Gagne, through his theory of learning and instruction, emphasized that different internal and external conditions or events are necessary for each type or level of learning. Internal conditions, according to him, are those capabilities which are already possessed by a learner on account of his previous learning, physical stamina, and mental and emotional make-up. External conditions represent those things and elements in his environment which affect his learning outcomes from outside. Good learning, in terms of its required outcomes, thus requires a proper organisation of these internal and external conditions of learning. As favourable internal conditions, we can consider the learner's interest, motivation, his mental and physical and emotional make-up, and previous learning (learning prerequisites that facilitate present learning). In terms of favourable external conditions, one should look for favourable teaching-learning strategies and environmental situations. For example, for learning cognitive strategies, a learner must be given

Table 13.2 Gagne's System of Learning

Hierarchical order	Type	Brief description of its nature
1.	Signal learning	A Learning of the nature that we are stopped at the red light and start driving our vehicle at the green. Here we learn to make a generalized response to a signal or stimulus (as happens with the classical conditioning of Pavlov and Watson).
2.	Stimulus-response (S.R.) learning	Learning based on S.R. type instrumental conditioning emphasized by Thorndike. Here a stimulus is properly discriminated for a mechanical alike response.
3.	Chaining	In this type of learning, two or more S.R. connections are joined together.
4.	Verbal association	In this type of learning the learner is made to emit chained responses of S.R. type by making verbal associations.
5.	Multiple discrimination	This is a stage of good discrimination, i.e. to learn making different responses to different (even having too much resemblance) stimuli.
6.	Concept learning	In this type of learning one learns to provide a common response to a class of stimuli.
7.	Rule learning	Also known as learning of principles. Principles are generated through the chaining of two or more concepts, e.g. if one is thirsty, one needs water to drink.
8.	Problem solving	In this type of learning, higher mental or cognitive abilities are involved for making use of the concept and rules for solving one or the other problem.

opportunities to enhance his thinking skills, and use novel methods for doing things and solving problems. Similarly, for learning attitudes, the learners may be exposed to a credible role model or persuasive arguments.

Events of Learning and Instructions

Gagne, while emphasizing the need for a proper theory of instruction, proposed that such a theory of instruction must be based on the hierarchical structure of the events of learning. How the information is processed by the learner may work towards planning the task of instruction (either for self-learning or through an instructor or teacher). What goes on inside the learner's mind (in the shape of various cognitive processes) during the teaching-learning process may be termed as *internal events*. These events must be fully taken into consideration (alongwith the external conditions or events in the shape of desired teaching-learning environment) while planning the corresponding instructional procedures. These learning events from the angle of a learner (also called as cognitive processes going inside the mind of the learner) along with the corresponding instructional events, may be well presented as follows (Table 13.3).

Table 13.3 Gagne's Learning Events along with their Corresponding Instructional Events

Learning event (cognitive process in a learner's mind)	Corresponding instruction event
Reception	Gaining attention
Expectancy	Informing learners of the objective
Retrieval	Stimulating recall of prior learning
Selective perception	Presenting the stimulus
Semantic encoding	Providing learning guidance
Responding	Eliciting performance
Reinforcement	Providing feedback
Retrieval	Assessing performance
Generalization	Enhancing retention and transfer

An instructional plan may thus be properly chalked out by following the sequences of learning events. For example, every learning requires its reception and acceptance from the learner. Thereafter, it should be realized with the assistance of a proper motivation. Every effort should therefore be made to seek his attention and make his learning goal and attainable purposeful. After being motivated to learn something, a learner is naturally inclined to depend on or associate it with previous learning and as such for this purpose, he has to undergo the process of retrieval in his mind. In tune with this requirement of the learner, the instructor or teacher has to make efforts to stimulate the recall of his previous learning. Similarly, we can judge the validity of the instructional events suggested by Gagne, well in tune with the requirements of the hierarchical sequence of the learning events (cognitive processes going inside the lerner's mind).

In this way, as Gagne puts the sequence of learning events (necessary conditions for learning) may serve as a useful and necessary base for designing instructions and selecting appropriate media for a teaching-learning process (Gagne, Briggs and Wager, 1992).

For the illustration of his views about the relationship between learning events and instructional events, Gagne (1985) has tried to provide examples of events for each category of learning outcomes. Here we can cite an example illustrating a teaching sequence related to the required instructional events for the topic, "Recognition of an equilateral triangle".

1. *Gain attention* – show variety of triangles (drawing figures illustrating models or computer generated figures).
2. *Identify the object* – pose question: "What is an equilateral triangle?"
3. *Recall prior learning* – review definitions of triangles.
4. *Present stimulus* – give definition of equilateral triangle.
5. *Guide learning* – show example of how to create an equilateral triangle.
6. *Elicit performance* – ask students to create five different examples.
7. *Provide feedback* – check all examples as correct/incorrect.
8. *Assess performance* – provide scores and remediation.

9. *Enhance retention/Transfer* – show pictures of objects and ask students to identify equilaterals.

Thus, Gagne, through his theory of learning, tries to provide a behaviouristic, eclectic approach to the psychology of learning. He proposes a set of events or conditions for the occurrence of learning and links them to a set of instructional events. The hierarchical order which he proposes for the learning types, outcomes, and the instructional designs, say much about his dynamic approach and efforts to integrate teaching well with the learning process. His theory almost covers all aspects of human learning and, therefore, it can be safely applied to the design of instruction in all domains of human behaviour.

Bandura's Social Learning Theory

Observation of other's behaviour may play a leading role in learning and acquiring various things concerning one's environment. The cognitive psychologists who appreciate the role of observation in learning are termed as social psychologists and the theory of learning they propagate is known as the social learning theory. Albert Bandura was a prominent American social learning theorist and the social learning theory is often designated as Bandura's social learning theory.

Introducing his theory Bandura (Lewin, 1978) writes:

> We do not blindly respond to environmental stimuli. Rather, we pick and choose from many environmental options, basing our decisions on our own insights and past experiences. This we do through vicarious or observational learning, by incorporating and imitating the behaviour of those around us.

Observational or vicarious learning (learning through indirect experiences) rather than the learning based on direct experiences is thus the base of the social learning theory. The advocates of this theory emphasize that most of what we learn is acquired through simply watching and listening to other people. The children from the very beginning keenly observe the behaviour of others, most commonly of the people nearest to them like parents, members of the family, teachers, the older members of society, etc. In turn, they try to imitate and do what they observe. The power of observational learning can be confirmed through laboratory experiments as well as through observation in our daily life. A child who sees his father throwing utensils around simply because he has not been served food of his taste, learns such behaviour and reproduces it in similar circumstances. He may also incorporate and imitate the behaviour of the characters he reads about in novels, hears about over the radio or sees on TV or in movies. The persons whose behaviour he observes and often imitates are known as models and observational learning is referred to as *modelling*.

Direct experiences no doubt constitute the most effective and powerful sources of one's learning but the role of indirect experiences leading to observational learning can also not be underestimated. In many cases, they prove more desirable, less expensive and more beneficial than the direct experiences. Commenting on this aspect Bandura (1977) writes:

> One does not teach children to swim, adolescents to drive automobiles, and novice medical students to perform surgery by having them discover the

appropriate behaviour through the consequences of their successes or failures. The more costly and hazardous the possible mistakes, the heavier is the reliance on observational learning from competent examples.

Observational learning can thus provide extra dimensions and opportunities for the learners in addition to their learning through self-experience and direct involvement with environmental consequences. It has certainly reduced the need of an individual going through every experience himself and thus helped him to learn from the examples of others.

How does learning take place?   According to the social learning theory, one learns through observations by incorporating and imitating the behaviours of others taken as models belonging to one's social environment. According to Bandura (1977), the following processes or steps are usually involved in this kind of learning:

1. *Attending to and perceiving the behaviour.*   In this step the learner is made to observe the behaviour of the person acting as a model. Here the total behaviour or a particular aspect of it may attract attention and become the subject of close attention.

2. *Remembering the behaviour.*   In this step, what the learner observes is filed away in his memory in the form of mental images.

3. *Converting the memory into action.*   In this step, a behaviour observed and remembered by the learner is analysed in terms if its acceptability to the learner with reference to the demands of his self and his environment. It is transformed into action only afterwards and thus the observed relevant and accepted aspects of the model's behaviour are imitated by the learner.

4. *Reinforcement of the imitated behaviour.*   In this final step, the behaviour of the model imitated by the learner is reinforced for proper adoption and further continuance.

Let us see how these steps may work in one's learning. Suppose a young girl happens to watch a T.V. programme concerning the preparation of some new dishes. She takes keen interest and is greatly influenced by the demonstration on the T.V. screen. She tries to keep in her memory all that she has observed on the screen and then enters her kitchen to convert the remembered observation into action. The new dishes are thus prepared by her in accordance with her observation of the performance on T.V. of the home science specialist. Her learning of the preparation of the new dishes may then be reinforced by the response she gets from the members of her family who taste the new dishes.

In this way, social learning i.e., learning through observation and modelling proves to be an effective means of learning many things concerning one's behaviour. How one displays love and anger, shows sympathy and prejudices, speaks and writes, dresses and eats, takes initiative or shies away, all depend upon what has been observed, remembered, imitated and reinforced in context of the vicarious or model learning as propagated by the social learning theory.

CARL ROGER'S THEORY OF EXPERIENTIAL LEARNING

The theory of experiential learning has been propounded by Carl Ransom Rogers, an American psychologist. It has its origin in his views about psychotherapy and humanistic approach to psychology. It was primarily employed to explain the learning mechanism of adult learners and then was applied to adolescent and school going learners also.

In his search for the basic nature of learning, Rogers tried to distinguish two types of learning—cognitive and experiential. He termed *cognitive learning* as meaningless in itself unless it is subjected to some use. Such learning is knowledge based and thus may include the learning of vocabulary, multiplication table, mathematical formulae, historical events and geographical facts. The experiential learning, on the other hand, is quite vital to one's progress and welfare. It is associated with the application of the acquired knowledge such as learning about engines in order to repair a car, learning psychological principles and methods in order to help the children get rid of bad habits. Thus experiential learning is learner-centered. That is to say, it cares for the needs, and wants of the learner. Carl Rogers has tried to enumerates these qualities of experiential learning in the following way:

1. Experiential learning is characterized by *personal involvement* of the learner.
2. It is *self-initiated.* The learner willingly takes initiative to engage in such type of learning.
3. It is characterized by *self-evaluation.* The learner himself is interested in evaluating the results and outcomes of such learning by applying it to the realization of learning objectives, i.e. he wants to test his knowledge of repairing an electrical gadget by actually doing the repair.
4. It leaves a *pervasive effect* on a learner. Whatever is learned through this method can be made into use when and where he needs.

Rogers, as a humanist, believes in the strength and potentialities of human beings. According to him, all human beings have a natural inclination for learning and a desire to grow and progress. The role of the teacher and the parents is thus to help their children in their inherent desire for personal change and growth. Teacher as well as the parents have to care for and facilitate such learning which helps the children to grow and develop according to their requirements. The attempts of the teachers and the parents in realising the objectives of experiential learning may, thus include the following provisions:

1. Arranging a favourable and positive climate for learning.
2. Helping the learner or learners to have clear-cut objectives and purpose of his/her learning.
3. Organising the learning resources and making them available to the learners.
4. Balancing intellectual and emotional components of learning.
5. Sharing feelings and thoughts with learners in a democratic way.

Thus, the primary responsibility of a teacher lies well in his sincerety as a helper, a guide and a facilitator in the ongoing teaching-learning process. He is not there to provide mere information or demonstrate his skills in any area of information or fact-finding. Through many tools and materials and his own characteristic ways, a teacher, while following the doctrine of experiential learning, has to play the role of a learning facilitator. For realising this objective, as Rogers points out, a learner must at least take care of the basic conditions that facilitate learning. According to him, learning is well facilitated when:

1. *threat* to the self of the learner is minimum;
2. learning resources and climate are in favour of the learner;
3. the learner participates completely in the learning process and has control over its nature and direction;
4. it is primarily based on direct confrontation with practical, social, personal or research areas.
5. self-evaluation is the principal method of assessing progress or success; and
6. the learner realizes the importance of learning and develops an openness as well as willingness to learn.

Thus, experiential learning is, in fact, a learner-centred enterprise. Here the learner is the key figure in the ongoing teaching-learning process. The role of a teacher is to facilitate such learning. The primary responsibility of learning and change in the behaviour of the learner for his personal and social development lies with him. However, he is to be properly helped, guided and kept on the proper track by the teacher as and when the need of doing so arises. The main thing is to help the learner realize the importance and significance of the learning task. If we can make him see the profit or gain of the learning task, we can very well realize the objectives of learning. Therefore, according to Rogers, learning must be linked with the motives, goals and ideals of the learner. Accordingly, for a learner who is interested in becoming rich in learning, pertaining to, say, such topics as economics, investment, financing, banking etc., the concept of learning may be of great importance. Decidedly he will take more genuine interest in the learning of topics and subjects which are helpful in realising his motives and ambitions, as compared to other students of his class who have significantly less interest in money matters.

Summing up, it can be easily concluded that Carl Rogers, through his theory of experiential learning, advocates a humanistic and learner-centred approach to be adopted in class rooms by the teachers, with the sole purposes of making the learning process more humane and suitable to the needs and interest of the learners, and turning it into more significant and purposeful event from the angles of their personal and social growth and development (by emphasizing more on application than on theory alone).

SUMMARY

Learning is defined as a process which brings relatively permanent changes in the behaviour of a learner through experience or practice. It can be classified into specific categories like trial and error, conditioning, insightful learning, serial learning, associate learning, chain learning, verbal learning, learning of motor skills, effective learning and cognitive learning, etc.

As its outcomes it helps in (i) bringing desirable modifications in behaviour (ii) attaining teaching-learning objectives (iii) achieving proper growth and development (iv) seeking balanced development of the personality (v) seeking proper adjustment and (vi) realizing the goals in life.

Learning is affected by so many factors that may be broadly classified as those associated with learner, the type of learning experiences provided to the learner, and the men and material resources available for learning.

The *theory of trial and error learning* propagated by Thorndike emphasizes that we learn through a trial and error mechanism. In trying to learn a correct behaviour, one tries hard in so many ways and may commit so many errors before striking upon a chance success. On subsequent trials we may learn to avoid the mistakes, repeat the correct moves and finally learn the proper way. Thorndike also propagated certain important laws of learning like the law of readiness (i.e. one can learn if one is ready to learn), law of exercise (i.e. learning needs repetition or drill) and law of effect (i.e. the effect or consequence decides the fate of one's learning).

Classical conditioning was first experimentally demonstrated by Ivan Pavlov through the conditioning of a dog to salivate when it heard a bell. Through this experiment Pavlov successfully demonstrated that the artificial stimulus (bell) become so strong as to produce salivation even when it was not accompanied by the natural stimulus (food). He referred to it as the conditioning of the dog resulting in its learning to get food with the ringing of the bell. Watson also demonstrated such conditioning by inducing fear in his eleven month old subject, Albert. Actually, most of our behaviour may be adjudged to be the product of conditioning. One who fears snakes may be seen to have a fear of any object which looks like a snake. Responding to the stimuli in such a generalized way is referred to as *stimulus generalization*. The opposite of generalization is *discrimination*. This is the process by which we learn to respond to one specific stimulus and to inhibit the responses to all other stimuli.

The phenomenon of *extinction* occurs when the subject learns to inhibit the conditioned responses i.e., accepting that the ringing of the bell is not always accompanied by food. In case the responses suddenly reappear on their own, the phenomenon is termed as *spontaneous recovery*.

In 'operant conditioning,' learning is dependent on its consequences. Behaviours which are reinforced are likely to be repeated and those which are not reinforced are unlikely to be repeated. The success of operant conditioning is dependent on the right choice of a reinforcement schedule. The appropriate reinforcement of the step-by-step successive approximation of the desired behaviour called *shaping,* may result in learning of the most complex behaviour. The techniques of operant conditioning have been found to be quite useful in the field of behaviour modification, programmed learning and computer-assisted instruction.

Insightful learning, advocated by the gestalists, emphasized that human learning is always purposeful and goal directed and is essentially based on one's cognitive powers. Köhler, on the basis of his learning experiments performed on apes concluded that, (a) a learner always perceives the situation in a gestalt form i.e., as a whole, (b) evaluates all the relationship and factors involved in the situation, and (c) then, arrives at an insightful solution.

Guthrie's *theory of continuous conditioning* is based on the principle of contiguity. According to it learning is based on association or the connection between a stimulus and a response and this association occurs simply because of contiguity or the occurrence of the stimulus and response together. Such association between S and R takes place in a single trial and this association tends to be continued until there is a change in stimulating conditions or a response is prevented from occurring.

Hebb's *neurophysiological theory of learning* provided a new dimension and paradigm to the approaches to learning in vogue at that time and attempted to explain the phenomenon of learning through a solid neuro-physiological base. It highlighted the role of the nervous system—senses, neural impulses and cortex etc. for explaining how learning takes place, how it is reinforced and retained, how the short-term memory is translated into permanent memory and what causes good and bad performance in a learning task in a particular learning situation.

Hull's *systematic behaviour theory* rejected the trigger-like function of stimuli-response advocated by the behaviourist theorists. It introduced the concept of intervening variables between stimuli and response and thus provided an amended formula S-O-R in place of S-R. Hull's theory is sometimes referred to as the *need or drive reduction theory* in the sense that it reduced learning to the function of need or drive reduction. One learns because one wants to satisfy one or other of one's needs and in case the learning results in reduction of one's need i.e. the state of tension, this automatically works as a reinforcer for repeating the S-R association and then makes one react in the same way in a particular situation.

Lewin's *field theory* considers learning to be a process of perceptual organisation or reorganisation of one's life space or field (the space in which one moves psychologically) involving insight. It attaches sufficient importance to motivation by equating it with the attraction towards a goal. One is supposed to structure one's life space into an appropriate pattern for achieving the desired goal. One's future behaviour thus depends upon the way one manages to bring about desirable changes in one's cognitive structure on the basis of previous learning and new insight.

Tolman's theory advocates that understanding and map-making, rather than conditioning or building up S-R connections, is the essence of learning. An individual does not learn specific response to specific stimuli but tries to learn about the places where things actually lie. Actually, in the path of learning one is always goal-oriented rather response-oriented. One constructs a mental map of the environment for reaching one's goal. This map-making ability is nothing but the ability to see and choose any one of the many alternative paths available. Tolman's theory also highlighted the existence of latent learning, learning which remains latent or unobservable in the individual until a happening in the environment requires him to make use of this hidden stockpile.

Gagne's theory of learning considers learning as a change in human performance or capabilities and depend upon certain internal and external conditions. The outcome of learning is thus the development of capabilities such as verbal information, intellectual and motor skills, cognitive strategies and attitudes. As a result of systematization of learning, he proposed eight types of learning arranged in hierarchy. Finally, in his process of operationalizing learning, he divided the learning act into eight distinct phases which start from motivation to learning and end in feed back for the performance. Each phase has internal processes and external events (conditions of learning) that influence it. In search of a proper theory of instruction, he also proposed that any instructional plan must be chalked out by following the sequence of learning events.

Bandura's *social learning theory* emphasizes the power of observational learning. It advocates that most of what we learn is acquired through simply observing and imitating the behaviour of others who are taken as models.

Rogers, through his theory of experiential learning, has emphasized on experiential learning (application of the knowledge) instead of a mere knowledge-getting-learning known as *cognitive learning*. Experiential learning, characterized as self-initiated and self-evaluative, thus stand for a learner-centered approach having a humanistic touch.

REFERENCES

Bandura, A., *Social Learning Theory*, Englewood Cliffs, N.J.: Prentice-Hall, 1977.

Biggie, M.L. and Hunt, M.P., *Psychological Foundations of Education*, New York: Harper & Row, 1968.

Crow, L.D. and Crow, A., *Educational Psychology*, New Delhi: Eurasia Publishing House, 1973.

Gagne, R.M., *The Conditions of Learning* (2nd ed.), New York: Rinehart & Winston, 1970.

_____, *Essentials of Learning for Instruction*, Hinsdele III: Dryden, 1974, p. 55.

Guthrie, E.R., *The Psychology of Learning*, New York: Harper & Row, 1935, p. 54.

_____, *The Psychology of Human Conflict*, New York: Harper & Row, 1938.

_____, Association and the law of effect, *Psychological Review*, 1940, p. 47.

Guthrie, E.R., Conditioning: A theory of learning in terms of stimulus, response and association, in N.B. Henry (Ed.), *The Forty-first Year Book of the National Society for the Study of Education, Part II*. The Psychology of Learning, Chicago: University of Chicago Press, 1942, p. 30.

_____, *The Psychology of Learning* (rev. ed.), New York: Harper & Row, 1952.

_____, Association by contiguity, *in* S. Koch (Ed.), *Psychology: A study of science*, Vol. 2, New York: McGraw-Hill, 1959.

Guthrie, E.R. and Horton, G.P., *Cats in a Puzzle Box*, New York: Rinehart, 1946, p. 78.

Hebb, D.O., *Textbook of Psychology* (3rd ed.), Philadelphia: Saunders, 1972.

Hergenhahn, B.R., *An Introduction to Theories of Learning*, Englewood Cliffs, New Jersey: Prentice-Hall, 1976.

Hilgard, E.R. and Bower, G.H., *Theories of Learning* (4th ed.), Englewood Cliffs, New Jersey: Prentice-Hall, 1975.

Hilgard, E.O., *Theories of Learning* (4th ed.), New York: Appleton-Century Crofts, 1976.

Hull, C.L., *Principles of Behaviour*, New York: Appleton-Century-Crofts, 1943.

————, *A Behaviour System: An introduction to behaviour theory concerning the individual organism*, New Haven, Conn: Yale University Press, 1952.

Kimble, G.A., in Hilgard and Marquis, *Conditioning and Learning* (2nd ed.), Englewood Cliffs, N.J.: Prentice-Hall, 1961.

Kingsley, H.L. and Garry, R., *The Nature and Conditions of Learning* (2nd ed.), Englewood Cliffs, New Jersey: Prentice-Hall, 1957.

Köhler, W., *The Mentality of Apes*, New York: Harcourt, 1925.

————, *Gestalt Psychology*, New York: Leveright, 1929.

————, *The Task of Gestalt Psychology*, Princeton, N.J., Princeton University Press, 1969.

Levin, M.J., *Psychology—A biographical approach*, New York: McGraw-Hill, 1978.

Lorenz, K., *King Soloman's Ring*, London: Methuen, 1952.

Murphy, Gardner, *An Introduction to Psychology*, New Delhi: Oxford & IBH, 1968.

Pavlov, J.P., *Conditioned Reflexes*, Oxford: Clarendon Press, 1927.

Pressey, Robinson and Horrocks, *Psychology in Education* (2nd ed.), Delhi: University Book Stall, 1967.

Skinner, B.P., *The Behaviour of Organisms*, New York: Appleton-Century-Crofts, 1938.

————, *Science and Human Behaviour*, New York: Macmillan, 1953.

————, *The Technology of Teaching*, New York: Appleton-Century-Crofts, 1968.

————, *About Behaviourism*, New York: Knopf, 1974.

Smith, H.P., *Psychology in Teaching*, Englewood Cliffs, New Jersey: Prentice-Hall, 1962.

Thorndike, E.L., *Animal Intelligence*, New York: Macmillan, 1911.

————, *Human Learning*, New York: Cornell University, 1931.

————, *The Elements of Psychology*, New York: Seiler, 1905.

Tolman, E.C., *Purposive Behaviour in Animals and Men*, New York: Century, 1932.

Woodworth, R.S., *Psychology*, London, Methuen, 1945.

SUGGESTED READINGS

Ausubel, D., *The Psychology of Meaningful Verbal Learning*, New York: Grune & Stratton, 1963.

Bandura, A. and Walters, R.H., *Social Learning and Personality Development*, New York: Holt, Rinehart & Winston, 1963.

Ellis, Henry, *Transfer of Learning*, New York: Macmillan, 1965.

Ellis, W.D., *A Source Book of Gestalt Psychology*, New York: Har Court Brace & World, 1938.

Holland, J.G. Skinner, *The Analysis of Behaviour*, New York: McGraw-Hill, 1961.

Horton, D.L. and T.W. Turnage, *Human Learning*, Englewood Cliffs, N.J.: Prentice-Hall, 1976.

Hulse, S.H., J. Deese and H. Egeth, *The Psychology of Learning* (4th ed.), New York: McGraw-Hill, 1975.

Mikulas, W.L., *Concepts in Learning*, Philadelphia: Saunders, 1974.

Nevin, J.A. and G.S. Reynolds (Ed.), *The Study of Behaviour: Learning, Motivation, Emotion and Instinct*, Glenview, Illinois: Scott, Foreman, 1973.

Peterson, L.R., *Learning*, Glenview, Illinois: Scott, Foreman, 1975.

Rachlin, H., *Introduction to Modern Behaviourism*, San Francisco: W.H. Freeman and Company, 1970.

Reynolds, G.S., *A Primer of Operant Conditioning* (2nd ed.), Glenview, Illinois: Scott, Foreman, 1975.

Sorenson, Herbert, *Psychology of Education*, New York: McGraw-Hill, 1948.

Stephens, J.M., *Handbook of Classroom Learning*, New York: Holt, 1965.

Watson, J.B., *Psychology from the Stand-point of a Behaviourist*, Philadelphia: Lippincott, 1919.

Chapter 14

Transfer of Learning or Training

WHAT IS TRANSFER OF LEARNING OR TRAINING?

Many of the things we do or perform in day-to-day life are often influenced by our previous experience of learning or training. The learning of addition and subtraction helps a child in learning multiplication and division. Learning of Mathematics helps in solving numerical problems in Physics. Similarly, if one has learned to play tennis one finds it easier to learn playing ping pong or badminton. In this way learning or training in one situation influences our learning or performance in some other situation. This influence is usually referred to the carry-over of learning from one task to another. The learning or skill acquired in one task is transferred or carried over to other tasks. Not only the learning of the tricks of a trade or the knowledge and skill acquired in a particular subject is transferred to other situations, but also the habits, interests and attitudes get transferred and try to influence the activities of the individual in future. According to Crow and Crow (1973):

> The carry-over of habits of thinking, feeling or working, of knowledge or of skills, from one learning area to another usually is referred to as the transfer of training . . . .

Sorenson (1948) also takes the same stand when he explains the meaning of transfer:

> Transfer refers to the transfer of knowledge, training and habits acquired in one situation to another situation.

The analysis of both these definitions may lead us to conclude that the term 'transfer of learning' stands for a special mechanism or process in which a person's learning in one situation is carried over or transferred to other situations and, as Bigge (1967) puts it,

> transfer of learning occurs when a person's learning in one situation influences his learning and performances in other situations.

Types of Transfer

Depending on the learning situations faced by the learner, the following three

246

kinds of transfer can occur: (i) Positive transfer, (ii) Negative transfer, (iii) Zero transfer.

Positive transfer.   Transfer of learning or training is said to be positive when the learning or training carried out in one situation proves helpful to the learner in another situation. Examples of such transfer are:

1. The knowledge and skills related to school mathematics help in the learning of statistical computation.
2. The knowledge and skills acquired in terms of addition and subtraction in mathematics in school may help a child in the acquisition of knowledge and skills regarding multiplication and division.
3. Learning to play badminton may help an individual to play ping pong (Table Tennis) and lawn tennis.
4. Learning to drive a particular brand of car, e.g. Maruti 800 may help an individual to drive other cars, e.g. Opel Astra.
5. Learning Hindi may help a student learn Punjabi or Gujarati.

Negative transfer.   Transfer of learning or training is said to be negative when learning or training in one situation hinders, interferes or weakens the learning in another situation. Examples of such transfer are:

1. Having learned to pronounce "But" correctly, the child may find it difficult to pronounce "Put" correctly.
2. One's regional language or mother tongue may create problems in one's learning the correct pronunciation and intonation related to one's national or foreign language.
3. One who is driving an auto-start kinetic Honda Scooter may find difficulty in driving Bajaj or Vespa scooter.
4. Having learned to drive on the right-hand side the tourists from Japan or USA may find it difficult to drive in India or UK where vehicles are to be driven on the left-hand side.

Zero transfer.   Transfer is said to be 'zero' when learning or training in one situation does not have any significant influence over the learning or training in another situation. Such a situation may arise when the learning activities and subject areas have nothing in common between them. In such cases, it is quite natural that possession of knowledge and skill related to one area may have no or quite minimal effect on the acquisition of knowledge and skill related to another area. Examples of such a transfer may now be cited:

1. Learning history may neither help nor hinder the learning of economics.
2. Learning to play football may not help or hinder learning to play volleyball.
3. Learning to play Guitar or Sitar neither helps nor hinders one's performance in her cooking or laundry class.

Experimental illustration of the transfer types.   Let us analyse the hypothetical experimental findings for illustrating the three transfer types. Suppose a group of students learn a task B, in 10 practice sessions. Another group of equivalent number of students, who previously had learned another task A, is found to reach the same level of performance on task B in only five practice sessions. Since the average number of practice sessions required to learn B was reduced from 10 to 5, transfer of training from task A to task B is said to be positive $(10 - 5 = 5)$.

Now, in case after learning task A, a group of students need 15 practice sessions to learn task B whereas only 10 sessions are required for those without any previous training in task A, then task A is said to lead to negative transfer of training on task B $(10 - 15 = -5)$.

In the third situation where for learning task B, students are found to require the same number of 10 sessions as were required by them in learning task A, the transfer is said to have a zero $(10 - 10 = 0)$ value, that is, signifying no transfer effect from task A to task B.

However, by the above categorisation it should not be concluded that transfer should always exhibit the extremes—positive, negative or zero. In many situations we may come across a mixed trend. Therefore, it may happen that learning in one situation partly help and partly interfere with the performance or learning in a new situation.

THEORIES OF TRANSFER OF LEARNING OR TRAINING

Theory of Mental Discipline (Faculty Theory)

This is the oldest of all the transfer theories. This theory assumes that the mind is composed of so many independent faculties, e.g. memory, attention, imagination, reasoning and judgement. These faculties, according to this theory, are nothing but the "muscles of the mind" and, like muscles of the body, can be strengthened or improved through exercise (practice and use). In this way, such properly strengthened or improved faculties later on function automatically in all the situations and areas in which they are involved. For example, if the memory of a person is strengthened or improved, to a great extent, through memorization of long and difficult passages, then it can prove useful in memorizing dates, names, formulae, figures and, in fact, anything and everything that involves memory. In the same way, propagators of the theory claim that reasoning and imaginative powers developed through the study of geometrical propositions can be used in solving various problems in life which demand a good deal of reasoning and imagination.

Mental discipline as an educational doctrine and as the basis for transfer of training was first seriously challenged by William James. He wanted to see whether daily training in the memorization of a poetry of one author would affect the learning of poetry of another author. For this experiment he acted as a subject for himself. He memorized 158 lines from Victor Hugo's *Satyr* in $131^5/_6$ minutes spread over eight days. He then worked for about 20 minutes daily memorizing the entire book of Milton's *Paradise Lost* (Book-I). This required 38 days. After this period of memory training, he returned to *Satyr* and memorized 158 additional lines. But now he could do so in $151^1/_2$ minutes as against $131^5/_6$ minutes in the first instance. William James therefore concluded that memory was not affected by training as claimed by the faculty theory.

The above findings of William James were later supported by psychologists like Dr. Sleight and Briggs, and others. Thorndike and Woodworth and others through their independent studies were able to conclude that the idea of finding any large difference in general improvement of the mind or its faculties from one type of mental activity or subject of study to another is absurd. As a result of all such studies and conclusions drawn by these latter-day psychologists, the theory of mental discipline or the faculty theory now-a-days stands almost rejected for explaining the mechanism of transfer of learning or training in one situation from other.

Apperception Theory of Transfer

This theory is based on the concept of *Apperception*. *Apperception* may be defined as a process of relating new ideas or mental states to a store of old ones. The storage of old ideas and experiences is called *apperceptive mass*. When a student sets himself to learn a subject, a new idea or to get experience, he learns it by assimilating it with ideas or experiences already acquired and present in his mind in the form of apperceptive masses. The pupils acquire various types of experiences in day-to-day life in informal encounters or through lectures, text books and other formal learning situations. These experiences help them have a huge build-up of apperceptive mass in their sub-conscious mind. That is why, apperceptionists like Herbart advocate the building up of a necessary apperceptive mass in the minds of the learners for promoting transfer. This reservoir or storage of ideas and experiences in the form of apperceptive masses may further help them utilize and carry over some or the other old ideas and experiences for being transferred to meet future situations in and outside the school boundaries. Hence what is stored in the form of ideas or mental states may lie in the sub-conscious mind in the form of apperceptive masses and this in turn may be utilised for further learning in the shape of transfer of memory images, dynamic perceptions and feelings etc. to the conscious layer of our mind. In this way much may be transferred from a person's apperceptive masses (the accumulated storage of ideas, experiences and mental states) to the learning of new ideas, facts, principles and performing of activities. Hence apperceptionists first lay emphasis on the building up of a huge mass of apperception (a powerful reservoir) related to a particular learning area into a person's subconscious mind and then try to strengthen it by repetition (bringing the past ideas more often into consciousness) for being automatically utilised in the relevant learning situations.

To obtain good results in the transfer of learning, apperception as a theory of transfer, advocates a rigidly planned and fixed order of teaching-learning. This leads one to the rigid employment of Herbartian's five steps in the planning and teaching of lessons by the teacher in a classroom.

Apperception, as a theory of transfer, thus gives a new turn to the cause and shape of transfer of learning from one situation to another. It brings into focus the role played by the accumulated ideas and experiences as well as the state of our mind. What is learned or performed in a new learning situation depends to a great extent on what is being transferred from the apperceptive masses lying in the subconscious mind. New experiences are always gained and interpreted in the light of this transfer. If a person possesses ideas and experiences related to a given area in an adequate manner, he may certainly make use of many of them in the new learning situations as and when the appropriate occasion arises. However, this theory, like the theory of mental discipline was also attacked, criticised and abandoned, on the grounds, such as the following:

1. It made the teaching-learning process a very routine and rigid affair, by advocating fixed steps of planning and delivery of lessons.
2. It encouraged memorisation and dependence on past learning by making the students completely docile and dependent on teachers and text books.
3. It discouraged problem-centred approach or class room interaction approach in seeking any transfer of learning.
4. It completely reduced the transfer mechanism to mechanical storage of ideas in an inert and inactive mind.

Theory of Identical Elements

The chief propounder of the theory of identical elements in transfer of training was Thorndike. Later on, Woodworth supported this theory and used the word 'components' in place of elements. Therefore, the theory is also called *Theory of identical components.*

This theory maintains that the transfer from one situation to another is possible to the extent that there are common or identical elements in the situations. For example, there is a possibility of transfer from the field of Mathematics to the field of Physics to the extent that there are some common elements like symbols, formulae, equations, numerical calculations etc. Similarly, transfer takes place from typing to playing a piano to the extent that such skills as eye–finger coordination are identical to both the activities. Thus, similarities in two situations with regard to the common elements of content, skill, attitude, method, aim, habits, interest etc. facilitate the process of transfer.

Theory of Generalization

The theory of generalization as an explanation of transfer of training or learning has been put forth by Charles Judd. The theory insists on a systematic organization and generalization of experiences in order to achieve the maximum transfer of learning or training. It also advocates the transfer of generalizations in new situations in place of identical elements as suggested by Thorndike. As a result of certain experiences, the individual reaches some conclusion or generalization. This conclusion or generalization can be applied by him to oncoming new situations. Thus generalization is nothing but a principle, a law or a rule which can be easily transferred to other situations.

According to this theory as Crow and Crow put it,

The developing of special skills, the mastery of specific facts, the achieving of particular habits or attitudes in one situation have little transfer value unless the skills, facts, habits are systematized and related to situations in which they can be utilized (1973).

Judd's experiments. Judd conducted a dart throwing experiment to test the transfer value of generalisation. He took (after matching them in terms of intelligence) two groups of children of fifth and sixth grades. He called one group as an experimental group and the other as control group. The purpose of experiment was to study the effect of instruction in the principle of refraction of light upon the ability of boys to throw darts at targets placed under water. The experimental group was given a full theoretical explanation of refraction and the other group was left to work without theoretical training. Both groups of boys were then asked to throw darts to hit a target placed 12 inches under water. Both the groups did not do well irrespective of the fact that the experimental group had a theoretical understanding of the phenomenon of refraction. Mere theoretical understanding of refraction could not help the experimental group to perform better than the control group. Again the situation was changed. The target was placed 4 inches under water. This time the experimental group showed much better results than the control group. Both the groups had an equal chance of practice but whereas the control group could not make use of its earlier experience to perform the task now, the experimental group derived maximum benefit out of it. The understanding of the principle of refraction (theoretically as well as practically) helped them hit the underwater targets which appear to be a little raised than their actual position.

On the basis of his experiment, Mr. Judd concluded that it is the generalization of the understanding of some relationships (a rule or a law) which is usually transferred from the earlier situation to the later one. Similarly the day to day generalized experiences of a child like—"By touching fire, we get burnt", "The green apples are sour in taste"—always get transferred to an oncoming new situation.

Therefore, one is largely benefited by the systematic and organised generalization of experiences and in this way, this theory lays stress on the generalization of specific experiences and formulation of some rules or principles so that they may be transferred from one situation to another.

Transposition Theory of Transfer

This theory has been propagated by Gestalt field psychologists. They brought into focus the role of insight and understanding in learning something or behaving in a particular way. Accordingly, they emphasized the role of insight in the mechanism of transfer of learning. They asserted that in transfer, the identical elements or generalizations do not get transferred automatically unless one has developed the proper insight of using and employing them and is desirous to transfer it at the right time. This process of gaining or developing insight into the use of concepts and generalizations in one situation and employing it afterwards in other situations is called transposition and it is this transposition of insight which can be a medium or a base for the transfer of learning from one situation to another.

This means that the key to transfer of learning from one situation to another lies in the development and transposition of proper insight. Hence, as the theory asserts, good results in the process of transfer of learning may be achieved if a person:

1. develops the attitude of throwing proper insight learning.
2. tries for a generalisation of the gained insight by perceiving common factors in different situations.
3. tries to understand how generalization can be used.

Theory of Ideals

This theory was put forward by W.C. Bagley. He tried to explain mechanism of transfer in terms of ideals. He asserted that generalizations are more likely to transfer if they are regarded as ideals—of some value—as desirable. There are two experiments on transfer of neatness which support Bagley's assertion.

In the first experiment the experimenter emphasized neatness in the preparation of arithmetic papers by pupils in the third grade. Nothing was said about neatness in the rest of the school subjects. Language and spelling papers were then compared with arithmetic papers for improvement in neatness. While the arithmetic paper showed clear proof of neatness, the language and spelling papers were rather less neat. It was concluded that specific training in neatness in one area did not transfer to other areas.

In the other investigation the experimenter insisted on neatness in all papers, and the children were told about the advantage of neatness in other respects of life inside and outside the school. In this way great effort was made to develop the ideal of neatness. The result showed an overall improvement in neatness in all subjects. The conclusion was that ideals do transfer.

Thus, the theory of ideals emphasizes that the ideals like love for wisdom, thirst for knowledge, tolerance for difference of opinions, spirit of enquiry etc. are transferable from one situation to another and therefore every attempt should be made to develop desirable ideals among the children.

All the above theories seem to hold divergent opinions regarding the explanation of transfer from one situation to another. But in actual sense these differences are probably more than real. All these theories are complementary and not contradictory. In one way or the other each one of them tries to explain the mechanism of transfer. By synthesizing the viewpoints of all these theories we can understand, how transfer of learning or training takes place from one situation to another.

Educational Implications of the Transfer of Training or Learning

The mechanism of transfer of learning or training has a wide educational implication in the following form:

1. Learning in one situation is capable of exercising positive or negative influence over the learning in another situation.

2. As far as possible efforts should be made to seek positive transfer value of the learned thing by avoiding the negative ones.

3. For seeking maximum positive transfer, the teachers while teaching, and the learners while learning, should try to draw proper lessons from the viewpoints of the theories of transfer like below:

   (a) identification of association, similarities and dissimilarities among the learning situations.

   (b) building generalizations and making their use in further learning.

   (c) developing proper understanding and insight for using them in further learning and problem-solving.

   (d) developing a proper apperceptive mass in the form of knowledge and experience for its future use.

   (e) developing proper ideals and imbibing them to perform things in future.

What should the learners do for achieving maximum positive transfer? The problem of transfer of training occupies a significant place in the process of education. It brings economy and effectiveness in the learning process. By realising transfer, what one learns or experiences in some previous situation can either be utilized for the learning in the new situations or it can be applied to find solutions for the day-to-day problems. Therefore, a wise learner should try to secure maximum transfer so that he may be benefited properly from his earlier experiences and training. The following suggestions can help in this direction:

1. What is being learned at present, should be linked with what has already been learnt in the past. What one already knows should form a basis for one's present learning. In this way one should try to take advantage of his past experiences or learning by seeking its proper transfer.

2. While engaging in learning, the learner should try to have integration of the theoretical studies with practical experiences.

3. The learner should always keep in mind the principle of correlated learning. What he is trying to learn should be properly correlated with his life experiences, environmental surroundings and other areas of study and knowledge.

4. Identical components between the two learning situations should be properly identified by the learner. Afterwards he should try to understand the relationship between these two situations. With the knowledge of such a relationship, he should try to transfer learning from one situation to another.

5. The learner should avoid rote learning. He must develop the habit of learning through proper understanding and insight.

6. He must try to take the help of multi-media and sensory aids for proper understanding and gaining of the required knowledge and skills.

7. As far as possible the learner should try to learn through his own efforts. He must make use of logical thinking for knowing and discovering things by himself.

8. The learner should try to seek unity in diversity by searching for

commonness and harmony among the different subjects and learning experiences. He should never hesitate to utilize the learning of one field in the learning of other fields.

9. Instead of learning discrete and isolated facts, the learner should concentrate on the learning of the principles, generalizations and rules. He should try to discover formulae, rules and principles on the basis of his experiences and then give sufficient time for their utilization and practice.

10. The learner, in all the situations, should be fully convinced about the importance and value of the transfer of learning or training. He may take the help of his teachers, elders and other experts for learning the art of transfer. As far as possible he should try to develop the skill of transferability so much so that he remains engaged in making conscious and deliberate efforts to transfer his learning and experiences from one situation to another.

11. Ideals as we have seen, possess a great transfer value. Therefore, the learner should try to imbibe desirable ideals to be transferred from one situation to another. For example one should try to imbibe the habit of cleanliness as an ideal in his life and should therefore to able to transfer it in all activities and spheres of life.

12. Learner should try to gain proper knowledge and insight into making distinctions between positive and negative transfer of his learning or training. As far as possible, he should seek the maximum positive transfer of his learning or training by saving himself from the ill-effects of negative transfer.

In this way, if one keeps in mind the above points, one may be able to get advantage of the mechanism of transfer of learning.

SUMMARY

Transfer of learning or training is a process by which learning or training in one situation is carried over or transferred to other situations.

Basically three types of transfer can occur—positive, negative and zero. Positive transfer occurs when learning in one situation helps the learning in other situation, negative when it hinders the other, and zero when it neither helps nor hinders.

Apart from such basic transfers, there may be a fourth possibility that learning in one situation may partly help and partly hinders the learning in another situation i.e. learning of English under the influence of Hindi or one's mother tongue.

The process of transfer from one learning situation to another can be explained on the basis of the theory of transfer of training or learning. According to the theory of mental discipline (faculty theory), our mind is composed of faculties like memory, attention, reasoning and judgement etc. These faculties can be trained and then strengthened like the muscles of our body and then they may be utilised in a quite automatic fashion in the other learning or practical situations in our life.

According to Apperception theory of transfer, learning results in the storage of ideas, experiences etc. (called apperceptive mass) into one's unconscious mind and their strengthening with repetition. Such strengthened apperceptive mass then leads automatically to its transfer in the relevant learning situation.

Theory of identical elements or components asserts that transfer from one learning situation to another do take place to the extent that there are common or identical elements involved in these situations.

Theory of generalization says that transfer do take place in the form of generalization (conclusions reached on the basis of experiences or experiments) instead of the isolated facts related to identical elements. As a result we usually employ principles, rules and laws for helping us transfer from one learning situation to another.

Transposition theory of transfer emphasizes on the development and transposition of proper insight for helping in the mechanism of transfer.

Theory of ideals says that neither the isolated facts nor the generalizations but the ideals get transferred from one learning situation to another. That is why it gives proper weightage to the development of desired attitudes and ideas about the things in the form of ideals for being transferred from one learning situation to another.

The mechanism of transfer carries wide educational implications for both the teachers and the learners as they come to realize that (i) transfer helps in better teaching and learning, (ii) it has positive and negative effects and therefore attempts should be made to seek maximum positive transfer by avoiding the negative ones, (iii) theory of transfer may help them in seeking maximum positive transfer.

A learner, whether in the class room situation or at the time of his self-learning may draw proper advantage from the lessons learnt through the mechanism of transfer of learning or training, if he is well motivated and prepared to do so. For this purpose he needs to keep in mind the principle of correlation, integration of the acquired experiences, development of proper attitudes and ideals, generalization of facts and principles and above all, the will and determination to seek maximum positive transfer of his learning or training from one situation to another.

REFERENCES

Bigge, Morris, L., *Learning Theories for Teachers*, Delhi: Universal Book Stall, (Indian Reprint), 1967.

Crow, L.D. and Crow, A., *Educational Psychology* (3rd Indian Reprint), New Delhi: Eurasia Publishing House, 1973, p. 319, 323.

Sorenson, Herbert, *Psychology in Education*, New York: McGraw-Hill, 1948, p. 387.

Thorndike, E.L., *Human Learning*, New York: Holt, 1965.

Woodworth, R.S., *Psychology*, London, Methuen, 1945.

SUGGESTED READINGS

Bigge, M.L. and Hunt, M.P., *Psychological Foundations of Education*, New York: Harper & Row, 1968.

Ellis, Henry, *Transfer of Learning*, New York: Macmillan, 1965.

Horton D.L. and Turnage, T.W., *Human Learning*, Englewood Cliffs, Prentice Hall, 1976.

Hulse, S.H., Deese, J. and Egeth, H., *The Psychology of Learning* (4th ed.), New York: McGraw-Hill, 1975.

Kingsley, H.L. and Garry, R. *The Nature and Conditions of Learning* (2nd ed.), Englewood Cliffs, New Jersey: Prentice Hall, 1957.

Peterson, L.R., *Learning*, Glenview, Illinois, Scott, Foresman, 1975.

Stephenes, J.M., *Handbook of Classroom Learning*, New York: Holt, 1965.

Woodworth, R.S. and Marquis, D.G., *Psychology*, New York: Henry Holt & Co., 1948 (5th ed.).

Chapter 15

Memory—Remembering and Forgetting

WHAT IS MEMORY?

Learning occupies a very significant place in one's life. It is the basis not only of the development and progress of human society but also of its survival. Learning, however, would be futile if its products cannot be utilized by us in the future. Whatever is learned needs to be somehow stored in the mind so that it can be utilized whenever required in the future. In psychological terms, this faculty of the mind to store the past experiences or learning and to reproduce them for use when required at a later time is known as 'memory'. Ryburn (1956) endorses this meaning of memory in the following words:

> The power that we have to 'store' our experiences, and to bring them into the field of our consciousness some time after the experiences have occurred, is termed *memory*.

An assessment of the strength of the power or quality of this ability can be made on the basis of performance in terms of the quality of the revival or reproduction of what has been learnt and stored up. In this sense, a good memory must reflect "an ideal revival" as Stout (1938) puts:

> So far as ideal revival is merely reproductive.... This productive aspect of ideal revival requires the object of past experiences to be re-instated as far as possible in the order and manner of their original occurrence.

However, the term 'memory', or the process of memorization, cannot be viewed merely in terms of reproduction or revival of past experiences or learning. It is quite a complex process which involves factors like learning, retention, recall, and recognition.

Mechanism of the Process of Memorization

Our mind possesses a special ability, by virtue of which every experience or learning leaves behind memory images or traces which are conserved in the form of 'engrams'. Thus what is learned leaves its after-effect which is conserved in the form of engrams composed of memory traces. This preservation of the memory traces by our central nervous system or brain is known as retention of the learned or experienced act. The duration of retention depends upon the strength and quality of the memory traces. When we try to recollect or repeat our past experiences or learning, we make use of the memory traces and if we are successful in the revival of our memory traces, our memory is said to be good. But if, somehow or the other, the memory traces have died out, we cannot reproduce or make use of our past experiences and learning. In this case it is said that we have been unable to retain what has been learned or that we have forgotten.

Learning is then the primary condition for memorization. If there is no learning there would be no remembering. At the second stage we have to ensure that these learning experiences are retained properly in the form of mental impressions or images so that they can be retrieved when the need arises. The third and fourth stages in the process of memorization can be termed as recognition and recall. Recognition is a much easier and simpler a psychological process than recall. The difference between these two terms can be illustrated by the following example:

Suppose, Ramnath had been your classmate for two years and you spent a fairly long time together. The old experiences would have been retained as memory traces. Now if, at the mention of his name, you are able to recollect all the experiences you shared with him, and describe him, it is said that you have a good memory, because the memory traces were stored or retained in a proper form. If, on the other hand, you can recall the mutual experiences only vaguely or not at all, the memory traces have either become weak or have disappeared.

In such cases 'recognition' is, however, possible because this requires only the awareness of having known an object or situation. Here the presence of the already experienced object or person aids the task of recollection. In the above example, a photograph or the actual presence of Ramnath may facilitate the task of recollecting the past experiences.

The process of memorization, thus, begins with learning or experiencing something and ends with its revival and reproduction. Therefore, memory is said to involve four stages, viz., learning or experiencing something, its retention, recognition, and recall.

Remembering and Memory

As discussed above, memory denotes the ability or power of mind to retain and reproduce learning. This power of ability helps in the process of memorization. Both the terms 'memorization' and 'remembering' carry the same meaning. While differentiating memory and remembering, Levin (1978) says:

> Memory can be likened to a giant filing cabinet in the brain, with data sorted, classified and cross-filed for future reference. Remembering depends on how the brain goes about coding its input.

However, in a practical sense, when we say that a person has a good or a poor memory, according to Woodworth and Marquis (1948): we always weigh it in terms of "remembering what has previously been learned". It is in this sense that the terms memory and remembering, in spite of their being noun and verb respectively, are used synonymously. In the present text, however, these words have been used interchangeably.

How Do We Remember—Models of Memory

Several theories and models have been devised by psychologists to explain how we remember or how memory works. Some of these are briefly discussed here:

Storage and transfer model. This model has been suggested by Atkinson and Shiffrin (1968, 1971). In connection with the working of memory, they have suggested three different memory storage systems: sensory stores, a short-term store, and a long-term store.

The process of memorization starts with the interaction of one's sense organs with one's environment. The sensory information is first picked up by the sense organs, then it travels through the nervous system and reaches the brain which interprets it. The sensory message or information must stay or linger in the nervous system briefly, to give the brain time to interpret it. This momentary pause of less than a second, or lingering or persistence of the sensory information, is referred to as sensory storage. According to Atkinson and Shiffrin (1971), there seems to be a sensory store for each sense—visual, auditory, smell, taste and touch (see Figure 15.1). However, only the visual and auditory storage systems referred to as *iconic storage* and *echoic storage* respectively have so far been studied extensively.

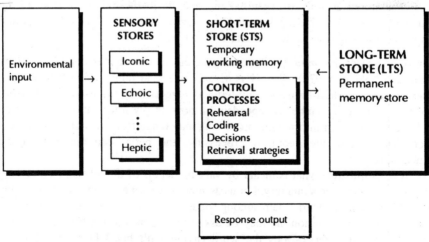

Figure 15.1   The model of memory storage.

Sensory information passing through the sensory stores (or registers) either disappears within a second or is transferred to the short-term store. This short-term store, according to Atkinson and Shiffrin, may be thought of as a stage of conscious activity. The information transferred from the sensory store to the short-term store may automatically stay for up to 20 seconds. However, it can be retained as long as an individual wants it in the short-term store through rehearsal, or repetition. In case the short-term store is able to hold or register the information up to 20 seconds, it may move into the long-term store. The short-term store, is thus responsible for the transformation of sensory information to the long-term store as well as its retrieval. It also decides which responses should be made. Actually for this reason, the short-term store is sometimes called the working memory, as this is the memory employed in much of one's mental work. For transferring information from the short-term store to the long-term store, one can make use of many control processes. Rehearsal is one such process while coding and other mental activities may aid long-term memory much more than simple repetition. In the retrieval (recalling what has been stored in the long-term memory) also, various control processes and retrieval strategies like decoding of stored information are put into use in the short-term storage.

The long-term store is used for storing the sensory information on a permanent basis, while the short-term store contains a limited amount of activated material in current use, the long-term store is assumed to have almost unlimited capacity for the storage of the encoded currently inactive material.

The sensory information is stored (or is transformed from short-term memory) in the coded form. At the time of reproduction or retrieval, this is again decoded. The different forms of such coding are linguistic (verbal), imaginal and motor.

In linguistic coding, the coding of the sensory information is done in the form of language or words. Imaginal coding makes use of images, mental picturization for the storage of information, and the third type of code, the motor code is employed for remembering physical skills like swimming, cycling, etc.

The stored as well as organised information in the long-term store in the coded form is transferred back to the short-term store where it is decoded and employed for response as desired and ordered by the brain.

Levels of processing model.   According to the model of memory designed by Craik and Lokhart (1972) memory is of only one kind rather than of three types (namely, sensory, short-term and long-term, as suggested by Atkinson and Shiffrin), and the ability to remember is dependent on how deeply information is processed by us. Levels of such information processing may range from very shallow to very deep. The greater the depth of processing, the better can the material be remembered.

Let us illustrate what is meant by varying depths of the levels of processing and how it affects one's memory. Let us assume that in one of the experiments, the subject is shown the word 'chair' among some other words on the screen. Later on as a test of his recognition, he may be asked to respond to questions like: Is the word in capital letters? Does the word rhyme with hair? Does it belong to something which may be used for sitting? It may be clearly seen that all of these three questions have been designed to control the level of processing of the word. The first question involves the subject's awareness of its sensory or structural feature of what the word looks. The level of processing at this stage is quite shallow. The next stage involves the subject's awareness of its sensory phonetic feature, the sound of the word. This may be termed as the intermediate level of processing. The last question concerns the task of making an association, i.e. assigning a meaning or use to the object. Here, the level of processing is deep, the kind that may help in forming the strong and more enduring memory trace. Experiments like this may reveal that one's memory performs best when it is processed to deeper levels. Apart from the memory of the verbal material, the theory of the levels of processing can be applied equally well to the memorization of non-verbal material. In one of their experiments, Bower and Karlin (1974) showed pictures of people to their subjects and asked them to (i) determine the sex of those persons shown, and (ii) assess whether they would like those persons.

It was found that the subjects were able to remember the faces better when they processed the information related to the second question, i.e. judgement of attraction. It was obvious that in judging person's likability, they had to go quite deeper (semantic and meaningful processing) than merely judging a person's sex— male or female.

As further application of the levels of processing model, Perfetti (in Cermak & Craik, 1979, pp. 159–180) has extended the levels of processing framework to language comprehension. He has proposed seven levels: acoustic, phonology, syntactic, semantic, referential, thematic and functional. The first three levels are normally transparent while the fourth level (semantic) is the conscious interpretation of an utterance or a sentence. Processing of the last three levels depend upon context and is likely to result in comprehension, provided there is no ambiguity. One has to go deeper and deeper in gaining comprehension of the verbal or written text. The levels of processing provide us the following significant principles:

1. The greater the processing of information during learning or memorization, the more it will be retained and remembered.
2. Processing from one to other levels will be automatic unless attention is focussed on a particular level.

TYPES OF MEMORY

Psychologists have tried to classify memory into certain types according to its nature and the purpose it serves.

Sensory, Short-term and Long-term Memory

One of the broad classifications consisting of sensory or immediate memory, short-term memory and long-term memory is based on the storage and transfer model of remembering which was discussed earlier in the previous pages of this chapter. Let us now discuss these types of memory in detail.

Sensory or immediate memory. Sensory or immediate memory is the memory that helps an individual to recall something immediately after it is perceived. In this type of memory, the retention time is extremely brief—generally from a fraction of a second to several seconds. Old sensory impressions disappear as they are 'erased' by new information.

Immediate memory is needed when we want to remember a thing for a short time and can then forget it. For instance, when we enter an auditorium, we see the seat number given on our ticket. Having occupied the seat, we forget the seat number. We took up a telephone number from the directory and remember it. But after making the telephone call, we usually forget it. In all cases of this nature, immediate memory is needed which helps us to learn a thing immediately with speed and accuracy, remember it for a short duration and forget it rapidly after use.

Short-term memory. This type of memory is also temporary, though not nearly as short-lived as immediate memory. In order to further distinguish it from short-term memory, the following factors should also be taken into account:

1. Where the retention time is less than one second in immediate memory, the information temporarily stored in short-term memory may last as long as thirty seconds even if the material is not being rehearsed.
2. Whereas the sensory images in immediate memory decay regardless of the learner's actions, rehearsal by the learner can keep material in short-term memory indefinitely.
3. The span of immediate memory exceeds the short-term memory span. Whereas five to nine items ("the magical number, seven plus or minus two") can be held in short-term memory at any one time, about 11–13 items are available for recall in the immediate memory for at least half a second. However, some people are able to retain much more information in their short-term memories by a process called *chunking,* which groups information by coding it, e.g. the number 143254376 can be remembered by listing under three heads: 143, 254, 376 and the number 149162536496481 can be arranged as: 1 4 9 16 25 36 49 64 81 (in groups of the squares of 1 through 9) for better remembering.

Long-term memory. Unlike short-term memory, long-term memory has a seemingly limitless capacity to store information with little or no decay and requires little, if any, rehearsal. In addition to these characteristics, long-term memory codes information according to meaning, pattern and other characteristics. It is this memory that helps us to remember a number of things on a relatively permanent basis. Remembering identifying data like one's name, father's name, date of birth, date of marriage, etc., is the simplest example of long-term memory. With the help of our long-term memory we can easily store, retain and remember most of the things in our life at a second's notice and thus easily conduct our daily life.

Episodic and semantic memory. Episodic memory is connected with episodes and events. It may consist of personal events and experiences associated with one's life. What even has happened during one's life is stored in the shape of episodic memory traces organised according to the time, space and other characteristics of the events. At the time of recall, these memory traces are reproduced in the manner and sequence in which they have been organised and stored in one's mental apparatus. For example, if a person has been on an excursion and, on his return, narrates all that he did or experienced, how he felt and enjoyed himself, he is able to do so by the exercise of his episodic memory. Also, when after hearing his account of the events or episodes you make inferences, that is the outcome of your episodic memory. Thus, episodic memory is the memory which depends on retrieving the particular events or episodes experienced by a person through his direct or indirect experiences. It should be considered as quite personal and individual in all its shades and nuances because what one experiences and how these episodes and experiences are organised in one's memory is totally an individual affair and thereby one individual's episodic memory of even common events is bound to differ from that of other person.

Semantic memory helps in storing as well as retrieving a collection of relationships between events or association of ideas. Examples of such collection may be found in one's ability to recall names of the capitals of different states of the Indian Republic, the meaning of the symbol CO_2, the formula for the computation of simple or compound interest, the rules for converting direct narrations into indirect narrations and vice versa, and so on. Semantic memory is thus based on general knowledge coupled with meaningful interpretation, generalized rules, principles and formulae. Semantic memory impressions are more or less permanent. Their recall does not necessarily depend on the retrieval of some specific episodes from the past and semantic memory is therefore, not as personal as episodic memory, e.g. the meaning of the symbol CO_2 and names of the capitals of the states, etc., are common to each individual's semantic memory.

Photographic memory. According to Haber (1979), the terrn 'photographic memory' stands for a kind of memory possessed by an individual who can remember a scene in photographic detail. The technical term used for such memory is *eidetic imagery*. Such people can 'see' a picture after it has been taken away, with their descriptions of objects from the picture stating the right colour and the proper locations.

Paranormal memory. This distinctive and unusual type of memory, popularly known as 'reincarnation' has emerged as a result of researches and findings in the field of para-psychology. It consists of the unusual memory traces concerning one's previous life or lives that can be partly or completely retrieved by the individual. In the language of psychoanalysis, such memory reflects an individual's regression not only in terms of time but also in terms of space and matter (from one place and one body to another). It is mostly connected with the phenomenon of rebirth, i.e. the belief that at the time of death one gives up one's body but not the soul which survives to acquire a new body much like one puts on new clothes after discarding old ones.

The Study of Memory

The experimental study of memory is aimed at learning the nature and process of memorization, the individual differences in memory, and the economical methods and best possible outcomes of the process of memorization. Let us discuss the materials, apparatus and techniques used for the study of memory.

Material. Simple verbal materials are used in most experiments on human memory, like serial list, paired-associate lists, and connected discourse.

A *serial list* is composed of words such as RAT, CAP, TENT and PAINT or numbers (e.g. 29, 57, 36, 72, . . .), or meaningless nonsense syllables (e.g. NAL, SOK, PAB, and KAZ).

A *paired-associate list* consists of a series of paired (but not necessarily related) words, digits or non-sense syllables presented sequentially (e.g. CORN-MUSIC, BOX-CAT, FOOD-BOOK).

In the material called *connected discourse,* we may include excerpts of actual blocks of language, either written or spoken. These might be entire sentences, paragraphs or longer passages from any piece of literature or a lecture.

Apparatus. Various techniques are used for the presentation of the memorization material to the learner. The experimenter himself may simply read it aloud or may use a tape-recorder for this purpose and the subjects may then be required to say or write what they remember. In most of the experiments, however, the verbal material is presented visually with the help of an instrument called a *memory drum* (see Figure 15.2). For example, the words of a serial list may be presented one at

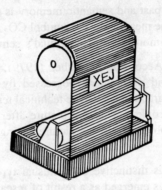

Figure 15.2   Memory drum.

a time for a specified duration through a window-like opening of this drum to be operated. The subjects are asked to recall as many words as possible. The list is presented again and again while the experimenter plots how long and how many trials it takes to learn a task. Recent technological developments have replaced the age old memory drum apparatus with sophisticated electronic computers.

Measures and criteria. Memory—good or bad—can be inferred from the retentivity, and the degree of retention may be measured directly if we know how much material was learned originally by using the formula:

$$\text{Amount of retention} = \text{amount learned} - \text{amount forgotten.}$$

What is actually retained by the learner can be ascertained by the experimenter if he tests the performance of the learner through reproduction, i.e. in terms of recognition and recall.

Two most commonly used procedures for measuring recognition are tests of simple recognition and multiple-alternative recognition. In simple recognition tests, the subject may be presented with a photograph or an item to decide whether or not he has seen it before. In a multiple alternate recognition test he has to recognize a particular person or item seen before out of several pictures or items presented to him.

The important methods employed in the measurement of recall are *free recall, probed recall,* and *serial recall.*

In the **free recall** method, a subject is asked to recall in any order as many items as possible from the list he has seen or recall anything in any way from a stanza or poem read. In **probed recall,** the subject may be given some hint or cue suggesting the appropriate item. For example, in a paired-associate list consisting of the pair BOX-CAT, he may be asked to say what word appeared with BOX in the list seen by him. When a **serial list** is used, the cue may be in the form of the location of a certain item in the list: top, bottom, middle and so forth. In serial recall, the subject is asked to repeat the items in exactly the same order as they were presented to him during the experiment.

In addition to employing tests of recognition and recall for measuring one's retention power, certain other methods may also be employed. Two such methods devised by the psychologist Ebbinghaus are the learning method and the saving method.

In the **learning method,** the subject is shown a list of verbal material (words or nonsense syllables). He tries to memorize this material by taking the syllables one by one over a number of trials. After each trial he is required to write down all the words of syllables he remembers. The subjects will differ in terms of the number of trials required to learn the list correctly. A subject's power of retention may then be judged in terms of the number of trials required to reproduce a standard list of verbal material (e.g., 12 nonsense syllables like NAL, SOK, BAP, in the Ebbinghaus' study). The better a person's retentive power, the lower would be the number of trials required by him for remembering the complete list.

The **saving method** is employed after the subject has learned all the words or syllables correctly after several trials. The subject may then be given a period of rest. Naturally, during this period, he may be expected to forget some of the material he has learned. He is now allowed further trials for relearning. Different individuals will differ in the number of trials they need for relearning and reproducing the complete list. The number of trials or repetitions saved in the second learning (relearning) are then considered to be the measure of the power of retention. If, for example, a subject had 10 trials to learn—all the 12 nonsense syllables correctly in the first learning and took seven trials to learn again in the second learning session, then he had a saving of three trials. His retention power will definitely be better than that of another who needed eight trials for relearning or one who has a saving of only one assuming, of course, that he too had 10 trials in the first learning.

Economy in Memorizing

The problem of bringing economy into memorizing something prompted several psychologists to devise various methods of memorization. All these methods aim at finding the best way of utilizing the available time in the most advantageous manner. Some of these methods are here discussed:

1. *Recitation method.* In this method one learner first reads the matter once or twice and then tries to recite and recall it without looking at the material. The recitation method thus provides continuous self-appraisal. The learner evaluates himself from time to time and makes notes of the points which he has been unable to recall. Due attention can be paid to these points and so he does not have to unnecessarily repeat the already memorized material. Moreover, the recitation method is more stimulating than the continued re-reading of the same material. It helps in detecting errors made earlier and avoiding them by paying closer attention.

2. *Whole and part methods.* There are two methods of memorizing a thing, say, a poem. One is to read the poem again and again from the beginning till the end as a whole. This is called the whole method of memorization. In the other method, viz. the part method, the poem is divided into parts and each part is memorized separately.

Both these methods have advantages as well as disadvantages and which of the two would prove more suitable and economical depends upon the prevailing conditions and the nature of the matter to be memorized. The 'whole' method is found to be better than the 'part' method for memorizing a thing which requires less time like a short poem for instance, while the part method proves more advantageous if the poem is a long one. In some cases a combination of the two methods has been found most suitable. In this combined method, the learner starts initially with the whole method and locates the areas of difficulty. These difficult portions are then attended to by the part method. After that the subject once again reverts to the whole method and is then able to remember the matter successfully.

3. *Spaced and unspaced methods (methods of distributed and massed practice).* In the spaced or distributed practice method of memorization, the subject is not required to memorize the assigned material in one sitting. Each time after memorizing the material for some time, a period of rest is provided and this principle of 'work and rest' is followed throughout. For example, if a subject has to memorize a piece of poetry by this method, he would be advised, in the beginning, to just go on repeating it for some time and then take a break. After this, he would be asked to resume reading and then take another break. In this way, with the alternate periods of reading and rest, he would be able to memorize the assigned piece.

On the other hand, in the unspaced or massed practice method of memorization, the subject has to memorize the assigned material at one sitting without any interval or rest until it is mastered.

Many experimental studies have been conducted to assess the relative values of these two methods. Although in case of short lessons it is not considered necessary to have any interval yet the spaced method has yielded better results. It has been observed that instead of working continuously without rest, it is better to distribute the hours of work in these sittings and introduce periods of rest between sittings. This helps in removing the monotony of long periods of study. Attention also does not flag and fatigue is avoided. The subject gets a fresh start after a period of rest and thus his interest in the task can be maintained. Which of these methods is better and more appropriate is a difficult question to answer. Definitely, all these methods are found to be useful and effective in one situation or the other. However, no single method has been found to be equally effective under all circumstances. In fact, success in the use of a particular method depends more on the abilities of the individual and the nature and range of the material to be memorized than on the method itself. Besides the adoption of a particular method of memorization, there are so many external and internal factors in the environment and the individual himself which affect the process of memorization and consequently help or obstruct a person's progress in memorization. Care should, therefore, be taken to ensure favourable conditions and situations for best results in memorization.

Training in Memory

Whether memory can be improved by training is a controversial issue though its improvement is desired by all. Every one of us is keen to improve his sense organs and muscles etc., but the improvement of memory as such is not possible. The opinion expressed by Morgan and Gilliland (1942) is relevant in this context:

> Memory training is not like muscle training. You can make a muscle develop by any kind of use. Memory is not helped by any kind of exercises.

Mere repetition of material for the sake of memorization in the form of mental exercise does not yield enduring and effective results. As stated earlier, memory consists of four factors—learning, retention, recognition and recall. Improvement in any one or more of these constituents is likely to improve memory as a whole. Therefore, to obtain a logical answer regarding the improvement of memory, its four different components have to be considered: Is it possible to improve learning, retention, recognition, and recall as independent functions? Let us examine these aspects and try to find an answer.

Retention, it is said, is native and inherited and, therefore, cannot be improved by training. We can, at the most, try to protect retentiveness by some measures but it is most hardly possible to improve it by training. In the case of recognition also, it is most difficult to say whether it can be improved by training as it happens to be a prompt and spontaneous act.

The remaining two constituents—learning and recall, have been observed to improve by training. Let us see how they can be improved.

1. While trying to recall something, you should be free from excessive anxiety, fear and other emotional factors which tend to block memory.
2. Have confidence in yourself and never think that you would not be able to recall something. Be calm, avoid nervousness, and concentrate on the task of recall.
3. Remember that association of ideas, connection and systematic thinking, are very helpful in the task of recall. If, for example, you need to recall the place where you have put the key of your drawer, and you should try to think systematically with the help of the principle of association: where was I just before this time, what was I doing. I was taking a bath, so I may have put it in the cupboard of the bathroom. Proceeding like this you can ultimately recall the exact place.
4. Do not strain yourself for too long to recall anything. If you find it difficult to recall something, give up for a while and after allowing yourself a little time to relax, try again later.

Learning is the most important factor of memory. Improvement of memory to a large extent rests upon this factor which can be improved by training. Improvement in learning is mainly influenced by (a) the techniques and methods of learning, (b) the learning situations and environment, and (c) the learner's state of mind.

Improvement in all these aspects calls for interest and earnestness on the part of the learner. Let us now examine some of the requirements and techniques which can lead to successful results.

1. *Will to learn.* There must be firm determination or strong will to learn effectively and successfully. Where there is a will there is a way. Materials read, heard or seen without genuine interest or inclination are difficult to be remembered for being recalled at a later time.

2. *Interest and attention.* Interest as well as close attention are essential for useful learning and memorization. A person who has no interest in what he learns, will not give due attention to it and consequently will not be able to learn it. Bhatia (1968) states this fact in the following words:

> Interest is the mother of attention and attention is the mother of memory; if you would secure memory, you must first catch the mother and the grandmother.

Every care should, therefore, be taken to create the necessary interest in the material by making its purpose clear and linking it with one's natural instincts and urges. All the factors causing distraction should be reduced to a minimum so that full attention can be paid to the material in hand.

3. *Adopting proper methods of memorization.* There are several efficient methods of memorization but not all are suitable on all occasions and for all individuals. Therefore, a judicious selection should be made in choosing a particular method in a given situation.

4. *Following the principles of association.* It is always good to follow the principle of association in learning. A thing should never be learnt in an isolated, insular manner. An effort should be made to connect it with one's previous learning on the one hand and with as many related things as possible on the other. Sometimes, for association of ideas, special techniques and devices are used that facilitate learning and recall, e.g., the letters VIBGYOR have proved to be a very effective aid to remembering the colours of the rainbow. Many such associations may be formed and the material to be learned easily remembered with their help.

5. *Grouping and rhythm.* Grouping and rhythm also facilitate learning and help in remembering. For example the telephone number 567345234 can be easily memorized and recalled if we try to group it as 567 345 234.

Similarly, rhythm also proves to be an aid in learning and memorizing. Children learn effectively the multiplication tables by reciting them in a sing-song. The arrangement of the material in verse with rhythm and rhyme is found very useful in this direction. The rhyme about the days of the months is well-known:

Thirty days hath September,
    April, June, and November,
All the rest have thirty-one,
    Excepting February alone,
To which they twenty-eight assign,
    Till a leap year gives it twenty-nine.

6. *Utilizing as many senses as possible.* Senses are said to be the gateways of knowledge and it has also been found that things are better learned and remembered when they are presented through more than one sense. Therefore, attempts should be made to take the help of audio-visual aid material and receive impressions through as many senses as possible.

7. *Arranging better learning situations.* Environmental factors also affect the learning process and due care should, therefore, be taken to arrange favourable learning situations and environment. A calm and quiet atmosphere and stimulating environment proves to be an effective aid to learning.

8. *The learner's internal factors.* Besides the various external factors there are things within the learner which affect his learning and capacity of recall. His physical and mental health and emotional state at the time of learning as well as reproduction of the material learnt counts a lot towards the effectiveness of his memory. Therefore, due attention should be given to the improvement of the student's health—physical as well as mental. His emotions should also be trained and emotional tensions removed as far as possible.

9. *Provision for change and proper rest.* Adequate provision for rest, sleep and variety in the work should be made as this helps to relieve fatigue and monotony. A mind which is fresh is naturally able to learn more and retain it for a longer period than a mind which is dull and fatigued.

10. *Repetition and practice.* Finally, repetition and continuous practice adds to the effectiveness of memorization. Intelligent repetition with full understanding always helps in making the learning effective and enduring and things repeated and practised frequently are remembered for a long time. Due attention should, therefore, be given to drill work, practice and review etc. in the process of memorization and learning.

11. *Making use of SQ 4 R technique.* Thomas and Robinson (1972) developed this strategy for effective learning and memorization. In this technique, the learners are taught to adopt a systematic approach to learning the desired material involving sequenced steps, i.e. survey, question, read, reflect, recite and review. These steps are named and remembered through the letters SQ 4 R.

- *Survey.* Initially, the material to be remembered is surveyed quickly to get an idea of what is going to be remembered.

- *Question.* In this step the learner asks himself questions like why, what, when, where and who, concerning the material surveyed in the first step.

- *Read.* The material is then read for mental comprehension and to learn the answers to the questions raised in the second step.

- *Reflect.* The information given in the required material is organized and made meaningful by (a) linking it with the previous knowledge, (b) comparing and contrasting the facts, (c) correlating the information with other similar facts, concepts and principles, and (d) attempting to make use of the material in solving simulated problems.

- *Recite and recall.* The information provided in the material is remembered through recitation and recall both orally and in writing.

- *Review.* In this final step, the material needed to be remembered is actively reviewed. The learner asks himself questions related to the information given in the material and in case he is unable to provide satisfactory answers, he reads the material again, recites and remembers it more carefully and then again evaluates his learning or remembering performance.

12. *Making use of mnemonics.* 'Mnemonic' is a Greek word meaning "aid to memory". In this sense, a device that helps us remember information is known as mnemonic and an entire system to improve or develop memory is called *mnemonics*. This system usually makes use of visual imagery to provide useful associations and connections for remembering the required material. Let us consider a few popular mnemonic devices.

(a) *The method of loci.* The word 'loci' means "locations" or "places" in Latin and the loci method is based on the assumption that location can serve as an effective cue for remembering the material. It consists of the following three steps:

   (i) Developing one's own route by identifying a set of places which occur in some natural or familiar order (i.e. 20 or 30 locations in one's own house).

   (ii) Converting each item one wants to remember into an image and storing it in a location (a stop on the decided route).

   (iii) During retrieval or reproduction, taking a mental walk by recalling what was placed or stored in each place falling on the familiar route.

(b) *The peg-word method.* In this method we have to memorize:

   (i) A set of peg-words rather than a set of locations as cues. The peg-words numbering 1–10 may be memorized with the help of a rhyme such as:

One is a gun	Six is sticks
Two is a shoe	Seven is heaven
Three is a tree	Eight is a gate
Four is a door	Nine is wine
Five is knives	Ten is a hen

   (ii) Each item to be remembered is then converted to an image so that it figuratively hangs on one or the other peg; such as the words gun, shoe, tree, etc. in the foregoing rhyme.

(iii) At the time of recall, the peg-words serve as cues. What one has to do is to simply follow the peg-words in numerical order.

(c) *The narrative-chaining method.* This method consists of making up a story built around whatever things one wants to remember. Here the plot or incidences of the story work as a clue for remembering the items.

(d) *Initial letter strategy.* In this strategy, the initial letters are the focus for remembering and association. Suppose one has to remember the order of the planets going away from the sun, what he has to do is to take the initial letters of the list of the planets and then make a more easily remembered word or phrase like: "Men very easily make jugs serve useful nocturnal purposes". This phrase can be helpful in making the proper associations and then remembering the order of planets i.e., mercury, venus, earth, mars, jupiter, saturn, uranus, neptune and pluto.

Similarly, for remembering the steps to simplify mathematical expressions one can make use of mnemonic BODMAS which stand for bracket (B), of (O), division (D), multiplication (M), addition (A), and subtraction (S) respectively.

(e) *The keyword method.* This method makes use of imagery for remembering the difficult, uncommon and unfamiliar words and items. For example, if one wants to learn 'golova' the Russian word for head, one looks for a keyword resembling and associated with the word golova. It may be Gulliver. Now a mental image can be built around this keyword making note of the other word 'head' of the desired pair for associate learning. For this purpose the learner may visualize Gulliver with his head tied down by the lilliputians and this portrait or mental image may now help him to remember the Russian word 'golova' associated with its English equivalent 'head'.

WHAT IS FORGETTING?

We frequently hear the expression: "I am sorry, but I have forgotten." A student feels ashamed of having forgotten what he had learned, a housewife feels embarrassed because she forgot to season the food she cooked, or a professional feels bad because he forgot to keep an appointment. We are thus generally quite well acquainted with the phenomenon of forgetting. Let us see how the eminent writers on the subject scientifically define "forgetting".

Munn (1967):

Forgetting is the loss, permanent or temporary, of the ability to recall or recognize something learned earlier.

Drever (1952):

Forgetting means failure at any time to recall an experiences, when attempting to do so, or to perform an action previously learned.

Bhatia (1968):

> Forgetting is the failure of the individual to revive in consciousness an idea or group of ideas without the help of the original stimulus.

In all these definitions, forgetting is termed a failure. Let us see how it counts towards the failure of an individual.

The power of long retention and rapid reproduction (recall and recognition) makes for a good memory. It counts towards the success of an individual in the task of learning or memorizing. Forgetting on the other hand, contributes towards failure. "I have forgotten" implies that I have failed to retain or have been unable to recall what was learned or experienced by me earlier. In this way, forgetting is just the opposite of remembering and is essentially a failure in the ability to reproduce experienced or studied material.

Ebbinghaus's Curve of Forgetting

Studies done by the psychologist Ebbinghaus (1885) represent the earliest systematic work in studying the phenomenon of forgetting. He himself worked as a subject for these studies and described his results by plotting a _curve of forgetting._

He memorized a list of non-sense syllables and then tested himself at intervals varying from 20 minutes to a month to see how much of the list he remembered. The results in terms of the percentage of material forgotten with the lapse of time were as follows:

Time elapsed	Amount forgotten
20 minutes	47%
One day	66%
Two days	72%
Six days	75%
Thirtyone days	79%

He plotted the data as a graph as shown in Figure 15.3 and he termed the

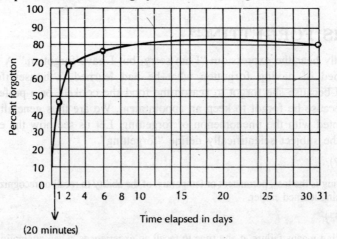

Figure 15.3   Ebbinghaus's curve of forgetting.

graph which he obtained by plotting the amount forgotten as a function of time, as the *curve of forgetting*. From his experimental data and the presentation in the form of the above curve of forgetting, Ebbinghaus concluded that: (a) the amount of learnt material forgotten depends upon the time lapsed after learning; and (b) the rate of forgetting is very rapid at first and then gradually diminishes proportionately as the interval lengthens.

Types of Forgetting

Forgetting may be described in a number of ways based on the nature of forgetting and the manner in which it occurs. It may be broadly classified as natural and morbid forgetting. In *natural forgetting,* forgetting occurs with the lapse of time in a quite normal way without any intention of forgetting on the part of the individual while in *morbid* or *abnormal forgetting* one deliberately tries to forget something. This type of forgetfulness, as Freud explains, results from repression and is wishful as one happens to forget the things which one does not wish to remember.

According to another view, forgetting may be classified as *general* or *specific*. In general forgetfulness, one suffers a total loss in one's recall of some previous learning, while in specific forgetfulness the individual forgets only one or the other specific parts of his earlier learning.

Yet another view related to the cause of its occurrence classifies forgetfulness as physical or psychological. In case a person loses his memory on account of the factors of age, diseases, biological malfunctioning of the brain and nervous system, accidents, consumption of liquor or other intoxicating materials, etc., it is termed as physical or organic forgetting. However, when loss of memory occurs on account of psychological factors like stresses, anxiety, conflicts, temper provocation, lack of interest, aversion apathy, repression or similar other emotional and psychological problems, the resulting forgetfulness is termed as *psychological.*

Theories of Forgetting

Whatever the nature and types of forgetting, it occurs more or less universally to all human beings. How and why it happens has been the subject of extensive research and investigation resulting in a number of theories. Some of the main theories are:

The trace decay theory.   According to some psychologists, time is the cause of much forgetting. What is learnt or experienced is forgotten with the lapse of time. The cause of such natural forgetting with the lapse of time can be explained through a process known as decay of the memory trace. They believe that learning results in neurological changes, leaving certain memory traces or engrams in the brain. With the passage of time, through disuse, these memory traces or learning impressions get weaker and weaker and finally fade away. Thus the older an experience, the weaker its memory and as time passes, the amount of forgetting goes on increasing.

Experimental results, however, as well as day-to-day experiences in the field of learning and remembering do not bear out the above-mentioned trace decay theory. The theory has proved a failure in many instances of forgetting and in long-tern memory such as learning to ride a bicycle where forgetting does not occur even after years of disuse. Similarly, the trace decay theory, through its disuse mechanism, has proved a failure in explaining the morbid or abnormal forgetting. However, this theory has provided good results in explaining forgetfulness in the context of short-term memory. Drill, practice, rehearsal or repetition of a learning always succeeds in preventing decay. The reverse is also true as, reading a poem once, for example, without repeating it or thinking about it, is likely to result in the death of the memory trace before its coding into long-term memory can occur.

The interference theory. The second major theory of forgetting holds the mechanism of interference responsible for forgetting. Interference is the negative inhibiting effect of one learning experience on another. This theory holds that we forget things because of such interference. The interfering effects of things previously learnt and retained in our memory with the things of more recent memory can work both backward and forward. The psychological terms used for these types of interference are retroactive inhibition and proactive inhibition.

In *retroactive inhibition* the acquisition of new learning works backward to impair the retention of the previously learned material. For example, a second list of words, formulae or equation may impair the retention of a first list. *Proactive inhibition* is just the reverse of retroactive inhibition. Here the old learning or experiences retained in our memory works forward to disrupt the memory of what we acquire or learn afterwards. For example, we may find it difficult to learn a second language when vocabulary or grammar from the first interferes; or learning a new formula may be hampered on account of the previously learned formulae in one's memory.

In both types of these inhibition, it can be easily seen that when similar experiences follow each other, they produce more interference than dissimilar experiences. Because in this latter case all experiences are so intermingled that a state of confusion prevails in the mind and consequently the individual faces difficulty in retention and recall.

The interference theory, as a whole, has successfully provided an adequate explanation of natural and normal forgetting for both, short-term and long-term memory. However, for explaining abnormal or morbid forgetting we need to look for explanation elsewhere.

The repression theory. Abnormal or morbid forgetting may be explained in the light of the repression theory put forward by Freud's psychoanalytic school of psychology. Repression, according to this school, is a mental function which cushions the mind against the impact of painful experiences. As a result of this function, we actually push the unpleasant and painful memories into the unconscious and so try to avoid, at least consciously, the conflicts that bother us. This kind of forgetfulness is motivated and intentional. We usually like to see ourselves—and to some extent, the world around us—as pleasant and reasonable. The memories that are in tune with this view are acceptable to us, but those that conflict with it are often pushed out and this explains why our forgetting, like our attention, is selective. Thus, as a result of repression, we forget the things we do not want to remember. In course of time, we forget about our closest relatives and friends who are dead. We forget to attend a marriage party which we do not want to attend. Similarly, most of us tend to forget the names of the people we do not like. In this kind of forgetting, however, some serious mental cases may also be encountered. People under a severe emotional shock are seen to forget even their own names, or the names of their wives and children.

Apart from causing abnormal forgetting, an impaired emotional state of an individual also plays a part in disrupting his normal memory process. A sudden excessive disturbance of emotions may completely block the process of recall. When one is under the influence of emotions like fear, anger, or love, one may forget all one has experienced, learned or believed earlier. When in the grip of these emotions one becomes so self-conscious that one's thinking becomes paralysed. For instance, a child fails to recall the answer to a question in the presence of a teacher whom he fears or dislikes. Similarly, many of us fail to do well before the interview board or in an examination because of interview or test-phobia. An actor, orator or musician may also fail miserably in his performance before an audience because stage fright may cause him to forget his prepared dialogue, lines or music.

SUMMARY

Memory is a special faculty of the mind to conserve or retain what has been previously experienced or acquired through learning and, then, at some later stage, to revive or reproduce it in the form of recall or recognition to enable us to utilise such learning in different situations of daily life.

How we remember can be explained through the models of memory. *The levels of processing model* suggested by Craik and Lokhart emphasizes that the ability to remember depends on the levels at which we process the information. The deeper the processing of the information, the longer it can be remembered. The other model, Atkinson and Shiffrins's *storage and transfer model,* put forward the concept of three separate kinds of storage for the three types of memory—sensory, short-term and long-term.

Sensory or *immediate memory* helps an individual to recall something a split second after he perceives it. It has an extremely brief retention span, i.e. from a fraction of a second to a few seconds. *Short-term memory* is also temporary, though not nearly as short-lived as immediate memory. Here, the time of retention may endure upto thirty seconds or so and may be further extended through rehearsal. *Long-term memory,* unlike short-term memory, has a seemingly limitless capacity to store information, undergoes little or no decay, and requires little or no rehearsal. It is also able to code information according to meaning, pattern and other characteristics.

Episodic memory is quite personal and connected with the episodes or events of one's life. The *semantic memory,* on the other hand, is public and related to the connection of the relationship between events or the association of ideas. It contains generalized ideas, principles, rules and facts concerned with general knowledge. *Photographic memory* helps the individual to remember a scene in photographic detail. It is quite rare and unusual. However, the most astonishing is *para-normal memory* (also known as reincarnation) through which an individual is able to remember the things or events related to his previous life or lives.

For performing experiments to study memory, one needs the use of simple *verbal materials* in the form of serial list, paired associate list and connected discourse. For the visual presentation of the memorizing verbal material an apparatus called a *memory drum* is generally employed in the laboratories. The material can be exhibited through a window-like opening in the drum to be operated rhythmically. Memory, good or bad, can be assessed by the amount actually retained by the learner which in turn, can be directly measured through certain tests of recognition and recall. Special methods like *learning* and *saving* devised by Ebbinghaus may also be used for this purpose.

Economy in memorizing may be achieved by utilising proper methods of memorization like recitation in place of continuous re-reading of the same material. Similarly, one may choose between the whole and the part methods and the distributed and the massed practice methods.

The aim of *training in memory* is to achieve a good memory. We can improve recall by freeing ourselves from harmful emotional factors, building up our self confidence and making use of different associations coolly and patiently. Moreover, proper memorization always results in long retention and easy reproduction. Therefore, factors like the learner's will, his interest and attention, the learning methods, use of the principle of association, grouping and rhythm, a suitable learning environment, repetition and practice, emotional and mental state of the learner, use of proper mnemonic devices, etc. always need to be attended to carefully for achieving best results in the process of memorization.

Forgetting is the temporary or long-term loss of the ability to reproduce things that have been previously learned. Depending upon its nature and intensity, it may be classified as natural or morbid (abnormal), general or specific, and physical or psychological.

The psychologist Ebbinghaus pioneered the experimental study of forgetting. He plotted the results of his study as a graph of the amount forgotten against the time elapsed. The curve so obtained was named as the 'curve of forgetting'.

Natural forgetting can be properly explained through the theory of *trace decay* which holds that we forget on account of decay of the memory traces with the lapse of time. The *repression theory* is held to be more applicable to explaining morbid forgetting. According to this theory, we forget the things we do not want to remember by burying them in our unconscious. The *theory of interference* is able to explain all types of forgetting. According to this theory, we forget things because of the interference of other things. *Proactive* inhibition occurs when earlier learning interferes with the later learning. *Retroactive inhibition* is the result of later learning coming in the way of earlier learning.

REFERENCES

Atkinson, R.C. and Shiffrin, R.M., Human memory: A proposed system and its control processes, *in* K.W. Spence and J.T. Spence (Eds.), *The Psychology of Learning and Motivation: Advances in research and theory*, Vol. 2, New York: Academic Press, 1968.

Bhatia, H.R., *Elements of Educational Psychology*, Calcutta: Orient Longman, 1968, pp. 144, 203.

Bower, G.H. and Karlin, M.B., Depths of processing pictures of faces and recognition memory, *Journal of Experimental Psychology*, Vol. 103, pp. 751–757, 1974.

Craik, F.I.M. and Lokhart, R.S., Levels of processing: A framework for memory research, *Journal of Verbal Learning and Verbal Behaviour*, Vol. 11, pp. 671–684, 1972.

Drever, James, *A Dictionary of Psychology*, Middlesex: Penguin Books, 1952, p. 99.

Ebbinghaus, H., *On Memory*, New York: Dover, 1964.

Haber, R.N., Twenty Years of Haunting Eidetic Imagery: Where's the ghost? *The Behavioural and Brain Sciences*, 1979, pp. 583–629.

Levin, M.J., *Psychology: A biographical approach*, New York: McGraw-Hill, 1978, p. 297.

Morgan, J.B. and Gillilend, A.R., *An Introduction to Psychology*, New York: Macmillan, 1942, p. 210.

Munn, N.L., *An Introduction to Psychology* (2nd ed.), Delhi: Oxford & IBH, 1967, p. 425.

Ryburn, W.M., *Introduction to Educational Psychology*, London: Oxford University Press, 1956, p. 220.

Stout, G.F., A *Manual of Psychology*, London: University Tutorial Press, 1938, p. 521.

Woodworth, R.S. and Marquis, D.G., *Psychology* (5th ed.), New York: Henry Holt, 1948, pp. 542–543.

SUGGESTED READINGS

Adams, J.A., *Learning and Memory: An introduction*, Homewood, Illinois: Dorsey Press, 1976.

Bartlett, F.C., *Remembering: A study in experimental and social psychology*, New York: Cambridge, 1932.

Cermak, L.S., *Human Memory: Research and theory*, New York: Ronald Press, 1972.

Collins, M. and Drever, James (Ed.), *Experimental Psychology*, London: Methuen, 1930.

Deese, J. and S.H. Hulse, *The Psychology of Learning* (3rd ed.), New York: McGraw-Hill, 1967. (Chaps. 8–11).

Higbee, K.L., *Your Memory: How it works and how to improve it,* Englewood Cliffs, New Jersey: Prentice-Hall, 1977.

Hunter, Ian, M.R., *Memory,* London: Penguin Books, 1964.

Klatsky, R.L., *Human Memory,* San Francisco: Freeman, 1976.

Paplia, D.E. and Olds, S.W., *Psychology,* New York: McGraw-Hill, 1987.

Roediger, H. L., Rushton, J.P. et al., *Psychology* (2nd ed.), Boston: Little Brown, 1987.

Skinner, B.F., *Verbal Behaviour,* New York: Appleton Century Crofts, 1957.

Wickelgren, W.A., *Learning and Memory,* Englewood Cliffs, New Jersey: Prentice-Hall, 1977.

Chapter 16

Intelligence

In our day-to-day conversation we often comment that a particular child or individual is very intelligent or is not intelligent. All such comments are based on our observation of the performance or behaviour of the individual concerned in comparison to others of his group. What makes an individual behave or perform well or not well in his group? Interest, attitude, the desire for knowledge, communicative skill and similar other attributes contribute towards his performance or behaviour. However, there is something else which is also responsible to a large degree. In psychology this is termed *intelligence*; in ancient India our great *rishis* and seers named it *Viveka*.

DEFINING INTELLIGENCE

Intelligence as a concept has been understood in different ways by different psychologists and has, therefore, a wide variety of definitions.

Stern (1914):

> Intelligence is a general capacity of an individual consciously to adjust his thinking to new requirements. It is the general mental adaptability to new problems and conditions of life.

Thorndike (1914):

> Intelligence may be defined as "the power of good responses from the point of view of truth or fact".

Terman (1921):

> An individual is intelligent in the proportion that he is able to carry on abstract thinking.

Wagnon (1937):

> Intelligence is the capacity to learn and adjust to relatively new and changing conditions.

Woodworth and Marquis (1948):

> Intelligence means intellect put to use. It is the use of intellectual abilities for handling a situation or accomplishing any task.

Jean Piaget (1952):

> Intelligence is the ability to adapt to one's surroundings.

Apart from the foregoing definitions, there are several more, but all of them, if taken separately, give an incomplete picture because each of them emphasizes a single aspect. For instance they define intelligence as the ability to learn, to deal with abstractions, to make adjustments, to adapt to new situations, or the ability or power to make appropriate responses to certain stimuli in a given situation.

In view of the lacunae in the existing definitions, David Wechsler (1944), who devised the adult intelligence test, tried to provide a somewhat comprehensive definition:

> Intelligence is the aggregate or global capacity of an individual to act purposefully, to think rationally, and to deal effectively with his environment.

Wechsler also provided a criterion for defining intelligent behaviour in terms of four characteristics, i.e. it involves awareness, is goal directed, rational and has value. Taking a cue from this criterion, Stoddard (1943) defined intelligence as:

> The ability to undertake activities that are difficult, complex and abstract and which are adaptive to a goal, and are done quickly and which have social value and which lead to the creation of something new and different.

However, both these so-called comprehensive definitions have also come under severe criticism due to difference of opinion among psychologists.

However, the terminology and language used in defining intelligence apart, there seems to be some agreement among the psychologists. They agree on the following:

1. Intelligence must be understood as the mental capacity or mental energy available with an individual at a particular time in a particular situation.
2. This mental capacity helps him in the task of theoretical as well as practical manipulation of things, objects or events present in his environment in order to adapt to or face new challenges and problems of life as successfully as possible.
3. His capacity or the fund of mental energy available with him can be judged only in terms of the quality of his behaviour or performance.

Keeping all these basic factors in mind, we may attempt a viable definition *of intelligence as a sort of mental energy, in the form of mental or cognitive abilities, available with an individual which enables him to handle his environment in terms of adaptation to face novel situations as effectively as possible.* In terms of definition, we can access a person's intelligence in proportion to his ability to use his mental energy to handle his problems and leading a happy and well-contented life.

THEORIES OF INTELLIGENCE

By studying the various definitions, we can understand how intelligence operates—what type of behaviour of an individual stamps him as intelligent or unintelligent. The theories of intelligence propagated by psychologists from time to time have tried to uncover the components or elements of intelligence. These theories can be grouped under two categories, namely, factor theories and cognitive theories.

Factor Theories of Intelligence

Unitary theory or monarchic theory. This theory, the oldest in origin, holds that intelligence consists of one factor, a fund of intellectual competence, which is universal to all activities of the individual.

A man who has vigour can move as much in one direction as he can in another. Similarly, if he has a fund of intelligence, he can utilize it in any sphere of life and depending on it, be as successful in one sphere as in any other. The ideas propagated by this theory are not, however, born out in real-life situations. It may be seen, for instance, that a child who is good in mathematics may not, despite genuine interest and deligence, be able to do as well in civics while an above-average performer in the laboratory may not exhibit comparable competence in learning a language. This goes to show that intelligence is not just a unitary factor and the unitary theory is, therefore, not acceptable.

Anarchic theory or multifactor theory. The main propagator of this theory was E.L. Thorndike. As its name suggests this theory, also called the atomistic theory of intelligence, considers intelligence to be a combination of numerous separate elements or factors, each one being a minute element of one ability. There is, then, no such thing as general intelligence (a single factor) and there are only many highly independent specific abilities which go into the accomplishment of different tasks.

Monarchic and anarchic theories thus hold two extreme views. Just as we cannot assume good intelligence to be a guarantee of success in all spheres of human life we cannot also assume that with certain specific types of abilities an individual would be entirely successful in a particular area and completely unsuccessful in other areas. In this context, Murphy (1968) says: "There is a certain positive relationship between brightness in one field and brightness in another and so on." Thus we conclude that there should be a common factor for all tasks. The failure to explain this phenomenon gave birth to Spearman's two-factor theory.

Spearman's two-factor theory. This theory was advocated by Spearman (1923). According to him, each intellectual activity involves a general factor 'g' which it shares with all intellectual activities and a specific factor 's' which belongs to it alone.

In this way, he suggested that there is something which might be called general intelligence—a sort of general mental energy, running through all the different tasks. The amount of 'g' in a person depends on the amount of cortical (cerebral cortex) energy present and the maximum quantum of this is fixed. How much of this energy one utilizes depends on the motivation, available environment and previous experiences etc. In addition to this general factor there are specific capabilities, which give an individual the ability to deal with specific problems. For instance, an individual's performance in Hindi is partly due to his general intelligence and partly due to some specific aptitude for language which he might possess, i.e. $g + s_1$ or in mathematics his performance may be the result of $g + s_2$; in drawing, it may be due to $g + s_3$ and so on. The factor g is thus present in all specific activities. The total ability or intelligence 'A' of an individual, thus, will be expressed by the following equation:

$$g + s_1 + s_2 + s_3 + ..., = A$$

This two-factor theory of Spearman has been criticized on various grounds:

1. Spearman held that intelligence may be expressed in terms of two factors, but as we have seen above, there are not only two but several factors ($g, s_1, s_2, s_3...$).
2. According to Spearman, each job requires some specific ability. This view was untenable as it implied that there is nothing common to different jobs except a general factor and professions such as those of nurses, compounders and doctors could not be put in one group. In fact, the factors $s_1, s_2, s_3, s_4 ...$ are not mutually exclusive. They overlap and give rise to certain common factors.

This idea of overlapping and grouping resulted in a new theory called the group factor theory.

Group factor theory.   For factors not common to all intellectual abilities but common to certain activities comprising a group, the term 'group factor' was suggested. Prominent among the propagators of this theory was L.L. Thurston, an American psychologist. While working on a test of primary mental abilities, he came to the conclusion that certain mental operations have a common primary factor which gives them psychological and functional unity and, which differentiates them from other mental operations. These mental operations constitute a group factor. So there are a number of groups of mental abilities and each of these groups has its own primary factor. Thurston and his associates have identified nine such factors. They are:

1. Verbal factor (V) is concerned with comprehension of verbal relations, words and ideas.
2. Spatial factor (S) is involved in any task in which the subject manipulates an object imaginatively in space.
3. Numerical factor (N) is concerned with the ability to do numerical calculations, rapidly and accurately.
4. Memory factor (M) involves the ability to memorize quickly.
5. Word fluency factor (W) is involved whenever the subject is asked to think of isolated words at a rapid rate.
6. Inductive reasoning factor (RI) is the ability to draw inferences or conclusions on the basis of specific instances.
7. Deductive reasoning factor (RD) is the ability to make use of generalized results.
8. Perceptual factor (P) is the ability to perceive objects accurately.
9. Problem-solving ability factor (PS) is the ability to solve problems with independent efforts.

The weakest aspect of the group factor theory was that it discarded the concept of the common factor. It did not take Thurston long to realize his mistake and to reveal a general factor in addition to the group factors.

Sampling theory.   This theory was propagated by G.H. Thompson (1939), a

British Psychologist. It assumes that the mind is made up of several independent bonds or elements. Any specific test or school activity samples some of these bonds. It is possible that two or more tests sample and utilize the same bonds, and a general common factor can be said to exist among them. It is also possible that some other tests sample different bonds, in which case the tests have nothing in common and each of them is specific.

The sampling theory combines several theoretical viewpoints in that it appears to be similar to Thorndike's multifactor theory except that he concedes to the practical usefulness of a concept like 'g', and at the same time Thompson seems to maintain that the concept of a group factor (G) is of equal practical usefulness.

Vernon's hierarchical theory. The British psychologist P.F. Vernon (1950) suggested a hierarchical structure for the organisation of intelligence as illustrated in Figure 16.1.

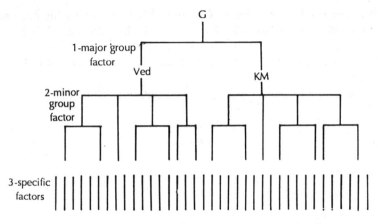

Figure 16.1 Vernon's hierarchical structure of human intelligence.

According to him, the mind is a kind of hierarchy in which 'G' is the most prominent mental ability, i.e., an overall factor measured through intelligence tests. Under 'G', we have two major group factors, termed as Ved and KM, representing two main kinds of mental abilities. While the first major group factor Ved is concerned with the verbal, numerical and educational abilities, the other major group factor KM is connected with practical, mechanical, spatial and physical abilities. These two major factors can be divided into minor group factors and ultimately these minor factors may be further sub-divided into various specific factors related with minute specific mental abilities.

Guilford's theory involving a model of intellect. Guilford (1961) and his associates, while working in the psychological laboratory at the University of Southern California, developed a model of intelligence on the basis of the factor analytical research studies conducted by them which involved a number of intelligence tests. They concluded that every mental process or intellectual activity can be described in terms of three different basic dimensions or parameters known as operations—the act of thinking; contents—the terms in which we think (such as words or symbols); and product—the ideas we come up with.

Each of these parameters—operations, contents and products—may be further sub-divided into some specific factors or elements (see Table 16.1).

Table 16.1 Division of Intellectual Activity into parameters and specific factors

Operations	*Contents*	*Products*
Evaluation (E)	Figural factor (F) (i.e. concrete	Units (U)
Convergent	material perceived through senses)	Classes (C)
thinking (C)	Symbolic (S) (i.e. material	Relations (R)
Divergent	in the form of signs and symbols)	Systems (S)
thinking (D)	Semantic (M) (i.e. material in the	Transformations (T)
Memory (M)	form of verbal meaning of ideas)	Implications (I)
Cognition (C)	Behavioural (B)	

Through his later researches Guilford (1967) expanded his cube-shaped model of intellect to include 150 factors (by dividing the figural factor of the contents into two separate categories—visual and auditory).

This model consisting of 150 factors may be diagrammatically represented as shown in Figure 16.2.

The structure of human intelligence, according to Guilford's model, can be

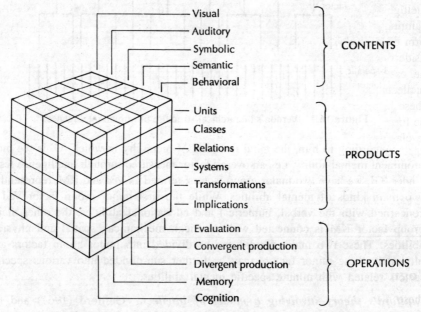

Figure 16.2 Guilford's model of the structure of intellect.

viewed in terms of the three basic parameters along with their divisions into a specific number of factors. There could be $5 \times 6 \times 5 = 150$ factors in all, which may constitute human intelligence. Each one of these factors has a trigram symbol, i.e. at least one factor from each category of the three parameters has to be present in any specific intellectual activity on mental task.

Let us illustrate this with an example. A child is asked to determine the day of the week on a particular date with the help of a calender. The task involves operations like convergent thinking, memory and cognition. In carrying out these operations, he has to make use of the contents. In this particular case, he will make use of semantics, i.e. reading and understanding of the printed words and figures indicating days and dates of a particular month in the calendar. By carrying out mental operations with the help of the contents he will finally arrive at the products. The day of the week to which the date in question refers represents the factor known as 'relations'. He may further transform and apply this knowledge to identify the days for contiguous dates or vice versa.

Conclusion

The theories discussed so far fall in the broad category of factor theories of intelligence as these employ factor analysis techniques for identification of factors or common abilities which constitute one's intelligence. These theories exhibit wide variations in terms of the number of factors that they consider important. The range of such factors goes from 1 (monarchic theory) to 150 (Guilford's intellect model).

Each of the above theories of intelligence attempts to provide a structure of intelligence in terms of its constituents or factors. The unitary theory is right in claiming that intelligence in its functional form is always used as a whole in the form of a total fund of mental energy. However, for understanding what goes on inside one's intelligence we must try to build an eclectic view by incorporating the essence of all the workable theories of intelligence. Consequently, any intellectual activity or mental task may be said to involve the following factors. These factors may be arranged in hierarchical order as suggested by Vernon or in the form of some model like the one designed by Guilford. These factors may also be classified as unlearned and learned as advocated by Cattell and Jensen.

1. General factor g (common to all tasks) as advocated by Spearman in his two factor theory.
2. Group factor G (common to the tasks belonging to a specific group) as advocated by Thurston and others in the group factor theory.
3. Specific factors s_1, s_2, etc. (specific to the task) as advocated by Thorndike in his multifactor theory.

Cognitive Theories of Intelligence

These theories of intelligence tried to analyse and describe intelligence in terms of certain fundamental cognitive processes. The important theories falling in this category are:

Cattell and Horn's Theory of Intelligence

Cattell (1965) and Horn (1978) proposed a theory of intelligence by distinguishing between two types of intelligence, i.e. *fluid intelligence* and *crystallized intelligence.* Although viewed as different and distinct, these two types of intelligence intermingle and interact to produce overall intelligence.

Fluid intelligence is considered to be the mental capacity of an individual, which is required for learning and problem solving. It is dependent on neurological development and is relatively free from the influences of education and culture. In other words, it is derived more from biological and genetic factors and is less influenced by training and experience. This type of intelligence is put to use when facing new and strange situations requiring adaptation, comprehension, reasoning, problem solving and identifying relationships etc. It reaches full development by the end of an individual's adolescence.

Crystallized intelligence, on the other hand, is not a function of one's neurological development and therefore is not innate or unlearned like fluid intelligence. Rather, it is specially learned and is, therefore, dependent on education and culture. It involves one's acquired fund of general information consisting of knowledge and skills essential for performing different tasks in one's day-to-day life. It can be identified through one's fund of vocabulary, general knowledge of the world affairs, the knowledge of customs, traditions and rituals, manner of behaving in the society, handling of machines and tools, craftsmanship and art, computation and keeping of accounts and various other such tasks requiring knowledge, experience and practice.

Thus, while fluid intelligence is characterized by a relatively high degree of culture, education, experience and training-free performances in abstraction, thinking, reasoning and imagination, crystallized intelligence is known for its evolution through experience, training and interaction with of one's environment over a number of years. That is why it is found to continue to increase throughout one's life span.

Jensen's Theory of Mental Functioning

Arthur Jensen (1969) propounded the theory of mental functioning. According to this theory, the functioning of one's mind depends upon the type and degree of intelligence one possesses. Jensen describes one's intelligence as being composed of two types of abilities, namely, associative abilities and conceptual abilities.

The first category includes one's ability to remember, reproduce, identify, discriminate, synthesize, associate, assimilate, transfer, and apply etc. Such abilities are usually measured by means of intelligence test items, or tasks involving free recall, recognition, serial learning, free and controlled associate learning, selection and discrimination, etc. Conceptual abilities on the other hand, involve one's ability to carry out higher order of thinking, reasoning, analysing and the capacity of problem solving. That is why this type of abilities are said to be measured through tasks and test items requiring the use of conceptual ability, abstract reasoning, novelty of situation and methods as also analytical and divergent thinking. According to Jensen associative abilities relate to biological maturation and show little variation among social classes and races. Conceptual abilities, however, are dependent on education and culture and are, therefore, responsible for the observed differences in conceptual reasoning and abilities among social classes and races.

This attribute of intelligence in an individual according to Jensen, is two-dimensional, having intellectual breadth and intellectual altitude. What is described as the breadth of one's intelligence consists of the intellectual fund of general information, vocabulary, practice and skill of handling tools and machines, ways and manners of behaving in society, etc. It usually depends upon one's interaction with one's environment, the attitudes, values, interests one possesses, the experiences and training one receives and the things and treatments one obtains from one's environment. Thus, described as a function of one's learning, education and culture, it is similar to Cattell's concept of crystallized intelligence.

The altitude component of one's intelligence, on the other hand, depends more on innate and neurological factors than or learning, training and environmental influences. It imparts altitude to one's intellectual structure by involving the relatively high-level cognitive abilities like abstract and divergent thinking, logical reasoning, imagination and conceptualization, problem solving, etc.

A person's intelligence is thus said to be built up on the base provided by his intellectual breadth and height maintained by his intellectual altitude. How intelligently he will function in a given situation thus depends upon his innate basic abilities and the required mental functioning.

Campion and Brown's Theory of Intelligence

The American psychologist Joe Campion and Ann Brown (1979) developed a theory of intelligence according to which one's intelligence is composed of a two-part system. The first part is a biologically based architectural system and the second, an environmentally influenced executive system.

The architectural system works as a base for one's intellectual functioning. It includes such basic mental abilities as memory capacity, the rate of loss of memory, the ability of proper information processing, etc. The executive system works as a store-house of knowledge and information and is said to include the cognitive abilities like cognitive schemata, cognitive learning strategies and meta-cognition (i.e. the awareness of one's abilities to plan, evaluate and regulate learning). The executive system works on a higher level and is thus responsible for higher order mental functioning and the abilities comprising this system are dependent on training and experience. The abilities comprising the architectural system, on the other hand, are innate and biological and are thus relatively independent of the education, culture and training influences.

Sternberg's Information Processing Theory of Intelligence

The most recent acceptable theory of intelligence has been put forward by the American psychologist Robert Sternberg (1985) by adopting an information processing approach to cognition or problem solving. The information processing approach is the manner in which one proceeds to perform a mental task or solve a problem from the time one comes across it, gathers information and makes use of this information for completing the task or solving the problem in hand. The theory propagated by Sternberg identified the following steps in the way one processes information:

1. Encoding (identifying the relevant available information in the mind)
2. Inferring (drawing the necessary inference)
3. Mapping (establishing the relationship between a previous situation and the present one)
4. Application (applying the inferred relationship)
5. Justification (justifying the analysed solution of the problem)
6. Response (providing the best possible solution)

Considering the way human beings process information in executing a mental task, Sternberg laid down a triarchic structure for his theory of intelligence based on three sub-theories, namely, (a) component sub-theory, (b) experimental sub-theory, and (c) contextual sub-theory.

(a) *Component sub-theory.* This is the core of Sternberg's theory. Sternberg advocates that a person's intellectual functioning is decided mainly by the components, i.e. elementary information processes operating on internal representation of objects or symbols. He listed three types of components serving distinct functions:

(i) *Meta components* which represent higher order executive processes employed for planning, monitoring and regulating the execution of a task such as analysis of the problem, selection of the strategies, monitoring of the possible solutions and interpretation of the feed-back about performance etc.

(ii) *Performance components* which represent the actual mental processes used for the execution of a task like task perception, concept identification and response making etc.

(iii) *Knowledge-acquisition components* which represent the processes used in acquiring new information such as synthesizing old ideas in some original and creative ways.

(b) *Experimental sub-theory.* By this sub-theory, Sternberg proposed that intelligence represents the ability or capacity of an individual to deal with new tasks, problems and situations by adopting an information processing approach with as little conscious effort as possible. This means that to assess the degree of intelligence of an individual, we must give him the opportunity to perform new tasks or face novel situations or problems. This sub-theory has thus led psychologists and researchers to identify specific tasks and situations which may be utilized as reliable yardsticks for measuring intelligence.

(c) *Contextual sub-theory.* While proposing this sub-theory, Sternberg (1985) declared that intelligence should be regarded as "*a mental activity directed toward purposive adaptation to, and selection and shaping of, real-world environments relevant to one's life*".

This declaration made out intelligence—to be a factor of a practical nature rather than a mere abstraction. He, in fact, sought the real function and purpose of human intelligence by considering it as a proper instrument for adaptation, and the selection and shaping of one's environment. The concept and structure of intelligence proposed by Sternberg thus went beyond the concept of I.Q. measurement and traditional cognitive processes as it gave greater-freedom and power to an individual to solve his day-to-day problems and to become the master of his destiny.

Gardner's Theory of Multiple Intelligence

Howard Gardner of Harvard University has propounded a unique theory of intelligence called the "theory of multiple intelligence". It first appeared in his 1983 book, *Frames of Mind: The theory of multiple intelligence.* Through his new theory, Gardner challenged the notion of general intelligence, "g" and then questioned the very basis of prevailing intelligence tests by asking how an individual's intellectual capacities could be captured in a single measure of intelligence. Indeed, he tried to give a broad base to the concept of intelligence and its measurement by providing a multiple frame. He asserted that human intelligence or cognitive competence can be better described as a set of an individual's multiple abilities, talents and mental skills related to a multiple number of domains of knowledge in a particular cultural setting. Elaborating his pluralistic view of intelligence further, he concluded that there are seven independent types of intelligence that grow and develop differently in different people, depending upon their hereditary characteristics or environmental experiences. By calling them independent, Gardner meant that each intelligence is a relatively autonomous intellectual potential which is capable of functioning independently of the others. These different types of intelligence have been named by him as linguistic, logical-mathematical, spatial, musical, bodily-kinesthetic, intrapersonal and interpersonal.

Linguistic intelligence. This type of human intelligence is responsible for all kinds of linguistic competence-abilities, talents and skills, available in human beings. It can be best broken down into components like syntax, semantics and pragmatics as well as more school-oriented skills such as written or oral expression and understanding. This type of intelligence is most visible in professionals like lawyers, lecturers, writers and lyricists, and a number of other professionals exploiting linguistic intelligence.

Logical-mathematical intelligence. This type of intelligence is responsible for all types of abilities, talents and skills in areas related to logic and mathematics. It can be broken down into components like deductive reasoning, inductive reasoning, scientific thinking including solving of logical puzzles, carrying out calculations and the like. Professionals like mathematicians, philosophers, physicists, etc. are found to exhibit this type of intelligence in abundance.

Spatial intelligence. This type of intelligence is concerned with the abilities, talents and skills involving the representation and manipulation of spatial configuration and relationship. Many of us as adults make use of this kind of intelligence in the sphere of our work. For example, painters may be seen to demonstrate spatial intelligence through their use of space when applying pigments to a canvas. This is also true of professionals like land surveyors, architects, engineers, mechanics, navigators, sculptures and chess players—who are found to rely upon the spatial intelligence in their own way.

Musical intelligence. This type of intelligence covers the abilities, talents and skills pertaining to the field of music. It may be well demonstrated through one's capacity for pitch discrimination, sensitivity to rhythm, texture and timbre, ability to hear themes in music; and in its most integrated forms, the production of music through performance or composition. It is visible in a quite large proportion in professionals like musicians and composers.

Bodily kinesthetic intelligence. This type of intelligence is concerned with the set of abilities, talents and skills involved in using one's body or its various parts to perform skillful and purposeful movements. A child may be seen to demonstrate such intelligence in moving expressively in response to different musical and verbal stimuli or bending different body parts in organised sports. Among professionals, dancers, atheletes and surgeons may be seen to demonstrate a high degree of bodily-kinesthetic intelligence in their respective fields.

Intra-personal intelligence. This type of intelligence consists of an individual's abilities to enable him to know his self. It includes knowledge and understanding of one's own cognitive strengths, styles and mental functioning, as well as one's feelings, range of emotions and skills to utilize one's fund of knowledge in practical situations. In brief, intrapersonal intelligence helps an individual to understand his own self by providing an insight into his total behaviour—what he feels, thinks or does. It is, therefore, said to be the most private of the intelligences that a person possesses. On account of its secret and private nature, the access to this type of intelligence in an individual is available only through self-expression, i.e. language, music, visual art and similar other forms of expression. In our practical life, this type of intelligence is demonstrated by yogis, saints and masters of Zen.

Inter-personal intelligence. The counterpart of intrapersonal intelligence in one's cognitive structure is interpersonal intelligence. It consists of the abilities to understand individuals other than one's self and one's relations to others. In addition, it includes the ability to act productively, based on the understanding of others. The knowledge and understanding of others is the quality that is needed for social interactions in one's day-to-day life. In practical life, this type of intelligence is most visible among psychotherapists, teachers, sales people, politicians and religious leaders.

In this way, Gardner's theory of multiple intelligence provides a broad and comprehensive view of human abilities, extending from linguistic and logical-mathematical abilities (the type of skills most addressed and valued in traditional school settings as also in majority of standardized intelligence tests) on the one hand, to intrapersonal and interpersonal abilities on the other. Out of these seven types of intelligence, whereas the linguistic, logical-mathematical and spatial abilities have been accepted widely as the types and components of intelligence, the last four have been the subject of great controversy as to whether they should be categorized as separate types of intelligence or as different talents. However, as far as the broader and global assessment of one's intellectual competencies and abilities is concerned, there is sufficient truth in the assertion of Gardner's theory that knowledge of all the seven types of intelligence is essential for the true assessment of one's level of intellectual functioning.

The other striking feature and contribution of Gardner's theory of multiple intelligence is its bold declaration that the concept of a measurable "g" is at best limited and at worst educationally misleading. It is not at all essential that an individual highly loaded with linguistic and/or logical mathematical abilities will also display exceptional ability (or even interest) in all or any remaining domains, i.e. spatial and musical abilities etc. It happens on account of a sort of autonomy maintained by each type of the seven different human intelligence which are said to be quite capable of developing independently of each other and also quite independently of an all-encompassing general intelligence, "g" .

NATURE OF INTELLIGENCE

The true nature of intelligence can be understood by first defining it to understand its meaning, discussing the various theories explaining its structure in terms of the several constituents and factors, and identifying the numerous other aspects and characteristics related to intelligence and its functioning. We have already covered the first two points in the present chapter, let us now concentrate briefly on last point through the following description.

Distribution of Intelligence

The distribution of intelligence is not equal among all human beings. It resembles the pattern of distribution of health, wealth, beauty and similar other attributes or endowments. It is a normal distribution that is governed by a definite principle which states that *the majority of people are at the average, a few very bright and a few very dull.*

Individual Differences in Intelligence

Wide individual differences exist among individuals with regard to intelligence. Truly speaking, no two individuals, even identical twins or individuals nurtured in identical environments, are endowed with equal mental energy. The assessment of intelligence by various tests has given reasons enough to believe that not only does intelligence vary from individual to individual but it also tends to vary in the same individual from age to age and situation to situation.

Intelligence and Changes in Age

As the child grows in age, so does the intelligence as shown by intelligence tests. The question which now arises is, at what age does this increase stop? The age at which mental growth ceases, varies from individual to individual. It tends to stabilize after the age of 10 and is fully stabilized during adolescence. The idea that intelligence continues to grow throughout life is not strictly true. Since intelligence is basically a function of neurons and neuroglia, its development or deterioration goes hand in hand with the development or deterioration of the nervous system. However, in the majority of cases, the growth of a person's intelligence reaches its maximum sometime between the age of 16 and 20 years after which the vertical growth of intelligence almost ceases. Horizontal growth i.e. achievement, the realization of the intelligence in terms of accumulation of knowledge and acquisition of skills etc. may continue throughout an individual's life.

Intelligence and the Sexes

Many studies have been conducted to find out whether men are more intelligent than women and vice versa but no significant difference has been found. It may, therefore, be stated that difference in sex does not contribute towards difference in intelligence.

Intelligence and Racial or Cultural Differences

The hypothesis whether a particular race, caste, or cultural group is superior to another in intelligence has been examined by many research workers. In the U.S.A. it has been a burning problem for centuries. The results of earlier studies which take the Whites to be a superior race in comparison to the negroes have been questioned. It has now been established that intelligence is not the birthright of a particular race or group. The 'bright' and the 'dull' can be found in any race, caste or cultural group and the differences which are found can be the result of environmental factors and influences.

INTELLIGENCE: THE ROLE OF HEREDITY AND ENVIRONMENT

Whether one's intelligence is largely dependent upon heredity—genetic materials and codes inherited from one's parents or is chiefly designed by one's life experiences or environmental factors has been a controversial issue. While geneticists in this debate attach all importance to heredity, the environmentalists give all credit to environment. In support of their viewpoints, both of them put forward the following experimental evidence.

Evidence in Support of the Role of Heredity

Family resemblance studies.   Bouchard and McGue (1981) reported a study based on the computation of coefficients of correlation and their comparison. The results of their studies can be summarised as follows:

Identical twins	0.86
Parents and children	0.56
Brothers and sisters	0.53
Half siblings	0.31
Cousins	0.15

Through this study they tried to establish that the closer the kinship or blood relationship between individuals, the more similar their I.Q. scores tend to be, leading to the conclusion that similarity from the point of view of heredity potential increases the probability of the intelligence potential being similar.

A similar conclusion has been arrived at by Teasdale and Owen (1984) through their comparative study of intelligence scores of full siblings, half siblings and individuals who were unrelated but reared together, and apart. This study demonstrates a very high correlation in the I.Q. scores of full siblings, whether they were raised together or apart in comparison to half siblings and unrelated individuals who demonstrated comparatively less correlation and no correlation respectively.

Further evidence of this theory of blood relationship and family resemblance may be seen in the studies reported by Jencks (1972) and Munsinger (1978). These studies demonstrate a positive correlation ranging from .40 to .50 between adopted children and their real parents in contrast to a very small correlation of +.10 to +.20 between the adopted children and adopted parents, leading to the conclusion that people closer to each other from the point of view of heredity potential have comparable I.Q.

Twins studies.   Twins are said to be genetically more closely related than normal siblings and among twins also, identical twins (having exactly the same genes) are said to be even closer in terms of heredity potential than fraternal twins (having different sets of genes). Many studies involving the separation of twins at birth and their rearing in different environments have been carried out.

In one such study, Wilson (1975) tried to test I.Q. of over 100 pairs of twins on the Wechsler scales at ages 4, 5 and 16 and found a strong correlation between the I.Q. scores of identical twins in comparison to the scores of fraternal twins.

In another study Bouchard and his colleagues (1984, 1987) located a number of identical twins (who were separated from their parents only a few days after their birth and reared in different homes) and subjected them to intelligence tests. This study demonstrated a very high correlation in the I.Q. scores of identical twins reared apart to almost the same degree as found in the case of identical twins reared together. Moreover, twins reared apart are found to resemble each other in other aspects of human personality—physical appearance, interests, aptitudes, habits and mannerism, etc. also.

In the light of the findings of such studies, psychologists like Arthur Jensen have taken a firm stand that heredity decides everything about the observed differences in human intelligence. Through a study of 1200 California school children in which blacks on the average were found to score 16 points lower on I.Q. tests than whites, he tried to establish that genetic factors are strongly responsible for measured differences in intelligence.

Evidences in Support of the Role of Environment

Family resemblance studies.   Many studies have indicated that the individuals (having same degree of blood relationship or family relationship) have more comparable I.Q. if they happen to be reared in the same environment in comparison to those raised apart and in different environments. The results of two such studies, Study 1: Loehlin, Lindzey and Spuhler (1975), and Study 2: Bouchard and McGue (1981) are given below:

Modes of relationship and rearing	Coefficient of correlation	
	Study 1	Study 2
Identical twins (reared together)	0.88	0.85
Identical twins (reared apart)	0.75	0.67
Siblings (reared together)	0.49	0.45
Siblings (reared apart)	0.46	0.24

Studies of environmental deprivation or enrichment. The adverse effects of environmental deprivation and positive, favourable effects of environmental enrichment upon the children's intellectual development have been demonstrated in many studies.

In one of his studies Gottfried (1984) concluded that if the children are subjected to certain forms of environmental stimulation early in life, their intellectual development gets adversely affected. Similar conclusions were drawn in another study conducted by Sherman and Key (1932) in an unpriviledged remote hilly area of U.S.A. to the effect that lack of language training and school experience accounted for the very poor scores of the children in the standardized intelligence tests.

However, when the children were provided with favourable environmental situations in the form of appropriate adoptive homes, better schooling, and learning facilities, etc., the results were quite encouraging in terms of intellectual development. A well known adoption study (Schiff et al., 1978) conducted in France is a good example. In this study, the investigators compared the I.Q. scores of the children who had been adopted by parents belonging to higher socio-economic class with those of their siblings who had not been adopted. The average score of the adopted children was 111 in comparison to the average score of 95 of their siblings (brothers and sisters) raised by their biological parents. The privileged environment may thus be said to be responsible for raising the average I.Q. score by 16 points.

Family structure and birth order studies. The environmental influences related to the composition and structure of the family even to the extent of the birth order of the child has been found to affect his intellectual growth. There have been many studies, e.g. those conducted by Belmont and Marolla (1973), and Robert Zajonc (1983), to demonstrate that (a) children from large families tend to have lower I.Q. scores than children from small families, and (b) later-born children usually score lower than early-born children.

Zajonc (1976, 1986) proposed the confluence theory to explain the difference in intelligence on account of order of birth. According to this theory one's intellectual development is dependent upon the intellectual environment available in one's family. A first-born child enjoys the benefit of the company of two parents—a relatively advantaged intellectual environment compared to the second-born child in whose case the attention of the parents is divided between the two. The first-born also has the initial advantage of a better intellectual environment in living only with adults rather than with both, adults and with their younger siblings. Consequently, in the matter of intellectual development, the second child is bound to suffer. Such effects become more apparent in the third-borns and continue to multiply as the number of children in the family increases.

Apart from the above mentioned considerations, the other things related to the family environment like education of the parents, economic and social status of the family, nutrition, physical and social surroundings of the home, etc., are also found to contribute significantly to the intellectual growth of the children. Enough experimental evidence bas been put forward by geneticists and environmentalists to support their respective view points. Prem Pasricha (1963) has made a very interesting observation regarding these experiments. According to her:

> It is quite customary for the psychologists wedded to either side, viz. heredity and environment, to perform experiments and quote findings in favour of either of the factors. It has also been found that the findings of these experiments can be interpreted either way and can be easily made to support the opposite view. When analysed in an objective manner, it indicates clearly that the two are so closely interwoven that it is difficult to separate the effect of one from that of the other.

Let us discuss why it is difficult to conduct actual experiments for the study of the impact of pure heredity or environment on the growth and development of intelligence.

To accurately study the impact of environment on intellectual development we have to have subjects with the same heredity. After keeping them in different environments, comparisons can be made. Conversely, for studying the impact of heredity, the environmental factors need to be identical and individuals belonging to different hereditary stock and brought up in exactly the same environments may be compared for this purpose.

The following difficulties arise while conducting these studies:

1. It is impossible to get individuals having the same heredity. Even identical twins are not supposed to have exactly the same genes and therefore, the same hereditary characteristics.

2. If we assume that identical twins at the time of conception, belong to approximately similar hereditary stock, then the question arises: Is it possible to experiment upon them from the moment of conception? Starting from the time of fertilization and division of the ovum, can these twins be exposed to different types of environment for studying the impact of environmental differences? This is obviously not possible and only after their birth—approximately nine months after their conception—is the pair available for experimentation. We cannot rule out the environmental effects inside the womb of the mother. Nor can these effects as a common influence upon the pair be ruled out. It may happen that one of the twins gets a major share of nourishment and is favoured by the inner environment in one way or the ·other while the other is to some extent neglected. It is, thus, difficult to ensure exactly identical heredity even in identical twins.

3. Further, the environmental influences cannot be identically controlled; hence it is very difficult to provide exactly the same environment for different individuals. Even the mother cannot show equal amount of love and affection to all her children. There are individual differences and as a result one individual may be favoured in comparison to another. In the same foster home or orphanage, the various individuals are subjected to different environmental conditions depending upon their own nature as well as the attitude of the officials and the people in charge.

The main reason for the failure to specifically control the hereditary or environmental factors is that the influence of both these factors on the growth of the individual's intelligence is inseparable. Right from the time of conception, the two factors are so intimately intermingled and interwoven that it is difficult to say whether the differences in intellectual capacities of different individuals are due to the genes or due to the environmental influences. It is obvious, therefore, that the claims of both geneticists and environmentalists are one-sided and exaggerated. However, there is no gainsaying the fact that a person's intellectual development at a particular age is the sum of what he inherited from his parents and his experiences as a result of interaction with the environmental situations. Since we cannot control or modify the hereditary factors, we need to direct all our efforts and resources towards providing the most conducive environmental situations for the proper intellectual development of the children in our charge.

Assessment of Intelligence

We can observe the intelligence of an individual only to the extent that it is manifested by him in one or more intelligence tests. Many such tests have been devised by psychologists for the measurement of intelligence. In reference to these, however, the term 'assessment' is preferred because, intelligence being only a concept or an abstraction rather than a substance, it cannot be measured in physical units like a length of cloth or temperature of the body.

In this context, Griffiths (1933) observes: "the standard of measurement is a group performance". Therefore, when we measure an individual's intelligence by means of an intelligence test, we try to interpret his score in terms of the norms set (group performance) by the author of the test. One's intelligence is thus determined in relation to the classified group to which one belongs. Thus, whereas a piece of cloth may be measured in absolute terms, relative measurement or assessment has to be resorted to in the case of intelligence.

Classification of Intelligence Tests

Intelligence tests may be classified broadly as follows:

1. *Individual tests* in which only one individual is tested at a time.
2. *Group tests* in which a group of individuals is tested at the same time.

Intelligence tests may also be classified on the basis of their form as *verbal or language tests* and *non-verbal or non-language tests*.

Verbal or language tests. In these the subjects make use of language in which the instructions are given in words, written, oral, or both. The individuals being tested are required to use language, verbal or written, for their responses. The test content is loaded with verbal material which may include varieties of the items listed below:

- *Vocabulary tests.* In these the subject is required to give the meanings of words or phrases. For example, what is the meaning of the word 'eventually'? What is the difference between bear, wear and bare? What does the phrase 'many roads to Rome' convey?

- *Memory tests.* These are designed to test the subject's immediate and long-term memory, and include recall and recognition type of items. He may be called upon to tell the full names of teachers who teach him different subjects; his phone number, the number of his vehicle, the dates of birth of his siblings and so on.

- *Comprehension tests.* By means of these, the subject is tested for the ability to grasp, understand and react to a given situation. The questions, for example, may be like: Why do big ships float in the sea while a small needle would sink in it? Why are the nights longer and the days shorter in winter?

- *Information tests.* The subject is tested on his knowledge about the things around him by means of these tests, e.g., Where is the Taj Mahal situated? Name the countries which surround Iraq.

- *Reasoning tests.* In these tests the subject is asked to provide answers which demonstrate his ability to reason—logically, analytically, synthetically, inductively or deductively as outlined below:
  Complete the series: 1, 2, 4, 7, 11, 16, 22, 29, ?, ?, ?
  A picture is to frame as an island is to . . .

- *Association tests.* Through these test items the subject is tested for his ability to point out the similarities or dissimilarities between two or more concepts or objects. For example:
  1. In what ways are animals and plants alike?
  2. Which of the items mentioned below is the odd one?
  —gold, silver, copper, iron, glass.

Non-verbal and non-language tests. These tests involve activities in which the use of language is not necessary except for giving directions. Performance tests are a typical example of such tests. The main features of these are:

1. The contents of the tests are in the form of material objects.
2. What is required of the subject is conveyed by the tester through oral instructions, or by pantomime and signs.
3. The subject's responses are assessed in terms of how he reacts or what he does rather than what he says or writes.
4. Generally these are individual tests. As Pillai (1972) observes: *"These cannot be used as group tests, chiefly because it is necessary to supervise the individual testee at work and give him necessary directions".*

A comprehensive representation of all kinds of intelligence tests is provided in Table 16.2.

Table 16.2   Classification of Intelligence Tests

Individual tests		Group tests	
Verbal test	Performance tests (a typical form of non-verbal tests)	Verbal tests	Non-verbal tests

Now we will discuss these types one by one.

INDIVIDUAL VERBAL TESTS

Tests involving the use of language, which are administered to one individual at a time belong to this category. The Stanford Binet scale, which is the revised form of the scale, is an example. It is the revised form of the original Binet-Simon test. Actually, French Psychologist Alfred Binet (1916) is the father of the intelligence tests construction movement. He, alongwith Theodore Simon, prepared a test as early as in 1905, consisting of 30 items (arranged in order of increasing difficulty) graded for different levels. The test included such items as:

At age 3—point out nose, eyes and mouth.

At age 7—say what is missing in the unfinished picture.

The first American revision of this test was published in 1931 by Terman at Stanford University and in 1937 another revision was carried out with the help of Maud A. Merril. This, as well as the 1960's revision is known as the Stanford Binet Scale and is widely used as an individual intelligence test.

The tests in this scale are graded into age levels, extending from age 2 to 22 years. The tasks to be performed by the subject in these tests range from simple manipulation to abstract reasoning.

The Binet tests have been adopted in India also. The first such attempt was made by C.H. Rice in 1922 when he published his "Hindustani Binet performance point scale". This was an adaptation of the Binet test with some additional performance tests. The State *manovigyanshala* of Uttar Pradesh has made a Hindi version of the Stanford-Binet test. This test is divided into several age groups and is known as, *budhi pariksha anushilan.*

The other common verbal individual intelligence test used in India is *Samanya budhi pariksha* (parts 1 and 2). This test is an Indian adaptation of the well known test of William Stephenson and has been prepared by the State Bureau of Educational and Vocational Guidance, Gwalior (M.P.).

Individual performance tests.   As stated earlier, the complete non-verbal or non-language tests of intelligence for testing one individual at a time come under this category. In these tests the contents and responses are in the form of performance and language is not used and include items which require responses in terms of motor activities. Generally the activities, on which the performance of an individual is tested are of the following types:

- *Block building or cube construction.* The subject is asked to make a structure or design by means of blocks or cubes supplied to him. The Merril Palmer block building, Koh's block design test, Alexander's pass-along test etc. are examples of tests involving this type of activity.

- *To fit blocks in holes.* Test material of this type provides numerous blocks and a board on which there are holes which correspond to these blocks. The subject has to fit the blocks in their corresponding holes on the board. The Seguin form board test and Goddard form board test belong to this category.

- *Tracing a maze.* The test material consists of a series of mazes of increasing difficulty, each printed on a separate sheet. The subject is required to trace with a pencil, the path from entrance to exit. The Porteus maze test is an example involving this type of activity.

- *Picture arrangement or picture completion.* In a picture arrangement test, the task is to arrange the given pictures in series, whereas in a picture completion test the subject is required to complete the picture with the help of given pieces cut out of each picture. The Healy pictorial completion test is a good example of such a test by which a good estimate of the intelligence of the subject may be obtained without the use of language.

As would be clear, these tests highlight one or the other type of performance. A group of performance tests organized into a scale or a battery is used in preference to just one or two tests in order to obtain a comprehensive idea of a person's mental ability. Some of the better known scales are:

1. The Pinter-Patterson scale.
2. The Arthur point scale.
3. Alexander's battery of performance tests.

The Pinter–Patterson scale. A popular scale in U.S.A., this was designed in 1917 mainly for the use of deaf and linguistically backward children. It is a comprehensive scale which includes 15 sub-tests, viz. mare and foal picture board, Seguin form board, the five figure board, the two figure board, the casuist board, the triangle test, the diagonal test, the Healy form board, puzzle test, Manikin test, the feature profile-test, the adaptation board, and the cube test etc. The performance on this scale is timed and marks are given for performance. These are added up and are compared with the established norms given in the manual to interpret the subject's general intelligence.

Arthur's point scale. This scale has been developed by Grace Arthur by adopting a point scale than the median mental age for the method of scoring. Its new revised version includes the Knox cubes, the Seguin form board, two-form figure board, casuist form board, Manikin test, feature profile, mare and foal picture board, Healy picture completion, and Koh's block design test.

Alexander's battery of performance tests. This scale was designed in Edinburgh University by W.P. Alexander. It consists of three tests—passalong, block designs, and cube construction. The passalong test consists of small blue and red cubes placed in differing numbers in small shallow wooden trays and the position of these cubes is to be reversed by moving them about but without lifting them from the trays. There are nine such patterns printed on cards and the subject is required to manipulate the cubes within the space of the wooden tray without lifting them so that their position is reversed, i.e. if originally placed on one side indicating blue colour, they have to be shifted to the opposite side indicated by red colour. Individual performance is evaluated in terms of success in the task and the time taken.

Koh's block design test at present consists of 17 graded patterns which are printed on cards and coloured cubes matching the colour of the patterns. The cubes are coloured half blue and half yellow, red or white. The subject is required to manipulate the cubes to match the patterns one by one within a time limit to earn the maximum marks or deductions in case the time limit is exceeded.

The cube construction test consists of 26 cubes; some coloured on three sides, some on two, some on one and only one on none. With the help of these cubes, the subject is required to assemble a square block consisting of nine cubes so that three sides are coloured and the top is colourless. Similarly, there is another square block of nine cubes in which all the sides are coloured but the top and the bottom faces have to be colourless, and the third block consists of eight cubes of which all four sides are colourless. The subject has to use his judgement to place the cubes in the right positions to arrange them in square blocks as quickly as possible and points are scored in terms of the time taken.

Bhatia's battery of performance tests.   Attempts have been made in India also to construct such batteries of tests. C.M. Bhatia's work in this regard deserves special mention. Bhatia's battery of performance tests developed by him contains Koh's block design test, Alexander's passalong test, pattern drawing test, picture construction test, and an immediate memory test for digits with an alternative form for the use of illiterate subjects.

The last three tests in this battery have been constructed by Bhatia himself while the first two are adaptations of the scales available in Alexander's battery.

Wechsler Bellevue intelligence scale.   This scale is available in two forms: i.e., WISC for children and WAIS for adults. It is an individual test which has the unique quality of being simultaneously a verbal as well as a performance scale.

The scale consists of eleven sub-tests. Six sub-tests make up the verbal scale and five others comprise the performance scale. These tests are listed below in the order in which they are administered.

Verbal scale:

1. Test of general information.
2. Test of general comprehension.
3. Test of arithmetic reasoning.
4. Test of distinction between similarities.
5. Test of digit span.
6. Test of vocabulary.

Performance scale:

    7. Digit symbol test.
    8. Picture completion test.
    9. Block design test.
  10. Picture arrangement test.
  11. Object assembly test.

    The scores on these sub-tests are added together to assess the subject's intelligence.

THE GROUP VERBAL INTELLIGENCE TESTS

The tests which necessitate the use of language and are applied to a group of individuals at a time come under this category. Some of the earlier tests belonging to this category are:

1. Army alpha test (developed during World War 1).
2. Army general classification test (developed in World War II).

    Several group verbal tests are in use these days; some of the popular Indian tests of this nature are:

1. C.I.E. verbal group test of intelligence (Hindi) constructed by Professor Uday Shankar.
2. The group test of general mental ability (Samuhik mansik yogyata pariksha) constructed by S. Jalota (Hindi).
3. Group test of intelligence, prepared by Bureau of Psychology, Allahabad (Hindi).
4. Prayag Mehta's group intelligence test (Samuhik budhi pariksha, Hindi). This test has been published by Mansayan, Delhi.
5. General mental abilities test, prepared by P.S. Hundal of Punjab University (Punjabi).
6. Group verbal intelligence test prepared by P. Gopala Pillai of Kerala University (Malayalam).
7. Samuhik budhi pariksha (Hindi), prepared by P.L. Shrimali, Vidya Bhavan G.S. Teachers College, Udaipur.
8. Samuhik budhi ki jaanch (Hindi), prepared by S.M. Mohsin, Educational and Vocational Guidance Bureau, Bihar, Patna.

GROUP NON-VERBAL INTELLIGENCE TESTS

These tests do not necessitate the use of language and are applicable to a group of individuals at a time.

    The difference between performance tests (used for an individual) and non-verbal tests (used for a group) is one of degree as far as their non-verbal nature is concerned. The individual performance tests require the manipulation by the subject, of concrete objects or materials, supplied in the test. The responses are purely motor in character and seldom require the use of paper and pencil by the testee (except in a case like the maze test etc.), whereas the test material in the non-verbal tests, used for group testing, is provided in booklets and requires the use of a pencil by the testee.

The test material does not, however, contain words or numerical figures. It contains pictures, diagrams and geometrical figures etc., printed in a booklet. The subject is required to fill in some empty spaces, to draw some simple figures, to point out similarities and dissimilarities, etc. In this way, although the subject uses paper and pencil he does not need to know words or numerical figures. What the subject is required to do is explained clearly by the examiner usually through demonstrations so as to make the least possible use of language.

Some examples of such tests are:

- *Army beta test.* This was developed in World War I in the U.S.A. for testing the intelligence of soldiers who were either illiterate or were not familiar with the English language.

- *Chicago non-verbal test.* This non-verbal test has proved most useful for young children aged 12 and 13 years.

- *Raven's progressive matrices test.* This test was developed in the U.K. It is a very popular non-verbal group test of intelligence. The test has been designed to evaluate the subjects' ability (a) to see the relationship between geometric figures or designs; and (b) to perceive the structure of a design in order to select the appropriate part for completion of each pattern.

C.I.E. non-verbal group test of intelligence. Originally designed by J.W. Jenkins, this test is printed by C.I.E. for adaptation in Hindi medium schools. The test contains items such as the one illustrated here.

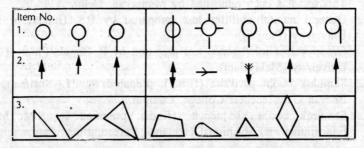

Figure 16.3 An item from C.I.E. non-verbal group test of intelligence.

Concept of Mental Age and I.Q.

Intelligence, assessed through the various intelligence tests is expressed in terms of Intelligence Quotient or I.Q. This term was first coined by the German psychologist, William Stern (1914), for the ratio of mental age and chronological age, which was then multiplied by 100 in order to eliminate the decimal point. The formula for calculation of I.Q. was expressed as

$$I.Q. = \frac{MA}{CA} \times 100$$

where MA stands for mental age and CA for chronological age of the individual whose intelligence is being tested.

The concept of mental age was earlier introduced by French psychologist Alfred Binet. It was based on the principle of the normal distribution of intelligence at the majority of children of a particular age are of normal intelligence and that they have a mental level approximating that age, which could be termed as their mental age. If some child excels in the performance of a certain task compared the performance of the majority of the children of his age, he was said to be of a higher mental age. If, for instance, the performance of an eight-years old on certain adequately determined tasks is equal to that of a majority of ten-year olds, then he has a mental age (MA) of ten years, whereas another child of eight years showing performance equal to that of the majority of six-year olds, on the same tasks would be said to possess a mental age of six years.

In any standard test of intelligence, there is provision of a table which shows the conversion of actual scores obtained on the test into respective mental ages in months. All one has to do is to read the mental age from this table on the basis of the scores earned by the subject on that test. This mental age divided by the chronological age in months (available from the identifying data) and multiplied by 100, then yields the intelligence in terms of I.Q.

The constancy of I.Q. As mentioned earlier, intelligence goes on growing up to the age of 16 to 20 years but the I.Q. for most individuals, remains constant. The I.Q. provides a ratio for determining how bright an individual is as compared to others of his age. Actually, it is an index which is independent not only of the particular score which an individual makes on a particular scale but also of the particular age at which he happens to make it. It is thus a measure which acquaints

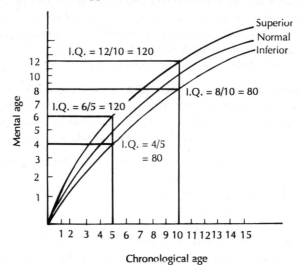

Figure 16.4 Hypothetical growth curves which give a constant I.Q.

us with the relative brightness or intellectual possibilities of an individual, more or less permanently.

It is true that not only an individual grows in intelligence but the whole group (other individuals of his age group) also grow at the same rate. Thus, the intelligence quotient, as a measure of defining relative brightness or intellectual possibilities of an individual remains practically constant. Under ordinary circumstances (accident or disease excepted) an individual's I.Q. is supposed to remain constant throughout life or at least throughout the age limits covered by the scale. This property of the I.Q. is referred to by psychologists as the constancy of I.Q.

Uses, Misuses and Abuses of Intelligence Tests

All intelligence tests—verbal, non-verbal and performance possess many merits and demerits and have been used, misused and abused in so many ways. Let us take a look at these aspects of intelligence testing.

Values of Intelligence Testing

Use in selection. Results of intelligence tests can be properly used for selection of suitable candidates for educational and professional activities such as the following:

1.   admission to a special educational programme or course of instruction.
2.   identification and offer of scholarships to gifted students.
3.   selection of students for assigning specific responsibilities in the school's academic and co-curricular programmes.
4.   selection of trainees for a vocational programme or job.

Use in classification. Intelligence tests help in classifying individuals according to their mental make-up. In the school, it is possible for the teacher to classify the students in his class as backward, average, bright or gifted and thus arrange for homogeneous grouping to provide them with proper educational opportunities according to their individual capabilities. Enrichment programmes for the gifted and remedial education for the backward and dull can thus be possible with the help of classification done through intelligence testing.

Use in assessment for promotion. The results of intelligence tests along with the achievement tests can be successfully used for promotion of students to the next higher grades of classes. Besides this, such tests can also be used in deciding the promotion of people in their chosen profession and social careers.

Use in provision of guidance. The results of intelligence tests may be successfully used in providing educational, vocational and personal guidance to students by teachers and guidance personnel. Problems like, what courses or special subjects one may study, how one should proceed on one's course of learning, what can be achieved by the removal of some learning or emotional difficulties, what profession or occupation should be aimed at by a particular individual, etc. may be successfully solved on the basis of the results of intelligence testing.

Use for improving the learning process. Results of the intelligence testing may prove helpful to teachers to plan the teaching-learning activities. In this connection, Crow and Crow (1973) write:

> Results of intelligence tests can help a teacher to discover what the child can learn and how quickly he can learn, as well as the teaching methods that should be applied and the learning content that should be utilized to guide the learner to use his mental potentialities to their utmost.

Use in setting proper level of aspiration. According to Sawrey and Telford (1964):

> One should aim for what one desires. In other words, one should very carefully set one's level of aspiration neither too high nor too low, if one ventures to be successful. It is possible only when one's potentiality can be properly assessed. Intelligence tests can serve this purpose, and hence they are found to assist the individual to establish a level of aspiration that is realistic in terms of intellectual potential.

Use for diagnosis. The other use of the intelligence testing relates with its capacity to diagnose, distinguish and discriminate the differences in the mental functioning of individuals. This potentiality of intelligence testing can be utilized for (a) identifying exceptional children like gifted, backward and the mentally retarded (both on a general or specific dimension); (b) assessing the degree of mental retardation or extent of giftedness; (c) diagnosing the cause of problematic behaviour and suggesting possible remedial action; (d) arranging suitable educational programmes in view of the varied individual differences found in the mental functioning of the learners.

Use in research work. Finally, the results of intelligence tests can be used in carrying out research in the fields of education, psychology and sociology. For example, to ascertain (a) whether individual differences in mental capacities are the result of heredity or environment or both; (b) whether delinquency or problematic behaviour is caused by inferior intelligence; (c) how mental capacities grow with age, experience or training; (d) how far scholastic achievement depends upon the results of intelligence testing or how far the I.Q. tests can predict one's school performance; (e) what is the interrelationship among mental traits and to discover definite mental or psyche types and; (f) the relationship of intelligence with creativity, anxiety, task performance, job satisfaction, adjustment or a number of other variables.

Misuse and Abuse of Intelligence Testing

Intelligence testing has sufficient scope for being misused which leads to unhealthy effects on the welfare of individuals and society. These effects can be briefly summarized as follows:

Ill-effect on students. The subjects whose intelligence is tested through intelligence tests may be adversely affected by the knowledge of their I.Q. The test findings may colour not only their interests and attitudes towards learning and work but also their total behaviour and personality in dealing with their environment. The dull or below average children prove clever enough to realise through the results of intelligence testing that they are inferior and slow to learn. This can give rise to disappointment and inferiority feelings and adversely affect their future. On the other hand, the label of high I.Q. may also be misutilized by the above average and gifted students. The awareness may make them careless, over-confident and too conscious and proud. Such an attitude may, in the long run, prove to be a potent factor in spoiling their otherwise good behaviour and turning them into problem children. The results of such testing may prove harmful even to the average children as they may lose interest in striving sufficiently to achieve higher goals only because of the knowledge that they are merely average. In this way, the knowledge of the result of intelligence testing may prove harmful to all types of students on account of its misutilization by them.

Misuse by teachers and parents.   The I.Q. labels tagged to the children are very carefully remembered and misutilized by their teachers and parents. They try to see them in the light of their I.Q. They tend to discourage students with lower I.Q. and to generate excessive confidence in students with higher I.Q. In fact, they begin to use the I.Q. as an excuse for their own slackness and inefficiency. They either make no effort to teach the child or humiliate him by saying that he is too dull to understand and, therefore, there is no point in wasting time on him. The gifted may be neglected because they are presumed to have enough intelligence to fend for themselves. In this way, the teachers who themselves are irresponsible may be tempted to use the knowledge of intelligence tests for their own convenience.

Misuse by society.   Not only students and teachers, but society in general has tried to misinterpret and misutilize the results of intelligence testing for upholding the theory of elitism resulting in segregation, sectarianism, casteism and racial discrimination in many societies, including the most developed societies of the west.

The most heat on this issue has been generated recently by some contemporary scholars like Arthur Jensen, a California professor of education (through his article "How much can we boost I.Q. and scholastic achievement" published in the *Harvard Educational Review* in 1969) and by the well-known psychologist H.J. Eysenck. They have proclaimed that the difference in I.Q. scores between different groups (i.e. the blacks and whites in U.S.A.) must also be hereditary. Although such a claim has been rejected by the vast majority of psychologists on the basis of studies conducted in different parts of the world, it has provided ground for the segregationists in America, Britain and other European countries for advocating and enriching separate systems of education and opportunities for whites and blacks. Similarly, the South African white government was maintaining for a quite long time its policy of apartheid only on account of such unproven and dubious arguments. It has also led to the belief that compensatory education is a waste of teachers' time and efforts and of the tax payers' money. Once Professor Jensen's assertion for giving 80% weightage to the genetic factors for determining one's intellectual output is accepted, certainly no need of enriching the environment will remain.

However, the picture is not as has been presented by staunch geneticists like

Jensen. It is impossible to rule out the influence of environment when the subjects are considered for the measurement of their intelligence. Adequate researches have been carried out and incidental evidences exist to demonstrate that the I.Q. level depends upon education, culture, income, social status, nutrition and many other environmental conditions. Therefore, it is quite wrong and unjustified to exploit the results of I.Q. tests to spread segregation and discrimination on the basis of caste, colour, creed and race.

Culture-free, Culture-fair and Culture-specific Intelligence Tests

It is often argued that intelligence tests contain items, verbal or non-verbal, highly loaded with the contents and experiences of one or the other culture, particularly the culture of the majority and the privileged class of society. Consequently, testing on such scales has put the children of the minority or unprivileged at a disadvantage on account of their ignorance of the relevant knowledge and experiences required in responding to the test items.

In order to eliminate such problems, it was thought to plan for *culture-free intelligence tests* by devising test items free of cultural content and eliminating those that are culturally loaded. Cattell (1933) first of all developed a test consisting of novel problem-solving items that do not occur in any culture. He called it a culture-free test of intelligence. Later on some other tests like Davis-Ell's tests of general intelligence or problem solving ability were also designed. However, the researches conducted on the basis of these tests demonstrated that it is not possible to devise culture-free tests. In planning the items one has to depend upon contents—verbal or non-verbal. In absolute terms, it is possible to design a test that does not require language, but how can we do away with the experience acquired or not acquired in our culture or way of thinking and behaving which is required for responding to the items of non-verbal or performance tests? Obviously, a subject who is familiar with the objects pictured will certainly be in an advantageous position. Similarly, the children of privileged parents, society and culture will certainly perform better.

In view of these considerations, attempts were made to devise culture-fair tests, i.e. tests containing items which are common to all cultures. However, in practice the use of such culture-fair tests has also been disappointing. It has been found that it is almost impossible to screen for culturally determined values and attitudes and the tests almost always favour people from the same culture as the test constructor. All tests are content or culture specific to some degree. An intelligence test is used for measuring the intelligence of an individual in terms of the successful performance with reference to a particular culture, and hence, if it is not related to any culture, it defeats its very purpose. A culture-fair or culture-free test is thus counter-productive.

The way out then, is to plan culture-specific intelligence tests in place of culture-free or culture-fair test. These tests may contain items related to a specific culture or sub-culture and validated in terms of their accuracy in predicting educational, vocational and social competence within those specific cultures and sub-cultures. However, in case one needs to predict success within the main stream of society, one has to depend upon the conventional tests based on the main-stream culture (Hobbs, 1975).

How Reliable and Dependable are the Intelligence Tests?

Not only intelligence tests but any test used for measuring human traits or characteristics should satisfy the criteria of reliability, validity, objectivity, comprehensiveness, practicability, etc. Moreover, it should have suitable standardized items relevant to local situations and should be essentially administered in conditions most favourable to the subject. The interpretation of the responses in the context of the provided norms should also be made with great caution.

However, one should not be over-enthusiastic about intelligence test findings on account of the following drawbacks:

1.   Intelligence cannot be measured in the way a cardiologist measures heartbeat or an occulist measures eyesight. No intelligence test by itself or in combination with others can ever measure the true psyche potential or mental functioning of an individual. At the most they can assess the I.Q. rather than the real cognitive ability of an individual.

2.   It is very difficult to find equal values of I.Q. with the help of different I.Q. tests. It is quite surprising and rather confusing when a child scores very high on one test and very low on another. Which of these scores should be taken as a measure of the child's I.Q.? The average value of the two may be quite misleading.

3.   No intelligence tests, including the most refined performance tests, can be claimed as culture-free or culture-fair tests. Moreover, these are not completely free of practice and coaching effects. A person brought up in a relatively healthy and rich environment and exposed to the monkey tricks of intelligence testing (due to practice and coaching effects) will surely fare better in an intelligence test and earn a higher score than warranted by his intelligence.

4.   In fact, intelligence tests are of little help in determining a child's overall potentiality because they do not go beyond the subjects' cognitive abilities. No conclusions can be drawn from these about one's aspiration, motives, aptitudes, attitudes, interests, likes and dislikes, and personal choices etc.

5.   The I.Q. scores of the testees are highly influenced by the conditions prevailing at the time the intelligence tests are administered. Physical conditions such as mental and physical fatigue, and ailments seem to interfere with performance. Test anxiety is another factor. Emotional and psychological factors may also present obstacles. Commenting on this aspect Crow and Crow (1973) write:

> The results of all such tests may be affected by many factors inherent in testing conditions, the child's background of experience and other favourable or unfavourable elements. Hence no administrator, teacher or student of education should accept test results as the only measure of an individual's ability to learn.

It may, therefore, be concluded that too much reliance cannot be placed on the results of intelligence testing. These should not be accepted as the sole measure of the likelihood of success in school achievements, profession and future life. In any case, these should not be made an instrument for creating complexes among the students and misunderstandings among the teachers. These need to be wisely planned, properly administered and intelligently interpreted for the welfare of students and the productive growth of society. The results of achievement tests, aptitude tests, interest inventory, attitude scale, motives measurement etc., should also be considered along with I.Q. scores while making any decision about the education, profession and future life of the subject.

SUMMARY

Intelligence may be understood to be a mental energy available with an individual which enables him to cope with his environment in terms of adaptation and dealing with novel situations as effectively as possible.

The factor theories of intelligence try to throw light on the structure of intelligence by pointing out the number of factors or constituents, e.g. the *unitary theory* holds that intelligence consists of only one factor, i.e. a fund of intellectual competence. Quite contrary to this, the *multi-factor theory* considers intelligence to be a combination of numerous separate elements or factors, each of which is a minute element of an ability. *Spearman's two-factor theory* advocates the presence of two factors—general intelligence 'g' and specific intelligence 's'. The *group factor theory* postulates that all intellectual tasks can be categorized in definite groups. Each group has a unique common factor known as the group factor. Thurston and associates had discovered nine such group factors. *Vernon's hierarchical theory* suggests a hierarchical structure for the organisation of intelligence in the shape of G, an overall factor branching into two major group factors and various specific factors. *Guilford's theory* lays down a model of the intellect involving three interrelated and interacted basic parameters—operations, contents and products for explaining the structure of human intelligence.

Cognitive theories of intelligence try to analyse and describe intelligence in terms of certain fundamental cognitive processes, e.g. *Cattell and Horn's theory of intelligence* states that intelligence is made up of two types of intelligence— fluid intelligence (derived more from biological and genetic factors and relatively free from the influences of education and culture) and crystallized intelligence (acquired fund of general information). The other cognitive theory, namely *Jensen's theory of mental functioning,* describes one's intelligence as being composed of two types of abilities, i.e. associative abilities (related to biological maturation differing little among social classes and races) and conceptual abilities (dependent on education and culture and responsible for observed differences in conceptual reasoning among social classes and races).

Campion and Brown's theory of intelligence suggests that intelligence includes a biologically based architectural system and an environmentally influenced executive system. While the former works as a base for one's intellectual functioning incorporating such factors as memory capacity, information processing etc., the latter is responsible for the higher order mental functioning. *Sternberg's information processing theory of intelligence* makes use of the information processing approach for explaining the individual's cognitive or problem-solving behaviour. It outlines our mental functioning as definite steps explaining what we do with information from the time we perceive it till the time we finish using it to slove our problem.

Gardner's *theory of multiple intelligence* challenges the notion of general intelligence, or g, on which most current models of intelligence testing are based. It defines intelligence as a set of abilities, talents, or mental skills that permit an individual to solve problems or fashion products that are of consequence in a particular cultural setting. This theory, while providing a comprehensive view of the human cognitive structure, believes that there are seven independent types of intelligence (developing differently in different people) ranging from linguistic and logical-mathematical abilities to intrapersonal and interpersonal abilities.

A more comprehensive picture of the concept of intelligence may emerge if, certain important factors about its nature are known; namely, that intelligence is normally distributed in nature; it is a product of both heredity and environment, it grows with age and its vertical growth ceases at the age of 16 to 20; it shows a wide variety of individual differences but factors like sex, race, culture, caste and colour etc. are not found to influence the degree of intelligence.

Intelligence cannot be measured in the same way as we measure a piece of cloth or the temperature of our body. It can only be assessed. This assessment is carried out through intelligence tests categorized as individual and group tests involving the use of verbal or non-verbal material.

In individual tests, we test one individual at a time whereas in group tests, a group of individuals may be tested at the same time. There are numerous individual and group tests, some of which are paper and pencil tests and thus essentially require the use of language, while others are language-free tests. Performance tests are a typical example of such non-language tests. In such tests an assessment of one's intelligence is made through the evaluation of one's performance on tests involving intellectual abilities. These tests are most useful in cases of individuals who have language handicaps such as foreign language speaking groups, illiterates, the deaf and dumb and mentally retarded or culturally deprived individuals.

The concept of mental age and I.Q. is used for interpreting the scores earned on intelligence tests. The *mental age* of a child signifies comparison with a particular mental level which is normal for the majority of children of his age. In a standardized test of intelligence, we can read the mental age of an individual (in months) directly from the table provided in the manual on the basis of the score.

REFERENCES

Belmont, L. and Marolla, F.A., Birth order, family size and intelligence, *Science,* Vol. 182, pp. 1096–1101, 1973.

Bouchard, T.J. (Jr.), Twins reared together and apart: What they tell us about human diversity, in S.W. Fox (Ed.), *Individuality and Its Determinism,* New York: Plenum Press, 1984.

Bouchard, T.J. (Jr.) and McGue, M., Family studies of intelligence: A review, *Science,* Vol. 212, pp. 1055–1059, 1981.

————, *Information about the Minnesota Center for Twin and Adoption Research,* Minneapolis: University of Minnesota, 1987.

Binet, A. and Simon, T., *The Development of Intelligence in Children,* Baltimore: Williams & Wilkins, 1916.

Cattell, R.B., *The Cattell Intelligence Test Scales 1, 2 and 3,* London: Harrap, 1933.

Campion, J.C. and Brown, A.L., Toward a theory of intelligence: Contribution from research with retarded children, *Intelligence,* (2), 1979.

Crow, L.D. and Crow, A., *Educational Psychology,* New Delhi: Eurasia Publishing House, 1973, p. 160.

Eysenck, H.J. and Kamin, Leon, *The Intelligence Controversy,* New York: John Wiley, 1981.

Gardner, H., *Franws of Mind. The theory of multiple intelligence,* New York: Basic Books, 1983.

Gottfried, A.W. (Ed.), *Home Environment and Early Cognitive Development,* San Francisco: Academic, 1984.

Griffith, J.H., *The Psychology of Human Behaviour,* London: George Allen, 1933, p. 138.

Guilford, J.P., *The Nature of Human Intelligence,* New York: McGraw-Hill, 1967.

Hobbs, N., *The Future of Children,* San Francisco: Jossey-Bass, 1975.

Horn, J.L., The nature and development of intellectual abilities, in R.T. Osborne, C.E. Noble, and N. Weyl (Eds.), *Human Variation,* New York: Academic Press, 1978.

Jencks, D., *Inequality: A reassessment of the effect of family and schooling in America,* New York: Basic Books, 1972.

Jensen, A.R., How much can we boost I.Q. and scholastic achievements? *Harvard Educational Review,* (39), 1969.

Loehlin, J.C., Lindzey, G. and Spuhler, J.N., *Race Difference in Intelligence,* San Francisco: W.H. Freeman, 1975.

Munsinger, H.A., The adopted child's I.Q.: A crucial review, *Psychological Bulletin,* Vol. 82, pp. 623–659, 1978.

Piaget, J., *The Origins of Intelligence in Children,* New York: International Universities Press, 1952.

Pillai, N.P., Pillai, K.S. and Nair, K.S., *Psychological Foundations of Education,* Trivandrum: Kalaniketan, 1972.

Schiff, M., Duyme, M., Dumaret, A., Steward, J., Tomkiewiezes and Feingold, Intellectual status of working class children adopted early into upper middle class families, *Science,* Vol. 200, pp. 1503–1504, 1978.

Sherman, M. and Key, C.B., The intelligence of isolated mountain children, *Child Development,* Vol. 3, pp. 279–290, 1932.

Spearman, C.E., *The Nature of Intelligence and Principles of Cognition,* London: Macmillan, 1923.

_____, *The Abilities of Man,* New York: Macmillan, 1927.

Stemberg, R.J., *Beyond I.Q.: A triarchic theory of human intelligence,* London: Cambridge University Press, 1985, p. 45.

Stern, W., *Psychological Methods of Testing Intelligence,* Baltimore: Warwick and York: Inc., 1914, p. 3.

Stoddard, G.D., *The Meaning of Intelligence,* New York: Macmillan, 1943, p. 4.

Teasdale, T.W. and Owen, D.R., Heredity and familial environment in intelligence and educational level: A sibling study, *Nature,* Vol. 309, pp. 620–622, 1989.

Tennan, L.M. and Merrill, M.A., *Measuring Intelligence,* Boston: Houghton Mifflin, 1937.

Thompson, G.H., *The Factorial Analysis of Human Ability,* London: London University Press, 1939.

Thorndike, E.L., *Educational Psychology* (Briefer Course), New York: Columbia University, 1914.

Thurston, L.L., *Primary Mental Abilities,* Chicago: University of Chicago Press, 1938.

Vernon, P.E., *The Structure of Human Abilities,* London: Methuen, 1950.

Wagnon, M.J. (Ed.), *Readings in Educational Psychology,* New York: Houghton Mifflin, 1937, p. 401.

Wechsler, D., *Wechsler Scale of Intelligence,* (WAIS, WISE), New York: Psychological Corporation, 1939.

_____, *The Measurement of Adult Intelligence* (3rd ed.), New York: Williams and Wilkins, 1944, p. 3.

Wilson, E.O., *Sociobiology: The New Synthesis,* Cambridge: Harvard University Press, 1975.

Woodworth, R.S., *Psychology: A Study of Mental Life,* New York: Century, 1932.

Woodworth, R.S. and Marquis, D.G., *Psychology* (5th ed.), New York: Henry Holt, 1948, p. 33.

Zajonc, R.B., Family configuration and intelligence, *Science,* Vol. 192, 1976, pp. 226–236.

_____, Validating the confluence model, *Psychological Bulletin,* Vol. 93, pp. 457–480.

_____, Mining new gold from old research, *Psychology Today,* Feb., 1986.

SUGGESTED READINGS

Brody, E.B. and Brody, N., *Intelligence: Nature, determinants and consequences,* New York: Academic Press, 1976.

Butcher, H.J., *Human Intelligence: Its nature and assessment,* London: Methuen, 1968.

Cronbach, L.J., *Essentials of Psychological Testing* (3rd ed.), New York: Harper & Row, 1970.

Drever, J. and Collins, M., *The Performance Tests of Intelligence,* Edinburgh: Oliver & Boyd, 1948.

Jensen, A.R., *Bias in Mental Testing,* New York: Free Press, 1980.

Sawrey, J.H. and Telford, C., *Educational Psychology* (2nd ed.), New Delhi: Prentice-Hall of India, 1964.

Wolfe, D. (Ed.), *The Discovery of Talent,* Cambridge (Mass.): Harvard University Press, 1969.

Chapter 17

Emotions and Emotional Intelligence

Our emotions play quite a signifcant role in guiding and directing our behaviour. Many times they seem to dominate us in such a way that we have no solution other than behaving as they want us to. On the other hand, if a person has no emotions in him, then he becomes crippled in terms of living his life in a normal way. In this way, emotions play a key role in providing a particular direction to our behaviour and thus shaping our personality according to their development. In the present chapter, we would like to throw light on the emotional aspect of our behaviour.

WHAT ARE EMOTIONS?

Etymologically, the word emotion is derived from the Latin word 'emovere' which means 'to stir up' or 'to excite'. Emotion can thus be understood as an agitated or excited state of our mind and body. Taking clue from its derivation, various psychologists have tried to define the term 'emotion' in their own ways. Let us reproduce a few of such definitions.

Woodworth (*1945*):

> Emotion is a 'moved' or 'stirred-up' state of an organism. It is a stirred-up state of feeling, that is the way it appears to the individual himself. It is a disturbed muscular and glandular activity, that is the way it appears to an external observer.

Crow and Crow (*1973*):

> Emotion is an affective experience that accompanies generalised linear adjustment and mental and physiological stirred-up states in the individual and that shows itself in his overt behaviour.

Charles G. Morris (*1979*):

> Emotion is a complex affective experience that involves diffuse physiological changes and can be expressed overtly in characteristic behaviour patterns.

McDougall (*1949*):

> Emotion is an affective experience that one undergoes during an instinctive excitement. For example, when a child perceives a bull coming towards him. (cognition) he experiences an affective experience in the form of the arousal of

314

accompanied emotion of fear and consequently tries to run away (conative aspect of one's behaviour).

McDougall discovered 14 basic instincts and concluded that each and every emotion, whatever it may be, is the product of some instinctive behaviour.

These instincts, with their associated emotions, can be listed as:

Table 17.1 Human instincts with their associated emotions

S. No.	Instinct	Emotion accompanying it
1.	Flight or escape	Fear
2.	Pugnacity or combat	Anger
3.	Repulsion	Disgust
4.	Curiosity	Wonder
5.	Parental	Tender emotion, love
6.	Appeal	Distress
7.	Construction	Feeling of creativeness
8.	Acquisition	Feeling of ownership
9.	Gregariousness	Feeling of loneliness
10.	Sex, mating	Lust
11.	Self-assertion	Positive self-feeling or elation
12.	Submission	Negative self-feeling
13.	Food-seeking	Appetite
14.	Laughter	Amusement

Thus, whatever may be the terminology used by all these different writers and psychologists, their definitions tend to describe emotions as some sort of feelings or affective experiences which are characterised by some physiological changes that generally lead them to perform some or the other types of behavioural acts.

NATURE AND CHARACTERISTICS OF EMOTIONS

From these definitions and discussions, we may be able to conclude following things about the nature and characteristics of emotions.

1. *Emotional experiences are associated with some instincts or biological drives.* Every emotional experience is associated with one or the other innate instinct. An emotion is aroused under the current or influence of an instinctive excitement. One can experience emotion of anger only after riding on the instinctive waves of pugnacity or combat.

2. *Emotions are the product of perception.* Perception of a proper stimulus (object or situation) is needed to start an emotional experience. The organic changes within the body (favourable or unfavourable) then, may intensify the emotional experience.

3. *The core of an emotion is feeling.* Actually every emotional experience, whatever it may be, involves feelings—a sense of response aroused in the heart.

Feelings and emotions—both are affective experiences. There is only the difference of degrees. After perceiving a thing or a situation, feelings like pleasure or displeasure can be aroused. There may be some intensity or degree of strength in these feelings. When the feelings are so strong as to disturb the mind and excite an individual to act immediately, they are turned into emotions. Therefore, the urge to do or act (conative aspect), is the most important emotional experience.

4. *Emotions bring physiological changes.* Every emotional experience involves many physical and physiological changes in the organism. Some of the changes which express themselves as overt behaviour are easily observable. For example, reddened eyes, flushed cheeks, beating of the heart, choke in the voice, or an attack on an emotion-aroused stimulus. In addition to these easily observable changes, there are internal physiological changes. Examples are, changes in the circulation of blood, impact on the digestive system and changes in the functioning of some glands like adrenal glands.

These changes become so specific and distinguishable in the human being that a simple glimpse can enable us to detect a particular emotional experience in an individual and we can see whether he is in anger or, suffers from fear and so on.

In addition to the above, emotions have some more specific characteristics. These are:

(a) Emotions are prevalent in every living organism.

(b) They are present at all stages of development and can be aroused in young as well as in old.

(c) Emotions are individualistic, and they differ from person to person.

(d) Same emotion can be aroused by a number of different stimuli—objects or situations.

(e) Emotions rise abruptly but subside slowly. An emotion once aroused, tends to persist and leave behind, an emotional mood.

(f) Emotions have the quality of displacement. The anger aroused on account of one stimulus gets transferred to another situation. The anger resulting from being rebuked by the boss, gets transferred to beating the children at home.

(g) One emotion can give birth to a number of similar emotions.

(h) There is a negative correlation between the upsurge of emotions and intelligence. Reasoning and sharp intellect can check sudden upsurge of emotions. Also, under emotional experiences, the reasoning and thinking powers are decreased.

KINDS OF EMOTIONS

If we try to analyse the impact of various emotional experiences on the well-being of an individual, we can come to the conclusion that emotions have both positive as well as negative effects. Whether an emotion will prove to be helpful or harmful to an individual, depends upon the following factors:

1. the frequency and intensity of emotional experience.
2. the situation, occasion and the nature of stimulus which arouses the emotion.
3. the kind of emotional experience or emotions.

The last factor—the kind of emotional experience—counts much in this direction. Emotions, in general, can be categorized into two—positive emotions and negative emotions.

Unpleasant emotions like fear, anger and jealousy which are harmful to the individual's development are termed as negative emotions, while the pleasant emotions like affection (love), amusement, curiosity and happiness which are very helpful and essential for normal development, are termed as positive emotions.

By their nature of being both positive and negative, it should not be assumed that all the positive emotions are always good, and the negative emotions, bad. While weighing their impact, other factors like frequency and intensity, nature of situations and the stimuli aroused, should also be considered. Excess of everything is bad. Emotions with too much of intensity and frequency, whether positive or negative, bring harmful effects. But, the so-called negative emotions are essential for human welfare. The emotion of fear prepares an individual to face the danger ahead. The child who has no emotion of fear is sure to get affected because it has not learnt to save itself against a possible danger.

Physiological or Bodily Changes Accompanying Emotions

When we are in the waves of positive or negative emotions, our behaviour is totally controlled and directed by that emotion. During this period, various types of internal or external changes occur in our body, which may be briefly summarised as follows:

1. *Internal bodily changes.* The internal structure and functioning of our body is very much influenced and affected by any emotional experience. Some of these bodily and physiological changes may be judged through outward observation or simple instruments but often, we have to make sophisticated special instruments like galvanic skin reflex instrument, electro encephalograph (EEG), sphygmo-manometer (blood pressure checking instrument) and polygraph (lie detector) etc. Some of these internal bodily changes can be mentioned as follows:

(a) Functioning of our heart is affected by emotional experience. Generally, the heart beat is increased under states of agitation and excitement aroused by the emotion.

(b) Blood circulation system is quite affected by emotional experiences. Generally it increases but in some cases as of fear, anxiety and shock, it may also reduce considerably.

(c) Rate of respiration and breathing is also deeply affected by emotional experience. Generally it increases, but in cases like excessive fear, happiness, shocks and excitements it may go down to the extent of becoming nil.

(d) Digestive system is adversely affected by emotions. Experimental studies have concluded that under the current of emotions, our stomach and intestines work quite slowly and sometimes become inactive. The secretion of the digestive glands including saliva, decreases considerably resulting in malfunctioning and inactivity on the part of our digestive system. That is why, most of the emotionally charged individuals are found to suffer from digestive problems.

(e) Emotions bring changes in the chemical composition of our blood like (i) increase in the amount of adrenal, (ii) increase in the amount of sugar level, (iii) changes in the number and proportion of red corpuscles.

(f) Normal body temperature fluctuates. At the time of intense excitement, it generally goes down.

(g) There are significant changes in the secretion of the duct and ductless glands. The flow of these secretions in the form of saliva, tears and sweat can be externally observed.

(h) There are significant changes in the electrical or galvanic skin responses. There is a decrease in the case of emotions like distress, disgust and anger which results into sweating or perspiration. On the other hand, there is increase in the case of emotions like fear, love, wonder, etc. which results into the *erection of the body hairs.*

(i) The muscles of our body are hardened and get tensed during an emotional current. It may bring destabilization and inequilibrium to our body functioning. The twisting and hardening of the muscles may be easily detected from external observation.

(j) Functioning of the brain is also adversely affected during intense emotional currents. The sensory and perceptual processes are influenced by these emotional experiences. Many times, emotions play quite a dominant role over reasoning resulting in sudden fits of anger and frustration.

2. *External or observable bodily changes.* Apart from the overt changes mentioned above, there are many other emotional currents outwardly expressed. These may be of the following nature.

(a) *Changes in facial expression.* Face, to some extent, is said to be the index of human behaviour. It equally applies to our emotional behaviour. Under the influence of an emotional current, there are significant changes in our facial expression that can be identified through simple external observation. By looking at a person's facial expression, we can identify his intended emotions as anger, laughter, fear, disgust, contempt, love, happiness or surprise. The basis for the correlation between facial expressions and emotions may be discovered both in one's innate dispositions and socio-cultural environment. Where the way of expressing emotions may vary from culture to culture, it may also be revealed in the form of responses to situations, say, jumping at the time of hearing a sudden noise and biting teeth when angry.

Behavioural expressions in the form of facial expressions and non-verbal communications, however, cannot be understood as sufficiently objective, reliable and valid instrument for the identification and measurement of one's emotions. One can easily hide one's feelings under an apparent mask of false facial expressions and other non-verbal communications and thus make the task of identification quite difficult and most unreliable.

   (b) *Changes in body postures.* Besides the changes in facial expression, there are significant changes in one's body postures during emotional experiences. For example, when one is angry, besides the redness of his face, his body postures and movements may exhibit his anger. He may begin to walk fast, tighten his fist, bang on the table, utter incomprehensible words and so on. His whole body and its movements, through their various forms and postures reveal the emotional state he is in. That is why, when one is trembling or trying to hide or run away in a bid to save one's life, we say that one is in the grip of fear. Similarly we can also identify other emotions like love, delight, disgust, wonder or distress.

However, there lies less reliability in this method of identification of the emotions through one's body postures. A person may be able to hide his emotional feelings by exhibiting different types of body postures other than those expected for the display of his actual feelings. Also, many of the emotions have similarities in terms of the observable body postures and movements.

   (c) *Change in voice or vocal expression.* There are significant changes in one's voice or vocal expression during an emotional current. Laughing, weeping, speaking in a loud voice with an unusual high pitch, crying, talking slowly with some hesitation, feeling difficulty in speaking, uttering abusive language, speaking in a very sweet and affectionate manner, whistling, murmuring, humming etc. are some of the examples and ways through which we demonstrate different emotions. That is why when we listen to the dialogues of actors in a play or programmes on the radio and television broadcast, we can very well say that at this particular time, a person is displaying the emotion of anger, fear, disgust, love and lust. However, it is also not a reliable method for the identification of one's emotional experience simply on the ground that many of the emotional expressions may demonstrate similarities in terms of voice or vocal expressions. Besides this, there may be individual differences with regard to the vocal expression of a particular emotional behaviour. In such cases, therefore, we don't get any idea about the vocal expression of the emotions and so we may tend to misinterpret the concerned person's behaviour.

Development of Emotions and Emotional Maturity

The process of maturation and learning play effective roles in the development of emotions in the human beings. As a child grows, he may acquire various positive and negative emotions through his environmental experiences and training. Emotions or emotional behaviour are in all sense, the learned and acquired pattern of our behaviour. Therefore, at the time of birth, a child does not show the presence of any specific emotions except a sort of general excitement in the form of crying or smiling. This state of general excitement showing pleasure or displeasure to the concerned stimuli remains with the infant up to 6 months. Therefore, it can be safely said that a child begins his journey towards the development of his emotional behaviour with the help of two distinct emotions i.e. emotion of distress (displeasure) and emotion of delight (pleasure). When an infant completes his six months, negative emotions (like fear, disgust, anger, jealousy etc.) take the lead and then the positive emotions (like elation, love, sympathy, enjoyment etc.) creep in. Generally, upto two years, almost all the emotions, positive and negative, take their shape and become quite distinct in children.

Emotional development, after the stage of infancy, is thus totally concerned with the development of the ways and manners of expressing various positive and negative emotions. These ways and means of emotional expressions are learned through environmental experiences, formal as well as informal education and specialized training given to an individual right from his childhood.

Whatever, experience, education or training a person may get for the expression of his emotional behaviour during his childhood and adolescence, we expect from him a quite mature behaviour in terms of his emotional expression during his adulthood. Besides attaining maturity in terms of his physical and mental development, an adult should also demonstrate adequate maturity in terms of his emotional development. In other words, he must be emotionally mature and must exhibit it in his behaviour.

Meaning of Emotional Maturity

Emotional maturity is that characteristic of emotional behaviour that is generally attained by an adult after the expiry of his adolescence period. After attaining emotional maturity, he is able to demonstrate a well-balanced emotional behaviour in his day-to-day life. A person may be said to be emotionally matured if he has in his possession almost all types of emotions—positive or negative and is able to express them at the appropriate time in an appropriate degree.

The Characteristics of an Emotionally Matured Person

An emotionally matured person demonstrates the following traits and charac-teristics in his behaviour.

1. Almost all the emotions can be distinctly seen in him and their pattern of expression can be easily recognised.
2. Manifestation of emotions is very much refined. Usually he expresses his emotions in a socially desirable way.
3. He is able to exercise control over his emotions. Sudden inappropriate emotional outbursts are rarely found in him. He is able to hide his feelings and check his emotional tide.
4. The person perceives things in their real perspective. He is not a day-dreamer and does not possess the desire to run away from realities.

5. His intellectual powers like thinking and reasoning are properly exercised by him in making any decision. He is guided more by his intellect than his emotions.

6. He does not possess the habit of rationalization i.e. he never argues in defence of his undesirable or improper conduct. Also he never shifts the responsibility of his mistakes on others. He is always honest in his behaviour.

7. He possesses adequate self-concept and self-respect. He never likes to do things or show such behaviour that can injure his self-respect and is adverse to his ideals.

8. He is not confined to himself. He thinks about others and is keen to maintain social relationships. He never engages himself in such a behaviour as is antisocial and can result in social conflicts and strain his social relationships.

9. He can exercise his emotions at a proper time in a proper place. If there is a danger to his self-prestige or if anyone is in distress, he can rise to the occasion by exercising his emotion of anger. But if he commits a mistake and is rebuked, he is equally able to check his emotion of anger. Matured emotional behaviour is characterised by greater stability. A person having such maturity does not sudden shift from one emotion to another.

In conclusion, regarding the meaning of emotional maturity, I would like to quote Arthur T. Jersild (1968). He is of the opinion that emotional maturity should not involve just simple restriction and control. It means much more. An adequate description of emotional maturity must take account the full scope of the individual's capacity and powers, and of his ability to use and enjoy them. In its broadest sense emotional maturity means the degree to which the person has realized his potential for richness of living and has developed his capacity to enjoy things, to relate himself to others, to love and to laugh; his capacity for whole-hearted sorrow when an occasion for grief arises . . . and his capacity to show fear when there is occasion to be frightened, without feeling a need to use a false mask of courage.

THEORIES OF EMOTIONS

Psychologists have propagated a number of theories on emotions. A few important ones are described below:

James–Lange Theory

One of the first psychologists to attempt a scientific explanation of emotion was a Harvard Professor, William James. Incidentally a few years later in 1885, a Danish physiologist Carl Lange also arrived at the same conclusion as propagated by James and consequently, the theory is jointly named as James–Lange Theory.

The James–Lange theory advocates that emotions spring from physiological reactions. The perception of a stimulus causes our body to undergo certain physiological changes and we experience emotion.

This theory, however, reversed the old common notion about the sequence of the arousal of emotions. The previous sequence was we see a bear, we feel afraid, we run. According to the new theory, the order is changed to we see a bear, we run, we feel afraid.

While commenting on his new theory, James (1890) writes: "My theory, on the contrary, is that the bodily changes follow directly the perception of the exciting fact, and that our feeling of the same changes as they occur in the emotion. Common sense says, we loose our fortune, are sorry and weep; we meet a bear, are frightened and run: we are insulted by a rival, are angry and strike . . . this order of sequence is incorrect and more rational statement is that we feel sorry because we cry, angry because we strike, afraid because we tremble."

Cannon–Bard Theory

In 1927, the American psychologist Walter Cannon unleashed an attack against the James–Lange theory. Later on reinforced by L.L. Bard's work on the 'thalamus', he proposed that the lower brain centres, specifically the thalamus and hypothalamus, are responsible for inciting emotional reactions. After perceiving a stimulus, the sensory impulses reach the thalamic–hypothalamic regions. From there they are carried simultaneously to the internal organs of the body and the cerebral cortex. The cerebral cortex, therefore, receives and experiences emotion at the same time when physical changes occur in the body.

Cannon–Bard theory tries to maintain that emotion and physiological responses occur simultaneously, not one after another. For example, when we encounter a frightening stimulus like a bear, the sequence of the arousal of emotion takes the form as, we perceive the bear, we run and are afraid, with neither reaction that is emotional response and emotional experience, preceding the other.

Schachter–Singer Theory

Around 1970, the American psychologists Stanley Schachter and Jerome Singer, while adopting an eclectic approach to both the earlier theories of emotion, introduced a new theory named Cognitive theory of emotion. They suggested that our physical arousal together with our perception and judgment of situation (cognition) jointly determine our emotions. In other words, our emotional arousal depends on both physiological changes and the cognitive or mental interpretation of those changes. One cannot work without the other. However, the necessary explanation for an emotional state always rests on the interpretation of situation. Since this interpretation is purely a subject of cognitive functioning, the cognitive factors are said to be the potent determiners of our emotional states.

The views expressed by Schachter and Singer were also supported by Magda Arnold who stated that cognitive processes control the way we interpret our feelings and the way we act on them. She used the term *Cognitive Appraisal* for the identification and interpretation of emotion-provoking stimuli.

Cognitive theory of emotion thus tried to emphasize the role of cognitive factors, a third element in understanding the relationship between physical reactions and emotional experience aroused on account of the perception of an emotion-provoking stimulus. Cognitive theory helped us learn that the emotional experience and physiological changes through which we pass are determined by the way we interpret a situation through the cognitive element of our behaviour in the form of our previous knowledge and our interpretation of the present situation.

Activation Theory

The implications of the Cannon–Bard theory in suggesting that "emotions serve an emergency function by preparing the organism for appropriate action" led the way to the modern Activation theory of emotion. The theory was actually propounded in 1951 by Donald B. Lindsley. In general, Activation theory refers to the view that emotion represents a state of heightened arousal rather than a qualitatively unique type of psychological, physiological or behavioural process. Arousal is considered to lie on a wide continuum, ranging from a very low level such as deep sleep, to such extremely agitated states as rage or extreme anger.

According to Lindsley (1951), emotion-provoking stimuli activate the recticular activating system in the brain stem, which in turn sends impulses both upward, towards the cortex and downward, towards the musculature. To evoke a significant emotional behaviour, the recticular system must be properly activated. However, the activating system tries to serve only a general function and the specific structures in the brain organise the input and determine the particular form of emotion to be expressed.

Conclusion about Theories

All these four types of theories discussed so far, have tried to provide explanation for emotional behaviour in human beings, their own ways. The James–Lange theory states that our bodily responses stimulate our perception of emotion. The body first responds physiologically to a stimulus, and then the cerebral cortex determines the emotional experience. The Cannon–Bard theory states that impulses from the emotion provoking stimulus are sent simultaneously to the cerebral cortex and the internal organs of the body. Thus the emotional experience and the bodily responses occur simultaneously, but independently. Cognitive theory brings into the limelight the dominant role played by cognitive factors stating that the emotions we experience and the physiological responses we give are both determined by cognitive functioning; the way in which our mind receives and interprets the stimuli. The Activation theory developed by Lindsley focusses on the role played by the recticular activating system for the arousal and display of emotions. If we try to evaluate the views proposed by these theories, we can come to the conclusion that none of these existing theories, can be termed as a comprehensive theory of emotional behaviour. However, to some extent it can be concluded, that emotional behaviour is surely a product of the process of activation. The biological structure of an individual influenced by environmental experiences, in one way or the other, must activate the internal organs and the cerebral cortex for the various physiological responses and affective experiences that are undergone by an individual, while going through an emotional behaviour.

EMOTIONAL QUOTIENT (E.Q.) AND EMOTIONAL INTELLIGENCE

Emotional Quotient represents the relative measure of a person's emotional intelligence similar to intelligence quotient (I.Q.).

We know that one's intelligence is an innate as well as acquired intellectual potential. Every child is born with some intellectual potential which grows and develops with the help of maturity and experiences. Similarly, one is also born with some innate emotional intelligence in terms of one's level of emotional sensitivity, emotional memory, emotional processing and emotional learning ability. This potential (unlike intelligence) is liable to be developed or damaged as a result of one's experiences. The difference here is between the development pattern of innate emotional intelligence and general intelligence as a result of maturity and experiences.

Where general intelligence is generally not subjected to decline or damage with life experiences (it always picks up the rising trend), the emotional intelligence can be either developed or destroyed depending upon the type of environmental experiences one gets in one's future life. More specifically, if a child starts with a certain level of innate mathematical abilities, he has generally almost no chance of getting his potential lowered through training or experiences since no teacher, parent or television programme teach him that $2 + 2 = 5$ or 3. However, here are enough chances that unhealthy environmental influences or lessons taught by the parents, teachers and other models may lead to the declining or damaging of one's innate or previously held level of emotional intelligence. In this way, whatever a person's emotional intelligence at a particular time in life is that level of his emotional intelligence which is with him at that time as a result of the ongoing emotional lessons or life experiences.

This level or potential of one's emotional intelligence is relatively measured through some tests of situations in life, resulting in one's emotional quotient (E.Q.), a relative measure of one's emotional intelligence or potential. Consequently, *the term emotional quotient (E.Q.) may be defined as a relative measure of one's emotional intelligence possessed by him at a particular period of his life.*

Emotional Intelligence—Meaning and Definition

Emotional intelligence, like general intelligence, is the product of one's heredity and its interaction with his environmental forces. Until recently, we have been led to believe that a person's general intelligence measured as I.Q. or intelligence quotient is the greatest predictor of success in any walks of life—academic, social, vocational or professional. Consequently, the I.Q. scores are often used for selection, classification and promotion of individuals in various programmes, courses and job placements etc. However, researches and experiments conducted in the 90s onwards have tried to challenge such over-dominance of the intelligence and its measure intelligent quotient (I.Q.), by replacing it with the concept of emotional intelligence and its measure, emotional quotient (E.Q.). These have revealed that a person's emotional intelligence measured through his E.Q. may be a greater predictor of success than his or her I.Q.

Historically speaking, the term emotional intelligence was introduced in 1990 by two American University professors Dr. John Mayer and Dr. Peter Salovey in their attempt to develop a scientific measure for knowing the differences in people's ability in the areas of emotions. However, the credit for popularizing the concept of emotional intelligence goes to another American psychologist Daniel Goleman (1995).

Let us now consider the views and definitions of the term emotional intelligence given by eminent psychologists and researchers in the field of emotional intelligence.

1. Although the term emotional intelligence has been defined in many best sellers including Dr. Daniel Goleman's 1995 book "Emotional Intelligence" in a number of ways, comprising many personality traits such as empathy, motivation, persistence, warmth and social skills, the most accepted and scientific explanation of the term emotional intelligence may be found in the following definition given by John D. Mayer and Peter Salovey (1995).

Emotional intelligence may be defined as the capacity to reason with emotion in four areas: to perceive emotion, to integrate it in thought, to understand it and to manage it.

According to this definition, every one of us may be found to have varying capacities and abilities with regard to one's dealing with emotions. Depending upon the nature of this ability, he or she may be said more emotionally intelligent or lesser, in comparison to others in the group.

A person will be termed emotionally intelligent in proportion if he is able to

(a) identify and perceive various types of emotions in others (through face reading, body language and voice tone etc.);

(b) sense his own feelings and emotions;

(c) incorporate the perceived emotions in his thought (such as using his emotions feelings in analysing, problem solving, decision making etc.);

(d) have proper understanding of the nature, intensity and outcomes of his emotions;

(e) exercise proper control and regulation over the expression and use of emotions in dealing with his self and others so as to promote harmony, prosperity and peace;

2. For further clarification and explanation of the terms emotional intelligence and emotionally intelligent person, I would like to quote the viewpoint of Mr. Yetta Lautenschlager (1997), a NIP teaching fellow of Hamden, Connecticut, U.S.A. He writes:

To be emotionally intelligent, I submit that you must become proficient in the Four A's of emotional intelligence i.e. Awareness, Acceptance, Attitude and Action. Awareness means knowing what you are feeling when you are feeling it. Acceptance means believing that emotions are a biological process taking place in the body and the brain and that is not always rational. It means being able to feel an emotion without judging it. Attitudes are beliefs that are attached to emotion. These are times when the emotion follows an attitude, or is colored by an attitude. Unless the attitude is challenged, the emotion will continue to be felt in the same direction. Action is the behaviour you take based on emotion and attitude.

The above viewpoint of Yetta Lautenschlager clearly emphasizes that, for developing as an emotionally intelligent individual, one must develop the ability of (i) emotional awareness (knowing the feelings of the self and the others), (ii) cognitive realization that emotional expression may be irrational or unhealthy and hence one should be cautious in utilising his emotions for action, (iii) have a fresh look or acquire a desired attitude for the proper utilisation of emotional feelings, (iv) resulting ultimately into proper behaviour for the progress of the self, in proper tune with others.

Based on these, *we may understand one's emotional intelligence as a unitary ability (related to, but independent of standard intelligence) helpful in knowing, feeling and judging emotions in close cooperation with one's thinking process to behave in a proper way, for the ultimate realize of the happiness and welfare of the self in tune with others.*

Importance of knowing about one's Emotional Intelligence (E.Q.). Knowing about one's emotional intelligence in terms of an emotional quotient has wide educational and social implications for the welfare of the individual and the society. This fact has now been recognized and given practical shape and implications all around the globe. The credit of giving due publicity and acquainting the world-wide population about the importance and significance of emotional intelligence goes to the famous American psychologist Dr. Daniel Goleman through his best selling books like *Emotional Intelligence—Why it can matter more than I.Q.* and *Working with Emotional Intelligence*, has stressed the following factors while showing the importance of emotional intelligence:

1. Emotional intelligence is as powerful, and at times more powerful than I.Q. While I.Q. contributes only about 20% of success in life, the other forces contribute the rest. We can infer that emotional intelligence, luck and social class are among those other factors.

2. Unlike I.Q., emotional intelligence, may be the best predictor of success in life. Emotionally intelligent people are more likely to succeed in everything they undertake in their life.

3. Unlike what is claimed of I.Q., we can teach and improve in children and in any individual, some crucial emotional competencies, paving the way for increasing their emotional intelligence and thus making their life more healthy, enjoyable and successful in the coming days.

4. The concept of emotional intelligence is to be applauded not because it is totally new but because it captures the essence of what our children or all of us need to know for being productive and happy.

5. I.Q. and even Standard Achievement Tests (SAT) scores do not predict any person's success in life. Even success in academics can be predicted more by emotional and social measures (e.g. being self assured and interested, following directions, turning to teachers for help, and expressing needs while getting along with other colleagues) than by academic ability.

6. In working situations too, emotional intelligence helps more than one's intellectual potential in terms of one's I.Q. or even professional skills and competencies. A professionally competent person having poor emotional intelligence may suffer on account of his inability to deal with his self or getting along properly with others.

7. A person's emotional intelligence helps him much in all spheres of life through its various constituents or components namely knowledge of his emotions (self awareness), managing the emotions motivating oneself, recognizing emotions in others (empathy), and handling relationships. The achievement of the end results in terms of better handling of mutual relationships is quite essential and significant in his life. It can only be possible through his potential of emotional intelligence and its proper development.

The viewpoints and ideas propagated by Daniel Goleman have brought a revolution in the field of child care, home, school and work place management. It has also provided sufficient support to guidance and counselling services including physical and mental health programmes. Although there may seem a bit exaggeration in the tall claim that emotional intelligence is a sure guarantee for unqualified advantage in life, there is no denying the fact that one's emotional make up counts quite substantially towards one's ability to live, progress and adjust to others. In all sense, emotional intelligence essentially reflects our ability to deal successfully with other people and with our own feelings. Since these qualities count significantly towards a person's success in his area of achievement, it may induce him likewise to achieve the required success. Most of the problems in our life, whether childhood problems, adolescent problems, home and family problems, work situation problems or political, regional or international problems are the results of misinterpretation of the involved sentiments, feelings and emotions of the concerned individuals, group of individuals, society and the nations. If proper efforts are made for training the emotions and developing proper emotional intelligence potential among the people right from their childhood, then it will surely help in bringing mutual emotional understanding, empathy, accompanied with right actions and behaviour on the part of the individuals and groups, to lead a better life in peace and cooperation.

To progress and let others progress and to live and let others live are thus the ultimate goals of any education or training provided for developing one's potential of emotional intelligence.

How to help in the proper development of emotional intelligence? The following measures may prove helpful in this direction.

1. Try to help yourself and the youngsters develop the ability to understand feelings in the right manners both in oneself and others.

2. Do not give away to misgivings and misinterpretations of feelings in others. It leads to a hostility and bias. Remember that love always begets love, while suspicion, hatredness and aggressions are rewarded with similar emotions.

3. In all situations, self-awareness of the feelings and emotions are important. Try to teach the children and help yourself know what you feel at a particular time.

4. For understanding others and their feelings develop the trait of a good listener. People who have a high E.Q. (emotional quotient) also have a high score on empathy and empathy occurs through effective listening.

5. Try to do away with the wrong notion that thought is most appropriate when not clouded by emotions. Try to learn the integration of thoughts and emotions, heart and mind for appropriate behaviour at the right time. Therefore, do not try to suppress emotions (as every feeling has its value and significance); strike a balance between rational thought and emotions.

6. Teach the children and yourself that all emotions are healthy (because emotions unite the heart, mind and the body). Anger, fear, sadness, the recalled negative emotions are as healthy as peace, courage and joy. The important thing is to learn the art of expressing one's feelings or emotions in a desirable way at the desirable time in a desirable amount. In this connection, the remark of the Great Greek Philosopher Aristotle can be referred to as a guideline:

Anyone can become angry—that is easy. But to be angry with the right person, to the right degree, at the right time, for the right purpose, and in the right way— that is not easy.

7. Try to practise and teach the children the art of managing the feelings and emotions as adequately as possible. This is especially important for the distressing emotions of fear, pain and anger.

8. Do not allow the emotions and feelings be obstacles in your path. Use them as a motivating agent or a force for achieving your goals.

9. Teach yourself and your children the lessons of empathy, i.e. developing a sense of what someone else is feeling.

10. Learn the methods of proper development of social skills for better communication and inter-personal relationship with others. Express your feelings with an equal sense of attending and listening to other's feelings for the better management of relationships.

11. Try to devote more time and take efforts to develop not only the cognitive professional skills but also the affective skills for the development of emotional intelligence.

12. Last but not the least is to provide yourself a model or a companion for maintaining proper emotional bonds. If you have developed yourself as an emotionally intelligent individual, you may inspire or lead others to become so. However, it is not essential to be perfect or complete or guide others as parents, teachers or bosses. You just need to see what others need, and be there to meet their needs.

The measurement of emotional intelligence. For the measurement of one's intelligence we make use of one or the other intelligence test (verbal or non-verbal). Similarly for the measurement of one's emotional intelligence we can make use of such measures called emotional intelligence tests or scales. These tests and measures are not available easily or in a sufficient quantity. A few references of such well-known measures of emotional intelligence may be cited:

1. Mayer Emotional Intelligence Scale (MEIS) constructed and standardized by Dr. John Mayer of the University of New Hampshire, U.S.A.
2. Mayer, Salovey and Caruso Emotional Intelligence Test (MSCEIT) constructed and standardized by Dr. John Mayer, Dr. Peter Salovey and Dr. David Caruso of U.S.A.
3. Bar-On Emotional Quotient Inventory (EQ-i) constructed and standardized by Dr. Reuven Bar-On and published by Multi-Health Systems, U.S.A. for the first time in 1996. This test covers five areas: intrapersonal, interpersonal, adaptability, stress management and general mood.

In addition to such well standardized measures, we may also come across some emotional intelligence measures which have a limited value or somewhat meant for just a fun or amusement. However, these may provide vital clue to what is expected from an emotionally intelligent person in an arbitrarily assumed emotional situation. The sample items of such tests are reproduced here to give an idea.

Test items of a scale type measure

1. I find myself using my feelings to help make big decisions in my life.

   Always   Usually   Sometimes   Rarely   Never

2. People do not have to tell me what they feel _____ I can sense it.

   Always   Usually   Sometimes   Rarely   Never

3. I have trouble handling conflicts and emotional upsets in relationships.

   Always   Usually   Sometimes   Rarely   Never

Test item of a multiple choice type measure

Item No. 1

Situation: You are hanging out with a group of friends when one of your friends starts to make negative comments about a friend who is not there.

Your response:

- You add a few negative comments about the friend who is not there.
- You say nothing at the moment and later you privately talk about your feelings to your friend who made the comment.
- You tell your friend that you do not feel comfortable talking about people who are not there, and change the subject.
- You keep quiet and beat yourself up for not saying anything to stop it.

Item No. 2

Situation: Your best friend has recently broken up with someone and is taking it hard.

Your response:

- You take him or her out for a wild night on the town to get his or her mind off the breakup.
- You start to worry about your own relationship and if you might get dumped.
- You bash your friend's mate and tell your friend that he or she is better left alone.
- You ask your friend what you can do to help him or her get through this.

SUMMARY

Our emotions play a significant role in directing and shaping our behaviour and personality. Whatever they may be, the form, frequency and intensity of our emotional experience, these can be categorized into two heads—positive emotions (like affection, amusement, curiosity, joy etc.) and negative emotions (like fear, anger, jealousy etc.). However, the development of both positive as well as negative emotions and the learning of their expression in a reasonable way is quite essential for our own and social well being.

Our emotions and emotional behaviour bring in us many typical physiological or bodily changes. These changes may be classified as internal physiological changes and external or observable bodily changes. Increase or decrease in our heart beat, rate of respiration and breathing, body temperature, changes in the chemical composition of our blood and functioning of glands, skin responses, muscles of the body and functioning of the brain may be termed as internal bodily changes accompanying the emotions. On the other side changes in facial expression, body postures, and voice or vocal expressions are termed as external observable bodily effects.

Regarding the development of emotions in the human beings, it may be attributed to the process of natural growth and development (maturity) and learning. Although the crying and laughing behaviour of a new born child show that the stimuli of emotional reactions to pleasant and unpleasant experiences exist in the child from very birth, the development of emotions or emotional behaviour, desirable or undesirable is in fact, a totally learned or acquired through experience.

However, a person is expected to show a reasonably emotional, matured behaviour after passing through the period of adolescence. The goal of one's emotional development is thus to attain emotional maturity in his behaviour by demonstrating possession of (i) all types of emotions—positive and negative and (ii) their experience in a reasonable amount at the right time in the proper way.

There exists a number of theories to explain emotions and emotional behaviour. While the James–Lange theory advocates that emotions spring from physiological reactions, the Cannon–Bard theory maintains that emotion and physiological responses occur simultaneously, not one after another. Cognitive theories on the other hand try to emphasize the role of the cognitive factors, a third element, in understanding the relationship between physical reactions and emotional experiences aroused on the perception of an emotion-provoking stimulus. Lastly, the Activation theories, the most modern in line, emphasize that emotion represents a state of heightened arousal. For the occurrence of a significant emotional behaviour, the recticular activating system located in our brain stem must be properly activated to reach in consultation with the higher structures of the brain.

A new concept, 'emotional intelligence' with its significance even more than one's general intelligence has emerged on the educational scene. It may be defined as one's unitary ability (related to independence of standard intelligence) to know, feel and judge emotions in cooperation with a person's thinking process for behaving in a proper way, with the ultimate realization of happiness in himself and in others. In view of its wide significance from the individual as well as social angles, it becomes quite imperative that serious efforts should be made for its proper development, right from the early childhood among the human beings. We must made to acquaint with the degree of its potential named as E.Q. (Emotional Quotient), present in an individual in the same way as we remain interested in knowing about a person's I.Q. (Intelligence Quotient). E.Q. can be computed on the basis of the results of standardized Emotional Intelligence tests to arrive at a judgement of a person's level of emotional intelligence in the same way as we use the intelligence test for knowing his I.Q., that is general intellectual potential.

REFERENCES

Bar-on Reuven, *The Emotional Quotient Inventory (EQ-i), A test of emotional intelligence*, Toronto: Multi-Health Systems, 1996.

Cannon, W.B., *Bodily Changes in Pain, Hunger, Fear and Rage* (2nd ed.) New York: Appleton-Century-Crofts, 1929.

Crow, L.D. and Crow, A., *Educational Psychology* (3rd Indian Reprint), New Delhi; Eurasia Publishing House, 1973, p. 83.

Goleman, Daniel, *Emotional Intelligence: Why it can matter more than IQ*, New York: Bantam Books, 1995.

————— , *Working with Emotional Intelligence*, New York: Bantam Books, 1998.

James, William, *Psychology: Brief Course*, Condon: Collier Macmillan Ltd., 1890, p. 450.

Jersild, A.T., *In Essentials of Educational Psychology*, (Ed.) by Skinner, C.E., Prentice-Hall Inc., 1968, p. 281.

Lautenschlager, Yetta, *The Four A's of Emotional Intelligence*, paper submitted at the ISNIP Conference, U.S.A., 1997.

Lindsley, D.B., Emotion in S.S. Stevans (Ed.) *Handbook of Experimental Psychology*, New York: John Wiley, 1951.

Mayer John D. and Salovey Peter, *Emotional intelligence and the construction and regulation of feelings*, Applied & Prevention Psychology, 1995, 4(3), 197–208.

McDougall, William G., *An Outline of Psychology* (13th ed.), London, Methuen, 1949.

Morris, Charles G., *Psychology* (3rd ed.), Englewood Cliffs, New Jersey: Prentice-Hall, 1979, p. 386.

Woodworth, R.S., *Psychology*, London: Methuen, 1945, p. 410.

SUGGESTED READINGS

Arnold, M.B., *Emotion and Personality* (2 Vols.); New York: Columbia University Press, 1960.

Darwin, C., *The Expression of the Emotions in Man and Animals* (reprint), Chicago: Chicago University Press, 1965.

Delgado, J.M.R., *Physical Control of the Mind: Towards a Psycho-civilized Society*, New York: Harper & Row, 1969.

Drever, J., *Instincts in Man*, Cambridge: Cambridge University Press, 1917.

McDougall, William, *An Introduction to Social Psychology* (28th ed.), London: Methuen, 1946.

Salovey, Peter & Mayer, John D., *Emotional Intelligence, Imagination, Cognition and Personality*, 1990, **9,** 185–211.

Schachter, S. & Singer, J.E., *Cognitive, Social and Physiological Determinants of Emotional State,* "Psychological Review", 1962, **69,** pp. 369–399.

Schachter, S., *Emotion, Obesity and Crime*, New York: Academic Press, 1971.

Selye, H., *The Stress of Life*, New York: McGraw-Hill, 1956.

Young, P.T., *Emotion in Men and Animal* (2nd ed.), Huntington: New York: Krieger, 1973.

Wood, J., *How Do You Feel?* Englewood Cliffs, New Jersey: Prentice-Hall, 1974.

Chapter 18

Creativity

INTRODUCTION

The Almighty God, the creator of the universe, is the supreme-mind who possesses the finest creative abilities. He has created all of us and all that is revealed in nature. We are elevated to be called His creation. According to Indian philosophy, we are constituents of the Supreme Power as the rays of the sun are the constituents parts of their creator, the sun. Therefore, every one of us ought to possess creative abilities—and has these abilities. Every one of us is a unique creation, but does not possess the same creative ability as his pears. Some of us are endowed with high creative talents and contribute to advancement in the fields of art, literature, science, business, teaching and other spheres of human activity, and are responsible for propounding new ideas and bringing about social and cultural changes. Mahatma Gandhi, Abraham Lincoln, Homi Bhabha, Newton, Shakespeare, Leonardo da Vinci were some of the creative individuals who left their mark in their chosen fields. Though they were undoubtedly gifted with creative abilities, the role of environment in terms of education, training and opportunities in their development cannot be ignored.

Good education, proper care and provision of opportunities for creative expression inspire, stimulate and sharpen the creative mind, and it is in this sphere, that parents, society and teachers make a significant contribution. They are required to help the children in nourishing and utilizing their creative abilities to the utmost. The educational process, therefore, should be aimed at developing creative abilities among children. This can be achieved by acquainting the teachers and parents with the real meaning of the creative process and the ways and means of developing and nurturing creativity.

DEFINING CREATIVITY

The terms 'creativity' or 'creative process' have been defined in many ways. Some of these definitions are as follows:

Stagner and Karwoski (1973):

> Creativity implies the production of a 'totally or partially' novel identity.

Drevdahl (1956):

> Creativity is the capacity of a person to produce compositions, products or ideas which are essentially new or novel and previously unknown to the producer.

Bartlett (1958):

Creativity is an adventurous thinking or a getting away from the main track, breaking out of the mould, being open to experience and permitting one thing to lead to another.

Spearman (1931):

Creativity is the power of the human mind to create new contents by transforming relations and thereby generating new correlates.

Wallach and Kogan (1965):

Creativity lies in producing more associations, and in producing more that are unique.

David Ausubel (1963):

Creativity is a generalized constellation of intellectual abilities, personality variables and problem-solving traits.

M.J. Levin (1978):

Creativity is the ability to discover new solutions to problems or to produce new ideas, inventions or works of art. It is a special form of thinking, a way of viewing the world and interacting with it in a manner different from that of the general population.

Paplia and Olds (1987):

Creativity is the ability to see things in a new and unusual light, to see problems that no one else may even realize exist, and then to come up with new, unusual, and effective solutions.

Wilson, Guilford and Christensen (1974):

The creative process is any process by which something new is produced—an idea or an object including a new form or arrangement of old elements. The new creation must contribute to the solution of some problems.

Stein (1974):

Creativity is a process which results in novel work that is accepted as tenable to useful or satisfying to a group of people at some point in time.

There seems, however, to be considerable lack of agreement among these scholars regarding the true nature and concept of creativity—its process as well as its product. Some of them consider it to be purely a function of the mind, a component of the congnitive behaviour while Ausuble and others maintain it to be an attribute of the person as a whole involving his total behaviour and functioning of his whole personality. Some like Stein use a cultural frame of reference and opine that besides being novel, a creative product must be useful from the cultural and social angles while yet others view it in a personal frame and hold that:

a product may be a creative one if it is new or novel to the individual involved, if it is his creation, if it is expressive of himself rather than dictated by someone else. It need to neither useful nor unique. Its social recognition and cultural impact may be zero, but if it is a unique personal experience, it is creative (Maslow, 1970 quoted by Telford & Sawrey, 1977).

By assigning the characteristic of "a unique personal experience" to the creative product, the scope has been so widened as to include any novel idea or thing including the rearrangement or reshaping of already existing and known ones. The definitions given above have considered creativity both as a process and a product, the thought as well as its result, but the central, essential condition of novelty or newness in the creation has not been overlooked by any one. By incorporating all these viewpoints, we may describe *creativity as the capacity or ability of an individual to create, discover, or produce a new or novel idea or object, including the rearrangement or reshaping of what is already known to him which proves to be a unique personal experience.*

Nature and Characteristics of Creativity

Creativity as a unique and novel personal experience, and on the basis of the experiences and findings of the various scholars, may be said to possess the following characteristics:

Creativity is universal. Creativity is not confined to any individual, groups of individuals, caste, colour or creed. It is universal and is not bound by the barriers of age, location or culture. Everyone of us possesses and is capable of demonstrating creativity to some degree.

Creativity is innate as well as acquired. Although many research findings and incidents favour the suggestion that creativity is a God-given gift and natural endowment, the influence of cultural background, experiences, education and training in the nurturing of creativity cannot be ruled out. Therefore, one's creativity may be correctly said to be a function of natural endowment as well as its nurturing.

Creativity produces something new or novel. Creativity denotes the ability of a person to produce something new or novel, but this novelty or newness does not necessarily imply the production of a totally new idea or object which has never been experienced or has never existed before. To make a fresh and novel combination of existing separate elements or to reshape or rearrange the already known facts and principles or to reform or modify previously known techniques, are as much acts of creative expression as the discovery of a new element in chemistry or a new formula in mathematics. The only precondition for naming an expression as creative is that it should not be repetition or reproduction of what has already been experienced or learned by an individual.

Creativity is adventurous and open thinking. Creativity is a departure from the stereotyped, rigid and closed thinking. It encourages and demands complete freedom to accept and express the multiplicity of responses, choices and lines of action. It is a kind of adventurous thinking, calling a person to come out in the open to express himself according to his will and to function unrestricted by routine or previous practice.

Creativity is a means as well as end in itself. Creativity as an urge inspires and persuades the individual to create something unique and thus acts as an impetus for expression. This creative expression proves to be a source of joy and satisfaction to the creator. No one other than the creator can experience the warmth, happiness and satisfaction which he receives through his creation. Creation is a source of happiness and a reward in itself. The creator expresses himself as fully as possible through his creation and has his own perceptions about his creation. It is, therefore, not essential that a creative work would arouse the same feelings or give the same joy and satisfaction in others as is experienced by the creator himself.

Creativity carries ego involvement.   There is complete involvement of one's ego in the creative expression. One's individuality and identity are totally merged in one's creation. One's style of functioning, philosophy of life and personality may be clearly reflected in his creation be it a work of art, or a piece of writing, etc. The creator takes pride in his creation and hence makes ego involved statements like, "it is my creation", "I have solved this problem", "it is my idea", etc.

Creativity has a wide scope.   Creative expression is not restricted by any limits or boundaries. It covers all fields and activities of human life, in any of which one is able to demonstrate creativity by expressing or producing a new idea or object. It is not restricted to scientific inventions and discoveries or the production of works of art but covers multifarious human accomplishments like the composition of poems; writing of stories and plays, performance in the fields of dance, music, painting, sculpture, political and social leadership, business, teaching and other professions as also the mundane activities of daily life.

Creativity and intelligence do not necessarily go hand-in-hand.   Research findings and observations have demonstrated that there is no positive correlation between creativity and intelligence. One is not the essential or necessary prerequisite of the other. Those found scoring high on intelligence tests may demonstrate little or no signs of creativity whereas individuals performing poorly in intelligence tests may sometimes create something very original.

Taking a consolidated view of the researches conducted on this issue, we may conclude that although intelligence and the creativity component of one's personality can function independently, a certain minimum level of intelligence is a necessary precondition for successful creative expression. Were it not so, a person of below average mental ability like a moron or an idiot could also be creative; but in actual-life situations we hardly come across any such instances. Conversely, although creative people generally tend to be relatively intelligent, beyond a certain level, a higher I.Q. does not necessarily predict creativity. In other words, as Kitano and Kirby (1986) state: "*an individual can be extremely bright but uncreative, or highly creative but not necessarily intellectually gifted*". Therefore, no clear relationship has been seen to exist between intelligence and creativity.

Creativity rests more on divergent thinking than on covergent thinking. Divergent thinking involves a broad scanning operation, enabling a person to evolve a general multiple possible solution and hence it is put into use when one is confronted with a problem which has many possible solutions. (Convergent thinking, on the other hand, requires a narrowing process leading the individual to pin point the one most appropriate solution or response.) It is involved with situations, which require the production of only one correct solution or answer as for example, a multiple-choice test.

Divergent thinking has been considered to be more characteristic of highly creative individuals rather than of those not rated as being highly creative. That is why, in the tests designed to test creativity one is required to list as many uses as possible for some common article such as a knife or a brick, provide as many solutions of a problem as possible, give as many innovative combinations as possible, etc. Tests of this kind, requiring divergent thinking are, therefore, scored for divergence, i.e. the number, diversity and uniqueness of the responses and not for the convergent outcomes in the form of one single correct answer as is usually done in tests of intelligence.

Creativity cannot be separated from intelligence. In spite of the fact that intelligence or creativity may function independently and creativity involves more of divergent thinking as opposed to the convergent thinking employed in the demonstration of intelligence, it is not possible to entirely separate creativity from intelligence. This is because thinking is neither purely divergent nor purely convergent and always has elements of both which are simultaneously involved in the creative and the intellectual process. It, therefore, follows that when a person is considered to be creative, he has to have a minimum level of intelligence certainly above the average.

Creativity and school achievement are not correlated. No significant correlation has been observed between an individual's creative talent and his school performance. One may be creative but score quite low on achievement tests and, similarly, a topper in school or in the Board examination may show little or no creative output. The reason for this is that in the usual achievement testing, assessment is done in terms of the quality of reproduction of the informational input while the creativity testing requires greater output than the input in terms of formal as well informal teaching.

Sociability and creativity are negatively correlated. Creativity requires creative individual to be more sensitive to the demands of a problem than the evaluation of his social environment. The creative individual is more inner—than outer-orientated. He likes to utilize his energy and potential more for the satisfaction of his creative urge than to care for the pleasant security of positive peer approval. It is for this reason that the creative individuals are usually not very sociable.

Creativity and anxiety often go together. It has been noted that creative people demonstrate an above average state of anxiety. However, the anxiety of the creative individual is quite different from that of the neurotic individual with a disturbed personality. The high anxiety of the creative individual may be the result of his craving for the satisfaction of his creative urge and discontent with his status or rate of progress in attaining his creative motive. But creative individuals are quite capable of keeping their anxiety within manageable limits and directing it into productive channels.

THEORIES OF CREATIVITY

A number of theories have been put forward to explain the nature of creativity: how it operates, why some of us show greater creative tendencies and others less. Let us now discuss some of the better known theories.

Divine Inspiration or God-given Gift Theory

According to this ancient theory, creativity is a gift from God to the human beings and is not universally distributed. Accordingly, some people get a large share while it is denied to others. An individual can then be creative to the extent to which he is endowed with this divine power. However, this theory of creativity being a gift according to one's luck, is quite irrelevant is these days of scientific thinking and understanding and we must surely look for some other convincing explanation.

Theory Describing Creativity Equivalent to Insanity?

Based on historical evidence and their own observations, some authors and scholars like Cesare Lambroso, have concluded that creativity and insanity go hand-in-hand. An insane person lives in his own world. His thinking, feelings and actions are concentrated and centred around his own interests and intentions. The states of mind of highly creative persons are somewhat similar and their behaviour may be considered quite abnormal and even insane. However, these findings are not based on objective and empirical studies. Certainly, no definite correlation has so far been established between insanity and creativity. The creative individual may seem to be far from normal because of his constant absorption in his creative pursuits, but that does not mean he is mentally abnormal or that his creative strivings can be taken as signs of madness.

Theory Describing Creativity as Native or Inborn

According to another viewpoint, creativity is regarded as something native, an innate or inborn trait, a special mental power or unique cognitive ability that cannot be acquired by learning or training. Thus, according to this theory, creatives are born and not made. One may have a special inborn sensitivity to sound, another may have extremely sensitive vocal chords, senses of touch, sight or smell to enable him to be highly talented or creative in any of these spheres. One may have been born with extraordinary intuitive power for a sudden or quick grasp of new things or phenomena in any field or a fine imagination and insight for discovering new things like scientists James Watt, Newton, Einstein or Mathematicians Gauss and Ramanujam.

Theory of Environmentally Acquired Creativity

According to this viewpoint, creativity is not only the result of one's heredity, inborn capacity of God's gift. It is acquired and nurtured like other human traits. A positive environment or situation that is open, democratic and free may be said to contribute positively to the release and development of creative potential. On the other hand, a closed society, culture or situation may act as a strong deterrent to the development of initiative within the individual. Arieti (1976) proposed the concept of creativogenic society to emphasize the influence of culture and environment on the development of creativity. According to him, the creativogenic society or environment is distinguished by its lack of emphasis on immediate gratification, its tolerance for and interest in divergent points of view, and its use of incentives and rewards for creativity. As a result of such favourable environment creativity may get full nourishment and creatives build up. Hence, it is the environment—favourable or detrimental—which is responsible for making one creative or non-creative.

Taylor's Level Theory of Creativity

According to the level theory enunciated by I.A. Taylor (1975), creativity may be described as existing at five levels in an ascending hierarchy. A person is said to be creative to the extent that he is able to reach these levels. The five levels are the following:

- *Expressive creativity.* This stands for spontaneous expression without reference to originality and quality of the product.
- *Productive creativity.* At this level, a person is able to produce something innovative.
- *Inventive creativity.* This level is marked by the presence of ingenuity with a clear emphasis on novel use of old things.
- *Innovative creativity.* At this level one is able to develop new ideas or principles with the help of highly developed abstract conceptualizing skills.
- *Emergentive creativity.* This fifth and highest level of creativity is rarely achieved. The most abstract ideational principles or assumptions underlying a body of art or science are made use of at this level of creation.

Hemisphere Theory of Creativity

According to this theory, creative acts are said to be the result of interaction between the two hemispheres of the individual's brain. It gives quite a predominant biological base to the upsurge and functioning of creativity. The researches into hemispheric functioning of Clark (1983) and Kitano and Kirby (1986) have demonstrated that creative individuals are usually right hemisphere-dominant while logical, rational thinkers are left hemisphere-dominant.

Psychoanalytical Theory of Creativity

The school of psychoanalysis considers creativity as a means and product of one's emotional purging, an opportunity for sublimation and catharsis. Freud, the father of this school, considers the creations of the creators as nothing but attempts for the expression of their repressed desires, mostly sexual in nature. Accordingly, most creative works of art, particularly ones portraying beautiful figures of men and women can be interpreted by Freudians as expressions of repressed sexual desires. Similarly, the compositions of many writers and poets like Tulsidas, Meerabai, Raskhan etc., would be viewed by them as attempts at sublimation, i.e., diversion of libidinal energy into a socially desirable and personally gratifying channels. Besides the role of libidinal or sexual energy, the unconscious was also described by the Freudians, to play a significant role in one's creative expression and output.

A somewhat different approach was adopted by the later psychoanalysts like Kris (1952), Kubie (1958) and Jung (1933) for explaining creative expression. They opposed the unconscious-seated and sex-dominated approach of Freud and advocated the use of preconscious rather than unconscious mental mechanisms in the creative act. Going further, Jung through his analytic or depth psychology brought out the concept of the collective unconscious, according to which, animation of the collective unconscious, the archetypes, explains the mechanism of the creative process. However, the views of these psychoanalysts have been under constant attack chiefly on account of their being over-generalised, their sole dependence on unconscious motivation and early conflicts for explaining all types of human behaviour including creative acts.

Arieti's Theory of Creativity

The theory of Arieti (1974, 1976) represents the contemporary views about the nature and meaning of the terms creativity, the creative process and creative output. The major theoretical notions underlying this theory are as follows:

1. Creativity and mental illness are parallel to one another in that both involve the transformation of reality. The distinction between them is that while creatives aim to change reality for broader and more useful social purposes and self-actualization, psychotics want to transform reality within the framework of their private world regardless of serving any useful purpose to their selves or society.
2. To say that a creative person is mentally ill is quite incorrect. He is, in fact, a person who enjoys good mental health which energizes his cognitive abilities to create something unique or novel.
3. The creative process is a 'magic synthesis' of the two modalities, the primary process and the secondary process and may thereby be termed the "tertiary process".

The primary process, as Freud maintains, originates in the primitive part of the mind called the 'id' and the archaic 'ego'. The secondary process is the outcome of the developed mind and involves logical and systematic thinking at the conscious level. In the words of Arieti (1976), "*in the creative process, both these primary and secondary processes work in the quite strange and intricate combinations, synthesizing the rational with the irrational and, thus, instead of rejecting the primitive, the creative mind integrates it with the normal psychological processes. It is from this magic synthesis that something new, novel, the unexpected and the desirable emerges.*"

From the foregoing theories of creativity, it seems that none of them provides a complete picture. Each one of them takes its own stand for explaining creativity either through the process approach or the product approach and hence each perception is, as Clark (1983) observes, only a fragment of the total. It is only through a holistic view, by the integration of the various divergent views of the different theories, that a meaningful picture of creativity may emerge.

INVESTIGATING CREATIVITY

Creativity, as Rock, Evans and Klein (1969) put it, may be satisfactorily investigated by adopting the following three basic approaches, namely, creativity as a process, creativity as a product and creativity as an attribute of one's personality.

The Creative Process

Many psychologists and scholars have studied the creative process in an effort to understand it. Let us summarize some of their findings.

1. Wallas (1926) described the process as consisting of four stages: preparation, incubation, inspiration or illumination, and verification or revision.

In the first stage—preparation—the conscious work on the problem is initiated and continued as long as possible. Initially, the problem is defined or analysed and the stage is set for its solution. The facts and material relevant to the solution are then collected and examined and the plan of action is formulated. Then, we start working to the set plan. In between, if essential, the plan of action is modified, we switch over to another method or take the help of other relevant data if those in hand fail to help us. In this way, a continuous and persistent effort is made. In case, it appears at some point that we cannot solve the problem, frustration leads us to set the problem aside for the time being.

This kind of deliberate or voluntary turning away from the problem is the beginning of the second stage, i.e. incubation. This stage is characterized by the absence of activity, or in many instances, even of thinking about the problem. We may rest, sleep or engage in other interesting activities. If this is done, ideas which were interfering with the solution of the problem tend to fade. In the absence of such interference our unconscious begins to work towards finding a solution of the problem Sometimes, the things we experience or learn in the meantime, may provide a clue to the solution (Archimedes found the solution of his problem when he was in his bath tub).

The stage of inspiration or illumination follows. During this stage the thinker is often presented with a sudden appearance of the solution of his problem. Such illumination may occur at any time, sometimes even while the thinker is dreaming.

The final stage, verification or revision comes next. During this stage the illumination or inspiration is checked out to determine whether the solution or idea which appeared through insight is in fact the correct one. In case it does not work out, fresh attempts are made to solve the problem. Sometimes, the earlier solution needs slight modification or change to become workable. The creative thinker does not, at any stage, accept a solution as perfect and holds it open to modification or revision in line with subsequent findings.

2. Rosman (1933) has mentioned the following seven stages in the creative process:

    (a) Observation of a need or difficulty
    (b) Analysis of the need
    (c) Survey of all the available information
    (d) Formulation of all the objective solutions
    (e) Critical analysis of these solutions
    (f) Birth of a new idea—the invention
    (g) Experimentation to test the most promising solution, and selection and perfection of the final embodiment by some or all of the previous steps.

3. Torrance and Myers (1970) have defined the process as consisting of the following stages:

    (a) Becoming sensitive to or aware of problems
    (b) Bringing together available information
    (c) Searching for solutions
    (d) Communication of the results

4. Stein (1974) has attributed the following stages to the creative process:

    (a) Preparation or education
    (b) Hypothesis formation
    (c) Hypothesis testing
    (d) Communication of the results.

However, the stages mentioned by each of the different scholars should not be considered to be rigid and fixed stages followed every time by every creative thinker. One person may arrive at the solution of the problem before experiencing all the previous stages. Another person, on the other hand, may not find the solution even after passing through all stages of the creative process and may need to repeat the cycle several times before producing anything creative or arriving at an acceptable solution of the problem.

The Creative Product

Creativity is investigated, understood and identified through the outcome of the process of creation or the creative products. How creative one is, can thus be determined through one's output in the form of ideas, works of art, scientific theories, or even building designs. However, for a product to qualify as creative, certain minimum criteria must be met. Telford and Sawrey (1977) and Mackinnon (1978) have proposed originality or novelty and relevance or appropriateness as the two main criteria for judging a creative product.

However, according to these authors, originality or novelty of a product should not be judged independently of the second criterion of relevance or appropriateness. To be creative, a so-called original or novel creation must fit or be useful within its relevant context. It must demonstrate proper relevance to a problem, situation or goal including the purposes of its creator.

In addition to these necessary and essential conditions, a creative product must also fulfil the following conditions:

1. It must be aesthetically pleasing and give joy and satisfaction to the producer as well as the user.
2. It should provide new perspectives in some areas of human experience and create new conditions of human existence.

The Creative Person

The creativity aspect can also be discussed on the basis of those personality characteristics of the creatives which distinguish them from the non-creatives. A number of researches have been done in this area and consequently different researchers have presented different lists of personality traits attributed to the creative persons. Reference in this connection may be made to the studies conducted by Cattell (1968), Torrance (1962), MacKinnon (1962) and Foster (1971), etc. These studies alongwith other personality studies have brought out the following behaviour characteristics or personality traits of a potentially creative individual:

1. Originality of ideas and expression.
2. Adaptability and a sense of adventure.
3. Good memory and general knowledge.
4. A high degree of awareness, enthusiasm and concentration.
5. An investigative and curious nature.
6. Lack of tolerance for boredom, ambiguity and discomfort.
7. Foresight.
8. The ability to take independent decisions.
9. An ambitious nature and interest in vague, even silly ideas.
10. An open mind with preference for complexity, asymmetry and incompleteness.
11. A high degree of sensitivity towards problems.
12. Fluency of expression.
13. Flexibility in thought, perception and action.
14. Ability to transfer learning or training from one situation to another.
15. A creative imagination.
16. Diversity and divergence of thought even in convergent and stereotype situations.
17. Ability to elaborate, to work out the details of an idea or a plan.
18. Absence of the fear of and even attraction to the unknown, the mysterious and the unexplained.
19. Enthusiasm for novelty of design and even of solution of problems.
20. Pride in creation.
21. Peace with his own self so that he has more time for creative pursuits.
22. High aesthetic values and a good aesthetic judgement.

23. Self-respect, self-discipline and a keen sense of justice.
24. Ebullient and easy nature with a relaxed attitude.
25. Awareness of obligations and responsibilities.
26. Ability to accept tentativeness and to tolerate and integrate the opposites.
27. Patterns of thought different from those of the less creative, particularly during creative activity.
28. Respect for the opinions of others and acceptance of disagreement and opinions different from one's own.
29. Spontaneity and ease of expression.
30. The capacity to fantasize and daydream.

Identification of Creative Potential

Although every one of us is endowed with some aspects of creativity, its distribution is neither equal nor universal and some individuals have greater creative potential than others. How can such high creative talent be recognized? Researches in this regard have established that creativity is not necessarily accompanied by a high level of intelligence. Guilford (1959) has clearly made the distinction by proposing the concept of convergent and divergent thinking, the latter being closely associated with creative thinking. Similarly, Getzels and Jackson (1962) have successfully argued that creativity was far more independent of I.Q., especially at the upper levels. Therefore, a genius or a gifted person may not have a very high I.Q. as creativity in its many shapes and forms is an expression of giftedness, and not of a high degree of intelligence. How then, can the creative individuals be identified.

Behaviour as we know is expressed through its cognitive, conative and effective components and creative behaviour is no exception. Consequently, an individual is creative to the extent to which he can demonstrate creative potential in his thinking, actions and feelings. For a total assessment of creative behaviour, we have to apply a multi-dimensional approach involving the use of the available creative tests and the multiple non-testing devices like observation, interview, rating scale, personality, inventory, situational tests, interest inventories, attitude scales, aptitude tests, value schedules and projective techniques etc. The characteristics and personality traits of the creatives mentioned earlier may also serve the purpose by providing reliable indications for the identification of creative potential which may be further verified by comparing the performance with standardized creativity tests.

Creativity Tests

Creativity tests may be used in the identification of the creatives in the same way as intelligence tests are used for the assessment of intelligence. There are many standardized tests available for this purpose in India and abroad. Some of these are now enumerated.

- *The tests standardized abroad*
  1. Minnesota tests of creative thinking.

  2. Guilford's divergent thinking instruments.
  3. Remote association tests.
  4. Wallach and Kogan creativity instruments.
  5. A.C. test of creative ability.
  6. Torrance tests of creative thinking.

● *The tests standardized in India*

  1. Baqer Mehdi's tests of creative thinking (Hindi/English).
  2. Passi's tests of creativity.
  3. Sharma's divergent production abilities test.
  4. Saxena's tests of creativity.

Creativity is a complex blend of a number of abilities and traits, and hence all the creative tests mentioned above attempt to measure several dimensions of one's creative behaviour through their test items—verbal and non-verbal. The factors or dimensions of creativity commonly measured through these tests are: (a) fluency, (b) flexibility, (c) originality, (d) unusual responses, (e) resistance to premature closure and (f) elaboration, etc.

Let us now try to illustrate components and functioning of the creative tests with the help of two creative tests, one developed abroad and the other in India.

Torrance Tests of Creative Thinking

Creativity tests developed by E. Paul Torrance, the eminent American psychologist, cover both verbal and non-verbal activities performed by the subjects and are claimed to be successfully used from kindergarten to graduate school. For testing the non-verbal performance, Torrance has developed Torrance test of creative thinking (figural forms A and B) and for the verbal performance, the Torrance test of creative thinking (verbal forms A and B).

Forms B are the equivalent alternatives of the forms A of these tests.

The figural forms (employed as a non-verbal testing device) make use of tasks that require drawing and picturization. The activities required in the non-verbal sub-tests are of the following nature:

● *Figure or picture completion test.* In this sub-test there are some incomplete figures (as shown in Figure 18.1). The subject is asked to complete these figures by adding new dimensions or lines for providing new ideas. He is also asked to give suitable titles for the completed figures or pictures.

● *Picture or figural construction test.* In this sub-test, the subject is provided with a piece of coloured paper cut in a curved shape and asked to think of a figure or picture of which this piece of paper may be a part. He is allowed to add new ideas to make this figure as interesting and meaningful as possible. He is also asked to provide a suitable title for this figure or picture.

● *Parallel lines test.* In this sub-test there are several pairs of straight lines. The subject is required to draw as many objects or pictures by

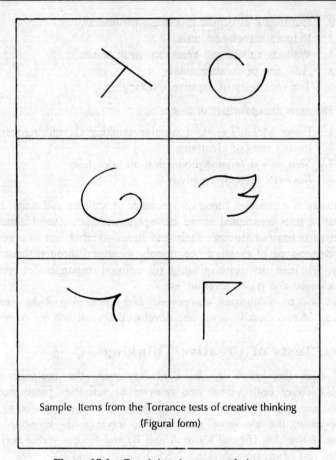

Sample Items from the Torrance tests of creative thinking
(Figural form)

Figure 18.1   Creativity picture completion test.

using each pair. He is also asked to provide a title for each of his drawings.

The verbal forms (employed as a verbal testing device) incorporate tasks which require the use of language. The subject is required to provide written responses to the questions put to him. The verbal activities asked to be performed are of the following nature:

- *Asking type.*   In asking type of activities, the subject is encouraged to reveal his ability to perceive all things which are not normally perceived by others. The help of some pictures may be taken for this purpose. In these activities the subject may also be asked questions that would enable him to fill in the gaps in his knowledge.

- *Guess causes and guess consequences type.*   Both these guessing type activities are aimed at revealing the subject's ability to formulate hypotheses concerning cause and effect. While being presented with a picture, the subject may be asked to guess what lies behind the situation in the picture and what its consequences may be.

- *Product-improvement type.* In these activities, the subject is asked to suggest ways and means of improving a toy, a machine or some other such product to make it as interesting and useful as possible.

- *Unusual uses type.* These devices are meant to test the subject's divergent thinking about the number of ways in which a product may be used. Here the subject has to enumerate as many unusual uses as he can think of, for instance, in how many unusual ways can a knife or brick be used?

- *Unusual questions type.* In these activities, the subject is required to ask as many unusual questions as he can about a picture, scene or verbal description.

- *Just suppose type.* In these activities, the subject is required to predict the outcomes of unusual situations, e.g., what would have happened had you been provided with another set of eyes at the back of your head?

All the activities mentioned above, both on figural and verbal forms, are evaluated in terms of the creative abilities such as originality, fluency, flexibility and elaboration, etc. An overall high score on the various sub-tests of the Torrance creative test gives the tester an idea of the overall creative potential of his subject. However, for a more reliable and valid appraisal of creative potential, one has to take recourse to other non-testing devices and personality assessment measures.

Baqer Mehdi's Verbal and Non-verbal Tests of Creativity

This test, developed by Dr. Baqer Mehdi has been published by the National Psychological Corporation, Agra. It consists of four verbal and three non-verbal sub-tests. The verbal and non-verbal forms are also available separately.

- *Consequence test* (Time allowed 12 minutes). Think for the following situations as many consequences as possible:
  1. What would happen if man could fly like the birds?
  2. What would happen if our schools had wheels?
  3. What would happen if man did not have any need for food?

- *Unusual uses test* (Time allowed 15 minutes). Write as many novel, interesting and unusual uses for the objects as you can think of, viz., a piece of stone, a wooden stick, water.

- *New relationship test* (Time allowed 15 minutes). Think of as many relationships between the following pairs of words, as possible:
  1. Tree, house.
  2. Chair, ladder.
  3. Air, water.

- *Product improvement test* (Time allowed 6 minutes). Suppose you start with a toy horse. Think of as many new things or features to make it more useful and interesting.

The non-verbal sub-tests

- *Picture construction test* (Time allowed 20 minutes). In Figure 18.2, there are two simple geometrical figures, viz., a semicircle and a rhombus.

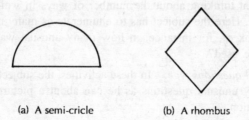

       (a) A semi-cricle   (b) A rhombus

Figure 18.2   Creativity picture construction test: (a) A semicircle, and (b) A rhombus.

You have to construct and elaborate pictures using each figure as an integral part. For each picture, you have to give a separate title.

- *Line figures completion test* (Time allowed 15 minutes). Ten incomplete line drawings are shown in Figure 18.3. You are required to draw meaningful and interesting pictures using each of them and also give appropriate titles.

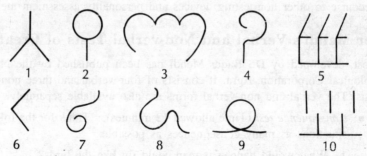

Figure 18.3   Creativity line figures completion test.

- *Picture construction test* (Time allowed 10 minutes). Seven triangles and seven ellipses are shown. You are required to construct different meaningful and interesting pictures by using these figures in multiple associations.

Nurturing and Stimulation of Creativity

Creativity, as a natural endowment, needs stimulation and nourishment. Most creative talent, unless it is given proper training, education and opportunities for expression, is wasted. Moreover, creativity as we have emphasized earlier, though not equal, is universal. It is not the monopoly of a few geniuses only. Every one of us possesses some creative abilities and it is not only the geniuses who are needed to create, manifest and produce.

It becomes essential, therefore, for teachers as well as parents to realize the need of creating an environment conducive to full growth and development of the creative abilities of children. Proper stimulation and nurturing of the traits which help to develop creativity, namely, originality, flexibility, ideational fluency, divergent thinking, self-confidence, persistence, sensitiveness, ability to see relationship and make associations etc. are essential for this and may be achieved through the following practices.

1. *Freedom to respond.* Most often teachers and parents expect routine, fixed responses from children and thus kill the creative spark by breeding conformity and passivity. We should allow adequate freedom to our children in responding to a situation. They should be encouraged to think out as many ideas as they can for the solution of a problem. We must also let them have their own way when they need a particular kind of novel expression strongly enough.

2. *Opportunity for ego involvement.* Feeling like 'this is my creation', 'I have solved it', give much satisfaction to children. Actually, a child can be expected to put in determined efforts into creative activities only when his ego is involved, i.e. when he feels that a particular creative work is the outcome of his efforts. We should, therefore, provide opportunities to children to derive satisfaction from identifying themselves as the cause of a product.

3. *Encouraging originality and flexibility.* Originality on the part of children in any form should be encouraged. Passive submission to the facts, unquestioning mimicry, and memorization by rote discourage creative expression and should, therefore, be checked as far as possible. If children seek to change their methods of learning a task or solving a problem, they should be encouraged to do so. Adequate training can also be given by making them answer problems like: how would you dig the earth if you don't have a spade or, how would you draw an angle if you do not have a proper instrument for drawing it or, how would you cross a river if there is no bridge over it?

4. *Removal of hesitation and fear.* In countries like India, there seems to be a great hesitation mixed with a sense of inferiority and fear in taking the initiative for creative expression. We, generally come across comments like "I know what I mean, but I cannot write (or speak) before others". The causes of such diffidence and fear should be discovered and removed as far as possible. The teachers and parents should encourage and persuade such children to express themselves by saying or writing something, anything, no matter how crude it may be.

5. *Providing appropriate opportunities and atmosphere for creative expression.* A healthy atmosphere, favourable for creative thinking and expression is essential for the stimulation and nourishment of creativity among children. The rate of learning must be balanced with its application, passive receptivity with challenging productivity, stable certainty with daring and adventure. The child should never be snubbed for his curiosity and creativity. There is need of a sympathetic atmosphere in school and at home. Cocurricular activities in school can be used for providing opportunities for creative expression. Religious festivals, and social get-togethers, exhibitions etc., can also provide the opportunity for creative expression. Even regular class-work can be arranged in such a way as to stimulate and develop creative thinking among children.

6. *Developing healthy habits among children.* Industriousness persistence, self-reliance and self-confidence are some of the qualities that are helpful in creative output. Children should, therefore, be helped to imbibe these qualities. Moreover, they should be encouraged to stand up against criticism of their creative expression. They should be made to feel that whatever they create is unique and expresses what they desire to express.

7. *Using the creative resources of the community.* Children should be made to visit the centre of art, scientific, and industrial creative work. This may stimulate and inspire them for creative work. Creative artists, scientists and creative persons from different fields may also be occasionally invited to the school to interact with the children in an effort to enhance the scope of knowledge of our children and kindle the spark of creativity in them.

8. *Avoidance of blocks to creative thinking.* Factors like conservation, faulty methods of teaching, unsympathetic treatment, fixed and rigid habits of work, anxiety and frustration, excessively high standards of achievement for low levels of work, over-emphasis on school marks, authoritarian attitude of teachers and parents etc., are known to be detrimental to the growth of creativity among children. As far as possible, parents and teachers should, therefore, try to avoid such factors in upbringing and educating the children.

9. *Proper organisation of the curriculum.* Learning experiences in the form of curricula should be so designed as to foster creativity among children. For this purpose, the school curriculum should be organized primarily on the basis of concepts rather than facts. It should also cater to the individual needs of each student rather than to the generalized needs of all students. It should also follow the general philosophy that truth is something to be sought after rather than something to be revealed. It should be quite flexible and make provision for studying and working without the threat of evaluation. In a nutshell, the curriculum should reflect what is expected from the creative children in terms of fluency, flexibility, originality, divergent thinking, inventiveness and elaboration etc.

10. *Reform in the evaluation system.* Our education system is totally examination oriented and appropriate reform must, therefore, be made in our evaluation system if creativity is to be nurtured. The emphasis on memorization by rote, fixed and rigid single responses, and convergent thinking etc. which kills creativity of the children should be abandoned and a proper evaluation system adopted for encouraging complete and balanced experiences in developing their creative behaviour.

11. *Use of special techniques for fostering creativity.* Researchers in the field of creativity have suggested special techniques and methods for fostering creativity among children. A few of these are:

   (a) *Brainstorming.* Brainstorming is a strategy or technique for allowing a group to explore ideas without judgment or censure. In practice, the children may be asked to sit in a group for solving a problem and attacking it without any inhibition from many angles: in fact, literally storming it with a number of possible ideas and solutions. To start with, the students may be provided with a focus e.g., a particular problem like 'student unrest', or the growing unemployment in India, or how to check truancy in our school, etc. The students are then asked to suggest ideas as rapidly as possible and the following norms are observed:

(i)   All ideas are encouraged and appreciated, therefore, no criticism is allowed during the brainstorming session.

(ii) Students are encouraged to come out with as many ideas as possible, even unusual and unorthodox ones.

(iii) They are not restricted to new ideas only but are also encouraged to enlarge upon ideas put forward by fellow students.

(iv) No evaluation or comment of any sort is to be made until the session is over. At the end of the session, all the ideas received (preferably written on the blackboard) should be discussed in a free, frank and open environment and the most viable ideas accepted for solution of the problem in hand.

(b) *Use of teaching models.*   Some of the teaching models developed by educationists may prove quite beneficial in developing creativity among children. For example, Bruner's concept attainment model helps in developing creativity in children for the attainment of various concepts. Similarly, Suchman's inquiry training model is very helpful in developing creativity among children in addition to imparting training in the acquisition of scientific inquiry skills.

(c) *Use of gaming technique.*   Gaming techniques, in a playful spirit, help the children in the development of creative traits. These techniques provide valuable learning experiences in a relaxed, spontaneous and evaluative situation. Both verbal and non-verbal stimulus material is used in such techniques. For instance, in verbal transaction of ideas, children may be asked to name all the round things they can think of, tell all the different ways a knife may be used, or all the ways in which a cat and a dog are alike.

In non-verbal transactions the children may be asked to build a cube, construct or complete a picture, draw and build patterns, interpret the patterns of drawings and sketches, and build or construct something or anything out of the raw material given to them.

12. *Teaching by example.*   There is truth in the saying that example is better than precept. Children are very imitative. The teachers and parents, who themselves follow the beaten track and do not show any originality for fear of being wrong or never experience the excitement of creating or doing something new, fail to stimulate creativity among the children in their charge. The teachers and parents must, therefore, themselves develop the habit of creative thinking. They should learn to believe in change, novelty and originality, and themselves experience the creative process. Their behaviour and style of teaching must reflect their love of creativity. Then, and only then, they can inspire the children to be creative.

SUMMARY

Creativity as the unique characteristic of the human mind may be defined as the capacity of an individual to create or produce an entirely new or novel idea or object or by the rearrangement or reshaping of what is already known. It is both innate as well as acquired and a process as well as a product. It is also characterized by qualities like universality, adventurousness and open-mindness a craving for change and novelty, ego involvement and divergent thinking. It does not necessarily have a positive correlation with school achievement and intelligence. It does, however show positive correlation with anxiety and negative correlation with sociability.

Various theories have been put forward for explaining the mechanism of creativity. The theory considering creativity as a God-given gift and the theory of insanity advocating positive correlation between insanity and creativity have been rejected outright. Similarly, theories describing creativity as being either inborn or an environmentally acquired characteristic are not accepted as exclusive of each other.

While Taylor's level theory of creativity is known to distinguish the existence of creativity at five levels in an ascending hierarchy, the hemisphere theory of creativity considers creative acts as a function of the interactions between the brain's hemispheres. A good explanation of creativity has been propounded by the psychoanalytical theory of creativity which defines creativity as a means and a product of one's emotional purgative, a medium for sublimation and catharsis. Recently Arieti through his own theory of creativity, described the creative process as a magic synthesis of two modalities:

1. The *primary process,* the outcome of the primitive part of the mind involving unconscious and irrational thinking and,
2. The *secondary process,* the outcome of the later developed mind involving rational thinking at the conscious level.

In studying creativity as a process we consider what happens in the creative process. Scholars have suggested various stages involved in the creative process to be from four to seven. The commonly employed stages are four, namely preparation, incubation, illumination and verification.

Creativity is also investigated through its outcome, i.e. the creative products. The degree of one's creativity may thus be judged on the basis of its originality, novelty and relevance. Creativity may also be described and understood through the personality characteristics of the creatives as distinct from those of the non-creatives. Who is creative and what should be expected from a creative mind can, therefore, be properly determined by referring to the lists of the characteristics framed by researchers and psychologists.

For objective identification of creativity, however, it is better to employ the standardized verbal as well as non-verbal creative tests in the same way as we utilize intelligence tests for the assessment of intelligence. These tests usually incorporate such items for testing the various components of factors of creativity as fluency, flexibility, originality, unusual responses, resistance to premature closure and elaboration, etc. The Torrance tests of creative thinking, Minnesota tests of creative thinking, and Baqer Mehdi's tests of creative thinking are examples of such tests.

There is a need for properly planned, deliberate and conscious efforts on the part of teachers, parents, members of the society, Government as well as the children themselves for the appropriate nurturing and stimulation of the creative urge and potential. It should, therefore be ensured that children are provided with the environment and facilities conducive to the nurturing and stimulation of all that which is helpful in the development of creative faculties and qualities like originality, flexibility, ideational fluency, divergent thinking, self-confidence, persistence, sensitiveness, the ability to see relationship and make association.

REFERENCES

Arieti, S., *Creativity: The magic synthesis,* New York: Basic Books, 1976.

Ausubel, D., The psychology of meaningful verbal learning, in *Introduction to School Learning,* New York: Grunc, 1963, p. 99.

Bartlett, F.C., *Thinking—An experimental and social study,* London: Allen & Unwin, 1958

Cattell, R.B., Quoted by B.S. Dagar, *Culture, Education and Creativity,* Delhi: Uppal Publishing House, 1989

Clark, B., *Growing up Gifted* (2nd ed.), Columbus, Ohio: Merril 1983.

Drevdahl, J.E., Factors of Importance for Creativity *J.Cl. Psy.* Vol. 12, 1956, p. 22.

Foster, Quoted by B.S. Dagar, *Culture, Education and Creativity,* Delhi: Uppal Publishing House, 1989.

Getzels, J.W. and Jackson, P.W., *Creativity and Intelligence,* New York: John Wiley, 1962.

Guilford, J.P., Three faces of intellect, *American Psychology,* Vol. 14, pp. 469–79, 1959.

Jung, C.G., *Modern Man in Search of a Soul,* New York: Harcourt Brace, 1933.

Kitano, M.K. and Kirby, D.E., *Gifted Education: A comprehensive view,* Boston: Little Brown, 1986, p. 192.

Kris, L., On preconscious mental processes, *Psychoanalytic Quarterly,* 19, p. 542, 1952.

Kubie, L.S., *Neurotic Distortion of Creative Processes,* Lawrence, Kansas: University of Kansas Press, 1958.

Levin, M.J., *Psychology: A biographical approach,* New York: McGraw-Hill, 1978, p. 311.

MacKinnon, D.W., *In Search of Human Effectiveness,* Buffalo, New York: Creative Education Foundation, 1978, p. 311.

Mehdi, Baqer, *Verbal and Non-verbal Tests of Creative Thinking,* Agra: National Psychological Corporation, 1989.

Paplia, D.E. and Olds, S.W., *Psychology,* New York: McGraw-Hill, 1987, p. 296.

Rock, D.A., Evans, F.R., Klein, S.P., Quoted by C.W. Telford and J.M. Sawrey, *The Exceptional Individual* (3rd ed.), Englewood Cliffs, N.J.: Prentice-Hall, 1977.

Rossman, Quoted by B.S. Dagar, *Culture, Education and Creativity,* Delhi: Uppal Publishing House, 1989.

Stein, M.I., Stimulating Creativity, Vol. I: *Individual Procedures,* New York: Academic Press, 1974, p. 8.

Stagner, R. and Karwoski, T.F., Quoted by L.D. Crow and A. Crow, *Educational Psychology*, New Delhi: Eurasia Publishing House, 1973, p. 314.

Telford, C.W. and Sawrey, J.M., *The Exceptional Individual* (3rd ed.), Englewood Cliffs, N.J.: Prentice-Hall, 1977, p. 193.

Taylor, I.A., A retrospective view of creative imagination, in I.A. Taylor and J.W. Getzels (Eds.), *Perspectives in Creativity,* Chicago: Aldine Publishing Co., 1975.

Torrance, E.P. and Myers, R.E., *Creative Learning and Teaching,* New York: Dodd, Mead, 1970.

Wallas, G., *The Art of Thought,* New York: Harcourt Brace, 1926.

Wallach, M.A. and Kogan, N., *Modes of Thinking in Young Children,* New York: Holt, Rinehart & Winston, 1965.

Wilson, R.C., Guilford, J.P. and Christensen, P.R., Quoted by N.K. Dutt, *Psychological Foundation of Education,* Delhi: Doaba House, 1974, p. 208.

SUGGESTED READINGS

Mangal, S.K., *Educational Psychology* (8th ed.), Ludhiana: Prakash Brothers, 1989.

Spearman, C.E., Quoted in Gowan, Demos and Torrance's *Creativity, its Educational Implication,* New York: John Wiley, 1967.

Taylor, I.A., The nature of the creative process, in P. Smith (ed.), Creativity: *An examination of the creative process*, New York: Hastings House, 1960.

Torrance, E.P., *Guiding Creative Talent*, Englewood Cliffs, N.J.: Prentice-Hall, 1962.

————— , *Torrance Tests of Creative Thinking: Norms Technical Manual,* Bensonville, Illinois: Scholastic Testing Service, 1974.

Chapter 19

Psychology of Thinking, Reasoning and Problem-solving

INTRODUCTION

Cognitive abilities like thinking, reasoning and problem-solving may be considered to be some of the chief characteristics which distinguish human beings from other species including the higher animals. Good poetry, a highly developed computer or a robot, a beautiful painting, or a magnificent building are all products of the thinking, reasoning and problem-solving capabilities of their creators and inventors. Even to understand, appreciate or put these into use, we have to employ our powers of thinking and reasoning. The challenges and problems faced by the individual, or by society, in general, are solved through serious efforts involving thinking and reasoning. The powers of thinking and reasoning may thus be considered to be the essential tools for the welfare and meaningful existence of the individual as well as society. We will now try to learn something about the processes involved in the thinking, reasoning and problem-solving behaviour of human beings.

THINKING

Definition

Thinking is an incredibly complex process and the most difficult concept in psychology to define or explain. However, it has not deterred the thinkers, and many different definitions exist. Some of them are given here.

Valentine (1965):

> In strict psychological discussion it is well to keep the *thinking* for an activity which consists essentially of a connected flow of ideas which are directed towards some end or purpose.

Ross (1951):

> Thinking is mental activity in its cognitive aspect or mental activity with regard to psychological objects.

Garrett (1968):

> Thinking is behaviour which is often implicit and hidden and in which symbols (images, ideas, concepts) are ordinarily employed.

Mohsin (1967):

> Thinking is an implicit problem-solving behaviour.

Gilmer (1970):

> Thinking is a problem solving process in which we use ideas or symbols in place of overt activity.

All the foregoing definitions fall into two categories: One class of definitions maintains that thinking is a process of internal representation of external events, belonging to the past, present or future, and may even concern a thing or an event which is not being actually observed or experienced by the thinker. The second category of definitions describes thinking in terms of problem-solving behaviour. These latter definitions are more concrete as well as more definite because they do not rely on unobservable internal representations and define thinking as problem-solving activity that can be readily studied and measured (Fantino and Reynolds, 1975).

Whatever the apparent difference may be, both classes of definitions actually tell the same story. The internal representation of external factors influences problem-solving behaviour and the problem-solving behaviour provides evidence for the existence of internal representation. Therefore, what is representational may be used as functional and vice versa. The process of thinking and the product of thinking are both actually assessed by what is obtained as a result of thinking. The lines along which individuals think must, therefore, always be inferred from the way they behave. Internal representation or mental explanation of the thing or events i.e., internal behaviour, should be made an essential aspect of the thinking process used in the problem-solving behaviour. Therefore, a workable definition of 'thinking' must combine internal behaviour and the product of thinking or the aims or purposes of thinking. *Thinking may thus be defined as a pattern of behaviour in which we make use of internal representations (symbols, signs etc.) of things and events for the solution of some specific, purposeful problem.*

Nature of Thinking

What we have discussed about the meaning of the term 'thinking' so far has brought out the following aspects of its nature:

1. Thinking is essentially a cognitive activity.
2. It is always directed towards achieving some purpose. In genuine thinking we cannot let our thoughts wander aimlessly as happens in the case of day-dreaming and fantasizing.
3. Thinking is described as a problem-solving behaviour. From the beginning till end, there is some problem around which the whole process of thinking resolves. But every problem-solving behaviour is not thinking. It is related only to the inner cognitive behaviour.

4. In thinking, there is mental exploration rather than motor exploration. One has to suspend one's overt or motor activities while engaging in thinking through some kind of mental exploration or the other.
5. Thinking is a symbolic activity. In thinking, a mental solution of the problem is carried out through some signs, symbols and mental images.
6. Thinking can shift instantaneously over a span of time and space.

Theories of Thinking

Various theoretical viewpoints have been put forward by different psychologists from time to time to explain the nature, mechanism and development of thinking. Let us now examine some of the more influential theoretical approaches.

Behaviouristic learning theory.   According to this theory, thinking behaviour is learned or acquired in much the same way as other modes of behaviour, interests, attitudes, knowledge and skills etc. J.B. Watson, an associationist, opined that there is association between the movement of one's tongue or vocal cords with one's thoughts. As an S-R mechanism, the response, an outcome of one's thinking is the product of the associated stimuli. The stimulus thus generates the process of thinking. The same stimuli generate the same type of thought and the organism thus becomes conditioned. Not only the classical conditioning propagated by Watson and Pavlov, but also the theory of operant conditioning propounded by B.F. Skinner viewed thinking as that private behaviour which was determined by stimulus control and reinforcement in the same way as overt behaviour.

The gestalt and holistic theory.   This theory emphasized the importance of the organisation of the perceptual field in the process of thinking leading to problem-solving behaviour. According to it, thinking behaviour is always purposeful and goal-oriented. While thinking, one gets to look at the whole field or context in which the thinking is occurring. With this wider perception, one is set for the reorganisation and restructuring of the perceived field for an optimal solution of the problem in hand. The acts of such restructuring or reorganisation of the perceptual field belong to the process and product of thinking.

Piaget's developmental theory.   Piaget tried to provide a satisfactory explanation of the development of thinking in man through the successive stages of cognitive development, the sensory-motor, pre-operational, concrete operational and formal operational stages. The thought processes evolved while passing through these stages have already been discussed in detail in Chapter 8. These are again briefly touched upon now for the sake of continuity. In the beginning, at the sensory-motor stage (up to 2 years) a child's behaviour exhibits more sensory-motor activities than the mental manipulation of objects. He cannot distinguish between animate and inanimate objects. Anything out of sight has no existence for him. He does not differentiate between the world and himself. The sun moves because he moves, the rain must stop because he needs to go out to play, etc. Gradually, he develops a sense of object permanence (a toy, though concealed, exists), the ability to categorize things and differentiate between his self and the world.

At the preoperational stage (2 to 7 years), the child begins to use words and symbols for representing things and events and also tries to form images of every thing he encounters.

At the concrete operational stage (7 to 11 years) he begins to think logically by learning some distinctive logical operations like combining, acquiring the basic cognitive concepts such as numbers, classification and conservation. However, at this stage he can only think in terms of concrete things.

The formal operational stage (12 years and after) is the last stage of one's cognitive development. The thinking at this stage is characterized by the development of the ability to think in abstract terms, test hypotheses and deal with problems that are not physically present in the environment. It is, in fact, the highest stage of intellectual functioning, the stage at which one's thought processes are said to be functioning to the maximum at the most advanced level.

Sullivan's basic modes theory. The leading psychoanalyst H.S. Sullivan has postulated three basic developmental stages referred to as the modes of thought process for explaining man's cognitive development. These are the prototaxic mode, parataxic mode and syntaxic mode.

In infancy, during the prototaxic mode, there is no evidence of any definite structure of the thought process of the individual. This is vaguely manifested mainly in the form of feelings such as pleasure at sucking the nipple and apprehension at being separated from the persons who take care of the individual.

During the parataxic mode, the child begins to differentiate between his self and the world. He is able to discriminate, distinguish and differentiate between the objects and the persons around him. His thinking at this stage is quite elementary and operative in the concrete manipulation of the things and objects. Moreover, while parataxic thinking makes sense to the individual, it is not necessarily logical to others e.g., the child may say that movement of the clouds causes the wind to blow, the sun moves because it is being pushed by the clouds and so on.

The final stage, comprising the syntaxic mode reflects the development of the logical thought processes, incorporating the use of symbolic representation, images, and abstract reasoning and involving the use of the developed logical operations commonly agreed to by a group of people.

Bruner's theory of cognitive development. Jerome S. Bruner, like the other developmentalists Piaget and Sullivan, hypothesized that one's thought processes evolve as a result of maturation, training and experiences through a series of sequential stages. The stages of cognitive development enumerated by him for this purpose were enactive, iconic and symbolic representation. The first *enactive representation stage* is characterized by the child's representation of things and events in terms of appropriate motor responses and activities. At this stage, he is unable to make use of language images or other symbolic representations for carrying out his thought processes and 'acts out' and represents them through non-verbal activities based on motor actions and movements.

The next *iconic representation stage* of cognitive development is characterized by the child's representation of things and events in terms of sensory images or mental pictures.

The final *symbolic representation stage* is that stage of one's cognitive development when thought about things and events is not necessarily dependent upon the motor activities or sensory images and mental pictures. During this stage, symbolic representations in the form of words, symbols and other imaginary abstract phenomena take the place of motor manipulation or concrete visualization. For instance, to understand a question like: "if a child has four apples and his sister has three, how many apples do they have between them?" One does not now need to actually have these apples (in physical terms) nor to draw a mental picture of these apples for the counting. One may just write the numbers 4 and 3 or mentally visualize these numbers to add them up.

The information processing theory. According to this theory, thinking is connected with the information one receives from the environment through one's senses and the nature of the thought process depends on how it is utilized by the individual from the time he perceives it until the time he processes it at various depth levels in solving his problem or chalking out a strategy or plan. This theory identifies a series of steps in the way we process the information. The salient stages of this processing may be: registering information, retrieving material related to this information from memory and using both kinds of knowledge purposefully.

Freud's psychoanalytic theory of thinking. The key concepts in Freud's psychoanalytic system may be described as the inherent desire for satisfaction of the sex urge and the role of the unconscious in moulding and shaping of one's behaviour. The thinking behaviour is also governed through these two factors. If the goal is pleasure through sex gratification, the thought process would be naturally coloured accordingly and since nine-tenths of one's psyche consists of the unconscious and sub-conscious, the major portion of one's thinking must emerge from it. The wish fulfilment, dreaming and unconscious morbid thinking, should thus be considered to be a major part and parcel of one's thought process influencing one's interests, attitudes and overall behaviour.

In the process of development of thinking, the new-born infant does not show any sign of thought-related activities. In fact, his mental life is chaotic at this stage and is driven by a set of psycho-physiological drives, for example, when he is hungry, he cries. Gradually, Freud maintains, the infant develops a kind of self-centred thinking termed as narcissistic thinking. His behaviour is almost entirely dominated by the Id and the pleasure principle and the thoughts of the infant are highly coloured by instinctual impulses demonstrating a total disregard of realities and logic. As the child grows older, another part of his personality, the ego comes into play. He then begins to pay attention to people and his environment in order to be able to cope with it effectively. He now begins to operate according to the reality principle and his thought processes become more rational and logical. Symbols and words also become involved in his thinking but he still remains ego-centric. With the entry of another component of his personality, the super-ego, his thinking is now fashioned in accordance with the mores and ideals of society. It becomes more objective. The development of creative thinking, enrichment of fantasy, imagination and abstract thinking is the outcome of emergence of the super-ego and the subsequent expansion of the child's thinking apparatus.

Elements of Thought (Tools of Thinking)

The various elements involved in the thinking process may be summarised as follows:

1. *Images.* Images, as mental pictures consist of personal experiences of objects, persons or scenes actually seen, heard and felt. These mental pictures symbolize actual objects, experiences and activities. In thinking, we usually manipulate the images rather than the actual objects, experiences or activities.

2. *Concepts.* A concept is a general idea that stands for a general class and represents the common characteristic of all objects or events of this general class. Concepts, as a tool, economise the efforts in thinking. For example, when we hear the word 'elephant' we are at once reminded not only about the nature and qualities of elephant as a class but also our own experiences and understanding of them come to the surface in our consciousness to stimulate our thinking at that time.

3. *Symbols and signs.* Symbols and signs represent and stand for substitutes for the actual objects, experiences and activities. In this sense, they are not confined to words, mathematical numerals and terms. Traffic lights, railway signals, school bells, badges, songs, flags and slogans are all forms of symbolic expression. These symbols and signs stimulate and economise thinking. They at once tell us what to do or how to act. For example, the waving of the green flag by the guard tells us that the train is about to move and we should get on to the train. Similarly, the mathematical symbol for subtraction (–) tells a child what he has to do. The following conclusion drawn by Boring, Langfield and Weld to emphasize the role of symbols and signs in the process of thinking is worthy of mention.

> Symbols and signs are thus seen to be the pawn and pieces with which the great game of thinking is played. It could not be such a remarkable and successful game without them.

4. *Language.* Language is the most efficient and developed vehicle used for carrying out the process of thinking. When one reads, writes or hears words, phrases or sentences or observes gesture in any language, one is stimulated to think. Reading and writing of documents and literature also help in stimulating and promoting the thinking process.

5. *Muscle activities.* Thinking in one way or the other shows evidence of the involvement of some incipient movements of groups of our muscles. It can be easily noticed that there are slight muscular responses when we think of a word, resembling the movements used when we say the word aloud. A positive correlation has been found between the thinking and muscular activities of an individual. The more we engage ourselves in thought, the greater is the general muscular tension and conversely as we move towards a state of muscular relaxation, our thought processes are also gradually lulled.

6. *Brain functions.* Whatever may be the role of the muscles, thinking is primarily a function of the brain. Our mind or brain is said to be the chief instrument or seat for the carrying out of the process of thinking. The experiences

registered by our sense organs have no meaning and thus cannot serve as stimulating agents, or instruments for thinking unless these impressions are received by our brain cells and properly interpreted to derive some meaning. The mental pictures or images can be stored, formed, reconstructed or put to use only on being processed by the brain. What happens in our thought process is simply the function or product of the activities of our brain.

Role of Rigidity, Set, Direction and Interest in Thinking

"Set" may be inferred either as a kind of habit or as the way in which we are accustomed to perceiving certain situations. Our thinking, reasoning and problem-solving behaviour are all largely influenced by our sets. What was registered earlier in our perception or experience provides the base for our present and future thinking. We usually tend not to deviate from this pre-set path of our thinking, which leads to much rigidity in our behaviour. As a result, we become victims of inertia and do not easily accept new facts or ideas. We always follow the beaten path (on the basis of the previous set), have the same likes and dislikes, biased or oversimplified ways of thinking, reasoning and problem-solving attitudes. The set that has been gained from previous experiences, surely interferes with our subsequent thinking behaviour. This reliance on a set way of thinking and habitual problem-solving interferes with comprehensive consideration of potential solutions that is required for effective problem-solving. It undermines the creative aspect of our endeavour. In brief, while the induction of a set in our thinking process may help us in initiating some constructive thinking, dependence on it, leading to rigid habits of thinking (fixation of the thinking behaviour) may kill the potential for effective problem-solving and creativity in our behaviour.

The sets induced in our process of thinking are quite often the result of our interests, directions, purposes and goals or our accomplishments. How we would think, reason or engage in problem-solving can be understood and predicted in the light of our interests, attitudes, emotions and life's goals. The limits within which a person thinks or reasons are influenced and circumscribed by his previous experiences, habits, interests and attitudes. This is an advantage as well as a drawback. The advantage is that the set procedures allow us considerable freedom and insulate us against mistakes because of the known alternatives and consequences. The drawback is that we persist in our old ways of thinking and this rigidity reduces the alternatives and choices which, in turn, results in stereotyped behaviour and constricted thinking, thus completely destroying initiative and the potential for adequate problem-solving and creativity.

Types of Thinking

Thinking, as a mental process, is usually classified into the following categories:

1. *Perceptual or concrete thinking.* This is the simplest form of thinking. The basis of this type of thinking is perception, i.e., interpretation of sensation according to one's experience. It is also called concrete thinking as it is carried out on the perception of actual or concrete objects and events.

2. *Conceptual or abstract thinking.* Unlike perceptual thinking, this does not require the perception of actual objects or events. It is an abstract thinking where one makes use of concepts; the generalised ideas and language. It is regarded as being superior to perceptual thinking as it economizes efforts in understanding and problem solving.

3. *Reflective thinking.* This is a somewhat higher form of thinking. It can be, distinguished from simple thinking in the following ways:

(a) It aims at solving complex rather than simple problems.
(b) It requires reorganisation of all the relevant experiences and the finding of new ways of reacting to a situation or of removing an obstacle instead of a simple association of experiences or ideas.
(c) Mental activity in reflective thinking does not involve the mechanical trial and error type of efforts. There is an insightful cognitive approach in reflective thinking.
(d) It takes all the relevant facts arranged in a logical order into account in order to arrive at a solution of the problem in hand.

4. *Creative thinking.* This type of thinking, as the name suggests, is associated with one's ability to create or construct something new, novel, or unusual. It looks for new relationships and associations to describe and interpret the nature of things, events and situations. It is not restricted by any pre-established rules. The individual himself usually formulates the problem and is also free to collect the evidences and to fashion the tools for its solution. The thinking of scientists, artists or inventors provides ideal examples for such type of thinking.

As a matter of definition, it has been defined by the famous psychologist Charles Skinner (1968) in the following way:

> Creative thinking means that the predictions and/or inferences for the individual are new, original, ingenious, unusual. The creative thinker is one who explores new areas and makes new observations, new predictions, new inferences.

The above views have been confirmed by another famous psychologist and scholar M.J. Levin (1978) in the following words:

> It is a special form of thinking, a way of viewing the world and interacting with it in a manner different from that of the general population. It is the ability to discover new solutions to problems or to produce new ideas, inventions or works of art.

Based on the analysis and understanding of the above two definitions, we may understand creative thinking as "that type of thinking which helps an individual to create, discover or produce a new idea or object including the rearrangement or reshaping of what is already known to him."

We can further substantiate and add a few points about the nature and characteristics of creative thinking:

(a) Creative thinking, in all its shapes and forms, is absolutely an internal mental process and hence should be considered as an important component of one's cognitive behaviour.

(b) Every one of us is capable of creative thinking and hence it is a universal phenomenon.

(c) Creative thinking results in the production of something new or novel (including a new form or arrangement of old elements).

(d) Any creative expression as a result of one's creative thinking is a source of joy and satisfaction for the creator.

(e) Although our creative abilities involving creative thinking are natural endowments, they can be nourished and nurtured by training or education.

(f) Creative thinking in all its dimensions involve divergent thinking instead of the routine and fixed type of convergent thinking. The mind must have complete freedom to wander around to create a new idea.

(g) The field of creative thinking and its output is quite comprehensive and wide. It covers all the aspects of human accomplishments belonging to an individual's life.

(h) Psychologists, on the basis of their researches, have agreed on the presence of following elements or factors in one's creative thinking:

(i) Ideational fluency, (ii) Originality, (iii) Flexibility, (iv) Divergent thinking, (v) Self-confidence and persistence, (vi) Ability to see and build relationships.

5. Critical thinking. It is a type of thinking that helps a person in stepping aside from his own personal beliefs, prejudices, and opinions to sort out the facts and discover the truth, even at the expense of his basic belief system. In this way it represents a challenging thought process which leads a person to new avenues of knowledge and understanding. It is in fact a structural approach of thinking to find ways and means for the improvement of thinking process itself. Here one resorts to a set of higher cognitive abilities and skills for the proper interpretation, analysis, evaluation and inference, as well as explanation of the gathered or communicated information resulting in a purposeful, unbiased and self-regulatory judgement. An ideal critical thinker is habitually inquisitive, well-informed, open-minded, flexible, fair-minded in evaluation, free from personal bias and prejudices, honest in seeking relevant information, skilled in the proper use of the abilities like interpretation analysis, synthesis, evaluation and drawing conclusions and inferences etc., interested in reasoned inquiry, prudent in making judgements, willing to reconsider, clear about issues, orderly in dealing with complex matters, persistent in seeking results which are as precise as the subject. In this way a critical thinker is supposed to imbibe certain specific critical thinking skills along with proper dispositions and attitudes of utilising these skills for his personal and social progress.

On the basis of what has been said above we can draw a conclusion about the nature of critical thinking, by terming it as *a higher order well-disciplined thought process, which involves the use of cognitive skills like conceptualization, interpretation, analysis, synthesis and evaluation for arriving at an unbiased, valid and reliable judgement of the gathered or communicated information or data as a guide to one's belief and action.*

Critical thinking may be distinguished from general or ordinary thinking in many ways. Its real value lies in its quality of being most skillful and responsible thinking that facilitates good judgement. It definitely sets some criteria for its own procedural advancement and is self-correcting and sensitive to the contemporary issues and circumstances. It proves to be a backbone and a reliable support for carrying out the process of problem solving. It does not teach or encourage the child to mug up things without proper understanding. Rather it makes him a self-reliant, independent inquirer and discoverer and a useful and progressive citizen as needed by a rational and democratic society. Therefore, all our efforts should be concentrated to develop the required critical thinking potential among the youngsters.

6. *Non-directed or associative thinking.* In the strict psychological sense what we have discussed so far concerning the types or categories of thinking encompasses real or genuine thinking. It is essentially *directed thinking* which pertains to reasoning and problem-solving procedures aimed at meeting specific goals. However, there are times when we find ourselves engaged in a unique type of thinking which is *non-directed* and without goal. It is reflected through dreaming, free associations, fantasy, delusions, day-dreaming and other free-flowing uncontrolled activities. In psychological language these forms of thought are termed as associative thinking.

Day-dreaming, fantasy and delusions all fall in the category of withdrawal behaviour that helps an individual to escape from the demands of the real world by making his thinking free, non-directed and floating placing him somewhere or doing something unconnected with his environment.

While there is nothing seriously abnormal in behaviour involving day-dreaming and fantasy, behaviour involving delusions definitely points towards abnormality. Day-dreaming and fantasy are also not quite the same: fantasy is more self-directed. Here one roams through one's own private world by engaging himself in thinking like, "If I could . . ." or "If I were . . .". In day-dreaming, on the other hand, our thinking unconsciously floats in unexpected directions. Day-dreaming and fantasizing have both positive as well as negative consequences. On the one hand, they reflect our repressed desires and are a kind of wishful thinking that occurs when our inner needs cannot be fulfilled in real life. This may lead to an individual withdrawing from his obligations and responsibilities. He may try to avoid facing the realities of life and waste his energy and talents in day-dreaming or fantasy. On the credit side, day-dreaming and fantasy can prove quite constructive by providing opportunities for building cognitive and creative skills and helping in problem-solving behaviour. They provide a respite from the harsh realities of life and are also a means of reducing internal tensions and external aggressive behaviour.

Delusions, characterising abnormality of behaviour, may be defined as persistent thoughts or false beliefs which the individual defends vigorously by accepting as absolutely true despite logical absurdity of such beliefs or proofs to the contrary, and despite their serious interference with his social adjustment. Individuals suffering from delusions refuse to accept any appeal to reason for correction of their thoughts or beliefs which have no basis in reality and are often inconsistent with the individual's knowledge and experience. A person under the influence of such delusions may think or believe that he is a millionaire, the ruler of the universe, a great inventor, a noted historian or even God. In the opposite case, a person in the grip of delusion may be inclined to consider himself to be the most incapable, unworthy and unwanted person and may develop guilt feelings or complain that he is the victim of some incurable physical or mental disease.

Training or Development of Thinking

Thinking is one of the important aspects of teaching-learning process. Our ability to learn and solve the problems, depends upon our ability to think correctly. It helps us in adjustment and is necessary for a successful living. Only the men who can think distinctly, consecutively and carefully, can contribute something worthwhile to the society. But one is not a born thinker. One has to learn to think, just as one has to learn to perceive. Learning to think is not an easy road. It requires a knowledge of the techniques and practice of proper thinking. Though it is difficult to list the measures for developing effective and correct thinking, the following discussion may prove fruitful in this direction.

1. *Adequacy of the knowledge and experiences.* We need some grounds for thinking. Thinking, no matter simple or complex, rests on the previous knowledge and experience of the thinker. Adequacy of knowledge and experiences brings adequacy in thinking. Lack of knowledge and experience or improper knowledge and faulty experience is the common cause of bad thinking. Therefore, care should be taken to equip the children with adequate knowledge and experiences. It may be done in the following ways:

(a) Knowledge and experiences are acquired through sensation and perception. It is very important therefore, that children should receive correct sensation and be able to interpret them correctly. Thus training in correct observation and interpretation should be given to children.

(b) A person should be provided with opportunities for gaining adequate experience and should be encouraged for self-study, discussion and participation in healthy, stimulating activities.

2. *Adequate motivation and definiteness of aim.* Thinking is a purposeful activity. Unless there is a definite aim or purpose, thinking cannot proceed on the right track. It is a problem-solving behaviour which ends in the satisfaction of felt needs and motives. A person does not think because he thinks, but because he has a need. Therefore, there is a motive behind any valid thinking. It helps in mobilizing our energy for thinking and makes us deeply absorbed in the task of thinking. It creates genuine interest and voluntary attention in the process of thinking and thus helps a lot in increasing the adequacy and efficiency of our thinking. Therefore, one should try to think on definite lines with a definite end or purpose. The problems we solve should have intimate connection with our immediate needs and basic motives. The aimless wandering of our thinking should be checked and our energy should be concentrated on creative and productive activities.

3. *Adequate freedom and flexibility.*   Thinking should not be obstructed by imposing unnecessary restrictions and narrowing of the field of thought process. Also, it should not get unbridled freedom as to tempt one to roam around the world of pure imagination. Actually a person should have flexible attitude towards himself so that he can set his thinking, according to the requirements of the situation. For example, if the past experiences or habitual methods do not help in solving the problem, he should strive for new association, relationships and possibilities for arriving at satisfactory results.

4. *Incubation.*   To bring adequacy in the process of thinking, use of the phenomenon of incubation is very helpful. When we set ourselves to solve a problem but fail to solve it in spite of our strenuous and persistent thinking, it is advisable to lay aside the problem for some time and release for a while or engage in some other activity. During this interval, the unconscious mind starts working on the problem and just as eggs are hatched by incubation, a solution is evolved through the efforts of our unconscious mind.

5. *Intelligence and wisdom.*   Intelligence is defined as the ability to think properly and thus proper development of intelligence is essential for bringing adequacy in thinking. Wisdom is also regarded as an effective instrument for carrying out the process of thought. It helps in thoughtful solution to any problem. Therefore, proper care should be taken to use intelligence, wisdom and other similar cognitive abilities for carrying out the process of thinking.

6. *Proper development of concepts and language.*   As discussed earlier, concepts, symbols and signs and words and language are the vehicles as well as instruments of thought. Without their proper development one cannot proceed effectively on the path of thinking. Their development stimulates and guides the thought process. Improper development and faulty formation of concepts and likewise, symbolic behaviour not only hamper a person's progress in thinking but also prove fatal, as they may give rise to perverted thinking and wrong conclusions. Therefore, proper care should be taken to develop right concepts and linguistic ability (using various symbols, signs and formulae, besides words and language) to be used in the process of thinking.

7. *Adequacy of reasoning process.*   Thinking is also influenced by the mode of reasoning one adopts. Illogical reasoning often leads to incorrect thinking. Logic is the science of correct reasoning which helps to think correctly. Therefore, we should cultivate the habit of logical reasoning among our children.

Besides the above considerations, we should be quite cautious to keep ourselves well-guarded against the elements that bring inadequacy in thinking. There are certain factors which either arrest one's thinking or hamper its progress. One of such factors is the state of emotional excitement. Under emotional current one loses one's balance of mind. Therefore, it is essential to train ourselves in exercising control over our emotions. Prejudices, superstitions and incorrect beliefs also arrest thinking and make it biased and one-sided. Valid and correct thinking needs elimination of all such obstructing factors.

REASONING

Meaning and Definition

Reasoning plays a significant role in one's adjustment to one's environment. It controls not only one's cognitive activities but may also influence the total behaviour and personality by the proper or improper development of one's reasoning ability. It is essentially a cognitive ability and is like thinking in many aspects.

1. Like genuine thinking, it has a definite purpose or goal.
2. It is also an implicit act and involves problem solving behaviour.
3. Like thinking, it involves the use of one's previous knowledge and experiences.
4. Like thinking, in reasoning also, there is mental exploration instead of motor exploration as it involves mental exploration of the reason or cause of an event or happening.
5. Like thinking, reasoning is a highly symbolic function. The ability to interpret various symbols, development of concepts and language aids reasoning.

In view of the foregoing points of similarity, it is not easy to clearly distinguish between thinking and reasoning as separate functions. Reasoning is said to be a productive and advanced stage in the complex process of thinking. In comparison to thinking it may be said to be a more serious and complex mental process which needs a well-organised brain and deliberate effort.

The following definitions given by some eminent scholars can throw more light on the meaning and nature of the process of reasoning.

Garrett (1968):

Reasoning is step-wise thinking with a purpose or goal in mind.

Gates (1947):

Reasoning is the term applied to highly purposeful controlled selective thinking.

Woodworth (1945):

In reasoning, items (facts or principles) furnished by recall, present observation or both; are combined and examined to see what conclusion can be drawn from the combination.

Skinner (1968):

Reasoning is the word used to describe the mental recognition of cause-and-effect relationships. It may be the prediction of an event from an observed cause or the inference of a cause from an observed event.

Munn (1967):

Reasoning is combining past experiences in order to solve a problem which cannot be solved by mere reproduction of earlier solutions.

A close analysis of the foregoing definitions may reveal that reasoning depicts a higher type of thinking which is a very careful, systematic and organised function. It may follow some logical systematic steps like:

1. Identification of the goal or purposes to which the reasoning is to be directed.
2. Mental exploration or search for the various possibilities, cause-and-effect relationships or solutions for realising the set goal or purposes based on the previous learning or experiences and present observations or attempts.
3. Selection of the most appropriate possibility or solution by careful mental analysis of all the available alternatives.
4. Testing the validity of the selected possibility or solution, purely through mental exercise and thus finally accepting or rejecting it for the actual solution of the problem.

Reasoning may thus be termed *as highly specialized thinking which helps an individual to explore mentally the cause-and-effect relationship of an event or solution of a problem by adopting some well-organised systematic steps based on previous experiences combined with present observation.*

Types of Reasoning

Reasoning may be classified into two broad type—Inductive reasoning and Deductive reasoning.

Inductive reasoning. In this type of reasoning we usually follow the process of induction. Induction is a way of proving a statement or generalizing a rule or principle by proving or showing that if a statement or a rule is true in one particular case, it will be true in all cases in the same serial order and it may thus be applied generally to all such cases. Therefore, in inductive reasoning one can formulate generalized principles and conclusions on the basis of certain facts and specific examples. For instance:

1. Mohan is mortal, Radha is mortal, Karim is mortal, Edward is mortal. Therefore, all human beings are mortal.
2. Iron expands when heated, water expands when heated, air also expands when heated. Therefore, all matter—solid, liquid and gas—expands when heated.

Inductive reasoning may thus be considered to be a type of specialized thinking aimed at the discovery or construction of a rule or generalized principle by making use of particular cases, special examples and identity of elements or relations.

The study of inductive reasoning. To find the extent to which one's reasoning is inductive, we can employ the three following types of problems:

1. Classification problems like:

   Mouse, wolf, bear, . . .   (a) rose, (b) lion, (c) run,
   (d) hungry, (e) brown, and so on.

2. Series completion problems:
   (i) 32, 11, 33, 15, 34, 19, 35, . . .
   (ii) 72, 43, 90, 71, 47, 85, 70, 51, 80, . . .

3. Analogy problems:

(i)   Sugar : Sweet :: Lemon : _____
(ii) 15 : 19 :: 8 : 12 :: 5 : _____
(iii) 28 : 21 :: 24 : 18 :: 20 : _____

(Note: Solutions are on page 381)

Deductive reasoning.   Deductive reasoning is the exact opposite of inductive reasoning. It may be defined as the ability to draw logical conclusions from known statements or evidences. Here, one starts with some already known or established generalized statement or principle and applies it to specific cases. The following statements are examples of deductive reasoning:

1. All human beings are mortal; you are a human being; therefore, you are mortal.
2. Matter expands when heated; iron being a form of matter, will expand when heated.

Henry L. Roediger and others (1987) in their book *Psychology* have mentioned three types of deductive reasoning—conditioned reasoning, categorical reasoning, and linear reasoning. Let us see what they mean.

Conditioned reasoning.   Conditioned reasoning is the reasoning tied down by some specific condition such as the following:

If there is a solar eclipse, the street will be dark. There is a solar eclipse. Therefore, the streets are dark.

Categorical reasoning.   This type of reasoning is based on some categorical statements like:

All Robins are birds.
All birds lay eggs. Therefore, all robins lay eggs.

Linear reasoning.   This type of reasoning involves straightforward relationships among elements, e.g.,

1. If Ram is taller than Mohan, and Mohan is taller than Sohan, Ram is the tallest.
2. If Sita is taller than Gita, and Gita is not as short as Rita, then Rita is the shortest.

PROBLEM-SOLVING

Meaning and Definition

From birth onwards, everybody in this world is beset with some problem or the other. There are needs and motives that are to be satisfied. For this purpose, definite goals or aims are set. In an attempt for their realization one experiences obstacles and interferences in one's attempt to achieve them. This creates problems and serious and deliberate efforts have to be made to overcome these impediments.

The productive work involved in the evaluation of the situation and the strategy worked out to reach one's set goals is collectively termed *problem solving*. This is an essential exercise for individual advancement as also for the advance-ment of society. The meaning and nature of problem solving is further clarified by the following definitions:

Woodworth and Marquis (1948):

> Problem-solving behaviour occurs in novel or difficult situations in which a solution is not obtainable by the habitual methods of applying concepts and principles derived from past experience in very similar situations.

Skinner (1968):

> Problem solving is a process of overcoming difficulties that appear to interfere with the attainment of a goal. It is a procedure of making adjustment in spite of interferences.

An analysis of the above definitions brings out the following observations about the meaning and nature of problem-solving behaviour:

1. In the satisfaction of one's needs and realisation of the set goals, problem-solving behaviour arises only when the goal is purposeful and essential for the individual, there is serious interference in the realisation of this goal, and this interference or obstacle cannot be overcome by simple habitual acts or mechanical trial and error methods.
2. One has to utilise one's thinking and reasoning powers and engage in serious mental work by systematically following some well-organised steps for the removal of the difficulties and obstacles.
3. The problem-solving behaviour involves quite deliberate, conscious and serious efforts on the part of the problem-solver.
4. Problem-solving behaviour helps in the removal of, or adjustment with, interferences and ultimately helps an individual to reach his goal and satisfy his motives.
5. Problem-solving behaviour helps an individual in the growth and development of his personality, making his life happier and wiser by appropriate adjustment. It also contributes significantly to the progress and development of society.

In view of the foregoing, problem-solving behaviour may be said *to be a deliberate and purposeful act on the part of an individual to realise the set goals or objectives by inventing some novel methods or systematically following some planned step for removal of the interferences and obstacles in the path of the realization of these goals when usual methods like trial and error, habit-formation and conditioning fail.*

Steps in Effective Problem-solving Behaviour

Psychologists have tried to study carefully, the behaviour involved in the process of problem-solving in animals as well as in human beings. They have suggested different steps involved in the process of problem-solving according to their respective findings and viewpoints.

John Bransford and Barry Stein (1984) advocated five steps that are basically associated with the task of problem-solving. They referred to these steps as 'IDEAL' thinking and arranged them in the following order:

I = Identifying the problem.
D = Defining and representing the problem.
E = Exploring possible strategies.
A = Acting on the strategies.
L = Looking back and evaluating the effects of one's activities.

Bourne, Dominowski and Loftus (1979), on the other hand, enumerated three steps or stages in problem-solving: preparation, production and evaluation, by proclaiming *"we prepare, we produce, and we evaluate in the task of problem solving."*

Problem-solving is an individual phenomenon and involves the exercise of cognitive abilities of a high order and continuous and persistent struggling on the conscious as well unconscious levels. Often, there is a considerable movement back and forth as one moves from one step to another in the task of problem-solving. In general the following steps may be followed in the task of problem-solving.

1. *Problem-awareness.* The first step in the problem-solving behaviour of an individual is concerned with his awareness of the difficulty or problem which needs to be solved. He must be faced with some obstacle or interference in the path of the realization of his goals, needs or motives and consequently he must be conscious of the difficulty or problem.

2. *Problem-understanding.* The difficulty or problem encountered by the individual should next be properly identified and analysed so that its exact nature becomes clear to him. This should be followed by relating the problem to his specific goals and objectives. Thus all the difficulties and obstacles in the path of the goal or solution must be properly named and identified and what is to be achieved through the problem-solving effort should be clearly known in very specific terms.

3. *Collection of the relevant information.* In this step, the individual is required to collect all the relevant information about the problem by all possible means. He may consult experienced persons, read the available literature, recall his own experiences, think of the numerous possible solutions, and put in all possible efforts to collect comprehensive data and knowledge concerning the problem.

4. *Formulation of hypotheses or hunch for possible solutions.* After understanding the nature of the problem and collecting all relevant information, one may start some cognitive activities to think out the various solutions to the problem.

5. *Selection of the correct solution.* In this important step, all the possible solutions, thought out in the previous step, are closely analysed and evaluated. Gates and others (1946) have suggested the following activities in the evaluation of the assumed hypotheses or solutions:

1. Identify the conclusion that completely satisfies all the demands of the problem.
2. Find out whether the solution is consistent with other well-established or accepted facts and principles.
3. Make a deliberate search for negative aspects which might cast any doubt upon the conclusion.

The above suggestions would help the individual to select the proper solution of his problem out of the numerous solutions that may be available. In the final analysis, however, he has to use his own discretion by utilising his higher cognitive abilities to properly identify the appropriate hypothesis or solution by rejecting all other hypotheses.

6. *Verification of the concluded solution or hypothesis.* The solution arrived at or conclusion drawn must be further verified by applying it in the solution of various similar problems and only if the derived solution helps in the solution of these problems, should one consider the solution to be acceptable. Such a verified solution may then become a useful product of one's problem-solving behaviour and be utilized in solving other future problems.

Factors Affecting Problem-solving

Every one of us in life faces one or other problem. We make our attempts with all the resources in hand in finding out solutions to these problems. In doing so, many times we get success but it may also go otherwise. There are factors which are attributed as causes for our success or failure in problem-solving behaviour. There are a number of such factors which may be broadly put into two categories. In the first category we may include the factors which are directly linked with the nature and type of the problem and in the second category we may include the factors which have a direct relation with the nature and capacities of the problem solver and his approach to problem solving. Let us discuss now the various things and factors affecting one's problem-solving behaviour under the heads of this two-fold classification.

1. *Factors inherent in the nature of the problem.* The problem-solving factors depend to a great extent on the nature of the problem. Some of them may be outlined as below:

(a) The simplicity or complexity of the problem.
(b) The size or shape of the problem.
(c) Appropriate or inappropriate definition of the problem.
(d) The nature of the definiteness of the problem.
(e) Its similarity or analogy with the problems experienced or solved in the past.
(f) The nature of the help available from the present circumstances and resources at hand.
(g) The effect of the unfavourable circumstances or lack of resources in the solution of the problem.

2. *Factors associated with the problem solver.* The problem-solving behaviour also depends much on the factors associated with the nature, capacities and many other things inherent in the problem solver. These factors may be outlined as follows:

(a) *The level of previous learning or training.* One can solve a problem easily if it has some connection with one's past experiences or specific training received for the solution of similar problems. Hence the level of proficiency gained through some learning or training of one or the other types of problems, always works as a deciding factor for the problem-solving behaviour of an individual.

(b) *Interest and motivational level of the problem solver.* Interest and motivation are known as the key factors and moving forces behind any activity or behaviour carried out by an individual. It equally applies to one's problem-solving behaviour. The nature of interest and motivation thus should always be regarded as important factors affecting a person's problem-solving behaviour. A person's interest and motivation in terms of seeking the desired goals, motives, satisfaction of needs, etc. induce him to do all that he can to find a solution to his problem.

(c) *Understanding and analysis of the problem.* Every problem needs a proper understanding and careful analysis before attempting to find a solution. However, the problem solver often tend to act in haste and rush to find solutions without understanding what the problem actually is. As an illustration, let us take the following simple problems:

1. Take three oranges from seven oranges. What have you got?
2. A poultry owner had 125 hens; all but 18 died. How many hens were left?

The answers are, of course, three oranges and 18 hens. In case you did not get them right, think what went wrong with your attempt. The basic reason will certainly be found that you did not care to completely understand and analyse the problem. A person, who does not care for an appropriate analysis of his problem, is bound to suffer in finding a solution to his problem. It is through the analysis of the problem that he knows what he needs essentially to solve the problem. What is the problem? What is its nature? What is given in the problem? What have we got to find out in the problem? In how many ways is it similar to other problems, solved in the past? What type of help is available for finding solution to the problem? In this way, there are many queries, the answers for which can only be found through a systematic and careful analysis of the problem. The individuals who care and know the techniques of proper analysis of a problem, thus may always get success in solving their problem, in comparison to others who either do not care or do not know the proper way of analysing a given problem.

(d) *Mental set.* Our problem-solving behaviour depends much on a particular type of mental set, woven around the ways and means of finding solutions to one or the other types of problems. It is our previous learning and experiences that go deep into our nature, giving birth to a certain fixed type of problem-solving behaviour. As a result we always try to solve a given problem in the light of a mental picture of its solution already set in our mind. Mental set may be regarded as a way of perceiving things in the light of their mental images already fixed in our mind based on past experiences. Consequently, influenced by our mental set, we try to solve a problem. Let us illustrate the effect of the mental set on problem-solving behaviour through an already referred illustration, in which you were asked "to take three oranges from seven oranges" and find the balance left. Obviously the correct answer was three but you arrived at the wrong answer, four. This is certainly because of the strong impact of your mental set up which forces you to make use of the process of mathematical addition or subtraction in finding out solution to such problems. Your mind is already set to work in a particular direction for finding out a solution to such similar computational problems by adding or subtracting. For finding out "the balance in hand" you just work according to the set direction—you find the result by subtraction and so end up with a wrong answer.

(e) *Functional fixedness.* Functional fixedness refers to our rigidity or fixedness in our functions or ways of behaving. As a result, we always tend to provide similar responses to the same stimuli. We have a fixed pattern of problem-solving behaviour to find solution for a particular type of problem. We cannot think of any alternative or a new solution other than habitually adopted by us for their solution. It may work somehow when the problems faced are quite similar to those faced earlier. However, the results are not always as desirable or satisfactory as there should be. Mere repetition or reproduction of such problem-solving behaviour cannot help us devise more suitable, economical and rewarding ways of problem solving. Moreover, in many situations, we may face a lot of difficulties and obstacles in finding solutions to the problems which are somewhat new or different from the old ones in some or other aspects (no matter how minutely it may be). Our functional fixedness does not allow us to experiment something new to find solutions to these problems and as a result, we are bound to waste our energy, time and resources. We cannot just see a new perspective for solutions to the problems which are more simple, practicable and rewarding only on account of the fixedness or rigidity of our problem-solving behaviour. One who can overcome such functional fixedness in such a situation, is sure to win the race. He may find a most appropriate solution of the given problem by adopting new ways and means by giving his rigidity or fixedness of the problem-solving behaviour. Hence we must always be careful about the obstruction mechanism of the rigidity or fixedness of our problem-solving behaviour and should always follow a dynamic and flexible approach for developing originality, creativity and inventiveness in our problem-solving behaviour.

(f) *Mental and physical states of the problem solver.* The mental and physical states of an individual at the time of solving a problem definitely exercise their favourable or unfavourable impact over the processes and products of his problem-solving behaviour. If he is alert, attentive, capable and active in using his physical and mental abilities to find a solution to the problem, he is sure to proceed properly on the path of problem solving. Otherwise, there will be a lot of difficulties in getting success in the task of problem solving. Take the case of anxiety, i.e. state of anxiousness. It may help the individual in his problem-solving task as an energiser of his otherwise motivated behaviour if it remains within his control. But if it exceeds and reaches out of control, it may prove a great obstacle in the path of problem-solving. The same is true with emotions. A person can cross many hurdles in the path of his problem solving with favourable emotions if he exercises desirable control over their manifestations and reactions. Untimely emotions at a dispropor-tionate or uncontrolled amount may cost dearly to an individual in his task of problem-solving. The other important cognitive factors that affect both the processes and products of a person's problem-solving behaviour may be named as (i) the ability to think and reason, (ii) the nature of attention and concentration and (iii) the power of retention and retrieval. One may get success or failure in his task of problem-solving depending upon the quality and nature of these cognitive factors. If one can think and reason well, pay proper sustained attention to his task, utilize his past learning and experiences on the basis of his good memory, he is sure to get success in his problem-solving task. Contrarily, with lack of attention, reproduction and ability to think and reason, he may struggle with his problem without any commendable results. In this way, not only the mental state but also the physical state of one's well-being affects his problem solving behaviour favourably or adversely. When one is suffering from headache, stomachache or any other problems in his body or feeling uncomfortable on account of the seating arrangement, light, ventilation, noise and extremes of weather and climatic conditions, then how can we expect him to have a control over his problem-solving behaviour? In such unfavourable physical states, his problem-solving ability is likely to be affected adversely resulting in failure in the task of problem-solving.

(g) *The time spent on solving the problem.* Every problem needs its own time for its solution. Hence the minimum desired time should be spent in its solution depending upon its nature and complexity, from the view-point of the problem solver. However, in case one is in a haste or does not care to give the required time to find a solution to his problem, he may not get the desired success.

The utilization of time in problem solving may also be considered from another angle. If we take some rest or get ourselves engaged in some recreational or other work activities, that period may also be counted as spent, although unconsciously, finding solution to the problem. This time-related phenomenon is named as 'incubation' in the language of psychology. It happens many times with us that we do not find a solution to our problem despite our constant efforts and struggling with it. What do we do then? We suspend or give up our attempts. As an alternative, we may take some rest, go for sleep, engage ourselves in some recreational or work activities and thus keep away physically from our problem. However, during this time, we mentally do not go away from our problem. Our unconscious mind may continuously work towards the solution of the problem and finally, we do arrive at it. The solution so found, through our unconscious attempts, is said to be the consequence of the mechanism of incubation.

In conclusion, we can say that there are many factors or things lying within the problem. However, much depends on the abilities and capacities of the problem solver including his interests, attitudes, level of aspiration and motivation, determination and will power to find a solution to his problem. If a person is set to reach his goal, he is bound to get success in spite of heavy odds and barriers in the path of his problem-solving.

Useful Strategies for Effective Problem-solving

The task of problem solving depends to a great extent upon the nature of the problem, the means and materials available for its solution and the ability and competency of the problem solver. However, psychologists and educationists, as a result of their extensive research in the field of problem-solving, have recommended a few special strategies and tactics that can help a lot in finding the ways of solving the problem in quite an economical and effective way. Let us have a look into the mechanism of a few useful devices.

1. *Algorithms.* Algorithm may be defined as a strategy for arriving at a solution. The method exhausts every possible step to land up at the correct solution. It is in fact a set of rules which, when followed, must lead to a solution because it is systematically applied in a specific order, to all possibilities and their outcomes. Let us illustrate the use of algorithm as a strategy to solve a problem.

Problem. There is an anagram UBC. You have to build up a meaningful word using the three letters U, B and C of this given anagram.

Solution. Using algorithms, we will put the three letters U, B and C in every possible combinations like, C B U, B U C, B C U, U C B until the correct order C U B (a meaningful word) is found.

However, the use and application of algorithm needs a very cautious approach. It has its own shortcomings and limitations like below:

(a) Algorithms cannot be applied to every situation as they do not exist for many problems.

(b) These are quite expensive in terms of the time and energy as one has to test all the available alternatives and hypotheses for arriving at the final solution. It may make the problem solver tired, bored, or fatigued, before reaching the final stage of the solution.

(c) Their use also may prove impracticable except for a few simple problems.

2. Heuristics. In comparison to algorithms, heuristics, as a strategy of problem-solving, are more economical in terms of time and labour. Their use and application are also simpler and less demanding. Heuristics represent such problem-solving strategies in which we make use of some mental short cuts or rules of thumb for restructuring a problem in a certain way to arrive at a quick solution.

The weakness of these heuristics lies in the fact that, there is no guarantee of finding the correct solution of the desired problem. One may or may not arrive at it with short cuts. The application is simple, less time consuming, least tiring or boring to the individual but the correctness of the solution is not so sure as in the use of algorithms. The use of algorithms, however, tiresome, lengthy and time consuming may be, always results in a hundred percent guarantee of correctness of the arrived solution. However, as a quick and fast means of finding a solution to the problems, the use of heuristics is quite commendable. The most commonly used heuristics as a problem-solving strategy, may be named as under:

- Sub-goal analysis
- Means-end analysis
- Working backward
- Using an analogy.

Let us discuss their application in problem solving one by one.

(i) *Sub-goal analysis.* In this strategy, the complex goal or target reached to find solution to a problem, is divided into easily attainable sub-goals. In other words, a complex problem is reduced to a series (or hierarchy) of smaller, more easily solvable problems. It is similar to covering a long, tedious and difficult journey by dividing it into short lengths instead of feeling tired trying to cover it at a single stretch.

(ii) *Means-end analysis.* While solving a problem, it is always better to have a proper analysis of the nature of the problem in perfect coordination with the means, materials and resources in our hand. Where we have to reach? What needs to be done? What type of solution the problem needs?—All these issues should be carefully analysed in relation to the means available for coping with these issues.

The means-end analysis strategy stands for:

(a) The identification of the difference between the current state and the one that is desired in relation to the nature of the problem and then (b) taking action to reduce this difference for arriving at the solution.

(iii) *Working backward.* Starting with the desired result (what is to be found out or aimed at) and trying to work backwards until the intial state is attained. For example, suppose we have a problem in geometry: to prove that the sum of the three angles of a triangle is equal to two right angles.

Here, while making use of 'working backward strategy' we will start from the end, the concluded result and then may proceed as under:

1. The three angles of a triangle are equal to two right angles.

2. Which one of the angles is equal to two right angles? Surely it is called a straight angle.
3. How can we demonstrate the three angles of a triangle through a straight angle?
4. Which one of three sides of the given triangle is to be extended for the construction of a straight angle?
5. How can this straight angle be proved as equal to the sum of three angles of the given triangle?

In this way, we can utilize such backward chaining for discovering the proof of a given geometrical theorem.

Similarly, we can utilize this working backward strategy in finding solutions to problems related to other areas of knowledge. Suppose, you have forgotten where you kept the key of a room, you can find its solution by working backward. You are at present here but where were you prior to your arrival at the present place, and thinking in retrospect about the place of your presence or working, you may certainly remember where you misplaced your keys. Let us further substantiate this by employing it in finding a solution to the following algebraic problem.

"Divide 100 into such four parts, that is (i) one part to be multiplied by four, (ii) second part to be divided by four, (iii) in the third we add four and (iv) from fourth subtract four—the results in all the four cases remain the same." For a solution to such problems, we always start from the end by following the sequence as under:

1. Suppose in the end we get x in all the four cases.
2. Here, working backward, the processes will be reversed and we will consequently rearrange the sign of the actual algebraic operation, i.e. × by ÷, ÷ by ×, + by − and − by + and in this way our final algebraic equation will be in the following form:

$$\left(\frac{x}{4}\right) + (4x) + (x - 4) + (x + 4) = 100$$

or $x + 16x + 4x + 4x = 400 - 16 + 16 = 400$

or $25x = 400$

or $x = 16$

In this way, we can divide 100 into the parts

$\left(\frac{16}{4}\right)$, (16×4), $(16 - 4)$, $(16 + 4)$, i.e.

4, 64, 12, 20 the sum of which is equal to the given figure 100.

- *Using an analogy.* In this strategy a person makes use of his own experiences, training and practice work carried out to find a solution for similar problems. Here, while solving a particular problem, one formulates or hypothesizes another problem, similar to that in hand, but with a known solution; and this known solution is then used to devise a solution for the current problem. We make use of this strategy to find a solution to any new problem faced by us. Every textbook of mathematics duly emphasizes this strategy. To begin with any topic, it provides certain problems with their proper solution as illustrations or examples for understanding the ways to solve these problems. Then it provides a number of similar problems as practice work. Students then try to adopt the analogy strategy for solution to these practice work problems. They simply search for the analogy between the problems at hand and the solved problem. The previous experience gained through understanding of the solved examples helps them to find out a solution for the current problem.

SUMMARY

Thinking refers to a pattern of behaviour in which we make use of internal representations of things and events for the solution of problems.

The important theories for understanding the nature, development, and mechanism of thinking are, the behaviourist's learning theory, Gestalt and holistic theory, Piaget's developmental theory, Sullivan's basic modes theory, Bruner's theory of cognitive development, the information processing theory and the psychoanalytical theory. Each of these theories explains the human thought processes according to the views held by their propounders, yet none of them has succeeded in giving a comprehensive and clear picture.

Tools employed in the process of thinking generally consist of *images* (mind pictures of the stimuli experienced), *concepts* (categories for classifying stimuli), *symbols* and signs (like +, and badges or flags), and *language*. In addition to these, thinking in one way or the other shows evidence of the involvement of a slight incipient movement of groups of our *muscles* and is guided and operated by the higher cognitive areas of the brain. Moreover, our thinking is largely affected through inducement by *sets*—habit or the way we habitually perceive certain situations. These induced sets are quite often the results of our interests, directions and purposes. This set induction may result in a kind of rigidity in our thinking behaviour.

What we consider as genuine thinking may be classified into certain types like, perceptual or *concrete thinking, conceptual thinking, reflective thinking, critical thinking*, and *creative thinking*. However, we can also add one more category in the form of *associative thinking*, including day-dreaming, fantasy and delusions, which is non-directed and without goals.

Measures for developing effective and correct thinking include one's adequacy of knowledge and experiences, motivation and definiteness of aim, adequate freedom and flexibility, incubation, intelligence and wisdom, proper development of concept and language and adequacy of reasoning process.

Reasoning is referred to as specialized thinking involving well-organised systematic steps for the mental exploration of a cause-and-effect relationship for solution of a problem. Reasoning is of two types—*inductive* and *deductive*—while in inductive reasoning we make use of many experiences and examples for arriving at a generalized principle or conclusion, in deductive reasoning we start by completely agreeing with some deduced results or principles and try to apply these to particular cases.

Problem-solving is a deliberate and serious act, involves the use of some novel methods, higher thinking and systematic planned steps for the realisation of set goals. The systematic steps involved in effective problem-solving may be identified as problem awareness, problem understanding, collection of relevant information, formulation of hypotheses and selection of a proper solution.

One's problem-solving behaviour, however, depends upon a number of factors broadly classified in two categories—factors inherent in the nature of the problem and factors associated with the problem solver like his level of previous learning, interest and motivation, way of solving the problem, mind set, functional fixedness, mental and physical status and the time spent by him in the problem-solving. We can adopt some useful strategies for effective problem solving in the shape of algorithms (strategy for generating a solution by exhausting every possible answer for ending up with the correct solution) and heuristics (rule of thumb for arriving at a quick solution) like sub-goal analysis, means-end analysis, working backward and using an analogy etc.

REFERENCES

Boring, E.C., Langfield, H.S. and Weld, H.P. (Eds.), *Foundation of Psychology*, New York: John Wiley, 1961, p. 199.

Bourne, L.E., Dominowski R.L. and Loftus, E.F., *Cognitive Processes*, Englewood Cliffs, N.J.: Prentice-Hall, 1979.

Bruner, J.S., Goodnow, J.J. and Austina, G.A., *A Study of Thinking*, New York: John Wiley, 1956.

Bransford, J.D. and Stein, B.S., *The Ideal Problem Solver: A guide for improving thinking, learning and creativity*, New York: Freeman, 1984.

Fantino, E. and Reynolds, G., *Introduction to Contemporary Psychology*, San Francisco: W.H. Freeman & Co., 1975, p. 166.

Garrett, H.E., *General Psychology*, New Delhi: Eurasia Publishing House, 1968, pp. 353, 378.

Gates, A.I., *Elementary Psychology*, New York: Macmillan, 1947, p. 428.

Gates, A.I. et al., *Educational Psychology*, New York: Macmillan, 1946.

Gilmer, B. Vonhaller, *Psychology* (International ed.), New York: Harper, 1970, p. 326.

Mohsin, S.M., *Elementary Psychology*, Calcutta: Asia Publishing House, 1967, p. 117.

Munn, N.L., *An Introduction to Psychology*, New Delhi: Oxford & IBH, 1967, p. 339.

Roediger, H.L., Rushton, J.P. et al., *Psychology* (2nd ed.), Boston: Little Brown & Company, 1987, pp. 288–289.

Ross, J.S., *Ground Work of Educational Psychology*, London: George G. Harrap & Co., 1951, pp. 196–197.

Skinner, B.F., *Verbal Behaviour,* New York: Appelton-Century-Crofts, 1957.

Skinner, C.E. (Ed.), *Essentials of Educational Psychology,* Englewood Cliffs, New Jersey: Prentice-Hall, 1968, pp. 529, 539.

Valentine, C.W., *Psychology and its Bearing on Education*, London: The English Language Book Society & Methuen, 1965, p. 278.

Woodworth, R.S., *Psychology*, London: Methuen, 1945, p. 523.

Woodworth, R.S. and Marquis, D.G., *Psychology* (5th ed.), New York: Henry Holt & Co., 1948, p. 623.

SUGGESTED READINGS

Bartlett, F., *Thinking*, New York: Basic Books, 1958.

Davis, G.A., *Psychology of Problem Solving*, New York: Basic Books, 1973.

Lindsay, P.H. and Norman, D.A., *Human Information Processing*, New York: Academic Press, 1972.

Piaget, J., *The Origins of Intelligence in Children*, London: Routledge & Kegan Paul, 1953.

Vinacke, W.E., *The Psychology of Thinking* (2nd ed.), New York: McGraw-Hill, 1974.

Wertheimer, M., *Productive Thinking* (Enlarged ed.), New York: Harper & Row, 1959.

Solutions to problems on pages 368–69

Solution to Classification problem	:	(b)	Lion
Solution to Completion problems	:	(i)	23, 36, 27, 37, 31, 38
		(ii)	69, 55, 75, 68, 58
Solution to Analogy problems	:	(i)	Sour
		(ii)	9
		(iii)	15

Chapter 20

Aptitude

MEANING AND NATURE OF APTITUDE

It is an observable fact that people differ from one another and within themselves in their performance in one or the other field of human activity such as leadership, music, art, mechanical work, teaching etc. Ramesh joins a commercial institute to learn typing and short-hand. He makes rapid progresses and in due course gets a diploma. Later on, when he is offered a steno-typist's job he carries it out satisfactorily. Suresh, although in no way inferior to Ramesh in general intelligence, also takes admission in this institute, progresses very slowly and even after getting the diploma proves to be an inefficient typist and stenographer. Similarly Radha profits from musical training while Sunita having almost the same intelligence as Radha under similar circumstances, makes little or no progress.

In many spheres of everyday life we come across individuals who excel over others, under similar conditions, in acquiring certain knowledge or skills and prove more suitable and efficient than their peers in certain specific fields. Such persons are said to possess a certain specific ability or aptitude in addition to intellectual abilities or intelligence, which helps them to achieve success in some specific occupations or activities.

Therefore, aptitude may be described as a special ability or specific capacity distinct from the general intellectual ability which helps an individual to acquire the required degree of proficiency or achievement in a specific field. However, to obtain a clear understanding of the term aptitude let us consider some of the definitions given by different scholars:

Bingham (1937):

> Aptitude refers to those qualities characterizing a person's way of behaviour which serve to indicate how well he can learn to meet and solve a certain specified kinds of problem.

Traxler (1957):

> Aptitude is a condition, a quality or a set of qualities in an individual which is indicative of the probable extent to which he will be able to acquire under suitable training, some knowledge, skill or composite of knowledge, understanding and skill, such as ability to contribute to art or music, mechanical ability, mathematical ability or ability to read and speak a foreign language.

Freeman (1971):

> An aptitude is a combination of characteristics indicative of an individual's capacity to acquire (with training) some specific knowledge, skill, or set of organized responses, such as the ability to speak a language, to become a musician, to do mechanical work.

All these definitions reveal the predictive nature of aptitudes. When we say that Ram or Radha has an aptitude for teaching we mean that they have the capacity or ability to acquire proficiency in teaching under appropriate conditions.

Similarly, when we say Mohan has an aptitude for music we mean that his present condition or ability reveals that if he were to learn music he would be successful. The knowledge of an individual's aptitude thus helps us to predict his future success in a particular field of activity, with appropriate training or experience.

Like so many other personality traits or characteristics, it is difficult to say whether a particular aptitude is an absolute product of heredity or of environment. Certain aspects of an aptitude may be inborn. For example, a person showing an aptitude for singing may have been born with a musical voice and a person showing aptitude for type-writing or watch repairing may have sensitive and dexterous hands. But this is one side of the picture. It is also equally possible that the musical person's aptitude may be the result of his living in the company of good musicians or the typist's aptitude may be the creation of his father or mother who also happens to be a typist.

It is safer to conclude, therefore, that the aptitude of an individual at a particular moment is in all probability, dependent upon heredity and environment both.

How Aptitude Differs from Ability and Achievement

Aptitude and present ability do not mean the same thing. A person may have no present ability to drive a car but may have an aptitude for driving—which means that his chances of being a successful driver are good provided he receives the proper training. Thus, while aptitude has a future reference and tries to predict the degree of attainment or success of an individual in an area or activity after adequate training, ability concerns itself only with the present condition—the potentiality or capability which one possesses at the present moment regardless of the past and does not try to make any assessment of one's future success or failure.

Contrary to the predictive nature of aptitude and the contemporary nature of ability, achievement is past-oriented, reflects on the past and indicates what an individual has learned or acquired in a particular field.

It does not follow, however, that we can forecast an individual's future accomplishment in any area of activity with the help of aptitude measurement. Aptitude tests, in all their forms, measure only the present ability or capacity of an individual on which a prediction of his future attainments may be based.

Difference between Intelligence and Aptitudes

The existing intelligence tests gauge the general mental ability of an individual while aptitude tests as we have seen, are concerned with specific abilities. Therefore, whereas with the knowledge of intelligence of an individual we can predict his success in a number of situations involving mental function or activity, the knowledge of aptitudes, on the other hand, acquaints us with the specific abilities and capacities of an individual to succeed in a particular field of activity. Therefore, in predicting his achievement in some specific job, training, course or specialized instruction we need to know more about his aptitudes or specific abilities rather than his intelligence or general ability.

Difference between Aptitude and Interest

In order to succeed in a given activity, a person must have both aptitude for the activity and interest in it. This does not mean that interest and aptitude are one and the same thing. A person may be interested in a particular activity, job or training but may not have the aptitude for it. In such cases, the interest shown in a particular occupation or course of study is often not the result of personal aptitude but of some other outside influence or reason such as the wishes of parents, the probability of getting a particular appointment or job, stipend or other financial help or the prestige associated with the work. Similarly, a person having long and dexterous fingers who makes a good showing on a mechanical aptitude test may have little or no interest in becoming a watch-maker.

A guidance or selection programme must, therefore, give due weightage to the measure of aptitude as well as of interest. Both are essential for the success of an individual in a given activity, job or course of instruction.

Aptitude Testing

Aptitude tests measure or assess the degree or level of one's special bent or flair much the same way as intelligence tests are employed for measuring one's intelligence. They are chiefly used to estimate the extent to which an individual would profit from a specific course or training, or to predict the quality of his or her achievement in a given situation. For example, a mechanical aptitude test would be able to determine whether an individual would do well as a mechanic after appropriate training and with the right motivation.

Two types (based on the specific purpose served) of aptitude tests are usually employed. These are, specialized aptitude tests and general aptitude tests.

Specialized Aptitude Tests

These aptitude tests have been devised to measure the aptitudes of individuals in various specific fields or activities. Generally, these tests can be divided into the following sub-types according to the specific aptitude tested by them:

1. Mechanical aptitude tests
2. Musical aptitude tests
3. Art judgement tests
4. Professional aptitudes tests, i.e. tests to measure the aptitude for professions like teaching, clerical duties, medicine, law, engineering, salesmanship, research etc.

5. Scholastic aptitude tests, i.e. tests to measure the aptitudes for different courses of instruction.

Let us now discuss these aptitude tests in detail.

Mechanical aptitude tests. Like intelligence, mechanical aptitude is also made up of many components. While explaining its meaning, Freeman (1971) writes:

> The capacity designed by the term 'mechanical aptitude' is not a single, unitary function. It is a combination of sensory and motor capacities plus perception of spatial relations, the capacity to acquire information about mechanical matters and the capacity to comprehend mechanical relationships.

The purpose of mechanical aptitude tests is to test the above-mentioned abilities and capacities of an individual in order to assess his chances of success in mechanical pursuits.

Some well-known mechanical aptitude tests are:

1. Minnesota mechanical assembly test.
2. Minnesota spatial relations test.
3. The revised minnesota power form board (1948).
4. Stenguist mechanical aptitude tests (Parts I & II).
5. L.J.O. Rourke's Mechanical Aptitude tests (Parts I & II).
6. Bennet tests of mechanical comprehension.
7. S.R.A. mechanical aptitude test.
8. Mechanical aptitude test battery by Dr. A.N. Sharma (published by National Psychological Corporation, Agra).
9. A battery of mechanical aptitude tests (Hindi) prepared by *Mano-Vigyanshala,* Allahabad.

These tests usually include the following items:

1. Asking the subject to put together the parts of mechanical devices.
2. Asking him to replace cut-outs of various shapes in corresponding spaces on a board.
3. Solving geometrical problems.
4. Questions concerning the basic information about tools and their uses.
5. Questions relating to the comprehension of physical and mechanical principles.

For instance, the Bennet mechanical comprehension test Form AA has 60 items in pictorial form. They present mechanical problems arranged in order of difficulty and involve comprehension of mechanical principles found in ordinary situations. As an example, two items of this test are shown below (Figure 20.1 and Figure 20.2).

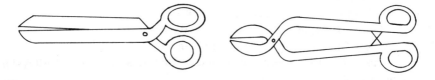

Figure 20.1   Which shear would be better for cutting metal?

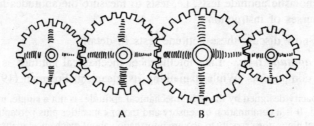

Figure 20.2   Which gear will make the most turns per minute?

Clerical aptitude tests.   Like the mechanical the clerical aptitude is also a composite function. According to Bingham, it involves several specific abilities namely,

- *Perceptual ability.*   The ability to register words and numbers with speed and accuracy.

- *Intellectual ability.*   The ability to grasp the meaning of words and symbols.

- *Motor ability.*   The ability to use various types of machines and tools like a typewriter, duplicator, cyclostyle machine, etc.

Some of the popular clerical aptitude tests are:

1. Detroit clerical aptitude examination.
2. Minnesota vocational test for clerical workers.
3. The clerical ability test prepared by the Department of Psychology University of Mysore, Mysore.
4. Clerical aptitude test battery (English and Hindi), Bureau of Educational and Vocational Guidance, Patna (Bihar).
5. Test of clerical aptitude prepared by the Parsee *Panchayat* Guidance Bureau, 209, Hornby Road, Bombay-400001.

Specimen item from a clerical aptitude test is as follows:

Samples of correctly matched pairs of numbers.
    79542   79542
    5794367   5794367
Samples of correctly matched pairs of names.
    John C. Linder   John C. Linder
    Investors Syndicate   Investors Syndicate
Now try the samples below:
    66273894   – 66273284
    527384578   – 527384578
    New York World   – New York World
    Cargil Grain Co.   – Cargal Grain Co.
    This is a test for speed and accuracy. Work as far as you can without making mistakes.
    Do not turn the page until you are told to begin.

(Reproduced from General Psychological test by H.E. Garrett, 1968, p. 477).

Musical aptitude tests. These tests have been devised for discovering musical talent. One of the important musical aptitude tests is described below:

Seashore measure of musical talent. It gives consideration to the following musical components:

- discrimination of pitch;
- discrimination of intensity of loudness;
- determination of time interval;
- discrimination of timbre;
- judgement of rhythm;
- tonal memory.

The test items in this battery are presented on phonograph records. The subject sits down, listens and attempts to discriminate. He is required to mark his responses on an answer form supplied to him by the examiner. The instructions in these tests are of the following nature:

> You will hear two tones which differ in pitch. You are to judge whether the second is higher or lower than the first. If the second is higher, record H, if lower, record L.

Aptitude for graphic art. These tests are devised to discover the talent for graphic art. Two important tests of this nature are:

- The Meier art judgement test.
- Horne art aptitude inventory.

In the Meier art judgement test there are 100 pairs of representational pictures in black and white. Figure 20.3 shows one such pair.

In this pair the subject is required to select the original and aesthetically superior work on the basis of the shapes of the bowls

Figure 20.3 Graphic art aptitude testing.

One item of each pair is an acknowledged art masterpiece while the other is a slight distortion of the original. It is usually altered in such a way that it violates some important principle of art. The examinees are informed regarding which aspect has been altered and are asked to choose from each pair the one that is better, more pleasing, more artistic, and aesthetically more satisfying. For example, in the above illustration, the examinees are required to select the original and aesthetically superior work on the basis of the shapes of the bowls. The number of correct responses is taken as a measure of the subjects judgement or aptitude for graphic art.

Another important test of measuring aptitude for graphic art is the Horn art aptitude inventory. It requires the subject to produce sketches from given patterns of lines and figures. The created sketches of the subject are then evaluated against the standard given by the author of the test.

Tests of scholastic and professional aptitudes. Many aptitude tests have been designed for the selection of students for admission to specific courses or professions like engineering, medicine, law, business management, teaching etc. Some of these aptitude tests are:

1. The American council of education scholastic aptitude test (ACE).
2. Scholastic aptitude test (SAT) developed in U.S.A.
3. Stanford scientific aptitude test by D.L. Zyve.
4. Science aptitude test (after Higher Sec. stage); N.I.E. Delhi.
5. Moss scholastic aptitude test for medical students.
6. Ferguson and Stoddard's law aptitude examination.
7. Tale legal aptitude test.
8. Pre-engineering ability test (Education Testing Service, U.S.A.).
9. Minnesota engineering analogical test.
10. Coxe-Orleans prognosis test of teaching ability.
11. Teaching aptitude test by Jai Prakash and R.P. Shrivastav, University of Saugar (M.P.).
12. Shah's teaching aptitude test.
13. Teaching aptitude test by Moss, F.A. & Others, George Washington University Press.
14. Teaching aptitude test battery (Hindi) by Dr. R.P. Singh & S.N. Sharma (published by National Psychological Corporation, Agra).

General Aptitude Tests

Instead of employing specialized aptitude tests for measuring specific aptitudes, the present trend is to use multiple aptitude test batteries to assess the suitability of persons for different professions on the basis of scores in the relevant aptitude tests in the battery.

Like intelligence tests, multiple aptitude batteries measure a number of abilities, but instead of a total score, they provide a suitable instrument for making intra-individual analyses through sectional scores. The General Aptitude Test Battery (GATB) and the Differential Aptitude Test (DAT) are two examples of such tests.

GATB, developed by the Employment Service Bureau of USA, contains 12 tests. Eight of these are paper-pencil tests for name comparison, computation, vocabulary, arithmetic, reasoning, form matching, test matching, and three-dimensional space. The other four require the use of simple equipment in the shape of moveable pegs on a board, assembling and disassembling rivets and washers. From the scores obtained by the subject, the experimenter is able to draw inferences about the nine aptitude factors: intelligence, verbal aptitude, numerical aptitude, spatial aptitude, form perception, clerical perception, motor coordination, finger dexterity and manual dexterity. The GATB has proved to be one of the most successful multiple aptitude batteries particularly for the purposes of job classification.

The DAT, developed by U.S. Psychological Corporation, has been adapted in Hindi for use in India by S.M. Ojha*. It is available in two forms. It includes tests for verbal reasoning, numerical ability, abstract reasoning, spatial relation, mechanical reasoning, clerical speed and accuracy and two tests for language: one for spelling and the other for grammar. DAT has proved very successful in predicting academic success and has been found specially useful for providing educational and vocational guidance to secondary school children.

The other notable multiple aptitude batteries commonly used for testing aptitudes are the comprehensive ability battery (1977) developed by Sheridian Psychological Services USA and the Guilford-Zimmerman aptitude survey (1956).

Utility of Aptitude Tests

Aptitude tests have wide areas of application. Firstly, they are the back-bone of the guidance services. The results of these tests enable us to locate with a reasonable degree of certainty, the fields of activity in which an individual would be most likely to be successful. Therefore, these tests are found to be very useful for guiding the youngsters in the selection of appropriate courses of instruction, fields of activity and vocations.

These tests can also be used for educational and vocational selection. They help in the systematic selection of suitable candidates for the various educational and professional courses as well as for specialized jobs as Munn (1967) puts it:

> chief value of aptitude testing is, in fact, that it enables us to pick out from those who do not yet have the ability to perform certain skills those who, with a reasonable amount of training, will be most likely to acquire the skills in question and acquire them to a desirable level of proficiency.

Aptitude tests thus properly anticipate the future potentialities or capacities of an individual (irrespective of whether he possesses those future capacities before the training or not) and thereby help us in selecting individuals who are best fitted for a particular profession and courses of instruction or those who are likely to benefit most from the pre-professional training or experiences.

It is clear then, that any purposeful guidance and counselling programme or entrance examination to specialized academic and professional courses or selection procedures for specialized jobs should give due importance to aptitude testing. Aptitude testing, combined with the other information received through interest inventory, personality tests, intelligence tests and cumulative record etc.,

---

*Ojha, S.M., The DAT (Hindi adaptation), National Psychological Corporation, Agra.

can help to a greater extent, in avoiding considerable waste of human as well as material resources by placement of individuals in places and lines of work in which they are most likely to be productive.

SUMMARY

Aptitude may be defined as a specific capacity or special ability, distinct from the general intellectual ability of an individual, indicative of his probable success in a particular field after receiving appropriate opportunity for learning or training. Like so many other personality traits, aptitudes have been adjudged to be the product of both heredity and environment.

Aptitude differs from ability and achievement in that it is forward looking in nature, i.e. it gives an indication of the future success of an individual whereas ability limits itself to the present performance of an individual. Achievement, with its past-oriented nature, merely indicates what an individual has learned or acquired.

Aptitude should not be confused with interest. One may show interest in a particular act or job but may or may not have the aptitude for it. The opposite is also true. However, to achieve the desired success in a given task, one must have both, interest as well as aptitude.

Measurement of aptitude is carried out by means of several relevant specific aptitude tests. For example, mechanical aptitudes test measure a person's aptitude for mechanical work; clerical aptitude tests are employed for measuring the aptitude for clerical work; musical aptitude tests like the Seashore measure of musical talent attempt to discover musical talent; the aptitude for graphic art is tested through tests like the Meier art judgement test. Similarly, we have various standardized aptitude tests for the measurement of scholastic and professional aptitudes of individuals for the relevant specific courses or professions like engineering, medicines, law, business management, teaching, etc.

Aptitude tests have a wide range of application. They have proved to be the backbone of all kinds of guidance services and selection programmes as they are very useful for predicting the suitability of individuals for specific jobs and lines of work.

REFERENCES

Bingham, W.V., *Aptitudes and Aptitude Testing*, New York: Harper & Brothers, 1937, p. 21.

Freeman, F.S., *Theory and Practice of Psychological Testing*, Bombay: Oxford & IBH, 1971, pp. 431, 444.

Guilford, J.P. and Zimmerman, W.S., *The Guilford-Zimmerman Aptitude Survey*, New York: McGraw-Hill, 1956.

Meier, C.N., *Meier Art Tests II Aesthetic Perception*, Iowa: University of Iowa, 1963.

Minnesota Clerical Test, New York: Psychological Corporation, 1959.

Munn, N.L., *Introduction to Psychology*, Delhi: Oxford & IBH, 1967, p. 117.

Seashore, C.E., *Seashore Measures of Musical Talents*, New York: Psychological Corporation, 1960.

Sheridian Psychological Services, Orange C.A.: Institute for Personality and Ability Testing, 1977.

Traxler, A.E. *Techniques of Guidance* (rev. ed.), New York: Harper & Brothers, 1957, p. 49.

U.S. Department of Labour, Employment and Training Administration; *Manual, USES General Aptitude Test Battery*, Washington, D.C.: U.S. Govt. Printing Press, 1980.

SUGGESTED READINGS

Anastasi, A., *Psychological Testing*, London: Macmillan, 1968.

Bennet, G.K., et al., *Manual of Differential Aptitude Tests* (5th ed.), New York: Psychological Corporation, 1974.

Hull, C.L., Aptitudes Testing, New York: Yonkers, World Book Co. 1928.

Long, L. and Mehta, P.H., *The First Mental Measurement Handbook of India*, New Delhi: NCERT, 1966.

Chapter 21

Personality

MEANING AND NATURE

The term "personality" is derived from the Latin word *persona*, which was the name given to the masks that actors wore and the characters they portrayed. The meaning of the word personality has changed little since classical times and comments like what does he see in her? She has such a poor personality", or "look at that young man, what a fine personality he has" are quite common. Remarks like this make us believe that personality is a thing or quality that is possessed by all of us and we can paste labels such as fine, good or poor on it on the basis of the physical make-up, manner of walking, talking, dressing and a host of other similar characteristics of individuals. However, this is a very limited view and the psychological concept of personality goes further and deeper than mere appearance or outward behaviour. The question of how best to interpret or define personality has long exercised the minds of psychologists.

Watson (1930), the father of behaviourism, on the basis of his behavioural studies, concluded:

> Personality is the sum of activities that can be discovered by actual observations over a long enough period of time to give reliable information.

In this way he tried to make the word personality synonymous with the consistent behaviour patterns of an individual. This, however, reflected a very narrow meaning of the term personality.

During the same years, Morton Prince (1929) tried to give personality a broader base by accepting the role of both environmental and hereditary factors in constituting what is termed as personality. In his words:

> Personality is the sum total of all the biological innate dispositions, impulses, tendencies, appetites and instincts of the individual and the dispositions and tendencies acquired by experience.

This definition of Morton Prince was criticised on the ground that it does not present an integrated and organizational view of personality. Personality cannot be described through merely summing up the various elements involved in it and if this definition is accepted, it would be like describing a house as a collection of bricks.

The inability of various existing definitions to describe personality in acceptable terms led Allport (1948) to engage in trying to discover some useful definition. After evaluating 49 such definitions, he concluded:

> Personality is a dynamic organization within the individual of those psycho-physical systems that determine his unique adjustment to his environment.

Although Allport tried to give a comprehensive definition of the term personality by recognizing its dynamic nature and organizational aspects and by emphasizing the role it can play in an individual's adjustment to his environment, his definition suffered from some serious defects. In emphasizing the dynamic organization within the individual he seems to view personality as somewhat different from the individual, residing within him, rather than as an integrated unity of mind and body. Personality to him is something put into the individual like water is put into a jug and it takes the shape of the jug. Contemporary psychologists like Cattell (1970), Eysenck (1971) are of the opinion that the true nature of personality cannot be understood by considering only the behavioural or dynamic aspects.

Cattell (1970):

> Personality is that which permits a prediction of what a person will do in a given situation

Eysenck (1971):

> Personality is the more or less stable and enduring organization of a person's character, temperament, intellect and physique, which determine his unique adjustment to the environment.

In Eysenck's definition character signified conative behaviour or will; physique meant bodily configuration and neuroendocrine endowments, temperament stood for affective behaviour based on emotions, and intellect implied the cognitive behaviour or intelligence.

The definition given by Eysenck has very strong points in its favour. *First,* it tries to provide personality with a physiological base and gives a balanced consideration to the role of heredity and environment in building the personality. *Secondly*, it gives a complete picture of human behaviour by involving all of its aspects—conative, cognitive and affective. *Thirdly,* it stresses the need of integration and organisation of the behavioural characteristics. *Finally*, it aims at making personality somewhat measurable and assessable, thus giving it a scientific base. However, on the other hand, it does have some weaknesses also in that human personality cannot be supposed to necessarily possess a physiological base and it cannot be considered to be as static and fixed as advocated by this definition. It is true that personality should be evaluated on the basis of generality of the behaviour but at the same time, changes cannot be denied. The person who is an extrovert may turn into an introvert depending upon so many intervening factors.

The following definition given by S.R. Maddi (1976), an American psychologist in his work, *Personality Theories—A Comparative Analysis*, views personality as an organized and integrated whole of definite characteristics and tendencies within the individual which make him correspond to the persons of his group, society, culture and nation and at the same time maintain the individuality and uniqueness of his personality:

> Personality is the stable set of characteristics and tendencies that determine those commonalities and differences in the psychological behaviour (thoughts, feelings and actions) of people that have continuity in time and that may or may not be

easily understood in terms of the social and biological pressures of the immediate situation alone.

These characteristics and tendencies (inherited as well as acquired) although stable to a large extent are subject to change and modification according to the needs of the time and the environmental situation for making one adjusted to one's self as well as to the environment. The causes of such modification and changes are not necessarily linked with present physical, biological and social situations, and may be connected with the earlier childhood experiences, genetic code and many other unknown factors. Thus, what a person presents in his totality is his personality.

Although this seems to be quite a comprehensive definition, the evolution of an ideal definition capable of explaining the meaning and nature of the term personality in all its aspects calls for further extensive research. In fact, concepts like personality are difficult to explain as they have the identity like sound and electricity etc., the impact of which can be felt but their real nature is always something of a mystery. Something can be known about them by their utility or the description of some of their characteristics and distinguishing features. Let us seek the meaning of the term personality along similar lines.

Distinguishing Features and Characteristics of Personality

The results of various experimental studies and observations have led to the identification of the following characteristics of personality.

1. Personality is something unique and specific. Every one of us is a unique person in oneself. Every one of us has specific characteristics for making adjustments. However, the uniqueness of an individual's personality does not mean that he has nothing to share with others in terms of traits and characteristics of personality. He may have certain characteristics which he may share with others and at the same time many others which are unique to him.

2. Personality exhibits self consciousness as one of its main characteristics. Man is described as a person or as having a personality when the idea of 'self' enters into his consciousness. In this connection Bhatia (1968) writes:

    We do not attribute personality to a dog and even a child cannot be described as a personality because it has only a vague sense of personal identity.

3. "Personality", as stated by Allport (1948):

    It is not only the assumed, the external and the non-essential but also the vital, the internal and the essential.

It includes everything about a person. It is all what a person has about him. Therefore, it includes all the behaviour patterns, i.e. conative, cognitive and affective and covers not only the conscious activities but goes deeper to the semi-conscious and unconscious also.

4. Personality is not just a collection of so many traits or characteristics. For instance, by only counting the bricks, how can we describe the wall

of a house? Actually, personality is more than this: it is an organization of psychophysical systems or some behaviour characteristics and functions as a unified whole. Just as an elephant cannot be described as a pillar only by examining its legs, an individual's personality cannot be judged by only looking at his physical appearance or his sociability. The personality of an individual can be assessed only by going into all the aspects that comprise his totality.

5. Although the personality of an individual remains stable to a large extent, it cannot be said to be static, it is dynamic and continuously in the process of change and modification. As we have said earlier, personality is the 'everything' that a person has about him. It gives him all that is needed for his unique adjustment to his environment. The process of making adjustment is continuous. One has to struggle with the environmental as well as the inner forces throughout one's life. As a result, one has to modify and change one's personality patterns and this makes the nature of personality dynamic.

6. Personality is sometimes subjected to disorganisation and disinte-gration, leading to severe personality disorders on account of factors and conditions like severe anxiety, stress, traumatic experiences, prolonged illness, infections, and damage to the brain and nervous system.

7. Every personality is the product of heredity and environment. Both these contribute significantly towards the development of the child's personality. A child is not born with a personality but develops one as a result of continuous interaction with his environment. Therefore, not only heredity but also factors like constitutional make-up, social and cultural influences as well as experience and training etc. all affect one's personality.

8. Learning and acquisition of experiences contribute towards growth and development of personality. Every personality is the end-product of this process of learning and acquisition.

9. The personality of an individual can be described as well as measured.

10. Personality should not be taken as synonymous with one's character. Character is an ethical concept. It represents a moral estimate of the individual, while personality as a psychological concept is a more comprehensive term which includes character as one of its constituents.

11. Personality may be further distinguished from temperament which can be termed a system of emotional disposition. This system of emotional disposition represents only the affective side of one's personality and so personality must be taken as being much beyond one's temperament.

12. Personality should also be viewed differently from the ego or the individual self. The word ego is generally used for that unified part of one's personality which in ordinary language we call "I". However, as the psychoanalytic view of personality advocated by Freud explains, it is only a small aspect of one's total personality. Personality, therefore, stands for more than what the ego carries.

13. Every person's personality has one more distinguishing feature, that is,

aiming to an end or towards some specific goals. Adler clearly asserts this view and is of the opinion that a man's personality can be judged through a study and interpretation of the goals which he has set for himself and the approaches he makes to the problems he faces in his life.

In view of the foregoing discussion regarding its characteristics and scope, as a practical definition, it may be said that, *personality is a complex blend of a constantly evolving and changing pattern of one's unique behaviour, emerged as a result of one's interaction with one's environment and directed towards some specific ends.*

THEORIES OF PERSONALITY

The search for understanding the meaning and nature of personality would be incomplete if we do not discuss some important theories of personality. These theories in one way or another, try to describe the basic structure and underlying entities or constructs involved in personality along with the processes by which these entities interact. The theories of personality in general can be classified into the following broad categories:

Theories adopting the type approach. The viewpoint of Hippocrates, Kretschmer, Sheldon and Jung belong to this category.

Theories adopting the trait approach. Theories like Allport's theory and Cattell's theory of personality are based on the trait approach.

Theories adopting the type-cum-trait approach. Theories like Eysenck's theory of personality can be put under this category.

Theories adopting the psycho-analytical approach. Theories like psycho-analytic theory of Freud, theory of individual psychology by Adler, analytical psychology of Jung, social relationship theory of Horney and Erickson's theory of psychosocial development may be included in this category.

Theories adopting the humanistic approach. Theories like Carl Roger's self theory and Maslow's self-actualization theory belong to this category.

Theories adopting the learning cpproach. Dollard and Miller's learning theory and Bandura and Walter's theory of social learning can be put into this category.

Let us now briefly discuss the viewpoints propounded in these theories.

Type Approach

Theories adopting the type approach advocate that human personalities can be classified into a few clearly defined types and each person, depending upon his behavioural characteristics, somatic structure, blood types, fluids in the body, or personality traits can be described as belonging to a certain type. Based on such an approach, the physician of ancient India broadly categorized all human beings into three types. This classification was based on the three basic elements of the body, namely *pitt* (bile), *vat* (wind), and *kuf* (mucus). An almost similar approach was followed by the Greek physicians like Hippocrates, one of the disciples of the great philosopher Aristotle. In the years that followed, many more scholars and psychologists tried to divide people into types depending upon their own specific criteria.

Ancient Indians (Ayurvedic) Classification

Even in India, the ancient system of medicine Ayurveda classifies man based on the presence of combination of elements of Nature. Ayurveda, advocates that the entire Universe (living and non-living) is made up of five elements: air, fire, water, earth and ether (space), collectively called "panchamahabhutas". Human body contains these elements as its constituents. However, their lie individual differences in human beings and as such the composition of these elements in the individual's differ. Where some are loaded with the combination of air and ether (space), others may have increased amount of the combinations like water and earth or fire and water. The presence of such combinations of the elements in the human bodies may group them into distinctive body types with a definite pattern of physiological and psychological characteristics depicted as below:

Ayurvedic's Classification of Personality Types

Dominance of the elements in the body	Personality type	Physiological/ somatic characteristics	Personality characteristics
Air & ether (space)	Vata	Slightly built, a little pigeon chested with dull dark hair and eyes, have dry rough and chapped skin, suffer from stiff joints, rheumatic problems and constipation.	Restless with active minds, indecisive and emotionally insecure, poor in memory, tendency towards insomnia depression and night marish dream, good artists and enjoy travelling, solitary and rebellious.
Water & Earth	Kapha	Big boned, often over-weight with a pale, smooth complexion, hairs are lustrous and wavy and eyes are wide and attractive, suffer from sinus problems, lethargy and nausea.	Need a lot of sleep, rational speak and move slowly, calm and loyal, emotionally secure, experience romantic and sentimental dreams.
Fire & Water	Pitta	Average build, have a ruddy complexion or red hair, with moles, freckles or acne, tendency to go grey and bald early in life and often have green or very piercing eyes.	Intense, argumentative and precise with a critical sharp intelligence, make good leaders, at their worst they can be passionately angry, enjoy sports, hunting and politics and have vivid dreams.

Hippocrate's classification. According to Hippocrates the human body consists of four types of humours or fluids—blood, yellow bile, phlegm (mucus), and black bile. The predominance of one of these four types of fluids in one's body gives him unique temperamental characteristics leading to a particular type of personality as summarized in Table 21.1.

Table 21.1   Hippocrates Classification of Personality Types

Dominance of fluid type in the body	Personality type	Temperamental characteristics
Blood	Sanguine	Light-hearted, optimistic, happy, hopeful and accommodating.
Yellow bile	Choleric	Irritable, angry but passionate, and strong with active imagination.
Phlegm (mucus)	Phlegmatic	Cold, calm, slow or sluggish and indifferent.
Black bile	Melancholic	Bad tempered, dejected, sad, depressed, pessimistic, deplorable and self-involved.

Kretschmer's classification.   Kretschmer classified all human beings into certain biological types according to their physical structure and has allotted following definite personality characteristics associated with each physical make-up (Table 21.2).

Table 21.2   Kretschmer's Classification

Personality types	Personality characteristics
Pyknic (having fat bodies)	Sociable, jolly, easy-going and good natured.
Athletic (balanced body)	Energetic, optimistic and adjustable.
Leptosomatic (lean and thin)	Unsociable, reserved, shy, sensitive and pessimistic.

Sheldon's classification.   Sheldon too, like Kretschmer, classified human beings into types according to their physical structures and attached certain temperamental characteristics to them as shown in Table 21.3.

Table 21.3   Sheldon's Classification

Personality types	Somatic description	Personality characteristics
Endomorphic	Person having highly developed viscera but weak somatic structure, (like Kretschmer's athletic type).	Easy-going, sociable and affectionate.
Mesomorphic	Balanced development of viscera and somatic structure, (like Kretschmer's athletic type).	Craving for muscular activity, self-assertive, loves risk and adventure.
Ectomorphic	Weak somatic structure as well as undeveloped viscera, (like Kretschmer's Leptosomatic).	Pessimistic, unsociable, and reserved.

The approach adopted by the above psychologists of classification on the basis of correlation between the structure of the body and personality charac-

Ectomorphy Mesomorphy Endomorphy

Figure 21.1 Sheldon's three basic somato-types.

teristic, is lopsided and somewhat misleading. No such perfect body-mind or body-heart correlation exists as the propagators of these approaches have assumed

Jung's classification. Jung divided all human beings basically into two distinct types—introvert and extrovert—according to their social participation and the interest which they take in social activities. Later on he further sharpened his twofold division by giving sub-types. In this process, he took into consideration the four psychological functions—thinking, feeling, sensation and intuition—in relation to his previous extrovert and introvert types. This division can be diagrammatically represented along with the main characteristics of each sub-type as already described in Chapter 7.

This classification has been criticised on the ground that in general, the different types or classes as suggested by Jung do not exist. On the basis of typical characteristics prescribed for the extrovert and introvert, most of us may belong to both categories at different times and may be called ambivert. This introduces a complication and hence the type approach does not give a clear classification or description of personality.

Trait Approach

In the trait approach the personality is viewed in terms of various traits. In our day-to-day conversation we ascribe traits to our friends and near one's as being honest, shy, aggressive, lazy, dull, dependent etc. Traits may be defined as relatively permanent and relatively consistent general behaviour patterns that an individual exhibits in most situations. These patterns are said to be the basic units of one's personality that can be discovered through observing one's behaviour in a variety of situations. If a person behaves honestly in several situations, his behaviour may be generalized and he may be labelled as honest and honesty is then said to be a behavioural trait of his personality. The psychologists who subscribe to this approach believe that the personality of an individual is but a combination or sum total of these personality or behavioural traits that can be discovered through the continuous and objective observation of his behaviour. Two personality theories namely, Allport's theory and Cattell's theory are said to be the best examples of the trait approach.

Allport's theory.   Gordon W. Allport (1897–1967) was the first theorist who by rejecting the notion of a relatively limited number of personality types adopted the trait approach for the descriptioon of highly individualized personalities.

Traits, according to Allport, are the basic units of personality. Each of us develops a unique set of such organised tendencies termed as traits in the course of our continuous and gradual development. Allport distinguished three types of traits namely, cardinal traits, central traits and secondary traits.

Cardinal traits are the primary traits so dominant is one's personal dispositon that they colour virtually every aspect of one's behaviour and attributes. These traits, if found in an individual, are limited in number to just one or two. For example, if a person has humorousness as a cardinal trait, he will bring a sense of humour into almost all situations irrespective of its actual demands. In fact, such cardinal traits although very few in number, overrule other traits and thus drift the whole personality of the individual along with them.

Central traits represent those few characteristic tendencies which can be ordinarily used to describe a person, e.g., honesty, kindness, submissiveness, etc. According to Allport, for knowing an individual's personality, we need to know only five to ten such central traits.

Secondary traits are not as dominant as the cardinal or central traits. They appear in only a relatively small range of situations and are not considered strong enough to be regarded as integral parts of one's personality.

Cardinal traits are thus central to the description of one's personality. These traits combined with a few central traits form the core of characteristic traits responsible for giving uniqueness to to one's personality. The other remaining traits, not so generalized and consistent may also be found in other people and may thus be categorized as common traits. These traits are the ones we may have in common with other people. Thus the trait theory propounded by Allport emphasized that an individual differs from others but also has common traits with others at least within the limits of cultural norms.

In order to find out how many traits are responsible for defining personality, Allport and one of his colleagues, Odbert (1936) analysed about 18,000 terms taken from a dictionary that could be used by people to describe each other and they finally came up with a total of 4541 psychological traits from describing human behaviour.

In this way, Allport focused on these large number of behavioural traits to describe personality instead of explaining it like other developmental and psychoanalytical theorists. To him personality was the dynamic organisation of all the behavioural traits that an individual possessed and it was that organisation which could be considered responsible for his behaviour in a particular situation.

Allport (1961) showed that traits lead towards the consistency in one's behaviour though this does not mean that trait of personality must be regarded as fixed and stable operating mechanically to the same degree on all occasions. Instances of inconsistency thus do not mean the non-existence of a trait. It is very much there in the behaviour of the person, but for the time being allows itself to be dominated by the demands of the situation. Allport's theory of personality is known not only for its emphasis on traits but also for its stress on concepts like functional autonomy, individualized approach in the study of personality, and the discontinuous nature of the development of personality, etc.

The concept of functional autonomy suggests that functions or means which once served a purpose may attain autonomy at a later stage. Though motives are goal-oriented to begin with, they become functionally autonomous when the goals are achieved. A behaviour that once satisfied some specific need later serves only itself. For example, what originally began as an effort to reduce hunger, pain or anxiety may become a source of pleasure and motivation in its own right. The drinks or intoxicating substances originally taken to reduce pain or anxiety may thus attain autonomy by becoming an end in themselves.

Regarding the method of investigation into behaviour, Allport was not interested in looking at large groups of people and identifying general principles of behaviour (a normative survey or dimensional approach to study personality) but rather in adopting an individual approach known as the idiographic approach. Such an approach demands the study of every individual separately and consequently through his methods of study and findings Allport always emphasized the uniqueness of the individual (having unique traits and unique aspects of personality functioning).

Allport also emphasized another important concept of the discrete and discontinuous nature of the development of personality. In his book "Pattern and Growth in Personality", he mentioned three stages in the growth and development of personality namely, the childhood, adolescence and adulthood personalities. He emphasized that these are not continuous. Personality is not a continuation from childhood to adulthood rather it is a discrete and discontinuous development. The past cannot decide the functions of the present. What matters during childhood is certainly different from the values during adolescence and adulthood and, therefore according to Allport, the adolescent's or adult's functioning is not constrained by his or her past. Only those aspects of the past, which are relevant to the present or for planning the future are thus recollected and utilized by the individual in his behaviour manifestation and development of personality.

In this way, Allport gave a new dimension to the explanation of human behaviour, personality, evolution of the behaviour and aspects of personality by taking traits as the basic units of behaviour. However, his theory has been criticised on the following grounds:

1. The theory does not give clear and specific consideration to a study of the pattern of growth and development from conception till the end of life as done by the other theorists.
2. His belief and assertion that personality is not a continuum between childhood and adulthood holds no ground as one's present cannot be delinked from one's past or future.
3. In the opinion of Pervin (1984), the division of traits into cardinal, central and secondary is somewhat confusing. He devised the idea of uniqueness of one's personality but did little research to establish the existence and utility of specific traits concepts.

Cattell's theory. The most recent advanced theory of personality based on the trait approach has been developed by Cattell (1973), a British-born American researcher. He has defined a trait as a structure of the personality inferred from behaviour in different situations and described four types of traits:

- *Common traits.* The traits found widely distributed in general population like honesty, aggression and cooperation.
- *Unique traits.* Traits unique to a person such as temperamental traits, emotional reactions.
- *Surface traits.* These can be recognised by manifestations of behaviour like curiosity, dependability, tactfulness.
- *Source traits.* These are the underlying structures or sources that determine behaviour such as dominance, submission emotionality, etc.

The theory propagated by Cattell attributes certain specific dimensions to personality so that the human behaviour related to a particular situation, can be predicted. Cattell has adopted factors analysis as a technique for this work. Let us see how this is done.

1. Cattell began by attempting to make a complete list of all possible human behaviours. In 1946, he compiled a list of over 17,000 traits and by eliminating similarities and synonyms reduced the list to 171 dictionary words related with personality and called these trait—elements.

2. His next step was to ascertain how they are related. He found that each trait element has high correlation with some traits and low with others. In this way, he identified some 35 specific groups and called them surface traits.

3. He further analysed these surface traits in terms of their interrelations and eliminated those which were overlapping. The removal of such overlapping gave him the desired basic dimensions which he called source traits, i.e. the real structural influence underlying personality.

4. After obtaining the source traits (which are 16 in number) he tried to use them to predict behaviour employing what is called the specification equation

$$\text{Response} = s_1T_1 + s_2T_2 + s_3T_3 + ..., S_nT_n.$$

The response or behaviour of an individual is thus predicted from the degree to which he exhibits each source trait (T) modified by the importance of the trait for that response (s).

Suppose, for example, that academic performance (AP) is predictable from two source traits namely intelligence (I) and Reading habits (R), then

$$\text{AP} = s_1I + s_2R.$$

Now also suppose that intelligence (I) is more important for this behaviour than reading habits (R) in the ratio of 5 : 3; this may be expressed as:

$$\text{AP} = 5I + 3R$$

Thus, in order to predict the academic performance (AP) of an individual we need to know his scores on intelligence and reading habits.

The 16 basic or source trait dimensions (arrived at through the process of factor analysis) were named as factors. Cattell regarded these factors as the building blocks of personality, i.e. the characteristics in terms of which one's personality can be described and measured.

These 16 basic trait dimensions or factors (the ways in which people may differ) are reproduced below along with explanatory descriptions of the related dimension:

Symbols	Trait Dimensions or Factors		
A	Reserved (detached, critical, aloof, stiff).	v/s	Outgoing (warm-hearted, easy-going, participating).
B	Less intelligence (concrete thinking.	v/s	More intelligent (abstract thinking, bright).
C	Affected by feelings (emotionally less stable, easily up set, changeable).	v/s	Emotionally stable (mature, faces reality, calm).
E	Submissive (mild, easily led, docile, accommodating).	v/s	Dominant (aggressive, stubborn, competitive).
F	Serious (sober, taciturn).	v/s	Happy-go-Lucky (enthusiastic).
G	Expedient (disregards rules).	v/s	Conscientious (persistent, moralistic, staid).
H	Timid (shy, fears threat, sensitive).	v/s	Venturesome (uninhibited, socially bold).
I	Tough-minded (self-reliant, realistic)	v/s	Tender-hearted (sensitive, clinging, over protected).
L	Trusting (accepting conditions).	v/s	Suspicious (hard to fool).
M	Practical (down-to-earth concerns).	v/s	Imaginative (bohemian, absent-minded).
N	Forthright (unpretentious, genuine but socially clumsy).	v/s	Shrewd (socially aware, astute).
O	Self-assured (secure, placid, complacent).	v/s	Apprehensive (self-critical, insecure, worrying, troubled).
Q_1	Conservative (respecting traditional ideas).	v/s	Experimenting (liberal, free-thinking).
Q_2	Group-dependent (a "joiner" and sound follower).	v/s	Self-sufficient (resourceful, prefers own decisions).
Q_3	Uncontrolled (careless of social rules, follows own urges).	v/s	Controlled (socially precise, exercising will power, compulsive).
Q_4	Relaxed (tranquil, unfrustrated, composed).	v/s	Tense (frustrated, drive, overwrought).

Source: Cattell (1973)

Cattell made use of his 16 factors of basic dimensions in the measurement of personality by devising a personality inventory known as Cattell's sixteen personality factors inventory (16 PF) consisting of suitable, multiple choice questions like:

I generally prefer persons who are:

1. somewhat reserved
2. somewhat outgoing
3. moderate

The trait theory of Cattell, thus, tried to describe and predict the behaviour of individuals on the basis of their personality traits (the fundamental building blocks of human personality). Basically, Cattell's work as a whole, involves the identification of basic dimensions of personality (by applying factor analysis techniques to the observable behaviour, i.e. traits) and then developing instruments to measure these dimensions.

However, Cattell's theory, as claimed by some, cannot be said to suggest that traits alone account for behaviour and that other motivational variables concerning a situation have nothing to do with it. In fact, for the prediction and measurement of one's personality, Cattell has taken clearly into account the motivational variables like urges (innate tendencies to react to goals in a specific way), sentiments, attitude states (the individual's moods), and the roles (the way one is presenting oneself) relevant to the situation and thereby his theory enjoys a good standing among the contemporary theories of personality. His theory has given equal importance to the role of both heredity and environment in the growth and development of personality and thus is able to demonstrate strong interaction between biological-genetic factors and the environmental influence for prediction of human behaviour.

Cattell's personality theory is, however, criticised as a trait theory on the grounds of (a) circularity of the trait concept (i.e. first defining trait in terms of observed behaviour and then using it to explain the same behaviour), (b) excessive emphasis on overt behaviour, and (c) projection of a static picture of human functioning. It is also criticised for not making full use of the factor analytical approach to yield higher order factors for identifying fundamental categories or dimensions of personality like the personality types listed by Eysenck.

Type-cum-Trait Approach

This approach tries to synthesize the type and trait approaches. Starting with the trait approach, it yields definite personality types. The Eysenck theory of personality reflects such an approach.

Eysenck's theory of personality.   While Cattell has tried to use the factor analysis technique to give some basic dimensions to personality by enumerating 16 basic traits, H.J. Eysenck, a German-born British psychologist, went a step further in the adopting factor analysis technique by extracting second order factors and grouping traits into definite personality types.

How individual behaviour is organised and acquires the shape of a definite type is revealed by the following illustration (Figure 21.2).

According to Eysenck, there are four levels of behaviour organisation:

1.   At the lowest level are the specific responses. They grow out of particular responses to any single act. Blushing, for example, is a specific response.

2.   Habitual responses form the second level and comprise similar responses of an individual, to similar situations. For instance, (a) the inability to easily strike friendships, or (b) hesitancy in talking to strangers are habitual responses.

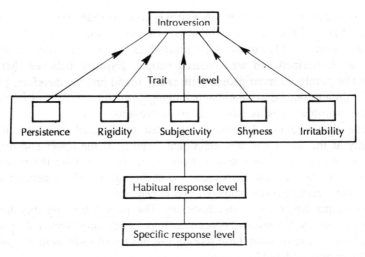

Figure 21.2   Organisation of individual behaviour.

3. At the third level is the organisation of habitual acts into traits. Behaviour acts which have similarities are said to belong to one group and are called traits. In the above example the habitual responses (a) and (b) etc., give birth to a group of traits called 'shyness'.

4. The fourth level is the organisation of these traits into a general type. A type is defined as a group of correlated traits. Traits which are similar in nature give birth to a definite type just as in Figure 21.2 traits like persistence, rigidity, shyness etc., have been grouped into a type termed as *Introversion*.

An ultimate, distinct type is obtained at this final stage. A person, can now be classified as an introvert if he has traits as described at the third level, habits and habit systems as described at the second level and responds specifically as described at the first level.

Eysenck's work has clearly demonstrated that human behaviour and personality can be very well-organised into a hierarchy with specific responses at the bottom and the definite personality type at the top. In fact, in this work, what was described as basic dimension in the form of personality traits by Cattell has been further regrouped yielding fewer dimensions for the description of human behaviour and personality. The three basic dimensions (defined as clusters or groups of correlated traits) derived by Eysenck through his work are:

1. Introversion–extroversion
2. Neuroticism (emotional instability–emotional stability)
3. Psychoticism.

These three basic dimensions refer to definite personality types i.e. introvert, extrovert, neurotic and psychotic. However, the term 'type' as applied by Eysenck stands clearly for a dimension along a scale with a low end and a high end for putting people at various points between the two extremes. While the high end on the first dimension introversion–extroversion, includes the highly extrovert recognized as sociable, outgoing, impulsive, optimistic and jolly people, the lower and typifies the highly introvert recognized as quiet, introspective, reserved, reflective, disciplined and well-ordered people. Eysenck believed that purely extrovert or purely introvert people were rarely found and he, therefore, preferred to use a dimension, i.e. a continuum ranging from introversion to extroversion instead of naming types as introverts and extroverts.

The second major dimension suggested by Eysenck involves emotional instability at the lower end and emotional stability at the upper end describing people as neurotic and not neurotic. Thus, at its lower end are the persons who are moody, touchy, anxious or restless and at the upper end are persons who are stable, calm, carefree, even-tempered and dependable.

The third dimension is psychoticism. The people high on this dimension tend to be solitary, insensitive, egocentric impersonal, impulsive and opposed to accepted social norms while those scoring low are found to be more empathic and less adventurous and bold.

Eysenck has also tried to make use of Cattell's basic dimensions for the measurement of one's personality by developing an appropriate set of questions in the form of two well-known inventories—the Maudsley personality inventory and the Eysenck personality inventory.

The contribution of Eysenck's theory to describing, explaining, and predicting one's behaviour and personality are notable and worthy of praise. He has presented a viable synthesis of the trait and type approaches, given personality a biological-cum-hereditary base, accepted the role of environmental influences in shaping and developing personality and exploded many myths and over-generalizations of psychoanalytical theory. In addition to its close focus on individual differences and principle of behaviour changes, his theory has contributed to the study of criminology, education, aesthetics, genetics, psychopathology and political ideology.

Psychoanalytical Approach

The psychoanalytic approach to personality was first created and advocated by Sigmund Freud (1856–1939) by viewing people as being engaged in a constant struggle to tame their biological urges. He propagated analysis of the psyche or mind by coining many new terms and used psychoanalysis as a method for under-standing behaviour and for treating mental illness. His school of thought is known as the school of psychoanalysis and the approach it adopted for understanding human behaviour and personality is known as the psycho-analytical approach.

Freud's psychoanalytic theory of personality. Freud's theory of personality is built on the premise that the mind is topographical and dynamic; there are provinces or divisions which are always moving and interrelated. The human mind has three main divisions namely, the conscious, semiconscious and unconscious.

These three levels of the human mind are continuously in a state of clash and compromise to give birth to one or the other type of behavioural characteristics resulting in a specific type of personality. Freud also believes that the anatomy of our personality is built around the three unified and inter-relating systems, namely, id, ego and superego (see Figure 21.3).

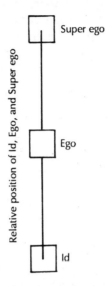

Figure 21.3 Relative positions of id, ego and superego.

The id is the raw, savage and immoral basic stuff of a man's personality that is hidden in the deep layers of his unconscious mind. It consists of such ambitions, desires, tendencies and appetites as are guided by the pleasure-seeking principle. It has no values, knows no laws, follows no rules, does not recognise right or wrong and considers only the satisfaction of its needs and appetites to be paramount.

Obviously, the id cannot be allowed to dominate and so a second system, the ego, functions, as a policeman to check the unlawful activities of the id. It is the executive unit with the power of veto. It follows the principle of reality and acts with intelligence to control, select and decide what appetites have to be satisfied and in which way they may be satisfied.

The third system of personality is the superego. It is the ethical or moral arm of the personality. It is idealistic and does not care for realities. Perfection rather than pleasure is its goal. It is a decision-making entity which decides what is good or bad to the social norms and therefore acceptable or otherwise.

Freud put forward a dynamic concept of personality by conceptualizing the continuous conflict among the id, ego and superego. While the id operating on the pleasure principle, continuously presses for the immediate discharge of bodily tension, the superego concerned with morality prohibits such gratification. Thus, a warlike situation is created between the id and the superego with the ego attempting to mediate. The extent to which the ego is able to discharge its responsibilities decides the personality make-up of the individual.

1. Individuals who have a strong or powerful ego are said to have a strong or balanced personality because the ego is capable of maintaining a balance between the superego and the id.

2.   In case an individual possesses a weak ego, he is bound to have a maladjusted personality. Here two situations may arise. In one situation, the superego may be more powerful than the ego, and so does not permit desirable fulfilment of the repressed wishes and impulses which results in a neurotic personality. If, on the other hand, the id is more powerful than the ego, the individual may indulge in unlawful or immoral activities leading to the formation of a delinquent personality.

In addition to the above structure of the personality, built around the concept of the id, ego and superego, Freud tried to provide an explanation of the development of human personality through his ideas about sex. He held that sex is a life energy. The sexual needs of the individual are basic needs which have to be satisfied for a balanced growth of the personality. A knowledge of the sex needs of a person and the status of their satisfaction is sufficient to tell us all about a person's personality. He will be an adjusted or maladjusted personality depending the extent to which his sexual needs are satisfied.

So much was his emphasis on sex, that he linked the whole development of the personality with the sex behaviour by putting his theory of psycho-sexual development. In this theory, he outlined the five different psycho-sexual stages for the development of personality namely, oral, anal, phallic, latency and genital. Here we would not provide the description or explanation about these stages as it has been already presented earlier in Chapter 5.

Alder's individual approach to personality.   Adler opposed the Freudians' structure of personality. He held that sex is not the life energy or the centre of human activities; the power motive is the central urge and human beings are motivated by the urge to be important or powerful. All of us strive towards superiority put each individual strives in a different way. He called it the style of life. Therefore, the kind of personality one possesses can be understood by studying one's style of life, i.e. the goals of life one has set for oneself and the way one strives to achieve these goals.

He thus initiated the individual approach to the study of personality patterns and maintained that there are no distinct personality types or classes. Each individual is unique in himself because everybody has definite goals and style of his life. Adler's concepts and ideas related to the description and understanding of personality development have already been discussed in detail in Chapter 6.

The Humanistic Approach

This approach to personality came from a group of psychologists subscribing to the humanistic school of psychology. Humanistic psychology, the so-called third force in psychology (the other two being behaviourism and psychoanalysis) reflects a humanistic trend in dealing with and understanding human behaviour. It believes in the goodness of man and reposes optimistic confidence in man's positive nature. Contrary to the unconscious of psychoanalytical psychology here, a person's conscious experience (what he or she feels and thinks) forms the basic structure of his or her personality. Consequently, the approach adopted by the humanists does not assume that personality is governed by biological forces from within or that destructive drives are inherent in human beings but instead points out that every one of us has the potential for self-actualization through spontaneity, creativity and personal growth. A number of theories, such as those of Godlstein, Angyal, Rogers and Maslow subscribe to the approach advocated by humanistic psychology. We shall now discuss the viewpoints of the highly influential humanistic thinkers, Abraham Maslow and Carl Rogers.

The self-actualization theory of Abraham Maslow. Abraham H. Maslow, an American psychologist, has been the major theorist adopting the humanistic approach for studying human behaviour and personality. According to his theory, human beings are basically good or neutral rather than evil and there lies in every one an impulse craving towards growth or the fulfilments of one's potentials. The goal is to seek self-actualization, that usually comes from the pursuit of knowledge, the appreciation of beauty, playfulness, self-sufficiency, insight into the truth or other constructive and creative expression. The behaviour or personality of a human being thus depends upon his style of striving towards the ultimate goal of self-realization. However, the path leading towards the ultimate goal may have sub-goals in the form of satisfaction of the lower-order needs. In this way, Maslow's theory of self-actualization suggests a hierarchy of needs for which reference may be made to 'Psychology of Motivation' in Chapter 11.

Thus, the pattern of human behaviour is always governed by the satisfaction of our needs from the lower, base level to the upper, top level. We have to satisfy our biological needs for our survival and for our social and psychological needs, we have to strive for the satisfaction in the socio-psychological context. The satisfaction of these need is, however, not the end of man's pursuit for excellence. His craving for the actualization of his inner potential continues till he reaches his ultimate goal of attaining fine humanistic values.

These values or characteristics of a self-actualized person to which one's efforts are directed in terms of the development of his personality have been enumerated by Maslow through sixteen basic characteristics. These characteristics have been arrived at by him through the study of a selected group of thirty-eight persons. This select group had included the well-known personalities past and present, e.g., Albert Einstein, Abraham Lincoln, Roosevelt etc., and also his own professors and persons who were known for self-actualization in their respective fields. From this study Maslow concluded that the self-actualized people have the following common characteristics which distinguish them the average person (Source: Maslow, 1962):

1. Ability to perceive reality accurately.
2. Willingness to accept reality readily.
3. Naturalness and spontaneity.
4. Ability to focus on problems rather than on themselves.
5. Need for privacy.
6. Self-sufficiency and independence.
7. Capacity for fresh, spontaneous, nonstereotyped appreciation of objects, events and people that they encounter.
8. Ability to attain transcendence.

9. Identification with humankind and shared social bonds with other people.
10. They may have few or many friends but have deep relationships with at least some of these friends.
11. A democratic, egalitarian attitude.
12. Strongly held values and a clear distinction between means and ends.
13. A broad, tolerant sense of humour.
14. Inventiveness and creativity with the ability to see things in new ways.
15. Resistance to confirm or succumb to social pressures.
16. Ability to go beyond dichotomies and bring together opposites.

Thus, the goal for personalty development according to Maslow's theory is self-actualization, i.e. realization of one's basic human potential to the maximum extent and as effectively as possible. The theory, thus, presents a very bright picture of human behaviour and personality by setting an ultimate motivating goal of self-actualization. However, it is criticised on account of its not being objective and scientific in its approach, especially in view of its subjective criteria for self-actualization.

Carl Roger's self theory. Carl Ransom Rogers, an American psychologist, in 1947 propounded a new theory of personality called the self theory quite distinct from the earlier theories of personality. He stressed the importance of an individual's self for determining the process of his growth, development, and appropriate adjustment to his environment. There are two basic systems underlying his personality theory—the organism and the self. Rogers considers them as systems operating in one's phenomenological field (a world of subjective experience, the personal and separate reality of each individual). The organism is an individual's entire frame of reference. It represents the totality of his experience—both conscious and unconscious. The second system, the 'self' is the accepted, aware part of experience. The self as a system of one's phenomenal field can perhaps be best understood in terms of our concept of I, me or myself.

What we recognize as the personality of an individual is the product of interaction between the above-mentioned systems of one's phenomenological field. The acquisition of the concept of self is a long and continuous process. Human beings have inherited the tendency to develop their self in the process of interpersonal and social experiences which they acquire in the environment. In other words, our inner world (in the form of our natural impulses) interacts with our total range of experience to form the concept of our self. For example, if one is told that one is a handsome person, one tends to include in the concept of one's self, the idea that one is handsome. We are in a continuous process of building the concept of our self in this manner. The concepts of self thus developed may differ from person to person as they are based purely on one's own personal experiences. The concepts of self are sometimes based more on personal needs than on reality, and at other times as Rogers believes, we develop an ideal self, i.e. the kind of person we would like to be.

Rogers does not advance a set of specific stages in the development of personality as proposed by Freud, rather, he advocates continuity of growth in terms of a continuous evolution of the concept of 'self'. Once a concept of self is formed, the individual strives to maintain it by regulating his behaviour. Whatever is consistent with the concept of his self is readily accepted and maintained at the conscious level while that which threatens that image may be totally ignored or buried deep in the unconscious.

The most unfortunate results in the development of personality occur in cases where an individual develops some false self-image. This false image is sometimes so strong that even indisputable reality is vehemently denied. Inconsistency between one's actual image and a false self-image, may then lead to abnormality in one's behaviour. Similarly, the development of an ideal self, too unreasonable and unattainable or too different from one's real self, may result in maladjustment and serious personality disorder.

An individual's adjustment, happiness, growth and development all depend upon the union and harmony between the image of his self and the organism i.e. the experience or situations he meets in his life. Stressing the psychological personality theory, Rogers emphasizes that a person normally possesses considerable capacity for growth and the realization of his individual potential and thus tries to advance continuously towards the development of his self (i.e. self-actualization) to lead to harmony between the concept of his self and his real life experiences resulting in feelings of self-integrity, self-fulfilment and a satisfying sense of psychological growth. The development, however, runs into trouble when the self fails for some reason to incorporate, and learns to live with its own new thoughts, feelings or behaviour. The goal of a therapist as Rogers advocates in his therapy, in such cases lies in bringing the individual in a unified way, from what he or she is not, to what he or she really is.

Learning Theories of Personality

The learning theories of personality depict a new developmental approach quite different from psychoanalytic and phenomenological theories of personality in the sense that they emphasize the importance of learning and objectivity to understand personality. The notable psychologists who are known to have developed personality theories are Pavlov, Watson, Guthrie, Thorndike, Skinner, Dollard & Miller; Bandura & Walters, etc. The theories developed by Dollard & Miller and Bandura & Walters are worthy of mention in this context.

Dollard and Miller's learning theory of personality. By combining the psychology of learning with aspects of psychoanalytic theory, John Dollard and Neil Miller (1950) in the institute of human relations at Yale University put forward their theory of personality. In this theory they tried to substitute Freud's concept of a pleasure principle with the principle of reinforcement, the concept of ego with the concept of learned drive and learned skills, the concept of conflict with competing reinforcers etc.

The theory of Dollard and Miller tries to describe the development of personality from simple drives to a complex function from a learning theory angle. It emphasizes that what we consider as personality is learned. The child at birth is equipped with two types of basic faculties: *reflexes and innate hierarchies of responses and a set of primary drives,* which are internal stimuli of great strength and are linked with known physiological processes which impel him to action. Thus impelled by drives (both conditioned and unconditioned) one acquires responses to the extent that they reduce the drives. Drive reduction results in reinforcements or rewards which in turn may give birth to many other drives or motives and impel the individual to learn new responses and new behaviour patterns. Since our social environment is a major source of reinforcement, it plays a key role in creating new drives and motives, our learning new responses and consequently developing our personality. Dollard and Miller's theory stressed the development of a personality on the basis of the responses and behaviour learnt through the process of motivation and reward. Dollard and Miller's theory of personality did not really ascribe any static structure to personality, and emphasized, instead, habit formation through learning as a key factor in the development of personality. Habits are formed by S.R. connections through learning. As one's fund of learning grows on the basis of experiences and interaction with one's environment, one's habits are reorganised, new habits are learned and consequently one's personality is modified and developed in terms of learning new behaviour and picking up new threads or styles of life.

Bandura & Walters' social learning theory. Albert Bandura and Richard Walters (1963) came out with an innovative approach to personality in the form of their social learning theory. They advanced the view that what an individual presents to the world at large as his personality, is acquired through a continuous process of structuring and restructuring of experiences, gathered by means of social learning and later imitated in corresponding situations. Social learning may involve real as well as symbolic models. Children, for example, pick up etiquette and attitudes by watching their parents and elders; viewers garner traits and mannerisms from popular actors and models whom they see on television or in films. The imitation of the model's behaviour is further reinforced in the viewer's mind by the recognition or reward the model receives as a result of his actions. An individual thus acquires numerous traits and modes of behaviour from many sources, and all these together contribute to the formation and development of his unique, distinctive personality.

Conclusions about the Various Theories of Personality

The theories of personality which we have so far discussed may be seen to have followed altogether different approaches to promote their viewpoints. Clearly, the difference lies in emphasis. The trait approach emphasizes behavioural consistencies and describes personality on the basis of certain basic personality traits while the type approach classifies people into definite types based on distinct personality characteristics or traits. The psychoanalystical approach emphasizes the unconscious motives and considers the nature of the human being to be basically animal nature. The humanistic approach, on the contrary, underlines the finer values of the human being and attaches maximum importance to the contents of consciousness. The social learning theorist, on the other hand, gives no credence to the heredity-cum-biological base of a person's personality for determining his behaviour but takes personality to be the function of one's social learning by focussing on the acquired variability of traits. All the viewpoints expressed, however, irrespective of their seeming differences, should not be viewed as entirely independent of each other, as all of them try to explain the nature, structure and functioning of personality and behaviour in their own way.

In fact, an eclectic approach to all the viewpoints propagated by the different psychologists may yield a clearer picture of personality and behaviour. The contents of the unconscious focused on by the psychoanalyst are as significant as the contents of the conscious underscored by the humanist. Similarly, behaviour may be described as consistent if interpreted by the trait approach; and equally plausible, as variable in various situations as maintained by the social learning theorists. It is advisable, therefore, to incorporate the views expressed in the main personality theories to obtain a comprehensive understanding of the nature, mechanism and dynamics of personality and the whys and wherefores of human behaviour.

Assessment of Personality

Why 'Assessment of Personality' rather than measurement of personality has been chosen as the title of this section is a question that needs to be answered. This has been done because the accurate measurement of personality is itself problematical. The accuracy of any process of measurement depends on the following:

1. The nature of the thing to be measured.
2. The instruments to be used.
3. The person who will do the measurement.

Let us now evaluate the measurement of personality in terms of these criteria.

1. *The nature of the 'thing'*. Personality is a complex characteristic that it is hardly possible to measure it. First, personality is not a 'thing'; it is an idea, an abstraction, and in an attempt to measure it, we would have to wrongly, try to give it a concrete shape. Secondly, since psychologists are not agreed upon the dimensions or content of personality, what would be measured? Thirdly, personality is not static. How can we accurately measure something which is constantly in the process of change and modification? Its measurement would vary from time to time and hence would not be the same from one moment to the next.

2. *The nature of the instruments*. The process of measurement requires appropriate tools and satisfactory units of measurement. In personality measurement, we encounter difficulties in this direction as well:

(a) There is no zero (starting point) for reference in case of personality. No child is born with zero personality.

(b) Length is measured in units like inches, centimeters etc., temperature is measured in degrees but in psychological measurement we do not have any such equal or regular units of measurement.

(c) Accurate measurement requires exact scales or measuring instrument. No such reliable instruments are available for measurement of personality.

3. *The nature of the person.*   The dependability, accuracy and validity of any process of measurement largely depends on the competence and detachment of the person doing the measurement. In the absence of standard tools or units of measurement, the results of any evaluation of personality are bound to be influenced by the subjective views and the norms, likes and dislikes of the person carrying out the measurement.

In this way the actual measurement (which defines itself in terms of objectivity, reliability and validity) of personality is not possible. Also, it is very difficult to go round in search for all the constituents or elements of personality, most of which are unknown. Moreover, prediction of the future status is the most essential aim of measurement. In case of a dynamic phenomenon like personality, such prediction is not possible and hence it is not justified to use the term measurement. We can only have the estimate or assessment of personality.

Techniques and Methods of Assessment of Personality

The methods used for the assessment of personality may be termed as subjective, objective or projective. As it is not possible, however, to clearly demarcate subjectivity from objectivity and even effectively insulate projective processes against the subjectivity and personal biases of the examiner, it is necessary to look for other ways to classify the techniques of personality assessment. The commonly employed assessment techniques may be classified as follows:

1.   Where an individual's behaviour in actual life situations can be observed, namely observation techniques and situation tests.
2.   Where the individual is required to speak about himself namely, autobiography, questionnaire and personality inventory and interview.
3.   Where other people's opinions about the individual whose personality is under assessment are ascertained. These are biographies, case history, rating scales and sociometric techniques.
4.   Projective techniques involving fantasy which aim at assessing the individual's reaction to imaginary situations.
5.   Indirect techniques in which some personality variables may be determined in terms of physiological responses by the use of machines or technical devices.

Let us discuss some of the important techniques in detail.

Observation

Observation is a popular method to study the behaviour pattern of an individual in an actual life situation. The observer decides what personality traits or characteristics he needs to know, and he then observes the relevant activities of the subject in real life situations. The observation can be done in two ways. In one the observer does not hide from the subject or subjects and even becomes more or less a part of the group under observation. In the other, he takes a position where his presence is least disturbing to the subject but from where he can clearly observe every detail of the behaviour of the individual under observation. He may also use a tape-recorder, photographic cameras, a telescope etc. To ensure reliability of the observed results, the observer may repeat the observations in the same situation several times, or the subject may be observed by a number of observers and the results may be pooled together.

Situational Tests

Here situations are artificially created in which an individual is expected to perform acts related to the personality traits under testing. For example, to test the honesty of an individual, some situations can be created and his reaction can be evaluated in terms of honesty or dishonesty. Does he feel the temptation to resort to copying? Does he try to pick up the ten-rupee note which is lying there? His behaviour would lead to an assessment of how honest he is.

Questionnaire

The nature of a questionnaire is explained by the description given by Goode and Hatt (1952):

> In general the word questionnaire refers to a device for securing answers to questions by using a form which the respondent fills in himself.

This definition makes it clear that in collecting information from the subject himself about his personality characteristics, a form consisting of a series of printed or written questions is used. The subject responds to these questions in the spaces provided in columns of yes, no or cannot say etc. These answers are then evaluated and used for personality assessment. Items, like the following, are included in the questionnaires:

	Yes,	No,	(Cannot say)
Do you enjoy being alone?	—	—	—
Do you enjoy seeing others succeed?	—	—	—
Do you laugh at a joke on yourself?	—	—	—
Do you get along well with your relatives?	—	—	—

This is the most popular method and is quite useful in collecting both quantitative as well as qualitative information.

Personality Inventory

While this resembles the questionnaire in many respects such as administration, scoring, interpretation etc., it is different in two ways. First, while the questionnaire is a general device and can be used for collecting all kinds of information not connected specifically with personality traits or the behaviour of an individual, personality inventory is specifically designed to seek answers about the person and his personality. Second, the questions, set in the questionnaire, are generally worded in the second person, e.g.,

Do you often feel lonely?   Yes,   No,

while in the personality inventory, they may be worded in the first person such as,

I often feel lonely   Yes,   No,

The best known personality inventory is the Minnesota Multiphasic personality Inventory (MMPI) developed by J.C. McKinley and S.R. Hathaway of the Minnesota Medical School. The items included in this inventory are such that their answers are known to indicate certain specific personality traits. It consists of 550 items some of which are:

I sweat very easily even on cool days.
There is something wrong with my sex organs.
I have never been in love with any one.
I like to talk about sex.

Each item is printed on a separate card. The subject reads the questions and then, according to his response puts it down as yes, no or doubtful in the space provided for the purpose. Evaluation of the important personality traits can then be done in terms of these responses.

The California personality inventory, the Eysenck personality inventory and the Sixteen personality factor inventory (16 P.F.) developed by Cattell are some of the other well-known inventories.

The questionnaire and personality inventory technique suffer from the following drawbacks:

1. It is difficult to get the responses to all questions.
2. The subject may give selective responses rather than genuine ones (hide his weaknesses etc.)
3. He may be ignorant of his own traits or qualities which he may possess.

Rating scale. The rating scale is used to assess where an individual stands in terms of other people's opinion of some of his personality traits. It reflects the impression the subject has made upon the person who rates him. There are three basic factors involved in this technique:

1. The specific trait or traits to be rated.
2. The scale on which the degree of possession or absence of the trait has to be shown.
3. The appropriate persons or judges for rating.

First of all, the traits or characteristics, which have to be evaluated by the judges are to be stated and defined clearly. Then a scale for the rating has to be constructed. How it is done can be understood from the example which follows:

Suppose we wish to rate the students of a class for the quality 'leadership'. We can rate the degrees of this quality as divisions such as very good, average, poor, very poor etc. Now the arrangement of these divisions along a line, on equal intervals, from high to low is termed as a rating scale for assessment of the quality of leadership. Usually the divisions of the scale are indicated by numbers, 1 to 3, 1 to 5 or 1 to 7, comprising a three-point, five-point or seven-point scale. The seven-point scale is of the following type:

7	6	5	4	3	2	1
Excellent	Very good	Good	Average	Below average	Poor	Very poor

Now the raters, who are in a position to properly rate the individuals may be asked to give them scores, ranging from 1 to 7, according to the degree of leadership they possess.

Rating techniques suffer from some obvious drawbacks like the error of central tendency, subjective bias and halo effect etc. In the former, the raters hesitate to give very high or very low ratings and tend to keep their ratings in the middle. Subjective bias leads to their own likes and dislikes, colouring their assessment of the individuals under rating, and under the halo effect, they may rate an individual (on the basis of general impression) to be more honest or the like, than he may actually be.

To bring some reliability into rating scale technique, it has been suggested that instead of having rating by only one judge, we an assign the rating work to more judges—for example to different teachers, classmates, parents etc.—the rating may be done by pooling the individual assessments.

Interview

Interview is a technique of eliciting information directly from the subject about his personality in face-to-face contacts. It gives an opportunity for mutual exchange of ideas and information between the subject and the psychologists. For this purpose, the psychologist tries to arrange a meeting with the person or persons under assessment. The face to face interaction in the interview is of two types viz., structured or unstructured.

An unstructured interview is an open interrogation. Here the interviewer asks the interviewee any question on any subject relevant to the situation. The interviewer here is not restricted to a particular set of predetermined questions but is free to drift along the paths opened up by the interviewee to explore any issue that may arise, and to clarify any dought that may emerge in the broad assessment of his personality. The structured interview on the other hand, adopts a systematic and predetermined approach instead of riding on the tides of the situation. Here the interviewer is definite about the personality traits or behaviour he has to assess and then plans accordingly. Usually, a list of questions, is prepared for this purpose and after taking the subject into confidence, the psychologist tries to seek answers to these pre-planned questions. He does not attend to only the content of the responses but also to the tone, behaviour and other similar factors, for the total evaluation in terms of the designated personality pattern of the individual.

The limitations of this technique are that it calls for a well-trained competent interviewer and is costly in terms of labour, time, and money. It also suffers from the subjective bias of the interviewer. Here also, like questionnaire and personality inventory, we cannot have any safeguard to prevent the subject from hiding his feelings or from giving selective responses. The points in favour of the technique are that answers are obtained to every question which is put to the subject. In fact, responses even to intimate questions, which subjects may hesitate to put in writing, can also be obtained. In fact, interview is a relatively flexible tool. It permits explanation, adjustment and variation according to the situation and thus has proved to be one of the essential and more important tools of personality assessment.

PROJECTIVE TECHNIQUES

We have so far discussed only those techniques which evaluate the overt of conscious behaviour of an individual. The covert or unconscious behaviour is in fact, not insignificant; rather, it is more significant than overt behaviour, as Freud believes that our conscious behaviour is only one-tenth of our total behaviour. There should, therefore, be some other techniques which do not stress only the observable part of human personality but can reveal a person's inner or private world and go deeper in the unconscious of an individual to dig out the repressed feelings, wishes, desires, fears, hopes and ambitions, etc.

These techniques, on account of their using projection phenomena are called projective techniques. The material used in these techniques or tests represents 'a sort of screen' on which the subject 'projects' his characteristics through processes, needs, anxieties and conflicts (Anastasi, 1976)

Projective techniques are devised to meet the challenge. They are to assess the total personality of an individual rather than in fragments. Let us see what these technique are.

The nature of projective techniques. In view of the declared objective of all such types of tests and techniques, relatively indefinite and unstructured stimuli (like vague pictures, inkblots, incomplete sentences, drawings etc.) are presented to the subject and he is asked to structure them in any way he likes. In doing so he unconsciously projects his own desires, hopes, fears, repressed wishes etc., and thus not only reveals his inner or private world but also gives indications on the basis of which his total personality may be assessed.

Some Common Projective Techniques are discussed here.

The Rorschach Inkblot Test

This technique was developed by Harmann Rorschach (1884–1922), the Swiss psychiatrist. The material used in this test consists of 10 cards on which there are ink-blots. Five of them are in black and white and five are multi-coloured. These ink-blots are completely unstructured—the shapes of the blots do not have any specific meaning (Figure 21.4).

Figure 21.4 An inkblot of the type used in the Rorschach test.

Administration of the test. The test is administered in the following sequence:

1. The cards are presented one at the time in a specified order. When the subject gets seated, the examiner gives him the first card with necessary instructions and asks him to say what he sees in it, what it looks like to him, etc.
2. The subject is allowed as much time as he wants for a given card and is permitted to give as many responses as he wishes. He is also allowed to turn the card around an look at it from any angle he wants.
3. Besides keeping a record of the responses of the subject concerning these inkblots on separate pieces of paper, the examiner notes the time taken for each response. The position in which the cards are being held, emotional expression and other factors of incidental behaviour of the subject during the test etc.
4. After all the cards have been presented, the second phase of inquiry which is intended to seek clarification or addition to the original responses follows.

Scoring, analysis and interpretation of the test. For the purpose of scoring, the responses are given specific symbols and are entered into 4 columns.

These scoring categories are marked as (a) location, (b) contents, (c) originality and (d) determinants.

Location refers to the part of the blot with which the subject associates each response. The symbols *W, w, D, d* and *s* are used for scoring the location responses as follows:

(*W*) indicates that the subject is seeing the card as a whole.
(*w*) indicates that the subject has failed to see the problems as a whole.
(*D*) indicates the major details.
(*d*) indicates minor details involving petty issues or less important matters.
(*s*) indicate the subject's response to the white spaces within the main outlines.

Contents column is concerned with the contents of the responses. It takes note only of what is seen by the subject and not the manner of its perception. Some of the symbols used for scoring the contents of the responses are:

Scoring Symbol	*Contents of the response*
H	human forms
A	animal forms
Ad	animal detail
Hd	human detail
N	natural objects like rivers, green fields etc.
O	inanimate objects like lamp-shade, pot etc.

In *originality* column for each of 10 cards, certain responses are scored as popular, by using the symbol P, because of their common occurrence while others which contain something new and thus indicate some type of originality are scored as original and represented by the symbol O.

Determinants column takes note of the manner of perception, i.e., the particular characteristics which helped the subject in deciphering the blot or deciding his manner of perception. The main determinants are (F), the form of the blot, (C), its colour, (M) its movement and (K), its shading.

For instance, if the subject responds to a blot as a butterfly, then, we can say that it is the "form" which led to this way of seeing it and we score the response as F. On the other hand, if the subject sees something like fire, blood etc., then the determinant is certainly the "colour" and we enter C in the fourth column.

The subject's responses on account of shading, e.g., perception of rough or smooth surfaces, smoke, cloud etc., are scored as K, whereas if the subject responds in terms of movements—(like a boy running, dancing etc.), an animal (like a dog barking), or inanimate objects like water following, cloth fluttering etc.), the symbols, M, F_m or m are entered in terms of C, F, K or M, etc. Alternatively, they may be noted by using mixed symbols like CF, FK etc.

Interpretation. Now, the different symbols in all the four columns are counted. This gives an idea of the relative frequencies of different kinds of responses. The score may be entered in terms of symbols in different columns as shown in Table 21.4.

Table 21.4 Recording of the subjects' Responses in Rorschach inkblot test

	I Column location	II Column contents	III Column originality	IV Column determinants	
Symbols	W D d	H A A$_d$ H$_d$ N O	P O	F C K M	Mixed category
Frequency					

The relative frequencies of the different symbols within the scoring categories, and among the several categories help the interpreter to decide the personality characteristics of the subjects. For example, if (a) the number of Ws is greater than d or D; then the person is said to be mature, intelligent and is expected to possess the ability to synthesize; (b) greater frequency of colour at the expense of human movement indicates an extrovert nature while domination of M over K characterizes an introvert; (c) dominance of shading responses expresses anxiety, depressed attitudes and feelings of inferiority; and (d) relatively greater emphasis on movement indicates the richness of the subject's imaginative life.

It is not only the relative importance or occurrence of certain kinds of responses which helps in interpretation but other factors like the time factor, behaviour of the subject at the time of reactions etc., also have their own significance.

It is, therefore, only through various kinds of relationships, observations, records and integration of results from various parts that a final global picture about a subject's personality can be drawn. The test demands a lot of training and skill in scoring and interpretation on the part of the examiner and, therefore, the work must be taken seriously and done only be an experienced and trained psychologist.

TAT or Thematic Apperception Test

This test consists of perception of certain picture in a thematic manner, i.e. revealing imaginative themes. It was first introduced by Henry Murray (1943) to measure the need for achievement. Later it was fully developed for the assessment of personality with the help of the psychologist C.D. Morgan.

Test material and administration. The test material consists of thirty pictures which portray human beings in a variety of actual life situations. Ten of these cards are meant for males, ten for females and ten are common to both sexes. The maximum number of pictures used on any one subject is thus, twenty. The test is usually administered in two sessions, using ten pictures in each session.

Figure 21.5   A sample picture from TAT.

The pictures are presented one at a time. They are vague and indefinite. The subject is told clearly, that this is a test of creative imagination and that there is no right or wrong response. He has to make up a story for each of the pictures presented to him, within a fixed period of time. He has to take care of the following aspects while knitting the story:

1. What is going on in the picture.
2. What has led to this scene.
3. What would likely happen in such a situation.

In making up the stories the subject unconsciously projects several characteristics of his own personality. There is no time to think. Therefore, the stories express his own natural life's desires, likes and dislikes, ambitions, emotions, sentiments etc. The special value of this test lies in its capacity to exploring the underlying hidden drives, complexes and conflicts of the subject's personality. A competent examiner can learn a lot about the personality of his subject by carefully analysing the given responses.

Scoring and interpretation. Originally Murray analysed the contents of the stories according to needs and pressures in the form of the environmental forces to which the subject is exposed. The terms of analysis have now been modified and the system of scoring and interpretation takes the following into account:

- *Hero of the story.* What type of personality does he have?
- *Theme of the story.* What is the nature of theme or plot used in making up the story?
- *The style of the story.* The length of the story, the language used, whether the expression is direct or indirect, forced or poor, organization of the contents, originality and creativity, etc.
- *The content of the story.* What interests, sentiments, attitudes they depict, whether behaviour has been expressed in real terms or as fantasy and what inner state of the mind the story reveals.
- *Test situation as a whole.* The subject's reaction is to be listed as a whole.
- *Particular emphasis or omissions.* The omissions, addition, distortion and attention to particular detail.
- *Subject's attitude* towards authority and sex.
- *Outcome.* Whether the ending of the story is happy, unhappy, funny etc.

As a whole, the recurring themes and features contribute more towards the interpretation than a single response. Moreover, the global view of one's personality should be based on the responses of all the twenty pictures shown to the subject. There are many chances of misinterpretation of the contents of the stories by an immature examiner. The future of TAT therefore, hangs more on the success in perfecting the interpreter than on success in perfecting the material. People entrusted with interpreting the test must be given adequate opportunities to acquire the necessary knowledge and training for this purpose.

CAT (Children's Apperception Test)

TAT works well with adults and adolescents but it is not suitable for children. Dr. Leopold Bellak developed this test for children between three and ten years of age.

Description. This test consists of 10 cards. The cards have pictures of animals instead of human characters since it was thought that children could identify themselves with animal figures more readily than with human figures. These animals are shown in various real life situations. All ten cards are used for children of both sexes. The pictures designed to evoke fantasies relating to the child's own experiences, reactions and feelings. The child's personality is reflected in whatever story emerges. It is a colour-free test but it demands some alterations according to the child's local conditions.

Administration and interpretation of the test. All the ten cards are presented one by one and the subject is asked to make up stories out of them. The examiner should try to develop such a rapport that the child treats the making-up of stories as a game.

Interpretation of the stories is centered around the following eleven variables:

- *The hero.* The personality traits of the hero as revealed in the story.
- *Theme of the story.* The nature of the theme selected for building the story.
- *The end of the story.* Whether the ending is happy, wishful, realistic or unrealistic?
- *Attitude towards parental figures.* Which of the following emotions has been depicted in relation to parental figures: hatred, respect, devotion, gratitude, dependence, aggression, fear?
- *Family role.* With whom in the family has the child identified himself?
- *Other outside figures introduced.* Objects or external elements have been introduced in the story which are not shown in the pictures.
- *Omitted or ignored figures.* Which figures has the child omitted or ignored should be noted as they may reveal the wish of the subject that the figures were not there?
- *Nature of anxieties.* Harassment, loss of love, fear of being left alone etc., should also be noted.
- *Punishment for crime.* The relationship between a crime committed in the story and the severity of punishment given for it should be noted.
- *Defence and confidence.* The type of defences, flight, aggression, passivity, regression etc., the child adopts the nature of compliance or dependence, involvement in pleasure and achievement, sex desire etc. should also be noted.
- *Other supplementary factors.* The language, the overall structure of the stories, the time taken for completing them and the reactions of the subject at the time of making up the story etc.

With all this knowledge an expert interpreter can form an assessment of the various aspects of the child's personality.

Word Association Test

A number of selected words, comprise this test. The subject is told that the examiner would speak a series of words one word at a time and he (the subject) should immediately say the first word which comes to his mind and that there are no right or wrong answers.

The examiner then records the reply to each word spoken by him, the reaction time and any unusual speech or behaviour manifestations which might accompany a given response. The contents of the responses along with the other items recorded in connection with them give clues for evaluating the individual's personality and thus help a psychologist in his work.

Sentence Completion Tests

These tests consist of a list of incomplete sentences, generally open ended, which require completion by the subject in one or more words. The subject is asked to go through the list and answer as quickly as possible (without giving a second thought to his answers). For example, we can have the following sentences:

I am worried over . . . . .
My hope is . . . . .
I feel proud when . . . .
My hero is . . . . .

The sentence completion tests are considered superior to word association because the subject can respond in more than one word and so it becomes possible to have great flexibility and variety of responses as a result of which a wider area of personality and experiences may be revealed.

In addition to the projective technique mentioned above, there are some others which may prove useful in several situations. They are, the *play technique, drawing and painting tests* etc. Both these techniques are very useful in the case of small children. In the former, the examiner observes the spontaneous behaviour of the children while playing with or constructing something from given material and in the latter, the natural free hand drawing and paintings of the children constitute the matter of study. Both these techniques offer the opportunity for careful analysis of a child's personality.

In spite of being criticised as being very difficult and subjective in interpretation the projective techniques discussed above have been found quite useful in the assessment of the personality of people belonging to different age groups including the older ones and the smaller children. Their use has been widely appreciated especially in rendering necessary advice to guidance personnel, clinical psychologists and even to the persons engaged in selection of personnel, their placement and promotion. The chief value of these tests lies in the fact that it is extremely difficult for the subject to give fake responses since there are no right or wrong responses which the subject may try to guess as in the non-projective techniques like questionnaire, inventory, interview etc.

These techniques, on account of their widespread use have now become available for use on people of all ages. Many attempts have been made to adapt the well-known projective tests like Rorschach inkblot test, TAT and CAT, for use on subjects of different cultural educational and social group. We have a number of adaptations for use with Indian subjects in our local situations. Some of these are,

1. Indian adaptation of senior apperception test developed by Uma Chaudhary.
2. Indian adaptation of thematic apperception test developed by Uma Chaudhary.
3. Indian adaptation of children's apperception test developed by Uma Chaudhary.
4. A pragmatic view of Rorschach inkblot technique developed by B.L. Dubey.
5. Mosaic test of personality developed by Dr. B.B. Chatterjee.
6. Sentence completion test developed by Dr. L.N. Dubey and Archana Dubey.

SUMMARY

An impressive personality is often taken to be synonymous with a good appearance, healthy physique, pleasing manners, a good character, a pleasant temperament, etc. Although personality includes all these aspects of one's self, it is far beyond each or even the sum of all these attributes. It may be defined as a complex blend of a constantly evolving and changing pattern of a person's unique behaviour, emerged as a result of his interaction with his environment, directed towards some specific ends in view.

Personality theories try to explain the structure of personality by adopting various approaches such as, type, trait, trait-cum-type and developmental approach etc.

Theories adopting the type approach try to classify people into categories or types according to certain characteristics. Hippocrates classified people according to the type of humour or fluid found in the body. Kretschmer described specific biological types based on body structures. Sheldon also identified three distinct types based on the relationship between a person's body physique and behaviour. Jung also adopted the type approach in classifying people in terms of introversion and extroversion.

Theories based on the trait approach try to describe people in terms of their unique pattern of traits. They define traits as relatively permanent and relatively consistent general behaviour patterns which an individual exhibits in different situations. Notable among these theories are the personality theories of Allport and Cattell. Allport identified three types of traits—cardinal, central and secondary; responsible for an individual's personal disposition. Cardinal traits are the primary traits so dominant as to cover virtually every aspect of a person's behaviour and attributes. Central traits represent those few characteristic tendencies that could be used to describe one and secondary traits are those displayed from time to time in a relatively small range of situations. Cattell used factor analysis to identify the surface traits and source traits and enumerated sixteen factors as the building blocks of personality.

Eysenck's theory of personality is based on a trait-cum-type approach towards personality and starting with the traits it yielded definite personality type.

Freud's psychoanalytic theory of personality postulated that there are three levels of mind—the conscious, the sub-conscious and the unconscious that operate to shape one's personality. Besides this, he was of the opinion that the anatomy of our personality is built on the three unified and interrelated systems, the id, ego and superego. He also held that sexuality is at the core of all human behaviour. According to him, in the development of personality, the child passes through five psychosexual stages namely, oral, anal, phallic, latent and genital.

Adler, while disagreeing with Freud, laid stress on the power motive and not sex as the life energy. He pioneered the individual approach in the study of personality. The self-actualization, humanistic theory of Abraham Maslow believed that individuals are motivated by their needs arranged in a hierarchical order from the lower base level of physiological needs to the upper top level of the need for self-actualization. The personality build up of an individual, therefore, depends upon his striving for the level of his needs and the extent to which he feels that he has been successful in his attempts.

The other important humanistic theory, Carl Rogers' self theory holds that personality to be a function of the interaction between the two systems (the organism and the self) of one's world of subjective experience. He linked the personality with the development and maintenance of the self-concept and the effort to achieve the ideal self.

Dollard and Miller in their learning theory of personality attempted to combine the learning theory with the psychoanalytic theory and viewed personality as a function of drive reduction. Bandura and Walters in their theory of social learning emphasized that people acquire personality characteristics by observing and imitating real life as well as symbolic models.

We can only make an estimate or assessment of personality as the true measurement of one's personality is not possible. This assessment can be made by means of a variety of techniques like observation, situation test, questionnaire, personality inventory, rating scale, interview, and projective techniques.

Projective techniques make use of ambiguous or unstructured stimuli in order to permit people to express their own perception of stimuli. The various techniques involved in this category are, the Rorschach inkblot test, thematic apperception test (TAT), children's apperception test (CAT), word association test, sentence completion test, play technique, drawing and painting test and others.

REFERENCES

Adler, A., *Practice and Theory of Individual Psychology,* New York: Harcourt Brace & World, 1927.

Anastasi, A., *Psychological Testing* (4th ed.), New York: Macmillan, 1976, p. 559.

Allport, G.W., *Personality—A psychological interpretation,* New York: Holt, 1948, pp. 28, 49.

———— , *Pattern and Growth in Personality,* New York: Holt, 1961, pp. 180–81.

Bandura, A., *Social Learning Theory,* Englewood Cliffs, N.J.: Prentice-Hall, 1977.

Bandura, A. and Walters, R.H., *Social Learning and Personality Development,* New York: Holt, 1963

Bhatia, H.R., *Elements of Educational Psychology* (3rd ed.) Calcutta: Orient Longman, 1968, p. 371.

Cattell, R.B., Personality Pinned Down, Psychology To-day, Quoted by H.L. Roediger et al. (1973), *Psychology* (2nd ed.), Boston: Little Brown & Co., 1987.

_____ , Quoted by C.S. Hall and G. Lindzey, *Theories of Personality* (2nd ed.), John Wiley, 1970, p. 386.

Dollard, J. and Miller, N.E., *Personality and Psychotherapy*, New York: McGraw-Hill, 1950.

Eysenck, H.J., *The Structure of Human Personality* (3rd ed.), New York: Methuen, 1971, p. 2.

Freud, S., *An Outline of Psychoanalysis*, New York: Norton, 1939.

_____ , *An Outline of Psychoanalysis*, London: Hogarth, 1953.

Goode and Hatt, *Methods of Social Research*, New York: McGraw-Hill, 1952, p. 33.

Hogan, R., *Personality Theory*, Englewood Cliffs, N.J.: Prentice-Hall, 1976.

Kretschmer, E., *Physique and Character*, New York: Harcourt Brace, 1925.

Maddi, S.R., *Personality Theories: A Comparative Assessment*, Homewood, Illinois: Dorsey, 1976, p. 9.

Maslow, A.H., *Toward a Psychology of Being*, Princeton N.J.: Van Nostrand, 1962.

Murry, H.A., *The Thematic Apperception Test*, Cambridge (Mass.) Harvard University Press, 1943.

Pervin, Lawrence, A., *Personality: Theory and Research* (4th ed.), New York: John Wiley, 1984, p. 269.

Prince, Morton, *The Unconscious* (2nd ed.), New York: Macmillan, 1929, p. 532.

Rogers, C.R., A theory of therapy, personality and inter-personal relationships, in S. Koch (Ed.), *Psychology: A study of science*, Vol. III, New York: McGraw-Hill, 1959.

_____ , *A Way of Being*, Boston: Houghton Mifflin, 1980.

Sheldon, W.H., *The Varieties of Temperament: A Psychology of Constitutional Differences*, New York: Harper, 1942.

Watson, J.B., *Behaviourism*, London: Kegan Paul, 1930.

_____ , *Behaviourism*, New York: Norton, 1970.

SUGGESTED READINGS

Abramson, Paul, R., *Personality*, New York: Holt, 1980.

Butcher, James, N., *Objective Personality Assessment*, New York: Academic Press, 1972.

Cohen, R. and Schaeffer, D.L., *Pattern of Personality Judgement,* New York: Academic Press, 1973.

Cronbach, L.J., *Essentials of Psychological Testing* (3rd ed.), New York: Harper & Row, 1970.

Eysenck, H.J., *Dimensions of Personality,* London: Kegan Paul, 1947.

Fordham, F., *An Introduction to Jung's Psychology,* London: Penguin Books, 1953.

Hall, C.S. and Nordby, V.J., *A Primer of Jungian Psychology,* New York: John Wiley, 1978.

Hall, C.S. and Lindzey, G., *Theories of Personality* (3rd ed.), New York: John Wiley, 1978.

Janis, I.L. and Mahl, G.F. et al., *Personality Dynamics,* Development and Assessment, New York: Harcourt Brace, 1969.

Jones, E., *The Life and Work of Sigmund Freud,* Lionel Trilling and Steven Marcus (Eds.), Garden City, New York: Anchor Books, 1963.

Klopfer, B. and Kelley, D., *The Rorschach Technique,* Yonkers: World Book Co., 1946.

Maslow, A.H., *Motivation and Personality* (2nd ed.), New York: Harper & Row, 1970.

Mischel, Walter, *Personality and Assessment,* New York: John Wiley, 1968.

_____ , *Introduction to Personality* (2nd ed.), New York: Holt, 1976.

Sherman, Mark, *Personality,* New York: Pergamon Press, 1979.

Vernon, P.W., *Personality Test and Assessment* (rev. ed.), London: Methuen, 1965.

Wiggens, J. et al., *Principles of Personality,* Reading (Mass.): Addison-Wesley, 1976.

Chapter 22

Educating Exceptional Children

INTRODUCTION

The word exceptional is used here to mean rare or unusual. It represents a kind of significant deviation from the usual, natural or normal happenings. In this sense, a boy standing seven feet tall would be termed quite a typical, exceptional and above average in a population of Indian adolescents. Similar would be the case with a boy having height of 4 feet 6 inches, as he would be exceptional at the lower end of the height scale. Thus, people are termed exceptional if they deviate considerably in one attribute to the other from what is supposed to be normal or average for their group. One person may be exceptionally beautiful and other extremely ugly, one a genius with an I.Q. of 200, the other an idiot with an I.Q. of 20. Such wide variations and deviations are found nearly in all attributes and traits of personality and patterns of human behaviour. Consequently, the term exceptional carries a very wide connotation as it covers the entire range and possibilities of the significant in deviations in every shades of human activity and personality trait. The term exceptional here stands for a separate and in many ways distinct category or class of children who have markedly above average or below average traits and characteristics which makes them fundamentally different from the general or average population of children. These children begin to demonstrate signs of their exceptionality from their very birth or during their developmental stages as they race ahead or lag behind in terms of natural growth and development in various dimensions—physical, mental, emotional, social and moral etc. to such an extent that they exhibit symptoms of maladjustment with average children and with the average ways and means of their upbringing and education.

Definition of the Term "exceptional children"

The term exceptional children has been defined in many ways by authors and researchers.

Crow and Crow (1973):

> The term 'atypical' or 'exceptional' is applied to a trait or to a person possessing the trait if the extent of deviation from normal possession of the trait is so great that because of it the individual warrants or receives special attention from his fellows and his behaviour, responses and activities are thereby affected.

Kirk (1984):

> An exceptional child is he who deviates from the normal or average child in mental, physical and social characteristics to such an extent that he requires a modification of school practices or special educational services in order to develop to his maximum capacity, or supplementary instruction.

Telford and Sawrey (1977):

> The term exceptional children refers to those children who deviate from the normal in physical, mental, emotional, or social characteristics to such a degree that they require special social and educational services to develop their maximum capacity.

These definitions highlight the following typical features or characteristics of the exceptional children:

1. Exceptional children are quite different and distinct from the so-called normal or average children.
2. Their deviation from the normal or average children is so great that they can be recognised and distinguished easily from average children.
3. This deviation in terms of their acquired traits or development may fall in any behavioural or developmental dimension, physical, intellectual, emotional or social etc.
4. The degree of deviation in any behavioural or developmental trait is so marked that these children experience unusual or peculiar problems and require special arrangements in terms of care and education for their proper growth and upbringing to meet the special conditions necessary for the full development and nurturing of their capabilities.

Thus defined, the following types of deviant or exceptional children in terms of different dimensions of human growth and development may be termed as exceptional:

1. The gifted backward and the creative children.
2. The crippled, orthopaedically handicapped, the hard of hearing and the deaf, the partially sighted and the blind, etc.
3. The mentally retarded or handicapped.
4. The emotionally handicapped ranging from those with minor personality maladjustments to those with serious problems—the neurotics and the psychotics.
5. The socially handicapped such as juvenile delinquents.
6. The learning disabled.

Let us know in detail about some of these children in the following pages.

GIFTED CHILDREN

Meaning and Definition

The term 'gifted child' has been defined by different scholars and psychologists in the following words:

Telford and Sawrey (1977):

> The intellectually gifted can be defined in terms of test scores or demonstrated performance, or as the upper 1 or 2 per cent of the general population as measured by some designated intelligence and/or achievement test.

Fleigher and Bish (1959):

> The term gifted encompasses those children who possess a superior intellectual potentiality and functional ability to achieve academically in the top 15 to 20 per cent of the school population; and/or talent of a high order in such special areas as mathematics, mechanics, science, expressive arts, creative writing, music and social leadership; and a unique creative ability to deal with their environment.

Witty (1940):

> The term gifted or talented stands for those whose performance is consistently remarkable in some potentially valuable activity.

Prem Pasricha (1964):

> The gifted child is the one who exhibits superiority in general intelligence or the one who is in possession of special abilities of a high order in the fields which are not necessarily associated with a high intelligence quotient.

Marland report (1972):

> The gifted are those who possess outstanding abilities or potential in the area of general intellectual capacity, specific academic aptitude, creative or productive thinking, leadership ability, visual or performing arts and psycho-motor activity.

Havighurst (1958):

> The talented or gifted child is one who shows consistently remarkable performance in any worthwhile line of endeavour.

Tannenbaum (1983):

> The term giftedness denotes their potential for becoming critically acclaimed performers or exemplary producers of ideas in spheres of activity that enhance the moral, physical, emotional, social, intellectual, or aesthetic life of humanity.

Analysis of the above definitions shows that various scholars and thinkers have adopted different approaches in defining the term giftedness. The first two definitions have tried to provide a statistical and operational definition by adopting scores on intelligence and achievement tests. Although the use of the I.Q. and achievement test score has the advantage of objectivity, it cannot be made a sole criterion for deciding giftedness. Moreover, there lies a difficulty in deciding the cut-off point i.e. the minimum score for labelling one as gifted as some may fix it as 140 (Terman and Oden, 1947) while others may lower it to 110 (Bentley, 1937).

Prem Pasricha's definition takes a proper stand by declaring that giftedness need not be necessarily associated with high performance on some general intelligence test. A person who shows outstanding or remarkable performance in other spheres of activity regardless of his average I.Q. or lower scholastic achievement may also be termed as gifted. This feature has been repeated in almost all the other definitions as well. However, while adopting demonstrated social performance as a criterion, these definitions have clearly stated that in order to qualify as an indication of giftedness, a person's performance must be consistent, outstanding, distinctive, remarkable and clearly above the average performance of others in the group. It should, at the same time, be useful and worthwhile and should contribute towards the welfare of society and also of humanity at large.

Consequently, on the basis of the above definitions we may draw the following conclusions about the meaning, nature and characteristics of gifted or talented children:

1. The gifted child is essentially an exceptional child.
2. In comparison to children of his own group, he is superior in some ability or group of abilities.
3. In most cases, the gifted child invariably exhibits superior performance only in the area or areas of his giftedness.
4. The appellation 'gifted children' is applicable to not only the academically talented but also to those who show promise in other spheres such as

   (a) music, dance, drama, painting, sculpture, writing and other creative arts,
   (b) mechanical work,
   (c) social leadership and human relationships,
   (d) creative scientific experimentation and exploration,
   (e) physical activities like games, sports and gymnastics.

5. A gifted child need not necessarily possess a very high intelligence quotient (I.Q.).
6. If he receives proper attention and opportunity for self-expression and development, the gifted child can make a noteworthy contribution to the welfare of society, the nation and humanity at large.

Needs and Problems of Gifted Children

Like other children, the gifted children have certain basic needs, the need for security, for love, for belonging and the need to be accepted as an individual. In addition to these basic needs the gifted children may have certain special needs like (a) the need for knowledge and understanding, (b) creativity and ingenuity, (c) the development of his exceptional ability or abilities, and (d) the need for self-actualization or self-expression.

The gifted child thus strives for the satisfaction not only of the basic needs but also has to have the opportunity and the facilities for the realization of the above-mentioned specific needs. In case he experiences difficulty in the accomplishment of these needs he becomes disturbed mentally as well as emotionally. This leads to a sort of maladjustment and he becomes a problem child.

The gifted child needs a proper environment for his development. He wants to be understood carefully in response to his different needs and problems. The gifted child is exceptionally curious and has a thirst for knowledge and is, therefore, in the habit of asking searching questions. The parents as well as the teachers who do not understand his urges, usually snub him. Sometimes, he wants appreciation for his ingenuity in a scientific field or creativity in the arts, but does not get it. Consequently, he feels insecure and rejected and any sort of mishandling or carelessness on the part of teachers or parents further aggravates the situation and he becomes a nuisance.

In case the gifted child gets undue attention and appreciation, he becomes too conscious of his superiority and develops a boastful and supercilious attitude. He cannot adjust with his fellow students. He considers them inferior and foolish and may even dislike them, while they, in turn become jealous of him. They do not accept his superiority and begin to reject him. The gifted child, in this way, does not get recognition from his peers and faces a sort of social rejection. This perturbs him and as a result, he either becomes withdrawn or aggressive and hostile.

From another angle too, the gifted children are faced with problems of adjustment in our usual system of class-room, instruction. We, in the class-rooms, plan work for an average child and the same task is assigned to all the children in the class. For the gifted child this is no challenge and he either finishes the assignment much ahead of the others or takes no genuine interest in it. As a result, he becomes restless, careless, inattentive and idle and often utilizes the extra time and surplus energy in making mischief and indulging in acts of indiscipline in the class-room and out of it.

In this way due to lack of adequate facilities, suitable environment and ignorance about their specific needs and problems, the gifted children are exposed to the risk of being turned into maladjusted or abnormal personalities. Under these circumstances, their superior talents go to waste. There is, therefore, a clear need for special care and proper education to be given to the gifted children.

The Identification of Gifted Children

The first step in the direction of planning special education for gifted children is to identify or separate them from the average children. In the absence of identification and adequate provision, many of the gifted children, like the flowers in the desert or diamonds in the earth, go unnoticed.

For the proper identification of the gifted children, we must make a distinction between the intellectually gifted children and children with special talents who show superior performance in one area or the other.

In the identification of intellectually gifted or academically talented children, intelligence tests are more often used as a screening instrument. Psychologists have differences of opinion regarding demarcation between the average and the gifted children on the basis of I.Q. Some consider children with I.Q. of 125 and above as gifted while others raise this limit to 135 or 140. The criterion is quite arbitrary and not universal. However, an I.Q. of 130 or above (as measured by an individual intelligence test) is usually accepted as the most agreed criterion for singling out the gifted children from the average population.

The following list of identifying characteristics prepared by De Haan and Kough (Dutt, 1974, p. 201) can be of great help in the identification of intellectually gifted or academically talented students:

1. Learns rapidly and easily.
2. Uses a great deal of common sense and practical knowledge.

3. Reasons things out. Thinks clearly, recognizes relationships, comprehends meanings.
4. Retains what he has heard or read without much rote drill.
5. Knows about many things of which most students are unaware.
6. Has a large vocabulary, which he uses easily and accurately.
7. Can read books that are one or two years in advance of the rest of the class.
8. Performs difficult mental tasks.
9. Asks many questions, has a wide range of interests.
10. Does some academic work one or two years in advance of the rest of the class.
11. Is original in his thinking, uses good but unusual methods.
12. Is alert, keenly observant and responds quickly.

As already mentioned, there are some gifted children who, although do not possess superior general intelligence, exhibit special abilities or talents in one field or the other. It is not possible to identify such children by intelligence tests. Such children need careful observation and study so that the specific areas of their giftedness can be spotted. Aptitude tests can render valuable help in this direction. Interest inventory, anecdotal records, opinions and reports of friends and teachers often help in exploring the latent gift. Self-analysis also sometimes helps in understanding the kind if giftedness a child possesses. In addition to this, the over-all behavioural assessment through personality tests and sociometric techniques also reveals the special abilities of a child. Some children show their talents when they are provided opportunities for self-expression and self-actualization. Some need a little more stimulation and encouragement. A wise and expert teacher should, therefore, try to put in an all around effort to detect and recognize the specific abilities and talents of these children so that they may be given appropriate help to achieve success in their specific fields.

The Education of the Gifted Children

At the present juncture students all over the world appear to be in revolt. They have been feeling that life is without any ideal or objectives to strive for. It is also an alarming fact that the leaders of these angry youths are found to be the most brilliant and the gifted. This makes one wonder what is wrong with the present system of education. Why is the stream of valuable human energy and the talents of such gifted individuals flowing in a negative direction?

Surely, there is an urgent need for a well thought-out programme or scheme of special education for the gifted children. The following plans have been put forward by different thinkers for this:

1. Separate schools.
2. Ability grouping or separate classes.
3. Acceleration or double promotion.
4. Enrichment programmes.

It is often suggested that there should be separate schools for gifted children and adequate facilities should be provided in these schools to help them in developing their specific abilities and potentialities. Such segregation is often criticized and labelled as undemocratic. The products of public schools, where there is provision for selective special education also justify our fears and doubts. The students educated in these schools develop a superior and conceited attitude and widen the gulf between the educated and the uneducated or the privileged and the unprivileged.

Similarly, segregation of gifted children into a separate section within the same school also involves the same danger. This plan is known as ability grouping. Here, a given grade is divided into different sections on the basis of ability, the range of ability within each section being relatively narrow. The non-feasibility of both these plans involving segregation is obvious in the Indian context. We can neither afford such segregation as it involves huge expenditure nor can it yield very fruitful results. The gifted child is gifted or talented in his area of giftedness only. He may or may not possess superior general intelligence and children who possess talents in a particular area may be as few as one or less per cent of the total population of their class. It is, therefore, impractical to think of having a separate section consisting of these few children. What is more, segregation on the basis of I.Q. is no guarantee to the maintenance of homogeneity in the grouping.

Another concept in the education of gifted children is 'acceleration', usually known as double promotion. According to this plan, the gifted child is allowed accelerated progress. He is either promoted to the next higher grade in midsession without completing the prescribed full term or is permitted to skip a grade or class at the end of the term. The plan, though quite feasible, suffers from a serious defect in that it creates a gulf between educational ability and experience. The children who get early promotion to the advanced grade usually find it hard to adjust among children who are senior to them in age. Though intellectually at par with them, they lag behind in emotional, social and physical spheres and thus fall victim to adjustment problems.

Another proposal for the education of gifted children is what is technically known as 'enrichment'. Basically, it involves the selection and organisation of learning experiences and activities appropriate to the child's adequate development. In this way the enrichment of education should be considered to be a need of all students. But in the case of gifted children it will definitely meet an urgent need of giving them a greater variety of experience or tasks at a more advanced level. Thus, enrichment programmes aim to provide additional educational opportunities to gifted children. For example, it may include, (a) special assignment (within or outside the syllabus), (b) work on independent projects, (c) preparation of reports and participation in panel discussions, (d) independent library reading, (e) visits to the sites to obtain first-hand information, (f) construction of models, aid material and improvised apparatus etc., (g) participation in the organisation of cocurricular activities, and (h) experimentation and independent research.

The learning experiences should thus, be so enriched that gifted children find come across new and challenging things. In this situation, they can get adequate opportunities for proper development. Enrichment of the learning experiences or programmes provided in the school in my opinion, is the most suitable plan for the education of gifted children in our country wedded as it is, to democracy and socialism. It not only provides facilities for the total development of the special abilities and potentialities of the child but also take care of the development of his overall personality. It tries to satisfy the basic needs of the gifted children and helps towards their proper adjustment. Moreover, it helps in evolving a school programme that is beneficial to both the average as well as the gifted children. Each of them can develop according to their own abilities and capacities without interfering in the development of the other. In this way, 'enrichment' provides all the essential facilities for a gifted child within the broad structure of our educational system and does not impose any extra hardship or financial burden on our educational institutions. In any scheme of education for the gifted in our country, therefore, adequate provisions should be made in the school curriculum for enrichment of the learning experiences according to the needs and requirements of the gifted children.

THE MENTALLY RETARDED

In the classification of exceptional children, the mentally retarded children belong to the lower end of the scale of intelligence and scholastic aptitude quite opposite and contrary to the gifted and creative who lie at the high end of this scale. As a matter of terminology such children are known by so many names other than mentally retarded such as, 'feeble-minded', 'mentally handicapped', 'mentally deficient', 'mentally subnormal' or 'mentally sub-average', etc. By whatever, name we recognize them, it connotes the sub-average mental functioning of a group of children which affects not only their behaviour and future development but also creates serious problems for the people responsible for their welfare. Who are these children? What are their specific characteristics and requirements? What can be done for them specially in the sphere of education?

Defining Mental Retardation or Mental Deficiency

The term 'mental retardation' or 'mental deficiency' has been defined in several ways. Some definitions of mental retardation are:

Page (1976):

> Mental deficiency is a condition of sub-normal mental development, present at birth or early childhood and characterized mainly by limited intelligence and social inadequacy.

Rosen, Fox and Gregory (1972):

> Mental retardation refers to a chronic condition present from birth or early childhood which is characterized by both impaired intellectual functioning as measured by standardized tests and impaired adaptation to the daily demands of the individual's social environment.

British Mental Deficiency Act (1981):

> Mental retardation is a condition of arrested or incomplete development of mind existing before the age of 18 years whether arising from inherent causes or induced by disease or injury.

American Association on Mental Deficiency (1983):

> Mental retardation refers to significantly sub-average general intellectual functioning existing concurrently with deficits in adaptive behaviour, and manifested during the development period.

Let us try to analyze and synthesize the viewpoint expressed in the above definitions. All these definitions agree that:

1. Mental retardation is a condition or state of mind.
2. It is related to the sub-normal development of the mind or brain.
3. It is not a disease nor a medical syndrome with a specific cause. A number of specific identified causes involving both the inherent and external factors may be responsible for it.
4. The deficiency may be observed at birth or manifested later during the course of development, generally before the end of the years of adolescence.
5. The mentally retarded, can be identified through:

    (a) their very low scores on some standardized intelligence tests.
    (b) the observation of their behaviour in the developmental period demonstrating impaired intellectual functioning.
    (c) their inadequacy to deal with the demands of environmental or deficiency and defects in adaptive behaviour.

However, as a matter of comparison, while the definition given by the British Mental Deficiency Act only mentions the incomplete development of the mind without reference to the state of the individual's adjustment to his environment or the nature of his adaptive behaviour or the difficulties he may face on account of his sub-normal intellectual functioning; the other definitions try to point out both, the state of the sub-normal's intellectual functioning and its effect on his day-to-day behaviour and environmental adaptation. While Page stresses inadequate social adjustment as a consequence of impaired intellectual functioning, Rosen, Fox and Gregory point out difficulties in meeting the daily demands of the environment.

Among all these definitions, the last definition put forth by the American Association on Mental Deficiency seems to be the most comprehensive. It is the latest in the sense that it reflects the modem viewpoints in the understanding, care and education of the mentally retarded. Let us consider the wording of this definition in some detail to understand the meaning and nature of mental retardedness.

Developmental period. The developmental period means the period of time between one's conception and the expiry of the period of adolescence, generally the 18th birthday.

General intellectual functioning. This is determined through the results obtained after individual administration of general intelligence tests such as the Stanford-Binet intelligence scale or the age-appropriate Wechsler scale.

Significantly sub-average. A person is described as significantly sub-average if his full-scale I.Q. does not exceed 70 on the Stanford-Binet test. However, a student with an I.Q. of 75 or even 79, could be classified as retarded if he demonstrates deficits in adaptive behaviour.

Adaptive behaviour. Adaptive behaviour is defined as "the effectiveness or degree with which the individual meets the standards of personal independence and social responsibility expected of his age and cultural group" (Grossman, 1983). These expectations differ from age to age. However, deficits with regard to these expectations may be manifested by slow, incomplete or arrested development.

According to the American Association on Mental Deficiency (AAMD) the deficits in adaptive behaviour during the different developmental stages may be reflected period-wise in the following areas:

1. During infancy and early childhood

    (a) Sensory-motor skills (turning, crawling, walking, manual manipulations).
    (b) Communication skills (social smiling, gesturing, speaking).
    (c) Self-help skills (eating, dressing, toilet, bathing).
    (d) Early socialization skills (playing imitatively, playing with others cooperatively or in parallel, depending upon age).

2. During childhood and early adolescence

    (a) Academic learning.
    (b) Judgement and reasoning in dealing with the environment.
    (c) Social skills (participation in group activities and effective interpersonal relationships).

In this way, the definition proposed by AAMD, has included criteria of both measured intelligence and adaptive behaviour for the identification of the mentally retarded. Consequently, a person cannot be designed as mentally retarded solely because of a low I.Q. A low I.Q. plus impaired or deficient adaptive behaviour originating before maturity is the essential requirement for a person to be described as mentally retarded. This definition deliberately does not consider the etiology of mental retardation simply because mental retardation may not be attributed to any specific cause or causes. The definition says nothing about the curability of the mental retardation. For many, mental deficiency or retardedness seems to be incurable in the sense that the deficiency cannot be overcome by a healthy nourishing diet, medicine or psychotherapy. The mentally deficient cannot be made intelligent and brought up to the level of average intellectual functioning. The remedy lies in the sincerity of the attempts relative to current medical, rehabilitative and educational efficiency of the measures adopted. By adopting the appropriate means, functional levels of the so-called mentally retarded can, no doubt, be significantly altered and improved to maximize their personal and social effectiveness. Considering its comprehensive scope, the AAMD definition appears to be the most acceptable and functional definition for further discussion on mentally retarded children.

Detecting or Identifying the Mentally Retarded

What are mentally retarded children like? Do they have so different a personality make-up from the normal as to be easily discernible? It is possible to some extent, that the physical appearance of the mentally retarded may give rise to some doubt about their normal intellectual functioning. This, however, is not always so, and in many cases the physical appearance gives no indication of mental retardation. In fact, the similarities between the mental retardates and the intellectually normal people exceed the differences. Therefore, great care must be taken for the proper identification and detection of mental retardedness among children. To correctly answer the question, what type of child should be labelled as mentally retarded, we have to consider the broader concept of the term 'mental retardation' or 'mental deficiency'. It is also clear in the light of our accepted AAMD definition, that a mere knowledge of a child's low I.Q. would not suffice for identifying him as mentally retarded. The following considerations would also have to be taken into account for the identification of mental retardedness among children.

1. The detection or identification must be carried out during the developmental period, i.e. from the embryonic stage to the end of adolescence.
2. Behaviour should be closely and objectively observed for detecting deficiencies in adaptive behaviour.
3. In case adaptive behaviour is judged to be indicative of possible mental retardation, it should be confirmed through intelligence testing or vice versa.
4. In all cases, the low I.Q. and deficient adaptive behaviour both, should be used as criteria for detecting mental retardedness.

Let us now discuss the procedures involved in identifying the mentally retarded.

Detection before birth. By means of certain tests in which a small amount of the fluid surrounding the developing foetus is examined, it is possible to screen metabolic diseases or the incurable chromosomal abnormalities affecting the developing foetus.

Detection at the time of birth. Most of the metabolic diseases and developmental defects causing mental retardation may be detected soon after birth. For example, phenylketonuria (PKU) may be easily diagnosed through the detection of phenylpyruvic acid in a newborn infant with the help of the urine test or a relatively simple blood test. Similarly, congenital cerebral defects causing bio-logical disorders leading to mental retardation like macrocephaly, microcephaly and hydrocephaly may be detected soon after birth.

Collecting history of the causation or development of mental retardation. Adequate information about the history of causation and development of mental retardation can help in the identification of disabilities among the retarded. This may be in the form of genetic information, prenatal history of the child and the mother's condition and experiences during pregnancy, history of labour and delivery, blood group incompatibility, exposure to infections and chronic diseases, happenings in the form of accidents, seizures and impairment in motor and intellectual development, emotional episodes and psychological stresses.

Assessment of intellectual functioning. Intelligence test scores in terms of I.Q. are used not only for identifying or segregating individuals with subnormal intellectual capacities but also for classifying the severity of their mental retardation into various categories such as moron, imbecile and idiot; or degrees like moderate, severe and profound. However, diagnosis of subnormal intellectual capacity cannot be made merely on the basis of a relatively low I.Q. The following characteristics should also be kept in mind:

1. Mentally subnormal children lack much in the power of observation, imagination, thinking and reasoning, and ability to generalize.
2. They are poor at abstraction and can only think in terms of concrete objects and situations.
3. They are slow learners. It has been found that they take longer to learn a skill.
4. They are poor at following general verbal instructions, unless these are repeated at frequent intervals.
5. Their rate of intellectual development is very slow in comparison with children of their age.
6. The areas of their interest, aptitudes and choices are limited.
7. The creativity aspect is almost absent in such children.

Assessment in terms of adaptive behaviour. In addition to the criterion of sub-normal intellectual capacities, an assessment of a child's deficiency in terms of adaptive behaviour and personality problems may also prove helpful in the diagnosis of mental retardation. Personality problems and deficiency in terms of adaptive behaviour may be assessed through close observation, or with the help of tests like adaptive behaviour scale and the Minnesota developmental programming system.

Classifying the Mentally Retarded

The mentally retarded constitute a group quite distinct from the normal and the above-normal. As elucidated in the AAMD definition, each mental retardate displays distinctly sub-average general intellectual functioning along with noticeable deficiencies in adaptive behaviour during the developmental stages. This does not mean, however, that they are all alike. In addition to the individual differences within the population, there are identifiable subgroups with characteristics in common. The mentally retarded can be classified into certain distinct subgroups on the basis of some criteria or systems of classification.

Medical System of Classification

This system is related to causalty, or medical diagnosis associated with mental retardation. According to this system, the mentally retarded can be classified into the following groups:

1. *Environmentally influenced or cultural—familial group.* This consists of the cases for which no precise etiology (causation of mental retardation) can be determined.

2. *Unknown prenatal influence-carrying group.* There are many unknown prenatal influences established by genetic factors or unknown influences operative inside the womb of the mother which are responsible for certain types of mental deficiency. This subgroup includes cases arising from unknown prenatal influences such as chromosomal abnormalities, including Down's Syndrome.

3. *Infections and intoxication-caused group.* This subgroup includes cases of mental retardation caused by severe infections and intoxicants like rubella, viral infections and maternal disorders.

4. *Trauma or physical-agent-caused group.* The cases arising out of physical damage to the brain including prenatal injury and hypoxia at birth are included in this group.

5. *Metabolic and endocrine disorder-caused group.* This group includes the cases arising from disturbances in metabolism and endocrine imbalances including phenylketonuria (PKU) and hypothyroidism.

6. *Gross brain disease-oriented group.* This group includes the mental retardation cases caused by gross brain diseases like brain tumours and other new growths.

7. *Prenatal conditions-caused group.* This group includes the cases arising out of perinatal conditions like extreme immaturity and foetal and/or maternal nutritional disorders.

The foregoing classification is used from the viewpoint of medical treatment, prevention programmes and research on prevention and treatment. For the purpose of designing a programme of education for the mentally retarded, however, we need to look for some other norms for the classification of mental retardation.

Intelligence Test as a Means of Classification

The scores on some standardized intelligence test, like the Stanford-Binet scale or the Wechsler scale have been used for classifying the mentally retarded into certain definite subgroups like morons, imbeciles and idiots. Consequently, the results of intelligence tests in terms of I.Q. became a standard for classification and the I.Q. of 70 was established as the common cut-off score for retardation and consequently the following subgroups based on the different levels of I.Q. emerged.

Table 22.1 Classification of mentally retarded on the basis of I.Q.

Subgroups of the mentally retarded	I.Q. on Stanford-Binet scale
Morons	51 to 70
Imbeciles	25 to 50
Idiots	Below 25

However, this approach to classify the mentally retarded solely on the basis of I.Q. was dropped following later researches in the field of mental retardation. It was felt that a certain level of I.Q. does not by itself characterise an individual as a mental retardate.

Adaptive Behaviour as a Norm for Classification

This criterion involves the comparison of an individual's adaptive behaviour, with the adaptive behaviour expected of people of his age and cultural group, as a means of assessment. Two aspects are considered for the assessment, namely the degree to which the individual is able to function and maintain himself independently, and the success with which he meets his cultural, social and personal responsibilities.

Attempts have been made to devise measures for the assessment of deficiency in adaptive behaviour by use of the Vineland social maturity scale, the adaptive behaviour scale (AAMD), and the Maxfield Buckholz social maturity scale etc.

The consideration of deficiency in adaptive behaviour together with the very low scores on an intelligence test resulted in the development of an altogether new classification of subnormality. The terms moron, imbecile, and idiot are now completely avoided for determining the level of retardation. The new terminology in terms of I.Q. scores on different test scales is shown in Table 22.2.

Table 22.2 Level of Retardation and I.Q.

Level of retardation	Intelligence quotient	
	Stanford-Binet	Wechsler scale
Profound	Under 20	Under 25
Severe	20–35	25–39
Moderate	36–51	40–54
Mild	52–67	55–69

A discussion of these categories of retardation in terms of the typical subnormal intelligence and deficient adaptive behaviour follows:

1. *Mild retardation.* A majority or approximately eightyfive per cent of the retarded are only mildly retarded. As grown ups, these individuals attain intellectual levels comparable to those of the average ten-year-old child. Their social adjustment may be compared with that of an adolescent. Here too, they lack the innovative and vigorous nature of normal adolescents. They show signs of delayed development early in life and learn to walk, talk, feed and toilet themselves one year later than the average. They may be identified in schools as slow learners and are frequently required to repeat early grades. Speech disturbances are also common among them.

In comparison to normal individuals, the mildly retarded exhibit immature behaviour, have poor control over their impulses, lack judgement, and fail to anticipate the consequence of their actions. Their sexual behaviour and adjustment, in spite of the normal sexual development and fertility, is unpredictable and leads to a variety of problems and difficulties.

The mildly retarded individuals generally do not show any organic pathology and require little supervision. They are considered to be educable. With early diagnosis, parental assistance, and help of special classes, they can be expected to reach a reasonable degree of educational achievement and to make an adequate social and economic adjustment in the community.

2. *Moderate mental retardation.* Approximately ten per cent of the total mentally retarded have moderate mental retardation. In adult life these individuals attains an intellectual level similar to that of the average six year old child. Physically, they appear clumsy, suffer from motor incoordination and present an affable, dull and somewhat vacuous personality. As a result of their inadequate development and deficient capacities and abilities they are regarded as 'trainable' instead of being 'educable' like the mildly retarded. They show signs of retardation in almost all areas of development from infancy or early childhood, and though they manage to speak, their rate of learning is too slow. They are unable to do any work that requires initiative, originality, abstract thinking, memory or consistent attention, and cannot be expected to acquire the basic skills of reading and writing.

With early diagnosis, parental help and adequate training and support, most of the moderately retarded can achieve considerable independence in all spheres of life. They require constant supervision and support, however, and need institutionalization depending on the general nature of their adaptive behaviour.

3. *Severe mental retardation.* Nearly 3.5 per cent of all retarded individuals—mostly children and adolescents—suffer from severe mental retardation. They never attain an intellectual level greater than that of the average four year old child. The mortality rate due to high susceptibility to disease is quite high among these individuals. They are grossly retarded in development from birth or infancy onward and show severe motor and speech deficiency. Sensory defects and motor handicaps are common. The majority of them display relatively little interest in their surroundings and many of them never master even basic skills and functions like feeding and dressing themselves, or bladder and bowel control.

The severe mental retardates are neither 'educable' nor 'trainable' and the majority of them remain dependent on others throughout their lives. They need care and supervision of others with a real need for institutionalization. They may profit from proper care, timely treatment and specialized training and managing their own physical well-being and doing manual labour.

4. *Profound mental retardation.* The profoundly retarded constitute 1.5 percent of the total mentally retarded population. It is characterized by the most severe symptoms of mental retardation. The individuals belonging to this category never attain in adult life an intellectual level greater than that of the average two year old child. They are severely deficient both in intellectual capacities and adaptive behaviour. The symptoms associated with them are retarded growth, physical deformities, pathology of the central nervous system, mutism, severe

speech disturbances, motor incoordination, deafness and convulsive seizures. They are unable to protect themselves against common dangers and are unable to manage their own affairs and satisfy their physical needs. Their life span, as a result of their low resistance, is very short. Such individuals are completely dependent on others and need the care and supervision normally given to an infant. Essentially, they need to be institutionalized, as their condition deteriorates on account of the biased attitude of the parents and stressful demands of their environment.

Common Clinical Types of Mental Retardation

The knowledge of well-known categories of mental deficiency or retardation based on a number of clinical symptoms and syndromes is useful in the identification, treatment and care of retardates.

1. *Mongolism.* The mental deficients whose facial characteristics bear a superficial resemblance to members of the Mongolian race are classified as mongols. The retardation in them ranges from moderate to severe (I.Q. approximately 20–25).

The mongoloids tend to be short in stature with small round heads, abnormally short necks, thumbs and fingers, slanting almond-shaped eyes, and short flat noses. They usually have a small mouth and fissured and dry lips and tongue. Their hands and feet are broad and clumsy, they have a deep voice and their motor coordination is awkward. They are handicapped in any learning or training, but most of them can learn self-help skills, acceptable social behaviour and routine manual skills.

The causes of mongolism are faulty heredity (possible chromosomal anomalies, and metabolic factors like glandular imbalance often involving the pituitary gland. It is irreversible and there is no effective treatment or workable preventive measures.

2. *Cretinism.* This mental deficiency ranging from moderate to severe retardation results from thyroid deficiency. The severity of the disorder depends on the age at which the deficiency occurs as well as the degree and duration of the deficiency.

The physical symptoms in the case of persons suffering from cretinism consist of a dwarf-like, thickset body, coarse and thick skin, short and stubby extremities, abundant hair of wiry consistency and thick eyelids that give a sleepy appearance. Other pronounced symptoms include a broad, flat nose, large and flabby ears, a protruding abdomen and failure to mature sexually. Early timely treatment in the form of injection of thyroid gland extract produces favourable results in all cases except those of long standing where the damage to the nervous system and to general physical development is beyond repair.

3. *Microcephaly.* This refers to mental deficiency associated with the failure of the cranium to attain normal size on account of impaired development of the brain. The microcephalic has an unusually small

head which rarely exceeds a circumference of seventeen inches, as compared with the normal of approximately twenty-two inches. In addition, he is short statured with the usual cone-shaped skull and receding chin and forehead. Depending upon the degree of severity of mental retardation, microcephalics fall into the profound, severe and moderate categories of mental retardation.

Both genetic as well as non-genetic factors impair development of the brain and thus cause microcephaly. There is no effective medical treatment available for microcephaly if there has been impaired brain development.

4. *Hydrocephaly.* This mental deficiency results from the accumulation of an unusually large amount of cerebrospinal fluid within the cranium, causing damage to the brain and enlargement of the skull. The degree of mental retardation in this disorder varies from moderate to profound depending upon the extent of neural damage which, in turn, depends upon the age at onset, the duration and also the size of the skull.

The main symptom in hydrocephaly is the gradual increase in the size of the skull. The causes seem to be genetic as well as non-genetic. In some cases, the disorder is present at birth or the head begins to enlarge soon after birth on account of prenatal disturbances. More often, the disorder develops during infancy or early childhood on account of intracranial neoplasm or acute inflammatory brain disease.

An early diagnosis and proper surgical treatment has been known to show favourable result in checking further damage to the brain tissue. The advanced, acute stage, however, does not respond to any treatment and eventually results in death.

5. *Phenylketonuria* (PKU). This disorder has a genetic base and is assumed to be transmitted through a recessive gene carrying metabolic disturbance. As a result the child, at birth lacks an enzyme needed to breakdown phenylalanine, an amino acid found in protein foods. Consequently, there is an abnormal accumulation of phenylalanine in the blood causing damage to the brain tissue.

Symptoms like vomiting, a peculiar musty odour, infantile eczema and seizures, motor incoordination, signs of mental retardation and neurological manifestations relating to severe brain damage are common with this disorder. However, the diagnosis of this disorder, however, is primarily made on the basis of the presence of phenylpyruvic acid in the urine.

The success of treatment of PKU depends on early detection. Special diet low in phenylalanine, is recommended for the affected infants. Timely treatment helps in restraining or preventing brain damage.

6. *Amaurotic idiocy.* This is a rare hereditary disorder of fat metabolism transmitted as a simple recessive characteristic. It is never transmitted directly from patient to offspring, because death generally occurs before puberty. The only mode of transmission is through the mating of persons who, although free of overt symptoms, are carriers of the defective gene.

This disorder has been described to occur in two different forms—infantile and juvenile—depending on the age at which it occurs.

The major symptoms of this disorder include muscular weakness, inability to maintain normal posture, loss of ability to grasp objects, visual difficulties leading to progressive blindness, seizures and neurologic manifestations.

Infantile amaurotic idiocy, also known as Tay-Sachs disease is common among infants. The disorder appears at about six months of age and death occurs between the ages of two and three years. Juvenile amaurotic idiocy occurs at five or six years of age and the patient may live up to thirteen years.

Causes of Mental Retardation

It is difficult to lay down the standard causes of mental retardation applicable to every such case. A number of factors are believed to cause mental retardation which may be divided into two broad categories:

1. Organic or biological factors
2. Socio-psychological factors

1. *Organic or biological factors.*   Causes listed in this broad category are:

(a) *Genetic factors.*   Mental deficiency may be established by genetic factors operative at the time of conception in two ways—either through transmission of some defective genes in the chromosomes of one or both parents, or on account of chromosomal aberrations.

The transmission of defective genes gives rise to many disorders causing mental deficiency. Mental retardation or deficiency attributable to a dominant gene is very rare because the persons affected are generally incapable of reproduction. It is often the result of the pairing of two defective recessive genes. When defective recessive genes are paired, as in PKU, the production of an enzyme, necessary for an important metabolic process, is disturbed. This, in turn, affects the development of the embryo and causes mental deficiency. In some cases, like Tay-Sachs disease, mental deficiency may also result from the pairing of single recessive genes.

Several chromosomal anomalies determine mental retardation at the time of conception. Down's synrdome or mongolism is one such disorder which is said to be caused by chromosomal aberrations. The majority of the Mongoloid children are found to have 47 chromosomes instead of the usual 46. The number of chromosomes increases as a result of tripling of chromosome 21 (during the fertilization of the egg the chromosome pair 21 become three instead of two). Another example of chromosomal abnormality is Klinefelter's syndrome in which an extra X chromosome is usually the culprit. This disorder occurs only in males and symptoms are usually noticed at puberty when the testes remain small and the body develops feminine secondary sexual characteristics such as enlarged breasts and round hips.

(b) *Infection.*   Mental retardation can also be the result of many infectious diseases like syphilis, rubella (German measles) toxoplasmosis, or encephalitis which can damage brain tissue and the nervous system resulting in severe mental deficiency or retardation. If the mother suffers from one or the other of these infectious diseases she may transmit infection to the developing foetus.

A child may at birth or afterwards be infected with diseases which cause life-long mental subnormality. Encephalitis and meningococal meningitis cause irreversible brain damage and even death if contracted in infancy or early childhood. Besides directly damaging brain tissues, such infectious diseases may indirectly lead to mental subnormality by causing congenital physical defects such as blindness, deafness, paralysis and epilepsy.

(c) *Intoxication.* Mental retardation may be caused by intoxication. A number of toxic agents like carbon monoxide, mercury, lead and various immunological agents like anti-tetanus serum or the use of small pox, rabies and typhoid vaccines may result in brain damage during development after birth. Similarly, large doses of X-ray in radio therapy in the abdominal region of the pregnant mother, drugs administered to the mother during pregnancy, incompatibility in blood types between mother and foetus, and overdose of drugs administered to the infant also lead to toxicity and brain damage.

(d) *Trauma.* Mental retardation may be caused by physical damage to the brain in the form of injuries prior to birth, at the time of delivery, or following birth.

Prenatal injuries adversely affect the brain and the nervous system of the foetus. One of the main causes of such damage is asphyxia which results from oxygen deprivation and consequently causes suffocation of the tissues. This may occur from compression of the umbilical cord which supplies the foetus with blood carrying oxygen and nutrition from the mother. Another example of prenatal injury is the damaging effects of irradiation on the uterus of the pregnant mother.

Abnormal delivery and birth injuries are another cause of mental retardation, Difficulties during labour may result in damage to the infant's brain. Any abnormal delivery involves the risk of brain injuries. An abnormal position of the foetus, breech extraction, the use of forceps and other obstetrical procedures may cause hemorrhage of the brain and thus lead to mental retardation.

Premature birth exposes the child to an increased risk of brain damage from mechanical trauma and anoxia (a condition associated with changes in oxygen supply). Similarly, postmature birth also results in an increased risk of anoxia for the child, during the later weeks of pregnancy and during birth.

Another birth trauma in the form of anoxia resulting from delayed breathing of the newborn infant or as a result of anesthetic accidents may also damage the brain. Anoxia may also occur after birth as a result of cardiac arrest associated with operations, heart attacks, gas poisoning or near-drowning.

Accidental brain injuries received in infancy, childhood or later in life, causing damage to the brain also lead to serious mental retardation.

(e) *Metabolic and endocrine disorders.* Mental retardation may be caused by various disturbances in metabolism in which body cells are built up and broken down, and by which energy is made available for their functioning. The chemical errors involving metabolism of fat cause the Tay-Sachs disease while disturbed protein metabolism causes PKU. Both these disorders lead to severe mental retardation. Similarly, metabolic disorders like galactosemia involving an inability to metabolize galactose and maple syrup urine disease, involving chain amino acids lead to mental retardation. Several metabolic disorders involving endocrine imbalances may also result in various degrees of mental retardation. Hypothyroidism (usually referred to as cretinism) is one such metabolic disorder.

(f) *Tumours.* Mental retardation may be caused by brain damage associated with brain tumours and other new growths. Tuberous sclerosis or epiloia is characterized by numerous nodules and tumours throughout the brain and other parts of the body. A butterfly shaped rash initially appearing on the face, spreads over a wider area. It may finally lead to convulsions and mental retardation. Similarly, macrocephaly (large headedness), microcephaly (small headedness) and hydrocephaly (accumulation of an abnormal amount of cerebrospinal fluid in the cranium) are some of the other conditions resulting in mental sub-normality that may be caused by tumours.

2. Socio-psychological factors. Psychological factors coupled with adverse socio-cultural environment play a leading role in the causation as well as perpetuation of mental retardation. Children who are denied the satisfaction of their psycho-logical and social needs become over-sensitive to psychological stress in the same way as the patient with vitamin deficiency is susceptible to infection. The early childhood deprivation like lack of adequate mothering and parental care results in a retarded rate of development.

In an inadequte socio-cultural environment, the children are deprived of the basic necessities of life for their proper physical, intellectual, emotional and social development. A poverty ridden, deprived, crowded and uncongenial family environment provides sufficient as well as necessary grounds for the germination and perpetuation of mental subnormality. The deprived individuals tend to marry spouses like themselves and their poverty compels them to suffer. The severe environmental deprivation in the form of physical, cultural, emotional and intellectual poverty especially during infancy and childhood results in the retardation of the child's intellectual development even when his potential at birth is normal. The child may have difficulty in developing verbal ability on account of such unfavourable environment or may suffer from lack of emotional and social maturity and thus may not be able to adapt to the needs of his environment.

In some cases, the failure of the school system has adverse effects. School maladjustment tends to retard the development rate of the child who, once labelled as a slow learner or retarded on the basis of speech, I.Q. scores, achievement test scores and observable behaviour, becomes subnormal on account of the perpetuation of inferiority feelings and complexes.

Prevention of Mental Retardation

Prevention is said to be better than cure. An attempt should, therefore, be made to adopt preventive measures for exercising control over the occurrence and development of mental retardation. Some preventive measures are listed here.

Genetic counselling and voluntary birth control. Genetic factors play a significant role in the causation of mental retardation. Chromosomal aberrations as well as pairing of defective recessive genes prove detrimental to normal brain development and functioning. This knowledge may be helpful for the caring parents. There are tests to identify parents who have chromosomal anomalies, or defective and inferior genetic material. For example, the fluorescent blood test can help to determine whether one or the other prospective parent is genetically normal or is a carrier of the recessive gene causing Tay-Sachs disease. Similarly, there are tests that reveal whether the developing foetus will be the victim of some specific mental retardation. These parents should be made aware of the problems to be faced in raising a mentally retarded child. They may be counselled about the risk they run in begetting children.

Proper care of the mother and child. Adequate care of the mother and the newborn infant is essential for the prevention of mental retardation. Generally speaking, it is essential that a balanced, adequate diet is provided to all expectant and nursing mothers. All routine health measures should be adopted for the mothers and the infants. Proper care should be taken for the prevention of possible physical damage in the form of injuries prior to birth, at the time of birth or immediately following birth.

Provision of normal and stimulating environment after birth. Uncongenial and unfavourable conditions present in one's socio-cultural environment and psychological deprivations especially in early childhood may cause or perpetuate mental retardation. For the prevention of such consequences, there is a great need for educating the parents and other responsible members of society. As far as possible, the children should be provided a normal, stimulating environment for the proper growth and development of their innate capabilities. Illiteracy and poverty of the parents, and poor or defective family environment should not come in the way of the satisfaction of their basic needs. Moreover, they should not be allowed to develop inferiority feelings, complexes, or frustrations on account of their limitations.

Provision of public education. Efforts should be made to arouse the public to adopt preventive measures for controlling mental retardation. For example, by giving the right information about the correlation of the mother's age and mongolism, public opinion may be built up in favour of avoiding children after forty. Similarly, retardation caused by toxic agents may be prevented by providing information and education to the public so that they may be saved from their adverse effects. In the field of environmental modification, and pollution control, programmes of public education may yield effective results which, in turn, may prevent and control mental retardation. Public education can also help in educating the masses about the need and importance of a nutritious and balanced diet, control of infectious diseases and the adoption of measures for the welfare of the mother and infants. The hazards of accidents may also be reduced if people are made aware of the relevant safety measures.

Remedial Measures for Mental Retardation

Whatever preventive measures we may adopt, it is neither possible nor feasible to completely eliminate the possibility of the occurrence of mental retardation. We can neither exercise much control over hereditary influences nor can we avoid accidental hazards, and traumas. Moreover, we are also handicapped in controlling the unfavourable influences of defective socio-cultural environment and are unable to overcome the deficiency arising from psychological deprivation. Therefore, cases of mental retardation are bound to exist and we have to think out and plan the treatment and remedial measures for the mental retardates.

One thing which has to be accepted while seeking treatment of mental retardation is that there is no cure for mental deficiency. Mental retardates are essentially incurable in the sense that they cannot be given more intelligence and made normal. No amount of training or medical care can transform a mental retardate into a normal individual. The mentally subnormal should not be confused with persons who are mentally ill or suffer from a mental disease. In this connection, the observation of Wechsler (1979) is worth quoting:

> Mental deficiency, unlike typhoid fever or paralysis is not a disease. A mentally
> deficient is not a person who suffers from a specific disease process but one
> who by reasons of intellectual arrest or impairment is unable to cope with his
> environment to the extent that he needs special care, education and
> institutionalization.

It will be appropriate to consider the treatment or remedial measures for the adjustment, rehabilitation and education of the mentally retarded, in the light of the above observations.

Medical or Physical Measures

Mental retardation, to some extent, is said to be a medical problem. The following medical measures may prove helpful in some cases:

- *Cretinism.* This mental retardation resulting from deficiency in thyroid secretion, if recognised at birth or in its early manifestations, may be corrected or controlled by the institution of thyroid therapy.

- *Congenital syphilis.* Children infected with congenital syphilis are usually found to be suffering from severe mental subnormality. Early detection and prompt penicillin therapy is found to be helpful in the prevention as well as control of many effects of congenital syphilis.

- *Phenylketonuria* (PKU). On early detection with the help of a simple urine test, PKU, a metabolic disorder causing mental retardation may be checked or controlled, to a great extent, by placing the infant on a special diet relatively free of phenylalanine found in most protein foods.

- *Hydrocephalus.* Hydrocephalus, resulting from the accumulation of an abnormal amount of cerebrospinal fluid within the cranium results in mental retardation. Surgical treatment is found to be very effective in the treatment of this disorder. It is aimed at the reduction of the normal production of cerebrospinal fluid or to the channelling of the fluid by removing the blockade or obstruction resulting from congenital malformations or post-natal infections.

- *Epileptic seizures.* In the case of patients subject to epileptic seizures, the administration of anticonvulsant medication may prove helpful in controlling and minimizing intellectual deterioration.

- *Controlling disturbed behaviour.* The administration of tranquilizers proves useful in controlling hyperactive and disturbed behaviour among mental retardates.

Psychological Treatment

Often on account of the link between mental subnormality and psychological factors, psychological treatment in the form of individual or group psychotherapy is found to be useful in providing remedial measures for mental retardation. Children can be helped in solving problems of emotional and social maladjustment and resolving their mental conflicts through psychological measures.

Educating the parents. Parents can also help in the welfare, care as well as treatment of the mental retardates. For this purpose, there is a need for proper counselling services for them. Moreover, on account of their emotional involvement the parents do not always realize the shortcomings and deficiency of their children and waste a lot of time and money in the hope that some magic cure will be found or the deficiency will automatically disappear with time. Sometimes, they become disturbed by the responsibilities of looking after their mentally retarded child. Such disappointed, insecure and guilt-ridden parents begin to demand behaviour and intellectual achievement beyond the abilities of the child who is often abused, snubbed and punished for no fault of his. Some parents adopt an over-protective approach in their effort to shield the child from challenging situations and thus make him completely dependent by interfering with the development of whatever abilities or capacities he may possess. It is therefore essential that parents should first realize the truth about their child. They should accept the child's limitations and the mental deficiency in the sense that the child cannot be given more intelligence and made normal.

Secondly, they should be educated to behave normally with their mentally subnormal child without being over-protective or rejecting the child.

Thirdly, the parents should be given training and education for handling the emotional and social adjustment problems of the retarded children. They should never compare their achievements and abilities with those of their normal siblings or other children in the home and neighbourhood. It should be seen that the retarded child is not unnecessarily criticised or ridiculed by others.

Fourthly, they should be educated to provide essential training at home to their mentally retarded child. How to train him to manage his affairs independently, how to help the child to develop and seek maximum utilization of his subnormal capacities are some of the areas where useful education and training can be provided by the parents.

Finally, the parents should be made to realise that if needed there is no harm in sending their children to special schools meant for the mental retardates. It is the best place for their education and training.

Provision of special education and training. It is a cardinal educational as well as psychological error to educate or train the mental retardates with normal children. The involved attitude of the parents at home also interferes with the development of the retarded child. The remedy lies in the provision of special education or training for them. The institutes or boarding schools meant for subnormal children serve a useful purpose in this direction. For better results, the special institutes or schools must be managed keeping the following considerations in mind:

1. There should be proper grouping and classification of the mentally retarded children on the basis of the degree of severity of their retardation.
2. The 'educable' should be educated and the 'trainable' should be trained. Those who are neither easily educable nor trainable should be cared for and efforts should be made to train them to manage their basic day-to-day needs.
3. The schools should provide the environment essential for maximum development of the abilities and capacities of all mental retardates. Curriculum, methods of teaching, and tools for evaluation should be adjusted according to their individual needs.
4. There should be provision for specially trained teachers, able to utilize latest materials and techniques for their education or training. They should be able to deal with the special problems of these children, understand them sympathetically, and help them to grow with their deficiencies.
5. In these schools greater emphasis should be placed on cocurricular experiences and the children should be provided opportunities for learning the ways for their emotional and social adjustment, imbibing moral virtues and desirable personal habits.
6. These institutions should make provision for vocational education and training. The mental retardates should be trained for manual work, crafts and specialized vocations in keeping with their abilities.

The general attitude towards the mentally handicapped needs to be changed. They are not to be sympathized with, protected or ridiculed but to be helped in growing and developing within their strengths and limitations. Their education or training should begin at home. Thereafter special schools or institutions may be involved in their education and training. The society and the state, then, should take responsibility for their rehabilitation and adjustment.

Planning Education according to the Levels of Mental Retardation

The mentally retarded, as emphasized earlier are not all alike. After segregation from the normal individuals they can be properly grouped into distinct categories. The most accepted classification based on the I.Q. as well as adaptive behaviour criteria enumerates the four levels of retardation i.e. mild, moderate, severe and profound. For educational care and programmes, the mentally retarded children belonging to these four levels of retardedness can be regrouped into educable (labelled as mild), trainable (labelled as moderate) and custodial (labelled as severe and profound). Let us now consider the specific educational programmes for these types of children.

Educational programmes for the educable mentally related (EMR). The educable mentally retarded (EMR) are considered educable in the sense that if the instructions and the atmosphere for learning are appropriate, they can be expected to acquire the basic academic skills of reading, writing and arithmetic. However, their maximum academic achievement can be expected to equal that of the average eight to twelve year old child. Most of them can easily learn vocational skills needed for future employment preferably of semi-skilled or unskilled nature. The following points should be specially taken into consideration for planning the educational programmes for them:

1. Schooling of these students may be delayed for 2 to 3 years.
2. During the earliest school years, they may be given instruction in simple arithmetical concepts, understanding of the home and community and early development of good work habits.
3. Formal reading and writing instruction must be started preferably at the age of 9 or 10.
4. The curriculum for these children should include the topics, contents and learning experiences related to basic academic skills as well as the basic skills for coping with the environment as children and as adults.
5. The school's curricular as well as cocurricular activities should lay stronger emphasis on experience than on abstraction.
6. In any case, in spite of their educability these children should not be expected to attain the level of accomplishment of the same chronological age as normal children.

Educational programmes for the trainable mentally retarded (TMR). The TMR children cannot be educated like the EMR. However, they can be trained to acquire certain basic skills so that they may lead their future dependent or semi-independent lives. The following aspects may be considered for planning appropriate training programmes for them:

1. They may be helped to acquire self-help skills like independent eating, dressing, toileting, washing and combing hair, brushing teeth, and using towels and handkerchiefs, etc. They may be gradually taught to follow directions and perform simple tasks.

2. They should then be trained to acquire social skills like greeting people, play with their companions, take turns and follow the rules of the road, observe common social courtesies and health rules, etc.

3. Necessary training should also be provided for the development of motor skills and improvement of sensory discrimination.

4. Necessary household skills like dusting and sweeping, washing of utensils and clothes, ironing, sewing, using household articles and appliances like the radio, television, telephone, and limited travelling in familiar areas etc. should also be taught to them.

5. The teaching of basic academic skills should not be started until early adolescence. The academic skills taught to them should be of very simple nature like learning to recognize common signs and symbols, learning to recognize and use coins and currencies, and telling the time to the half or the quarter hour.

6. The curriculum should then include activities for teaching unskilled occupational jobs. It should also include activities related with leisure skills.

7. Throughout their training and acquiring learning experiences, the training programme should be based on the use of concrete lesson materials rather than on any abstract thinking or lecturing (i.e. real objects rather than two-dimensional representations on paper, careful modelling rather than heavy emphasis on verbalized directions).

8. In addition to providing concrete and real experiences, the training programmes for these children must be based fundamentally on principles of reinforcement like token economy, contingency management and other concepts of behaviour modification.

Educational programmers for the custodial mentally retarded (CMR). The severely retarded (I.Q. range about 20 to 35) and profoundly retarded (I.Q. below 20) children can neither be educated nor trained like the educable or the trainable children. No public school system or voluntary organisation exists in India for their schooling and rehabilitation and such children have, of necessity, to be admitted into government or semi-govemment residential institutions. Educationally both the severely retarded and the profoundly retarded have no hope and custodial treatment provided in the residential institutions is the only avenue open to them. A proper custodial programme whether run in residential institutions, day hospitals, day-care centres or boarding and nursing homes must take care of the following:

1. Educational programmes for these children must lay strong emphasis on self-help skills like feeding, toilet training, washing and cleaning of their body parts and dressing up etc.

2. They must be taught to protect themselves from health and weather hazards, harmful insects, animals, fires, etc.

3. The children suffering from behavioural problems should be helped in making their life as smooth and free of trouble for themselves as well as for others.

4. Application of the reinforcement theory, specially the principles of operant conditioning used in training lower animals may be found more suitable in teaching them the basics regarding self-help skills, household skills, performance of routine tasks involved in the residential institutional management and in some cases simple, routine unskilled occupational skills.

BACKWARD CHILDREN

Definition and Meaning of the Term Backward Child

The term 'backward children' and 'backwardness' has been defined in many ways. We give below, some of the well-known definitions.

Barton Hall (1947):

> Backwardness in general, is applied to cases where their educational attainment falls below the level of their natural abilities.

Schonell (1948):

> Backward pupil is one who, compared with other pupils of the same chronological age, shows marked educational deficiency.

Burt (1950):

> [A backward child is] one who in midschool career is unable to do the work of the class next below that which is normal for his age.

All the definitions quoted above lead to the following conclusions about a backward child.

1. He is a slow learner and finds it difficult to keep pace with the normal school work.
2. Educationally, he is not able to attain what he should and his educational attainment falls below his natural abilities.
3. He falls far behind other children of his age in matters of study. Usually, such children remain in the same class for a number of years.
4. Not only is he unable to learn at the same level as other children of the same age but also finds it difficult to keep pace with children in lower classes who are younger to him in age.
5. He is necessarily a failure in the academic field and shows educational impoverishment.
6. Unlike the mentally retarded and mentally handicapped children we cannot call a child backward merely on the basis of his low I.Q. That is why no definition suggests an I.Q. level below which a child can definitely be called backward.

In fact, intelligence is no guarantee against backwardness nor does a lower I.Q. alone necessarily make a child backward. Consequently, the backward child should not be misunderstood and labelled as mentally retarded or dull. Barton Hall (1947) has emphasized this fact in these words: *A child may be both dull and backward but he is not necessarily backward because he is dull.* A child can be really termed backward only if his attainment falls below his natural ability. In order to decide whether a child with a low I.Q. is backward or not, he should be compared with children possessing the same. I.Q.

Another striking feature concerning backward children is that they may, in fact, possess very superior intelligence, special skill or talents and may be inattentive or indifferent towards schoolwork due to many environmental and psychological reasons and so lag behind in achievement. Backwardness, therefore, is not necessarily a characteristic confined to dull, mentally deficient or retarded children. An average, superior child, even a prodigy may also show backwardness. Truly speaking, any child who does not progress at a rate corresponding to his abilities may be said to be backward. A superior child possesses better abilities and potentialities and may, therefore, be expected to display intellectual superiority, and may be said to be backward if he fails to do so. By the same reasoning, a dull child cannot be termed backward if his achievement is below that of a superior or even an average child. He may be termed backward only if his progress falls short of what he is supposed to achieve according to his abilities.

Kinds of Backwardness

Backward is supposed to be of two kinds, general and specific. The child suffering from such general backwardness is weak in all the subjects of the school curriculum. The child suffering from specific backwardness on the other hand, lags behind in one or two specific subjects only, while in others his progress may be satisfactory or even extraordinary.

Causes of Backwardness

It is difficult to list the general causes of backwardness as it is an individual problem and every individual problem is unique. But it is certain that the roots of backwardness of a child must lie within him or outside him in the environment. Moreover, it is also found that usually, many factors or causes operate together in a particular case of backwardness. Let us try to ascertain some possible causes or factors resulting in backwardness.

Inherent Factors

Physiological or physical factors. The physiological and physical condition of the child affects his educational attainment at every stage. The studies of Burt, Schonell and others have shown that a majority of the educationally backward children suffer from some kind of developmental or physical retardation. They are either born with poor health, lack of vitality and physical deformities or become victims of poor environment and thus suffer from physical ailments, chronic diseases and bodily defects. The resultant drawbacks like poor eyesight, faulty hearing, defective speech etc., make them deficient and they perforce develop as backward. Physical ailments or generally poor health may also seriously interfere with such children's attendance at school and study at home. These problems may also undermine their health to such an extent that they may as a result, be unable to devote adequate time and energy to their studies and so become educationally sub-normal and end up being termed backward.

Intellectual factors. Intellectual inferiority is also found to be an important contributory factor. Some children are born with some inherent defects in their brain system or with some intellectual subnormality. These mentally handicapped or intellectually inferior children cannot keep pace with the normal school curriculum and prove to be very slow in learning. Burt (1953), on the basis of his studies, asserts:

> in majority of the cases defective intelligence or lower I.Q. has been found to be the sole cause of the backwardness.

It is generally seen that students whose intellectual powers like thinking and reasoning, concentration, observation and imagination, are, for some reason, not properly developed generally drift towards educational subnormality. Such children are not only affected in terms of quick understanding and grasp of meaning or remembering but also suffer emotional imbalance and social maladjustment which impedes their progress in school subjects.

Environmental factors. Apart from the above innate factors, environmental forces, especially the home, neighbourhood and school atmosphere significantly influence the educational attainment of an individual. Let us discuss some of these environmental factors.

Home influences. The parents, family relationships and home atmosphere have a direct relationship with the child's educational attainment.

1. The privileged homes and well-to-do families are able to provide the best amenities of life and good education to their children. Children belonging to poor families on the other hand, leave alone proper education, are denied even the basic necessities of life. Their health suffers as a result of malnutrition and unhygienic living conditions. This impairs their capacity for learning and they become backward. In such an atmosphere the child is also deprived of the elementary fund of general knowledge and experiences. He does not get the opportunities to acquire experience in the form of varied social contacts, outings and excursions etc. Consequently, he faces difficulty in grasping ideas related to these experiences and becomes educationally subnormal. In poor homes the children are often required to help with many household chores or to augment the family income. As a result, they can devote less time to their studies. They also become tired with the household work and thus are unable to devote proper attention to their studies at home as well as at school.

2. Besides poverty, the intellectual inferiority and illiteracy of the parents also contribute towards sub-normal educational attainment of the children. Such parents have neither a positive attitude towards education nor the ability to guide and help the children in their studies.

3. The family relationships and the behaviour of family members also contribute to the child's achievements. Strained relationships and

improper behaviour not only disturb the harmony of atmosphere at home, but also create many emotional and social problems. In homes where the parents are divorced or the child has a father or step-mother or where the parental attitudes are either too harsh or too indulgent or where there are unusual conflicts and quarrels, the child's psychological and social needs are not satisfied. In this kind of environment, the child neither feels secure nor gets enough love, affection and guidance from his parents and hence becomes educationally sub-normal.

School influence. An inappropriate school atmosphere and unfavourable environmental conditions also contribute to the problem of backwardness. Irregular attendance or prolonged absence from school contributes to the scholastic subnormality of a child. Additionally, the following factors operating in school may also affect the educational attainment of the children:

1. Defective, uninteresting and ineffective teaching.
2. Lack of equipment, facilities and provision for revision, experimental and creative work, cocurricular activities and varied experience etc.
3. Defective curriculum and examination system.
4. Lack of guidance and wrong choice of subjects by the children.
5. Poor administration and indiscipline.
6. No regular checking of home assignment and lack of proper incentives and stimulation.
7. Improper attitude of the teacher and interpersonal relationships among the staff and students.

Influence of neighbourhood and other social agencies. The social environment of the child is not confined within the boundary walls of his home or the school. The neighbourhood where the child lives, the companions with whom he plays and the gang with whom he associates himself, the members of the society he comes in contact with, the press, radio, cinema, clubs, religious and social places that he visits, all contribute to the problem of educational subnormality. Any or all of these may colour his attitude towards life, work or study and also divert his attention to other socially undesirable activities in place of studies and consequently causes scholastic backwardness.

In this way, environmental forces greatly influence and direct the scholastic progress of a child. His interests, attitudes, habits of work and study, thought and reasoning processes, understanding and observational powers—all get affected by the kind and nature of environment in which he lives and consequently, he attains what his environment allows him to attain.

The Education of Backward Children

Backward child, as we have seen above, suffers from mental, emotional and social problems. Besides a defective intelligence and inherited physical characteristics, this condition is the result of maladjustment and maltreatment. Like other children, he also needs security, love, affection and the satisfaction of his urges of construction, self-assertion etc. If for any reason, the satisfaction of his social and emotional needs is denied, he becomes mentally and emotionally disturbed and suffers from serious adjustment problems. As a result of this he fails to pay necessary attention to his studies and becomes educationally subnormal or backward. After being termed backward, he again becomes the victim of serious maladjustment and behavioural problems. He becomes conscious of his backwardness and develops an inferiority complex, he feels socially isolated and may become a delinquent child. Thus his backwardness not only becomes a problem for him but it affects the adjustment and progress of other children in his class or group. The backward, therefore, need proper care and there is urgent need of special attention for the backward if wastage and stagnation of human resources and increase in the number of problem children is to be checked. The following steps may be helpful in this direction:

Diagnosis of the cause or causes. The primary task in planning for the education of the backward child is to ascertain the possible and more probable causes of his backwardness. This can be done in the following ways:

1. Attainment tests as well as the diagnostic tests may be used to assess the extent and nature of backwardness in specific subjects.
2. The intellectual level of the backward child can be assessed by any standard test of intelligence. As far as possible both verbal and performance type tests should be used for this purpose.
3. The child's special abilities should also be ascertained by means of other psychological tests.
4. The child's overall behaviour and his behaviour in specific situations should be judged through situational tests and by the observation method. His emotional characteristics, social relationships and temperamental traits should also be carefully assessed.
5. A thorough physical and medical examination is also essential to determine the physical and physiological condition of the backward child. The child's developmental history from early childhood should also be studied with special reference to physical ailments, disabilities and defects etc.
6. The socio-economic status of the child's family, their living conditions, education of the parents, size of the family, birth order, relationship within the family, the nature of the gang influence and the social environment in which the child is living should also be carefully studied.
7. The school environment including methods of teaching, courses of instruction, the facilities available for cocurricular activities, and student-teacher interaction should be carefully evaluated.
8. The scholastic history of the child should be properly studied and his day-to-day individual and group behaviour should be carefully assessed.

Educational guidance or treatment of backwardness. After diagnosing the probable cause or causes of backwardness, conscious efforts should be made to help the child to get rid of his backwardness. The remedy of backwardness lies entirely in its nature and extent as well as the causes which produce it. Moreover, there is no single or simple remedy applicable alike to every case of backwardness. Each case is unique in itself and, therefore, needs individual attention and planned treatment depending upon the kind of backwardness. The following points may however prove helpful in planning educational programmes, or suggesting possible remedial steps for the backward children:

1. *Regular medical check-up and necessary treatment.* In cases of backwardness where physical defects and ill-health are found to be contributing factors, there is need for proper arrangement for regular medical check-ups. The school authorities with the cooperation of the parents and government should take steps for the correct treatment of such children.

2. *Readjustment in the home and the school.* As a consequence of several environmental factors, backward children have temperamental and emotional problems, and suffer from mental conflicts. They should be helped in their readjusunent in the home as well as at school. Such emotionally starved and mentally perturbed children need tender love, affection and security. They should be properly understood and encouraged. There is a need of close contact with parents so that the root causes of emotional and mental disturbances can be discovered. Parents also need education for the proper handling of these children. The social agencies and government should come forward not only for educating the parents but also for giving proper attention to remove the miserable handicaps which the children are faced with due to their poverty and other social maladies.

3. *Provision of special schools or special classes.* The provision of special education for the backward child is also a basic remedial step. Under this provision, backward children are segregated from other children and kept in small groups either in special classes or in special schools. Emphasizing the need of such segregation, Professor Udai Shanker (1958) writes:

If they are kept with normals, they will be pushed back and the backward will become more backward with children of their own level. But they will be less conscious of their drawbacks and they will feel more secure in a group of their own type where there will be more encouragement and appreciation and less competition.

However, the complete segregation of backward children in separate schools is often criticized as it does no t provide them the opportunities of mingling freely with children of superior intelligence and deriving rich experiences in their company. Therefore, a via-media should be adopted. These backward children should get the opportunity of mixing with the average and gifted children. As far as possible, they should be taught in the same schools but special care and attention should be paid to them.

4. *Provision of special curriculum, methods of teaching and special teachers.* The children suffering from acute backwardness rightly

deserve special care. These children should have a special curriculum, special methods of teaching and also suitably trained teachers. Their curriculum should cover less ground than the curriculum meant for the normal children. It should include more practical and concrete aspects so that they may be made competent workers and intelligent citizens rather than scholars. The methods of teaching such children should be accordingly modified. They require short and simple methods of instruction based on concrete living experiences with concrete materials. There is a need of using appropriate aids and providing rich direct experiences to such children. Also, the backward children should be taught by competent and specially trained teachers so that they may be properly understood and their difficulties removed.

5. *Special coaching and proper individual attention.* When the area and nature of the weakness is being identified through proper diagnostic tests in various subjects, arrangement for special coaching should be made for backward children individually or collectively as the situation demands. This may be given in the form of more practice, drill, repetition, review or explanation etc. By providing such special coaching their deficiencies and lacunae can be filled up.

6. *Checking truancy and non-attendance.* Backwardness in some cases may be the result of irregular attendance, truancy or long absence from school. The causes for such lapses should be determined and the required steps should be taken to remove them.

7. *Provision of cocurricular activities, rich experiences and diversified courses.* In some cases the backwardness is caused by lack of interest in the school studies or in a particular subject. The child sometimes does not find anything challenging or stimulating in the routine class instruction or does not get the opportunity of studying the subject or performing activities which he likes. Adequate provision should, therefore, be made for diversified courses and rich experiences in the form of varied cocurricular activities and instructional programmes.

8. *Maintenance of proper progress record.* The examination and testing programme of the school needs essential modifications. There should be a well-planned and regular evaluation of the progress of the children in all curricular or cocurricular aspects. The record of their regular evaluation should be maintained properly. For this purpose, progress charts and cumulative record cards can be kept. This helps in keeping track of the children's attainment level and their rate of progress.

9. *Rendering guidance services.* Lack of guidance for making proper choices in the selection of courses of instruction and field of work is also considered to be one of the contributory factors of backwardness. Proper guidance services should, therefore, be organised and made available in every school. State authorities should also pay due attention to making the parents conscious of their children's abilities, interests and aptitudes so that their aspirations for the careers of their children may be realistic.

10. *Controlling negative environmental factors.* The social surroundings and gang or peer group influences play a dominant role in colouring one's interests, attitudes and vision of life. Due care should, therefore, be taken to remove or at least reduce the influence of these negative environmental factors which are responsible for the backwardness of the children.

11. *Taking the help of experienced educational psychologists.* Services of an experienced educational psychologist can also prove valuable in the planning of the education of backward children. He may give valuable guidance to the teachers as well as parents in taking remedial steps for removing the causes of backwardness in their children.

The measures mentioned above are guidelines for teachers, but the problem is so complicated and intricate that it needs to be attacked from many directions. Not only the teachers or school authorities but parents, educational psychologists, social workers and the relevant departments of government should join hands to identify and rectify the conditions and remove the causes of backwardness. Only then can the malaise be properly eradicated and the millions of our future citizens given the proper opportunities for self-development and self-realization.

Juvenile Delinquency

Delinquent children belong to that category of exceptional children who exhibit considerable deviation in terms of their social adjustment and are consequently also labelled as socially deviant or socially handicapped. They are found to possess criminal tendencies and usually indulge in antisocial behaviour. In this sense, they are very much like criminals and antisocial elements. In legal terminology, however, they are referred to as delinquents and not as criminals. Let us try to clarify the distinction between the two terms 'delinquency' and 'crime'.

Delinquency and crime. 'Crime' and 'delinquency' are legal terms and their meaning varies from country to country, from one state to another in the same country. In India, any person 21 years or more of age convicted by a court for violating the provisions of Indian Penal Code (IPC) and the Criminal Procedure Code (CrPC) is termed as a criminal. Of course, there are state laws which vary from state to state. In some states or part of a state, for instance, liquor consumption, except for medical reasons, is considered a crime, whereas in others it may not be so.

Similarly, if a minor individual in the age group of seven to eighteen is convicted by a court for violating the provisions of the Children's Act, the IPC and the CrPC, he is termed a delinquent.

Individuals between the ages of 18 and 21 who violate the provisions of IPC and CrPC are midway between criminals and delinquents and are labelled 'young' or 'youthful' offenders. After the trial by the court, they are sentenced to be sent either to an institution or to prisons depending on the seriousness or the nature and circumstances of their crimes.

The individuals below the age of seven—even if they commit such offences as are covered legally by the term delinquency, are not labelled as delinquents and are termed problem children, because it is felt that they are not mature enough to distinguish between the legal and the illegal and between right and wrong.

Who are juvenile delinquents? As pointed out above, criminal behaviour or the tendency to commit crime is not restricted only to adults, and is found in minor children and adolescents also. These individuals are known as juvenile or young delinquents, (juvenile delinquents, therefore, are criminals minor in age legally from seven to eighteen in our country) and usually referred to as 'minors with major problems'. They violate the law of the land and commit offences like theft, gambling, cheating, picking pockets, murder, robbery, dacoity, destruction of property, violence and assault, intoxication, vagrancy, begging, kidnapping, abduction, and sexual offences. The term 'juvenile delinquent' or 'young delinquent' means a child or minor who deviates seriously from the norms of his culture or society and commits murder and robbery or other offences that are strictly age related such as drinking liquor and indulging in sexual activities. Juvenile delinquency should, therefore, be considered to be a serious challenge to the well-being of society. The young delinquents, if not handled properly, become a source of serious concern for society.

Causes of Delinquency

1. *Hereditary factors.* The early researches held heredity to be the main cause of delinquency. The claim of hereditarians like Henry, Maudsley, Tredgold and Dugdale that delinquency is inherited was tested by William Healey, Cyril Burt, Conrad and Jones, Wingfield and Sandiford. They concluded that delinquency is not inherited and, therefore, it is wrong to blame heredity for delinquent behaviour.

2. *Constitutional or physiological factors.* A defective constitution or glandular systems were also thought to be the causes of delinquent behaviour. Udai Shanker (1958) observes:

   Poor health, too short or too big stature of some deformity which gives rise to feelings of inferiority, disposes one to more aggression, as a compensatory reaction for his inadequacies. This observation seems to be well-founded but it is not so, for not much scientific evidence has been reported in its support so far. It may, however, be taken to be one of the causes of delinquent behaviour.

3. *Intelligence factor.* While earlier writers like Lombroso and Goddard emphasize that the most important cause of delinquency and crime is low grade mentality. Burt, Healey, Bronner, Merill and others deny that delinquents are mentally retarded. In fact, a direct causal relationship between lack of intelligence and delinquency is doubtful. High intelligence is no guarantee of good behaviour. Often, persons with superior intelligence have been found to be the leaders of notorious gangs, and antisocial organisations. On the basis of statistics, it is sometimes argued that since the majority among the delinquents have low intelligence, defective intelligence causes delinquency. This

conclusion, however, is not well-founded. The statistics, collected in such cases, may present an unreal picture. An intelligent individual may not be caught red-handed, while a delinquent with low intelligence is more likely to be apprehended. Moreover, defective intelligence may lead to delinquency in one situation and may be a barrier to it in another situation. Hence, low intelligence alone cannot be said to be responsible for delinquent behaviour.

4. *Environmental and social factors.* It has been proved that delinquent behaviour is a learned reaction. Delinquents do not inherit delinquent characters from their parents or anscestors but are made so by the uncongenial environment and social conditions. Udai Shanker (1958) observes:

> delinquency is not inherited: it is the product of social and economic conditions and is essentially a coefficient of the friction between the individual and the community. The most important causes of antisocial behaviour are environmental and sociological in character.

It is, therefore, the uncongenial family, school, neighbourhood and society, social environment which should be blamed for the delinquent behaviour of the child since he picks up delinquent traits in such situations. We shall now consider how environment influences delinquent character formation among minors.

A defective and deficient family environment is a fertile ground for the germination of delinquency. As a matter of fact, family life and delinquency are closely related. The findings of various studies indicate that the family environment, in which the following relationships or conditions prevail, is most susceptible to delinquency.

1. A broken home where the family is incomplete due to death, desertion, separation or divorce;
2. Improper parental control;
3. Unusual jealousy and rivalry among siblings or children within the family and reactions like "My parents gave him more love than they gave me";
4. The delinquent and criminal behaviour of the parents or other family members;
5. Domestic conflicts;
6. Economic difficulties and poverty of the family;
7. Dull, monotonous and uninteresting home environment;
8. Denial of reasonable freedom and independence to the youngsters;
9. Maltreatment and injustice to the youngsters;
10. Lack of proper physical and emotional security.

In these situations and environment the child does not get the opportunity for the satisfaction of his basic needs. He falls victim to emotional problems like inferiority, insecurity, jealousy or suppression which lead to maladjustment and consequently turn him into a hostile, rebellious and antisocial personality. Thus, uncongenial home conditions are entirely to blame for juvenile delinquency and in all circumstances the root cause of delinquent behaviour must be looked for in the family background and home environment.

5. *Uncongenial environment outside the home.* Whereas the home environment provides the base for delinquent behaviour, the social environment outside the home nourishes it by supplying substitutes for the satisfaction of unsatisfied basic needs and urges. For example, the peer-group or gang presents itself as a substitute for family love and belonging. It also satisfies the need for recognition and gives an individual the opportunity for self-dependence and adventure. Delinquent acts of the peer group lead him to and engage in delinquent behaviour. The neighbourhood and the place of social contacts and situations where senior members of society engage in antisocial activities, or the mass media like newspapers, books, magazines and cinema that acquaint children with immoral and anti-social acts may also provide temptations for the youngsters to become delinquent.

6. *Maladjustment in school.* In many cases of delinquency, uncongenial school environment may be a significant stimulating factor. It brings about serious maladjustment and consequently increases the probability of delinquent character-formation. Such environment may involve the following elements:

- Defective curriculum.
- Improper teaching methods.
- Lack of cocurricular activities.
- Lack of proper discipline and control.
- Slackness in administration and organisation.
- Antisocial or undesirable behaviour of the teachers.
- Maltreatment and injustice done to the child.
- Failure or backwardness.

To conclude, delinquency is an environmental and social disease. Delinquent acts are learned and acquired. No child is born delinquent nor is delinquent behaviour the product of the genes. Thus, delinquents are not a specific type of human beings born with any such innate, physical, mental or emotional characteristics. They are normal individuals with normal needs and desires. Like other normal children, they also want to love, to be loved, and to satisfy the need for security and recognition. The denial of these basic needs leads to mal-adjustment and results in their becoming hostile and rebellious. Thus, delinquent behaviour is a reaction to, or resentment against the prevailing social and environmental conditions. It is a revolt against parents, teachers or social organisations which do not provide them with an environment congenial to the satisfaction of their basic needs and urges.

Prevention and treatment. Delinquency, besides being a legal problem, is basically a psycho-social problem. All delinquents are essentially maladjusted personalities and the result of faulty upbringing and maltreatment. The solution of the problem requires preventive as well as curative measures.

Preventive measures. Initially these involve improvement of the social or environmental conditions which stand in the way of the satisfaction of the basic needs of the individual. The following suggestions may work well in this direction:

1. *Parental education.* Parents should be aware of the psychology of delinquency so that they may treat and handle their children with understanding and provide them an appropriate environment for the satisfaction of their basic needs and urges. This requires parental education which may be provided through guidance services, clinics and voluntary social organizations.

2. *The child's company.* Parents, family members and school authorities should keep a close watch on the activities and social environment of the children and take care to see that they do not fall into bad company. Antisocial elements and criminals often seek out youngsters for their nefarious purposes. Active efforts should be made to save the children from them and they should be educated in staying away from such elements.

3. *Substitute environment.* Should it be difficult to bring about change in the defective family environment or the influences of the neighbour-hood and peer group, the children should be removed from their original environment and placed either in foster homes or well-managed reformatories and special schools so that they may be provided with a healthy environment for their emotional and social adjustment.

4. *Rectifying school education and environment.* The school environment should be healthy and congenial. The curriculum, methods of teaching, discipline, class-room behaviour of the teacher and the social atmosphere of the school should be rectified so that children do not get involved in problems of emotional and social maladjustment. The attitude of teachers who impose their authority on children without understanding their basic needs should be changed. The headmaster as well as the teachers should be familiar with the psychology of individual differences and delinquency.

Curative measures. The problem of juvenile delinquency should not be regarded as penal problem. It is an educational and welfare problem. Juvenile delinquents should not be put behind bars and treated through the penal system. In fact, they require rehabilitation and re-education for which special legal provisions should be made. The legal processes dealing with juvenile delinquents have been changed in the progressive communities of the world. The children's and Young Person's Act of Britain can be adopted with some modifications in India. Its essential features are:

1. Establishment of special juvenile courts with trained magistrates to deal with juvenile delinquents.
2. Appointment of trained social workers or probation officers for taking charge of delinquent cases.
3. Taking the help of clinical psychologists and psychiatrists for understanding the delinquent behaviour of children.

4. Establishment of special schools where special education, correction and rehabilitation is possible.
5. Provision of keeping the children in the custody of responsible persons or social agencies.
6. Establishment of remand homes where delinquent children may be lodged while awaiting trial or placement in an approved school or in the custody of a responsible person; or if so directed by a probation officer prior to employment or on discharge from an approved school.

The provision of 'special schools' or 'approved schools' needs particular mention in this programme. These schools have specially trained staff. The curriculum is flexible and provides opportunities for self expression, recreation, manual work and learning of useful crafts. Provisions are made to satisfy the basic needs and urges of the children and thus they are helped in their social and emotional readjustment. Thus helping them to overcome their delinquent behaviour and learn to, respond meaningfully to social situations and conditions.

The attitude towards delinquency in our country also is changing. It has now been realized that children who are called delinquents are ill, primarily in terms of their inability to conform to the social milieu. Consequently, in most of the states, the Children Act has been enforced and some have gone ahead in the work of rehabilitation and re-education of young offenders. Separate child welfare boards have been established to deal with the problem of delinquency and approved schools have also come into existence. Some states encourage voluntary organisations to take custody of delinquent children. Provisions for the care of neglected and destitute children are also made so that they do not become delinquents. Some states have started foster care programmes which envisage the court giving custody of a child to a responsible person. There is, however, the need to arouse public consciousness of this problem. No government can solve a social problem without public cooperation. Therefore, there is a need for a change in our attitude towards delinquents so that they may be helped in their readjustment and rehabilitation.

SUMMARY

The term *exceptional children* stands for all those children who deviate considerably in terms of their natural and normal growth and development in various dimensions of their personality to the extent of requiring special attention and education for their upbringing, welfare and adjustment.

Gifted children are those children who are quite above average in terms of their intellectual growth and development. They consistently demonstrate outstanding, praiseworthy and remarkable performance in any worthwhile field of human endeavour. However, the giftedness needs to be identified and nurtured from the very outset. Among the various techniques or measures for better educational possibilities, the enrichment programmes (enriching the already existing system of education in view of the needs of the gifted) are the best suited for our country's democratic socialism.

Mentally retarded children are those children who, besides possessing a low I.Q., demonstrate impaired or deficient adaptive behaviour originating from conception and continuing into maturity. According to this criterion, mental retardation can be classified into four levels, namely mild, moderate, severe and profound. From the educational angle where the mildly retardate are considered educable and the moderately retardate trainable, the severe and profoundly retardate are considered neither educable nor trainable. They are termed as custodial, remaining dependent on others throughout their lives and thus needing custodial care and supervision by others.

Backward children are slow learners whose educational attainment falls below their natural abilities. They are considered failures in their field of accomplishment. However, they are not mentally retarded or dull nor does a lower I.Q. necessarily make a child backward. The causes of backwardness lie in the children themselves (in the shape of physiological and intellectual subnormality) and also in their environmental forces, home, neighbourhood, school situations and other social agencies. In planning better education for these children, the regimen must be started with the diagnosis of the extent, nature and causes of backwardness and a suitable remedial programme must then be chalked out depending upon the findings of such investigation.

Juvenile delinquents are those children and adolescents who are minors i.e., below 18 years of age. They deviate seriously from the norms of their culture and society and commit offences which are crimes in legal terms. The causes of delinquency do not lie in one's genetic or biological makeup. Delinquent behaviour in all its shades is a learned reaction. It is the product of improper and uncongenial environment of family, neighbourhood, school and society. All delinquents are essentially maladjusted personalities and this maladjustment is the result of faulty upbringing, improper environmental influences and maltreatment. The remedy lies in both prevention as well as treatment. While implementing preventive measures, an effort should be made to organise and improve the social or environmental conditions in such a way that the children do not feel maladjusted, get involved in the company of antisocial elements or turn into rebels against society. Curative measures involve that if a child commits an offence, he should not be put behind bars or treated as a criminal but should be tackled psychologically and sympathetically through the special rehabilitative, educational and correction programmes.

REFERENCES

Barton, Hall, *Psychiatric Examination of the School Child*, London: Edward Arnold, 1947, p. 102.

Bentley, J.E., *Superior Children*, New York: W.W. Norton, 1937.

British Mental Deficiency Act, Quoted in T.E. Shanmugam, *Abnormal Psychology*, New Delhi: Tata McGraw-Hill, 1981, pp. 197–198.

Burt, C., *The Causes and Treatment of Backwardness*, London: University of London Press, 1953, p. 77.

Burt, C., *The Backward Child*, London: University of London Press, 1950.

Burt, C., *The Young Delinquent* (3rd ed.), London: University of London Press, 1953.

Crow, L.D. and Crow, Alice, *Educational Psychology*, New Delhi: Eurasia Publishing House, 1973.

De Haan and Kough, Quoted by N.K. Dutt, *Psychological Foundation of Education*, Delhi: Doaba House, 1974, p. 202.

Fleigher, Louis, A. and Bish, C.E., Summary of research on the academically talented children. *Review of Educational Research*, 20, December, 1959, p. 409.

Grossman, H.G. (Ed.), *Classification in Mental Retardation*, Washington, D.C.: American Association on Mental Deficiency, 1983, p. 1024.

Havighurst, R.J., Quoted in N.B. Henry (Ed.), Education for the gifted, *Fifty-Seventh Year Book of National Society for the Study of Education, Part II*, Chicago: University of Chicago Press, 1958, p. 19.

Kirk, S.A., Educating Exceptional Children, Quoted in S.S. Chauhan, *Advanced Educational Psychology* (7th ed.), New Delhi: Vikas Publishing House, 1984, p. 435.

Marland, S., Education of the Gifted and Talented, Report of the Subcommittee on Education, Committee on Labour and Public Welfare, Washington, D.C.: U.S. Senate, 1972.

Page, James, D., *Abnormal Psychology*, New Delhi: Tata McGraw-Hill, 1976, p. 354.

Pasricha, Prem, *Educational Psychology*, Delhi: University Publishers, 1963, p. 301.

Rosen, E., Fox and Gregory Ean, *Abnormal Psychology*, Saunders International Student Edition, III, 1972, p. 356.

Schonell, F.J. (Ed.), *Backwardness with Basic Subjects*, Edinburgh: Oliver and Boyd, 1948, p. 54.

Shanker, Udai, *Problem Children*, Delhi: Atma Ram & Sons, 1958, pp. 70–71.

_____, *Exceptional Children*, New Delhi: Sterling Publishers, 1976.

Tannenbaum, A.J., *Gifted Children Psychological and Educational Perspectives*, New York: Macmillan, 1983, p. 86.

Terman, L.M. and Oden, M.H., *The Gifted Child Grows Up*, Stanford, California: Stanford University Press, 1947.

Telford, C.W. and Sawrey, J.M., *The Exceptional Individual* (3rd ed.), Englewood Cliffs, N.J.: Prentice-Hall, 1977, pp. 10, 11.

Tredgold, A.F. and Soddy, K., *Mental Deficiency* (9th ed.), Baltimore: William & Wilkins, 1956.

Warren, S.A., Article on mental deficiency, in C.E. Reynolds and Lester Mann (Eds.), *Encyclopaedia of Special Education, Vol. II*, New York: John Wiley, 1987.

Wechsler, D., Cited by N.K. Dutt, *Psychological Foundations of Education* (2nd ed.), Delhi: Doaba House, 1979, p. 186.

Witty, P.A., A Genetic study of fifty gifted children, *Year Book of the National Society for the Study of Education* 39, 1940, p. 402

SUGGESTED READINGS

Dettaan, F. and Havighurst, R.J., *Educating Gifted Children*, Chicago: University of Chicago Press, 1957.

Dunn, L.M. (Ed.), *Exceptional Children in the Schools*, New York: Holt, Rinehart & Winston, 1963.

Gunzburg, H.C., *Social Competence and Mental Handicap*, London: Bailliere Tindall, 1973.

Heck, A.O., *The Education of Exceptional Children*, New York: McGraw-Hill, 1953.

Hildreth, G.H., *Educating Gifted Children*, Hunter College Elementary School, New York: Harper & Brothers, 1952.

Hutt, M.L. and Gibby, R.G., *The Mentally Retarded Child* (2nd ed.), Boston: Allyn & Bacon, 1965.

MacMillan, D.L., *Mental Retardation in School and Society* (2nd ed.), Boston: Little Brown, 1982.

Masland, R.L., Sarason, S.B. and Gladwin, T., *Mental Subnormality*, New York: Basic Books, 1958.

Robins, L.N., *Deviant Children Grow up*, Baltimore, Md: Williams & Wilkins, 1966.

Robinson, H.B., and Robinson, N.M., *The Mentally Retarded Child* (2nd ed.), New York: McGraw-Hill, 1976.

Sumption, M.R. and Lucking, E.M., *Education of the Gifted*, New York: Ronald Press, 1960.

Verma, S.C., *The Young Delinquents*, Lucknow: Lucknow Pustak Kendra, 1970.

Wortis, J., *Mental Retardation and Developmental Disorders*, New York: Brunner Mazel, 1973.

Chapter 23

Learning Disabilities and Learning Disabled Children

MEANING AND DEFINITIONS

Learning disabled children are those children who suffer from serious learning disabilities. These children exhibit exceptionally inferior qualities and capacities in terms of learning and understanding in comparison to the normal children of their age or class. In fact, learning disability is nothing but a sort of handicap or helplessness that can be felt by the sufferer in terms of his academic performance (learning or understanding something) in the same way as experienced by a physically handicapped person in terms of his physical functioning or by a mentally handicapped in terms of his mental functioning. Let us try to know more about the terms learning disabled and learning disabilities with the help of some well-known definitions given below:

The Association for Children with Learning Disabilities USA, 1967:

> A child with learning disabilities is one with adequate mental ability, sensory processes and emotional stability who has a limited number of specific deficits in perceptual, integrative or expressive processes which severely impair learning efficiency. This includes children who have central nervous system dysfunctions which is expressed primarily in impaired learning efficiency.
>
> *(Telford & Sawrey, 1977)*

USA National Advisory Committee to the Education for the Handicapped, 1969:

> "Specific learning disability" means a disorder in one or more of the basic psychological processes involved in understanding or in using language, spoken or written, that may manifest itself in an imperfect ability to listen, think, speak, read, write, spell or to do mathematical calculations. The term includes such conditions as perceptual disabilities, brain injury, minimal brain dysfunction, dyslexia and developmental aphasia. The term does not apply to children who have learning problems that are primarily the result of visual, hearing, or motor disabilities, of mental retardation, of emotional disturbance, or of environmental, cultural, or economic disadvantages.
>
> *(Federal Register, 1977)*

471

S.A. Kirk (1971):

> The term learning disability is not meant to be used for children with minor or temporary difficulties in learning but with a severe discrepancy between ability and achievement in educational performance and such severed discrepancy described as learning disabilities with significant learning problems that cannot be explained by mental retardation, sensory impairment, emotional disturbance or lack of opportunity to learn.

National Joint Committee on Learning Disabilities USA:

> "Learning disabilities" as a generic term refers to a heterogeneous group of disorders manifested by significant difficulties in the acquisition and use of listening, speaking, reading, writing, reasoning or mathematical abilities. These disorders are intrinsic to the individual presumed to be due to central nervous system dysfunction and may occur across the life span. Problems in self-regulatory behaviors, social perception and social interaction may exist with learning disabilities but do not by themselves constitute a learning disability. Although learning disabilities may occur concomitantly with other handicapping conditions (for example, sensory impairment, mental retardation, serious emotional disturbance or social maladjustment) or with extrinsic influences (such as cultural differences or lack of opportunity to learn), they are not the result of those conditions or influences.
>
> *(McLoughlin & Netick, 1983)*

Kavale & Forness (1966):

> People with learning disabilities belong to a group of very diverse individuals but they do share one common problem: They do not learn in the same way or as efficiently as their nondisabled peers. Although most possess normal intelligence, their academic performance is significantly behind their classmates. Some have great difficulty learning mathematics, but most find the mastery of reading and writing to be their most difficult challenge.

A close analysis of all these definitions may reveal the following things concerning meaning and concept of the term learning disabilities and learning disabled.

1. Learning disabilities refer to certain kinds of disorders in the basic psychological processes of an individual.
2. These disorders are mainly caused by the intrinsic factors (the things lying within the individual) like central nervous system dysfunction (some brain or neurological damage impeding one's motor or learning abilities), specific deficits in information processing or the ability to learn.
3. Although one or the other learning problems may be caused by extrinsic factors like mental retardation, sensory impairment, emotional disturbance, cultural differences, lack of educational opportunities, poverty etc., learning disability is not the direct result of such external factors or conditions.
4. Disorders associated with learning disabilities are usually manifested into some specific severe learning problems confined to one or two cognitive areas like inability to grasp or understand the things, difficulty in language related areas such as communication, written language or reading, or handicap in terms of acquiring mathematical or social skills.

5. Individuals with minor or temporary difficulties in learning are not termed as learning disabled. Only those who have severely impaired learning inefficiency and serious learning problems are included in this category.

6. The learning disability may allow an individual to have intelligence scores within the normal range but it essentially makes them substantially delayed in academic achievement. He always lags behind in terms of his educational progress in comparison to the peers of his age and class.

7. The impaired learning inefficiency coupled with serious learning problems in one or the other cognitive areas leads to a distinctive gap between an individual's potential and actual educational achievement and as a result he becomes disabled or handicapped in one or the other learning areas so much so that he needs special care, attention and educational services for his adjustment and welfare.

In this way learning disability provides a lot of obstacles and difficulties in the path of learning. Gradually the learning problems become so acute as to cause severely impaired learning inefficiency in one or the other cognitive areas. It leads to a distinctive gap between one's potential and actual educational achievement which require special care, attention and remedial measures and when it happens the learner is labelled as learning disabled.

Nature and Characteristics of Learning Disabled

Researches in the fields of education and psychology have brought into notice a number of significant behavioural and personality characteristics as well as general outcomes of the nature and characteristics of the learning disabled children. Let us mention a few important ones.

1. Learning disabled children essentially suffer from serious learning problems or disorders for a number of reasons.

2. Their problems and disorders are usually manifested by significant difficulties in the acquisition and use of language (listening, speaking, reading, writing, etc.), reasoning or mathematical ability or of social skills.

3. They may exhibit symptoms of hyperactivity and impulsivity.

4. Most of them may suffer from emotional problems and demonstrate signs of anxiety, moodiness or ups and downs in their behaviour.

5. Their learning disability is not apparent in the physical appearance or not demonstrable through their I.Q. Scores. They may have robust body, good vision, sound ears, and normal intelligence.

6. They essentially suffer from severely impaired learning inefficiency, or a handicap, which is just as real as crippled leg.

7. All of them essentially exhibit a significant educational discrepancy i.e. a wide gap between their learning potential and actual educational achievement.

8. Some of them may demonstrate equivocal neurological signs and EEG irregularities.
9. They may exhibit disorders of memory, thinking, attention, general coordination, perception and motor functioning, etc.
10. The main problem for all these children lies in their observable deficiency in learning and mastering academic tasks. They are handicapped in learning and acquisition in the same way as physically and mentally handicapped are, in physical and mental performance.
11. They usually exhibit the following learning characteristics responsible for their learning impairment (i) lack of motivation, (ii) inattention, (iii) inability to generalize, and (iv) lack of adequate ability in problem-solving, information processing and thinking skills, etc.
12. Their learning impairment is so severe that they essentially require special attention, care and remedial programmes for the rectification of their learning problems and disabilities:

Causes of Learning Disabilities

Depending on the types of learning disabilities found in the children a number of researches have been conducted to find out the possible factors or causes of learning disabilities. Generally the factors causing learning disabilities may be found to fall in the following three categories:

1. Genetic or heredity factors
2. Organic or physiological factors
3. Environmental factors.

1. *Genetic or heredity factors.* In some cases, the genetic or heredity factor is found to be the major cause for generating learning disabilities among the children. On the pattern "Like begets like" it has been found that many characteristics commonly found in learning disabled are transmitted from generation to generation. This relationship between inheritance and disabilities has been established on the basis of the following results:

(a) Nearly 20 to 25 percent of hyperactive or impulsive children have been found to have at least one parent of this nature.
(b) Emotional imbalances, disorders of memory and thinking, speech and learning have been found to run in families.
(c) Going deep into the genetic research, the USA scientists and psychologists have attained success in identifying particular genes that may be held responsible for reading and other learning problems.

2. *Organic or physiological factors.* Study of most learning disabled cases reveals that they suffer from malfunctioning or dysfunction of their central nervous system consisting of brain, spinal cord and message carrying nerves etc. This dysfunction, how ever minimal it may be, is caused by the factors like below:

(a) Brain damage caused by an accident or by a lack of oxygen before, during or after birth resulting in neurological difficulties that may affect their ability to learn.

(b) Damage of injury caused to the spinal cord and message carrying nerves etc. leading to their malfunctioning and subsequent learning difficulties.

(c) Dysfunction of the central nervous system may be caused by bio-chemical imbalances generated by the factors like below:

　(i) Colourings and flavourings in many of the food items consumed by the children may cause hyperactivity, impulsivity, emotional imbalance etc. leading to malfunctioning of the central nervous system.

　(ii) Vitamin deficiency may cause inability of a child's bloodstream to synthesize a normal amount of vitamins essential for normal functioning of the central nervous system.

In short it can be concluded that one's learning capacities and abilities are very much dependent on proper functioning of one's central nervous system. Dysfunction of the central nervous system in any form may thus affect and cause serious learning difficulties and hence any factor that can cause neurological damage to our central nervous system may lead to its malfunctioning and subsequent learning difficulties.

3. *Environmental factors.* In many cases, learning disabilities may be caused by the improper and uncongenial conditions and factors present in an individual's physical, social, cultural and educational environment. Some of these factors may be cited as under:

(a) The poor nourishment and defective environment received by the foetus for development in the mother's womb.

(b) Pre-mature delivery, uncongenial and improper environmental settings at the time of birth or a defect in the central nervous system.

(c) Diet deficiency in the early age, severe diseases, accidents and injuries that may cause central nervous system dysfunction.

(d) Children who do not receive proper medical care and attention and as a result suffer from any impairment in their senses of hearing, sight, taste, touch, smell and other neurological functioning become handicapped in terms of learning.

(e) Insufficient early experiences and stimulation in terms of learning and acquisition received on account of defective educational set-up.

(f) Poor or inadequate instructions received on account of their own family set-up or lack of motivation, skill and ability on the part of teachers.

(g) Emotional disturbance and lack of motivation on account of so many factors persent in a person's environment and even on account of malfunctioning of his physiological processes.

(h) Inadequate and improper development of language skills, lack of concentration and adequate attention.

(i) Use of drugs and intoxicating substances like consumption of alcohol.

(j) Imitation and the company of defective learning models present in one's cultural, social and educational environment.

(k) Social and cultural deprivation.

Identification of Learning Disabled Children

Identification of the learning disabled children may be done mainly in two ways—the employment of non-testing and testing devices.

1. *Non-testing devices.* In non-testing devices we may include techniques like observation, rating scale, check list, interview etc. By employing these devices, we try to identify the learning disabled in relation to their general personality and characteristics. We may find a list of these characteristics common with the learning disabled and then weigh the observed child in relation to these for the identification of the degree of disability. We may also seek the opinion of the teachers and other persons regarding the learning abilities, mental level, scholastic potential etc. through such devices for the diagnosis and identification of learning disabilities of the children.

2. *Testing devices.* Testing devices include different types of tests that can be used as diagnostic measures for the identification and assessment of children with different kinds of learning disabilities. Generally, the following types of tests fall into this category:

(a) *Standardized diagnostic tests.* These are many such tests available in our country as well as abroad. With the help of norms given in these tests we can assess the relative educational standard of the children of same age or grade and thus may be acquainted with the educational deficits and deficiency of a particular child. As a result we can have a reliable and valid diagnosis of the learning difficulties in various areas of scholastic performance especially in language, mathematics, social and experimental skills etc. As examples of such available standardized diagnostic tests we may name the following:

    (i) *Diagnostic test in Decimal Systems and Percentage by V.P. Sharma and Shukla.*

    (ii) *Durrell Analysis of Reading Difficulty by Durrell.*

    (iii) *The Stanford Diagnostic Arithmetic Test by Betty, Madden and Gardner.*

    (iv) *The Spache Diagnostic Reading Scales by Spache.*

    (v) *The Gates Mckillop Reading. Diagnostic Test by Gates and Mckillop.*

(b) *Ability tests or process tests.* Learning disabled suffer from the inability or incapacity in their process of learning and understanding. The ability tests or process tests are so designed as to assess the degree of their inability or poor ability to understand and learn. Since the learning of a child is processed through his abilities of visual perception, auditory perception, eye motor coordination, psycho-linguistic understanding etc. the ability tests or the process tests are designed to test the abilities of the children related to these areas. As example of such tests we may cite the following:

    (i) *The Marianne Frosting Developmental Test of Visual Perception by Frosting, Lefever and Whittlesey.*

(ii) *Illinois Test of Psycholinguistic Abilities by Kirk, McCarthy and Kirk.*

(c) *Achievement tests.* These tests are designed to assess the degree of achievement of the children in various knowledge, skills and performance process areas. These may be of two types, namely *Standardized achievement tests and Teacher made tests.* While the former are structured by an outside agency and are readily available for administration, the latter are constructed by individual teachers in their respective subjects or areas for assessing the degree of the children's achievement or diagnosing their learning difficulties and disabilities. The performance of the individual students in these tests may reveal many things about the nature and extent of the learning deficiencies and deficits related to various learning areas.

(d) *Daily assessment system.* There can be a systematic, well planned regular daily assessment system in schools for recording the children's achievement on various specific knowledge, skill and performance areas. This process of continued information may bring into limelight many important things related with the nature and extent of learning deficiencies and deficits of individual learners particularly, in relation to the processes of their learning and understanding.

Educational Provisions for the Learning Disabled

Let us think what can be done to the learning disabled children once we identify them as such. Their identification clearly reveals that they suffer from somewhat a severe learning inefficiency, deficiency or deficit resulting into a serious gap between their potential and actual educational achievement. One or the other factors lying within them or their environment may cause it. We can find diversity in terms of their learning disabilities, their nature, types, degree of handicapness and etiology. As a result it is not proper to treat them as a group for their learning deficiencies and disabilities. Everyone of them is unique. Therefore no uniform treatment or remedial measure can be prescribed to all the learning disabled. Each one of them is to be cared and treated as a separate and individual case. This is why great care should be taken for the proper identification of the nature and amount of learning disability or disabilities of a particular child. The treatment then should be given on the basis of proper analysis and evaluation of the identification data. The researchers in this field have advised many ways. Let us discuss a few of such measures.

1. Provision of specialized schools or classes.
2. Provision of special remedial and educational programmes.
3. Structuring and improving the existing environmental set-up.

Let us discuss these one by one.

1. *Provision of specialized schools or classes.* This provision is based on the assumption that learning disabled children are quite distinct from other children of their schools or classes. They cannot be taught along with others as they suffer from severe learning deficiencies and deficits. Hence there should be special schools or at least separate classes for them where they can be taught by specialized teachers through special methods and techniques essentially on the same curriculum with greater care and attention.

In the specialized schools, learning disabled children thus find a complete-specialized-segregated setting. However, in the specialized classes in a regular school there is somewhat less segregation in comparison to the specialized schools. Here there is a provision for special instruction by special teachers for overcoming the learning deficiencies of the sufferers. In this task the help of the regular class teachers may also be counted for providing assistance in teaching subject matter. Along with instructions related to academic subjects experiences related to social and co-curricular activities are also provided along with the other normal students.

However, the segregated settings, whether in the form of separate schools or classes, suffer from serious defects and limitations. In fact, such segregation is neither feasible nor practicable. It is far from ground realities and may prove futile as we can't arrange segregation or separation based on the individualized learning inefficiencies and deficits. Each of the learning disabled is a unique case in itself. He or she needs individualized attention, care or even different methods, techniques and treatment for the rectification of his or her deficiency and overall adjustment. Therefore, the provision of putting the learning disabled in separate schools or classes cannot work well and hence we should now try to evaluate the other two provisions mentioned earlier.

2. *Provision of special remedial and educational programmes.* This provision can work well in the existing school and educational set-up. Here the beginning can be made with the proper identification of the nature, type and amount of learning difficulties, deficiencies or deficits. Then proper special remedial and educational programmes may be made out of the readymade programmes available in the market of at other places having provision for such educational services. The Resource Center of the Colleges of Education, DIETS, SCERT, NCERT, Extension Department of Universities and many other social and community organisations usually provide such educational services and thus we may obtain the necessary help from these centres simply on the institution to institution transaction basis. The remedial programmes, material and guidance available through such sources may definitely help the cause of learning disabled. For example, if the deficiency and deficits of the suffering children are related to the neural impairments in sensory-motor system, we can follow remedial programmes like (i) The Strauss-Lehtinen-Cruickshank Perceptual Motor Programme, (ii) Getman's Visuo-Motor Programme etc. Similarly if their deficiencies and deficits are related to their psycho-linguistic ability, these can be rectified through standardized remedial programmes like (i) Witmer's Psycho-Educational, (ii) The Fernald Kinesthetic Remedial Reading Method, (iii) The Pragmatic General Dignostic Remedial Approaches by Blanco or Morgan etc.

3. *Structuring and improving the existing environmental set-up.* Many of learning difficulties and deficiencies of the children are caused by the uncongenial, improper and negative factors present in their physical, social, cultural and educational environment. Therefore, attempts should be properly and honestly made for the adequate structuring and improving the existing environmental set-up. It will definitely help in reducing the cases of learning disabled by providing them due assistance, care and guidance for rectification of their learning disabilities. The task requires the joint efforts of all who are concerned with the brought up, education and welfare of the children. The parents, members of the family, teachers, guidance and counselling workers, educational authorities, social and community agencies etc. all should join hands for providing due care, attention and remedial and educational programmes to the learning disabled. They should help them in acquiring desirable personality traits in overcoming their deficiencies with regard to their educational progress and behavioural drawbacks. What can be expected from them can be summarized in the following way.

(a) Great care should be taken by the parents and teachers, to pick up proper methods of learning, communication, perceptual motor movements and general coordination etc.

(b) Efforts should be made to restructure and improve the men-material facilities provided in the school as to suit the individual learners according to their needs, interests and abilities. There must be proper integration of theory with practice as well as curricular with co-curricular activities. Methods of teaching as well as the handling of the students should be so structured as to cater to the needs and difficulties of the learning disabled present in a particular group, a section or as class.

(c) If the learning disabilities are so severe as to demand very special care and attention then learning disabled should be placed in a full time special learning setting under the guidance of a specially trained teacher. Here they must be given full opportunity and training for improving their poor study habits, methods of improper learning and modifying their undesirable and in appropriate socio-emotional and psycho-educational behaviour. After putting the learning disabled into a highly structured environment and getting satisfactory results he should be moved back into a less isolated setting and then into a normal classroom setting.

(d) Whether we employ specialized trained teachers or the usual classroom or subject teachers with some extra knowledge and training to deal with learning disabled, the one thing which is most important is their behaviour and attitude towards these children. One should not lose patience as these children are essentially slow learners, underachievers and far from satisfactory in their socio-psychological behaviour. They should be accepted with all their weaknesses and deficiencies. Snubbing, ridiculing, or punishing these children in any form brings negative and harmful results. The parents, elders and teachers all should exhibit love and care while dealing with them. Our approach towards them, as far as possible, should be very constructive, pleasant as well as encouraging so that these disabled children may learn the proper method of learning and behaving and develop required self-confidence and positive attitude of their educational progress by getting rid of themselves with some or the other learning difficulties and deficiencies in their behaviour.

(e) In schools as well as in community setting there should be a proper arrangement with regard to a well-structured educational setting or resource centre with adequate learning material equipment and some trained specialized teachers, experts in guiding and helping the learning disabled. With the help of men and material resources available the learning disabled should be helped in overcoming their deficits and deficiencies in skills like spelling, handwriting, memory, verbal expression, comprehension, mathematical skills, experimentation and observation, thinking and reasoning skills, visual and auditory perception, sensory motor development and social skills etc.

Let us now think about some special measures that can be adopted for the rectification of the deficiencies and difficulties pertaining to specific learning abilities and skills.

Remedial Measures for Some Specific Learning Deficiencies

1. *Handwriting.* Poor handwriting may be one of the major learning deficiency found in the learning disabled. It may cost them heavily in terms of academic achievement or may create inferiority feelings; lack of confidence and similar other things. Hence steps should essentially be taken for improving their handwriting right from the early diagnosis and identification of such deficiency among them. Some of the following measures can work well in this direction.

(a) Since lack of proper motor control may be one of the causes for their poor handwriting we must try to overcome it by adopting the following means:

(i) Using manipulative exercises to strengthen muscles. For this purpose it is better that before resorting to paper and pencil writing, the children should be provided opportunities in writing letters by doing manipulative exercises like writing in sands, modelling through clay games, doing chalkboard practice etc.

(ii) Helping them learn a proper position and form for writing. For this purpose they must be made to learn that while writing on the paper with a pencil or pen

• The paper should not be kept slant while writing and
• The writing instrument should be held between thumb and middle finger with index finger applying pressure.

(b) Children should be made to learn proper figuring of letters. For this purpose, sufficient practice can be provided through manipulative activities as well as through individualized assistance as described now.

  (i) Tape alphabet forms to the floor and ask them to reproduce the forms with coloured chalk.
  (ii) Ask the children to form letters in wet fingerprint or in the sand.
  (iii) Make use of coloured directional cues such as green arrows and red dots.
  (iv) Try to help the children in building some useful associations for the shape of letter so that they may never go astray in the process of writing that letter in its proper form.
  (v) When necessary they should be helped actively just like supporting their hands and providing them due direction etc.

(c) The children should be given sufficient practice and help for writing in straight lines. Use of lined paper or even graph paper can be recommended for providing them due practice.

(d) The children should be made to use good quality of ink; paper and pencil for providing them needed confidence in producing better results in their writing.

(e) They should be made to write legibly by maintaining proper links and gaps between the lines and curves of the letter as well as words and sentences.

(f) There should not be any overwriting, cutting or overlapping in their manuscript.

2. *Spelling*.   Many of the learning disabled may suffer from difficulties in writing words with the correct spelling. To help them in this direction start framing a list of words usually missspelt by a child and make the child learn the correct spellings—one word at a time.

(a) Write the word with correct spelling on the chalkboard or paper, ask the child to look at the correctly spelt word and compare it with the one he has written. Ask him to pronounce the word with its correct spelling. Ask him to repeat its pronunciation. The correctly spelt word may then be covered and the child asked to write it on his own on the paper or chalkboard spelling out all letters. He may then be asked to compare his spelling with the one already written on the chalkboard or paper. He may then be asked to write this word twice or thrice as the need may be for learning its proper spelling. For further practice, he may be given for writing a text or manuscript in which this particular word is repeated sufficient number of times.

(b) The child may be given opportunity to read and compare his misspelt word or words with the correctly spelt word or words from a standard text or manuscript. He may then be asked to write them first by copying and then without the aid of the text, using their memory.

3. *Reading skills*.   Learning disabled children may exhibit their weakness and poor performance with regard to reading and comprehension of text material or manuscript. Their difficulties and deficiencies in respect of reading skills are quite varied and diversified. Therefore while dealing with the children suffering from reading skill disabilities, a diagnostic-prescriptive approach must be adopted and hence any remedial programme for bringing improvement in their reading skills must be in tune with their individual needs and abilities like below.

(a) The children who can't pronounce a word, letter or sound correctly should receive phonetic guidance and drill to overcome their deficiency.

(b) The children who have some medical or psychological problem should be properly diagnosed for proper identification of their problems and accordingly, remedial measures should be taken with the help of medical or psychological experts.

(c) The children suffering with inadequacy or improper style of reading should be provided with model reading. A teacher, a model student or a recording device may be used for this purpose. The children should be asked to copy or imitate the model reading pattern.

(d) The children who feel difficulty in comprehension should be treated with multi-sensory techniques. Use of stories, narration of personal experiences, oral discussions, use of necessary multimedia facilities etc. prove useful in overcoming such deficiencies and they can be made to read and comprehend the material of their reading level. Gradually, they can be given material of some advanced level. The difficult words, the meanings of which they do not know should be clarified to them. The meaning of these words or sentences should be explained to them by adopting a suitable learning situation. Sometimes oral explanation may be sufficient, other times the teacher has to seek the help of some picture, tell a story or narrate personal experience etc.

4. *Thinking and reasoning abilities.* Thinking and reasoning abilities are essential instruments in the process of learning. The learning disabled mostly suffer from lack of proper reasoning and thinking ability. To overcome this, they may be helped to adopt the procedures given below.

(a) Initially, they may be asked to collect data by reading, listening, observing or doing.

(b) Then they may be asked to analyze this data. Find the similarities and dissimilarities. Here they may be helped and promoted by asking questions, giving examples etc. for learning how to discriminate and weigh out similarities or dissimilarities.

(c) They may be persuaded to classify the data into different groups.

(d) At later stage they may be persuaded to find some other ways of categorizing and classifying this data. In this way they may be directed to free thinking, develop broader outlook and an inclination to creative and divergent thinking etc.

(e) At the next stage, they may be persuaded to integrate this new information and new experience to their existing mental structures. In this way, they may be helped in the acquisition of the ability for continuous reorganization and restructuring of their learning experiences.

(f) At the next stage, they may be helped to build a generalization on the basis of their reorganization and restructuring of experiences. They may also be helped in acquiring the ability of making predictions based on the collected data and its analysis etc.

(g) They may also be helped in making alternative predictions, hypotheses and test the validity and prediction for arriving at some valid conclusion in order to help them in the acquisition of useful knowledge, skills or art and techniques for better learning.

5. *Social skills.* Many of the learning disabled exhibit poor performance and inadequate behaviour related to the use of essential social skills. They may remain aloof, isolated or feel maladjusted in social interaction, cooperative learning and other social group events.

These children may be helped in some of the following ways:

(a) It is to be remembered that the task of development of social skills can go well with the general setting. Special settings comprising of only the disabled children, cannot provide the needed training conditions, situations or experiences for the development of social skills.

(b) There must be adequate provision of co-curricular activities, hobbies classes, curricular areas of diversified interest for working in the group and get together situations.

(c) Children should be given proper opportunities, help and due encouragement for building up their self-confidence and self-respect to help them overcome their shyness, resistance and rigidity etc. and involve in group and social activities.

(d) They must be helped in sharing their thoughts and actions with others. Initially they may be helped in making friendship, joint efforts and group ventures with the help of some of their peers who are more active, cooperative and social.

(e) They must be helped in learning the art of social skills, group participation and social interaction with the help of pre-arranged and structured learning situations. Here through oral communication, charts and pictures, slides and films, they should be made to learn the essential things regarding expression of emotions, body language and symbols, desirable or undesirable behaviour in social encounters and social interaction.

(f) After identifying their area of interests in curricular and co-curricular areas, they should be given opportunities for discussion, group work and other social participation with their peers, school mates and neighbours.

(g) Teachers, with the help of useful instructional material and developed technology should try to transmit useful personal social experiences and skills to these children so as to improve their social behaviour and social interaction.

6. *Attention deficit.* Most of the learning disabled suffer from what is known as attention deficit or inattention. These children do not concentrate or focus on the task of learning or are in the habit of paying attention to unimportant details of the task. These children may be helped in some of the following ways:

(a) These children should be made the focus of the teachers, by making their seating arrangement at the centre of the classroom. Individual attention and extra care is to be given for observing their actions and movements in the class. They should be given enough opportunities for classroom interaction by asking them to cooperate in the display of aid material, experimenting etc.

(b) The method of advanced organizers may work well with these students. That is, we can provide an introductory overview of the material to be presented. This overview may acquaint the learners why the information they are going to be provided is important and what are the crucial elements of presentation.

(c) A highly structured learning environment providing direct instruction and incorporation of following features is very much recommended by educationists and researchers:

(i) Have a calm and cool environment by neutralizing the factors causing distraction or inattention.

(ii) Give clear and precise instructions.

(iii) Use appropriate and interesting methods to provide information.

(iv) Involve the students in teaching-learning process.

(v) Make use of reinforcements, appreciations and rewards etc.

(vi) Make the practice work, homework and assignment more interesting and purposeful.

(vii) Provide instruction that meets their individual needs.

(viii) Teach the students to practice self-restraint and overcome inappropriate behaviour.

Specialized Approaches and Techniques for Helping the Learning Disabled

There are several specific and specialized techniques and approaches that have been evolved through long experiences and researches while working with the learning disabled children. Let us discuss in brief some of them.

1. Behavioural approach. In this approach, attempts are made to modify the behaviour of the learning disabled by restructuring and reorganizing the environmental conditions, providing opportunities for modification or change in behaviour, properly reinforcing their changed behaviour and thus helping them to acquire desirable learning behaviour.

2. Psychoanalytic approach. In this approach, attempts are made to analyse the behaviour of the disabled child and find out the root cause or causes of his learning deficiency. Accordingly, a remedial programme is planned and administered by establishing proper rapport with him.

3. Individualized instructional approach. This approach advocates the use of small groups or even individuals for helping them rectify their learning deficiencies. Peer tutoring (making use of competent and good peers) has proved to be successful technique for providing individual assistance to the affected ones. The learning disabled feels quite safe and secure for receiving needed assistance in such a set-up and are then able to come up on the satisfactory learning level.

4. *Self-instructional approach.* In this approach, learning disabled children are required to adopt self-learning and self-improvement measures for treating their learning deficits and deficiencies. For this purpose, remedial programmes present in the form of programmed learning text, computer-assisted instructions, teaching machines, tape-recorder and video disc etc. can be put into use. Self-learning questionnaire and instructional modules can also be prepared and made into use with the help of teachers. In this approach, the learning disabled can avail valuable opportunities and means for rectifying their deficits and deficiencies by their own pace, needs and learning capacities. For a better out put, their progress can also be supervised and guided by the specialized or trained classroom teachers.

5. *Multi-sensory approach.* In this approach, learning disabled children are taught by appealing to their multiple senses—visual, auditory, touch, smell, and taste etc. depending upon the nature of the subject material and its learning objectives. For example, to provide wholesome language experiences, a multi-sensory approach named VAKT (providing visual, auditory, kinesthetic and tactile experiences to the children) has been devised. This is a step-by-step approach where a learner is first acquainted with the letters of a word and then slowly familiarized with the word. The learner is then made to see, say, hear and feel the experiences woven around this particular word. Once the word is mastered, the learner is asked to make use of it in a sentence. After the learning of words and sentences the learner may be given a storywriting test. Then, finally, they are provided reading practices. It can also be done through vicarious experiences provided through multi-sensory aid materials and equipments.

6. *Technological approach.* In this approach, advanced technology is used for providing remedial instructional programme to the learning disabled. Some of them are:

(a) *Audio tape and tape-recorder.* Use of audio tape and tape-recorder can work well with the learning disabled. They may able to rectify many of their language learning difficulties particularly related to pronunciation, proper intonation and way of speaking etc. Reading, speaking and conversation skills can be better developed with the help of audio tape and tape-recorders.

(b) *Video-disc instruction.* This type of remedial instruction provides high quality visual and auditory presentation. It can work well for arranging properly planned remedial programmes to all types of learning disabilities. The learning disabled can watch useful and interesting academic as well as social presentations on the video discs in the form of continuous motion pictures and simultaneously listen to the carefully prepared narration for providing useful instruction.

(c) *Computer-assisted instruction.* The use of computer has opened a vast field of remedial instruction for the learning disabled of all types. With the use of computer technology, we can arrange self-instructional or individualized instructional as well as group instructional remedial programmes to the learning disabled. The deficiencies regarding reading, writing, conversation, mathematics, science and other practical oriented subjects and social skills can well be treated by this method.

Let us take the case of students with learning disabilities in the field of writing. The programmes having provision of speech out-put can help them know whether the word or sentences they wrote matches with the word or sentences they hear. Computer generated list of words called word banks may help the students to know alternative words and their proper use. Also, they can be helped to evaluate their written composition in terms of grammatical errors, proper sentence structures or even identifying the proper meaning of whatever they write.

In the field of mathematics and sciences, it can provide best opportunities for the demonstration of knowledge and skills. The practical work in science can be better demonstrated by the use of CD-ROM technology. The students deficient in mathematical skills can be provided excellent opportunities with the help of computer-aided instructions. For achieving the objectives of knowledge, application, skill, attitude and interests related to all types of teaching subjects specially with children having learning difficulties, the computer-assisted instructions (CAI) have proved quite useful. Here, the advanced developments in CAI like Hypertext and Hypermedia have proved more useful in the following way.

(d) *Hypertext technology* uses pop-up text windows for desired further explanation and understanding of a traditional textbook material. Learning disabled usually feel difficulty in following their textbooks as properly and swiftly as their normal classmates. For them computer's hypertext makes the things quite simple. It may give definitions or illustrations of difficult words, may reword or rewrite the confusing or complicated language of the text, provide additional, useful hints for solving the problems, give diagrams, pictures and maps etc., for proper understanding of the text material, concepts and generalizations. All this simplification and extra understanding are available for the learning disabled children at their own convenience with the simple press of a key or moving of the mouse.

(e) *Hypermedia technology* of the computer makes use of a variety of formats to supplement and enrich text by merging computer and media technologies. One can listen, watch, store, locate, and search the needed information through the application of multimedia application of the computer technology.

In this way, the advanced technology related with the use of computers and multimedia, can be well utilized for providing useful remedial education to the learning disabled.

SUMMARY

Learning disabled children are those children who suffer from serious learning disabilities. Learning disability is nothing but a sort of handicap or a helplessness that can be revealed by the sufferer in terms of his academic performance (learning or understanding something) in the same way as experienced by a physically handicapped person in terms of his physical functioning or by a mentally handicapped in terms of his mental function.

Characteristically, learning disabled children (apparently not distinguished from their physical appearance or I.Q. scores) essentially suffer from severely impaired learning inefficiency to the extent that they essentially require special attention, care and remedial programmes for the rectification of their learning problems and disabilities.

Causes of their learning disabilities may be attributed to (i) genetic or heredity factors on the pattern of "Like begets like", (ii) organic or physiological factors causing malfunction or dysfunction of their central nervous system consisting brain, spinal cord and message carrying nerves etc., and (iii) improper and uncongenial conditions and factors present in one's physical, social, cultural and educational environment.

The identification of learning disabled children may be carried out by means of (i) non-testing devices like observation rating scale, check list, interview etc., and (ii) testing devices employing standardized diagnostic tests, ability tests or process tests, achievement tests and daily assessment system.

For adopting educational measures for the learning disabled, we should not emphasize segregation in terms of separate schools or classes for them but try to provide due care and attention within the existing educational set-up by adopting special remedial and educational programmes and restructuring and improving the existing environmental set-up to meet the special needs of these children.

Much attention needs to be paid in terms of devising and adopting special educational measures for rectification of the deficiencies and difficulties pertaining to specific learning abilities and skills like below:

— Steps should be taken to improve the handwriting right from its early diagnosis.
— The learning disabled who suffer with the difficulty to spell words correctly should be given proper training.
— Reading skills, social skills and thinking and reasoning abilities should be adequately developed and improved so that the children do not suffer academically on account of their deficits and deficiencies in these areas.
— Children suffering from the disability or deficit known as attention deficit or in attention should be helped in overcoming such deficit.

In addition to these special measures some more specialized approaches and techniques like below may also be adopted for helping the learning disabled:

— Behaviour modification through behavioural approach.
— Psychoanalytic approach for analysing and correcting the defective behaviour.

— Individualized instructional approach for providing individual assistance.
— Self-instructional approach for bringing self-improvement.
— Multi-sensory approach by appealing to the multiple senses of the learning disabled.
— Technological approach for providing remedial instructions through technological means like audio tape and tape-recorder, video-disc, computer and hypertext and hypermedia technologies etc.

REFERENCES

Kavale K.A. and Forness, S.R., *The Science of Learning Disabilities*, San Diego, CA: College-Hill, 1985.

Kirk, S., McCarthy, J., and Kirk, W., *Illenois Test of Phycholinguistic Abilities* (rev. ed.), Urbana, IL, University of Illenois Press, 1968.

Kirk, S.A. and Kirk, W.D., *Phycholonguistic learning disabilities; Diagnosis and Remediation*, Urbana, IL, University of Illenois Press, 1971.

Federal Register, Washington DC: U.S. Government Printing Office, Jan. 19, 1977.

McLoughlin, J.A. and Netick, A., *Defining Learning Disabilities: A New and Cooperative Direction*, Journal of Learning Disabilities, 1983, 16, p. 21–23.

Lerner, J.W., *Children with Learning Disabilities*, Boston; Houghton Mifflin, 1976.

Lerner, J., *Learning Disabilities: Theories, Diagnosis and Teaching Strategies*, Boston: Houghton Mifflin, 1985.

Telford, C.W. and Sawrey, J.M., *The Exceptional Individual*, New Jersey, Prentice-Hall, 1967.

Woodcock, R.W., *Woodcock Reading Mastery Test* (Revised), Circle Pines, MN: American Guidance Service, 1987.

SUGGESTED READINGS

Alley G. and Deshler, D., *Teaching the Learning Disabled Adolescent*, Denver Co. Love, 1979.

Cruickshank, W.M. and D.P. Hallahan (Eds.), *Perceptual and Learning Disabilities in Children*, Syracuse, N.Y., Syracuse University Press, 1975.

Curtisk and Sharer, J.P., *The Education of Slow Learning Children*, London; Routledge and Kegan Paul, 1980.

Deniel, P.H., James M.K. and John, W.L., *Introduction to Learning Disabilities*, N.Y., Allyn and Bacon, 1996.

Eving, A., *Aphasia in Children*, New York: Oxford University Press, 1930.

Fernald, G.M., *Remedial Techniques in Basic School Subjects*, New York: McGraw-Hill, 1943.

Frostig, M., *Manual for the Marianne, Frostig Developmental Test of Visual Perception*, Palo Alto, California, Consulting Psychologists Press, 1961.

Gearheart, B.E. *Learning Disabilities; Educational Strategies*, St. Louis; C.V. Mosby, 1973.

Gerald, H., *Teaching Slow Learners*, London: Temple Smith, 1977.

Hallahen, D.P. and W.M. Cruickshank, *Psycho-educational Foundations of Learning Disabilities*, Englewood Cliffs, N.J., Prentice-Hall, 1973.

Hallahan, D., Kauffman, J., and Llyod, J., *Introduction to Learning Disabilities* (2nd ed.), Englewood Cliffs, N.J., Prentice-Hall, 1985.

Haring, N. and E.L. Phillips, *Educating Emotionally Disturbed Children*, N.Y., McGraw-Hill, 1962.

Herman, K., *Reading Disability*, Springfield, IL; Thomas 1959.

Koppitz, E.M., *Children with Learning Disabilities*, A Five Year Follow up Study, N.Y., Grune & Stratton, 1971.

McCarthy, J.J. and J.F. McCarthy, *Learning Disabilities*, Boston: Allyn & Bacon, 1969.

Translay and Guilliford, *The Education of Slow Learning Children*, London: Routledge & Kegan Paul, 1962.

Torgesen, J.K. and Wong, B.W.L. (Eds.), *Learning Disabilities: Some new perspectives*, New York: Academic, 1986.

Torgesen, J.K., *Memory Processes in Reading Disabled Children, Journal of Learning Disabilities*, 1985, 18, 350–357.

Wallace, G. and McLoughlin, J.A., *Learning Disabilities: Concepts and Characteristics* (2nd ed.), Columbus, OH: Merrill, 1979.

Wug, E.H. and Semel, E., *Languages Assessment and Intervention for the Learning Disabled* (2nd ed.), Columbus, OH: Merril, 1984.

Chapter 24

Psychology of Adjustment

MEANING AND DEFINITIONS

The dictionary meaning of the word 'adjustment' is, to fit, make suitable, adapt, arrange, modify, harmonize or make correspondent. Thus, when we make an adjustment between two things, we adapt or modify one or both of them to correspond to each other. In some situations, one of the factors may not be changeable and so the one which is, has to be modified in some way to suit the other. The extension of a ladder by a suitable length to reach an upper story window is a good example of such an adjustment. Wearing of clothes according to the requirements of the seasons is another such example as ordinarily, it is beyond our capacity to change the seasons according to our clothes. Modern technology has, of course, made it possible to adjust the temperature inside dwelling houses and workplaces to harmonize with our needs.

There has been a continuous struggle between the needs of the individual and the external forces since time immemorial. According to Darwin's (1859) theory of evolution, those species which adapted successfully to the demands of living, survived and multiplied while others who did not, died out. Therefore, the adaptation or changing of oneself or one's surroundings according to the demands of the external environment became the basic need for our survival. It is as true today with all of us as it was with the Darwin's primitive species. Those of us who can adapt or adjust to the needs of changing conditions can live happily and successfully, while others either vanish, lead miserable lives or prove a nuisance to society. However, the concept of adjustment is not so simple as adaptation. Psychologists and scholars differ considerably in interpreting its meaning and nature as can be seen from the following definitions:

James Drever (1952):

Adjustment means the modification to compensate for or meet special conditions.

Webster (1951):

Adjustment is the establishment of a satisfactory relationship, as representing harmony, conformance, adaptation or the like.

Carter V. Good (1959):

Adjustment is the process of finding and adopting modes of behaviour suitable to the environment or the changes in the environment.

Warren (1934):

> Adjustment refers to any operation whereby an organism or organ becomes more favourably related to the environment or to the entire situation, environmental and internal.

Shaffer (1961):

> Adjustment is the process by which a living organism maintains a balance between its needs and the circumstances that influence the satisfaction of these needs.

Gates and Jersild (1948):

> Adjustment is a continual process in which a person varies his behaviour to produce a more harmonious relationship between himself and his environment.

Vanhaller (1970):

> We can think of adjustment as psychological survival in much the same way as the biologist uses the term adaptation to describe physiological survial.

Crow and Crow (1956):

> An individual's adjustment is adequate, wholesome or healthful to the extent that he has established harmonious relationship between himself and the conditions, situations and persons who comprise his physical and social environment.

Let us try to analyse these definitions for understanding the meaning and nature of the term adjustment.

In the first definition, James Drever takes adjustment to be the ways and means to help the individual to meet the demands of changed conditions by adapting or modifying his previous ways of doing or facing things. The other three definitions also agree with this opinion that one is required to change one's mode of behaviour to suit the changed situations so that a satisfactory and harmonious relationship can be maintained keeping in view the individual and his needs on the one hand, and the environment and its influence on the individual, on the other. In doing so, as Good's definition states, the individual can either change himself according to the needs of the environment or change his environment to suit his own needs.

Shaffer's definition underlines one's needs and their satisfaction. Human needs are vital, indispensable and urgently requisite. One feels adjusted to the extent that one's needs are gratified or are in the process of being gratified. The individual tries to bring about changes in his circumstances in order to overcome the difficulties in the fulfilment of his needs. Sometimes, he reduces his needs and as a result he may feel satisfied within the limits of his environment. He thus tries to maintain a balance between his needs and his capacity of realising these needs and as long as this balance is maintained, he remains adjusted. As soon as this balance is disturbed, he drifts towards maladjustment.

Gates and Jersild as also Crow and Crow define adjustment as the maintenance of a harmonious relationship between man and his environment. An individual needs to change or modify himself in some way or the other to fit into or accommodate himself with his environment. As the conditions in the environment are changing all the time, adjustment is also a continuous process. For instance, if a girl from the city marries into a rural family and has to live in a village, she would have to change her behaviour, her habits and her attitude in order to accommodate herself to the changed environment.

Vonhaller's definition takes the clue from Darwin's theory of evolution. Darwin maintained that only those organisms most fitted to adapt to changing circumstances survive. Therefore, the individuals who are able to adjust themselves to changed situations in their environment can live a harmonious and happy life. Adjustment as a psychological term may thus be said to be another name for the term 'adaptation' used in the biological world. Adjustment, in all its meanings implies a satisfactory adaptation to the demands of day-to-day life. From the foregoing discussion it may be concluded that adjustment is a process that helps a person to lead a happy and contented life while maintaining a balance between his needs and his capacity to fulfil them. It enables him to change his way of life according to the demands of the situation and gives him the strength and ability to bring about the necessary changes in the conditions of his environment.

In addition to his own basic needs, an individual is also subject to certain demands of society. If he thinks only in terms of satisfying his own needs without thought of the norms, ethics and cultural traditions of society, he will not be adjusted to his environment. Adjustment does not cater only to one's own demands but also to the demands of society. It may, therefore, be stated that in its comprehensive connotation, *adjustment is a condition or state in which the individual's behaviour conforms to the demands of the culture or society to which he belongs and he feels that his own needs have been, or will be fulfilled.*

Adjustment involves the gratification of a person's needs as governed by the demands of various environmental situations. This is not, however, a one-way process: an individual maintains the balance between himself and his surroundings either by modifying his own behaviour or by modifying the environment. In this context, as Arkoff (1968) states:

> Adjustment is the interaction between a person and his environment. How one adjusts in a particular situation depends upon one's personal characteristics as also the circumstances of the situation. In other words, both personal and environmental factors work side by side in adjustment. An individual is adjusted if he is adjusted to himself and to his environment.

Adjustment as Achievement or Process

Adjustment can be interpreted as both, process and the outcome of that process in the form of some attainment or achievement. When a poor child studies under the street light because he has no lighting arrangement at home he is said to be in a process of adjustment. What he attains in terms of success in his examination or the fulfilment of his ambition or pride in his achievement is nothing but the result of his adjustment to his self and his environment. Thus, adjustment as an achievement means how the effectiveness with which an individual can function in changed circumstances and is, as such, related to his adequacy and regarded as an achievement that is accomplished either badly or well (Lazarus, 1976).

Adjustment as a process describes and explains the ways and means of an individual's adaptation to his self and his environment without reference to the quality of such adjustment or its outcome in terms of success or failure. It only shows how individuals or a group or groups of people cope under changing circumstances and what factors influence this adjustment. Let us now consider some salient features of adjustment as an interaction between a person and his environment.

Continuous process. The process of adjustment is continuous. It starts at one's birth and goes on without stop till one's death. A person as well as his environment are constantly changing as also are his needs in accordance with the demands of the changing external environment. Consequently, the process or terms of an individual's adjustment can be expected to change from situation to situation and according to Arkoff (1968), there is nothing like satisfactory or complete adjustment which can be achieved once and for all time. It is something that is constantly achieved and reachieved by us.

Two-way process. Adjustment is a two-way process and involves not only the process of fitting oneself into available circumstances but also the process of changing the circumstances to fit one's needs. Emphasizing this two-way nature of the adjustment process, Robert W. White (1956) writes:

> The concept of adjustment implies a constant interaction between the person and his environment, each making demands on the other. Sometimes adjustment is accomplished when the person yields and accepts conditions which are beyond his power to change. Sometimes it is achieved when the environment yields to the person's constructive activities. In most cases adjustment is a compromise between these two extremes and maladjustment is a failure to achieve a satisfactory compromise.

Areas of Adjustment

Adjustment in the case of an individual should consist of personal as well as environmental components. These two aspects of adjustment can be further subdivided into smaller aspects of personal and environmental factors. Adjustment, although seeming to be a universal characteristic or quality may have different aspects and dimensions.

Through the numerous efforts at measuring adjustment through inventories and other techniques, these aspects have been identified and various tests have been constructed to assess their dimensions. For example, Bell (1958) has taken five areas or dimensions in his adjustment inventory namely, home, health, social emotional and occupational.

Arkoff (1968) in his book: *Adjustment and Mental Health* has enumerated the family, school or college, vocation and marriage as the important areas of adjustment.

Recently, Joshi (1964) and Pandey in their research study covering school and college students, have given 11 areas or dimensions of an individual's adjustment:

1. Health and physical development.
2. Finance, living conditions and employment.
3. Social and recreational activities.
4. Courtship, sex and marriage.

5. Social psychological relations.
6. Personal psychological relations.
7. Moral and religious.
8. Home and family.
9. Future—vocational and educational.
10. Adjustment to school and college work.
11. Curriculum and teaching.

In this way, adjustment of a person is based on the harmony between his personal characteristics and the demands of the environment of which he is a part. Personal and environmental factors work side by side in bringing about this harmony.

Measurement of Adjustment

Measurement as an instrument of inquiry is now frequently used in behavioural sciences. At a general level of classification in behavioural science, the following five different types of measuring techniques are used:

1. Testing techniques;
2. Projective techniques;
3. Inventory techniques;
4. Sociometric techniques; and
5. Scaling techniques.

In the area of measurement of adjustment, inventory techniques are the most popular because they have many advantages compared to other techniques. Testing techniques can only be used to assess the characteristics of individuals at the conscious, and projective techniques only at the unconscious level. The adjustment behaviour, the adaptation to changed circumstances involves both conscious as well as unconscious behaviour. Therefore, the two techniques separately are unable to give a proper assessment of an individual's adjustment.

Sociometric techniques are used in the measurement of social relationships. They can provide clues to the level of social adjustment. Social adjustment is only one part of an individual's total adjustment. The other aspects of his adjustment like physical, mental, emotional, social and occupational are not explored by the sociometric techniques and they cannot, therefore, be used for the accurate assessment of an individual's total adjustment.

In scaling techniques opinions are collected from some other person or persons about the adjustment pattern of a particular individual known to the respondents. Adjustment as a wide phenomenon carries so many things with it that one cannot judge the adjustment pattern of another individual from his overt behaviour and the inner private world or reactions of an individual cannot be assessed by the use of scaling techniques.

Some important inventories and measures of adjustment:

1. Bell's adjustment inventory developed by Hugh M. Bell.
2. Edward's personal preference schedule (EPPS) published by Psychological Corporation, New York.

3. The Heston personal adjustment inventory developed by Joseph C. Heston.
4. The Mooney problem checklist.
5. Asthana's adjustment inventory developed by H.S. Asthana.
6. Vyaktitva parakha prashnavali developed by M.S.L. Saxena.
7. Sinha's adjustment inventory developed by A.K.P. Sinha and R.P. Singh.
8. Joshi's adjustment inventory developed by M.C. Joshi and Jagdish Pandey.
9. Adjustment inventory for older people devised by P.V. Ramamurti.
10. Teacher adjustment inventory developed by S.K. Mangal.

Characteristics of a Well-adjusted Person

A well-adjusted person is supposed to possess the following characteristics:

1. *Awareness of his own strengths and limitations.* A well adjusted person knows his own strengths and weaknesses. He tries to make capital out of his assets in some areas by accepting his limitations in others.

2. *Respecting himself and others* The dislike for one-self is a typical symptom of maladjustment. An adjusted individual has respect for himself as well as for others.

3. *An adequate level of aspiration.* His level of aspiration is neither too low nor too high in terms of his own strengths and abilities. He does not try to reach for the stars and also does not repent over selecting an easier course for his advancement.

4. *Satisfaction of basic needs.* His basic organic, emotional and social needs are fully satisfied or in the process of being satisfied. He does not suffer from emotional cravings and social isolation. He feels reasonably secure and maintains his self-esteem.

5. *Absence of a critical or fault-finding attitude.* He appreciates the goodness in objects, persons or activities. He does not try to look for weaknesses and faults. His observation is scientific rather than critical or punitive. He likes people, admires their good qualities, and wins their affection.

6. *Flexibility in behaviour.* He is not rigid in his attitude or way of life. He can easily accommodate or adapt himself to changed circumstances by making necessary changes in his behaviour.

7. *The capacity to deal with adverse circumstances.* He is not easily overwhelmed by adverse circumstances and has the will and the courage to resist and fight odds. He has an inherent drive to master his environment rather than to passively accept it.

8. *A realistic perception of the world.* He holds a realistic vision and is not given to flights of fancy. He always plans, thinks and acts pragmatically.

9. *A feeling of ease with his surroundings.* A well-adjusted individual feels satisfied with his surroundings. He fits in well in his home, family, neighbourhood and other social surroundings. If a student, he likes his school, school-mates, teachers, and feels satisfied with his daily routine. When he enters a profession, he has a love for it and maintains his zeal and enthusiasm despite all odds.

10. A balanced philosophy of life. A well-adjusted person has a philosophy which gives direction to his life while keeping in view the demands of changed situations and circumstances. This philosophy is centred around the demands of his society, culture, and his ownself so that he does not clash with his environment or with himself.

Theories or Models of Adjustment

Why do some people adjust to their environment and others do not? What are the factors that make an individual adjusted or maladjusted? There are several theories and models describing the pattern of adjustment for answering such questions. Let us discuss some of the important models.

1. The moral model. This represents the oldest view-point about adjustment or maladjustment. According to this view, adjustment or maladjustment should be judged in terms of morality i.e. absolute norms of expected behaviour. Those who follow the norms are adjusted (virtuous or good people) and those who violate or do not follow these norms are maladjusted (sinners). Evil supernatural forces like demons, devils, etc. were blamed for making one indulge in behaviour against the norms (committing sins) while the religious gods, goddess and other saintly great souls were responsible for making one a happy, healthy, prosperous and pious person (adjusted in the modern sense). However, as the medical and biological sciences advanced and scientific reasoning gained a firm footing in the nineteenth century, the moral model was replaced by the medico-biological model.

2. The medico-biological model. This model holds genetic, physiological and biochemical factors responsible for a person being adjusted or maladjusted to his self and his environment. Maladjustment, according to this model, is the result of disease in the tissues of the body, especially the brain. Such disease can be the result of heredity or damage acquired during the course of a person's life—by injury, infection, or hormonal disruption arising from stress, among other things. In the opinion of Lazaras (1976), the correction of adjustive failures or disorders requires correction of the tissue defect through physical therapies such as drugs, surgery and the like.

This model is still extant and enjoys credibility for rooting out the causes of adjustive failure in terms of genetic influences, biochemical defect hypotheses, and disease in the tissues of the body. However, it is not correct to assign physiological or organic causes to all maladapted and malfunctioning behaviour, especially when there is no evidence of physiological malfunction. Such a situation certainly calls for other explanations, viewpoints or models.

3. The psychoanalytic model. This model owes its origin to the theory of psychoanalysis propagated by Sigmund Freud (1938) and supported by psychologists like Adler, Jung and other neo-Freudians.

(a) *Freud's views.* Freud's system of psychology and psychoanalysis has been discussed in Chapter 5 of this text. We will, therefore, confine the present discussion to only those factors which are relevant to success or failure in adjustment.

    (i) The human psyche or mind consists of three layers, the conscious, the sub-conscious and unconscious. The unconscious holds the key to our behaviour. It decides the individual's adjustment and maladjustment to his self and to his environment. It contains all the repressed wishes, desires, feelings, drives and motives many of which are related to sex and aggression. One is adjusted or maladjusted to the degree, extent or the ways in which these are kept dormant or under control.

    (ii) According to Freud, man is a pleasure seeking animal by nature. He wants to seek pleasure and avoids pain or anything which is not in keeping with his pleasure loving nature. The social restrictions imposed by the mores of society and his own moral standards dictated by his superego come in conflict with the unrestricted and unbridled desires of his basic pleasure seeking nature. These pleasures are mostly sexual in nature. One remains adjusted to the extent that these are satisfied. An individual drifts towards malfunctioning of behaviour and maladjust-ment in case such satisfaction is threatened or denied. Freud postulated the imaginary concepts of 'id', 'ego' and 'superego' for the adjustive and non-adjustive behaviour patterns and formulated the following conclusion:

A person's behaviour remains normal and in harmony with his self and his environment to the extent that his ego is able to maintain the balance between the evil designs of his id and the moral ethical standard dictated by his superego. In case the ego is not strong enough to exercise proper control over one's id and superego, malfunction of behaviour would result. Two different situations could then arise:

- If the superego dominates then there is no acceptable outlet for expression of the repressed wishes, impulses and appetites of the id. Such a situation may give birth to neurotic tendencies in the individual.
- If the id dominates, then the individual pursues his unbridled pleasure seeking impulses, without care for the social and moral norms. In such a situation the individual may be seen to be engaged in unlawful or immoral activities resulting in maladaptive, problem or delinquent behaviour.

    (iii) Freud also uses the concept of libido, i.e., a flow of energy related to sex gratification. He equates it with a flowing river and maintains that:

- If its flow is outward causing sex gratification and pleasurable sensation from outside objects, the individual remains quite normal and adjusted to his self and the environment.

- Its inward flow leads to self-indulgence and narcissism.
- If its path is blocked, this results in its arrest leading to regressive behaviour, a kind of abnormality.
- If the flow of the libido is dammed up, condemned or repressed through the authority exercised by the ego in association with the superego, it may cause severe maladjustment. When the ego is weak and the superego is rigid, this may lead to psychotic personality disorders. However, when the ego is weak and the superego also is not too rigid it may result in relatively simple disorders like neurosis or still simpler maladaptive behaviour characterized by restlessness, sleeplessness, headache, stomachache, backache, vomiting, lack of appetite etc.

(iv) According to Freud, adjustment or maladjustment should not be viewed only in terms of what the individual may be undergoing at present and what happened to him in his earlier childhood is even more important. What he may have experienced as a child, what types of gratification to his sex urge he has achieved, what has been repressed in his unconscious, how he has passed through the distinct stages of sexual development etc. are, thus, quite important for making him adjusted or maladjusted to his self and the environment.

(b) *Adler's views.* Adler disagreed with his teacher, and substituted the sex motive with the power motive or desire to attain superiority and perfection to explain human behaviour. He maintained that:

(i) There is an inherent strong urge in all human beings to seek power and attain superiority. Besides this as a child, one is helpless and dependent which makes one feel inferior and in order to make up for the feelings of inferiority, one takes recourse to compensatory behaviour, i.e. indulges in a struggle for power. Environmental situations, constitutional deficiency and many other factors may also make one feel inferior and to get away from these feelings one learns to struggle for achieving power. An individual's efforts for seeking power or attaining perfection may also be the result of his need for creative expression, the urge to do something new, to enhance his status in the eyes of his colleagues and others.

(ii) Stimulated thus by the urge to seek power or attain superiority and perfection, one adopts a distinctive lifestyle suited to one's environmental situations. One continues to strive for superiority by emulating and exploiting the ways and means provided by one's lifestyle. Adjustment or the lack of it would depend on whether one's efforts end in success or failure to achieve one's goal. Thus, the following three situations may arise:

- Success in seeking gratification of one's power motive or attaining superiority may lead to good adjustment to one's self and the environment.
- In the case of partial failure, if one is successful in bringing about a

slight modification in one's life's goals or style of life one may be able to reconcile with one's self and the environment and may feel adjusted and remain normal.

- In case of failure to obtain gratification of the power motive and to changing one's goal or style of life, one may drift towards non-adjustive or maladjustive behaviour leading to mild or severe mental illness.

(c) *Jung's views.* Jung's system of analytical psychology advocated the idea of the self-actualization motive instead of Feud's sex gratification motive and Adler's power seeking motive for explaining the why and how of human behaviour. According to him, one has a strong inner urge or motive to exhibit one's talents or abilities or seek self-actualization. Accordingly one utilizes one's life energy, i.e. the flow of libido as a channel for self-expression to satisfy the urge for self-actualization. The degree of adjustment of one's personality depends on the extent to which one is successful in actualizing oneself. Libido, the life energy as Jung maintains may flow both ways—inward or outward, turning an individual into an introvert or extrovert personality. In the introvert, thinking is predominant while sensations and feelings are suppressed. In the extroverts, on the other hand, the feelings or sensations are more predominant and the thinking is suppressed. Generally speaking, however, an individual is neither purely introvert nor a purely extrovert. He is ambivert, i.e. while showing the symptoms of an introvert, he possesses some characteristics of the extrovert and vice versa. As long as a person can maintain a proper balance between his thinking and feeling he remains adjusted to his self and the environment. But lopsided behaviour, i.e. laying too much emphasis on thinking at the cost of feelings or giving too much consideration to feelings at the cost of thinking may disturb the balance of one's psyche. It may lead to maladaptive behaviour causing mild or severe mental illness.

Another criterion for normal or properly adaptive behaviour, according to Jung's theory, is the reconciliation between one's conscious and unconscious behaviour. Failure on one's part to maintain or achieve such reconciliation may lead to maladaptive behaviour and mental illness. When one's conscious is not in tune with the unconscious or when the unconscious turns hostile on account of being not properly understood by the conscious it is bound to create imbalances in one's mind and make one's behaviour quite hostile to one self and to one's environment. If this hostility or aggression is directed inward, one becomes neurotic but when it overflows outwards, one turns into a psychotic or delinquent character. In some severe forms of insanity, as claimed by Jung, we find a complete autonomy of the unconscious, a type of complete control or bombardment of the conscious mind by the unconscious contents in the shape of disturbing and unusual ideas. Harmony or discord between one's conscious and unconscious may thus proves to be a deciding factor for one's personality to be termed as adjusted or maladjusted to one's self and the environment.

The views of other neo-Freudians and later psychoanalysts. The other followers of the psychoanalysis school also tried to put forward their own viewpoints explaining the why and how of human behaviour. Notable among them were Karen Horney, Erich Fromm, wilhelm Reich and Erik H. Erickson. Let us briefly discuss their views.

(d) *Karen Horney's views.* While Adler thought the need for power (to counter the feelings of inferiority) to be the root cause of human behaviour, Horney (1937) placed emphasis on the need for security (to offset the feelings of anxiety). She postulated that an individual as a child feels helpless and isolated in a potentially hostile world. This creates some basic feelings of anxiety and the craving for security in him. A reasonable concern with security is normal. But if an individual is obsessed with security to the exclusion of self-development, he is likely to drift towards maladaptive or abnormal behaviour.

The anxious child, she further theorizes, may ultimately move *towards* people and become dependent upon them, move *against* people and become hostile and rebellious, or move *away* from people and withdraw into himself. If a person can integrate these three attitudes or responses, sometimes giving, sometimes fighting and sometimes keeping to himself, he may remain adjusted to his self and his environment. But in case he turns too much to one of these directions, regardless of the appropriateness in specific circumstance, he is bound to become maladjusted ending up with mild or severe mental illness or delinquent behaviour.

The other reason for maladjustment, according to Horney's theory, may be the denial or obstruction in the way of realizing one's need for self-esteem or self-realization. Anxiety is the result of situations where one starts by not valuing oneself highly enough. A conflict then arises between one's ideal self and the real self. An individual can remain adjusted and normal to the extent that the balance between these two selves is satisfactorily maintained and may drift towards abnormal or maladaptive behaviour if this is disturbed.

(e) *Erich Fromm's views.* Like Horney, Fromm also emphasizes the need of security and feels that as a child one may feel the necessity for belonging to offset the fear of isolation and aloneness. Consequently, the individual in his childhood may desire to live in the family, belonging to the members of the family and provided with love, affection and security by them. In due course, however, when he attains maturity he is impelled by an inner craving for freedom and as a result he tries to escape from the very bonds which provided him the security he needed. In this kind of situation he may be confronted with the inner conflict of being dependent for the satisfaction of his need for security and his urge for freedom. This conflict is further heightened when parents and other members are also caught in the situation in the form of allowing independence to their progeny to play their roles as mature persons or trying to hold them back as a guarantee of their own future security. The extent to which this crisis of dependence versus independence or security versus freedom is resolved by the children with the help of their parents and elders, governs the degree to which their behaviour and functioning remain adjusted and normal. In case this crisis is not resolved satisfactorily, maladjustment and maladaptation followed by mental illness and delinquent character formation may result.

(f) *Wilhelm Reich's views.* In agreement with Freud's views on the importance of sexuality, Reich firmly believed that an individual's health, both physical and psychological, depends on the liberation of the sex drive, all the way to orgasm. However, from the day of birth, the release of libido or sexual energy is blocked by parents, teachers and society in general. Reich considers the term "sexual energy" in a wider connotation calling it "orgone energy" a life force energizing the total behaviour of an individual and responsible for all types of self expression. If this energy is properly channelized and flows along normal and natural ways, the individual remains adjusted and enjoys good physical and mental health; but in case the flow of this energy is blocked it may lead first to somatic or physical discomfort and then to the physiological and psychological disorders leading to mild or severe maladjustment and mental illness.

(g) *Erickson's views.* This contemporary psychoanalyst, born in 1902, views adjustment as a function of the conflict between inborn instincts and societal demands. He has divided the entire human life span into eight distinct stages. At each stage, the society characterized by a particular culture puts up a specific demand which may or may not suit the urges or instincts manifested at that specific stage by the individual. In this way, at each stage of life one is faced with a crisis the resolution of which can have either a good or bad effect on one's adjustment. For example, during the stage of infancy, the individual is confronted with the problem of resolving the crisis peculiar to this stage, i.e. trust (enabling him to form intimate relationships) versus mistrust (enabling him to protect himself in the hostile world) for his proper growth and development. The outcome of his behaviour depends upon the success or failure of the satisfactory resolution of this crisis and consequently he may grow into a wholesome healthy personality or a defective and deviant personality.

4. *The sociogenic or cultural model.* According to this model, the society in general and culture in particular affects one's ways of behaving to such an extent that behaviour takes the shape of adaptive or non-adaptive behaviour turning one into an adjusted or maladjusted personality. The society and culture to which one belongs does not only influence or shape one's behaviour but also sets a standard for its adherents to behave in the way it desires. Individuals behaving in the manner that society desires are labelled as normal and adjusted individuals while deviation from social norms and violation of role expectancy is regarded as the sign of maladjustment and abnormality. Although, society or culture plays a significant role in shaping and influencing human behaviour, yet it should not be regarded as the only factor in the adjustment process. Moreover, the societies or cultures may themselves, rather than the individual be maladaptive and sometimes even destructive to the individual's adjustment like Nazi Germany. It is not proper, therefore, to depend solely on the sociogenic or cultural model for the labelling of one's behaviour as adjusted or maladaptive.

5. *The sociopsychological or behaviouristic model.* The sociopsychological or behaviouristic model in general emphasizes that

(a) Behaviour is not inherited. Competencies required for successful living are largely acquired or learned through social experience by the individual himself.

(b) The environmental influences provided by the culture and social institutions are important but it is the interaction of one's psychological self with one's physical as well as social environment which plays the decisive role in determining adjustive success or failure.

(c) Behaviour, whether normal or abnormal is learned by obeying the same set of learning principles or laws. Generally, every type of behaviour is learned or acquired as an after-effect of its consequences. The behaviour once occurred, if reinforced, may be learned by the individual as normal. As a result, one may learn to consider responses which are labelled normal, as abnormal.

(d) Not only is normal and abnormal behaviour learned, the labelling of behaviour as normal or abnormal is also learned. Whether or not an individual is considered abnormal or maladjusted for a particular type of behaviour depends upon the observer of the behaviour and also upon the social context of the behaviour.

(e) Maladaptive behaviour may be treated by applying the principle of behaviour modification, unlearning, deconditioning and correcting environmental situations responsible for its occurrence.

Conclusion about the Models

All the models described above are true to certain extent (except the primitive moral model) for providing explanation for one's adjustive success or failure. But none of them is complete or adequate in itself for providing satisfactory explanation. Although medical or biological model provides a sufficient basis for understanding mental illness or maladaptive behaviour resulting through organic causes, physical damage to the brain and genetic factors, yet it cannot be applied to the disorders due to psychological causes and societal factors. Adjustment must always be considered as a continuing product of one's interaction with the biological and social determinants lying in one's biological and genetic make-up and environmental set-up. It is, therefore, innate as well as learned. For its analysis the analyst has to probe into not only how an individual is interacting with his environment at present but also in the past and how he has resolved his conflicts and crises in the past. It is, therefore, feasible to take a synthetic view of the above models for explaining and understanding one's success or failure in adjustment. All the factors, biological as well as social, the past as well as the present experiences, innate as well as learned patterns of behaviour, societal influence on the individual and vice-versa should be taken into consideration for understanding adjustment or maladjustment of the individual with his 'self' or environment.

Methods of Adjustment

In order to lead a healthy, happy and satisfying life one has to learn the various ways of adjustment, i.e. coping with one's environment as effectively as possible. Also he has to safeguard his self against turning into a maladjusted and abnormal personality. How can it be done? What are the different ways of coping with one's environment? How does one handle and face the conflicts, anxieties, pressures and stresses of one's life? To seek answers to these questions the description of possible modes, ways and methods used by the individual in his adjustment process is necessary.

The methods used for keeping and restoring harmony between the individual and his environment can be grouped into two categories, direct methods and indirect methods.

1. *Direct methods.* Direct methods are those methods which are employed by the individual intentionally at the conscious level. They are rational and logical and help in getting permanent solution of the problem faced by the individual in a particular situation. These methods include the following:

    (a) *Increasing trials or improving efforts.* When one finds it difficult to solve a problem or faces obstacles in the path, to cope with his environment he can attempt with a new zeal by increasing his efforts and improving his behavioural process.

    (b) *Adopting compromising means.* For maintaining harmony between his self and the environment one may adopt the following compromising postures:

        (i) He may altogether change his direction of efforts by changing the original goals, i.e. an aspirant for I.A.S. may direct his energies to become a probation officer in a nationalized bank.

        (ii) He may seek partial substitution of goal like selection for the provincial civil service in place of the I.A.S.

       (iii) He may satisfy himself by an apparent substitute for the real thing, e.g., in the case of a child, by a toy car in place of a real car and in the case of a young boy desirous of getting married by a doll in his arms.

    (c) *Withdrawal and submissiveness.* One may learn to cope with one's environment by just accepting defeat and surrendering oneself to the powerful forces of environment and circumstances.

    (d) *Making proper choices and decisions.* A person adapts himself to, and seeks harmony with, his environment by making use of his intelligence for the proper choices and wise decisions particularly when faced with conflicting situations and stressful moments.

2. *Indirect methods of achieving adjustment.* Indirect methods are those methods by which a person tries to seek temporary adjustment to protect himself for the time being against a psychological danger. These are purely psychic or mental devices—ways of perceiving situations as he wants to see them and imagining that things would happen according to his wishes. That is why these are called defence or mental mechanisms employed in the process of one's adjustment to one's self and the environment. A few important mental mechanisms are:

(a) *Repression.* Repression is a mechanism in which painful experiences, conflicts and unfulfilled desires are pushed down into our unconscious. In this way one unconsciously tries to forget the things that might make him anxious or uncomfortable. One tries to get temporary relief from the tension or anxiety by believing that the tension producing situation does not exist.

(b) *Regression.* Regression means going backward or returning to the past. In this process, an individual tends to regress to his early childhood or infantile responses in order to save himself from mental conflicts and tensions. A man failing in his love affair resorts to regression when he exhibits his love for dolls. Similarly an elder child may regress and start behaving like an infant when a new sibling is born and he feels neglected.

(c) *Compensation.* This is a mechanism by which an individual tries to balance or cover up his deficiency in one field by exhibiting his strength in another field. For example, an unattractive girl who becomes a bookworm to secure a position in the class is making use of such mechanism in order to attract attention which she is unable to do with her looks.

(d) *Rationalization.* This is a defence mechanism in which a person justifies his otherwise unjustified behaviour by giving socially acceptable reasons for it and thus attempts to defend himself by inventing plausible excuses to explain his conduct. A child makes use of rationalization when he tries to extend lame excuses for his failure. He may blame the teacher or parents or his poor health and thus try to disguise his own weakness and deficiency.

(e) *Projection.* Through projection one tries to see or attribute one's own inferior impulses and traits in other persons or objects. An awkward person sees and criticizes awkwardness in others. Similarly, a student who has been caught in the examination for cheating may satisfy himself by saying that others had also cheated. A person with strong unsatisfied sexual impulses may denounce others for their sexual aims or may try to think in terms of sex for every thing in the world around him. In this way one tries to overlook or defend one's shortcomings and inadequacies by emphasizing that others are worse than he is.

(f) *Identification.* In using this mechanism an individual is found to achieve satisfaction from the success of other people, groups or institutions by identifying himself with them. An artist who has not yet achieved success in his field may identify himself with a well-known, well-established artist. One may identify oneself with one's school and feel proud of its fame and reputation. Similarly, hero worship is also a sort of identification where an individual identifies himself with a popular leader or cine actor. He imitates his characteristics, dress and mannerisms and tries to revel in his accomplishments and successes.

(g) *Seclusiveness or withdrawal.* In using this mechanism an individual tends to withdraw himself from the situation that causes frustration or failure. He makes himself feel safe and secure by running away from the problem. For example, a child, may refuse to participate in games for fear of failure and deceive himself by believing that he could have done well if he had participated. Daydreaming or fantasy also is a sort of withdrawing behaviour in which one withdraws oneself into a world of fantasy or make believe. Thus, instead of feeling threatened by the realities one may become satisfied with unreal, imaginary success in the world of make-believe and imagination.

(h) *Sympathism.* Sympathism is a defence mechanism in which an individual tries to get satisfaction by seeking sympathy and pity for his own failures and inadequacies. Such persons always magnify the difficulties or obstacles in the path of their success and thus convince others to feel sorry for them. For example, a housewife who is not bringing up her children well may try to evoke others, sympathy by telling them how overworked she is because the members of her family do not cooperate with her or how the family is passing through hard times.

All the foregoing defence mechanisms are used unconsciously by a person to protect himself (although only for the time being), against psychological dangers. They are not permanent cures of the trouble as Morgan (1961) observes, *"They merely conceal or disguise the real problem. It is still there, ready to produce anxiety again and again".* A defence mechanism may thus be regarded as a temporary defence against anxiety and inadequacies. Moreover, the use of such a mechanism may create new difficulties for the individual who uses it. It is a situation similar to the one in which a person tells a lie to save himself from a difficult situation and obtains a temporary respite, but subsequently finds himself in an awkward situation because of his false statement. Therefore, we must keep a close watch on our children to see that they do not make frequent use of such defence mechanisms.

SUMMARY

Adjustment is not a simple term like adaptation or accommodation. It is actually a condition or state of mind and behaviour in which one feels that one's needs have been, or will be, gratified. The satisfaction of these needs, however, must lie within the framework and requirements of one's culture and society. As long as this happens, the individual remains adjusted; failing this, he may drift towards maladaptation and mental illness.

Adjustment can be interpreted in both ways, as a process as well as the outcome of that process in the form of some attainment or achievement. While adjustment as an achievement implies the effectiveness (good, satisfactory or bad) with which an individual can function in changed circumstances, adjustment as a process shows how an individual adjusts under changing circumstances and what influences this adjustment.

Adjustment, although a universal phenomenon, can be studied through its various aspects or dimensions like health adjustment, emotional adjustment, social adjustment, home adjustment and school or professional adjustment. Its measurement, the degree to which one may be described as adjusted or not adjusted, is possible through standardized adjustment inventories like Bell's adjustment inventory, Heston's personal adjustment inventory etc. The results and findings of these inventories may also be utilized to ascertain the personality traits and characteristics of well-adjusted persons.

Various theories and models of adjustment have been advocated by research scholars and psychologists to explain the phenomenon of adjustment. The *moral model* (the oldest and now discarded) views adjustment or maladjustment in terms of morality, the absolute norms of expected behaviour. The *medical, biological model* holds genetic, physiological and bio-chemical factors to be responsible for one's adjustment or lack of it. The *psychoanalytic model* incorporates the viewpoints of Freud, Adler, Jung and other neo-Freudians like Horney, Fromm, Reich and Erickson. According to this model, one is adjusted to the extent that one's needs are gratified or are in the way of being gratified. While Freud opines that these needs are predominantly sexual in nature, Adler replaces them by the motive to seek power or attain superiority and perfection and Jung by the urge of self-expression and self-actualization. Karen Horney, the neo-Freudian, places emphasis on the need for security and Erich Fromm on the need for security and freedom. Reich considers the release of sexual energy (which he terms Orgone energy responsible for all types of self-expression) as the basis of one's adjusted or maladaptive behaviour, and Erickson holds one's success or failure in resolving the crises of one's life at various stages to be the index of one's adjustment or maladjustment.

The sociogenic or cultural model, makes adjustment a function of the behaviour norms of one's culture and society. The *socio-psychological or behaviouristic model* on the other hand, makes adjustment a function of the interaction between one's self and the environment (physical as well as social). According to it behaviour whether adaptive or maladaptive is generally learned as an after-effect of its consequences.

The methods employed for keeping and restoring harmony between the individual and his environment may be described as direct or indirect. Direct methods are used by the individual intentionally at a quite rational and conscious level. These may include one's efforts to increase the number of trials, improve efforts or adopt comprises by resetting the goal or level of aspiration etc. Indirect methods of achieving adjustment are used at the unconscious level. Their aim is to provide temporary adjustment to the individual by protecting him against the psychological dangers. Various types of mental or defence mechanisms like compensation, rationalization, projection, identification, repression, regression, withdrawal, sympathism, etc. are indirect methods which provide temporary relief from the psychological tension, conflicts and stresses and make one able to seek adjustment for the time being.

REFERENCES

Arkoff, Abe, *Adjustment and Mental Health*, New York: McGraw-Hill, 1968, p. 6.

Asthana, H.S., *Manual of Direction and Norms of Adjustment Inventory*, Varanasi: Rupa Psychological Corporation, 1968.

Bell, Hugh M., *The Adjustment Inventory (Adult form)—Manual Alto*, California Consulting Psychologist Press, 1958.

Crow, L.D. and Alice Crow, *Understanding Our Behaviour*, New York: Alfred A. Knoff, 1956.

Drever, James, *A Dictionary of Psychology*, Middlesex: Penguin Books, 1952, p. 10.

Edward, A.L., *Edward's Personal Preference Schedule—Manual*, New York: Psychological Corporation, 1959.

Freud, S., Psychopathology of Everyday Life, *The Basic Writings of Sigmund Freud*, New York: Modern Library, 1938.

Freud, S., *An Outline of Psychoanalysis*, New York: Norton, 1949.

Gates, A.S. and Jersild, A.T., *Educational Psychology*, New York: Macmillan, 1970, pp. 614–15.

Good, Carter, V. (Ed.), *Dictionary of Education*, New York: Macmillan, 1959.

Heston, Joseph, C., *Heston Personal Adjustment Inventory*, Hudson: World Book Company, 1949.

Horney, K., *The Neurotic Personality of Our Time*, New York: Norton, 1937.

Joshi, M.C. and Pandey, Jagdish, *Adjustment Inventory* (Mimeographed information), New Delhi: NCERT.

Lazarus, R.S., *Patterns of Adjustment*, Tokyo: McGraw-Hill (3rd ed.), 1976, p. 15.

Mangal, S.K., *Teacher Adjustment Inventory* (short and long version), Agra: National Psychological Corporation, 1987.

Morgan, C.T., *Introduction to Psychology*, New York: McGraw-Hill, 1961, p. 143.

Ramamurti, P.V., Adjustment Inventory for Aged, *Indian Journal of Psychology*, 1968, Vol. 43, pp. 27–29.

Saxena, M.S.L., *Vyaktitva Parakha Prashnavali, Siksha*, Vol. 23, July, p. 127, 1962.

Sinha, A.K.P. and Singh, R.P., *Manual for Adjustment Inventory for College Students*, Agra: National Psychological Corporation, 1971.

Shaffer, L.F.'s Article in Boring, Longfield & Welb (Eds.), *Foundations of Psychology*, New York: John Wiley, 1961, p. 511.

Vonhaller, Geuner, B., *Psychology*, New York: Hougton International, 1970, p. 426.

Warren, Howard, C., *Dictionary of Education*, Boston: Houghton Mifflin, 1934, p. 6.

Webster, A. Merrian, *Webster's New Collegiate Dictionary*, London: G-Bell & Sons, 1951, p. 12.

SUGGESTED READINGS

Adams, H.E., *Psychology of Adjustment*, New York: Ronald, 1972.

Carroll, H.A., *Mental Hygiene: The dynamics of adjustment*, N.J.: Prentice-Hall, 1967.

Darwin, C., *The Origin of Species*, London: Murray, J., 1859.

Katkowsky, Walter and Leon Corlow (Eds.), *The Psychology of Adjustment*, New York: McGraw-Hill, 1976.

Lahner, George, F.J., and Ella Kube, *The Dynamics of Personal Adjustment*, New Jersey: Prentice-Hall, 1964.

Mangal, S.K., *Dimensions of Teacher Adjustment*, Kurukshetra: Vishal Publications, 1985.

_____ , *Abnormal Psychology*, New Delhi: Sterling Publishers (rev. ed.), 1987.

Maslow, A.H. and Michaelmann, B., *Principles of Abnormal Psychology*, New York: Harper, 1941.

McKinney, Fred, *Psychology of Personal Adjustment*, New York: John Wiley, 1961.

Patty, W.L. and Johnson, L.S., *Personality and Adjustment*, New York: McGraw-Hill, 1963.

Rivlin, L., *Education for Adjustment*, New York: Appleton Century, 1936.

Sawrey, J.M. and Telford, C.W., *Dynamics of Mental Health: The Psychology of Adjustment*, Boston: Allyn & Bacon, 1963.

Shaffer, L.F., *The Psychology of Adjustment*, Boston: Houghton Mifflin, 1936.

Symonds, P.H., *The Dynamics of Human Adjustment*, New York: Appleton Century, 1946.

Author Index

Subject Index